THE COMPLETE POEMS OF
A. R. AMMONS

VOLUME 1

THE COMPLETE POEMS OF A. R. AMMONS

VOLUME 1

1955–1977

Edited by Robert M. West

Introduction by Helen Vendler

W. W. NORTON & COMPANY

Independent Publishers Since 1923

New York   London

For information about permission to reproduce selections from this book, write to
Permissions, W. W. Norton & Company, Inc., 500 Fifth Avenue, New York, NY 10110

For information about special discounts for bulk purchases, please contact
W. W. Norton Special Sales at specialsales@wwnorton.com or 800-233-4830

Manufacturing by LSC Communications Harrisonburg
Book design by Helene Berinsky
Production manager: Julia Druskin

Library of Congress Cataloging-in-Publication Data

Names: Ammons, A. R., 1926–2001. | West, Robert, 1969– editor. |
Vendler, Helen, 1933– writer of introduction.
Title: The complete poems of A. R. Ammons / edited by Robert M. West ;
introduction by Helen Vendler. Other titles: Poems
Description: First edition. | New York : W. W. Norton & Company, [2017] | Includes
bibliographical references and index. Contents: v. 1. 1955–1977.
Identifiers: LCCN 2017047332 | ISBN 9780393070132 (hardcover : v. 1) |
ISBN 9780393254891 (hardcover : v. 2)
Classification: LCC PS3501 .M6 2017 | DDC 811/.54—dc23
LC record available at https://lccn.loc.gov/2017047332

W. W. Norton & Company, Inc., 500 Fifth Avenue, New York, N.Y. 10110
www.wwnorton.com

W. W. Norton & Company Ltd., 15 Carlisle Street, London W1D 3BS

1 2 3 4 5 6 7 8 9 0

Contents

EXPRESSIONS OF SEA LEVEL (1964)

Corsons Inlet (1965)

TAPE FOR THE TURN OF THE YEAR (1965)

NORTHFIELD POEMS (1966)

UPLANDS (1970)

BRIEFINGS: POEMS SMALL AND EASY (1971)

Previously Uncollected Poems
from Collected Poems 1951–1971 (1972)

SPHERE: THE FORM OF A MOTION (1974)

DIVERSIFICATIONS (1975)

The Snow Poems (1977)

HIGHGATE ROAD (1977)

Preface to Volume 1

The Complete Poems of A. R. Ammons aims to offer authoritative texts of all the poems for which Archie Randolph Ammons arranged publication, as well as a body of mostly late work that first saw print in the decade following his death. The edition's two volumes thus present the 966 poems gathered in his books, including those from three limited-edition chapbooks most of his readers have likely never seen. This first volume begins with his debut collection, *Ommateum with Doxology*, published in 1955, and ends with the long poem *The Snow Poems* and the chapbook *Highgate Road*, both of which appeared in 1977. The second volume begins with the 1978 chapbook *Six-Piece Suite* and continues through the collection *Bosh and Flapdoodle*, which appeared posthumously in 2005; the second volume's appendices add 127 previously published but hitherto uncollected poems.

In this volume and its counterpart, the text of each poem has been established after careful consideration of the manuscripts and other prepublication materials in the two major archives of Ammons's writing: the Archie Ammons Papers held by the Cornell University Library's Division of Rare and Manuscript Collections, and the A. R. Ammons Papers in the Reid and Susan Overcash Literary Collection, a holding of the Special Collections Division of East Carolina University's J. Y. Joyner Library. Also helpful were the A. R. Ammons Papers at the University of North Carolina at Chapel Hill's Southern Historical Collection, and the poet's marked copies of his books, held by his widow, the late Phyllis Ammons, and their son, John Ammons.

The archives include many interesting unpublished poems, drafts, and fragments that deserve to see print—and perhaps in the future there will be an edition dedicated to that unpublished manuscript material, clearly presenting it as such. In this edition, however, only two previously unpublished poems appear, both in this volume: "Finishing Up," from 1985, serves as a proem to the entire edition, and "Bookish Bookseller," an undated comment on *Sphere: The Form of a Motion* (1974), is included with the notes to that long poem.

As a rule, this edition defers to Ammons's final judgment, insofar as that could be determined, with regard to each poem. Those revised and reprinted in his retrospective volumes (the three *Selected Poems* published during his lifetime, plus the *Selected Longer Poems*, the *Collected Poems 1951–1971*, and *The Really Short Poems of A. R. Ammons*) appear here as sequenced in the books where they originally appeared, but as revised for those retrospectives.

For his *Collected Poems 1951–1971*, the three *Selected Poems*, and the *Selected Longer Poems*, Ammons ordered his work chronologically, by date of first composition; he seems to have thought that date the one most worth preserving, as he very rarely recorded dates of revision. Although he did not date some of his earliest poems, nearly all those from his second book, *Expressions of Sea Level* (1964), through *Collected Poems 1951–1971* (1972) are dated precisely, with the month, the day, and the year. The poems of his later books, however, are dated more sporadically: exact dates are attached to many, but many others have no dates at all. For this edition, then, arrangement of all the poems by chronology of composition was impossible. Especially since most of the early books have been out of print for some time, the best approach seemed to be to present the poems as originally sequenced, book by book.

No poem appears twice in this edition: in this volume, therefore, only the poems first gathered in *Collected Poems 1951–1971* represent that book, and the same is true of *The Really Short Poems* (1990) in Volume II. Readers interested in considering the sequencing of all the poems in those two books will find that information in the notes to them. The sequences of poems in the three *Selected Poems* and the *Selected Longer Poems*, books that include no previously uncollected work, are given in Volume II at the notes' conclusion.

Each poem Ammons dated is here followed immediately by the year of composition, outside parentheses; the endnotes give the complete date, as specifically as the poet recorded it. Each poem that appeared in a periodical, anthology, or other venue before being collected in one of the poet's books is followed here by the year of that first publication, *inside* parentheses; the notes give detailed information about those appearances. Ammons's books sometimes credit with first publication little magazines not indexed by print or electronic resources; a few of those have remained elusive, and so for half a dozen poems the notes give only the title of the venue the poet credited.

Lines are numbered here for convenient reference, but the poems sometimes complicate the issue of what should be included in that numbering. As one would expect, titles are generally not included in the line count, but the titles of poems within poems *are* counted. The one exception to this rule is *The Snow Poems*, which, despite the book's plural title, Ammons regarded as one long poem: it is divided into titled sections, but in each case the title is nothing but a heading that exactly repeats the section's first line, and so it is not included in the overall line count. In poems Ammons divided into numbered sections, the section-heading numbers are generally not counted—but if a poem *within* a poem is divided into numbered sections, those numbers *are* counted. The long poems sometimes use special characters to mark off passages; some seem no more than boundary markers, but some invite further consideration, and so all are included in the line numbering.

In assembling, editing, and annotating the *Complete Poems*, I have depended on the resources of several institutions and the assistance and advice of many people. A Humanities and Arts Research Program (HARP) Senior Fellowship from Mississippi State University's College of Arts and Sciences funded research travel. English Department Head Rich Raymond approved a helpful semester-long sabbatical leave and also granted me a second semester's release from teaching; for that and the many other ways he and his successor, Daniel Punday, have supported my work, I am deeply grateful. For their generous hospitality and fellowship during my research trips to New York and North Carolina, I thank Marlene Elling, Robert and Nancy Morgan, Margaret Bauer and Andrew Morehead, Maury and Dru York, and Stephen Craig and Joanne Promislow.

The research for this edition would have been impossible without the holdings, database subscriptions, and services of at least five libraries, and so I offer thanks to the deans, librarians, and other library staff of the Cornell University Library, East Carolina University's J. Y. Joyner Library, the University of North Carolina at Chapel Hill Library, Wake Forest University's Z. Smith Reynolds Library, and the Mississippi State University Libraries. For assistance with the A. R. Ammons Papers in the Overcash Literary Collection at ECU's Joyner Library, thanks to Jonathan Dembo, Special Collections Curator; Ralph Scott, Curator for Printed Books and Maps; Dale Sauter, Manuscripts Curator; and Maury York, then Head of the Special Collections Division. For assistance with the Archie Ammons Papers at Cornell's Division of Rare and Manuscript Collections, thanks particularly to Elaine Engst, University Archivist and, for most of my time there, Director of the RMC; Katherine Reagan, Assistant Director for Collections and Ernest L. Stern Curator of Rare Books and Manuscripts; Patrick J. Stevens, Curator of the Fiske Icelandic Collection; Laura Linke, Senior Reference Specialist; Ana Guimaraes, Head of Reference Services and Reproductions Coordinator; and Hilary Dorsch Wong, Reference Coordinator. For assistance with the A. R. Ammons Papers in the Southern Historical Collection at UNC–Chapel Hill, thanks go to Manuscripts Research and Instruction Librarian Matthew Turi; thanks also to Robert Anthony, Curator of UNC–Chapel Hill's North Carolina Collection. For help locating previously published but uncollected poems not found in the aforementioned collections, thanks to Ellen Daugman, Humanities Librarian at Wake Forest; Amanda Clay Powers, then Coordinator of Research Services for MSU Libraries; and Ben Nagel, Library Associate with MSU Libraries.

Four graduate research assistants also provided essential help with gathering materials, in addition to helping me study Ammons's revisions, set up electronic texts, proofread, and identify dedicatees and others mentioned in the poems: Tyler Trimm, Christie Collins, Jessica Burton, and Carol Hogan-Downey. Further assistance came from Academic Research Services' Mary L. White, who photographed for me some manuscript material held at Cornell, at a juncture when I could not travel to Ithaca.

Others have offered valuable information and perspective, as well as important encouragement: Alex Albright, Ted Atkinson, John Burt, the late Kathryn Stripling Byer, Seth Dawson, Joe R. Farris, Jesse Graves, William Harmon, Holly Johnson, Nancy Jones, Matthew Little, Kelly A. Marsh, Michael McFee, Kevin McGuirk, Robert L. Phillips, the late Noel Polk, Shelby Stephenson, Malvern and Nancy West, and the many other friends, colleagues, and students who have in one way or another contributed to the work and its progress. I owe a great deal to Roger Gilbert, Ammons's Cornell colleague and an essential scholar of his life and poetry, for his generous responses to my many queries.

For help with research and preparation of the manuscript, as well as much good counsel, I am deeply indebted to my wife and colleague, the always clear-thinking and resourceful Laura West. Our daughter Lena has my gratitude too, for her interest in the work and for understanding when it required me to spend time away from home.

Special thanks to Glen Hartley of Writers' Representatives, for his good advice and good humor; to Emily and Ed Wilson, for their sustaining friendship and support; and to Helen Vendler, for her wisdom and cheerful collegiality. I am very grateful to Jill Bialosky at W. W. Norton for her interest in this manuscript, her patience through its long assembly, and her editorial guidance. Thanks also to Maria Rogers and Drew Weitman, for their efficiency and camaraderie; to Becky Homiski, for all her work as Norton's project editor for both volumes; to Amy Robbins, for her eagle-eyed copyediting; and to everyone else who contributed to this edition's production..

Final thanks go to Phyllis and John Ammons for their support and their trust. I met Phyllis in 2001, at a memorial event for her husband at Wake Forest. In that first conversation, she volunteered that some had suggested to her that there should be a *Complete Poems*, but she was unsure how she felt about that possibility. Eight years later, we were meeting in Ithaca and discussing the contents of this edition. I wish she could have seen its publication—and offer it now to John, in her memory.

RMW
June 2017

INTRODUCTION

by Helen Vendler

ARCHIE RANDOLPH AMMONS (1926–2001) became one of the great American poets of the twentieth century. He remained less widely known than his contemporaries because he avoided reading his poems in public ("I get stage fright," he wrote), and even when he received the National Book Award in 1993, his intimidating anxiety forbade his appearing in person to accept the award: "As you'll recall," he wrote to me, asking me (as one of the judges) to read aloud his acceptance speech, "I show off but not up." In spite of that intense and lifelong emotional fragility, he wrote tirelessly, ever seeking to reinvent lyric poetry for contemporary America, deliberately suppressing overt mention of the poetry of England while feeling free to allude to it often—almost invisibly—within his own work. In the perpetual stand-off between tradition and the individual talent, Ammons chose to exhibit the individual talent more openly than poetic tradition. Eliot, with his allusive multilingual poems, chose to display an open recognition of the European and English tradition, establishing his individuality against it. Ammons, however, declared with every volume that he defined himself explicitly as an American poet writing of American places and American people.

Yet Ammons's America stretched from the magma underneath the American continent to the expanding universe above, ranging from the invisible subatomic particles of the laboratory to the constant proliferation of the innumerable galaxies. He extended Whitman's America by incorporating into his own work not only the vocabulary and formulae of modern scientific discovery but also the imaginative revolution that has followed in the wake of modern science. He became a writer of Whitmanian amplitude and excess, but he adopted a geometrical idea of poetic structure rather than Whitman's more geographic one. Each volume published in his lifetime revealed a new and surprising phase of Ammons's creative experimentation. He had the great good luck of remaining a striking poet into old age.

But when I read Ammons's posthumously published last volume, with its self-mocking authorial title *Bosh and Flapdoodle*, I at first could not understand—in spite of the transparency of the language—what he was up to as a poet. That bewilderment had also been present in the late seventies when I first encountered Ammons in *The Snow Poems*: who was this poet of dazzling language who so insouciantly filled up his page any way he liked—with doodles, with word lists, with a careening progress from personal events to weather reports to sublime testimony? Ammons regarded *The Snow Poems* as a single long poem in spite of its plural components because he made the sequence cohere as a grim and comic calendrical chronicle of Ithaca's near-interminable snow, from the first flakes in the fall to the last sleet in the spring. From *The Snow Poems* I read backward to Ammons's first volume, *Ommateum*, and forward through every subsequent volume. I became more and more moved and delighted by Ammons's inventiveness, humor, and daring as he expanded lyric possibility. Under his accounts, short and long, of personal and cosmic comedy, meditation, satire, elegy, and wonder, lay tragedy, first encountered at the age of four.

I lamented, with others, the absence of any comprehensive volume after the 1972 *Collected Poems*. Now, at last, under Robert West's expert and learned editorship, Ammons's volumes have all been assembled in this *Complete Poems*, together with a gathering of poems published in journals during Ammons's lifetime but never collected in volume form. Another smaller group of poems saw periodical publication after Ammons's death. West includes only two unpublished poems: one, "Finishing Up," opens the collection, and the other, "Bookish Bookseller," appears in the notes for *Sphere*. There remains a large amount of writing not yet in print, including letters and journals (some of which are reprinted in the raw and revealing collection of youthful documents called *An Image for Longing*).[1] But at last, in West's helpfully annotated edition, we have a properly ample register of Ammons's life-work as a poet. It will no doubt generate a new *Selected Poems*.

We will also have in the future a stirring comprehensive biography of Ammons now being written by Roger Gilbert of Cornell University, an expert on Ammons and the Ammons archive. It will shed light especially on

---

1 *An Image for Longing: Selected Letters and Journals of A. R. Ammons, 1951–1974*, edited by Kevin McGuirk (Victoria, BC, Canada: ELS Editions, 2013). Henceforth parenthetically referred to as *Image*.

Ammons's obscure rural beginnings, including his unpublished early work. With gratitude for his permission, I have drawn on Professor Gilbert's early chapters for some of the biographical information below.

Ammons, of Scots-Irish descent, grew up poor, the child of William Ammons (a farmer known as Willie) and his wife Della. They lived near Whiteville, North Carolina, in a frame house with no electricity (they had kerosene lamps) and no indoor toilet, scraping by at first as subsistence farmers with a mule and a plow, raising pigs and chickens. (Later, they attempted commercial tobacco farming, but fell into debt and lost the fifty-acre farm when Ammons was seventeen.) Willie and Della's first child, a daughter, died at five months, before Archie was born; and a few years later, when Archie was four, he suffered the decisive trauma of his life when his little brother Elbert died of a fever. The poet-to-be underwent a kind of breakdown, related in the unforgettable elegy "Easter Morning" and narrated more specifically in the volume *Glare*. It was Archie's first encounter with irremediable tragedy and personal guilt: the little brother had eaten raw peanuts while Archie was nearby, and "a rupture" caused the baby's death. (The family's last child, a son, was stillborn; Archie and his sisters Mona and Vida survived.)

When Archie's dramatic childhood Christianity (experienced chiefly in the charismatic Pentecostal Fire-Baptized Holiness Church) failed him, he found in his late teens a system he could credit intellectually—the universal and inflexible laws of the universe in disciplines from the bacteriological to the astronomical. The conflict between those lofty (and inhuman) laws and the physical life of the body generated much of Ammons's poetry. As he wrote in 1970 to the Yale critic Harold Bloom, his first academic admirer, "I think what I've tried to bring off is a further . . . secularization of the imagination. . . . [T]he spiritual has been with us and will remain with us as long as we have a mind. . . . I don't feel the desertion Stevens felt [when the gods disappeared], but how could I, I never felt the comfort he imagines before the desertion" (*Image*, 362). What Ammons had chiefly felt during his early exposure to religion was terror—the dread of Hell and the fear of the Rapture.

In his childhood house, the poet said, there were only three books: the family Bible and two others. And there were as well (who knows how) eleven pages of *Robinson Crusoe*, which, along with sermons and hymns, helped form his literary imagination. In the eighth grade, Ammons's teacher, Ruth Baldwin, recognized his verbal gift and highly praised his first composition; he wrote to her in gratitude until her death. He began to read voraciously, and read copiously throughout his life in various fields—the sciences, anthropology, ancient history, and of course poetry. After high school, he worked in a shipyard in Wilmington; when the war began, he enlisted in the Navy to avoid being drafted into the Army. (He did not see combat, but as his ship sailed into the harbor at Tokyo, a mine exploded near it.)

His ship was the USS *Gunason*, a destroyer escort in the Pacific theater. Archie began to keep a journal, to amass vocabulary lists, and to study the materials available from the Navy for courses in speech and composition. (After being trained as a sonar man, he became a yeoman, was assigned to a clerical job, and had his first access to a typewriter, a machine later indispensable to some of his poetic effects.) During night watches, he wrote his first groups of poems, inept pieces in standard rhyme and meter, varying from the sentimental to the comic. More essential to him than these early attempts at verse was his awed realization of the dynamics of sea and land: these earthly phenomena replaced the biblical account of creation and separated Ammons forever from denominational Christianity:

> The whole world changed as a result of an interior illumination: the water level was not what it was because of a single command by a higher power but because of an average result of a host of actions—runoff, wind currents, melting glaciers. I began to apprehend things in the dynamics of themselves—motions and bodies. . . . I was de-denominated.[2]

The multiple separate actions absorbed into ocean swells and affecting the bordering shore tutored the young sailor in the vexed relation between multiplicity and unity, an absorbing lifelong theme.

After the war, the G.I. Bill enabled Ammons to enroll in Wake Forest University, taking premedical and English courses, and graduating with a BSc in General Sciences. After his graduation, he married his young Spanish teacher, Phyllis Plumbo; we know from his letters to her before their marriage the agony he felt in trying to arrange his adult life so as to support a family and still write. The young couple went to Cape Hatteras, where for a year Ammons taught and acted as principal in an elementary school. Finally deciding to risk the uncertainty of a poet's life, he enrolled in an MA program (which he left unfinished when his father fell ill) at the University of California at Berkeley. There, for the first time, he received ongo-

---

2 From "The *Paris Review* Interview," conducted by David Lehman, in Ammons, A. R., *Set in Motion: Essays, Interviews, and Dialogues*, edited by Zofia Burr (Ann Arbor: University of Michigan Press, 1996), 95.

ing encouragement from the poet Josephine Miles, to whom he showed his work (although he silently chafed under the friction of their incompatible poetic tastes). After he left Berkeley, his wife's father offered him a job as a salesman in his New Jersey scientific glassware business: in a very dignified letter Archie explained that he could not betray his own nature by taking a position that would threaten his resolve to write poetry. However, not long after, realizing that he and Phyllis could not live on his writing, he accepted the job, and for the next nine years, somewhat to his surprise, was by his own account a successful sales manager, rising to be Executive Vice-President. He seems not to have been beset in that role by the anxiety always attending his self-presentation as a poet.

Even while holding the job, Ammons continued to compose poems and send them out to literary journals. The poems were almost uniformly rejected (except by the *Beloit Poetry Journal* and *The Hudson Review*), and he became so discouraged that in 1955, at the age of twenty-nine, he self-published with Dorrance (a vanity press in Philadelphia) a small book called *Ommateum*, the word for the compound eye of an insect. Motivated by a profound distrust of ideological prescriptiveness, whether religious or political, he explained his perspectivism in a letter to *The Hudson Review*:

> [In] the complex eye of the insect, each facet . . . perceives a single ray of light, the whole number of facets calling up the image of reality. Each of the poems is to be a facet, of course, and the whole collection to call up the stippled outlines of the image of truth, truth, from the human point of view, as a growing thing, filling out. (*Image*, 59)

Ommateum did not sell (the royalty for the first year was, he told me, four four-cent stamps), and Ammons humbly decided that he needed further instruction in how to write. The Chicago poet John Logan was offering a correspondence course in poetic composition, and in 1956, from New Jersey, Ammons sent him *Ommateum*: in this lucky moment of his life as an author, he found an enthusiastic reader who understood his achievement. Logan wrote, "I have read your book several times and I find it completely beautiful" (*Image*, 103). Subsequently, through the sponsorship of the poet Milton Kessler (met at the Bread Loaf Writers' Conference in 1961), Ammons's second book, *Expressions of Sea Level* (1964), was published by the Ohio State University Press; on the basis of its success he was appointed to the faculty at Cornell University and moved to Ithaca, in upstate New York, where he lived for the rest of his life. After the move to Cornell, books came in a cascade: in 1965, both *Corsons Inlet* and *Tape for the Turn of the Year*, and in 1966, *Northfield Poems* (all published by Cornell). His publisher then became W. W. Norton, with *Uplands* in 1970, *Briefings* in 1971, and in 1972 the premature *Collected Poems 1951–1971*. Volumes subsequently came out from Norton at frequent intervals until Ammons's death (and even after his death, in the case of *Bosh and Flapdoodle*). Although the poems won increasing recognition—a Guggenheim Fellowship in 1966, the National Book Award in 1973 for the *Collected Poems*, a MacArthur Fellowship in 1981, and a second National Book Award in 1993 for *Garbage*—Ammons never again issued a *Collected Poems*. This edition of the poetry offers the first complete record of Ammons as a poet of singular originality and insight.

In a 1960 journal entry, Ammons reported the crucial change in his idea of poetry, tracking his evolution from an overintellectual poet to one who had come to respect feeling. This passage marks the watershed in the poet's poetry between an "objective," abstract, scientific language of thought and a broader language in which feeling—the larger entity summoned by experience—*incorporates* the intellect:

> I wish I could put into words the coming-round I have experienced (intellectually) the last few years. I once despised feeling as worthless, evanescent, of no "eternal significance." I thought only of the "permanent" outside, the revolving galaxies, the endless space, and man on his tiny speck seemed meaningless. Can I now make the shift to humanity? Can I feel again? Can my blood stir at last? I now see feeling as incorporating the intellect—I once thought them separate. Intellect is the slow analytic way—the unexperienced way to action: feeling is the immediate synthesis of all experience, intellect as well as emotion. (*Image*, 165)

"Can I now make the shift to humanity?" the poet asks himself. A decade later, in a 1971 letter to Harold Bloom, he put his creed somewhat differently. When he gave up the neo-Platonic philosophical One—a "saving absolute"—in favor of the Many—the vicissitudes of human life—existence took on luster, presence, significance:

> I ran my motor fast much of my life seeking the saving absolute. There is no such item to be found. I had known these thoughts for a long time, and they meant very little, until I *experienced* them. I remember the hour I

experienced them. Nothing changed, and yet everything changed. Grief, fear, love, life, death, everything goes on just as before, but now everything seems lifted, just a bit, into its own being. (*Image*, 375)

As we pursue Ammons's poetry from its early scientific phase to its most explicitly human phase in *Bosh and Flapdoodle*, we cannot represent either end of the continuum as sovereign, nor could Ammons himself. The most solid proof of his vacillation between the One and the Many is his vacillation between short poems and long ones. He could publish a volume (*Briefings*) full of short poems; or he could publish a volume (*Garbage*) consisting of one book-length meditation. The worry he felt about the long poems—into which he deliberately inserted as much manyness as possible—arose from the doubt that he could carry off such a degree of arbitrariness and multiplicity and still call the result a poem. His fretfulness about the short poems arose from the contrary doubt that they could represent the grand inclusivity of thought and language to which he aspired. And—for Ammons was musical, played the piano, and had a fine singing voice—he worried about what sort of music the lines would convey. That restlessness drove his perennial reinvention of style.

Ammons's first two books were uncertain ones. *Ommateum* (1955) indeed found a style, philosophical but colloquial, which allowed appealing dialogues with items in nature—the indispensable sun, the poetic moon:

> I went out to the sun
> where it burned over a desert willow
> and getting under the shade of the willow
> I said
>   It's very hot in this country
> The sun said nothing so I said
>   The moon has been talking about you
> and he said
>   Well what is it this time
>
>   She says it's her own light
> He threw his flames out so far
> they almost scorched the top of the willow
>   Well I said of course I don't know

(*1, 6–7*)

Comic diffidence before supreme items of nature remained a part of Ammons's psyche, as did the Emersonian truculence of the moon, here rebelliously (however incorrectly) declaring her light to be her own, not borrowed from the sun. Poetry—immemorially connected to the moon—existed side by side with solar nature, and claimed its own inspiration.

Ammons never forsook the delights of the colloquial; his last book, like his first, makes ordinary speech a fundamental principle of style. Nonetheless, he was—as he must have known—the first American poet to whom the discourse of the basic sciences was entirely natural. He had been saturated in it as an undergraduate at Wake Forest, and it had for him a moral intimation as well as an intellectual one: it spoke provable truth, and so became an object of alliance in his disaffection with Christianity. His second book, *Expressions of Sea Level*, contained some rather unintegrated science-speak:

> honor the chemistries, platelets, hemoglobin kinetics,
>> the light-sensitive iris, the enzymic intricacies
> of control,
>
> the gastric transformations, seed
>> dissolved to acrid liquors, synthesized into
> chirp, vitreous humor, knowledge
>
> *(1, 56)*

Yet in both *Ommateum* and *Expressions of Sea Level*, there were, besides scientific declarations, poems of tender pathos, among them "Nelly Myers," commemorating a mentally disabled woman who lived with the Ammonses, and "Hardweed Path Going," an achingly sorrowful poem commemorating the young Archie's pet hog, Sparkle, slaughtered by his father. "She's nothing but a hog, boy," says the father, holding the axe, but to the boy she is a friend, her execution horrifying:

> Bleed out, Sparkle, the moon-chilled bleaches
>> of your body hanging upside-down
> hardening through the mind and night of the first freeze.
>
> *(1, 67)*

It was in his third book, *Corsons Inlet*, that Ammons developed the two central tenets of his poetics: that life is motion, and that there can be no finality, no absolute vision. (In this, he resembles Wallace Stevens, one of whose poems is entitled "Life is Motion.") Walking the Jersey shore, Ammons realizes that he is not satisfied with "narrow orders, limited tightness," but hopes to describe the "widening scope" of perception, rejoicing in his new freedom:

> enjoying the freedom that
> Scope eludes my grasp, that there is no finality of vision,
> that I have perceived nothing completely,
> that tomorrow a new walk is a new walk.
>
> (1, 95)

Various structural experiments occur on the page, as the poet prolongs a single sentence into an entire poem ("Prodigal," "The Misfit") or, as in "Configurations," turns to writing in columns down rather than in links across:

> when
> I
> am   bringing
> singing   those   home
> ,   two   again
> summer   birds
> comes
> back
>
> (1, 110)

Such an arrangement provokes a reader's question: Does this patterned sentence truly differ from its prose replication—"When I am singing, summer comes back bringing those two birds home again"—and if so, how and why? The erratic comma, the lowercase spelling, and the absence of end-punctuation speak of E. E. Cummings; the careful downward progress of the words resembles the tentative cat steps in Williams's "Poem." Such lines directly contest the Whitmanesque long lines to which Ammons was so attracted. And although both choices of line—short and long—offer freedom from ordinary lineation, still Ammons is not truly free. He has not yet learned that his poetics will not permit poems to end with conventional summings-up: he is still relying on such assertive conclusions as "I faced // piecemeal the sordid / reacceptance of my world" (1, 138). Such a conclusive termination is incompatible with the ever-anticipated "new walk" promised tomorrow. And although the poet celebrates the casual tone of the placid "new walk," he has yet to accept, intellectually, that violence will perpetually break out as one of the indispensable and inevitable ingredients of his lyric world, confronting the pastoral of the seashore with a furious wind: "Song is a violence / of icicles and / windy trees: . . . violence / brocades // the rocks . . . a / violence to make / that can destroy" (1, 119). Acknowledging hostility in himself, and seeing an equivalent violence in nature, Ammons is preparing for the emotional explosions in his later poems.

In 1965, Ammons publishes the first of his winter diaries, *Tape for the Turn of the Year.* Convinced that a poem aspiring to true manyness must be cut off, in both breadth and length, at a perfectly arbitrary place, he shapes his journal-poem to the narrow breadth and unforeseeable length of an adding-machine tape fed into his typewriter, his truncated lines confined between the left and right edges of the tape. A portion of Ammons's winter improvisation, at its most extreme, becomes a concrete poem:

❋

❋ ❋ ❋

❋ ❋ ❋ ❋ ❋

❋ ❋ ❋

❋

clusters!
    organizations!

❋ ❋ ❋ ❋ ❋

❋ ❋ ❋ ❋ ❋

❋ ❋ ❋ ❋ ❋

shapes!

)/((/)/)/((/)/)/(

designs!

(1, 191)

Since Ammons saw forms visually, as shapes, we can take it that these instances represent, first, a single module (❋) repeated in diamond shape (succeeded by an excited interpretation declaring such assembled forms "clusters!"); there follows a rectangular form composed of identical repetitions of the same module (preceded by a new triumphant announcement, "organizations!"). Then there arrives a more complicated and varying pattern of four ingredients—(concave parenthesis, convex parenthesis, virgule, and underline) upon which the poet bursts out in sheer pleasure, declaring them "designs!" (a word implying a mind behind such configurations, as the words "clusters" and "organizations," which arise in nature, do not). We deduce from this visual example that this is the way Ammons views the accreting form of his poems: first an intelligible module in a recognizable shape; then a repetition of the same module in a new shape; then a more complex set of new modules, unintelligible at first glance but interpretable as a whimsical and intended design. Substituting for such abstract module-arrangements traditional poetic shapes (alliteration, anaphora, quatrain, paradox), we can see sentences embodying them as they construct themselves in *Tape for the Turn of the Year.*

Sitting down once again at the turn of the year in 1970–71, Ammons opens a new winter diary, *Hibernaculum*, with a Keatsian landscape ("I see a sleet-filled sky's dry freeze"), and later, parodying Keats's "On First Looking into Chapman's Homer," the hibernating poet (now in his mid-forties, married and with a son) narrates his "studies" of a comically comprehensive world always assembling itself into design:

54

much have I studied, trashcanology, cheesespreadology,
laboratorydoorology, and become much enlightened and
dismayed: have, sad to some, come to care as much for

a fluted trashcan as a fluted Roman column: flutes are
flutes and the matter is a mere substance design takes
its shape in: take any subject, everything gathers up

around it:

(1, 618)

Although *Hibernaculum* exhibits Ammons's preferred end-punctuation, the colon (representing the unbroken continuity of sentence-thoughts in a stream of consciousness), the poem still appears relatively conventional, with 112 stanzas, each containing nine broad lines laid out as three tercets, with the stanza breaks completely arbitrary. Without an artificial container—the unchanging nine-line tercet-stanzas of *Hibernaculum*—Ammons fears that shapelessness will overtake his poetic diaries. Toward the end of *Hibernaculum*, he mocks his own irrepressible inclusiveness that can't decide what to leave out:

<blockquote>
if there is to be
no principle of inclusion, then, at least, there ought
</blockquote>

<blockquote>
108

to be a principle of exclusion, for to go with a maw at
the world as if to chew it up and spit
it out again as one's own is to trifle with terrible

affairs: I think I will leave out China[.]
</blockquote>

(1, 638–39)

Pursuing such reflections, he begins in 1976 to compose another winter diary, *The Snow Poems*, where his flirtation with the page creates the most unconventional poem he ever wrote, the one that charmed me into being a lifelong reader of his poetry.

Ammons wrote memorable long poems, including the single-sentence *Sphere* (1974) and the tragic *Glare* (1997). They continued his pursuit of improvisation—a form of art known to every pianist, long accepted in music. About the eighty-page *Garbage*, he wrote:

> I've gone over and over my shorter poems to try to get them right, but alternating with work on short poems, I have since the sixties also tried to get some kind of rightness into improvisations. The arrogance implied by getting something right the first time is incredible, but no matter how much an ice-skater practices, when she hits the ice it's all a one-time event: there are falls, of course, but when it's right, it seems to have been right itself.[3]

---

3 "On *Garbage*," *Set in Motion*, 125.

Ammons is speaking here of the constant will-to-form in the maker's mind, a will that seems to come from within the object itself rather than from "outside." Of course, as the will to form changes, the creative results change with it. The elated reader always wants more of the same, while the transforming writer always writes under a new imperative. The extraordinary geography of Ammons's inner world alters as the reader reads the *Complete Poems*: there are hills and declivities, creeks and snowstorms, dark weathers and brilliant ones, high altitudes and swamps. Although the actual geography of the world always came first, Ammons's symbolic world grew from the natural one. Whether the original impulse of the poet was a technical one—"a vague energy"—or an intellectual one—"an intense consideration"—the impulse moved always toward a fusion of nature and sensibility:

> Nature is not verbal. It is there. It comes first. I have found, though, that at times when I have felt charged with a vague energy or when I have moved into an intense consideration of what it means to be here, I sometimes by accident "see" a structure or relationship in nature that clarifies the energy, releases it. Things are visible ideas.[4]

Although Ammons, with his complex eye, has become one of America's most compelling nature poets, one must not forget that a geometrical "seeing" creates his templates. In a strange essay, "Figuring,"[5] published only posthumously in 2004 but probably written, according to Roger Gilbert, in the late sixties, Ammons startles the reader by admitting to a prior geometrical element in everything he writes: "Since I 'see' what to say and then attempt to translate the seen into the said, and since any translation distorts, I thought I might try by figuring here to get close to the given mental images themselves" (*F*, 535). "Mental images" follow, of which the first is a straight line going in a single direction indicated by its final arrowpoint: Ammons comments,

> This is flow, movement, motion. . . . The flow here is unidirectional, one-dimensional, unbounded: it is uncontested, unobstructed flow. It is motion "homogeneous," meaningless. It is what the poetic line

---

4 "On 'The Damned,'" *Set in Motion*, 124.
5 "Figuring," in "This is Just a Place: An Issue Devoted to the Life and Work of A. R. Ammons," *Epoch* 52.3 (2004), 535–44. Henceforth parenthetically identified as *F*. Roger Gilbert, in an email to me, says of it: "It was written in an undated notebook, actually a 'travel sketch diary.' . . . Based on the content alone, I would guess it was written in the late 60s or early 70s, perhaps around the time of 'Essay on Poetics.'"

(except for special effect) should never be—loose, fluent, uninformed, unstructured. (*F*, 535)

(This linear forward motion is of course the basic motion of prose, "meaningless" in the realm of lyric.) After the repudiated figure of the advancing straight line, Ammons offers a succession of fascinating geometrical alternatives, all directed against conclusiveness: "The poem, if it is to stop, must carry heterogeneity all the way to contradiction" (*F*, 538). The final geometrical shape, too complex to reproduce here, is a two-layered sphere with five named radii, providing Ammons with his ultimate belief and reassurance:

> If the earth, the mind, and the poem share a common configuration and common processes within that configuration, then it ought to be possible for us to feel at home here. (*F*, 543)

"Figuring" will eventually modify critical discussions that fasten chiefly on the immediately appealing thematic dimensions of Ammons's poems—emotional, philosophical, and epistemological. The dilatory "progress" of the long poems can seem exasperating until one recalls the active geometry of utterance subtending the poet's utterances; one knows that he wishes, at all costs, to avoid complacency, conclusiveness, and conclusion. Weather, as he realized in *The Snow Poems*, is his perfect aesthetic counterpart: it cannot be arrested, never repeats itself exactly, and remains unpredictable in its changes. But underneath the geometry, underneath the metaphorical correspondences, lie the strata of personal suffering that the poet must understand and transform. Poetry, Ammons wrote in 1989, moves "the feelings of marginality, of frustration, of envy, hatred, anger into verbal representations that are formal, structuring, sharable, revealing, releasing, social, artful. . . . Poetry dances in neglect, waste, terror, hopelessness—wherever it is hard to come by."[6] Every reader of Ammons will recognize the dance of geometry among feelings.

I had thought in the past that by reading all of Ammons, from epigrammatic "Briefings" through shapely lyrics through "epic" meditations (embodying "minor forms within larger motions")[7]— I had seen all his qualities. Then, in 2005, after Ammons's death, there appeared *Bosh and Flapdoodle*—

---

6 "Making Change," *Set in Motion*, 118.
7 "On 'Motion Which Disestablishes Organizes Everything,'" *Set in Motion*, 116.

composed in the late nineties but not published by Ammons, who by retaining his last book kept his poetry alive, cryopreserved, so that he would not be dead as a poet while still living in the flesh. That last volume so disconcerted me that I could not for some time find a way to write about it. Its subject (not a new one) is death, faced now not conceptually but directly and epigrammatically and dismissively: "Fall fell: so that's it for the leaf poetry" (2, 713). *Bosh and Flapdoodle* is the most transparent of Ammons's books: although airy on the page because printed in couplets, it is generated by a bizarre poetics, one where pathos is bathos and vice versa, all often confined to an arrantly simple diction. Why? I asked when I read it. I can answer only by giving a wonderfully original sample of bathos, pathos, humiliation, and primer-language, as we see old age (with heart trouble and diabetes) recalling an interview with a cheery hospital nutritionist. With barefaced inclusiveness Ammons ostentatiously names the poem "America": everyone in America is dieting and backsliding, fasting and slipping. I can't refrain from quoting from the superb comedy of the rebellious hungry self's dialogue with itself:

America

Eat anything: but hardly any: calories are
calories: olive oil, chocolate, nuts, raisins

—but don't be deceived about carbohydrates
and fruits: eat enough and they will make you

as slick as butter (or really excellent cheese,
say, parmesan, how delightful): but you may

eat as much of nothing as you please, believe
me: iceberg lettuce, celery stalks, sugarless

bran (watch carrots, they quickly turn to
sugar): you cannot get away with anything:

eat it and it is in you: so don't eat it: &
don't think you can eat it and wear it off

———

> running or climbing: refuse the peanut butter
> and sunflower butter and you can sit on your
>
> butt all day and lose weight: down a few
> ounces of heavyweight ice cream and
>
> sweat your balls (if pertaining) off for hrs
> to no, I say, no avail: so, eat lots of
>
> nothing but little of anything: an occasional
> piece of chocolate-chocolate cake will be all
>
> right, why worry:
>
> (2, 688–89)

The preposterousness of dieting when one is dying (or nearly so) suits Ammons's gift for social satire. But by including himself with the rest of us, he writes a humane satire, not a scornful one.

Ammons's final aesthetic aim, as he says outright in *Bosh and Flapdoo-dle*, is to say the most with the fewest words: this sparse poetry, which he wryly named "prosetry," can express the hellish as well as the comic. The rage and frustration that was so constitutive of Ammons's earlier years never vanished; it was in fact the fire from which the poems erupted, poems that warmed readers while consuming the author:

> did I take my bristled nest of humiliations
> to heart: what kind of dunce keeps a fire
>
> going like this: what do people mean coming
> to hell to warm themselves: well, it *is*
>
> warm: . . .
>
> (2, 696–97)

Yes, it *is* warm, but it has innumerable other qualities as well: sympathy, anger, love, irritability, patriotism, sadness, humor, risk—and most of all, original perceptions, rhythms, and cadences. Ammons's poems, first to last, are a record of American life, speech, and imagination in the twentieth century, a master inventory of the vicissitudes of human life, worked by genius into memorable shapes. In one of the most touching poems in *Bosh and Flapdoodle*, the inescapable paradigm for Ammons's own style of writing— a colloquial commentary on unceasing change—becomes the Ammonses' address book. Everyone, it seems, lives life pell-mell, with addresses that change as friends move away or die:

> The people of my time are passing away: . . .
>
> it was once weddings that came so thick and
> fast, and then, first babies, such a hullabaloo:
>
> now, it's this that and the other and somebody
> else gone or on the brink: . . .
>
> . . . our
>
> address books for so long a slow scramble now
> are palimpsests, scribbles and scratches: our
>
> index cards for Christmases, birthdays,
> Halloweens drop clean away into sympathies:
>
> *(2, 689–90)*

Ammons's style—one of wind and dynamics, of nature's ebb and flow, as rapid and rapacious as time itself; a style of elemental views as it journeys over hills of drama and through valleys of lull; a style as stormy and as beatific as weather, expressed in constant humorous intimacy in everyday language—this inconclusive but powerful accreting of words in a singing current, shaped by a changing geometry of structure and producing torrents of unexpected words, is Ammons's paradigm of the motion that is life. A voice of the rural South, modified by scientific modernity, observant and sardonic, he sounds like nobody else, his idiosyncrasy inimitable.

THE COMPLETE POEMS OF
A. R. AMMONS

VOLUME 1

Finishing Up

I wonder if I know enough to know what it's really like
to have been here: have I seen sights enough to give
seeing over: the clouds, I've waited with white
October clouds like these this afternoon often before and

5   taken them in, but white clouds shade other white
ones gray, had I noticed that: and though I've
followed the leaves of many falls, have I spent time with
the wire vines left when frost's red dyes strip the leaves

away: is more missing than was never enough: I'm sure
10   many of love's kinds absolve and heal, but were they passing
rapids or welling stirs: I suppose I haven't done and seen
enough yet to go, and, anyway, it may be way on on the way

before one picks up the track of the sufficient, the
world-round reach, spirit deep, easing and all, not just mind
15   answering itself but mind and things apprehended at once
as one, all giving all way, not a scrap of question holding back.

1985

OMMATEUM WITH DOXOLOGY (1955)

To Josephine Miles

⌒⌒⌒

So I Said I Am Ezra

So I said I am Ezra
and the wind whipped my throat
gaming for the sounds of my voice
    I listened to the wind
5   go over my head and up into the night
Turning to the sea I said
          I am Ezra
but there were no echoes from the waves
The words were swallowed up
10   in the voice of the surf
or leaping over the swells
lost themselves oceanward
     Over the bleached and broken fields
I moved my feet and turning from the wind
15   that ripped sheets of sand
     from the beach and threw them
     like seamists across the dunes
swayed as if the wind were taking me away
and said
20   I am Ezra
As a word too much repeated
falls out of being
so I Ezra went out into the night
like a drift of sand
25   and splashed among the windy oats
that clutch the dunes
of unremembered seas

1951

The Sap Is Gone Out of the Trees

The sap is gone out of the trees
in the land of my birth
and the branches droop
    The rye is rusty in the fields
5   and the oatgrains are light in the wind
The combine sucks at the fields
    and coughs out dry mottled straw
The bags of grain are chaffy and light

The oatfields said Oh
10   and Oh said the wheatfields as the dusting
combine passed over
and long after the dust was gone
    Oh they said
and looked around at the stubble and straw
15   The sap is gone out of the hollow straws
and the marrow out of my bones
                They are
    brittle and dry
    and painful in this land

20   The wind whipped at my carcass saying
How shall I
    coming from these fields
water the fields of earth
    and I said Oh
25   and fell down in the dust

1951

In Strasbourg in 1349

In Strasbourg in 1349
in the summer and in the whole year
there went a plague through the earth
    Death walked on both sides of the Sea

5   tasting Christian and Saracen flesh
and took another turn about the Sea
In a black gown and scarlet cape she went
skipping across the Sea
freeing ships to rear and fly in the wind
10   with their cargoes of dead
         Vultures whipped amorous wings
in the shadow of death
and death was happy with them and flew swiftly
whirling a lyrical dance on hidden feet
15   Dogs ate their masters' empty hands
      and death going wild with joy
      hurried about the Sea
and up the rivers to the mountains

The dying said
20   Damn us
      the Jews have poisoned the wells
and death throwing her head about lifted
the skirts of her gown
and danced wildly

25   The rich Jews are burning on loose platforms
in 1349
      and death jumps into the fire
setting the flames wild with her dancing

So I left and walked up into the air
30   and sat down in a cool draft
my face hot from watching the fire
      When morning came
I looked down at the ashes
and rose and walked out of the world

1951

I Broke a Sheaf of Light

I broke a sheaf of light
    from a sunbeam
that was slipping through thunderheads
drawing a last vintage from the hills
5   O golden sheaf I said
and throwing it on my shoulder
brought it home to the corner
    O very pretty light I said
    and went out to my chores
10   The cow lowed from the pasture and I answered
yes I am late
already the evening star
The pigs heard me coming and squealed
From the stables a neigh reminded me
15   yes I am late having forgot
I have been out to the sunbeam
and broken a sheaf of gold
    Returning to my corner
I sat by the fire with the sheaf of light
20   that shone through the night
and was hardly gone when morning came

1951

Some Months Ago

Some months ago I went out early
to pay
    my last respects to earth
        farewell earth
5   ocean farewell
lean eucalyptus with nude gray skin
    farewell

    Hill rain
pouring from a rockpierced cloud

10   hill rain from the wounds of mist
                        farewell

        See the mountainpeaks gather
        clouds from the sky
        shake new bright flakes from the mist
15   farewell

        Hedgerows hung with web and dew
        that disappear at a touch
            like snail eyes
                        farewell
20   To a bird only this
                        farewell
        and he hopped away to peck dew
        from a ground web
            spider running out of her tunnel to see
25   to whom I said
                        farewell
        and she sat still on her heavy webs

        I closed up all the natural throats of earth
        and cut my ties with every natural heart
30   and saying farewell
            stepped out into the great open
                                        1951

I Went Out to the Sun

        I went out to the sun
        where it burned over a desert willow
        and getting under the shade of the willow
        I said
5   It's very hot in this country
        The sun said nothing so I said
            The moon has been talking about you

6

and he said
    Well what is it this time

10   She says it's her own light
He threw his flames out so far
they almost scorched the top of the willow
    Well I said of course I don't know

The sun went on and the willow was glad
15   I found an arroyo and dug for water
which I got muddy and then clear
so I drank a lot
and washed the salt from my eyes
and taking off my shirt
20   hung it on the willow to dry and said
        This land where whirlwinds
walking at noon in tall columns of dust
        take stately turns about the desert
        is a very dry land
25   So I went to sleep under the willow tree

When the moon came up it was cold
and reaching to the willow for my shirt
I said to the moon
        You make it a pretty night
30   so she smiled

A night-lizard rattled stems behind me
and the moon said
        I see over the mountain
        the sun is angry
35   Not able to see him I called and said
        Why are you angry with the moon
        since all at last must be lost
        to the great vacuity

1951 (1954)

At Dawn in 1098

At dawn in 1098
the Turks went out from the gates
of Antioch
and gathered their dead

5   from the banks of the river
the cool ones
they gathered in

Bathing in the morning river
I said Oh

10   to the reapers
and stepping out gave
my white form to morning
She blushed openly
so twisting I danced

15   along the banks of the river
and morning rushed up over the hills
to see my wild form
whirling on the banks of the river
Saying O morning

20   I went away to the hills

With cloaks
and ornaments
arrows and coins of gold
the Turks buried their dead

25   and sealed the tombs with tears
But the Christians rising from the fields
broke open the cool tombs
and cut off heads
for a tally

30   Taking morning in my arms
I said Oh
and descended the eastern hills
and all that day
it was night in Antioch

1951

The Whaleboat Struck

The whaleboat struck
and we came ashore
to the painted faces
    O primitives I said
and the arrow sang to my throat
Leaving myself on the shore
I went away
and when a heavy wind caught me I said
    My body lies south
    given over to vultures and flies
and wrung my hands
so the wind went on
Another day a wind came saying
    Bones
    lovely and white
    lie on the southern sand
    the ocean has washed bright
I said
    O bones in the sun
and went south
The flies were gone
The vultures no longer searched
the ends of my hingeless bones
for a trace of lean or gristle
Breathing the clean air
I picked up a rib
    to draw figures in the sand
till there is no roar in the ocean
no green in the sea
till the northwind flings no waves
across the open sea
I running in and out with the waves
I singing old Devonshire airs

1951 (1954)

Turning a Moment to Say So Long

Turning a moment to say so long
    to the spoken
    and seen
    I stepped into
5   the implicit pausing sometimes
on the way to listen to unsaid things
At a boundary of mind
    Oh I said brushing up
    against the unseen
10   and whirling on my heel
    said
    I have overheard too much
Peeling off my being I plunged into
the well
15   The fingers of the water splashed
    to grasp me up
    but finding only
    a few shafts
of light
20   too quick to grasp
    became hysterical
    jumped up and down
    and wept copiously
So I said I'm sorry dear well but
25   went on deeper
finding patched innertubes beer cans
and black roothairs along the way
but went on deeper
till darkness snuffed the shafts of light
30   against the well's side
    night kissing
    the last bubbles from my lips

1951

Turning

Turning from the waterhole I said Oh
to the lioness whose wrinkled forehead
showed signs of wonder
O beautiful relaxed animal I said
5   The tall grass shivered up and down
and said
What a looseness is in her body how
limp are the wet teats of her belly
The grass sang a song I had never
10   heard before to the red sun
so I said cool evening with a wind
in the rushes
The lioness dropped loosely to the ground
and I said O tired lioness
15   you love the evening
She came to my chest and we fell into
the waterhole
                    to which
since the grass had stopped singing and
20   was watching the sun sink
                    I said
water is like love in tranquillity
my soul has wings of light and
never have I seen
25   more beauty
than is in this evening
Her paw touched my lips as if
she loved me passionate and loud
so I said
30   Loose lioness
and her lips took the words from my throat
her warm tongue flicking the living flutter
of my being
So I fumbled about in the darkness for my wings
35   and the grass looked all around at the evening

1951

Dying in a Mirthful Place

       Dying in a mirthful place
       I looked around at the dim lights
       the hips and laughing throats
       and the motions of the dance
5   and the wine the lovely wine
       and turning to death said
           I thought you knew propriety
       Death was embarrassed and stuttered
       so I watched the lips
10   and hurried away to a hill in Arizona
       where in the soil was such a noiseless
       mirth and death
       that I lay down and placed my head
           by a great boulder
15   The next morning I was dead
           excepting a few peripheral cells
       and the buzzards
       waiting for a savoring age to come
       sat over me in mournful conversations
20   that sounded excellent to my eternal ear

1952

When Rahman Rides

       When Rahman rides a dead haste in a dusty wind
       I wait for him and look for him coming over the desert
       blustering through the tough unwaving leaves
       and trembling behind a tall saguaro say
5   O Rahman
       and he says
           what what
      It's like this
           what what
10   so when I saw you coming I thought perhaps
       There was the rush of dust and then farther on
       a spiral whirlwinding

as if he had stopped too late and drawing up his wings
looked back at the saguaro's lifted arms

15 Unspiralling
he swept on across the desert
leaving me the ocotillo in a bloomless month

1952

With Ropes of Hemp

With ropes of hemp
I lashed my body to the great oak
saying odes for the fiber of the oakbark
and the oakwood saying supplications
5 to the root mesh
deep and reticular in the full earth
through the night saying these
and early into the wild unusual dawn
chanting hysterical though quiet
10 watching the ropes ravel
and the body go raw
　　while eternity
greater than the ravelings of a rope
waited with me patient in my experiment
15 Oh I said listening to the raucous
words of the nightclouds
how shadowy is the soul
how fleet with the wildness of wings

Under the grip of my bonds
20 I say Oh and melt beyond the ruthless coil
but return again saying odes in the night
where I stand splintered to the oak
gathering the dissentient ghosts of my spirit
into the oakheart
25 I in the night standing saying oaksongs
entertaining my soul to me

1952

My Dice Are Crystal

My dice are crystal inlaid with gold
and possess
    spatial symmetry
about their centers and
5   mechanical symmetry and
      are of uniform density
and all surfaces have equal
coefficients of friction for

my dice are not loaded
10   Thy will be done
whether dog or Aphrodite

Cleaning off a place on the ground
    I patted it
      flat and
15   sat back on my legs
        rattling the bones
Apparitionally god sat poker-faced
silent on the other side
    When the ballooning
20   silence burst I cast
and coming to rest
the dice spoke their hard directive
    and melting
left gold bits on the soil

Having Been Interstellar

Having been interstellar
    and in the treble clef

by great expense of
    climbing mountains

lighting crucible fires
in the catacombs

among the hunted
and the trapped in tiers
seeking the distillate
10 answering direct
the draft of earthless air

he turned in himself
helplessly as in sleep

and went out into the growth of rains
15 and when the rains
taking him
had gone away in spring

no one knew
that he had ever flown
20 he was no less
no more known
to stones he left a stone

Coming to Sumer

Coming to Sumer and the tamarisks on the river
I Ezra with unsettling love
rifled the mud and wattle huts
for recent mournings
5 with gold leaves
and lapis lazuli beads
in the neat braids loosening from the skull
Looking through the wattles to the sun
I said
10 It has rained some here in this place
unless snow falls heavily in the hills

to do this
       The floor was smooth with silt
and river weeds hanging gray
15   on the bent reeds spoke saying
Everything is even here as you can see
       Firing the huts
I abandoned the unprofitable poor
unequal even in the bone
20   to disrespect
       and casual with certainty
watched an eagle wing as I went
to king and priest

I Assume the World Is Curious About Me

I assume the world is curious about me
                              the sound
                  and volume of hell
where brittle grace polished as glass
5   glazed in fire glints
and pliant humility
furls coiling into itself
like an ashen abnegation
       for sin
10   you will want to see it
even without god is a hot consumption

I assume that when I die
going over and under without care
leaves will wilt and lose all windy interest
15   some ration of stars will fall
for my memorial

A simple thrust brings vomit
but a reduction
and retained separation has love in it

20 and love burns on itself
   while hate
 is a cold expulsion and devastation

 I assume many will crowd around me
 to praise my unwillingness to simplify
25 then turning
 assist in raising me to my outstanding tree
 someday unhang my sinews from the nails
 let down the gray locust from the pine

I Struck a Diminished Seventh

 I struck a diminished seventh
 and sat down
 to wait
   for the universal word
5 Come word
 I said
 azalea word
 gel precipitate
 while I
10 the primitive spindle
 binding the poles of earth and air
 give you
 with river ease
 a superior appreciation
15 equalling winged belief
   It had almost come
 I perishing for deity stood up
 drying my feet
 when the minor challenge was ignored
20 and death came over sieving me

Gilgamesh Was Very Lascivious

Gilgamesh was very lascivious
and took the virgins as they ripened
from the men that wanted them
To the men Gilgamesh gave wall building
5   brick burning and gleaning of straw
for a physical expression
    yielding more protection
for the virgins the men wanted
than long hours in jogging beds
10   with the walls crumbling before
who knew what predators
    seeking wine
virgins
long fields of wheat
15   and spearshafts wrapped in gold

Because he sought the mate
    of his physical divinity
Gilgamesh
let many usurp the missing one
20   and went
singly in his tragic excellence

At his going by
the men in mud and sweat
saw virgins yielding to his eyes
25   and turned to work with dreams
no virgin would ever give to them

Climbing the wall
and walking up and down upon it
I said
30   Fools fools
but they kneaded slowly
the muscles of their glassy backs
    worms working in the sun

When I Set Fire to the Reed Patch

When I set fire to the reed patch
that autumn evening
the wind whipped volleys of shot
from the bursting joints
5   and armies bristling defensive interest
rushed up over the fringing hills
and stared into the fire

I laughed my self to death
and they
10   legs afire
eyelashes singed
swept in flooding up the lovely
expressions of popping light
and hissing thorns of flame

15   Clashing midfire
the armies quite unwound
the intentions of the fire
and snuffed the black reeds smoking out
but like destroyed mountains
20   left deposits
that will insure
deep mulch for next year's shoots
the greenest hope
autumn ever
25   left this patch of reeds

The Grass Miracles

The grass miracles have kept me down all autumn
purpose turning on me like an inward division
The grasses heading barbed tufts
airy panicles and purple spikes
5   have kept me stalled in the deadends

of branching dreams
    It is as though I had started up the trunk
and then dispersed like ant trails
along the branches
10   and out on the twigs
and paused dipping with a golden thought
at the points of the leaves

A black stump hidden
in grass and old melon vines
15   has reined my hurry
and I have gone up separately
    jiggling like a bubble flock
in globes of time

I have not been industrious this autumn
20   It has seemed necessary
to accomplish everything with a pause
    bending to part the grass
to what round fruit
becoming entangled in clusters
25   tying all the future up
in variations on present miracles

I Came in a Dark Woods Upon

I came in a dark woods upon
an ineffaceable difference
and oops embracing it
felt it up and down mindfully
5   in the dark
prying open the knees to my ideas
    It was slim and hard
with a sharp point
and stood up
10   its shaft shot deep as a pile

———

Who will extract I said desiring
a public value this erect
difference from the ground
     and the dryads
15   shifting in the limbs
dipped leaves
blotting the angels' roofeyes out

Taking the neck below the barbs
I eased the wet shaft up into my hands
20   Everything retired
The dryads took body in the oakhearts
The angels shuttered their wintry peepholes
and flew off throneward across the fields
and the trees arms-up leaned as in wind away
25   and casting the difference
I splintered
     the whole environment

and somewhat dazed with grief ran
catching it up hot in my hands
30   and hurled it far into the seas
a brother to Excalibur

A Treeful of Cleavage Flared Branching

A treeful of cleavage flared branching
through my flesh and cagey
I sat down mid-desert
and heaping hugged up between my knees
5   an altarcone from the sand
and addressed it with water dreams

The wind
chantless of rain in the open place
spun a sifting hum
10   in slow circles round my sphere of grief

and the sun
inched countless arms
under the periphery of my disc of sight
eager for the golden thing

15 There must be time I said
to dream real these dreams
and the sun
startled by the sound of time
said Oh
20 and whirling in his arms
ran off across the sky
Heaping the sand
sharpening the cone of my god I said
I have oracles to seek

25 Drop leaf shade
the wet cuticle of the leaf tipped in shade
yielded belief
to the fixed will and there
where the wind like wisdom
30 sweeps clean the lust prints of the sun
lie my bones entombed
with the dull mound of my god
in bliss

[Behind the I]

Behind the I
    I is
  an I
        elated
5   leaves
  into
        separables

Falling too through scopes of
      variables

10   I
                          in the
                      I-beam is some
            for the moment accidental mote
            Behind the I
15   I discloses
                  flows
                              winds and seas
            of particles

            while he conceived outside
20   is whole
            beyond realities
                      I
                      never wants to lose

One Composing

One composing seminal works sat oblivious
by a brothel
and gave leaflets to the functions of the wind
saying
5   Time is a liquid orb
where we swim loose
timeless in a total time
pursuing among the nuclear sediment
the sweet pale flakes of old events
10   Stopping I watched the leaflets rock upward
from the windy alley
            and brought him a mug of stout
The contemporary he said
turning into the brothel
15   is an orb's shell
                  of light
            within the liquid orb
and fertility came into him like a virtuoso
and mounting pubic realms
20   he rode galloping through the night

sweetsap and rain playing marbles
on the wind's speed of his outstretched shirt
One
weeping beads of ice
25   down the cold deserts of his brain
cried from the street O Jezebel
and the seminal one rose wiping saying
In exhaustion's death are dregs of wanted sleep

In the Wind My Rescue Is

In the wind my rescue is
in whorls of it
like winged tufts of dreams
bearing
5   through the forms of nothingness
the gyres and hurricane eyes
the seed safety
of multiple origins

I set it my task
10   to gather the stones of earth
into one place
the water modeled sand molded stones
from
the water images
15   of riverbeds in drought
from the boundaries of the mind
from
sloping farms
and altitudes of ice and
20   to mount upon the highest stone
a cardinal
chilled in the attitude of song

But the wind has sown loose dreams
in my eyes
25   and telling unknown tongues

drawn me out beyond the land's end
　　　and rising in long
　　parabolas of bliss
borne me safety
30　　from all those ungathered stones

1954

[I should have stayed longer idle]

I should have stayed longer idle
and done reverence
to it
　　　　　waterfalls
5　　　　　　humbling in silent slide
the precipice of my effrontery
　　　poured libations of arms
like waterwheels
toward the ground but
10　knowing the fate of sunset things
I grew desperate and entertained it
　　with sudden sprints
　　somersaults
and cartwheels figuring eight

15　It would not stay
　　　　　Ring of cloud I said
high pale ringcloud
ellipsis of evening moment's miracle
where will I go looking for your return
20　and rushing to the rim
I looked down into the deep dissolution

I should have held still
before it
　　and been mute
25　cancelled by an oak's trunk
and done honors unseen
and taken the beauty sparingly

as one who fears to move and
shatter vision from his eyes

A Crippled Angel

A crippled angel bent in a scythe of grief
mourned in an empty lot
    Passing by I stopped
amused that immortality should grieve
5   and said
It must be exquisite

Smoke came out of the angel's ears
        the axles
      of slow handwheels of grief
10   and under the white lids of its eyes
bulged tears of purple light
Watching the agony diffuse in
         shapeless loss
I interposed a harp
15   The atmosphere possessed it eagerly
and the angel
saying prayers for the things of time

let its fingers drop and burn
the lyric strings provoking wonder

20   Grief sounded like an ocean rose
        in bright clothes
and the fire
breaking out on the limbs rising
caught up the branching wings
25   in a flurry of ascent
Taking a bow I shot transfixing
the angel midair
all miracle hanging fire
        on rafters of the sky

Dropping Eyelids Among the Aerial Ash

Dropping eyelids among the aerial ash
I ascending entered the gates of cloud
westward where the sliver moon
     keeled in sun was setting
5   and sat down on a silver lining to think
my mind splintered with spears of glass
and errors of the cold
         Below
the gorged god lay on the leveled city
10   and suburban bandaged
and drowsily tolled the reckonless waste
The clouds mushrooming rose
     and held about his head
like old incense of damp altars

15   Oh I said in the mistral of bleached
and naked thought
blood like a catalyst is evil's baptismal need
before the white rose and benefactions
rise
20   thin curls of hope from cooling lakes of ruin
and chiseled stone wins
     from the spout of human sacrifice
powers of mercy

Darkness pushed the sliver moon
25   from my silver lining and I arose
the high seed clouds fading
and went back down into the wounds and cries
and held up lanterns for the white nurses
moving quickly in the dark

I Came Upon a Plateau

I came upon a plateau
where mesquite roots

crazed the stone
      and rains
5   moved glinting dust
down the crevices
      Calling off rings
            to a council of peaks
I said
10   Spare me man's redundancy
and putting on bright clothes
sat down in the flat orthodoxy

Quivering with courtesy
a snake drew thrust in sines
15   and circles from his length
rearing coils of warning white
      Succumbing in the still ecstasy
sinuous through white rows of scales
l caved in upon eternity
20   saying this use is colorless

A pious person his heart
looted and burnt
      sat under a foundation
a windy cloak clutched round his bones
25   and said
When the razed temple cooled
I went in
and gathered these
relics of holy urns

30   Behold beneath this cloak
      and I looked in
at the dark whirls of dust

The peaks coughing bouldered
laughter shook to pieces
35   and the snake shed himself in ripples
across a lake of sand

Doxology

I

Heterodoxy with Ennui

Should I bold in a moment intrude
upon a silence, hold my hands properly,
crossed, in a mock eternity,
would someone use my lips
5   for an expiation?

I have heard the silent owl near death
sees wildly with the comprehension of fire;
have drunk from those eyes.

Transplanted my soul to the wind, wound
10   my days round the algae of rapid streams,
wedded my bones to the throat of flame,
spirited.

You have heard it said of old time
the streets shall flow blood, but the streets
15   swept out with the flood
shall be deposited upon sand.
You have this word for a fulfillment.

An unconstrained fluidity prevails, abides;
whole notes are rocks
20   and men *thirty-seconds*,
all in descending scales,
unvigiled bastardies of noise:
the motion of permanence.

Marble, pottery, signs endure,
25   support fluency, scrollwork,
where violins ornament, fingers,
offended with needles of care,

articulate poised domes.
This love for the thin and fleet
30   will race through the water-content
of my heavy death.

I die at the vernal equinox
and disorder like a kissing bug
quaffs my bonds: if I ascend,
35   I shall be congratulatory,
but if they fawn, desire
a season before immortality.

Detain me among the spiral designs
of an ancient amphora: fulfillment
40   comes before me like spiral designs
on an ancient amphora in which detain me,
fixed in rigid speed.

II

Orthodoxy with Achievement

Silent as light in dismal transit
through the void, I, evanescent,
45   sibilant among my parts,
fearing the eclipse of a possible glance
and not glancing, shut-eyed,
crouch froglike upon my brain,
hover and keep dark,
50   fervor opposed by dread,
activity numbed by its mixed result,
till some awaited drop falls
upon the mound and chaos
perfects the eternity of my silence.

55   I cannot count the forms,
thrown upon the wheel, delineated,
that have risen and returned
without accretion; but the spirit

drops falling upon wings
60   and preens the day with its call:
none say where in the silence it sleeps.

Though the sound of my voice
is a firmamental flaw, my self, in the rockheart,
in southern oakmoss blown tangled,
65   its supple pincers snaring
new forks of life, braiding thin limbs
of the wateroak on gooseberry hills
beside swamps where the raccoon runs
and dips his paw in the run-of-the-swampin
70   musky branchwater for darting crawfish
scuttling a mudwake before them; my self,
voluble in the dark side of hills
and placid bays, while the sun grows
increasing atmosphere to the sea,
75   correcting the fault of dawn; my self,
the drought of unforested plains,
the trilobite's voice,
the loquacity of an alien room troubled
by a blowfly, requires my entertainment
80   while we learn the vowels of silence.

III

Paradox with Variety

The temple stands in a rainforest
where bones have a quick ending.

Ephemeral as wings in fire
transparent leaves droop in the earth-steam;
85   growth and decay swallow the traces
of recent paths.

I went in. On one side sat the god of creation; on the other,
the god of destruction. Hatred held their eyes. Going deeper
to the next chamber, I found the god of destruction and the

90   god of creation tangled sensually on the floor; they gnawed
      and procreated. In the next chamber was majesty: one god
      sat staring at his golden walls.

      I hear an organ playing through the morning rain;
      it sounds like the memory of quilting women.
95   Between the organ and me, California poppies furl
      like splotches of conceit
      in the light and silent rain.
      A robin peeks up from the grass
      and rattles a ladybug in his beak.
100   Mr. Farnham says
      life is fearfully complex.

      When I was lustful I drew twenty maidens
      from the Well of Sacrifice
      and took them to Cozumel.
105   The priests of the steep temples
      longed to smear my body
      with blue ointment.
      We've all died since
      and all has been forgotten.
110   Strangers drop pebbles
      into the Hole of Water:
      it is too still.

      Should I mistake khaki blood on foreign snow
      for cherry ices, my mind would freeze;
115   but Red blood is interesting:
      its vessels on the snow
      are museums of eternity.

      When stone and drought meet in high places,
      the hand instructed by thirst
120   chips grace into solidity and Hellas,
      like a broken grape upon marmoreal locks,
      clarifies eternity. Had I come in the season
      when sheep nibble windy grasses,

I would have gone out of the earth
125 listening for grasses
and the stippling feet of sheep
on sinking rocks.

I like to walk down windowless corridors
and going with the draft
130 feel the boost of perpendicularity,
directional and rigid;
concision of the seraphim,
artificial lighting.

Sometimes the price of my content
135 consumes its purchase
and martyrs' cries, echoing my peace,
rise sinuously like smoke
out of my ashen soul.

1952

EXPRESSIONS OF SEA LEVEL (1964)

to Phyllis

❧

Raft

I called the wind and it
went over with me
    to the bluff
      that keeps the sea-bay
5   and we stayed around for a while
trying to think
      what to do:

I took some time to watch
the tall reeds
10   and bend their tassels
      over to my touch
      and
as the lowering bay-tide left
      salt-grass
15   combed flat toward the land
tried to remember
what I came to do:

in the seizures,
I could not think but
20   vanished into the beauty
    of any thing I saw
and loved,
pod-stem, cone branch, rocking
      bay grass:

25   it was almost dark when the wind
breathless from playing
with water
      came over and stopped

resting in the bare trees and dry grass
30   and weeds:

I built a fire in a hollow stump
and sitting by
wove a disc of reeds,
  a round raft, and

35 sometime during the night
   the moon shone but
it must have been the early night
for when I set out
   standing on my disc
40 and poling with a birch
   it was black dark
of a full tide:
the wind slept through my leaving:
I did not wake it to say goodbye:

45 the raft swirled before day
and the choppy, tugging bay
   let me know
I had caught the tide
and was rushing through

50 the outer sea-banks
into the open sea:

when dawn came
   I looked
and saw no land:

55 tide free and
without direction I
gave up the pole,
   my round raft
having no bow,
60 nowhere to point:

    ———

I knelt in the center
to look for where the
    sun would break
and when it started to come
I knew the slow whirl
of my ship
which turned my back to the east
    and
brought me slowly round again:

at each revolution
    I had
new glory in my eyes
and thought with chuckles
    where would I be at noon
and what of the night
when the black ocean
might seem not there

though of course stars
    and planets rise and
east can be known
    on a fair night
but I was not
certain
I wanted to go east:
it seemed wise
    to let
the currents be
whatever they would be,
allowing possibility
to chance
where choice
    could not impose itself:

I knelt turning that way
    a long time,
glad I had brought my great
    round hat
for the sun got hot:

65

70

75

80

85

90

95

                at noon
                I could not tell
100   I turned
                for overhead the sun,
                        motionless in its dome,
                spun still
                and did not wobble
105   the dome
                or turn a falling shadow
                        on my raft's periphery:

                soon though that symmetry
                eased
110   and the sun
                was falling
                and the wind came
                        in an afternoon way

                        rushing before dark to catch me.

                                                    c. 1955–60 (1963)

Hymn

        I know if I find you I will have to leave the earth
        and go on out
                over the sea marshes and the brant in bays
        and over the hills of tall hickory
5   and over the crater lakes and canyons
        and on up through the spheres of diminishing air
        past the blackset noctilucent clouds
                where one wants to stop and look
        way past all the light diffusions and bombardments
10   up farther than the loss of sight
                into the unseasonal undifferentiated empty stark

        And I know if I find you I will have to stay with the earth
        inspecting with thin tools and ground eyes
        trusting the microvilli sporangia and simplest

                                                                        37

15   coelenterates
        and praying for a nerve cell
        with all the soul of my chemical reactions
        and going right on down where the eye sees only traces

        You are everywhere partial and entire
20   You are on the inside of everything and on the outside

        I walk down the path down the hill where the sweetgum
        has begun to ooze spring sap at the cut
        and I see how the bark cracks and winds like no other bark
        chasmal to my ant-soul running up and down
25   and if I find you I must go out deep into your
            far resolutions
        and if I find you I must stay here with the separate leaves

1956 (1957)

Risks and Possibilities

Here are some pretty things picked for you:

        1)   dry thunder
            rustling like water
            down the sky's eaves

5   is summer locust
            in dogfennel weed

        2) the fieldwild
            yellow daisy
                focusing dawn

10   inaugurates
            the cosmos

        3) the universe comes
                to bear
            on a willow-slip and

15   you cannot unwind
                   a pebble
               from its constellations

        4)   chill frog-gibber
               from grass
20   or loose stone
               is

               crucial as fieldwild
               yellow daisy:

        such propositions:
25   each thing boundless in its effect,
               eternal in the working out
        of its effect: each brush
        of beetle-bristle against a twig
               and the whole
30   shifts, compensates, realigns:
        the crawl of a slug
               on the sea's floor
        quivers the moon to a new dimension:
        bright philosophy,
35   shake us all! here on the
        bottom of an ocean of space
        we babble words recorded
               in waves
        of sound that
40   cannot fully disappear,
               washing up
        like fossils on the shores of unknown worlds:

               nevertheless, taking our identities,
               we accept destruction:

45   a tree, committed as a tree,
               cannot in a flood
                    turn fish,
               sprout gills (leaves are

a tree's gills) and fins:
50   the molluscs
dug out of mountain peaks
are all dead:

oh I will be addled and easy and move
over this prairie in the wind's keep,
55   long-lying sierras blue-low in the distance:
I will glide and say little
(what would you have me say? I know nothing;
still, I cannot help singing)
and after much grace
60   I will pause
and break cactus water to your lips:

identity's strict confinement! a risk
        and possibility,
granted by mercy:
65   in your death is the mercy of your granted life:
        do not quibble:

dry thunder in the locust weed!
the supple willow-slip leafless in winter!
the chill gibber of the frog
70   stilled in nightsnake's foraging thrust!
how ridiculous!
grim:
enchanting:

repeating mid night these songs for these divisions.

1959 (1960)

Terrain

The soul is a region without definite boundaries:
    it is not certain a prairie
can exhaust it

                    or a range enclose it:
5   it floats (self-adjusting) like the continental mass,
                where it towers most
        extending its deepest mantling base
                    (exactly proportional):
        does not flow all one way: there is a divide:
10   river systems thrown like winter tree-shadows
        against the hills: branches, runs, high lakes:
                    stagnant lily-marshes:

        is variable, has weather: floods unbalancing
                gut it, silt altering the
15   distribution of weight, the nature of content:
                    whirlwinds move through it
        or stand spinning like separate orders: the moon comes:
                there are barren spots: bogs, rising
        by self-accretion from themselves, a growth into
20   destruction of growth,
        change of character,
                    invasion of peat by poplar and oak: semi-precious
        stones and precious metals drop from muddy water into mud:

        it is an area of poise, really, held from tipping,
25   dark wild water, fierce eels, countercurrents:
        a habitat, precise ecology of forms
                    mutually to some extent
        tolerable, not entirely self-destroying: a crust afloat:
                a scum, foam to the deep and other-natured:
30   but deeper than depth, too: a vacancy and swirl:

        it may be spherical, light and knowledge merely
                the iris and opening
        to the dark methods of its sight: how it comes and
                    goes, ruptures and heals,
35   whirls and stands still: the moon comes: terrain.

                                                    1959 (1960)

Nelly Myers

I think of her
        while having a bowl of wheatflakes
(why? we never had wheatflakes
or any cereal then
except breakfast grits)
           and tears come to my eyes
and I think that I will die
because

        the bright, clear days when she was with me
and when we were together
(without caring that we were together)

can never be restored:
        my love wide-ranging
    I mused with clucking hens
and brought in from summer storms
at midnight the thrilled cold chicks
        and dried them out
           at the fireplace
and got up before morning
unbundled them from the piles of rags and
    turned them into the sun:

    I cannot go back
        I cannot be with her again

        and my love included the bronze
sheaves of broomstraw
she would be coming across the fields with
before the household was more than stirring out to pee

and there she would be coming
    as mysteriously from a new world
and she was already old when I was born but I love
the thought of her hand
wringing the tall tuft of dried grass

and I cannot see her beat out the fuzzy bloom
again
35 readying the straw for our brooms at home,
I can never see again the calm sentence of her mind
        as she
measured out brooms for the neighbors and charged
a nickel a broom:

40 I think of her
        but cannot remember how I thought of her
as I grew up: she was not a member of the family:
I knew she was not my mother,
                not an aunt, there was nothing
45 visiting about her: she had her room,
        she kept her bag of money
(on lonely Saturday afternoons
    you could sometimes hear the coins
spilling and spilling into her apron):
50   she never went away, she was Nelly Myers, we
        called her Nel,
small, thin, her legs wrapped from knees to ankles
in homespun bandages: she always had the soreleg
                and sometimes
55 red would show at the knee, or the ankle would swell
and look hot
    (and sometimes the cloths would
dwindle,
        the bandages grow thin, the bowed legs look
60 pale and dry—I would feel good then,
            maybe for weeks
                there would seem reason of promise,
        though she rarely mentioned her legs
and was rarely asked about them): she always went,

65 legs red or white, went, went
through the mornings before sunrise
                covering the fields and
woods

looking for huckleberries
70 or quieting some wild call to move and go
            roaming the woods and acres of daybreak
    and there was always a fire in the stove
    when my mother rose (which was not late):

    my grandmother, they say, took her in
75 when she was a stripling run away from home
    (her mind was not perfect
            which is no bar to this love song
                for her smile was sweet,
            her outrage honest and violent)
80 and they say that after she worked all day her relatives
    would throw a handful of dried peas into her lap
                for her supper
    and she came to live in the house I was born in the
    northwest room of:

85 oh I will not end my grief
            that she is gone, I will not end my singing;
    my songs like blueberries
    felt-out and black to her searching fingers before light
    welcome her
90 wherever her thoughts ride with mine, now or in any time
        that may come
    when I am gone; I will not end visions of her naked feet
    in the sandpaths: I will hear her words
            "Applecandy" which meant Christmas,
95 "Lambesdamn" which meant Goddamn (she was forthright
            and didn't go to church
        and nobody wondered if she should

    and I agree with her the Holcomb pinegrove bordering our
    field was
100 more hushed and lovelier than cathedrals
        not to mention country churches with unpainted boards
    and so much innocence as she carried in her face
    has entered few churches in one person)

                        ———

and her exclamation "Founshy-day!" I know no meaning for
105   but knew she was using it right:

and I will not forget how though nearly deaf
she heard the tender blood in lips of children
and knew the hurt
      and knew what to do:

110   and I will not forget how I saw her last, tied in a chair
lest she rise to go
and fall
            for how innocently indomitable
      was her lust
115   and how her legs were turgid with still blood as she sat
and how real her tears were as I left
      to go back to college (damn all colleges):
         oh where her partial soul, as others thought,
roams roams my love,
120   mother, not my mother, grandmother, not my grandmother,
slave to our farm's work, no slave I would not stoop to:
I will not end my grief, earth will not end my grief,
I move on, we move on, some scraps of us together,
      my broken soul leaning toward her to be touched,
125   listening to be healed.

1961 (1963)

Bridge

A tea garden shows you how:

      you sit in rhododendron shade
at table
on a pavilion-like lawn

5   the sun midafternoon through the blooms
and you

———

watch lovers and single people
go over the steep moonbridge at the pond's narrows

where flies nip circles

10   in the glass
and vanish in the widening sight except for an uncertain

        gauze memory of wings

and as you sip from the small thick cup
        held bird-warm
15   in the hands

        you watch
the people
rising on the bridge

descend into the pond,
20   where bridge and mirrorbridge merge

        at the bank
returning their images to themselves:
        a grove
of pepper trees (sgraffito)
25   screens them into isolations of love or loneliness:

it is enough from this to think in the green tea scent
and turn to farther things:

when the spirit comes to the bridge of consciousness
and climbs higher and higher
30   toward the peak no one reaches live
but where ascension
        and descension meet
completing the idea of a bridge

————

think where the body is,
35   that going too deep

it may lose touch,
          wander a ghost in hell
          sing irretrievably in gloom,
and think

40   how the spirit silvery with vision may
break loose in high wind

          and go off weightless

body never to rise or spirit fall again to unity,
to lovers strolling through pepper-tree shade:

45   paradise was when
Dante
regathered from height and depth
          came out onto the soft, green, level earth
into the natural light, come, sweat, bloodblessings,
          and thinning sheaf of days.

1959 (1960)

Requiem

1.

Mind

The strawberries along the roadbank in the hills bloomed,
the starwhite petals brilliant and melty in the sun as frost:
a glimmer of angels through the pines
          rained fine needles, blanketing the rich fruit.

5   On Rome's hills stand Respighi's musical pines,
aural columns of light, beingless but with minds.

Rising from banana trees in Mexico one, beyond
        the clouds, comes into skies of pines on rocky tops.

Thus when I saw the strawberries, I rose into the singing trees
10   and the angels, white
sharks in a glittering sea,
        massacred me.
My blood drops still to the red pulp of wild strawberries
whose white shark flowers
15   will call any man into the waters of the boughs.

Oh my mind runs down the moon's glass tears
and plucks them up (tektites) frozen from the land.

        No creation equals a moment's consciousness.
        No cymbal cones and crashes peaks so.
20   No white shark stabs so.

Along the blade the dune thistle blows,
opening thorny hemispheres
of yellow florets half-deep in purple stain,
        and spears of onion grass rise sleek and clean
25   from the gray and gritty sand.
To stand with landward hair enduring these
requires sharks in the eyes, the backing of seas.

The coffin-carrier cries and the crow "cars" over the salt creeks.

2.

Event

        The day after,
30   after the golden culminations and unfuneraled dead,
after the nuclear trees drifting
        on cloudy stems,
and the fruits of knowledge
and the knowledge of those golden high-capped trees,

35   flaking, settling out,
after the transfigurations
and dark visitations,
        groans and twitching resentments,
after the golden culminations
40   and the trunks of violent trees stalking the vacant land,
        there rose an irrelevant dawn:

the white shell lay spiraled on the beach as it had lain
and the surf, again unheard,
        eased to primal rhythms
45   of jellyfishing heart, breaking into mind;
ants came out and withered in the sun;
        the white shark
sucked at the edge of the sea on the silent, scarlet morning;

and all the white souls sailing
50   sailed, funneling out into eternity;
        by the wharf, dolphin bobbled
belly-up with his poet, all his nudging sea-cleaning done;
briery the earth, iced
        with bones, rolled into time.

3.

Contraction

55   Repenting creation, God said,
        As you know, I Am,
God,
because I do not have to be consistent:
what was lawful to my general plan
60   does not jibe
with my new specific will;
what the old law healed
is reopened
        in the new.
65   I have drawn up many covenants to eternity.

Returning silence unto silence,
the Sumerian between the rivers lies.
His skull crushed and moded into rock
    does not leak or peel.
70   The gold earring lies in the powder
of his silken, perished lobe.
The incantations, sheep trades, and night-gatherings
    with central leaping fires,
roar and glare still in the crow's-foot
75   walking of his stylus on clay.
Under surgery the sick man rolls and
    vomits on the temple floor,
the anesthetic words of reciting priests
licking grooves through his frantic mind.
80   The dust has dried up all his tears.
    He sleeps out the old unending drug of time.

The rose dies, man dies, the world dies, the god
grows and fails, the born universe dies
    into renewal,
85   and all endures the change,
totally lost and totally retained.

1957 (1959)

Guide

    You cannot come to unity and remain material:
in that perception is no perceiver:
    when you arrive
you have gone too far:
5   at the Source you are in the mouth of Death:

you cannot
    turn around in
the Absolute: there are no entrances or exits
    no precipitations of forms

10   to use like tongs against the formless:
            no freedom to choose:

to be
            you have to stop not-being and break
off from *is* to *flowing* and
15   this is the sin you weep and praise:
origin is your original sin:
            the return you long for will ease your guilt
and you will have your longing:

            the wind that is my guide said this: it
20   should know having
                given up everything to eternal being but
direction:

how I said can I be glad and sad: but a man goes
            from one foot to the other:
25   wisdom wisdom:
                to be glad and sad at once is also unity
and death:
            wisdom wisdom: a peachblossom blooms on a particular
tree on a particular day:
30   unity cannot do anything in particular:

are these the thoughts you want me to think I said but
            the wind was gone and there was no more knowledge then.

                                                    1959 (1960)

Expressions of Sea Level

        Peripherally the ocean
        marks itself
            against the gauging land
        it erodes and
5   builds:

——————

it is hard to name
the changeless:
speech without words,
    silence renders it:
10   and mid-ocean,

sky sealed unbroken to sea,
    there is no way to know
the ocean's speech,
intervolved and markless,
15   breaking against

    no boulder-held fingerland:
broken, surf things are expressions:
the sea speaks far from its core,
far from its center relinquishes the
20   long-held roar:

of any mid-sea
speech, the yielding resistances
of wind and water, spray,
swells, whitecaps, moans,
25   it is a dream the sea makes,

an inner problem, a self-deep
dark and private anguish
    revealed in small,
by hints, to
30   keen watchers on the shore:

only with the staid land
is the level conversation really held:
only in the meeting of rock and
    sea is
35   hard relevance shattered into light:

upbeach the clam shell
    holds smooth dry sand,
remembrance of tide:

water can go at
40   least that high: in

       the night, if you stay
to watch, or
if you come tomorrow at the right time,
you can see the shell caught
45   again in wash, the

sand turbulence changed,
new sand left smooth: if
the shell washes loose,
flops over,
50   buries its rim in flux,

it will not be silence for
a shell that spoke: the
       half-buried back will
tell how the ocean dreamed
55   breakers against the land:

into the salt marshes the water comes fast with rising tide:
an inch of rise spreads by yards
       through tidal creeks, round fingerways of land:
the marsh grasses stem-logged
60   combine wind and water motions,
       slow from dry trembling
to heavier motions of wind translated through
cushioned stems; tide-held slant of grasses
       bent into the wind:

65   is there a point of rest where
       the tide turns: is there one
       infinitely tiny higher touch
on the legs of egrets, the
skin of back, bay-eddy reeds:
70   is there an instant when fullness is,
       without loss, complete: is there a
       statement perfect in its speech:

how do you know the moon
is moving: see the dry
75   casting of the beach worm
       dissolve at the
delicate rising touch:

that is the
      expression of sea level,
80   the talk of giants,
of ocean, moon, sun, of everything,
spoken in a dampened grain of sand.

1962 (1963)

Unsaid

Have you listened for the things I have left out?
I am nowhere near the end yet and already
      hear
    the hum of omissions,
5   the chant of vacancies, din of

silences:

there is the other side of matter, antimatter,
      the antiproton:
    we
10   have measured the proton: it has mass: we
have measured the antiproton: it has negative mass:

you will not

hear me completely even at this early point
unless you hear my emptiness:
15   go back:
    how can I
tell you what I have not said: you must look for it

———

yourself: that

side has weight, too, though words cannot bear it
20   out: listen for the things I have left out:
            I am
            aware
of them, as you must be, or you will miss

the non-song

25   in my singing: it is not that words *cannot* say
what is missing: it is only that what is missing
                cannot
            be missed if
spoken: read the parables of my unmaking:

30   feel the ris-

ing bubble's trembling walls: rush into the domes
these wordy arches shape: hear
            me
            when I am
35   silent: gather the boundaried vacancies.

                                1959 (1963)

Mechanism

Honor a going thing, goldfinch, corporation, tree,
            morality: any working order,
        animate or inanimate: it

has managed directed balance,
5   the incoming and outgoing energies are working right,
        some energy left to the mechanism,

some ash, enough energy held
            to maintain the order in repair,
        assure further consumption of entropy,

10   expending energy to strengthen order:
              honor the persisting reactor,
              the container of change, the moderator: the yellow

bird flashes black wing-bars
              in the new-leaving wild cherry bushes by the bay,
15   startles the hawk with beauty,

flitting to a branch where
              flash vanishes into stillness,
              hawk addled by the sudden loss of sight:

honor the chemistries, platelets, hemoglobin kinetics,
20   the light-sensitive iris, the enzymic intricacies
              of control,

the gastric transformations, seed
              dissolved to acrid liquors, synthesized into
              chirp, vitreous humor, knowledge,

25   blood compulsion, instinct: honor the
              unique genes,
              molecules that reproduce themselves, divide into

sets, the nucleic grain transmitted
              in slow change through ages of rising and falling form,
30   some cells set aside for the special work, mind

or perception rising into orders of courtship,
              territorial rights, mind rising
              from the physical chemistries

to guarantee that genes will be exchanged, male
35   and female met, the satisfactions cloaking a deeper
              racial satisfaction:

heat kept by a feathered skin:
>   the living alembic, body heat maintained (bunsen
>   burner under the flask)

40   so the chemistries can proceed, reaction rates
>   interdependent, self-adjusting, with optimum
>   efficiency—the vessel firm, the flame

staying: isolated, contained reactions! the precise and
>   necessary worked out of random, reproducible,
45   the handiwork redeemed from chance, while the

goldfinch, unconscious of the billion operations
>   that stay its form, flashes, chirping (not a
>   great songster) in the bay cherry bushes wild of leaf.

1959

Batsto

>   After two gray sunless days of warm
>   noreaster windy rains the sun breaking
>   clear this morning, over the bayside
>   field the sparrowhawk foraging in the
5   oval air, we took Route 9 north through
>   Pleasantville, past the pleasant
>   inviting cemetery crisp with light,
>   over the railroad, crosstown to the
>   Absecon meadows and into the sycamore
10   leaf-letting hills beyond and through
>   the housing development with groves
>   of old leaf-keeping darker oaks and

>   northward past Seaview Country Club
>   with the high round dining room and
15   young rich men in casuals crossing the
>   street to the golf-links and on past
>   fields and hedges, the scarlotry of

maple leaves, sassafras and skinny
birch resplendent in the clean sun,
20 the winding flat highway, empty
but for slight local traffic, and onto
Garden State Parkway to bridge the
wide-mouthed Mullica River that spreads
out in brown still meadows to the sea,
25 an occasional gull, the skeletal
cedar upriver against the land, off
to secondary roads not too well marked
and along the north bank of the
Mullica westward into the Wharton
30 Tract, now a state park, with ghost
towns and endless acres in neglect,

stopping at a pinerise to see the
cemetery of the French family, death
after more than a century light as
35 the morning sun, where Thomas French,
a year older than his wife, lies since
1844, his wife three years later
giving up her heavy grief, lying
down beside him, their secret union
40 invisible in the green needles of
the great pine that branches now
into their rest, looking where Levi
Scott, four years old in 1800, went
down beneath his thin tall slab, may
45 the child keep innocent of treason, and

on to Crowley Landing on the left
between river and road, now a campsite
and picnic ground, where we took
pictures, wild mullein starring the
50 grounds, a yucca group with dead
flower-spears off in a clearing, in
the center a mound of old chimney
bricks with wasp dust and gold grasses
and a yard tree, broken off, with

55   slender sprouts nude, swamp cedar
        standing around in clumps like persons
        edging the openings, by the river now
        narrower twists of white birch
        thin-twigged and leafless, and

60   around two curves to Batsto, the
        tower of the mansion house first seen,
        like the towers of shore women gazing
        the sea's return, a confluence of
        roads and streams, the bog-iron works
65   and Revolutionary cannon balls, iron
        hearths and iron oxen-shoes, seeing
        a nail made and headed from nail rod,
        the company store, and men from
        Trenton writing the place up for the
70   Sunday paper, wasps drunk with fall
        warmth, a beautiful November noon by
        the grist mill and the meal-honed
        wood, the carriage house and small
        seats, the sty with the iron-bowled
75   furnace for scalding, on the third
        floor of the mansion a strict stairway
        to the slaves' underground railroad,
        and

        weakening to the presence of a foreign
80   past and to the keeping of old things,
        back home by Route 30 and the White
        Horse Pike, by the farmers' stands,
        Naval Air Base and to the sea's edge.

1957 (1961)

Mansion

So it came time
    for me to cede myself
and I chose

the wind
5   to be delivered to

The wind was glad
         and said it needed all
the body
it could get
10   to show its motions with

and wanted to know
         willingly as I hoped it would
if it could do
something in return
15   to show its gratitude

When the tree of my bones
         rises from the skin I said
come and whirlwinding
stroll my dust
20   around the plain

so I can see
         how the ocotillo does
and how saguaro-wren is
and when you fall
25   with evening

fall with me here
         where we can watch
the closing up of day
and think how morning breaks

1959 (1960)

Close-Up

Are all these stones
         yours
I said

and the mountain
5 pleased

but reluctant to
admit my praise could move it much

shook a little
and rained a windrow ring of stones
10 to show
that it was so

Stonefelled I got
up addled with dust

and shook
15   myself
without much consequence

Obviously I said it doesn't pay
to get too
close up to
20   greatness

and the mountain friendless wept
          and said
it couldn't help
itself

1958 (1959)

Mountain Liar

The mountains said they were
      tired of lying down
and wanted to know what
      I could do about
5 getting them off the ground

———

Well close your eyes I said
    and I'll see if I can
by seeing into your nature
    tell where you've been wronged
10   What do you think you want to do
    They said Oh fly

My hands are old
    and crippled keep no lyre
but if that is your true desire
15   and conforms roughly
with your nature I said
    I don't see why
we shouldn't try
    to see something along that line

20   Hurry they said and snapped shut
    with rocky sounds their eyes
I closed mine and sure enough
    the whole range flew
gliding on interstellar ice

25   They shrieked with joy and peeked
    as if to see below
but saw me as before there
    foolish without my lyre
We haven't budged they said
30   You wood

(1958)

Prospecting

Coming to cottonwoods, an
orange rockshelf,
and in the gully
an edging of stream willows,

———

5   I made camp
and turned my mule loose
to graze in the dark
evening of the mountain.

Drowsed over the coals
10   and my loneliness
like an inner image went
out and shook
hands with the willows,

and running up the black scarp
15   tugged the heavy moon
up and over into light,

and on a hill-thorn of sage
called with the coyotes
and told ghost stories to
20   a night circle of lizards.
Tipping on its handle
the Dipper unobtrusively
poured out the night.

At dawn returning, wet
25   to the hips with meetings,
my loneliness woke me up
and we merged refreshed into
the breaking of camp and day.

1958 (1960)

Jersey Cedars

The wind inclines the cedars and lets
snow riding in
bow them

       swaying weepers
5   on the hedgerows of
        open fields

black-green branches stubby fans under snow
bent spires dipping at the ground

Oh said the cedars will spring let us rise
10   and I said rain
will thawing
          unburden you
        and will
          they said
15   we stand again green-cone arrows at the sun
The forces I said are already set up

but they splintering in that deep soft day
could not herd
their moans
20   into my quiet speech
        and I bent
      over arms

dangling loose to wind and snow to be
with them assailing the earth with moans

1958 (1960)

Hardweed Path Going

      Every evening, down into the hardweed
going,
the slop bucket heavy, held-out, wire handle
freezing in the hand, put it down a minute, the jerky
5   smooth unspilling levelness of the knees,
      meditation of a bucket rim,
lest the wheat meal,
floating on clear greasewater, spill,
down the grown-up path:

10   don't forget to slop the hogs,
            feed the chickens,
            water the mule,
            cut the kindling,
            build the fire,
15   call up the cow:

            supper is over, it's starting to get
dark early,
better get the scraps together, mix a little meal in,
nothing but swill.

20   The dead-purple woods hover on the west.
I know those woods.
Under the tall, ceiling-solid pines, beyond the edge of
field and brush, where the wild myrtle grows,
            I let my jo-reet loose.
25   A jo-reet is a bird. Nine weeks of summer he
sat on the well bench in a screened box,
a stick inside to walk on,
            "jo-reet," he said, "jo-reet."
            and I
30   would come up to the well and draw the bucket down
deep into the cold place where red and white marbled
clay oozed the purest water, water celebrated
throughout the county:
            "Grits all gone?"
35   "jo-reet."
Throw a dipper of cold water on him. Reddish-black
flutter.
            "reet, reet, reet!"

            Better turn him loose before
40   cold weather comes on.
            Doom caving in
            inside
            any pleasure, pure
            attachment
45   of love.

Beyond the wild myrtle away from cats I turned him loose
and his eye asked me what to do, where to go;
he hopped around, scratched a little, but looked up at me.
Don't look at me. Winter is coming.
50 Disappear in the bushes. I'm tired of you and will
be alone hereafter. I will go dry in my well.
    I will turn still.
Go south. Grits is not available in any natural form.
Look under leaves, try mushy logs, the floors of pinywoods.
55 South into the dominion of bugs.

    They're good woods.
But lay me out if a mourning dove far off in the dusky pines
    starts.

    Down the hardweed path going,
60 leaning, balancing, away from the bucket, to
Sparkle, my favorite hog, sparse, fine black hair,
grunted while feeding if rubbed,
scratched against the hair, or if talked to gently:
got the bottom of the slop bucket:
65   "Sparkle . . .
   You hungry?
   Hungry, girly?"
blowing, bubbling in the trough.

    Waiting for the first freeze:
70 "Think it's going to freeze tonight?" say the neighbors,
the neighbors, going by.

   Hog-killing.

Oh, Sparkle, when the axe tomorrow morning falls
and the rush is made to open your throat,
75 I will sing, watching dry-eyed as a man, sing my
    love for you in the tender feedings.

She's nothing but a hog, boy.

Bleed out, Sparkle, the moon-chilled bleaches
      of your body hanging upside-down
80   hardening through the mind and night of the first freeze.

1958 (1960)

Bourn

    When I got past relevance
    the singing shores
    told me to turn back

    but I took the outward gray
5   to be
    some meaning of foreign light

    trying to get through and
    when I looked back I saw
    the shores were dancing

10   willows of grief and
    from willows it was not far to
    look back on waves

    So I came to
    the decimal of being,
15   entered and was gone

    What light there
    no tongue turns to tell
    to willow and calling shore

    though willows weep and shores sing always

1958 (1960)

Grassy Sound

It occurred to me there are no
    sharp corners
      in the wind
and I was very glad to think
5   I had so close
      a neighbor
to my thoughts but decided to
    sleep before
      inquiring

10   The next morning I got up early
      and after yesterday had come
        clear again went
down to the salt marshes
    to talk with
15   the straight wind there
I have observed I said
    your formlessness
      and am

enchanted to know how
20   you manage loose to be
      so influential

The wind came as grassy sound
    and between its
      grassy teeth
25   spoke words said with grass
    and read itself
      on tidal creeks as on
the screens of oscilloscopes
    A heron opposing
30   it rose wing to wind

turned and glided to another creek
    so I named a body of water

                    Grassy Sound
            and came home dissatisfied there
35   had been no
                direct reply
            but rubbed with my soul an
                apple to eat
                    till it shone

                                        1958 (1959)

Silver

        I thought Silver must have snaked logs
            when young:
    she couldn't stand to have the line brush her lower hind leg:
    in blinded halter she couldn't tell what had loosened behind her
5   and was coming
    as downhill
    to rush into her crippling her to the ground:

    and when she almost went to sleep, me dreaming at the slow plow,
    I would
10 at dream's end turning over the mind to a new chapter
                let the line drop and touch her leg
                and she would
    bring the plow out of the ground with speed but wisely
    fall soon again into the slow requirements of our dreams:
15 how we turned at the ends of rows without sense to new furrows
    and went back
                flicked by
            cornblades and hearing the circling in
    the cornblades of horseflies in pursuit:

20   I hitch up early, the raw spot on Silver's shoulder
    sore to the collar,
    get a wrench and change the plow's bull-tongue for a sweep,
    and go out, wrench in my hip pocket for later adjustments,
                down the ditch-path

25   by the white-bloomed briars, wet crabgrass, cattails,
                 and rusting ferns,
    riding the plow handles down,
       keeping the sweep's point from the ground,
    the smooth bar under the plow gliding,
30   the traces loose, the raw spot wearing its soreness out
    in the gentle movement to the fields:

          when snake-bitten in the spring pasture grass
    Silver came up to the gate and stood head-down enchanted
           in her fate
35   I found her sorrowful eyes by accident and knew:
    nevertheless the doctor could not keep her from all
    the consequences, rolls in the sand, the blank extension
          of limbs,
         head thrown back in the dust,
40   useless unfocusing eyes, belly swollen
    wide as I was tall
    and I went out in the night and saw her in the solitude
          of her wildness:

    but she lived and one day half got up
45   and looking round at the sober world took me back
        into her eyes
    and then got up and walked and plowed again;
    mornings her swollen snake-bitten leg wept bright as dew
    and dried to streaks of salt leaked white from the hair.

1958 (1960)

Concentrations

I.

By the ocean
dawn is
more itself,

———

nets hung like
5 mist on
      pole-racks or

spread out for mending, weed-picking, corking—

      landreefs of gray
      waves
10   between the poles:

      and the gray
      boats, turtle-nosed,
         beached, out

      of element, waiting,
15   salt-bleached,
         keels, hauled

      across the sand,
      ground to
         wood-ghosts,

20   sand-ghost gray:
      and if there
         is fog,

dawn, becoming itself as reeds, dunes, sheds,

      transfuses it,
25   opening
         dune-rose-wise

petal by petal—wave, net, boat, oar, thole:

II.

under the reedthatched or pineboughed sheds
dawn men,
30 opening gray eyes to gray light,

yawn out of the silver nets of dreams
and harden as entities,
their minds hardening the entities they seek:

III.

  how you catch a fish, slime-quick
35 with dart and turn,
  loose in the medium:

  remove the water,
  letting down dams: in pike pools,
  maybe looking for bait, dip

40 the water out,
  concentrate the residue, increase
  the incidence (you can

  catch fry
  with your hands then, clutching
45 the silver lights against the mud:)

  if you can't remove
  the water, change it, as
  by muddying: swamp

  ponds yield their fruit to this:
50 churn up the bottom,
  suffocate the brim,

  bluegills, "flowers," so they
  rise to breathe:
  seining

55 then is good: it
  ridding lets the water through,
  thickens the impermeables:

        (you round-up a tiger,
        isolate a compound, the same way:
60   surrounding, eliminating the habitat and

        closing in
        on a center or pass
        or tiger-run along a river:)

                        IV.

        the men rise from sand and sleep,
65   wheel the boat,
        strung like a turtle
            under a giant cart,
        to the sea's edge:

        dropped free,
70   the oared boat
        leaps, nosing into the surf,
            and spilling
        the net astern,
            semicircles back
75   to land:

        hauled in, the net is
            a windrow of fish,
        gathered into thin, starving air,
            the ocean, sucking, returned whole
80   to itself, separation complete,

        fish from sea, tiger
            from jungle, vision from experience.

                                    1959 (1962)

                    River

        I shall
            go down

          to the deep river, to the moonwaters,
     where the silver
5   willows are and the bay blossoms,

     to the songs
        of dark birds,
           to the great wooded silence
     of flowing
10   forever down the dark river

     silvered at the moon-singing of hidden birds:

     27 March

     the forsythia is out,
        sprawling like
15   yellow amoebae, the long
           uneven branches—pseudo-
     podia—
        angling on the bottom
     of air's spring-clear pool:

20   shall I
        go down
           to the deep river, to the moonwaters,
     where the silver
     willows are and the bay blossoms,

25   to the songs
        of dark birds,
           to the great wooded silence
     of flowing
     forever down the dark river

30   silvered at the moon-singing of hidden birds.

                                    c. 1955–1960 (1960)

Motion for Motion

Watched on the sandy, stony bottom of the stream
the oval black shadow of the waterbeetle, shadow

larger than beetle, though no blacker, mirroring
at a down and off angle motion for motion, whirl, run:

5   (if I knew the diameters
      of oval and beetle, the
      depth of the stream, several
            indices of refraction
            and so forth

10   I might say why
      the shadow outsizes the
      beetle—

      I admit to mystery
      in the obvious—

15   but now that I remember some
      I think the shadow
      included the bent water where
      the beetle rode, surface

      tension, not breaking, bending
20   under to hold him up,

      the deformation recorded in shade:
      for light, arising from so far away,

      is parallel
      through a foot of water
25   (though edge-light
      would

      make a difference—a beetle can
      exist among such differences
      and do well):

30   someone has a clear vision of it all,
         exact to complete existence;
         loves me when I swear and praise
         and smiles, probably, to see me
         wrestle with sight

35   and gain no reason from it, or money,
         but a blurred mind overexposed):

caught the sudden gust of a catbird, selfshot
under the bridge and out into my sight: he splashed
into the air near a briervine, lit:

40   I don't know by what will: it was clear sailing
on down the stream
and prettier—a moss-bright island made two streams
and then made one and, farther, two fine birches
and a lot of things to see: but he stopped

45   back to me,
didn't see me, hopped on through the vines, by some
will not including me . . .

and then there were two beetles, and later three at
once swimming in the sun, and three shadows,
50   all reproduced, multiplied without effort
or sound, the unique beetle—and I—lost to an

automatic machinery in things, duplicating, without
useful difference, some changeless order extending
backward beyond the origin of earth,

55   changeless and true, even before the water fell, or
the sun broke, or the beetle turned, or the still
human head bent from a bridge-rail above to have a look.

1961 (1963)

Identity

1)   An individual spider web
identifies a species:
an order of instinct prevails
through all accidents of circumstance,
though possibility is
high along the peripheries of
spider
webs:
you can go all
around the fringing attachments

and find
disorder ripe,
entropy rich, high levels of random,
numerous occasions of accident:

2)   the possible settings
of a web are infinite:

how does
the spider keep
identity
while creating the web
in a particular place?

how and to what extent
and by what modes of chemistry
and control?

it is
wonderful
how things work: I will tell you
about it
because

———————

30   it is interesting
and because whatever is
moves in weeds
        and stars and spider webs
and known
35   is loved:
      in that love,
      each of us knowing it,
      I love you,

for it moves within and beyond us,
40   sizzles in
winter grasses, darts and hangs with bumblebees
by summer windowsills:

         I will show you
the underlying that takes no image to itself,
45   cannot be shown or said,
but weaves in and out of moons and bladderweeds,
        is all and
      beyond destruction
      because created fully in no
50   particular form:

          if the web were perfectly pre-set,
         the spider could
    never find
    a perfect place to set it in: and

55   if the web were
perfectly adaptable,
if freedom and possibility were without limit,
        the web would
lose its special identity:

———————

60   the row-strung garden web
  keeps order at the center
 where space is freest (interesting that the freest
    "medium" should
   accept the firmest order)

65 and that
  order
      diminishes toward the
 periphery
   allowing at the points of contact
70   entropy equal to entropy.

             1961 (1963)

What This Mode of Motion Said

  You will someday
 try to prove me wrong
 (I am the wings when you me fly)
 to replace me with some mode
5   you made
 and think is right:

  I am the way by
  which you prove me
   wrong,
10   the reason you
  reason against me:

 I change shape,
 turn easily into the shapes you make
  and even you
15   in moving
 I leave, betray:

   ———

what has not yet been imagined has been
imagined by me
    whom you honor, reach for—
20 change unending though
slowed into nearly limited modes:

        question me and I
        will give you an answer

narrow and definite
25 as the question
        that devours you (the exact

is a conquest of time that time vanquishes)
        or vague as wonder
by which I elude you:

30   pressed
            for certainty
I harden to a stone,
lie unimaginable in meaning
        at your feet,

35   leave you less
certainty than you brought, leave
        you to create the stone
as any image of yourself,
shape of your dreams:

40   pressed too far
I wound, returning endless
inquiry
for the pride of inquiry:

            shapeless, unspendable,
45   powerless in the actual
            which I rule, I

            ———

will not
make deposits in your bank account
or free you from bosses
50   in little factories,
will not spare you insult, will not
protect you from
men who
      have never heard of modes, who
55   do not respect me
or your knowledge of me in you;
            men I let win,
their thin tight lips
humiliating my worshippers:

60   I betray
him who gets me in his eyes and sees
            beyond the fact
to the motions of my permanence.

1961

Still

I said I will find what is lowly
      and put the roots of my identity
      down there:
each day I'll wake up
5   and find the lowly nearby,
      a handy focus and reminder,
a ready measure of my significance,
the voice by which I would be heard,
the wills, the kinds of selfishness
10   I could
freely adopt as my own:

but though I have looked everywhere,
      I can find nothing

to give myself to:
15   everything is

magnificent with existence, is in
surfeit of glory:
nothing is diminished,
nothing has been diminished for me:

20   I said what is more lowly than the grass:
             ah, underneath,
             a ground-crust of dry-burnt moss:
             I looked at it closely
      and said this can be my habitat: but
25   nestling in I
      found
             below the brown exterior
             green mechanisms beyond intellect
      awaiting resurrection in rain: so I got up

30   and ran saying there is nothing lowly in the universe:
      I found a beggar:
      he had stumps for legs: nobody was paying
      him any attention: everybody went on by:
             I nestled in and found his life:
35   there, love shook his body like a devastation:
      I said
             though I have looked everywhere
             I can find nothing lowly
             in the universe:

40   I whirled through transfigurations up and down,
      transfigurations of size and shape and place:
             at one sudden point came still,
             stood in wonder:
      moss, beggar, weed, tick, pine, self, magnificent
45   with being!

1962 (1963)

The Golden Mean

What does
wisdom say:
wisdom says
do not put too much stress
5   on doing; sit some and wait,
if you can get
that self-contained:
but do not sit too much;
being can wear thin
10   without experience:
not too much stress on thrift
at the expense of living;
immaterial things like
life must be conserved against
15   materiality: however,
spending every dime you make
can exhaust all boundaries,
destroy resources and
recovery's means:
20   not too much stress on knowledge;
understanding, too, is a
high faculty
that should bear pleasurably on facts;
ordering, aligning,
25   comparing,
as processes, become diffuse in too
much massiveness:
but the acquisition
of thinking stuff is crucial
30   to knowledge
and to understanding:
wisdom says
do not love exceedingly:
you must withhold
35   enough to weather loss;
however, love thoroughly
and with the body

so women will respect and fear the little
    man: though dainty
40   they will scoff
when not profoundly had: not too much
    mind over body or
      body over mind;
they are united in this life and should
45   blend to dual good or ill:
      and do not stress
wisdom too much: if you lean neither
    way, the golden
      mean narrows
50   and rather than a way becomes a wire,
    or altogether
      vanishes, a
hypothetical line from which extremes
    perpendicularly begin:
55   and if you do not
violate wisdom to some extent,
    committing yourself fully,
      without reserve,
and foolishly, you will not become *one*,
60   capable of direction,
      selected to a single aim,
and you will be notable for nothing:
    nothing in excess is
      excessive nothingness:
65   go: but wisdom says do not go too far.

1959 (1960)

Nucleus

How you buy a factory:
    got wind of one for sale in

Montreal,
    Hochelaga

5   where Cartier, amicably received,
               gave the squaws and children

tin bells and tin paternosters
and the men knives
               and went up to the nearby
10   height and
               called it Mt. Royal
from which the view was
panoramic,
               an island 17 × 40
15   miles,
                    good trees (good as France)
                    and, below, thick maize:

Montreal,
               got "The Laurentian" out of New York
20   first morning after the strike ended
and rode up parlor-car (expense account)
               along the solid-white Hudson
               and on up into hilled
graybirch country, through the Adirondacks
25   and along the high west bank of Lake Champlain
               (on heavy ice
               men in windhuts fishing)

               and read Bottom
               and "gives to airy nothing
30   A local habitation and a name":

               met the vice president
in the lobby at 8 next morning, ascended
(étage de confrères, troisième étage, s'il vous plaît,
               third floor, please)
35   to the 22nd floor
               to "The Panorama"
for breakfast: sight to see: St. Lawrence over there,
Windsor Hotel remodeling, where the Queen stayed,

cathedral, replica (but smaller)
40   of St. Peter's:

Montreal,
and left center city by cab,
     through the French Quarter, out near Westmont,
long stairs from street to second floor,
45   said it was typical,
with metal viny rails,

       and on through streets, bilingual
traffic signs, turn left, left again: there:
Linden Sreet: 807, a local habitation and a name,

50   four walls, a limited, defined, exact place,
        a nucleus,
solidification from possibility:

       how you buy a factory:
determine the lines of
55   force
leading in and out, origins, destinations of lines;
determine how
       from the nexus of crossed and bundled lines
        the profit is
60   obtained, the
forces realized, the cheap made dear,
and whether the incoming or outgoing forces are stronger
and exactly why,
and what is to be done:

65   raw material inventory is
in winter
high: river frozen, must make half-year provisions,
squirrel-like, last till thaw, is
a warehousing problem: comes from England,
70   Germany (West):
        important to keep a ready

stock of finished goods—customers won't wait, will
order from parent companies in England, Germany:

    property taxes: things are
75   changing, you may get a rail siding here soon:
        profit and loss sheet, cash flow, receivables:
       large lot, vacancy providing for the future:
good machineshop and
         here are the production lines:
80   how many heads on those machines: pcs per hr:
          wages, skilled
unskilled: cut-off machines, annealing ovens, formers:
      "I'll say! 15 below this morning."

order backlog: "I would say we have
85   an edge,
growth possibility: 50 good customers, pharm-
aceutical houses: you have to understand the background."
      Perspective.

"Eight years ago . . . finally, I had to go to
90   Ottawa . . . left good man here, Oh, yes, he's done
fine . . . Swiss, later in Johannesburg;
      you understand, management
         wouldn't consider
selling him out, too much of himself": un-

95   favorable points: competition, international market,
low tariffs,
unprotected, only advantage personalized service
      to local
accounts, could
100   buy elsewhere,
large firms in States have bigger machines, faster,
more production per hour

(more overhead, too)

———

"being small's our advantage . . . can adapt, work with
105   short runs of specialties—customers want
            their own designs, premium,
        made-to-order prices . . ."

        Montreal,
            "sure to see McGill U., ice sculpture front of
110   each dorm, emblem"
        cornless lawns,
                Cartier going through the motions of worship,
        Indians looking up at sky, too,
        can't see what:

115   "We'll get that information to you"
                further study
        and in the deep cold night boarding train, bedroom,
        Yassuh,
        and heat connections broken, cold, next morning
120   going uptrain for toast and coffee,
        that's where East River turns—Manhattan:
        lines of force, winding, unwinding,
            nexus coiling in the mind:
                balance, judge: act.
                                                    1961

CORSONS INLET (1965)

for Family, for Friends

❧

Visit

It is not far to my place:
you can come smallboat,
pausing under shade in the eddies
    or going ashore
5   to rest, regard the leaves

or talk with birds and
shore weeds: hire a full grown man not
late in years to oar you
    and choose a canoe-like thin ship:
10   (a dumb man is better and no

costlier; he will attract
the reflections and silences under leaves:)
travel light: a single book, some twine:
    the river is muscled at rapids with trout
15   and a birch limb

will make a suitable spit: if you
leave in the forenoon, you will arrive
with plenty of light
    the afternoon of the third day: I will
20   come down to the landing

(tell your man to look for it,
the dumb have clear sight and are free of
visions) to greet you with some made
    wine and a special verse:
25   or you can come by shore:

———

choose the right: there the rocks
cascade less frequently, the grade more gradual:
treat yourself gently: the ascent thins both
    mind and blood and you must
30   keep still a dense reserve

of silence we can poise against
conversation: there is little news:
I found last month a root with shape and
    have heard a new sound among
35   the insects: come.

1961 (1962)

Moment

He turned and
stood

in the moment's
height,

5   exhilaration
sucking him up,

shuddering and
lifting

him
10   jaw and bone

and he said
what

destruction am I
blessed by?

1963 (1963)

Winter Scene

There is now not a single
leaf on the cherry tree:

except when the jay
plummets in, lights, and,

5   in pure clarity, squalls:
then every branch

quivers and
breaks out in blue leaves.

1963 (1964)

Corsons Inlet

I went for a walk over the dunes again this morning
to the sea,
then turned right along
    the surf

5   rounded a naked headland
    and returned

    along the inlet shore:

it was muggy sunny, the wind from the sea steady and high,
crisp in the running sand,
10   some breakthroughs of sun
  but after a bit

continuous overcast:

the walk liberating, I was released from forms,
from the perpendiculars,
15   straight lines, blocks, boxes, binds
of thought

into the hues, shadings, rises, flowing bends and blends
of sight:

I allow myself eddies of meaning:
20 yield to a direction of significance
running
like a stream through the geography of my work:
you can find
in my sayings
25 swerves of action
like the inlet's cutting edge:
there are dunes of motion,
organizations of grass, white sandy paths of remembrance
in the overall wandering of mirroring mind:

30 but Overall is beyond me: is the sum of these events
I cannot draw, the ledger I cannot keep, the accounting
beyond the account:

in nature there are few sharp lines: there are areas of
primrose
35 more or less dispersed;
disorderly orders of bayberry; between the rows
of dunes,
irregular swamps of reeds,
though not reeds alone, but grass, bayberry, yarrow, all . . .
40 predominantly reeds:

I have reached no conclusions, have erected no boundaries,
shutting out and shutting in, separating inside
from outside: I have
drawn no lines:
45 as

manifold events of sand
change the dune's shape that will not be the same shape
tomorrow,

———

so I am willing to go along, to accept
50 the becoming
thought, to stake off no beginnings or ends, establish
   no walls:

by transitions the land falls from grassy dunes to creek
to undercreek: but there are no lines, though
55 change in that transition is clear
   as any sharpness: but "sharpness" spread out,
allowed to occur over a wider range
than mental lines can keep:

the moon was full last night: today, low tide was low:
60 black shoals of mussels exposed to the risk
of air
and, earlier, of sun,
waved in and out with the waterline, waterline inexact,
caught always in the event of change:
65 a young mottled gull stood free on the shoals
   and ate

to vomiting: another gull, squawking possession, cracked a crab,
picked out the entrails, swallowed the soft-shelled legs, a ruddy
turnstone running in to snatch leftover bits:

70 risk is full: every living thing in
siege: the demand is life, to keep life: the small
white blacklegged egret, how beautiful, quietly stalks and spears
   the shallows, darts to shore
     to stab—what? I couldn't
75 see against the black mudflats—a frightened
  fiddler crab?

   the news to my left over the dunes and
reeds and bayberry clumps was
   fall: thousands of tree swallows
80   gathering for flight:
   an order held
   in constant change: a congregation

rich with entropy: nevertheless, separable, noticeable
        as one event,
85   not chaos: preparations for
flight from winter,
cheet, cheet, cheet, cheet, wings rifling the green clumps,
beaks
at the bayberries:
90   a perception full of wind, flight, curve,
     sound:
     the possibility of rule as the sum of rulelessness:
the "field" of action
with moving, incalculable center:

95   in the smaller view, order tight with shape:
blue tiny flowers on a leafless weed: carapace of crab:
snail shell:
        pulsations of order
        in the bellies of minnows: orders swallowed,
100   broken down, transferred through membranes
to strengthen larger orders: but in the large view, no
lines or changeless shapes: the working in and out, together
        and against, of millions of events: this,
           so that I make
105   no form of
           formlessness:

orders as summaries, as outcomes of actions override
or in some way result, not predictably (seeing me gain
the top of a dune,
110   the swallows
could take flight—some other fields of bayberry
        could enter fall
        berryless) and there is serenity:

        no arranged terror: no forcing of image, plan,
115   or thought:
no propaganda, no humbling of reality to precept:

———

terror pervades but is not arranged, all possibilities
of escape open: no route shut, except in
   the sudden loss of all routes:

120   I see narrow orders, limited tightness, but will
not run to that easy victory:
       still around the looser, wider forces work:
       I will try
   to fasten into order enlarging grasps of disorder, widening
125 scope, but enjoying the freedom that
Scope eludes my grasp, that there is no finality of vision,
that I have perceived nothing completely,
     that tomorrow a new walk is a new walk.

                          1962 (1963)

Dunes

     Taking root in windy sand
        is not an easy
     way
     to go about
5   finding a place to stay.

     A ditchbank or wood's-edge
        has firmer ground.

     In a loose world though
        something can be started—
10   a root touch water,
        a tip break sand—

     Mounds from that can rise
        on held mounds,
     a gesture of building, keeping,
15   a trapping
     into shape.

     Firm ground is not available ground.

              1963 (1963)

Street Song

Like an
eddying willow leaf
I stand

on the street
5   and turn:
people,

both ways coming
and going
around me, swirl:

10   probably I
am no stiller—
detached; but

gold is
coming
15   into my veins.

1963 (1964)

Lines

Lines flying in, out: logarithmic
    curves coiling
toward an infinitely inward center: lines
    weaving in, threads lost in clustral scrawl,
5   weaving out into loose ends,
wandering beyond the border of gray background,
    going out of vision,
        not returning;
or, returning, breaking across the boundary
10   as new lines, discontinuous,
        come into sight:
fiddleheads of ferns, croziers of violins,
    convoluted spherical masses, breaking through

                    ditchbanks where briar

15   stem-dull will

                leave and bloom:

                        haunch line, sickle-like, turning down, bulging, nuzzling

                    under, closing into

                        the hidden, sweet, dark meeting of lips:

20   the spiraling out

                    or in

                        of galaxies:

                            the free-running wavy line, swirling

                    configuration, halting into a knot

25   of curve and density: the broken,

                            irreparable filament: tree-winding vines, branching,

                    falling off or back, free,

                        the adventitious preparation for possibility, from

                            branch to branch, ash to gum:

30   the breaker

                hurling into reach for shape, crashing

                    out of order, the inner hollow sizzling flat:

                the longnecked, uteral gourd, bass line

                    continuous in curve,

35   melodic line filling and thinning:

                    concentrations,

                        whirling masses,

                            thin leaders, disordered ends and risks:

                    explosions of clusters, expansions from the

40   full radial sphere; return's longest chance:

                        lines exploring, intersecting, paralleling, twisting,

                    noding: deranging, clustering.

                                            1960 (1963)

Coon Song

                I got one good look

                        in the raccoon's eyes

                                when he fell from the tree

                        came to his feet

5   and perfectly still

seized the baying hounds
in his dull fierce stare,
in that recognition all
decision lost,
10 choice irrelevant, before the
battle fell
and the unwinding
of his little knot of time began:

Dostoevsky would think
15 it important if the coon
could choose to
be back up the tree:
or if he could choose to be
wagging by a swamp pond,
20 dabbling at scuttling
crawdads: the coon may have
dreamed in fact of curling
into the holed-out gall
of a fallen oak some squirrel
25 had once brought
high into the air
clean leaves to: but

reality can go to hell
is what the coon's eyes said to me:
30 and said how simple
the solution to my
problem is: it needs only
not to be: I thought the raccoon
felt no anger,
35 saw none; cared nothing for cowardice,
bravery; was in fact
bored at
knowing what would ensue:
the unwinding, the whirling growls,
40 exposed tenders,
the wet teeth—a problem to be
solved, the taut-coiled vigor

of the hunt
ready to snap loose:

45   you want to know what happened,
you want to hear me describe it,
  to placate the hound's-mouth
    slobbering in your own heart:
I will not tell you: actually the coon
50   possessing secret knowledge
     pawed dust on the dogs
and they disappeared, yapping into
  nothingness, and the coon went
    down to the pond
55 and washed his face and hands and beheld
  the world: maybe he didn't:
    I am no slave that I
should entertain you, say what you want
  to hear, let you wallow in
60   your silt: one two three four five:
one two three four five six seven eight nine ten:
    (all this time I've been
     counting spaces
while you were thinking of something else)
65   mess in your own sloppy silt:
    the hounds disappeared
yelping (the way you would at extinction)
  into—the order
   breaks up here—immortality:
70 I know that's where you think the brave
  little victims should go:
   I do not care what
you think: I do not care what you think:
  I do not care what you
75   think: one two three four five
six seven eight nine ten: here we go
  round the here-we-go-round, the
    here-we-go-round, the here-we-
go-round: coon will end in disorder at the
80   teeth of hounds: the situation

will get him:
spheres roll, cubes stay put: now there
one two three four five
are two philosophies:
85   here we go round the mouth-wet of hounds:

what I choose
is youse:
baby

1959 (1963)

Portrait

Dry-leaf life
curls up on
lobe toes

and like a lost
5   or haunted crab
skitters

across the street,
fretting at
the wind,

10   or curled forward
tumbles down or
even up a

rise, gay and
light as a
15   spring catkin,

or boatlike strikes
a stream or, wet,
flattens

———

out stream-bottom
20   in windless
black: come,

wind, away from
water and let
song spring &

25   leap with this
paper-life's
lively show.

1963 (1964)

Jungle Knot

One morning Beebe
found on a bank of the Amazon
an owl and snake
dead in a coiled embrace:

5   the vine prints its coil too deep into the tree
and leaved fire shoots greens of tender flame
rising among the branches,
drawing behind a hardening, wooden clasp:

the tree does not
10   generally escape
though it may live thralled for years,
succumbing finally rather than at once,

in the vine's victory
the casting of its eventual death,
15   though it may live years
on the skeletal trunk,

termites rising, the rain softening,
a limb in storm

falling, the vine air-free at last, structureless as death:
20   the owl,

    Beebe says, underestimated
the anaconda's size: hunger had deformed
      sight or caution, or
anaconda, come out in moonlight on the river bank,

25   had left half his length in shade: (you
        sometimes tackle
more than just what the light shows):
      the owl struck talons

        back of the anaconda's head
30   but weight grounded him in surprise: the anaconda
      coiled, embracing heaving wings
and cry, and the talons, squeezed in, sank

killing snake and owl in tightened pain:
      errors of vision, errors of self-defense!
35   errors of wisdom, errors of desire!
        the vulture dives, unlocks four eyes.

1961 (1963)

Dark Song

    Sorrow how high it is
    that no wall holds it
    back: deep

    it is that no dam undermines
5   it: wide that it
    comes on as up a strand

    multiple and relentless:
    the young that are
    beautiful must die; the

10   old, departing,
can confer
nothing.

1963 (1964)

Resort

Beautiful nature,
say
the neuter lovers

escaping
5   man/woman nature,
man

fierce competitive,
woman
taunting

10   treacherous:
regenerative nature,
they say

fingering the cool
red-dotted lichen
15   on an old

water-holding
stump:
sweet neutrality,

a calm love where
20   man and woman
are fang & fury.

(1964)

Upright

He said
I am mud
in a universe of stone and fire,

neither hard
5   enough to last
nor expressed
    in one
of those imperishable fires.

Be something
10   the grassblade said
rising whitegreen

from common swamp.
I am he
said

15   nothing &
feel better that
way.

The grassblade
said
20   be like us

grass stone
and fire and
pass.

Mud is
25   nothing
and eternal.

1963 (1963)

Catalyst

Honor the maggot,
supreme catalyst:
he spurs the rate of change:
(all scavengers are honorable: I love them
5   all,
will scribble hard as I can for them)

he accelerates change
in the changeless continuum;
where the body falls completed, he sets to work:
10   where the spirit attains
        indifference
he makes his residence:
in the egg on wing from mound
to mound he travels,
15   feeds, finds his wings,

after the wet-sweet of decay,
after the ant-sucked earth has drunk
the honey-fluids,
after
20   the veins
lie dried to streaks of tendon
inside the meat-free, illuminated skull,

lofts, saws the air, copulates in a hung
rapture
25   of riding, holds the sweet-clear
connection
through dual flights, male and female,
soil's victory:
(dead cell dross transfigured
30   into gloss,
iridescence of compound eyes,
duck-neck purple of hairy abdomen)

––––––––

                    O worm supreme,
             transformer of bloated, breaking flesh
35   into colorless netted wings,
             into the wills of sex and song, leaving
                    ash on odorless ground, the scent
                          of pinestraw
             rising dominant from the striking sun!

                                        1960 (1963)

Loss

             When the sun
             falls behind the sumac
             thicket the
             wild
5   yellow daisies
             in diffuse evening shade
             lose their
             rigorous attention
             and
10   half-wild with loss
             turn
             any way the wind does
             and lift their
             petals up
15   to float
             off their stems
             and go

                                        1964 (1964)

World

Breakers at high tide shoot
spray over the jetty boulders
that collects in shallow chips, depressions,

———

evening the surface to run-off level:
5 of these possible worlds of held water,
most can't outlast the interim tideless

drought, so are clear, sterile, encased with
salt: one in particular, though, a hole,
providing depth with little surface,

10 keeps water through the hottest day:
a slime of green algae extends into that
tiny sea, and animals tiny enough to be in a

world there breed and dart and breathe and
die: so we are here in this plant-created oxygen,
15 drinking this sweet rain, consuming this green.

1963 (1964)

Butterflyweed

The butterfly that
named the weed
drank there, Monarch,
scrolled, medallioned—
5 his wings lifted close
in pale underwing salute

occasionally would
with tense evenness
open down

10 hinged coffers
lawned against the sun:
anchored in
dream, I could hardly
fall when earth
15 dropped and looped away.

1963 (1964)

Configurations

1

when November stripped
    the shrub,
        what stood
        out
5   in revealed space was
a nest
      hung
      in essential limbs

2

    how harmless truth
10   is
    in cold weather
    to an empty nest

3

dry
leaves
15   in
the
bowl,
        like wings

4

    summer turned light
20   into darkness
    and inside the shadeful
    shrub
      the secret
      worked
25   itself into life:

———

icicles and waterpanes:
recognitions:

>at the bottom, knowledges
>and desertions

5

30 speech comes out,
>a bleached form,
nestlike:
>>after the events of silence
>>the flying away
35 >of silence
>into speech—

6

>the nest is held
>off-earth
by sticks;

40 >so, intelligence
>stays
>out of the ground

erect on a
brittle walk of bones:

45 >otherwise
>the sea,

>empty of separations

7

leaves
like wings

50   in the Nov
            ember nest:

wonder where the birds are now that were here:
wonder if the hawks missed them:
wonder if
55   dry wings
                lie abandoned,
            bodiless
            this
            November:

60   leaves—   out of so many
                             a nestful missed the ground

                                8

I am a bush
I am a nest
I am a bird
65   I am a wind
I am a negg

        I is a bush, nest, bird, wind, negg
        I is a leaf

if I fall what falls:
70   the leaves fell and the birds flew away and winter came and

                                9

when
I
am   bringing
singing   those   home
75   ,   two   again
summer   birds
comes
back

10

80   so what if
lots of

        unfathomable stuff
        remains,
        inconceivable distances,

        closed and open infinities:
85   so what if
all that, if

        thunderstorms spill the eggs,
        loosen the nest, strew it across
        galaxies of grass and weeds:

90   who cares what remains when
only the interior

        immaterial
        configuration—

        shape—
95   mattered, matters, immaterial, unremaining

11

there is some relationship between
proximity
to the earth and permanence:

        a shrub puts itself into and out of
100   the earth at once,
earth and air united by a stem's
polar meshes of roots and branches:

        earth
        shrub
105   nest
        leaf
        bird

———————

the bird is somewhere south, unoriented
    to these roots:
110   the leaves
       though they may not have wandered so far
    are random:

       earth
       shrub
115   nest

goodbye, nest, if wind lifts you loose
goodbye, shrub, if ice breaks you down
goodbye,
goodbye

12

120   the shrub is nothing
       except part of my song:
the bird I never saw is part of my song and
       nothing else:
(the leaves are a great many little notes I lost
125   when I was trying to make the song
      that became my silence)

13

the cockbird longs for the henbird
which longs for the nest
    which longs for the shrub which
130   longs for the earth
which longs for the sun which longs for

14

inside there the woodmeat is saying
      please, please

              let me put on my leaves
135   let me let the sap go

      but the zero bark is saying
                    hush, hush
                          the time is not right
                          it's not the right time

140   the woodmeat is always right
      but bark is knowing

                                        1963

Glass

              The song
              sparrow puts all his
              saying
              into one
5   repeated song:
              what

              variations, subtleties
              he manages,
              to encompass denser
10   meanings, I'm
              too coarse
              to catch: it's

              one song, an over-reach
              from which
15   all possibilities,
              like filaments,
              depend:
              killing,

              nesting, dying,
20   sun or cloud,

figure up
and become
song—simple, hard:
removed.

1963 (1964)

Morning Glory

Dew was
heavy
last night:

sun-up broke
5   beads
into running

water: under
over
and

10   against,
the mockingbird
fluffing

amorously
bathes
15   in leaves

1963

The Strait

At the oracle
I found the
   god
though active
5   recalcitrant

———

unliteral as air:
the priestess
    writhed
and moaned
10   caught

in the anguish
of some
    perishable
event:
15   birds flew by:

the urns
hummed: the
    columns
glazed with
20   sun; on the

inside lit wet with
fire: another, not
    capable
of the inner
25   speech,

read the priestess
and said,
    "The
god wants honor,
30   desires in you

honor's attitude:
honor him and
    your
venture will
35   go well":

cannot, I said,
the god be
    more

specific? will
40   I honor

him? come again
safe to this
    grove?
the reader said,
45   "The

descent of the
god is
    awkward,
narrowing and
50   difficult; first

he is
loose in the
    air,
then captured,
55   held, by

holy fire: the
circle of columns
    binds
him and from
60   the columns

the priestess
gathers him,
    seized
by her struggling
65   mouth into

a speech of
forms: it is
    speech
few can read,
70   the god

violent to
over-reach the
definite:
why should
75 he, who is

all, commit
himself to the
particular?
say himself
80 into less

than all? pressed
too far, he
leaves
wounds that are
85 invisible: it

is only as
she becomes
him
that the priestess
90 cannot be hurt

or can be hurt:
should she
break
her human hold
95 and go too far

with him,
who could bring
her
back, her eyes
100 lost to the

visible? step
by step into the
actual,

truth descending
105   breaks,

reaches us as
fragmentation
    hardened
into words":
110   but, I said, isn't

it convenient
the priestess is
    general
and inexact, merely
115   turning and wailing?

if the god fails
me, whom shall I
    blame?
her? you who may
120   have read her wrong?

and if all goes
well, whom shall I
    thank?
the god
125   with honor,

you with the
actual coin?
    "Night
falls," the reader said,
130   "the priestess lies

god-torn, limp: the
freed god
    flies
again blameless as
135   air: go

to your fate:
if you succeed, praise the
      god:
if you fail,
140   discover your flaw."

1960 (1964)

Spindle

Song is a violence
of icicles and
      windy trees:

rising it catches up
5   indifferent
            cellophane, loose

leaves, all mobiles
into an organized whirl
      relating scrap

10   to scrap in a round
fury: violence
      brocades

the rocks with hard silver
of sea water and
15   makes the tree

show the power of its
holding on: a
      violence to make
      that can destroy.

1963 (1964)

The Yucca Moth

    The yucca clump
is blooming,
    tall sturdy spears
spangling into bells of light,
5   green
in the white blooms
    faint as
a memory of mint:

I raid
10   a bloom,
spread the hung petals out,
    and, surprised he is not
a bloom-part, find
    a moth inside, the exact color,
15   the bloom his daylight port or cove:

though time comes
    and goes and troubles
are unlessened,
    the yucca is lifting temples
20   of bloom: from the night
    of our dark flights, can
we go in to heal, live
    out in white-green shade
the radiant, white, hanging day?

1962 (1964)

Anxiety

    The sparrowhawk
flies hard to

stand in the
air: something

5   about direction
lets us loose

into ease
and slow grace.

1963 (1964)

Four Motions for the Pea Vines

1.

the rhythm is
   diffusion and concentration:
in and out:
    expansion and
5   contraction: the unfolding,
    furling:

    the forces
     that propel the rhythm,
the lines of winding-up,
10 loosening, depositing,
    dissolving:

the vehicles!

light, the vehicle of itself, light
surrounding
15 we are made and fed by:
water, the solvent, vehicle
of molecules and grains,
the dissolver and depositor,
the maker of films
20 and residues,
the all-absorbing vessel uncontained!

———

the rhythm is
out and
in,
25   diffusion and concentration:

the dry pea from the
ground
expands to vines and leaves,
harvests sun and water
30   into
baby-white new peas:

the forms that exist
in this rhythm! the whirling
      forms!
35   grief and glory of
this rhythm:
the rhythm is

2.

for the expansions (and concentrations) here
is the five-acre
40   Todd Field:

seeding, too, is gathering,
preparation to collect
      mineral, rain, and light, and
between the corn-rows,
45   the broadcast field peas
fall into soft, laying-by soil:

dry beads of concentration
      covered by the moist
general ground:

50   and the general moisture, the rain's
held shadow, softens, breaks

down, swells
and frees
         the hard incipience that
55   generalizes outward toward extension;
the root reaching with gravity,
the stalk opposing
crazing through the black land upward to the light

3.

fat and sassy
60   the raucous crows
            along the wood's edge
            trouble the tops of
yellowing pines
            with points of dipping black;

65   cluster into groups
from summer,
         the younglings in their wings
poised,
careful,
70   precise,

the dazed awkwardness of heavy nest birds
hardened lean into grace;

assemble along the edge of the field and
            begin winter talk,
75   remembrances of summer and separations,
         agree
         or disagree
            on a roost,
            the old birds more often silent,

80   calmer and more tolerant in their memory,
         wiser of dangers
         experienced or conceived,

less inclined to play,
irritable,
85   but at times

exultant in pitched flight,
as if catching for a moment
     youth's inexperienced gladness, or as if
          feeling
90   over time and danger
          a triumph greater than innocent joy:

to turn aside and live with them
     would not seem
          much different—

95   each of us going into winter with gains and losses,
dry, light peas of concentration nearby
     (for a winter's gleaning)
          to expand warmth through us

4.

slow as the pale low-arcing sun, the women move
100   down windy rows of the autumn field:
the peavines are dead:
cornstalks and peapods rattle in the dry bleach
          of cold:

the women glean remnant peas
105   (too old to snap or shell) that
got past being green; shatter from skeletal vines
          handfuls of peapods, tan, light:

bent the slow women drag towsacks huge
     with peas, bulk but little
110   weight: a boy carries a sack on his
     shoulders to the end of the rows:
he stoops: the sack goes over his head

to the ground: he flails it with a tobacco stick,
    opens the sack, removes the husks, and
115   from sack to tub winnows
        dry hard crackling peas: rhythms reaching through
seasons, motions weaving in and out!

1962 (1964)

Hymn II

    So when the year had come full round
    I rose
    and went out to the naked mountain
    to see
5   the single peachflower on the sprout

    blooming through a side of ribs
        possibly a colt's
    and I endured each petal separately
    and moved in orisons with the sepals

10   I lay
        said the sprouting stump
    in the path of Liberty

    Tyranny though I said is very terrible
    and sat down leeward of the blossom
15   to be blessed
    and was startled by
    a lost circling bee

    The large sun setting red I went
    down to the stream
20   and wading in
    let your cold water run over my feet

1954 (1958)

Hymn III

In the hour of extreme

    importance

when clots thicken
in outlying limbs and
    warmth retreats

to mourn
the thinning garrison of pulse

keep my tongue loose
to sing possible

    changes

that might redeem

might in iron phrases
    clang the skies

bells and my jangling eyes
ringing you in
    to claim me

shriven celebrant
your love's new-reasoned singer

    home

dead on arrival

(1958)

Open

Exuberance: joy to the last
pained loss
   and hunger of air:
life open, not decided on,
5   though decided in death:

        the mind cannot be
rid
while it works
   of remembered genitals
10   beautiful, dank, pliant,

of canyons, brush hills, pastures, streets,
     unities and divisions,
meetings,

exact remembrance of liquid buttocks,
15   navel, ellipse of hand,

magnified territories of going down
and rising,
the thin tracing saliva line,

   joy's configurations:

20   serendipity: the unexpected,
the
possible, the unembodied,
     unevented:

the sun will burst: death
25   is certain: the future limited
    nevertheless is
limitless: the white knotted

———

groin,
the finger describing
30   entrances!

the dark, warm with glowing awareness, the
hot dis-
    missals of desire
until the last last tear of pain:

35   until the end nothing ends, lust
forward, rushing;
    pillars of ice wet-bright in melt,
warm

with always-yielding joy: yes
40   yes
yes, the loose mouths hiss in the mornings of death.

1960 (1963)

Epiphany

Like a single drop of rain,
    the wasp strikes
the windowpane; buzzes rapidly
away, disguising

5   error in urgent business:
    such is the
invisible, hard as glass,
unrenderable by the senses,

not known until stricken by:
10   some talk that
there is safety in the visible,
the definite, the heard and felt,

———

pre-stressing the rational and
    calling out with
15   joy, like people far from death:
    how puzzled they will be when

going headlong secure in "things"
    they strike the
intangible and break, lost,
20   unaccustomed to transparency, to

being without body, energy
    without image:
how they will be dealt
hard realizations, opaque as death.

1959 (1960)

Prodigal

After the shifts and dis-
continuities, after the congregations of orders,
    black masses floating through
    mind's boreal clarity, icebergs in fog,
5   flotillas of wintering ducks weathering the night,
    chains of orders, multifilamentous chains
    knobbed with possibility, disoriented
chains, winding back on themselves, unwinding,
    intervolving, spinning, breaking off

10   (nomads clustering at dusk into tents of sleep,
disorganizing, widening out again with morning)
    after the mental

blaze and gleam,
the mind in both motions building and tearing down,
15   running to link effective chains,
    establish molecules of meaning,

frameworks, to
　　　perfect modes of structuring
　　　(so days can bend to trellising
20　and pruned take shape,
　　　bloom into necessary event)

　　　after these motions, these vectors,
orders moving in and out of orders, collisions
　　　of orders, dispersions, the grasp weakens,

25　　　the mind whirls, short of the unifying
reach, short of the heat
　　　to carry that forging:
　　　after the visions of these losses, the spent
seer, delivered to wastage, risen
30　　　into ribs, consigns knowledge to
　　　approximation, order to the vehicle
of change, and fumbles blind in blunt innocence
　　　toward divine, terrible love.

　　　　　　　　　　　　　　　　1959 (1964)

Motion

　　　The word is
　　　not the thing:
　　　is
　　　a construction of,
5　　a tag for,
　　　the thing: the
　　　word in
　　　no way
　　　resembles
10　the thing, except
　　　as sound
　　　resembles,
　　　as in *whirr,*

sound:
15 the relation
between what this
as words
is
and what is
20 is tenuous: we
agree upon
this as the net to
cast on what
is: the finger
25 to
point with: the
method of
distinguishing,
defining, limiting:
30 poems
are fingers, methods,
nets,
not what is or
was:
35 but the music
in poems
is different,
points to nothing,
traps no
40 realities, takes
no game, but
by the motion of
its motion
resembles
45 what, moving, is—
the wind
underleaf white against
the tree.

1962 (1964)

The Misfit

The unassimilable fact leads us on:
round the edges
    where broken shapes make poor masonry
the synthesis
5   fails (and succeeds) into limitation
    or extending itself too far
becomes a different synthesis:
law applies
    consistently to the molecule,
10   not to the ocean, unoriented, unprocessed,
it floats in, that floats in it:
    we are led on

to the boundaries
where relations loosen into chaos
15   or where the nucleus fails to control,
fragments in odd shapes
expressing more and more the interstitial sea:
    we are led on

to peripheries, to the raw blocks of material,
20   where mortar and trowel can convert
    diversity into enlarging unity:
not the million oriented facts
but the one or two facts,
    out of place,

25   recalcitrant, the one observed fact
that tears us into questioning:
    what has not
joined dies into order to redeem, with
loss of singleness extends the form,
30   or, unassimilable, leads us on.

1961

The Watch

When the sun went down and the night came on
coming over the fields and up the driveway
to the rose arbor and the backporch posts

I gathered myself together from dispersing dark
5   and went up into the mountains
and sitting down on the round rock beyond the trees

kindled my thoughts
blowing the coals of my day's bright conscious
and said

10   all across the plains my voice going silently and down
among the stumps where the swamp cuts through
and in between among the villages of hill country

Now close your eyes
Sleep
15   Shut out the world from the dark sweet freshening
       of your quiet hearts
Lie loose in the deep waters
Do not be afraid to
give yourselves up to drowning in undefended rest

20   If a dust storm blows up out of the West I will run
down the mountain and go through all the homes
and wake you up

If a new fire appears in the sky I will let you know
in time
25   so you can know it should it claim you

I will have all your beings in mind burning like a watchfire
and when the night has grown thin and weak
and the full coyotes have given up their calls

———

I will move up close to the eternal and
30   saying nine praises
commend you to it and to the coming sun

1956 (1957)

Libation

I have been throughout the world sleuthing,
drawing back goatheads
and from the writhing throats bloodletting,
watching the harassed religious eyes
5   whirl and freeze.

Earth drinks
the blood of fawns: jasmines
bloom in lions' eyes.

Breath and heat I have returned O Earth to your freedoms.
10   Now keep me virile and long at love:
let submission kiss off
the asking words from my lips.

1951 (1964)

The Wide Land

Having split up the chaparral
blasting my sight
the wind said
    You know I'm
5   the result of
forces beyond my control
I don't hold it against you
I said
It's all right I understand

10   Those pressure bowls and cones
the wind said

are giants in their continental gaits
I know I said I know
they're blind giants
15   Actually the wind said I'm
        if anything beneficial
            resolving extremes
filling up lows with highs
No I said you don't have
20   to explain
It's just the way things are

Blind in the wide land I
turned and risked my feet
to loose stones and sudden

25   alterations of height

1957 (1958)

Thaw

Winter over, ice-bound
mind better not
rush to a spring-meet fast;
might trip, stiff thoughts,
5   shatter:
better not warm up too
close to sun;
might melt, run, gullies
caking off the good
10   firm country of the brain.

Better go slow,
bend with the gradual movement,
let sap flow but
keep an eye on any
15   thermal swell rising at
        glassy mind.

———

If it gets loose wind
will take it
riddling through the underbrush,
20   but if it stays
solid brilliant ice
tulip root
    warm in coming
will splinter it.

1958 (1959)

Whose Timeless Reach

I Ezra the dying
portage of these deathless thoughts
stood on a hill in
the presence of the mountain
5   and said wisdom is
too wise for man it
is for gods and gods have little
use for it so I do not know what
to do with it
10   and animals use it only when
    their teeth start to fall and it
is too late to do anything
else but *be* wise and stay
out of the way
15   The eternal will not lie
down on any temporal hill
    The frozen mountain rose and broke
its tireless lecture of repose
and said death does
20   not take away it
ends giving halts bounty and
    Bounty I said thinking of ships
that I might take and helm right
out through space
25   dwarfing these safe harbors and
their values

taking the Way in whose timeless reach
cool thought unpunishable
by bones eternally glides

1955 (1956)

Ritual for Eating the World

At a bend in the rocks there hung
inexplicably a rope
and musing I said
When I die don't bury me
5   *under no weeping willer tree*

It's I thought a hangman's loop
provided by my warmer ghoul to
raise me out of care

or god's own private fishing hook
10   for glaring people
who sit wasted in the sun
on rocks

But put me up in a high dry place
unavailable to the coyote's face

15   It's what I said old mountain
climbers left
dangling

The wind rides blade on mesa tops

Oh when I die don't bury me
20   *under no weeping willer tree*

and there being besides old bush
and distance nothing but a rope
I engaged myself with it but

it broke
25   and all through the heaving night
making day I faced

piecemeal the sordid
reacceptance of my world

1957 (1958)

Driving Through

In the desert midnight I said
taking out my notebook I
    am astonished
though widely traveled having
5   seen Empire State and Palestine, Texas
and San Miguel de Allende
to mention extremes
and sharpened my pencil on the sole
    of my shoe

10   The mountains running skidded
over the icy mirages of the moon
and fell down tumbling
    laughing for breath
on the cool dunes
15   The stone mosaics of the flattest
places (parting lake-gifts) grouped
    in colors and
played games at imagery: a green
tiger with orange eyes, an Orpheus
20   with moving fingers
    Fontal the shrubs flooded
everything with cool
water

I sat down against a brimming smoketree
25   to watch and morning found the

desert reserved
trembling at its hot and rainless task
   Driving through
you would never suspect
30   the midnight rite or seeing my lonely house
guess it will someday hold
laurel and a friend

1955 (1956)

March Song

At a bend in the stream by willows
I paused to be with the cattails
   their long flat leaves
and tall stems
5   bleached by wind and winter light

and winter had kept them
   edged down into the quiet eddy of the bend
tight with ice

O willows I said how you return
10   gold to the nakedness of your limbs
   coming again out of that country
into the longer sun

and Oh I said turning to the fluffy cattails
loosened to the approaching winds of spring
15   what a winter you leave in the pale stems
   of your becoming

1957 (1959)

Gravelly Run

I don't know somehow it seems sufficient
to see and hear whatever coming and going is,

losing the self to the victory
of stones and trees,
5   of bending sandpit lakes, crescent
round groves of dwarf pine:

for it is not so much to know the self
as to know it as it is known
by galaxy and cedar cone,
10   as if birth had never found it
and death could never end it:

the swamp's slow water comes
down Gravelly Run fanning the long
stone-held algal
15   hair and narrowing roils between
the shoulders of the highway bridge:

holly grows on the banks in the woods there,
and the cedars' gothic-clustered
spires could make
20   green religion in winter bones:

so I look and reflect, but the air's glass
jail seals each thing in its entity:

no use to make any philosophies here:
I see no
25   god in the holly, hear no song from
the snowbroken weeds: Hegel is not the winter
yellow in the pines: the sunlight has never
heard of trees: surrendered self among
unwelcoming forms: stranger,
30   hoist your burdens, get on down the road.

1958 (1960)

TAPE FOR THE TURN OF THE YEAR (1965)

for Josephine Jacobsen and Elliott Coleman

⤳⤳

6 DEC:

today I
decided to write
a long
   thin
5   poem

    employing certain
classical considerations:
      this
part is called the pro-
10   logue: it has to do with
   the business of
   getting started:

   first the
   Muse
15   must be acknowledged,
saluted, and implored:
I cannot
write
    without her help
20   but when
her help comes it's
water from spring heights,
warmth and melting,
    stream
25   inexhaustible:
I salute her, lady
of a hundred names—
   Inspiration
   Unconscious
30   Apollo (on her man side)

Parnassus (as her
          haunt)
Pierian spring (as
          the nature of her
35   going)
Hippocrene
Pegasus:
most of all she's a
woman, maybe
40 a woman in us, who sets
fire to us, gives us no
          rest
          till her
          will's done:

45 because I've decided, the
Muse willing,
to do this foolish
          long
          thin
50   poem, I
specially beg
assistance:
help me!
a fool who
55 plays with fool things

so fools and play
can rise in the regard of
the people,
provide serious rest
60 and sweet engagement
to willing minds:

and the Muse be manifest:

I'm attracted to paper,
visualize
65 kitchen napkins

scribbled
with little masterpieces:
    so
it was natural for
70   me (in the House &
        Garden store one
night a couple weeks
ago) to contemplate
    this roll of
75   adding-machine tape, so
narrow, long,
unbroken, and to penetrate
    into some
    fool use for it: I
80   thought of the poem
then,
but not seriously: now,
two weeks
have gone by, and
85   the Muse hasn't
rejected it,
seems caught up in the
    serious novelty:

I get weak in
90   the knees
(feel light in the head)
    when I look down
    and see
    how much footage is
95   tightly wound in that
roll: once started,
can I ever get
free
of the thing, get it in
100   and out of typewriter
and mind? one
rolled end, one
dangling, coiling end?

———

　　　　　　will the Muse fill it
105　　　up immediately and let me
　　　　　loose? can my back
　　　　　muscles last? my mind,
　　　　　　　　can it be
　　　　　　　　as long as
110　　　a tape
　　　　　and unwind with it?

　　　　　the Muse takes care of
　　　　　　　that: I do what I
　　　　　can:

115　　　may this song be plain as
　　　　　day, exact and bright!
　　　　　no moonlight to loosen
　　　　　　　shrubs into
　　　　　shapes that
120　　　never were: no dark
　　　　　　　nights to dissolve
　　　　　　　woods into one black
　　　　　　　depthless dimension:
　　　　　may this song leave
125　　　darkness alone, deal
　　　　　with what
　　　　　light can win into clarity:

　　　　　clarity & simplicity!

　　　　　no muffled talk, fragments
130　　　of phrases, linked
　　　　　without logical links,
　　　　　strung
　　　　　together in obscurities
　　　　　supposed to reflect
135　　　density: it's
　　　　　a wall

to obscure emptiness, the
talk of a posing man who
must talk
140   but who has nothing to
say: let this song
            make
complex things salient,
saliences clear, so
145   there can be some
understanding:

7 DEC:

today
I feel a bit different:
my prolog sounds phony &
150   posed:
            maybe
I betrayed
depth
by oversimplification,
155   a smugness,
unjustified sense of
security:
                last
                night I
160   read
                about the
geologic times
of the Northwest, the
periodic eruptions into
165   lava plateaus,
forest grown, stabilized,
and drowned
between eruptions:
in the
170   last
10,000 years (a bit of

time) the
glaciers have been
melting, some now unfed,
175   disconnected, lying dead
and dissolving in
high
valleys: how strange
we are here,
180   raw, new, how ephemeral our
          lives and cultures,
      how unrelated
      to the honing out of
      caves and canyons:
185   the lands, floating, rise
and fall, unnoticed in the
                rapid
          turning over
      of generations:

190   we, rapids in a valley
that millennially sinks:

nothing's simple, but
should we add
verbal complexity?

195   is there a darkness
dark words should
imitate?

I mean to stay on the
crusty
200   hard-clear surface: tho
          congealed
it reflects the deep,
the fluid, hot motions
and intermotions where,
205   after all, we
    do not live:

———

10,000 yrs

    Troy
        burned since then:
210   but the earth's been
        "resting"—entering
        a warm
        cycle: the Sumerians
        had not, that long ago,
215   compiled
        their
        holy bundle of
        the elements of civil-
            ization, nor
220   had one city-state stolen
        it from another:

        ten thousand years: how
        many Indians is that,
        fishing the northern
225   coast, marrying, dying?
        coming & going, they
        left no permanent sign
            on the warming
            trend:

230   I hadn't meant
        such a long prolog: it
        doesn't seem
        classical to go ahead
        without a plan:

235   wonder what plan
        the Indians had
        10 M years ago: the
            thought defines
            our sphere:

———

240 why should a world be
 bigger than what a man
 can reach
 and taste and strike &
  burn & hunt & hold?
245 bigger than

 that is metaphysics which
 tho entertaining
 is inedible
 and unsurrendering: what's

250 10,000 years to us,
 blips on
 radar screens?

 in the blip is all
 imperishable possibility:
255 not unity, not all—
 but the full,
 complete: we can
 in moments have
 that
260 but when we
 surround mind & world
 to say all
 in a single word,
 we kill advantage with
265 the cost of gain:
 can't we break loose
 and live?

 I wish I had a great
 story to tell: the
270 words then
 could be quiet, as I'm
 trying to make them now—
 immersed in the play

                    of events: but
275   I can't tell a great
                    story: if I were
                    Odysseus, I couldn't
                    survive
                    pulling away from
280   Lestrygonia, 11 of
                    12 ships lost
                    with 11 crews: I couldn't
                    pull away with
                    the joy of one
285   escaped with his life:
                    I'd search myself pale
                    with
                    responsibility, tho I'd
                    be in the wrong: that
290   we can't predict what
                    our actions will lead to
                    absolves us, tho not
                    altogether: we're held
                    to right deeds
295   and best intentions:

                    my story is how
                    a man comes home
                    from haunted
                    lands and transformations:
300   it is
                            in a way
                            a great story:
                    but it doesn't unwind
                    into sequence: it stands
305   still
                    and stirs
                            in itself like
                    boiling water
                    or hole of maggots: foam
310   or crust

can rise and
            sweep away into
            event: but not
            much of that:
315   mostly inner resolutions,
       countermotions
       that may work themselves
            out
            into peace,
320   bring the man
       home, to
       acceptance of his place
                        and time,
       responsibilities and
325   limitations: I mean
          nothing mythical—
       Odysseus
       wandering in a ghost-deep
       background—I mean only
330   or as much as
       restoration
       which takes many forms &
       meanings:

       but the story, tho
335   contained,
       unwinds on this roll
       with time & event: grows
       like a tapeworm, segment
       by
340   segment: turns
          stream corners: issues
       in low
       silence
          like a snake
345   from its burrow: but
       unwinding and unwound, it
       coils again on

          the floor
          into the unity of its
350   conflicts:

                  8 DEC:

          the way I could tell
          today
          that yesterday is dead
          is that
355   the little gray bird
          that sat
               in the empty
                 tree
          yesterday is gone:
360   yesterday and
          bird are gone:
          I know there's no use
          to look
          for either of them, bird
365   running from winter,
          yesterday
          running downstream
          to some ocean-pocket of
          rest
370   whence it may sometime
          come again (changed), new
          as tomorrow:
          how like a gift
          the memory
375   of bird and empty tree!
          how
          precious
          since we may not have
          that configuration
380   again:
          today is full of things,
          so many,

                how can they be managed,
                received and loved
385   in their passing?
                    on the bridle path
                this morning
                yellow horse-turds
                glistened
390   with the moisture of
                intestines:
                a purple leaf occupied a
                bush—a dozen kinds of
                lichen on an oak:
395   eelgrass stood straight
                up
                on underwater banks:
                someone told an
                elephant joke: how do
400   you kill a blue elephant?
                    with a
                blue-elephant gun: how
                do you kill a white
                elephant? with a
405   white-elephant gun? no,
                you tie a string around
                his trunk and when it
                turns blue
                you shoot him with a
410   blue-elephant gun:
                a little boy said, "Up,
                up," begging to ride his
                daddy's shoulders, and the
                morning was warm and
415   winter-bright:
                from completeness
                should one turn away?
                so they drank wine
                        and ate meat
420   and slept:

the shores fled
under the wind's weight:

why does an elephant lie
on his back? to trip the
425   birds:

tonight, so
  compressed is
  change,
  we're having
430 warm weather and windy
rain: the house, however,
smells of
  fruitcakes baking and
merriment curls along the
435   ceiling,
giggles down the walls,
and tickles the floor:

the inexhaustible
multiplicity & possibility
440 of the surface: while the
depths are
  generalized into a
  few
  soluble drives,
445 interesting, but to be
   returned from:

the crust keeps us: the
volcano-mind
emits
450 this ribbon of speech,
smoke & heat
that held
would bust the cone off,
inundate the house

455   with direct melt:
but let off, there's
easing, mind cool, the
slow accretion of hard
rock:
460   doesn't matter how much
the core shifts
long as we have these
islands to live on: we're
in a
465   solid, hard, exact world
that tells all we
need to know of depth:

art casts into being, the
glow-wobbling metal
470   struck by a
difference of ice:

both necessary:
without flow, there's no
resource for crust:
475   without ice,
no sharp steel:
death is life's
    prerequisite:

this is that & that is this
480   & on and on: why can't
every thing be just itself?
what's the use of the
vast mental burden
of correspondence? doesn't
485   contribute to the things
resembled:

except in the mind: except
in the mind: there's

the reality that needs to
490   hold:

9:35 pm: lightning! what,
in December? just flashed
   blue-bright and
   thunder, moving slowly
495   and rumbling hard into
deep bursting depressions,
went all the way out over
the Atlantic: now, will
   the ground, shaken
500   loose, turn green,
loam to new roots?
the old people say it's
a use
of thunder: but this time
505   of year, the seeds asleep,
thunder's sterile
disturbance runs dreams
through the meat of the
future, a prophecy: no,
510   fancy,
never satisfied with
wonderless things as
they are: it's the
return of air upon
515   itself, following an
electrical discharge and
separation: the grass
seeds, hanging
in clumps on soaked stalks,
520   paid no attn &
thought of nothing:

wind and rain have
stopped: the
thunder was a gigantic

525   period, punched over &
over: or do I hear now
a submissive, unwilling
drizzle?

    sequence: events
530   stalled in their
occurrence: a
running with, fleet
recorder at the crest of
change: a plane is in
535   this: it rumbles in the
distance, a chord through
my circular knowledge: it
is out in the rain:

9 DEC:

sunny again:

540   last night a plane
over Delaware struck the
storm
& 80 lives descended in
flames: it's

545   the nature of flame to
rise, celebrant, spirit
to whirl upward:

80

    11111111111111111111111
550   11111111111111111111111
    111111111111111111111111
    11111111111

    and he plucked two men
and broke fast:

---

555   grieved, we
      rejoice
      as a man rejoices saved
         from death: we beg
      that men be spared
560   calamity & the hard turn:
      we make an offering of our
      praise: we reaccept:

         our choice is
               gladness:

565   give us an idea!
      let us be sorted out and
         assembled: let a new
      order occur
      from the random &
570   nondescript:

      let thoughts & emotions
      fall behind into rank: or

      return us from all idea to
      undifferentiated
575   sensation—paradise:

      1 pm:

      had the storm last night
      come half a mile farther
      east, it would have
580   taken my roof off and
      wet my poem
            (and my pants): it

      "had a little twister in
         it," the man at the
585   Esso station said, came

right up the parkway,
took off
his plate-glass windows,
shattered the
590 outdoor movie's tall
wooden marquee,
 took the roof off
the concession and off
the Circle Diner and
595 busted a window in
Kinney's: "must have been
a sucker," he said, "lifted
oil cans right off the
shelves"

600 reality last night was
more than I apprehended:
is far more today
than feebleness lets me
know:
605 wind ruined several dead
weeds and rain
de-seeded a lot of grass:

the cloud patterns
must have been fine,
610 dark roils
hidden by rain:

I wonder what all did
 happen? but
 the record
615 can't reproduce event:
even if I could know &
describe every event, my
account would
 consume the tape & run
620 on for miles into air:

those who rely on facts
  have not heard:

those who rely on
arrangements—are
625   sometimes unwilling
    to surrender them:

those who rely on any shore
foolishly haven't faced
it that
630   only the stream is
        reliable: get
   right up next to the
break between
what-is-to-be and
635   what-has-been and
dance like a bubble
held underwater by water's
pouring in: when the grass
moves on the hill,
640   it's impossible to tell
whether it has moved or
   will move:

my "mind" is trying to
keep every cell
645   in my body
happy: yes, it says, we
understand that you need
so-and-so but we're
   temporarily (we hope)
650   out of that and are having
a substitute manufactured—
this will be released to
   you as soon as
possible: be sure to alert

655 your receiving dept: it
  gets an alarm from a group
  of injured or invaded cells:
  we are
  sending several divisions
660 & several kinds of
   divisions to help you:
  and so on:
  catalysts, enzymes &
  membranes, functions,
665 trades & forces, the
  in-coming, out-going:
  this mind that I turn
  outwardly—how thin by
    comparison—
670 the body releases from
  inner concerns and
  gives few commands: get
  food, water, sex: then
  reality brings its
675 interference in
  and the simple outward
  mind, complicated by
  postponements, symbols,
   prerequisites, proofs,
680 nearly loses in
  metaphysics &
   speculations its
  contact with the
  original commands: get
685 food, water: sex
  is put upon you as the lust
  of generations:
   it has been made to
   seem pleasurable
690 but is subservience
  to the cry of flesh to
   endure: the inner

mind says—do that for
the cells, for us, and we
695 will free you to the
pleasures of the
outer mind:

get food, get water: sex
is a fire we send you:
700 quench it into
generations:
be brought low of the fire:

I've
given up hope of
705 understanding for
what good is
understanding?
understanding
what?

710 the conversion of
currencies:
the multiplication tables:
IQ:
quantum theory & baby's
715 formula
and how to replace the
shingles & whether to put
the money in SKF or
Xerox, and the clauses in
720 insurance plans &
the "political
situation":

plenty of food & water in
paradise but some
725 confusion about sex:
anything so sweet

should come hard
as bread & water: so
   they were given the
730   gate: and
Eden survives in the mind
as half a solution:

analyze and project:
experience teaches
735 but stands to be
taught:

4:50 pm: the checker at
   the A & P said
he was returning from
740 Philly about 9:15 last night
and saw it: said the sky
   lit up,
he didn't know why
till the radio sd later:
745 said it wasn't hit by no
      lightning: said
   they have things
hanging from the wings:
said
750 he thinks it was
   turbulence, wind
turbulence—can take a
plane apart: woman
said
755 she's been up there & it
"gives her a funny feeling":

   one night I saw
something come apart
over Vineland: it
760 streaked in, glowed, &
   slowly tore apart:

I thought it was a
    satellite
       re-entering:
765   but next day read in the
papers it was seen from
Virginia to Connecticut:
    too big to land, as
    I thght it wd
770   in Millville: was no
small potatoes:
first there was this blue
flash:

    here are "motions"
775   that play in and out:
    unifying
correspondences that
suggest we can approach
unity only by the loss
780   of things—
a loss we're unwilling
to take—
since the gain of unity
   would be a vision
785   of something in the
continuum of nothingness:
we already have things:
    why fool around:
    beer, milk,
790   mushroom cream sauce,
eggs, books, bags,
telephones & rugs:
    pleasure to perceive
correspondences, facts
795   that experience is
holding together, that
what mind grew out of
is also holding together:

otherwise? how could we
800   perceive similarities?
                    but all
the way to unity is
too far off: we have
a place:

805   at dusk a deep blue
sweeping smooth
cloud mass went just
between us
          and the ocean:
810   but the night is
clear and full of stars:

10 DEC:

sunshine & shade
    alternate at 32: winter
seems about to, but hasn't
815   quite decided how to
              happen:
(ideas give direction
but sometimes the wrong . . .)

when the first
820   horizontal haze of
sunlight struck the sumac
thicket this morning,
        bluejay flew in
        and sat on an outside
825   limb, his
appreciation, meditative
but imperfect, troubled
        by starlings:
        no place to stop:
830   the pure moment
self-centered & posed:

―――――――

I heard of a little girl
who wrote not
  "poems," but
835 "feelings"—some tissue
resulting from
things & feelings
at interplay:
to make a world
840 we need out of the reality
that is
and is indifferent:

  but play
removing us—we must be
845 careful—a point away
  from reality, though
  an uncreated, unspecific
reality—that is, in a
sense, no reality at all:
850 what *is* out there? beyond
the touch of what
  we make?
whatever,
  stars shine through it
855 & bring us up
short:
we make a context
that lets us out, permits
fullest life: we must
860 care for ourselves,
  assume that, beyond,
we are cared for:

rely on feeling—
till it goes too far:
865 then
on sweet reason which

recalls, restores, and
levels off: we must all
die, it's quite
870   remarkable—
nevertheless, true:
but breakfast, and getting
off to school & work, and
what color to paint the
875   second bedroom is
meaningful: it's
           no
           great
joy to me
880 that I plunge deeply
(I think) into things:
eternal
significance is of some
   significance to me: I
885 don't know just how: but
temporal significance is
a world I can partly make,
loss & gain:

the social order obtains
890 identity
at the cost of certain
exclusions: unity
by the elimination of
difference: the pleasure
895 of the order is shared by
many, but the cost
   falls on a few: should
the many
be denied to relieve
900 the suffering of the few?
should the few pay
and not enjoy?
     if it's the few
who, alive to suffering,

905 advance the mind, do they
have their reward? and
the callous many? is
smugness the cost of their
pleasure?
910 motions of
society & psyche: what's
to be done?
ever been done?
greater tolerance of random
915 without obliterating
identity?
relieve the suffering of
the few & enrich the
many with difference?
920 if the oppressed are
freed, will they become
callous
and unfruitful?
will you have the secure
925 few and the oppressed
many?
is freedom
identity without
identity?

930 who's not working, slashing,
sweating, devising,
cheating to
surpass the many and
rise into
935 the Few: (only a few
who pride
themselves on being the
Bottom Few?): is the
fight for the Top
940 the true mystique? first dibs
on food & sex:

                    I know you,
        man:
            am grateful to the
945   order, however imperfect,
        that restrains you,
            fierce, avaricious: the
        Top: Olympus,
        the White House, the Register:
950   many lesser peaks in the
        range: choose one and
            fight:
        that's equality: if
        inequality, must
955   be a few hills even
            there:

        what's the way home?

        home?
        what's wrong with these
960   deserts, excitements, shows:
        excursions:

        home is every minute,
        occurring? just like this?

        man, you're sweet &
965   gentle to
                    those who are
                    no
                    threat to your
                    mt

970   but are
                    evidences that
                    you occupy one:

        I have your #: it's
        me first after you:

975   Odysseus screwed a lot but
         never got screwed: or
         if he did, he screwed back
           harder, first
         chance he got: he never

980   "took nothing lying down":

         my song's now
         long enough to screw a
         right good-sized article
         with:
985   flexible to vault me
         to the Top:
         I hope it will lift me into
           your affections:
         that's what I need:
990   the top I've chosen,
         the mt I wd climb:

         the nest I've pro-
                vided
                for this
995   song to wind into is
         the wastebasket: that's
         symbolic: the roll, tho,
           unwinds from the
           glazed bottom of an
1000   ashtray: I don't
           know what to make
           of that:
           phoenix?

         why always
1005   make something out of
           everything?
           maybe this song
         will be about getting

home
1010 and figuring out some
excuse to leave again:
that wd be gd bth cmng &
gng:

the clouds, continuous,
1015 are creased with light
between furrows: like a
forehead, opposite with
shadow:

just sat down
1020 to smoke, and the sun cast
my hand against the
wall, and my cigarette,
plus the lively shadow of
cigarette smoke:
1025 that vast, immediate, hot
body
touching me:
    the sustaining
    chemistries that
1030 separate it from me:
plankton, grass, pears,
apples, cows: steaks
holding heat,
the vessels of heat;
1035 lambchops, chickenwings,

green peas, mushrooms,
cornflakes, coffee, pecans,
storers & storages of
heat: the warmth
1040   on my hand,
inside my hand: I
wonder
I don't

think about it more often:
1045 transfigurations, touch:
    touches
everything and leaves a
shadow: kelp & birds &
pebbles even & each
1050 individual blade of grass
& outhouses & mountains &
dead trees: even clear
water, toward the bottom,
accumulates some shadow:
1055   intimate,
        necessary
        & hardly ever
        mentioned: often
complained of, "the
1060   sun's in my eyes":
this burning while imprtnt
theories are discussed &
business goes forward:
"goods were shipped
1065 last Thurs via PP"
ASAP, CIF, & FAS: & the
    lemon industry:
the sun, riding a moment-
to-moment crest: I
1070   hope it will keep on
riding: it's not a
        fixture:

noticed how
some nights the stars
1075 are raw & brand new?
        make you feel
        slightly
        uneasy?
        it's the size
1080   & distance

unwinds you,
pulls you out
attenuating you
into
1085   nothingness
till you grasp
around
at star-straws:

anybody doesn't believe in
1090   reality should
try to start a dead car
on a 10-degree
morning:

maximum definition of
1095   detail along
with
assumptions of symmetry:

I feel ideas—as forms of
beauty: I describe
1100   the form as
you describe a pear's
shape:
        not idea as ideal—
ideas are human products,
1105   temporal & full of
process:
but
idea as perception of form,
outside form that
1110   corresponds
to inner form, & inner to
outer:

(chaos at the bottom of
things & mind: only ideas

1115 lift up from
      there: only
   groupings, saliences
   of similarity &
      difference, only
1120 clustering rises into
   intelligence—instinct
   itself an ordering,
   overcoming great odds:)

   a few flies are still
1125 hanging around
   the front porch:
      they're big blue:
      when the door opens
      they stir
1130   in the sun:
   they remember or
   still have the scent
      of the cat that was
      rotting behind my
1135   blue spruce: it's
      been below freezing
   I don't know how many
   nights: I thought that
   was supposed to lay them
1140   but it ain't laid'em
         yit:
   looks like it ain't
   agonna: we can
   know only so much & even
1145 explanations
   that hang round long as
   flies
      have a way of going off:
      one of these days
1150 a snow's crusty freeze
   will draw'em a line

fiercer
than cat scent:
   catch them
1155   napping at night
under leaves: turn
into some nap: long,
rich, bluegreen
   dreams:
1160   beautiful, healthy-
looking flies, ate good,
long as the cat lasted:
had their day in
   the sunny nooks
1165   with lovely buzzes:

11 DEC:

they changed the forecast
today from
partly sunny to
mostly cloudy: not by
1170   prophecy:
   stuck their
heads out the window &
tho the instruments
didn't agree reduced
1175   the gap between
prophecy & existent fact:
the direct
yields abundance, while
calculation
1180   drags upon the event:

I beg that my eyes that are
open
be opened, that the
   drives, motions,
1185   intellections, symbologies,

myths—lift,
            expose me
to direct
sight: seeing, I
1190   color, alter, hide, accent:
but what is there, naked
        & nonhuman?
or here, deep &
terrifyingly human?
1195   are we confined in an atom
with fiery nucleus? is
there too much room,
the ego under threat of
        dispersion?

1200   you—who are you? how do
I feel about you?
do I hate it that I love
to be tied to you by love?
        untied, wd I be free
1205   or lost?

but for
your own sake: who
                are you?
can I help? is there any
1210   thing I can do:
are things
working out
all right for you? what
are those black areas?
1215   are they parts
            of you that can't
                fall into place,
        come into light?
        are they longings &
1220   fears only dreams whisper?

———————

I love you the best
I know how:
encounter me with
belief:

1225 are you getting yours?
  getting & giving
yours, mine, & ours,
are we resolving most of
the areas, are we touching
1230 on elation
  enough?
do I love you mostly, or
the thought of us
   together?

1235 are you hoping that
giving will make up for
not getting? that wd
be the course of saints:
  get, too: get it
1240 from me: I have it
  and having
  it for you, I get mine:

who are you, deeper?
have I sounded you? was
1245 that
bottom I struck? but oh
up in the heart & around
your breasts
  and to speak of the deep
1250 in your eyes, have
I come into your
   measure? are
you getting yours? have
you been had?
1255 you've had me: I float:

every cell
comes to this:
you are
beautiful: you are
1260 just beautiful:
beautiful: thank you:

11:16 a.m: a blur of light
just came into
the room,
1265 lived a few seconds, then
died away:
my crown-of-thorns,
waiting, got the benefit,
struck across the middle:
1270 the instruments were
right in a way:
emphasis distinguishes
partly sunny from mostly
cloudy: if it don't
1275 snow it's gonna miss
a good chancet: I'll
say that:
lagging behind the event:
running to catch up: to
1280 be at the
crest's break, the
running crest,
event becoming word:

anti-art & non-classical:
1285 in art, we do not run
to keep up with random
moments, we select
& create
the moment
1290 occurring forever:
timelessness held

at the peak of time:
(just went to take a leak:
jay on the back lawn,
1295   hopping, looking around,
        turning leaves)

but this may turn back on
itself, motion by motion,
a continuum, held in
1300   timelessness
    racing with time,,,,like
a napkin
burnt in the ashtray, red
beads, flameless, racing
1305   around, splitting, dying,
turning fiber into ash:
    held activity:

let's have faith to go
    ahead & see if anything
1310   will happen:
maybe the tape will run out:

(looks a long way off:
    Muse! Muse! fiery
    woman, what
1315   you got to tell me?
tell me:
I feel weak so
much tape remains:
my back's getting sore:
1320   I don't sleep good
with this going on—slept
    pretty good last night:
woke up once
    into a country of dreams:
1325   wanted to remember them:
but mostly cloudy was

             too bright, even,
             for them: it *was*
          a country, I think: great
1330   many people: & no news
          of my book at the pstffce
          again this morn: so I
             don't feel
             strong about
1335   things: I
             need plenty of help:
             the crusty world
             takes no notice:
             Muse, what must we
1340   do to hit the top:
             it'd better
          be good: give a little,
          will you, please?) (I'm
                      bushed:)
1345   but you can do worse
          than be a singer of verses:

          (I'm the biggest
          fool that ever was—
             assertion's not the
1350   way to the top, you're
             a little round fool—
          to follow you off into
          these woods: who are you
          anyhow? some kind of a
1355   prickteaser?)

             & so & so & so &
             so & so
             &
             so & so & so & so so

1360   (some kinuva sans merci?)

          ———

lunch: hot dogs and baked
beans again: swell:
2/23: 11½¢ a can: cheap:
hotdogs run you around—
1365   oh let's see:
this morning's coffee &
a chocolate fudge cookie:
maybe 30¢ altogether:
& all
1370   that energy
turned into verse
will bring
you
about
1375   four condemnations:

transformations!
metamorphoses!
mitochondria!
hell's bells!

1380   how my back hurts: even
by concentrating, I can't
feel any presence
to my balls: missing:

wd it be masturbatory if
1385   I if I
touched the area
briefly
just to make sure?

two cool tight weights!
1390   thank you:
thank you very much:

if I had a flute: wdn't
it be fine

to see this long thin
1395   poem
rise out of the waste-
                basket:
the charmed erection,
stiffening, uncoiling?

1400   anyways, that wastebasket
is coiled full: wonder if
I should stomp
        in it?

in & out: weaving in &
1405   out: a
tapestry, looking for all
the world
as if it were alive:

(break we that watch up)
1410   just took a ride out
to the refuge: 100,000
birds: mallards, grebes,
teals, herons, Canada
           geese &
1415   two excellent flyers
    from which there is
        no refuge:
one, the short-necked,
long-tailed red hawk: he
1420   browses the marshes &
for the little bird,
little bird
he is carefully looking:
& way overhead, turning,
1425   the quiet, black
vulture:
two avenues flesh
can take: the tight red

                    & the loose dark meat:
1430   red ambulance
                        & black hearse,
                    brazen reminders: and the
                    birds fly among, regarding
                    & regardless:

1435   the trash collectors came
                    while I was gone &
                        took the
                    week's waste away: we
                        are purged: even
1440   a house has the incoming &
                    outgoing energies
                    & losses by which it
                        is maintained:
                    the garbage truck
1445   says on the back
                    "We aim to serve,
                        not disturb":
                    sophisticated
                    assonance

1450   &&&&&&&

                    intellections are
                        scaffolds, trellises
                    we wish some vine of
                        feeling would take to
1455   & possess
                    completely:
                        spider build
                        a circle
                    hung in
1460   the squares of: bird
                    light on & sing from
                    the top of:
                        we build them even

for the windsong's
1465   tenuous life:
chance
    a vine will ramble up it
busting into leaves & roses,
giving the robin a place
1470   & making all the air
    around
    fragrant: we build these
structures because we
have hope, at least:
1475   we're
    flat & lifeless,
    but these erections,
they have hollow spaces,
room: we mean
1480   to change—that is,
a sprouting is going
to go on: good, bad, &
indifferent are gonna
clutter up all around,
1485   rise through the
    lattices
    of held space
    and sing all
together, rose,
1490   thorn,
    smear of birdshit:
    gonna rise
right up out of the
            ground
1495   where the dreams wait
and be red & gold
and laughing to beat the
            band:

intellections are
1500   bowls we hope to fill:

motions on the
prowl:
don't
cut them
1505 down or bust them up so
the water spills
& the vine hunts
aimlessly over the ground:

do
1510 not be impatient with us:
we're coming along &
meantime
entertain yourselves with
the dry beauty of our
1515 joists & timbers, slats
& designs:
if nothing ever breaks
into leaf
still we
1520 meant to encourage
the vine: we like
the call of the
robin & his early visit &
the color of his hen's
1525 eggs &
the way he stands on the
lawn, erect—
dressed for a wedding:

intellections have a use,
1530 don't think they don't:
if the vine couldn't
find a natural tree, what
would become of it? if
structure without life is
1535 meaningless, so is
life without structure:

we're going to make a
dense, tangled trellis so
   lovely & complicated that
1540   every kind of variety will
find a place in it or on
it: you just be
      surprised: &
      forgive us:
1545   who mean song
direct & fierce:

(this day
   ended
    in spite of all
1550   mostly sunny)

a dark night of stars
ensuing:

help me:
I have this &
1555   no other comfort:
   the song,
the slight, inner
unmistakable song you
give me
1560   and nothing else! what
    are you,
some kind of strumpet?
will you pull out on me?
look: I have faith: I
1565   have faith: come or go:
I'll always love you:
I have nothing else:
I have
nothing else besides you:
1570   will you tear me
   to pieces? I'll go

on without you, until
you come again:
                              then
　　　　in the flare of song
1575
we'll make a common flame:

if it ain't one fantasy
it's anothern: where
　　are you, reality?
1580　　come out of there:
you drift around in the
background, drooping
like a suckegg dog:
probably I'd like you
1585　　　all right
if I could get up close
enough to know you:
are you pieces of things
not quite fastened?
1590　what's your face like?
　　　　frowns &
　　　　bitters?
　　　　witchy?
　　　　scrawny?
1595　　　warty?
　　　　withery?
maybe I've given you a
horrible mask
and behind that you're
1600　　beautiful: or
is this another dream,
reality's dream?
　　then, is reality to be
free of fantasies, those
1605　I hang between us,
　　those I cast on you?

fact is, I'm having
this conversation with a

piece of paper!
1610   and "you" are a figment
of imagination and "you"
have no mask
& if you did
no face
1615   wd be behind it:
all this is just coming
out of my head:
the factory of fantasies:
some beautiful, some
1620   terrifying,
some this, some that—but
all, paper & thin air!
    a hundred dragons
and furies, satyrs &
1625   centaurs—and one
Muse!
        get food:
        get water:
        get sex:
1630   bank account, nice car,
good address, retirement
plan, investment portfolio,
country-club membership,
monogrammed shirts, summer
1635   home, cabin cruiser, big
living room (furnished
modern)
        Money
        Power
1640   Food
        Water
        Sex—and who needs
paper conversations,
words revved up in a
1645   fine motion and a headful
of dragons?

———————

reality, I've got a feeling
you can be awful nice! but
if the only reality
1650   I can get is a spare,
           hard-bought one, why
turn on the fantasies and
let there be gorgeousness,
color & motion,
1655   red & gold fabrics
and fine illusioning silks!

the man with bills to pay
dreams with a Muse!

reality is
1660   knowing what you want
and how
to get it:

12 DEC:

clouds came in soon after
dark last night, and today
1665   broke fact & prophecy
as snow turning into rain:
           the starlings sit
           like rainsheds,
           vertical in the gray
1670   trees: two jays
search the ground:
as
it neared midnight last
night, I felt
1675   pulled to go out
and hunt the roosts of
birds, flush them & hear
the shrieks of panic,
           blind beating wings:

1680   I wanted to know
    what birds do at night,
    how they
    handle surprise, of
    weasels, foxes, snakes:
1685   I wanted to know
    if they're adequate
    to the night:
    I wanted to hear them
    settle down
1690   as I turned away, feel
    the sweet emptiness
    of their panic:

    yesterday at the refuge, I
    saw a fingerling,
1695   crosswise
    in a rising gull's beak
    shiver at both ends:

    and last night, after
    anger & a family tiff, I
1700   suffered a loss & breakage
        of spirit, blankness
    as of plateaus: my "poem"
    turned to incontinent
    prose, unburned by spirit,
1705   and this occupation
        with a rolled
        strip of paper
    blackened to
    obsession, senseless,
1710   slightly mad: the Muse
    cleared out, leaving an
    empty house:

    but she's back with me
    today, I think: I hear

1715 a little voice
    singing
    under my brain, and I know
    she's there,
     modest & faithful:

1720 at the postoffice, no news:
    nothing is out there
    in the world: or it's
     all turned to concrete:
    I've won no battles & lost
1725 none:
     am engaging no
      realities:

    cause enough to stop &
     tear: cause enough
1730 to sleep today, rest my
    back & brain: except
    that song itself
     is enough, needs no
    appeals beyond itself,
1735 tightens fantasy
    into matter
    to outlast
    this day's real concerns:

    soundless mist,
1740   collecting, sounding
    in the gutterspouts:
    the saliva bed sucking in
    my pipe, the moaning suck
    of a dying bird:
1745 the burry buzz of a
    distant, peripheral plane:
    the yellow, octagonal
    pencil, rocking as I write:
    the air & surface burn
1750 of cars on Tilton Rd—heat

kicking on & off, baseboard
cracking, freezer
wheezing—silence,
broken by keys:

1755   ✿

              ✿ ✿ ✿

            ✿ ✿ ✿ ✿ ✿

              ✿ ✿ ✿

               ✿

1760 clusters!
    organizations!

            ✿ ✿ ✿ ✿ ✿

            ✿ ✿ ✿ ✿ ✿

            ✿ ✿ ✿ ✿ ✿

1765 shapes!

   <u>)/((/)/)/((/)/)/(</u>

designs!

close suspension of
cloud: not a break or
1770   beam: the jay
jumps around in the naked
sumac thicket, squalls,
complains, stares at a
     head of sumac-seed,
1775 pecks it violently, as
with contempt: what a
jar, moist rattle: the
seed-head comes still
again, indifferent:
1780 the crown-of-thorns has
had so little sun, the
flour-flowered spike,

                                        opening, is
                                        pale pink
1785   that in an outside
                 summer sun would be
                      blood red:
                 not much green
                 on the walls of
1790   the aquarium: the snails
                      are sluggish (!)—

                 the sky is like
                 neon lighting, a
                      ceiling of light
1795   without origin, no
                 fierce disc
                 radiant, recognizable
                 source: equal diffusion:
                 and when
1800   the Florentines painted
                 radiant populations in
                      the heavens, they were
                                not wrong:
                                each of
1805   us,
                 says modern science, is
                 radiant,
                                tho
                                below the
1810   visible spectrum:
                 paradise will
                 refine our radiance
                 or give us better sight:
                      we're fallen
1815   now:
                 we may be raised into
                 knowledge & light:
                 lower would be
                 longer & longer wavelengths
1820   to dark's undisturbed constant:

may we
not go there
but ever & ever up
    singing into shining
1825 light:
but not too high:
there's a zone we
    do best in: beyond
    on either side, we
1830 go by instruments
and artificial atmospheres:
a stark way:

we are, as bodies,
"localizations"
1835 supported by barriers,
        holding in &
        shutting out:
systems of
exclusion, permitting
1840   certain inlets, outlets:
we are
"held together":
minerals—such as
            calcium—
1845   selected, refined
    & deposited to high
    purities
            give support:
specialized tissues
1850 bind us to the bones: an
outer cage
protects softer organs:
        lovely
        loose mesenteries—
1855   permitting digestion's
        roil & change—
hold intestines in place:
    so

                the exchanges can go
1860   on, the trades in
                    blood, lymph,
                food, waste, water:
                traffic through
            barriers, each selective,
1865   responsive:
            if you have condemned the
            body, you have
            condemned a miraculous
                residence—
1870   temple
                we should try to keep
            the right spirit in:
            the aggregates! the
            widening accumulations,
1875   providing the molecules,
            proteins, triggers
            we need:

            imperfect, tho beautiful,
            body: when it can
1880   no longer defend, repair,
            grow—when mineral
            ash (that could not be
            processed away) stiffens
                the cell walls
1885   so they lose flexibility
            & effect—then the balance
            turns
            to invasion and
                disintegration:

1890   nothing permanent is old:
            what is forever has no
            youth or age: if you
                could choose, how
                wd you choose?

1895   the biochemist, first
seeing how
two molecules select each
other & interlink
  must think he
1900   beholds
  a face of God:
& from the center of all
these balances,
  coordinations,
1905   allowances,
integrations—waves
register & float away into
nothingness: there is
  mind:
1910   before you desecrate this
place, study its
architecture:
    but the mind doesn't
    insist we know all
1915   this: its commands
are few:
    reproduce this temple
    before it falls:
    food, water:

1920   barriers!
what is it, exactly, that
exists
when I see fish
travel in water & birds
1925   in air?
resemblance
  tying high above
  difference:
wings, fins: air, water:

13 DEC:

1930   my book came today, Friday
        the 13th
        wooooooooooooooooooooooo
        wooo wooo wooooooooooooo

        6:35 pm: we went
1935   Christmas shopping at
        Korvette's and
        Cherry Hill:

        had dinner just now
        over to Somers Point at
1940   Mac's: fried shrimp—
        & Phyllis had
        crab:
        they have a good salad
        dressing there: don't
1945   know what it is
        (on the
        order of French) but
        they call it "Mac's":

        bought Aristophanes's
1950   complete plays, very
        saxy (I hope)—I'd read
        Frogs & *Clouds* (no, it ws
        Birds) before:
        mostly, I walked
1955   around carrying my
        bk:

14 DEC:

today
came in an
opposite way

1960	of rain turning into snow:
	when I woke up
	the gutterspouts were
	dripping musical flutes:
	the tones dangled &
1965	broke &
	ran together with
	inexhaustible variety of
	mood & shape:
	but now (10:50 a.m.) the
1970	same colorless, closed sky
	turns weight
	into fluff, fast pellets
	into slow blurs
	that touch rainpools with
1975	many-fingered hiss
	& melt into silence: &
	the grass seems
	to rise up &
	cushioning bring down
1980	the flakes:
	as if a god slept hereabouts
	and meant to make a winter
	of his sleep:
	(snow, a servant to
1985	Agathon, cloistered up
	with odes)
	soft prisons are the
	worst kind: bars
	& stones are
1990	honest, exact,
	but this insinuation,
	insisting it's not itself,
	this deepening
	with universal touch: not
1995	a path, road

left: only circles of
    melt-stain under naked
    trees (the flakes
        caught in a
2000   foliage to
        branches) as if
the roots
sent up a warmth of
protest
2005 or stirred radiating
    summer dreams:

and (it's not very cold)
the foliage melts & hangs
rainbeads
2010   on twigs & branches—
points of clarity
concentrating light
    into sources:

no birds this
2015 morning: they
fear these white bodies
that fly into a still
white starvation:

a few seed, hung on
2020 weeds & grasses, fall
& pepper the snow:

the reason I write so much
is
that I can't do anything
2025 else:
poem must be now
close to 40 feet long: I
can't get it out
to write letters or

2030   postcards or anything:
              well
              if
              it
              must
2035   be
              onward
              to
              the
              end,
2040   let's
              get
              there
              in
              a
2045   hurry: or
is that cheating?
every time the roll turns
it speeds up: as the
diameter decreases, the
2050   revolutions per foot (rpf)
increase, so the poem
should rise to a pitch of
unwinding
              at the end: a
2055   spinning of diameter into
nothingness:

exclusions:
lepers on their islands,
drunks imprisoned in
2060   drunkenness,
the disappearances (un-
noticed—the streets
seem always full,
lively & young enough)
2065   into illness, stiff bones,
strokes, graves:

the silent child that stays
indoors,
unable to connect:
2070 I feel the bitterness of
fate: I feel the
bitterness of fate:

what it means to
drive away from the
2075 house: take a walk
down the street:
join the daylight
world's clean going:

are we as innocent of our
2080 joy
as they are of their
despair?

must do what we can,
accept the rest:
2085 God, help us: help us:

we praise Your light:
give us light to do what
we can with darkness:

courage
2090 to celebrate Your
light
even while the
bitterdrink
is being drunk:

2095 give us the will
to love
those
who cannot love:

———

a touch of the dark
2100 so we can know how one,
hungry for the light,
can
turn away:

we're here together:
2105 is it known,
has it been determined
what is right to do?

give us a song
sanctified
2110 by Your divinity
to make us new
& certain of the right:

should I sacrifice
myself for
2115 others? would
they, alarmed,
turn in confusion
against me?

should I care for
2120 myself only,
bring to its fullest
enunciation
what fate says in me?

we're here together,
2125 though:
let us know when
to reach out &
when to withdraw:

& so & so
2130 the snow has
turned to grit: I had

lunch after
"who cannot love"—
soup, sandwich, milk,
2135 chocolate fudge cookie, &
coffee (my wife's home
today)—most
of the week she
works,
2140 while I sit
home in
idleness:

I'm waiting to hear if
Cornell will give me
2145 a job: I need
to work &
maybe I write
too much:

silenced by
2150 exclusion: we
don't hear the
suffering: it
doesn't exist
and we are untroubled:

2155 prisons!
constellations!
shapes that possess
&
entangle the mind!

2160 run yourself through
Beethoven's
Sonata Pathétique &

exist like a bush!
willing entrapment
2165 of cell walls &

                    diamonds, a giving
               of the self
               over
               into shape, structure
2170   played upon
               by motion & flesh!

               they say there are
               water molecules in the
                         void—

2175   then it's not empty!—
               motions racing
               through, particles &
               drifts, a structure
                    woven
2180   beyond the
               diaphanous:

               but here
               around the roots of trees,
               a black engendering:
2185   prisons,
               hold fast!

               safe in these cages, I
               sing joys
               that never were
2190   in any thorough jungle:

               but betimes & at times
               let me out of here:
               I will penetrate into the
               void
2195   & bring back
               nothingness
               to surround all these
                         shapes with!

               ————

closing in
2200   without closing:
         running through
without filling:
opening out
    with walls:

2205   run my poem through
                your life & it will
                exist in you
                like a protein
                    molecule:

2210   clothes to try on, wear,
       abandon or keep:
       put away in the closet,
            a memory ectoplasmic
       with gone joys:

2215   what am I doing?
       what are my innermost
            feelings?
       do I know what I'm doing
            or am I waiting
2220   for it to
            be done?

       my innermost feeling is
       a silky pouring of
            semen, a rich
2225   disturbance
       in the groin,
       broken loose, flowing free:

       I remember a stallion
       had been stalled for wks:
2230   in the lot surrounding
       him were mules & mares:
            someone let down the

                     gate &
                     he hit the nearest
2235   bony old mule and gave
                     her a rapt opening,
                            invasion & filling,
                     & in a slick moment he
                     was shot: as if shot,
2240   dropped to the ground
                            and the loose wobbling
                            weight
                            poured & poured on the
                            ground
2245   & he came up & took her
                     again: she braced
                     herself and groaned:

                     the rich pouring
                     of this verbal
2250   itch:

                            I fall back:
                            shot:
                            winded:
                            God, relieved, sweet
2255   floating relief:

                     imprisoned in marvelous
                     desire
                     and set free! beautiful
                     bth gng in & cmng out:

2260   the men, embarrassed,
                     joked & hid
                     their hard-ons against
                            the fence: they

                     knew the stallion
2265   stalled in the prison of
                     his honest lust: you,

find the exit,
   the wooly
         entry
2270   and go free & take an
honest part
in the community: many
things to be
accounted for,
2275   to take into account:

oh this poem is long:
the tape's still thick
& slow:
Muse, come & take my
2280   riding, rouse my riding:
we got a long long way
      to go: present

      the cage men will
dwell in, design the
2285   gleaming city:

cars hiss on the highway:
typewriter clicks:
   the thermostat snaps:
(sounds like a motorcycle
2290   out there)
the day's unchanged—gray
undivided clouds:
but the
snow's stopped:

2295   we went out after "& we
are untroubled" up there:
I unpacked my mother-in-law's
new dishes
& Phyllis helped wash them:

2300   (forbidden, theirs is
        forbidden suffering:
        they turn inward & inward
        calls hopelessly
        to inward: song, poor
2305   song, lift them outward
        if you can)

        an object,
        exactly perceived
        & described is
2310   when entered in the
                        tapestry
        somewhat compromised:
        part strength flows
        from it
2315   to its
        compositional environment:
        no tapestry
        without
        this clustering,
2320   giving up of strength:

        no tapestry then! if it
        impose what may
        enter! forget it!

                but no exact
2325   thing, either,
                unless it
        calls & calls away to
        kindred things:

                the job is
2330   honest,
        full as a suspected
        reality

of tensions: to keep
the object clear as
2335   it can be (& itself),
the
tapestry "one" as it can
be,
without tyranny:

2340   partial solutions: men
feared
at the end of the 19th
century
that they were going to
2345   solve the universe: no
more need of physicists!

        just as the
        whole fell
        together it
2350   fell apart:

innocent again,
the physicists are
    re-employed:
(I'm glad somebody's
2355   working:
wish I were making some
money myself)

        @

back off there, populace!
2360   the poet will have a little
    room!
disburden the area: hey,
you: git off da stage!
    the poet will take
2365   a little distance on:

what?
can you think these
　　"private" things are
　　private?
2370　they were got from
jokes & dirty books:
the poet, lawsee, but
sings to the general
　　& claims
2375　but the murmur in the words:
have at you, sir!

the poor employee of the
ruling queen, the listener
to lies that
2380　they may become truth:
the raiser of halcyons
into storm: the public
voice
that has no pleading of
2385　its own: but, indeed,
bends to the great,
will take coins
　　to th'amusement:
that will, cold as a
2390　　　　　　glass, give
the hag the hag,
the beauty beauty, the
evildoer his face:
to the courts with your
2395　　disgraceful shows!
　　here
　　the poet lolls, suckled
up in the rapture of his
sacred saying:

2400　a nerveless creature
　　because all nerves:

odd-one-out
because he stands aside to
see: fool that makes
2405   foolishness a law:
will you be ruled,
sir, metered out?
the poet implores you to
get the hell off his back:
2410   he will have
room
and a universe
to cry all day
the trampling of a weed:

2415   go you the hell all on
back home: or stand off:
the music *descends*: look
up: there, now: there:
        thank you, gentlemen:

2420   and goodnight: it's past
twelve and a
        cold, freezing, windy
        night:

%

15 DEC:

2425   my poem went for a ride
today: I
        backgutted it all
the way out
of the typewriter,
2430   rewinding the roll:
stuck it in a paper
bag, then in the
        glove compartment:

we all went to York, Pa.
2435   to visit relatives:

I was reluctant to give
the day to myself & not
to the poem: but
   the thing I couldn't
2440   do was separate us:
what if the house caught
fire while I was gone?
unh, unh: took it with me:

but mightn't you have had
2445   a car accident & ruined it?
mebbe but bebbe I'd
have ruined myself, too,
    past caring about
    poems,
2450   mebbe:

took it with me: & have
returned (10 pm) &
reinserted & rewound:

I'm beat: drove
2455   there & back & drove
a lot while there,
   looking the city over,
the place my nephew
goes to school & where his
2460   daddy works & shopping
centers, bowling alleys
& the ritzy section,
mansions way up
on the highest ridge—
2465   overlooking:
    the Top:

———

but it's late:
excuse me, I'm tired: &
the cold drops—
2470 they say to 5 or 10 above
tonight:

16 DEC:

first I heard
on the radio this morning
it was
2475 19 degrees:
but it's bright sunny
and
believe it or not
   there're a couple of
2480 flies
out on the porch, still
okay, doing fine
on "areas of warmth":
   but doing I don't
2485 know what at night:
a one-legged starling
was hopping around on the
porch when I just drove
up: and a catbird was
2490   sitting
in the green-withered
rhododendron bush,
warming:

the joy of the crest,
2495 riding & writing
in the going making
single stream: but I
   can't always live
   there:
2500 obstructions:
frustrations:

frazzling reality,
　　many-fingered &
　　dividing: what
2505　self-acceptance, strength
of self, is
needed to meet it:
the gain's in doing
little things: but

2510　wherever you turn, someone
beat you there, is
in your way
obstructing you: some
　　idiot pulls out
2515　　in front of you,
without notice or
hesitation: someone pops
on his brakes: another
drags along:
2520　somebody behind you blasts
his horn:

here, the obstructions
continue: the flow
lost, the crest gone: the
2525　self not
pulling all together:

if things were easy
they'd be valueless:
wd they?
2530　this is easiest when it
rides highest
& when it's difficult
nothing can be done:

this fantasy: with
2535　faith, unity, I

may turn it into a
　　pleasing reality:
wdn't that be a blast:
　　wdn't that break up
2540　pragmatism:

　　(there you go
　　picturing yrself
　　worldwide again: easy,
　　boy: you
2545　dooky like
　　everybody else)

it's a loss of love:
I love all those
people (provided
2550　they get out of my way)

hostility, thrust, that
drives one to this
　　thrashing of keys:
violence of vowels:

2555　prisons of hostility,
gleaming as Manhattan
plate-glass towers:
solitude—so as not to
　　　　strike!

2560　death's
the maximum-security
prison: take a lot of
practice
to spring
2565　that one: too secure:
turn our faces into
cold wind &
risk's hard fact:

———

I feel like running:
2570 & wd:
except there's no
place to
run to: prisons to let
ourselves into
2575 and out of:

what kind of mess
am I in today?
Muse, if you
want anything out
2580 of me, you'll have
to do a little
fixing-up:

this tape is too damn long:
I'll tell you that:
2585 terrible task:
then you go off & whore
around:

10 pm: we've just
finished addressing the
2590 Xmas cards (policy:
send one to people
who sent one last year—
with some eliminations
(somebody has to make the
2595 first move:) some additions:)
stars, angels, snow,
donkeys, trees, bells, arches,
windows, children: not
a bad context, though
2600 reality
has a
way

of
wandering around the edges
2605 of
it: I'd take a liking to
it if it wasn't for
still having the stamps
to lick:
2610 next yr I intend to send
a card to everybody
I know (I think)—
that's not a bad context &
it says a lot about peace:

2615 just went to Tony's to
get a pack of cigs: it's
colder than you
can imagine: must be
around 8: yipe!

17 DEC:

2620 Sisyphus
   struggling
    with his
     immortal
      rock: some say this
2625 is all man's work,
crumbling castles, decay-
ing systems—absurdity:

but Sisyphus
knew each upward strain
2630 & groan
soaked into the hard
potential of the stone,
that the sweat burned in
deep:

———

2635   mountaintop, he released
weeks of energy
and saw—each time as
miracle—the
gravity-bound, difficult
2640   rock
leap & lollop
like a deer,
feather-light, bird

awing: & he let out a
2645   cry of joy that
rang through the
valley
mixing with stone-thunder:

the people—who'd
2650   forgotten Sisyphus & his
breadless labor—screaming
jumped out of bed
& ran
out into the night:

2655   Sisyphus took
light, jerky
steps downward
and resolving came,
luminous with explanation,
2660   among the people:

they cheered &
thanked the gods
for the return of reason

& Sisyphus, the
2665   groans all vented from
his rock
turned to the empty, easy

thing & rolled it like
a playball over the even
2670 ground
up to the bottom of the
rise:
the people, smiling, went
to bed & through
2675 the black morning hours
the rock,
breaking branches, began
to take on
again its difficult majesty:

2680   çç

got
    to leave Sissy Fuss
    & go
    pick out the Christmas
2685   tree:
    keep it cold in
    garage: so it don't
turn stiff & sheddy:
    cut'em around October:
2690   why
    they cut'em so soon?
    transportation:
    it's merchandising:
dealerships to work out:
2695 farmers to contact: red
        tape: whatd'ya
think?
they can just appear up
down here
2700 fresh
two days before Christmas?
sheez!
some kindova nut:

218

                    grows on a tree,
2705   a tree is part of
                    Nature,
Nature is beautiful &
thank you for the
                    compliment:

2710   why don't we go cut
our own?
cut our own!
where?
but we don't own that land:
2715   whatd'ya mean they don't
care?
I know they're beautiful:
grow right up in the
fallow land,
2720   taper up nice, standing
out half-deep in
        Indian grass, right
out in the middle of
        the field:

2725   when I was a boy:
or a bit more:
used to go get the
        Christmas tree: lived
way out in the country
2730   down in Carolina
in a time
& place
that seem so long ago,
everything different
2735   now & sort of loused up:

an only boy & I would get
the axe &

follow the paths over the
fields & back of the
2740   fields come into
hill-woods (hickory,
   lush-leaved tree,
      covering the ground each
year with
2745   thick-shelled nuts)
& then into the swamp woods:
   for
in the South
cedar grows deep
2750   in the damp swampwoods
and then it's sparse, so
sparse, where I come from:
& walk & walk, roaming and
nearly lost:
2755   there's one! already
   topped: and found
another, shaggy, topped
years ago: & finally
finally finding one
2760   bushy, full, &
      pointed:
climbing and with that
awkward, ungrounded swing,
hacking away at the
2765   trunk:
dragging it home, the limbs
obliging, flowing with
the motion:

we had no electricity but
2770   we had pinecones &
      colored paper &
      some tinsel: it
was beautiful enough:
it was very lovely:
2775   & it's lost:

—————

though there's no
　　　returning (and
shd be little desire
to return) still we shd
2780　keep the threads looped
tightly with past years,
the fabric
taut
& continuous, past growing
2785　into present so present
can point to future:

where am I now?
in a house with
no acres around it—don't
2790　　even own an axe—
plenty of electricity but
no hickory nuts,
no rummaging the swamp
for the scented green,
2795　the green-green, moist,
growing right on the tree:
now, a tree from
somewhere—maybe Vermont—
got by handing over
2800　　two or three green
pcs of paper:

$$\$\$\$\$\$\$\$\$\$\$\$\$\$$$

do you hear me, Sisyphus,
durn you? do you hear me
2805　groan:
　like:
　wow:

2:29 pm: (still sunny)

—————

I better get out of
2810   here & go
          get that tree:
the good ones are
gonna be gone:

&

2815   Snow

The little tree
on the hill
could surely be
bright & still

2820   except the wind
round the hill
has a mind
that isn't still

&

2825   I decided not to get the
tree:
instead, I lay down on the
couch
& nearly fell asleep
2830   & then sat up
& then
the little tree
      came to me:

4:30 pm: the sun's sunk:
2835   we approach the shallows
of the year: short
      days with the sun
      gone south:
      the light will

2840   lengthen, break through
           plate-glass ice,
           stir roots & bees:

           in a maze prison, you're
           free: every wall
2845   opens:
           you move around with
           trial:
           you know there's a way
           out:

2850   the mind turns & fails:
           and turns & fails: loss
           of bearings & origins:

           the maze shrinks into the
           head, paralyzing: unwind
2855   it, un-
           wind it!

           speaking of memries,
           I member
           this little spring
2860   that came mouthing out
           of sand at the foot
           of the pasture:
           I dammed up a good-sized
           pond around it,
2865   black mud walls
           maybe 6" high:
               held the flow,
           gave it structure:
           still the little mouth
2870   kept talking
           in the clear pond: clear!
           you could read the grain
           in the bottom mud,

kind of fluffy:
2875 frogs laid eggs in it:
messy eggs
with little black eyes:
beautiful & sticky:

they say the night will be
2880 cold
with increasing cloudiness:

probably: snow tomorrow:
flurries:

18 DEC:

today
2885 broke as if under water:
horizons & dome diffused
with completely
increased cloudiness:

a set of four thumb-size
2890 birds
flicker in the sumac
grove:
the sun's a silver bead
behind the clouds:
2895 flurries expected:

Christmas trees come
stout, stubby, tall, lean,
bunchy, lopsided, scrawny—
besides the kinds—cedar,
2900   pine, fir:
my wife & I diverge
    at scrawny-bunchy: she
likes bunchy ones (even a

little stubby): I like
2905   scrawny, open trees:
like to get inside the
tree
and hang it full of
      ornaments:
2910   I
      don't
      like
those bunchy ones that
thrust you out, accept only
2915   peripheral trim:

chacun à chacun, tho: that
is, the devil with it:
      husband & wife hold
      each other off
2920   by digging
chasms of difference:
then they have a hell of a
time bridging them: it's
important that a male be
2925   different from a female—
the greater the difference
the higher the charge—
      but if the
difference gets too wide,
2930   the two halves
drift off into alienations:

ever noticed how
dark it is
inside those bunchy trees?
2935   they hover-in the
dark, withholding, secret,
mysterious:
what? have a system of

                    darkness
2940   standing in the living
        room, recalcitrant,
        impenetrable? the devil
        take it!

                    —or—

2945   I cd think of it as
        protected darkness,
            boundaried by
        ornament & light:

        maybe that's a deeper
2950   response

        than my fully exhausted
            open tree:

        everybody to his own taste,
        said the old man as
2955   he kissed the cow: (and
        every little bit helps,
        said the old lady as
            she peed in the ocean)

        10:29 a.m: the bead's gone:

2960   11:40 a.m: fine, hurrying snow:

        12:48 pm: everything white:

        3:20 pm: still snowing: I
            went to the
        cleaner's, egg-lady's,
2965   & mailbox & just got in:
        trucks are whirling red
        gravel over the roads:
        the snow is holding,

packing down: tires aren't
2970 breaking through:

the children, let out of
school, run testing
mounds that look all
snow but are only surfaced,
2975   scraping up handfuls—
      not yet enough
      snow for
      huge
      crunchy handfuls—

2980 muffled, the highway's
stopped burning:

9:41 pm: we've just come
    in from being out:
it's a wicked white
2985   icy night:
cars slipping, wheels
      spinning: bushes
sparkle in the headlights:

imagine being out
2990 for a night
restless & wakeful with
cold, some child
coughing—or crying
with fever:

2995   who are we
    on this globe?
    how & at what cost
    have we survived?

    deer & birds:
3000 are they cold?

—————

maybe one way of
coming home is
into silence,

restfulness from words,
3005   freedom from the mill
that grinds
reality into sound:

why do I need to throw
this structure
3010   against the flow
which I cannot stop?
is there something
unyielding in me that
can't accept
3015   the passing away of days
and birds
flowers & leaves?
it's always never return
for them:
3020   that way, day by day, for
me & you:

acquiescence, acceptance:
the silent passage into
the stream, going along,
3025   not holding back:

I try to transfigure these
days
so you'll want to keep
them:
3030   come back to them: from
where?
        from the running honey
        of reality & life?
come back:

———

3035 I hold these days aloft,
    empty boxes
    you can exist in: but
    when you live in them
    you hurry out of your own
3040 life:
      if my meaning is
      to befriend you,
      must I turn you
        away?

3045 I stop to fasten, and
    currents
    swirl around, over
    me, wearing my
    structures away, teaching
3050 me not to grasp, not to
    try to keep:

    why does a man sit alone
    and question
    the answerless air where
3055 no blood stirs
    and no lips move?

    this love, fashioned
      into acts,
      might bring a lonely
3060 person
    purpose enough:
      what's the nature
    of this carrying-on?

    generations to come: are
3065 they more precious,
      estimable, than these
      that are?

can a lip quiver with
more need
3070   then than now?

I have a notion to be
wordless, but
    active with immediate
    deed, open
3075   with the glance of my
    need, direct,
        humble in my going,
glad
as the thoughtless are:

3080   are we creators in fact
or collectors of relics:
    do we make grow
    or cast into stone?

19 DEC:

this ole world could be
3085   one
    if it wusn't
for hate
    bustin it apart,
    keeps
3090   crackin it
into little pieces:

love, I mean, could
    rise up there love
and make all the
3095   children dance
    shaking breasts & hips,
pelvis
shooting in & out
and all kine of sanging
3100   going on:

summer coming back just
like it hadn't been
    nowhere:

and the bees
3105   bumbling
in the hollyhocks:

calves kicking up their
heels &
the spring roosters
3110   crashing into crows:

in Praxagora's perfect
world, tho,
the maiden could be had
only after the hag
3115   was served:

and what would we do with
our hate?
turning hate outward, we
keep dense & pure
3120   our inward love:

can we incorporate our
enemies?
can we maintain a high
degree of difference
3125   within unity's cluster?

give room, latitude, widen
the band
    of acceptance: we live
in strictures of hate
3130   & suspicion, intolerance
        & doubt:

absorb the margins:
enlarge the range:
give life room:

20 DEC:

3135 today is cold: hit
    ten last night:
    and it not winter
    yet:

    the sun comes high
3140 into the room: strikes
  the inside wall
  three feet up from the
  floor:

  we're going to Philly tdy:
3145 little more shopping:

  7:19 pm: oh it was a cold
   windy day, jaw-tight,
  ear-numb, nose-runny, cold
  windy day: the sun
3150   seemed to do no good
    (pigeons hovered
  in the morning sun
  along the steel trusses
  of overpasses) and the
3155 wind burst
  from intersections down
  the dark street-canyons:
  concrete, stone, steel,
  hard & cold:

3160 having shopped for hrs,
  I sat a
  few minutes

                in the waiting room (on
                    the balcony) at
3165   Wanamaker's:
                (or do they call that
                the gallery?):
                mostly old folks:
                some dozed: the eyes of
3170   some begged
                    out of strictures:

                the circles of reach:
                in the womb, confinement:
                then, opening, the
3175   bassinet: the cradle,
                playpen, the house, to
                school, enlarging always
                the widening circle: then
                away to college
3180   or military service, the
                    circle so large
                    now as to be
                    congruent with earth—
                the total openness:
3185   then the gradual
                    shrinking,
                    stiffening, the star-
                brittle bones,
                eyes fading,
3190   arm-reach,
                    and the last
                    confinement:

                my, my: & nothing to be
                    done:
3195   nothing to be done!
                is any time left?
                carpe diem, snatch, grab,
                hasten, do, jump, go:

get the rose, da
3200   rose, da rosa baby: see
that girl? when
she turns her head

& stands lost, her eyes
blank with something forgot,

3205   universes
crack up into little
pieces & blow away

and something quite
silvery
3210   starts singing—right

out in public
and whoever said men can't
be blossoms because

looking at her,
3215   near her,
they

bloom warm,
they just rise up,
something liberally
3220   extending itself,
expanding

and they turn to hot jelly
& freezing little bits
of ice

3225   and say "God" under their
breaths
and under the burden of

something too much
to have or lose:

3230 it's go: go & green:

the day we went to York
 I saw
a black&white cow
 standing close to
3235   the sunny side of a barn:

animals know a good many
things: they'd
 take over if
 they had hands:

21 DEC:

3240 the jay was out
  before sunrise
wheeling & dealing

& around noon
a covey of quail
3245 enjoyed (apparently)
 the sunlit margin
between the back lawn
and the sumac grove:

now, at 3:58 pm the
3250 sun is yellow,
coming into its
  horizontal: about
a half hour to go:
they used to say
3255 "half hour sun":
 I used to tell

sun-time, right
out of the burning clock:
have a gold watch, now,
3260   that takes its heat
from me: times change:

our tree, which I just
put up, was
    "Grown in Canada"
3265   &
comes via
Puyallup, Washington:
the tag says:

22 DEC:

we lost our mule Kate in
3270   the fall
to a chattel mortgage:
    men backed the truck
    up into a shallow
ditch, dropped the ramp,
3275   & with twitch & whip
loaded her on:

it seemed, rather than
    justice,
violation, breakage:
3280   tearing into
a mule's knowledge: &
I stood by, a boy,
violated & hard:

Kate was small, willing
3285   at a touch of straw
to run a wagon harder than
you meant:

she lunged in the
high-boarded truck:
3290   her ears flicked, her
eyes set back, blank &
reasonless: she
drowned from herself & us
when the motor, roaring
3295   over all meaning,
tore into gear:

farm with no mule:
the corn she made
   to lie all winter
3300   in a barn's weevil-dust
& rat droppings:

in the spring, a tragic
mule, bony,
   majestical
3305   came to us:

never forget first time I
saw her, coming down the
Chadbourn road: my
   father went to town
3310   in the morning:
late that afternoon,
sitting on the washbench,
waiting, I saw him
   coming, new wagon &
3315   new mule:
she seemed hardly to be
walking,
but the legs went out &
out in a reach
3320   that covered ground:

———

I called her Silver—O
loved beast,
dead & gone,
not to be lost from mind
3325 & song—
because
though huge & tired, she
wd rise to her hindlegs
at a touch of heels to
3330 her sides
and run stiff & fast: like
the Lone Ranger's horse:
& Silver was black:
she possessed the
3335 mark of play,
a liveliness silly,
inappropriate & great:

10:17 pm:
we went to church at 4
3340 this afternoon:
I held a lighted candle
in my hand—as all the
others did—and helped
sing "Silent Night": the
3345 church lights were doused:
the preacher lit his
candle & from his the
deacons lit theirs &
then the deacons went down
3350 the aisles & gave light to
each row
& the light poured
down the rows &
the singing started:
3355 though the forces
have different names
in different places &

times, they are
real forces which we
3360 don't understand:
        I can either believe
        in them or doubt them &
        I believe:

I believe that man is
3365 small
& of short duration in the
great, incomprehensible,
& eternal: I believe
it's necessary to do
3370 good
as we can best define it:
I believe we must
discover & accept the
        terms
3375   that best testify:
I'm on the side of
whatever the reasons are
        we are here:

        we do the best we can
3380 & it's not enough:

23 DEC:

I was thinking when I woke
up how much more I wanted
ice cream than breakfast:
        the wake-up radio was
3385 saying
the most dread terror is
        fire at sea
(ship burning in the
Atlantic with 800 aboard)
3390 and that forecast for

today was snow, turning
    along the coast into
    sleet & rain:

release us from mental
3395   prisons into the actual
        fact, the mere
        occurrence—the touched,
tasted, heard, seen:
        in the simple event is
3400   the scope of life:
let's not make up
categories to toss ourselves
around with:
        look: it's snowing:
3405   without theory
& beyond help:
I accept:
I can react with
        restlessness & quiet
3410   terror, or with
        fascination &
        delight: I choose the
side of possibility:

the snow's angling
3415   into the sumac thicket:
I see black &
        white, every twig
highlighted: if I were
looking with the snow,
3420   I'd see
all white:

4:48 pm: the vowels are
lifting around here: breve
a is becoming breve *i*:
3425   "I c'int stind it."

mansion is *minson*: *palace,*
    pillice:
    O Chaucer:

    Muse, you're an
3430   eagle in the mind: when
        you fly away
        the air's relaxed
        & empty:

            come back:
3435   maybe you're sick of
        domestic details & long
        for some swept
        transfigurations,
    leading, transforming
3440   ideas, details
        lifted into a
        marshaled whirl:

        I had
        decided to
3445   give up all
        but details:
        decision
    is sandhouse without you:

    I acknowledge you, am
3450   miserable without you:
    come again
    and make your will in me:

    or are you here now
    whipping a tired spirit
3455   the best you can?
    I admit
    I've shot my load:

but I can't stop: give
    me a second wind:

3460   it's there, I'm sure
of it, somewhere in the
mind—another valve to
    open:

    let it open &
3465   fill this tape
    plentifully up: let
the brim break: tear
thru surface tension
to the spring:

3470   the volcano shoots &
rests, gathering: the
man shoots &
    gathers: give me
a continuous, smooth
3475   shooting, rich
uninterrupted flowing:

do you want me to
wrestle & beg, testify
    your absence: I've
3480   made a long
piece of it:

26 DEC:

today is bright, warm:
supposed to go up to 40:
    ice in shade:
3485   sidewalks & walkways
slippery:

———

look what small beach
animals have made: a
   ruddy bird
3490   with curved beak
that turns stones
looking for
small beach animals!

(the consumed sustains the
3495   consuming form)

thought, too, is voracious:
Berenson sd
   the Gothic arch
ground three centuries of
3500   design
into gothic arches: a
   dominant form,
consuming insistence:

(here I'm probably
3505   converting the fine,
       shaped,
   differentiated world
   into
undifferentiated grist)

3510   I devour the sunlight off
     leaves,
the sound out of jet
    engines, I devour
    the whistle out of
3515   the bird,
     bust his
     guts open
     and devour
their churning:

3520   where is the
                  source?

        I eat the wind, frilly as
            a nap, off the
            mossbeds: I get down
3525   & close-up consume
        the sense of velvet
        off green winter moss:

        my heart eats the shape of
        your face:

3530   tell me, tell one
        moorless in the drift
            of broken forms, who is
        the conceiver who
        will pour this
3535   regurgitated pab
            into the
            transfigured
        saucepans, winejars,
        breadbaskets, garages,
3540   space stations
        of the new time?

        you've heard the larva
        chew
        in the wood?
3545   grit, grit, grit,
        metronomic?
        tell me—after
            wood's passage through
            guts,
3550   who will recall the tree?

            something's cooking in
            this life!

can you get on to it?
(will you need to
3555   be helped off?)

integrations &
  disintegrations:
    nothing that goes in
    comes out the same
3560   & nothing that comes out
has ever been the same
before:

small beach animals make
ruddy turnstones &
3565   wood meat makes larvae:
but where did the
    turnstone
    get the shape
by which he consumes? &
3570   how
the larva
find that special
    form of stridence?

things are related by
3575   opposition & similarity:
but the periphery
vanishes into nothingness,
the stabilizer:
    interior-ward
3580   is the going in & out
of shape,
    substance running
through shapes of itself,
itself the running:
3585   the container & the
  contained are
      somewhere

contained by the
universal noncontainer:

3590   frogs & snakes
keep the hawk's shrill
   whistle greased!

   thought jails!
keep us out!

3595   but
if we get too free,
all the way
into unrelated,
fractured sensation,
3600   call us back, jail,
occasionally
so we can get a good
   night's sleep:

since there are feelings
3605   (& thoughts) I can't
express
   through the forms of
society,
here I make other forms,
3610   play-forms,
to express them through:
that's the center:
maybe you're listing with
hidden passions, too: you
3615   can work
them off through
   play-shapes, as I
do:

use mine:
3620   get all the good
out of them you can:

clean up:
you have to take your
place
3625   at dinner: make decent
    conversation:

we have certain forms:
reality is to accept them
    at face cost & value,
3630   change them
    at peril
& if you do change them
stay awake
all night
3635   wondering what worse forms
will take their place:

careful how you go fooling
around with things: or
like me
3640   make sure you're
fooling:
      fooling takes
      instinct off:

(it's nice to
3645   have a good, quiet dinner:
wonderful to sleep,
    the cop on duty—
better look out
before you
3650   get dissatisfied, you may
be in for a real
gypping)

can I have that virgin?
nope:
3655   why?

she's taken:
who says?
'ciety:
I want her!
3660   sorry:
I can't stand it!
sorry:

better be careful, bub:
ever thought of taking
3665   up a little painting?
          ever been
interested in "expressing"
yourself in words?
          think you'd like it:

3670   jever think of taking up
mountain climbing:
          beautiful sport!
          dangle from
shocking heights, shoot
3675   off at peaks:
like babes!

like cool it: run it
into approved
    channels:
3680   irrigation
    in reverse: run it off:
lower the pressure
on the dam:

nice hobbies?
3685   stead of making that
married lady with the
          biggies,
jever think of making
chairs?
3690   photography is nice:

248

sing a song for sweet
society: keeps
ballocks in a row,
    where if you can't
3695   have every gal
      still—obey
the rules—
    there's one you can
have
3700   all your own
and nobody can take her
away from
you

or he'll wind up in
3705   court or behine bars:

sat simple:

think you could have one
  of your own
without not having all the
3710   others?

see that man's house?
I want it:
you can't have it:
why can't I?
3715   it ain't yourn:
why?
because:
I'll take it:
you can't:
3720   why can't I?
because:

there *is* a way:
get good marks in

kindergarten &
3725   discipline yourself so
the teacher likes you
& praises you & tells the
whole community how
    wonderful you are:
3730   & on up through college:
& don't get in any
trouble:
& then invent something or
start a business, and if it
3735   fails, start another:
    or work your way up
    through
a corporation: or start
saving early—invest wisely:
3740   someday you may get
    a house very much
    like that one—you
    may be able to buy
that very one
3745   if your tastes
haven't changed in
the meantime:

sheez!

it's called "coming to
3750   one's senses":

10:15 pm:

it's been a beautiful
day: warmth
made the light
3755   glossier: the cedars
and firs
stood

sprung into freedom,
snowless:
3760   the windy morning
      moved a trillion
      waves & branches:

streams
ran clear in the gutters
3765   from opaque
ice:
gutters running under
bright skies,
silent,
3770   ripples unpeopled
by raindrops, oiled
ripples of motion:

    energy
released from the sun
3775   made the gutters
      run: a fact,
ordinary & miraculous:
touch over great
distance: the cool melt
3780   from a vast,
      frying body:

that it's there:
that we're here!
    we, dependent,
3785   helpless, doing the best
      we can:

bacteria multiply by
simple division:
    changeless transmission:
3790   but also
they multiply sexually,

testing conditions
with mutant
possibilities:

3795   we must keep the
tradition &
modify it
so we stay resilient to
change:
3800   too traditional is loss of
change: too changing is
loss of meaning & memory:

27 DEC:

today is
cloudy
3805   in several ways:
details of pain,
causes of shivering: but
this must be done:

it's fairly warm,
3810   tho—speaking now
entirely of the weather:
may rain:
could turn cold
enough to snow again
3815   (none of my business)

I saw the jay
before breakfast:
he looked a little
grimy, gray,
3820   like old blue snow:
has had rough

times lately:
rough times is ordinary,

                    will not make
3825   the news:

                    the sun, screened dim by
                    clouds, enters the room,
                    strikes my typewriter,
                        throws shadow on
3830   the wall,
                        just touches
                    the flower-tip of a
                    crown-of-thorns branch:

                    ecology is my word: tag
3835   me with that: come
                    in there:
                        you will find yourself
                    in a firmless country:
                        centers & peripheries
3840   in motion,
                        organic,
                            interrelations!

                    that's the door: here's
                    the key: come in,
3845   celebrant,
                        to one meaning
                    that totals my meanings:

                        the circular lichen
                        spotting the tree
3850   trunk
                    is
                    like a moral order: there
                    is a center
                    where with threads the
3855   lichen knits in, the
                        "holding-on" point
                        that gathers stability
                        from bark: and there

                    is
3860   the outward multiplication
        of forms (cells & patterns)
        to an unprescribed
        periphery
        that marks the
3865   moment-to-moment edge
                of growth:

        the cougar, big in
                size & appetite,
        ranges widely:
3870   he won't turn
                a square mile
                into desert:
        travels out into the
        country of his sustenance,
3875   incorporating herds of
        deer
        within his trails
        and how thin
        the tissue of his going
3880   is! one month in
                the northwest of his
                range,
                a month in valleys,
                a month at
3885   higher altitudes:
        he's adapted to travel:
                it's not in his
                interest
                to exhaust
3890   the deer population, as
        it's not our interest
        to exhaust the host earth:
                the predator
        husbands his prey:

                ————

3895   at the center,
        the predatory gathering
        of energy done,
        the female drops her litter,

        new seeds of possibility:
3900   new animal-plants
                to take root,
                    spread out the wide
        thin tissue
        of life:

3905   tapestries! figures
            overlapping:

                at the dwindling of green
        a percentage of
        aphids begins to be
3910   born with wings: time

        to fly away &
        make trials of new centers:

        ecology out of balance
        turns tilt into
3915   direction:

        when the milkweed
        seed
        rises into the wind
        on down,
3920   the soft beauty
        means conquest:

        let's establish ourselves,
        send out our tokens:
                as I am I
3925   I will change you,

drop seeds of myself
in your ground:
watch out for me:
I mean to prevail:

3930   you think of yourself:
        I may welcome some
        thought of yours: I
        may give it ground:
          or I may not yield
3935   to it: I may find
it lacking,
    not able to survive
    my country,
    & cast it out
3940   as
    already withered
in potentiality:

the plains Indians centered
their lives
3945   on the chase: rooted in
    a moving herd
    of buffalo!
    a center
stabilized
3950   in instability:

    or the reverse: the
barnacle
on a rock, stationary,
    depends on the sea
3955   to bring it food:

where is the center
    that holds?
    it was the Earth,
became the sun, then
3960   the center of our

galaxy (Sagittarius?)
   then farther &
   farther out:
   no
3965   imaginable center: except
the one
the lichen makes:

my other word is
   provisional:
3970   we'll talk about that
someday,
   tho you may guess
the meanings from *ecology*:

don't establish the
3975   boundaries
first,
   the squares, triangles,
boxes
of preconceived
3980   possibility,
and then
   pour
life into them, trimming
off left-over edges,
3985   ending potential:
   let centers
proliferate
from
self-justifying motions!

3990   the box can't bend
without breaking:
   but the center-arising
form
adapts, tests the
3995   peripheries, draws in,
finds a new factor,

utilizes a new method,
   gains a new foothold,
responds to inner & outer
4000   change:

28 DEC:

today
is dim
again:

the sun makes diffuse
4005   shadows
that go
in & out
of focus:

      (just now, the
4010   thorns
      are black
      against the wall)

maybe it's gonna clear off:
not very cold:

4015   there comes the exactness
again:
pulsing:

gaits:
short/quick-stepping Kate:
4020   Silver,
      long & languorous:
      what

to do in case of fall-out:
put it
4025   back in & use
      shorter strokes:

　　　　　　　brushstrokes:
　　　　　　　short, straight, narrow
　　　　　　strokes
4030　　　　that blend & move
　　　　　　　into vague scenes:
　　　　　　　the broad, long
　　　　　　swash of color:

　　　　　　　the paroxysmic:
4035　　　　the full, slow
　　　　　　inner & outer reach:

　　　　　　　wavelengths:
　　　　　　　distance, elapse of time
　　　　　　from crest to crest, from
4040　　　　point of highest
　　　　　　　stirred feeling
　　　　　　to highest point: the
　　　　　　　silky, fiery
　　　　　　considerations
4045　　　　　down the hills
　　　　　　　and shallows and up
　　　　　　　the rises
　　　　　　　　of repeating motions:

　　　　　　rhythm, pace:
4050　　　　Silver, majestical,
　　　　　　　slow but sure: the
　　　　　　　turn-plow
　　　　　　　turned earth
　　　　　　　to overturning rivers:
4055　　　　smooth, rockless,
　　　　　　alluvial country,
　　　　　　　free of stumps:

　　　　　　　stump-holes, tho—still
　　　　　　in the pasture: the

4060   hollow shells—inside
       the crater lake
       of ancient wood-ambered
       rain, wriggling larvae,
       hanging head-down from
4065   the surface,
           breathing through
       their tails, & tiny green
       frogs
       hidden in crevices
4070   over canyons of wood:
           the thick, grazed
       carpet grass
       smooth in patches
           around inedible
4075   wire-grass clumps:

       worlds:
       the only longleaf pine
       left
       stood tall & spare-boughed
4080   as land-corner:
           marker between
       neighbor & us:
       mystical tree:
           half ours,
4085   half his, neither
       able to take his half
           without loss of all

       & in addition
       transfigured by
4090   boundary-meaning,
           entered in the record
               (history in the
       courthouse)
       a sign:

4095   spared: let us take on
         meanings to
         keep us:

         standing alone in the
         edge of the pasture,
4100   near the road
         (the road when it came
         through
         cut off a sliver of the
         neighbor's land
4105   so it was worthless to
         him—our pasture
         fence included his
         sliver &
         the tree stood in from the
4110   road—is the way it really
         was: and the road &
         tree became symbols
         of two kinds of truth,
         competing:
4115   the tree, ideals of
         truth:
         the road, the use of
         this world
         & compromise)
4120   high sparse
         branches
         sang
         thin songs:
         (one of my uncles, I
4125   heard said, used to
         go into the woods to pray,
         always to a
         particular tree:
         a praying tree—

4130   must have had
              meanings
              in it)

              if you don't think
              mechanisms work
4135   in the green
                becoming
                of
                the
              lichen, I don't care
4140   what you think: it's
              one-sided,
              unaware that
         crystals, even,
         exist
4145   as fluids:

         thallophyte & green
              alga
              living together,
              with
4150   necessary exchanges:

         abstraction may
         sight far
         over the facts
         & fall
4155   short or broken
       but meantime it shows
      saliences of going:
         its spare thin
         beauty
4160   is relating:

         reason & feeling
         living together, with
         necessary exchanges:

———

guidelines—but readiness
4165   to adjust
    to changed
    environments:

what is it that persists
through generations,
4170   throwing its pattern
    ahead?

    an earth-product,
I don't represent
all my wills:
4175   others, not mine, are
    in me:

    still, when the
    feelings are working
    right, knowledge
4180   is redundant: one
    doesn't analyze
    the good
      condition: one
      accepts,
4185 without consciously
accepting, and enjoys:
      let's
      reach out
      from this
4190   loneliness with
      as much love as
      we can:
      grief is on us:
      we're not
4195   just right:
      we are hurled
      away by
      exaggeration:

———

line us up!
4200   that's our directed,
undirected, or misdirected
wish:
give us an earth
between these frozen poles:

4205   gates:
entrances: doorways:
     wombs:

outward gates: exits:
     broken walls,
4210   bridged rivers & fallen
mountains:

     give us the being
whole
     wherever we are:
4215   intellect has
cast
     temporary resolutions:
pity—it's not
all intellect's fault—
4220   that now we see
breakage
(fragmentation & high
entropy)

but
4225   high entropy
is not loss of pattern:
we can't see:

     the man who feels good
has a shortage of
4230   problems:
     he's cabbage-cool
& -sweet:

we must—since
there's only one universe—
4235   bear the tearing up
before we can enjoy the
putting together,
the adjusted putting
          together
4240   that gives us
       fuller touch
       of what we know:

tho the crust
floats with under- &
4245   over-seas, it's hard
       as rock

       & anchorages
       in motion are
solider than rock:
4250   rock wears:
       motion is the full
openness of possibility:

       our existence is
         evidence
4255   of more
than we can imagine: much
we can't see
is working right:
       let's celebrate
4260   that part of our
       ignorance
       & keep on
till we learn better how to
praise:

4265   will you leave
         the Lord

                    & sit down
                in a man-made misery?
                then
4270   you've postulated a lot
                for yourself
                & lost:

                that we're going is
                reason to be going on:
4275   (the dance
                & warm red dry wine!)

                dance! you splendid
                    creatures!
                        your heel-strings

4280   sing like plucked
                instruments!
                    your skirts whirl
                    worlds
                    with inner secrets!

4285   swing!
                your partner,
                promenade (and when
                            you can
                            get laid
4290   get laid)
                first to the right, then
                to the left, right, left

                        (get lawfully
                        laid)

4295   Muse, no mortal
                    can have
                    enough of you:
                he wants bigger &

bigger draughts: he wants
4300   to get drunk on
        and in you:
he wants to consume you:

can you stand to be
nibbled on, Parnassus, by
4305   a million nibblers?
        wonder there's any
        chance I could
        chew off a big
        hunk of you?
4310   would you
                    mind
                    more than
                    the
                    tickle of
4315   tiny
                    teeth?
from the gouge I made in
you
would gush springs up,
4320   too, Pierian,
            bread washed down
            with wine:

(better confine myself
to steak)

4325   the immortal body
            replenishes itself,
the constant banquet:

so they did eat & drink:

and you keep giving me
4330   juice,
        I may drive through

all this
raillery
& come on
4335   the vine-water of truth,
the slot
of hazeless sight:

and you give me the ole
steam, baby,
4340   I may get all these
gargoyles up,
lined around the high
edges,
and then you may give
4345   me
two or three columns
& a plain wall:

and I can keep bringing this
stuff up,
4350   every fool thing
shining in
the light of its
foolishness,
I may get
4355   cleaned out
good,
worthy to taste your
simple fare:

oh wash all the crap out!
4360   I want to tremble with
need
when I reach for yr bread:
let lust for yr wine
parch my tongue
4365   so

the bread sticks:
    I hate hungering
    & thirsting,
    yet will I
4370   hunger & thirst
and go to the foot
of the table,
    pinch crumbs
    off the floor—if you
4375 will grant me
wide arm-reach
    & lifted
    voice
    so the table shakes
4380   & the people enter
the maze of yr presence!

    come on, now, f'god's
sake, what're you saving
it for?

4385   the light
reclines:
of a brightness not yet
gold: white gold:
    Bach runs in his high
4390   rant
    from the record
        player:
        we're going
        out
4395   to dinner:

30 DEC:

today is 19 &
    sunny:

                    the still-warm tide
                    comes in
4400   &
          the shallowing marshes
          freeze & keep it:
                    increments of
                    continental shelf:
4405   ocean loss:
          we may sink:

                    the gulls fly inland
          looking:
                    the dump swarms with
4410   gulls & smoke:

                    yesterday I gave
          to the memory of

          William Carlos Williams

                    (reception in NY
4415   for Mrs. Williams)
                    sat in the back of
                    the bus up
          & the motor ground my
          head to dust (gray,
4420   graphitic)
                    & a man fell
          in a fit
          in the bus station: three
          men held him till
4425   he jerked still:
                    a crowd circled &
                    watched:

          (we're monkeys, scratching
          our heads

4430   & asses &
dumb with joy & tragedy)

so many people
with bodies only:
so many bldgs with
4435   mere addresses:
buses, subways, cabs,
somebody everywhere:

fragments: faces never to
be seen again: isolations:

4440   poets, peaks of need,
loose cold
majesties,
sizing heights, cut off
from the common
4445   stabilizing ground of their
admirers:

peaks relate across
thin
&
4450   icy air:

how good to be back
here
with ruin's blue-bottle fly,
whole fields wasted with
4455   grass,
an empty cherry tree
& one jay:
sunlight on the wall
with precise
4460   black thorn:

———

5 pm:

       some rosy drifts
       still in
the west:
4465   are the days
         gathering moments at
the edges?

         every moment
         of light
4470   nudges
         my cold
         rhododendron &

         every inch
of this rising tape
4475   ruffles my blood
for the gathered product,

the heaping hamper,
accomplished florescence:

         empty places
4480   make room
         for
         silence to
         gather:

         high-falutin
4485   language does not
         rest on the
         cold water
         all night
         by
4490   the luminous
         birches:

is too vivid
for the eyes
of pigeons,
4495   heads tucked
under wings in
first
patches of sunlight:

is too noisy to
4500   endure
the sleep of buds,
the holding in
of the huckleberry
blossom:

4505   too voracious
to spin,
rest
& change:

is too clever
4510   for the frank
honey-drop
of the lily-pistil:

I hear the
porkchops frying!
4515   ah,
there's the sweet, burnt
smell!
sounds in the kitchen,
pots lifted
4520   with empty
hushing ring,
the plunger of the icebox
door

snapping loose: the
4525 sizzling roil of
porkchops turned:
protest, response:

flashes of aluminum
light
4530   as the pots work, the
glint of tines
   as the table
   dresses: the
   holy
4535   slow
    lifting & turning
in the spinach pot:
rituals, hungers,

   motions over
4540   fire,
   the stance &
   tending:

   I hear & visualize
   & the drop
4545 under the tongue
bulbs clear
& pressing:

what's that sound?
mashed potatoes being
4550   whipped?
   there, a chop turned:
   cups winding up
still in saucers:

   the grasping snip of
4555 celery stalks:
the high whir of

the garbage disposer,
chewed clear:
  a rough, troubled sound
4560   now
  of another charge, maybe
  the grapefruit rinds:

    "You
    can
4565   come
    sit
    down
    now
    if
4570   you
    want
    to."

  6:08 pm:

    no vegetables at all:
4575   (the grapefruit I had
    earlier—is that
    a vegetable?) we had
  porkchops & rice &
    a salad (pecans, raisins,
4580   apples, celery, lettuce):

  so wonderful to be just
  the outside edge of
    painfully full:
    then coffee!

4585   I wish my words could
    be quiet
    as if
  waiting for a mt to
  dissolve:

4590   or for a burnt woods
        to make
      cones and acorns:

      just north of here's
      the pine-barrens—maybe
4595   30 × 50 miles:
      hasn't been underwater
      since the Miocene,
        when it was an
        island: has a
4600   fern
        found
      nowhere else in the world:
      and a fox there
      has a modified kidney:

4605   all around deciduous
      forests
      took over the rising land
      so that's why
      the barrens
4610   is still an island
        (botanical):

      our woods, mostly
      scrub oak
      & pine,
4615   have three levels:

      the lowgrowth of
      floor shrubs:

      then laurel,
      Quercus marylandicus, and
4620   tall shrubs:

then oak & pine:

pine used to be
dominant here: but
when pine is cut
4625 oak takes its place:
        when oak is burned
        over, it
        sprouts,
five- and six-trunked:
4630 determined:

one day last summer I was
driving long the road
over by Gravelly Run and I
        seen this turtle
4635   just going
        in the bushes: so
I stopped (because my
            nephew loves 'em)
and when I stooped to pick
4640 up the turtle,
I seen a sight: his back
        was hazy with
        mosquitoes, thick
        as they could
4645   stick,
bumming a, now mind you,
ride on a turtle's back!
        saving their wings
        & certain
4650 sometime they'd be
brought to water:
        didn't see anything
like that in NY:
        economy, full use
4655   of possibility:

————

　　　　　　　　　(if you were
　　　　　　　　　sitting on a
　　　　　　　　　distant strand,
　　　　　　　longing for home,
4660　　　　　you'd have to
　　　　　　　conjure up things to
　　　　　　　occupy the time,
　　　　　　　too)

　　　　　　　　　　9:15 pm:
4665　　　　　　　but is it
　　　　　　　　　possible to
　　　　　　　　　talk the chaff
　　　　　　　　　away? can
　　　　　　　windy vowels
4670　　　　　brush off all the bits of
　　　　　　　paper
　　　　　　　& leave a clean place for
　　　　　　　　the simple design?

　　　　　　　　screens
4675　　　　　between us & memories
　　　　　　　　we can't bear:
　　　　　　　　what unmentionables
　　　　　　　of guilt & terror!
　　　　　　　go back & see
4680　　　　　terror as fantasy,
　　　　　　　guilt as innocence?

　　　　　　　　but we've
　　　　　　　　purposely lost
　　　　　　　　the road back:
4685　　　　　take it on
　　　　　　　faith
　　　　　　　we knew no better
　　　　　　　then, did the best we
　　　　　　　could,
4690　　　　　　　　& are repentant

for wrongs
imagined or real:
instinct protects us:
let's accept this
4695   provided & open
      possibility & go
ahead:
we may redeem ourselves:

feelings, troublesome,
4700   volcanic:
   disturbances held
down, deep as control
can reach:

should we let go a little?
4705   is it our fear of feeling
    & not feeling itself
that pours concrete slabs
across our lives?
     can we open a valve
4710   & let ourselves go
flat like a tire?
    or must we have that
pressure for our riding?

11:15 pm: my wife says if
4715   you put soft
cookies with
crisp cookies the
crisp cookies turn soft:

bad apples with
4720   good apples: bad
   potatoes with good
potatoes:
(2nd Law Thrmdnmcs)
soilage spreads

4725 &
nature is trying to get
everything back
        into the mill:

we exist because we're
4730 afire (& burning out):

31 DEC:

today the dry burn in
my nose of a cold
coming on:
I should have known:
4735   that bus back
        from NY the
        other night
had no heat—I'd put my
coat in the rack—and the
4740 guy beside me fell asleep:
        (he woke up in pain:
had had a few
beers
before boarding the bus—
4745 said
they were the longest miles
he'd ever ridden: express,
        sir, we don't make
        stops)

4750 little girl ahead of me
kept trying to push her
seat back, hitting me
        in the long-legged
        knees:
4755 she waited till I seemed
asleep: then, ram! wow:

people:

her mother, beside her
in the aisle seat, was
4760   rather attractive:
scratched her daughter's
head: daughter said, that
        feels good: & scratched
        her mother's head:
4765   (grooming: no lice
        to pop in teeth as
                reward)

energy transformations:
how do
4770   porkchops make
my body turn?

energy, conserved, weaves
in & out (perhaps not
        as a
4775   separation—structure
& function
are
inextricably
intertwined) is
4780   stored, released,
transformed—
        still continuum:

        what is the
subcellular machine
4785   in the eye that
converts
radiant to electrical
        energy?
        in the chloroplast,
4790   radiant to chemical
        energy?
        how do fireflies

turn
chemical into
4795   radiant energy?
the nerve,
chemical
into electrical energy?

mechanisms: necessary
4800   exchanges:
worked out & perfected
(proved
practical) long
before we stood
4805   by the shores of
incredibly ancient sea:

if we looked only by
what we know,
we couldn't turn our
4810   heads:
if we were at the
mercy of what
we understand,
our eyes couldn't see:

4815   discovery is
praise &
understanding is
celebration:
but understanding
4820   is to see itself
fallen short:

our proud words
(that possibly
tear & defame what
4825   is)—why

we don't know
how porkchops
give us the mouth!

but speech
4830   potential was
there
& we realized it: we
speak:
cabbage
4835   releases energy in us
that trembles
our vocal cords
to tangle with air
& give it shape!

4840   Lord, I'm in your
hands: I surrender:
it's your will
& not mine:
you give me
4845   singing shape
& you turn me to dust:

undefined &
indefinable, you're
beyond reach:

4850   what form should my
praise take?
this long thin
song?
to be
4855   simply & completely
human?
to unite
everything that has

been made
4860   with
                       tenderness?

                   we've made
                   miracles of our own!
                   spaceships
4865   abstract as the laws of
            motion:
                       the pure design of
                       wooden bowls:
                           wonders & matters
4870   of fact: but

            where did everything that
                   is
            come from?

                       while we can't
4875   understand, we can
            feel
            and
            that's a fine essence,
            astonishing as the
4880   mitochondrion—
                       if
                   not
                   more
                   so:

4885   leave structure
            to the Maker
            & praise
            by functioning:

            1:26 pm:

4890   I feel a little
                shivery:

                    the cold's making—
                 forgive me—headway:
                 but I just had a baked ham
4895   sandwich, glass of milk &
                 coffee,
                       that to be
                       transformed into
                       whatever ammunition
4900   it can:

                       after this,
                 this long poem, I hope I
                 can do short rich hard
                          lyrics: lines
4905   that can incubate
                 slowly
                 then fall into
                 symmetrical tangles:
                       lines that can be
4910   gone over (and over)
                 till they sing with
                 pre-established rightness:

                    here, I plug on:
                 whatever the Muse
4915   gives, I release
                 for
                 this is one possible kind
                 of song
                 & has one kind of veracity:

4920   I've been
                       looking for a level
                       of language
                       that could take in all
                       kinds of matter
4925   & move easily with
                       light or heavy burden:
                    a level

that could,
without fracturing, rise
4930   & fall
        with conception &
        intensity:
        not be completely
outfaced
4935 by the prosaic
& not be inadequate
    to the surges:

        I've hated at times the
self-conscious POEM:
4940   I've wanted to bend
        more, burrowing
with flexible path
into the common life
    & commonplace:

4945   the denominator
here may be too low: the
lines may be
too light, the song
    too hard to hear:
4950   still, it's not been
    easy: it's
    cost me plenty:

last day of the year:
I've been at this
4955   25 days—this
idle tendance
of typewriter & Muse—
nearly a month of Sundays:
    I'll miss the
4960   hovering over time,
the watchfulness—an idea
about to take hold,
an image reach for shape:

I'll miss the
4965 gathering up into days:
but not all art runs
along: it sometimes
 stands by,
 selects, stores,
4970 alters,
hardens till
 like a boulder it
nearly halts the running on:

I anticipate: the
4975 empty tape is still
 imposing,
 frightening:
 the unconscious will
have to act out
4980 several more shows
before the marginal red
ink
warns it's time
 for a new tape:

4985 poetry has
one subject, impermanence,
which it presents
with as much permanence as
possible:

4990 the moon was I suppose full
last night:
it cast exact shadows:
 9 degrees this morning
with the highest
4995 atmospheric pressure
recorded since 1927:
 something like 30.82
 and mostly sunny
 today:

5000   clabbering up now
          (3:50) though:
          thank it's agonna snow
          some:
          don't keer if it do:

5005   memories, tapestries:
          a huge
              wild cherry tree
              grew
              in the bank
5010   of the old deep ditch
              that cut
              all across the farm
              from road to swamp:
                field-tree, shady
5015   & cool: big roots, turned
          gnarled as bark,
          stuck out deep down,
          dark
          with damp:
5020   vines o vines
              running here & there all
              over the place tangling—
              jasmine vines or some
          kind of honeysuckle
5025   (not the shrub honeysuckle
          of open woods)
                but deep down in the
                ditch, crawled into,
                an opening, cool,
5030   vineless,
          with somber trickle of
          clear water:
          that's where I used to
                find the
5035   diamondback
          turtle: yellow stars on
          black shell: cool &

288

                    mysterious,
          with ruddy-yellow spotted
5040   mouth: a hold of
                    wildness
                         leaping in the veins—
          like a fountain, or,
          prolonged, excitement
5045   moderate & lingering
          as a spring
          oozing into the ditch:

                    a full tree, alone,
          that took on space far &
5050   high as it could reach:
                    corn wdn't grow
                    anywhere around:
                    would yellow,
          shrivel, never come
5055   to tassel:

                    that's why
                    one May
                    we girdled
                         the tree, a narrow
5060   belt of white meat
          showing and then
          the old heavy branches
          lightened
                    and all the stiff
5065   fingers
                    pierced black pleas
                    into the empty sky:

          in my memory all is
          white with blossom: the
5070   ground is
          purple with
          blackcherry stain:
                    and green

leaves hold
5075   way up into the day
an oasis of cool,
    settling air:
    the turtle swims
in my hand:
5080   water nearly declares its
running on:

times so far gone: a
new nakedness
    at the ends of rows:
5085   a new nakedness
of need:

how can these
pictures stay
in my head:
5090   how, after lying 30
yrs in darkness, can
they be brought up,
looked at, and
resubstantiated?
5095   what we don't
know's a scare:
& comfort:
how could we react
if we heard the machinery
5100   of our reactions?

there is a silence
in us:

here
I
5105   will
make
room

for
more:

5110   the record the surf leaves
on the shore
    relates tenuously to
    any given wave.

    yet is an exact
5115   history:

        I can't hear
        all the waves
        lapping
        back in my life
5120   still
        there's a song
running through,
wanting to come out here:

      country darkness:
5125   no street-corner light:
a yellow kerosene
lamp
across the fields, blown
out:
5130   stars
        in an uncompromised
clarity
rush into, dusting
    the heavens:
5135   see that?
        where?
over there—cat-eyes:
        two little stars:
look at that
5140   luminous dust,
the thick axis of the

galaxy:
                on
                this cool
5145   sandpath
I'm experiencing
the galaxy?

human concern in
country darkness is
5150   narrow
                & short of range
in a wide
rangeless house!

1 JAN:

raining:
5155   at the borderline &
promise
        of snow:
        gale warnings up
along the coast:
5160   no small craft to
                enter heavy water:

(the gulls are safe:
on the ground, they stand
erect into the wind
5165   that divides from
            the beak around them:
            in the air—why, the
wind can't harm what's
on the wing)

5170   too much stability
can't prepare
for the day
        resilience is the style:

                  go up with the wind,
5175   fall sideways,
                     wings taut to balance,
               into the wind:
               handling
               (winging) what disturbs,
5180   use of & victory over:

               took down the tree:
               undressed it:
                  stripped off
                  bright red
5185   & frosted yellow balls
                  & blue bells: unwaved
               draping ropes of tinsel:
               lines of twinkle-lights
                  falling straight from
5190   a top circle
               like bars in a hoop,
                  disbranched:

                  heaved it,
               stiff, shriven, out the
5195   back door
               into the rain:

                  silly tree:
                     lying there, shorn
               of meaning, some
5200   strips of tinsel
               glistering
               with sorrow of old joys:

                     an old woman
               glittering
5205   with jewels &
                  timeless paint:

                  ————

beauty that's been used
    can't comprehend
the special contempt
5210   of loss: lifts its
    wrinkled chin
    & lets
tears dance,
    held in a stubborn
5215   survival of will:

        or

        maybe

        the tree,

naked,
5220   caught with a ragged
        glitter on,
welcomes
    the return of its own
    dead
5225   branches
to their natural
configuration
    and loves the cold
    beading
5230   & hanging on
of rain,
in that remnant truth,
alive:

or maybe
5235   knew
better than the beholders
    and even at the moment
    of its highest shining
a perishing
5240   that drove rain
among its ornament:

———————

           (I forgot what
           I was going to write
           about today)

5245   (it was going to start out
           something like—wise up,
           you guys)

           have I prettified the
               tragedies,
5250   the irrecoverable
                   losses: have I
           glossed over the
           unmistakable evils:
           has panic
5255   tried to make a flower:

               then, hope distorts
               me:
               turns wishes into lies:

           I care about the statement
5260   of fact:
               the true picture
               has a beauty higher
               than Beauty:

           minds
5265   that have made so much
                   effort,
                   learned all over
                   again
           the alphabets,
5270   the battles,
                   architectures,
                       vegetables,
           monarchs,
           philosophies—

5275   minds
unique with memories,
    of conversations,
       bodies,
          homesteads,

5280   degenerate, wear thin,
wear out,
    and the woven,
worked fabric
    disperses:
5285   the fragments
        lose meaning:
the light
that was on each fragment
goes out:

5290   I know
the standing on loose
        ground:
         I know the
violence, grief, guilt,
5295   despair, absurdity:
      the sky's raw:
      the star
refuses our wish,
obliterates us with
5300   permanence,
      scope of its
      coming & going:

I know what it is
    to feel around in
5305   the dark
    for a hold
    & to touch
    nothing:

———

                    we must bear
5310   the dark edges of
                    our awareness:

                    taken in our measure,
                        we're unexcelled:
                            perceptions:
5315   appetites & satiations:
                    beside the terror-ridden
                        homeless man
                            wandering through
                            a universe of horror
5320   dwells
                    the man at ease
                            in a universe
                            of light:

                            let's tend our
5325   feelings &
                            leave the Lord
                            His problems
                                (if any): He
                    got us this far on His own:
5330   & millions have come
                    & gone in joy
                            (predominantly):

                            2 JAN:

                    today
                    feels above freezing & is
5335   sunshiny: so
                            bright on the tape, I
                            squint,
                    inhibited & frustrated:

                    don't want to close the
5340   blinds: three plants

in here
(besides the
crown-of-thorns): they'll
use the sun
5345   soon as it moves over
a little:

    feels good on my back:
I thought I'd thrown off
that cold yesterday (plenty
5350   of grapefruit
& water)
but I feel stuffy again
this morning:
ragged vocal cords:

5355   the soul accepts areas of
reality
that are machineries to
       gratification: income,
praise, sexual pleasure:
5360   but when the areas
      return
frustration &
loss of self-esteem, the
soul shrinks back into
5365   detachment, cold &
        uncommitted:

    no one questions
pleasure or the
reality of its
5370   source:

mazes here: shifts,
compensations, balances,
impositions, demands,
dislocations, exchanges:

5375   working together,
out, & against:
some areas clearing into
resolution:

one fellow says, get
5380   money: the wealthy are
excused: wealth, in a
    hard world, is
    proof:

    another says, do
5385   what you're here
to do: money's
  secondary:

    success or failure:
terms of definition:
5390   another fellow says,
    be successful:

when authority is
    multiple &
self-contradictory, look
5395   inside,
formulate & defend
your own authority:
    many different sets
of things can work out
5400   right:

they say creation is
thwarted unless
a man accepts & realizes
himself, stands open
5405   & finished
as a flower:

———

what of the evil man?
is he evil because he
realized himself
5410 or because he didn't?

conflict between
self-realization &
society:
    how's the adjustment
5415   to work out?
    can society cut its
individuals down? can it,
without crumbling, bend
to accommodate them?

5420 complicated, inconclusive,
organic,
working itself out: so
the center,
    strongly rooted,
5425 is rooted in motion:
a nexus
always becoming, its
    strength
    relatedness:

5430 poured into an axiomatic
box
one pays the cost of his
security:
    (may be a fair
5435   buy—depends)

earth holds in motion
    by poise
    between gravity
    & centrifugal
5440 force:
    the lichen's safe

with the tree:
the tree lasts a long
    time in the earth:
5445   the ground
keeps still:

motion holds us
apart, related:

I send this ahead:
5450   can you
    take a liking
to the song?

when we meet,
    will you shake hands,
5455   offer me a drink?
will you tell me
how you're moved by
fears & dreams & what
    your plans are
5460   & exactly
what you think about
when you wake up at night?

if I seem aloof
will you spot it as a
5465   guard
    & help me down? if I
    act insincere,
will you know it's my fear
you will expel me from
5470   your sincerity?

    see the roads I've
    traveled
    to come to you:
    monsters I've engaged:

———

5475   have I earned the grace
            of your touch?

            and if I sit blank,
               hearing the high
                  conversation of
5480   the Muse, listening
            hard
            to get the words right,
            will you understand
            I've not scorned you?
5485   and if the song she
               gives,
            pressing in its naked
            insistence, repels you,
            will you
5490   still allow me to serve
               one
            higher than your praise
            or blame?
               will you care for me
5495   specially because of
               that?
            can you tolerate another
            woman in the house?

            high in the mid-forties:
5500   mostly sunny & mild:

               quantum physics
               in human affairs:
                  the laws work
                  about the same
5505   in bodies, morals, or
            politics (or art)
               but
               the law
               you can't pin down is
5510   the one coming:

ancient laws with
the built-in
possibility of novelty:

fellow said
5515   everybody says "when my
ship comes in"
says
"they never sent one out"
one smart cookie:
5520   says his ships return now
from so many directions
        he can't keep up:
        &
every
5525   one
loaded
with
money:

pure
5530   money:

the economic forecast will
increase his fleet
if it comes true:

thirty yrs ago he didn't
5535   have nothing:
now there's nothing he
    can't have:
        (can't have the
        thirty yrs back,
5540   but neither can
            you)—
trouble is, he says, if
you can buy something you
don't want it:

5545   doesn't want anything &
has a million bucks to
prove it:

he sacrificed & sent the
ships out:
5550   I think he's glad:
       he's a glad,
independent man: loves
a lot of inexpensive
things—bushes, roses,
5555   maypops:
        loves them with
        complete ease,
not having to run
somewhere to do something:
5560   apologize he
should be working: unh-unh:
       talks with you in
       detail
       about rosehips (home-
5565   grown)
       as if nothing else in
       the world mattered:

I knew another man who
worked just as hard,
5570   spent every dime and now
is old & in a kind
of rant:

       don't ask me what you
       should do:
5575   if you decide to
sacrifice, you'll
do the sacrificing—&
there're no guarantees:
it's your business:

5580   figure it out
          for yourself:

          if you don't look out
          for yourself, who else
          has the time?

5585   11:10 pm:

              the eleven o'clock news
          says
          the plane that went down
          in the early December
5590   storm
          was hit by lightning:
              the pilot said
          something like, "This is
          flight 214: we are
5595   going down in flames":
          & the tower said something
          like,
          "Flight 214: we have
          your message":

3 JAN:

5600   today is warm & sunny:
          may go up to 50:
              the light seems
          to have body,
          & the crown-of-thorns
5605   that lost nearly all
          its leaves is
              sprouting green tips
          along the branches:

          (one way of standing aside
5610   from the fight
              is to win it:

failure's more despised
than cruelty)

my cold's worse:
5615   in the chest:
feel puffed &
weak: but
gotta keep moving along:
it's impossible
5620   there's not an end to this
tape:
move along, little
dogies:
Wyoming must be somewhere:
5625   don't throw your heads
back to lick
shoulder flies:
don't put that front leg
out
5630   & bend to graze:
git on, for God's sake:
that mountain's
been ahead three days:

the sun strikes my
5635   coffee & puts
a ring of light, like
Saturn, on the wall:
two poles
with bobbing center:
5640   jiggling design:

(the conservation of
angular momentum:
transfers of energy
of motion:
5645   there're many levels &

at some of them
　　abstraction works:
like a charm)

the vine that (still
5650　　　green) tangles under
　　the cherry tree
reminds me of a brain:
why?
it's a vine:
5655　or of a bed of sexual
　　nerves
　　intermingling:
　　　　or it's the
　　　　held green,
5660　the durable freshness, of
what keeps low,
　　undercover
　　(cherry tree & sumac
　　　grove): or
5665　it reminds me how
reality can go so many
　　ways
　　at so many levels
& still keep the "roundness"
5670　of a clump:
　　discernible unity:
but it's vine:
　I put mirrors in it
　& behold myself:

5675　　　given mind, we became
strangers here:
with mind, we convert
　strangeness
　to humanness:
5680　　we unnaturalize:

4 JAN:

3:20 pm: today is near-
ly shot aready:
   got up ear-
ly & drove
5685   mother- & father-in-law to
Philly for train to Fla:
Phyllis & Mary came, too:

stopped on way back at
Korvette's & traded in two
5690   records Phyllis gave me
for Christmas—Elizabethan
& Jacobean songs: ugh:
   I got 3 of Bach's
   cantatas instead:
5695   somebody may have written
music before
or after Bach but
it wasn't necessary:

& I like all kines of
5700   music:

        the day
        dwindles
        down:
     warm again:
5705   mid-fifties:
gladioli blades up,
scorched at the edges:
when came they up?
     warm spell first part
5710   of Dec:
     too tall—5"—to've
     sprung up in couple
     days:

———

an ant reconnoitering
5715   the kitchen counter:
        is't that hot?
        & a squirrel out:

the fool sayeth there is
no God
5720   because he can't tell
        what He is:
the wise man sayeth there is
a God
        because he can't tell
5725   what He is:

        there's unity,
but objects don't
describe it:
nor do words:

5730   if you go east on an
east-west highway
        this time of year
you will find dirty
snow
5735   on the right (by woods)
and a sunny bank (by
woods) on the left:
        the reason is,
with the sun low south,
5740   the trees
turn their shadows
on one side:
        that's a fact:
        caught up
5745   in an abstract
        configuration:

a further reason is, the
highway's wider

than the length
5750   of the shadows:
          wouldn't work with
          footpaths or woods roads:
          the proposition is:
          when the width of the
5755   highway exceeds the length
          of the tree shadows (depends
                  on the kind of
                  forest—sequoias
                  would require a
5760   vast
          thoroughfare) then one
          roadbank will be
          sunny
          (providing it isn't cloudy)
5765   :

              or night:

                          :

              unless there's
              a moon:
5770   :

                  in which case
                  it would be
                  moony: etc:

              now, predict
5775   yourself some things with
          high probability:

          of course, it must have
          snowed:
          & mostly melted:

5 JAN:

5780   today is sunny & it may
          be warm again:
                  the jay was in

                    the cherry
            tree
5785   breastward to the sun &
            he jumped up & opened his
            underwings
                    to the warmth,
                        looped & flew away:

5790   went to dinner last
                    night (jayless)
            at Copsey's
                    with Tom & Mary
                    & we all
5795   had lobster tails:
            feller said was the best
            tail he ever had anywhere:

            program & comment in most
            music:
5800   not
                    in
                    Bach
                    or
                    Mozart:
5805   there, the clear-cut
            lofty
            motions of musical forms:
            no knights thundering
            through woods, as in Mahler:
5810   no mania cross-country-in-
            the-clouds
            of Beethoven's Ninth:
                in Bach & Mozart
                the meanings are
5815   detached, exist among
            themselves:
            emotion lifts
            to intellectual feeling:

            ———————

without abstraction,
5820   fact is
meaningless with isolation:
    but abstraction by
the loss of fact
is "out of this world":

6 JAN:

5825   today is splennid again:
    sunny as to leave no
    clouds to be excused:
    how I coughed
through black time-gaps
5830   & time-emergences
    last night:
        red-eyed & indoors
        today:

        coming home:
5835   through spotted round
    stones with
    egg-careful feet:
    through thornbrush
    across emery sand:

5840   who was that I was?
    who's that from
    rumblings, dark baffles,
    trying to
    break, overriding
5845   into song?

give me some imago I can't
become:
        steadfast in the
        unrealizable:

    ———

5850   when we solve, we're
saved by deeper problems:
    definition is death:
       the final box:
hermetic seal:

5855   relieve our hunger, then,
for forms:
    give us the
inexhaustible feed: the
box is full outside:

5860   (a drop forms at the
icicle-tip, tapers, pulls
free, rounds-up (slightly
flattened falling-side)

breaks free (little
5865   explosion of fact)—
the precise event
    (sometimes audible)
when it hits the ground)

    jever watch a leaf
5870   trying to turn over?
      one edge may be
caught
by the projection of a
stonelette
5875   from hard ground:
the wind
whiffs
and the free edge lifts:
falls back:
5880   trembles a little
    in steady, low wind:
      gusts way up,
       nearly vertical,

nearly flop-overable,
5885   but falls back—
      oops, caught
        still at a
45-degree angle
by a sheet of steady,
5890   higher wind (higher
than the low):

the action seems no way
intended to satisfy
you—that is, complete
5895   itself
by flopping over:
    sometimes after hours
    of agonizing
    expectancy,
5900   the wind,
suddenly & inexplicably,
will die down:

    maybe, it'll be
rain finally that turns
5905   the leaf over
or floats it off its
      hang-up:
    or a
    completely
5910   unanticipated deer
may step
right next to it
& so disorder the ground
    as to shift the
5915   stonelette
1/64" away: so should a
    wind rise
    then
    why the leaf would have

5920   time to gain momentum
        before it struck the
        hang
        & so, whirling,
      somersaulting,
5925   wd vault right over:

        but the leaf may
        jam &
        leap free all in a
            second!
5930 breathlessly satisfying:
      nature's entertaining
      but makes no effort:
      go thru life: some things
          you see, some you don't:

5935 they told me the
      small world was concrete,
          inexhaustible, & where
          to dwell:
          so I dwelt there:
5940   & went smaller &
      smaller till
      everything turned into a
          wave-particle
          dilemma:
5945 nothing to hold, taste,
      hear, or see:

      11:08 pm:

        day exhausts:
            night renews:

5950 forms of thought
      please or terrify, but
      tire:

            the mind
            in its strife
5955   for completion
            pales, blurs, dries &
                crinkles up:
                sleep turns
                another way: to the
5960   spring: what's the source
            of that fresh water?
            how
            does it come up into our
            days?

7 JAN:

5965   today is rainy:
            started around 7 last nite:
            a quiet
                warm rain,
            musical in the gutterspouts:
5970   I woke up a lot
            coughing last night
            and my awareness would
            break into
            the rain's-song—a segment of
5975   consciousness—right on
            key & phrase: rain's never
            out of tune: a ragged
            range of sound, small &
            large events, assuming
5980   a low, bell-like
            resonance:
                random averaging
            into clusters of random:

            there's a blur-shadow of
5985   sun:
            it's clearing up:

the window edges on the
wall are sharpening:
what's going to happen?
5990   no, the blur dies:
the window disappears from
the wall:
    not now, not yet:

two jays in the sumac
5995   grove: they make
        no patterns:
as would three or four:
from branch to ground
to cherry tree
6000   to lawn: always two
       poles
of an invisible world,
shrinking, enlarging,
dipping, twisting its
6005   axis:
two points of radiation:
    two sources
with magnetic field:
close in
6010   and the emotions rise—
       anger
       or affection—
and then one jay flies
away:
6015   even so, the magnetic
lines hang
with tenuous hold:

sometimes you can keep
track
6020   of the patterns five birds
make in a woods edge or
       open tree:

                    beyond that,
                you start to have the
6025   large round
                    congregations,
                individuals
                lost to the general
                    symmetry:

6030   random flocks with overall
                    direction:

                facts are that way: more
                than a few
                & the facts are lost
6035   in a round hypothesis:
                    while one fact
                    or two,
                though surprising & concrete,
                can't make a meaning:

6040   another haze of sun
                and a quail calls from the
                    field:

                only the lively use of
                    language lives:
6045   can live
                    on dead words
                        & falsehood: the
                truths poetry creates
                    die with
6050   their language:
                        stir any old
                language up,
                feel the fire in it &
                its truths come true

6055   again:
the resource, the
creation, and the end of
    poetry is
    language: the
6060   mead-mad bard
did not
depend
on nuclear physics for his
    song,
6065   but on mead & word:

other elements are:
1)   isolated perception
2)   related perception
3)   imagination: word &
6070   image in surprise
4)   transfiguration
5)   dream: ego &
transfiguration

& there's feeling,
6075   invisible matrix: &
music!
    the going tension
    that holds us,
suspends, rises & falls,
6080   the going on:

poetry is art & is
    artificial: but it
realizes reality's
potentials:

6085   Channel 12 (NET) just gave
this list of common
nouns, with plurals:

quarrel	quarrels
shelf	shelves
6090 study	studies
donkey	donkeys
canary	canaries
goose	geese
speech	speeches
6095 knife	knives
ditch	ditches
deer	deer

    hear the sounds,
note the ir-
6100 regularities, the vagrancies
& rules:
a language is a particular
instrument
with possibilities
6105 peculiar to itself: bring
    out the facts:
      utilize & heighten
them into untranslatable
sound:

6110 which is the other element:
    (the substance of
music: tho music is an
    integration higher than
    pure sound—oriented
6115   into waves)

poetry has no use, except
this entertaining play:
    passion is
    vulgar when not swept up
6120 into the cool control
of syllables:

sorrow is brown & empty
unless
ocean vowels thunder
6125   from it in
organizations like surf:

then is sorrow that never
was,
come in an ocean
6130   that cannot reproduce
itself:

11:10 a.m:
    the sun's bright
    through the window:
6135   hits the right side of
the thornbush,
    illuminating half a
    dozen
    green leaves:

6140   they'll make food
& pass it around
to limbs that got no sun
today:

thornbush island: sits
6145   in an old
    triangular ashtray
    in a red round
    ceramic pot:

ashtray sits on a dry rug:
6150   removes from nature
    & the sweet ground:

in the pot, a soil,
reticular with roots:

———

add water
6155 &
leaves sprout:
blossoms blossom:
    where's the living part
that transfigures this?

6160 under the rug is a mat:
under the mat is
oak floor & subfloor:
under the floor is
    7 feet of space
6165 &
    under that
12 inches of concrete
and under
that
6170 the ground:

            o island!

                how distant you
                are
                from the true hold!

6175 (& earth will send out
seed
in self-sufficient ships,
beading
space with possibilities—
6180 what a separation)

                (somewhere
                they
                may
                take
6185   hold
                again!)

          ———

how many levels of drought
    & stone
    have I put
6190   between
    my soil & flower?

    poetry's my
    false water, black
      soil,
6195   dry blossom:

get out of boxes, hard
forms of mind:
go deep:
penetrate
6200   to the true spring:
        give up
      these islands:
(they're safely apart—
    but apart:
6205   take the risk of
    moving in)
merge with coming &
    going common life:
    drink
6210   the average
      drink:

the system apart, complete:
    add water
    & serve the bloom:

6215   bloom that doesn't
    come to seed,
no need throughout the
    rooms
    answering the need:

6220   2:18 pm: didn't
          stay sunny long:
          say it may
       rain again: but then
       tonight clear off
6225   & turn cold:

                    8 JAN:

       today is sunny & warming:
       last night the temperature
       must have dropped lower
       than the predicted 30:
6230   because yesterday's
            rainpools were
            frozen half an
       inch deep this morning:
       (see where the tires broke
6235   through)
               sunny & cheerless:
       no mail (as usual) at the
       box: three requests
       for subscriptions from
6240   magazines: thrown out
       unopened:

       lonely, isolated business:
       since what one sez or duz
            means nothing, one is
6245   free to sa & du
       what one likes: nobody
            will get very jarred or
            pleased: one
       acquires the
6250   indifference & moderation
       of neglect:
               it's out of order to
               be passionate with

concrete:
6255   or try to lift a
water-spiral from the sea:
turn in anguish, scream
          & sprout leaves of song
          & generally work up
6260   a good deal of
dust—the placid
world returns
cool sky & glassy
          concern: what
6265   must I do
          to reach
          the top?

          something else:

years ago, I had a way of
6270   thinking about
truth (again):
          how to determine the
          topography of
the ocean's floor:
6275   soundings: one here,
one there: a sample
depth of an area wide as
a steel cable:
          the more soundings,
6280   the more clearly (& truly)
the stippled terrain
          begins to appear:

soundings twenty miles
apart
6285   will approximate reality:
          (tho you could miss
          a fabulous cleft
          or cone):

———

only infinite (impossible)
6290   samplings could
produce a map symbolic
of the truth: & then the
map would be too small,
every sounding translated
6295   into a different
dimension:

the only representation
of the sea's floor
is the sea's floor itself:

6300   we take soundings & we
get schemas, approximations,
but we can't come
to the whole truth:

     then I'd turn the method
6305   to the mind, make soundings
on & on, get some vague
stippled configurations:

realized the mind can't be
rendered up:
6310   say what you please
(or I please) about me:
it's partial
   & schematic: I'm
free
6315   &
unknown:
the only me that is
is the me that is:
tho there are
6320   organizations,
saliences, directions
   approximately
   perceivable & reliable:

———————

long as we can't exhaust
6325   ourselves, we can
grow & change:

1:31 pm:

unity & diversity: how
to have both: must:
6330   it's Coleridge's
definition of a poem:

   somewhere, far off,
things come together,
hope rising from and
6335   moderating strength:
   somewhere, far off,
there's no expense to the
part
in the whole:
6340   somewhere
the ideal, the abstraction,
takes on flesh:

what a celebration! our
little earth
6345   united, shining in peace,
   hate managed,
   rerouted:
   the direction thru
   history is clear:
6350   unity amassing larger
& larger territories,
   till now
neighborhoods of nations
meet
6355   under the name "United
         Nations":
   the cost has been

                    great in
                    time & slaughter, it seems
6360   we've already earned
                    the prize:
                        let it be:

                        these are the
                    motions: listen to
6365   their music: improve
                        their economies:
                    atoms make molecules &
                    molecules make
                        matter & matter
6370   makes a universe: go
                    that way:
                    rise:
                        rather than
                        abolish the
6375   particle (individual)
                    unity, strong, self-assured,
                    may afford the
                        individual
                        more comfortably than
6380   division could:

                    7:38 pm:

                        deep down inside are
                        fireworks
                        & a whole mess of rivers:
6385   very interesting
                        country:
                    rip-roaring violences &
                    someone solicitous
                        fanning an angry one
6390   in the shade:
                            one over by a rock
                            making up songs

328

as if there were no
world at all:
6395 a wiry, fur-ragged lecher
running with
lawless hard-on,
whickering, leering, &
licking his lips:
6400   one
writhes, a beautiful lady
with high
feathery hat
doing a spike-heeled dance
6405 on his heart,
tossed clear
into the merciless open:
two squabble,
vicious geese,
6410 rending each other with
verbal knives
of disappointment:
& one,
prisoned by contrary
6415   winds, sits rigid,
distant:
two
young lovers
give & receive, fall
6420 asleep, wake into
mysteries, no world
beyond their reach, no
further completion:

I'm afraid to visit:
6425   wd take another tape to
get there: & reliable
trip ticket &
return ticket in advance:
& a lot of

6430   time to think it over:
                    thinking's safer:
                    (not as much fun, prhps:)

                            ✳ ✳ ✳

                    a man's center is his
6435   woman,
                    the dark, warm hole
                        to which he brings
            his meaning,
            offering & receiving:
6440   other meanings take
            wider orbits: many orbits
                of meaning:
                    that's the nucleus:

            you been lookin for a
6445   center to the universe?
            's it:

                        11:06 pm:
                    was out by
            the refuge
6450   again this afternoon:
                    froze up:
                    birds gone:
                    cept Canada geese:

                    they were
6455   waterborne
            at a melting edge along a
            bank:
                    I scared'em out
                    & they
6460   slipped & skidded on the
            ice! threw their wings
                    out

to right themselves
with air:

6465   two bald iggles
      been sighted out
      there:
      tell me:
      can you beat that?
6470   I looked for any but
    couldn't find some:

9 JAN:

today ben
    der clouds
downwashen
6475   die rainingdroppes
      und
tickleticklen
der puddlepoolens

      und
6480   all around ben der wind
upswelling
    und sideswashing
      dem glitterglassen
windowpanen:

6485   und smalle foules haben
    der tails
    downgedroppen
      for offdrippen
    der raingingdroppes:
6490   und die upshouten mouths
      ben upshuten gehaben:

    Muse, let
    my blood

stir!
6495 and, you, hear
arteries & veins
bring song
bridging heart to heart:

the tenderspoken
6500 assurer: the gentle
  enlightener &,
till enlightened,
  protector: arrive:
  say you're
6505 going on a journey
& need one to teach:
teach me,
father:
  behold one whose
6510 fears
are the harnessed
mares of his going!
fiery delights,
  pounding hoof
6515 & crystal eye:
where before
dread
& plug-mule
  plodded:

6520 clod:
mere earth:

  how the cornroots
  lift
  earth out of the
6525 ground:
clod,
I'll infuse you
  with blood:

                    show how many ways you
6530   can be
            unlike a clod:
            quiver with incredible
                    fire—oh, burn,
                        transfigured sod!—
6535   squeeze
            your slick cold hands
            in the fear
            & pleading of death:
                    clods are
6540   dispassionate, come
            in geometries &
            configurations most
            beautiful—you, tho,
                    with how much
6545   ferocity,
            what violence of outrage,
            can you defend your
            woman?
            unto a clod, how unlike:
6550   dance!
                    throw in:
                    throw yourself
                        into the river
                        of going:
6555   where the banks also flow:

                    yesterday at
                    the refuge:
            red hawk,
            sprung up from dike reeds,
6560   in each claw
                    held
                    a shoulder-wing of a
                        robin-size
                        bird,
6565   the parts clinging

together, empty spaces,
threads, the raked,
    ragged body:

    I don't know what
6570   Canada geese think:

    they see the
    little bird
fly by
under the hawk
6575   (last
            flight—
the ground covered unseen:
the feather-molding
    wind unfelt,
6580   cold air
rushing in
where a heart was,
        rushing
        through
6585   where was
back muscle of wingbone)

                ❊ ❊ ❊

    tho you have wronged me,
    still I love you:
6590   (that ought to put
            the squeeze on you
            good)
                (see you get out
                of that one):

6595   don't do anything specially
    moral: I may want to
    shed you:
        wrong me:
        with the wrongs you

6600   do me, I unlock myself
from the prison
of your tenderness:

            the clean fight
            in bed
6605   turns
            into children!

            I will consume
            you: consume
                  me:

6610   I break away
into my gratified self:
leave me alone:
don't smother me with
    unrequited concern:

6615   you cushion &
            absorb my thrust!
            be a wall, for my sake!
            resist
            so I can plunge you
6620   down:
                this soft way
                unmans me:

                ah, but sweet
                rest, that pliable
6625   wall
surrendered, loose:
that hairy stone
rocking with my given
             pool!

6630   who are you?
            come out in the open:
            let me see you:

your breasts, the
pellets
6635   afloat in warm white seas:

I will eat your
mouth:
crush the
numb of love
6640   out of my
lips:

who are you I have not
figured you out: you
shift: you're here
6645   & there:
changing, yielding,
presenting;

stand in one place:
let me anchor
6650   my connection: do
not fight me to death
by swimming
away, side to side:
don't drive me crazy:
6655   be still:
the ache possesses
me:

let's fight it out:

turn this strife &
6660   celebration
into infants:
there's the warless
love,
the giving that receives:

6665   Muse, provide:
          entangle me beyond sense
      or need of place:
        let me far & richly in
        so
6670   the words pour:

        we have yet a while
      to fill this tape: it's
      getting small:
      it turns fast:
6675   before long
        the red edge will
        rise
      from the floor: it'll
      climb,
6680   go under the roller, then
      turn up
      & out into the light:

      how glad I'll be then!
      I'm so tired
6685   you can't imagine:
      I want to do other things:

        and you, O supposed
      (& actual maybe)
      reader: how
6690   weary you are!
      I've bludgeoned you
      with every form of
        emptiness: you've
        endured my
6695   wrestling need:
        may something accrue
      to satisfy you:

      let's sit down & exchange
      tenderness of speech:

6700   have I deserved the
        engagement of your eyes?
      may I take your
      time?
    this noise & length
6705   says
    I honor your moments
    of silent understanding:
    let's sit down on
    a parkbench
6710   & talk how the world
    appears & disappears,
    sung through
    by light we have the
    tune to:

6715   if you find me
    dropped in a corner
        from the circles of
      conversation,
      come in continuous
6720   motion, without breakage
    of barriers,
    & confer the touch of yr
    speech upon my lips:
        I'll reward you
6725   with secrets of
      hands &
    dandelions, money-needles
    & moonlit nights: the
      weeds
6730   have given me
    their bitter song:

      come with need
      to a specialist
        in need:
6735   we'll exchange

gaps,
  fulfilling:
    our spaces will
    let us
6740   come close:
    intermingle:

if suddenly I
  get up
  & blow the joint—
6745 1 haven't forgotten you:
  don't think it for a
  moment: please:
sometimes, when I'm
off-balance &
6750 unsuspecting, the
Muse takes my mind:
    if I'm not to lose it
    & her
    I have to follow,
6755 clear out in a hurry:

  at another time,
  you'd be surprised
  how much I can
  remember & care:

6760 der greyische skies ben
    maken
    sidewalkens
      into mirrorshiners
mit mistyfoggendroppes:

10 JAN:

6765 today is windy as March
  & sunny:
    a window whines like

boring bees:
　　the outside lid
6770　　of the exhaust fan
　　in the kitchen
　　flaps:
the wind's muffled weight
falls against the end of
6775　the house:
whipping branches
　　in whistling trees:

　　we turn away from
　　galaxies
6780　to the warm knot
in the dark:

　　somehow in taking
　　pleasure
　　　from yr body,
6785　　I have given you
　　my heart:
　　I care now
　　more for you than for
　　the pleasure you give
6790　　me:
　　　you, your total
self, my anchorage:
the universe shifts its
center:
6795　it turns about you:
　　who are you?
　　will you destroy
　　me?

　　went to a
6800　party last
　　night:
　　& the living room was

large:
the guests sat around
6805   the walls
in a periphery of beads:
some beads clustered into
groups:
    but it was too far
6810   to cast a line
    across the room's
vacant center:
lack of unity:
disintegration overall
6815   with random
integrations:

    fun, tho: beads
shift,
regrouping the periphery:
6820   combinations:

my plants are in full sun
now,
the chloroplasts
    are working around the
6825   peripheries of cells:

    look!
    there's the red
    ink!
    rising from the
6830   floor:

Muse, I've done the best
I could:
    sometimes you ran out
    on me
6835   & sometimes I ran out
    on you:

I know you better now:
you've come closer:
will you
6840 confer the high
grace of your touch?
come & live enduring with
me:
I'll be faithful:
6845 I won't trick you:
I'll give you all
I've got:
bestow tendance &
concern:

6850 help me to surrender
myself:
I'll be the
fingers & keys
of your song:
6855 I'll ask nothing
but the sound
of yr voice:

reader, we've been thru
a lot together:
6860 who are you?
where will you go
now?

     ***

coughed a lot last night:
6865 round
4:20 a.m. got up &
took a shot of
brandy:

               numbed the tickle
6870   some:
                    slept better:

                    just had lunch:
          cold baked ham:
          coffee: chocolate fudge
6875   cookie:

                    last night had duck
          (Bobby's favorite) at
          Mary's: conversation:
                    hearing people
6880   talk, how marvelous:
          I'm alone too much: get
          to think
          other people
                    aren't people:

6885   the 200-inch glass
          shows a
          billion-billion galaxies:
          what is God
                    to this grain of sand:

6890   dispersions:
                    it's as brave to accept
          boundaries,
          turn to the center given,
          & do the best you can:

6895   think of other
                    people: devise some
                    way of living
                    together:

          get some fun out of life:

6900 how about the one who sez:
  it's too late
  for me to start: I
  haven't got anywhere:
  I can't get anywhere:

6905 how do the hopeless
  get some fun out of
  life?

  apes get
 something out of life:
6910 they don't ask what is:
   bamboo shoots,
 tender, cool:
 they have a head man:
  they pair off
6915 & raise babies:
  they defend:
  they sometimes rest in
 clearings
 and groom themselves
6920 in sunlight:

 have our minds taken us too
 far, out of nature, out of
 complete acceptance?

 we haven't remembered our
6925 bodies:
  let's touch, patiently,
  thoroughly: beyond
  vanity:

 but for all our trouble
6930 with the mind,
 look what it's done:
  a fact at a time:

                a little here (there's
                the red ink
6935   turned into the light!)
                a little there:
                let's be patient: much
                remains
                to be known: there may
6940   come
                re-evaluation:
                        if we don't have
                        the truth, we've
                        shed
6945   thousands of errors:

                        haven't seen the
                        jay:
                        a sparrowhawk
                can stand still
6950   in a high wind, too:

                coming home:
                        how does one come
                        home:

                        self-acceptance:
6955   reconciliation,
                a way of
                going along with this
                world as it is:

                nothing ideal: not as
6960   you'd have it:
                testing, feeling the way:
                    ready to
                    readjust, to make
                                amends:

6965   self, not as you would
                have it:

nevertheless, take
it:
   do the best you
   can with it:

I wrote about these
days
the way life gave them:
   I didn't know
   beforehand what I
   wd write,
whether I'd meet
anything new: I
showed that I'm sometimes
blank & abstract,
sometimes blessed with
song: sometimes
silly, vapid, serious,
angry, despairing:
   ideally, I'd
   be like a short poem:
   that's a fine way
   to be: a poem at a
time: but all day
life itself is bending,
weaving, changing,
adapting, failing,
   succeeding:

   I've given
you my
emptiness: it may
not be unlike
   your emptiness:
   in voyages, there
   are wide reaches
of water
with no islands:

———

I've given you the
interstices: the
7005　　　space between
electrons:
I've given you
the dull days
when turning & turning
7010　　revealed nothing:
I've given you the
sky,
uninterrupted by moon,
bird, or cloud:
7015　　　　　I've given
you long
uninteresting walks
so you could experience
vacancy:

7020　　old castles, carnivals,
ditchbanks,
　　bridges, ponds,
　　　steel mills,
　　　cities: so many
7025　　interesting tours:

the roll has lifted
from the floor &
our journey is done:
thank you
7030　　for coming: thank
you for coming along:

the sun's bright:
the wind rocks the
　　naked trees:
7035　　so long:

1963–1964

NORTHFIELD POEMS (1966)

to Blanche and W. M. Ammons

じあぞ

Kind

I can't understand it
   said the giant redwood
      I have attained height and distant view,
      am easy with time,

5   and yet you search the
      wood's edge
for weeds
that find half-dark room in margins
      of stone
10   and are
as everybody knows
      here and gone in a season

      O redwood I said in this matter
I may not be able to argue from reason
15   but preference sends me stooping
seeking
      the least,
      as finished as you
      and with a flower

1964 (1964)

Height

There was a hill once wanted
to become a mountain
    and
forces underground helped it

5 lift itself
  into broad view
  and noticeable height:

  but the green hills around and even
  some passable mountains,
10   diminished by white,
  wanted it down
  so the mountain, alone, found
   grandeur taxing and
   turned and turned
15 to try to be concealed:

  oh but after the rock is
  massive and high . . . !
    how many centuries of rain and
  ice, avalanche
20 and shedding shale
   before the dull mound
  can yield to grass!

1964 (1964)

Joshua Tree

  The wind
   rounding the gap
 found me there
   weeping under a
5   Joshua tree
  and Oh I said
 I am mortal all right
   and cannot live,
    by roads
10   stopping to wait
 for no one coming,
   moving on
    to dust

and burned weeds,
15 having no liturgy,
no pilgrim
from my throat
singing wet news of joy,
no dome, alabaster wall,
20 no eternal city:
the wind said
Wayfaring and wandering
is not for mortals
who should raise
25 the cock
that cries their
dawns in and
cannot always be coming to un-
broken country:
30 settle here
by this Joshua tree
and make a well:
unlike wind
that dies and
35 never dies I said
I must go on
consigned to
form that will not
let me loose
40 except to death
till some
syllable's rain
anoints my tongue
and makes it sing
45 to strangers:
if it does not rain
find me wasted by roads:
enter angling through
my cage
50 and let my ribs
sing me out.

1958 (1959)

Reflective

I found a
weed
that had a

        mirror in it
5   and that
        mirror

looked in at
a mirror
in

10   me that
        had a
        weed in it

1963 (1965)

Landscape with Figures

When I go back of my head
       down the cervical well, roots
          branch
thinning, figuring
5   into flesh
and flesh
glimmers with man-old fires
and ghosts
hollowing up into mind
10   cry from ancient narrowing
          needle-like caves:

a depth of contact there you'd
       think would hold, the last
          nerve-hair
15   feeding direct from
       meat's indivisible stuff:

but what we ride on makes us ride
and rootless mind
in a thundering rove
20   establishes, disposes:
            rocks and clouds
                take their places:

or if place shifts by a sudden breaking
            in of stars
25   and mind whirls
where to go
    then like a rabbit it
freezes in grass, order
as rock or star, to let whatever can, come,
30   pass, pass over: somewhere another human
figure moves or rests, concern
            for (or fear of) whom
                will start and keep us.

1963 (1965)

The Constant

When leaving the primrose, bayberry dunes, seaward
I discovered the universe this morning,
            I was in no
mood
5   for wonder,
            the naked mass of so much miracle
already beyond the vision
of my grasp:

along a rise of beach, a hundred feet from the surf,
10 a row of clam shells
            four to ten feet wide
            lay sinuous as far as sight:

———

in one shell—though in the abundance
there were others like it—upturned,
15 four or five inches across the wing,
a lake
three to four inches long and two inches wide,
all dimensions rounded,
indescribable in curve:

20 and on the lake a turning galaxy, a film of sand,
coordinated, nearly circular (no real perfections),
an inch in diameter, turning:
turning:
counterclockwise, the wind hardly perceptible from 11 o'clock
25 with noon at sea:
the galaxy rotating,
but also,
at a distance from the shell lip,
revolving
30 round and round the shell:

a gull's toe could spill the universe:
two more hours of sun could dry it up:
a higher wind could rock it out:

the tide will rise, engulf it, wash it loose:
35 utterly:

the terns, their
young somewhere hidden in clumps of grass or weed,
were diving *sshik sshik* at me
then pealing upward for another round and dive:

40 I have had too much of this inexhaustible miracle:
miracle, this massive, drab constant of experience.

1962 (1964)

Contingency

Water from the sprinkler
collects
in street-edge gravel and
makes rocky pools: birds
5   materialize—puff, bathe
and drink: a green-black

grackle lopes, listing,
across the hot street, pecks
a starling, and drinks: a

10   robin rears misty with
exultation: twittering comes
in bunches of starts and
flights: shadows pour
across cement and lawn: a
15   turn of the faucet
dries every motion up.

1963 (1965)

One:Many

To maintain balance
between one and many by
    keeping in operation both one and many:

    fear a too great consistency, an arbitrary
5   imposition
        from the abstract *one*
        downwardly into the realities of manyness:
    this makes unity
not deriving from the balance of manyness
10   but by destruction of diversity:
    it is unity

unavailable to change,
cut off from the reordering possibilities of
            variety:

15   when I tried to summarize
                a moment's events
        along the creek shore this afternoon,
        the tide gathering momentum outwardly,
        terns
20   hovering
        dropping to spear shallow water,
            the minnows
        in a band
        wavering between deep and shallow water,
25   the sand hissing
        into new images,
                the grass at its sound and symmetry,
                scoring
                semicircles of wind
30   into sand,
        the tan beetle in a footprint dead,
        flickering to
            gusts of wind,
                the bloodsucking flies
35   at their song and savage whirl,
        when I tried to think by what
        millions of grains of events
            the tidal creek had altered course,
                when I considered alone
40   a record
        of the waves on the running blue creek,
            I was released into a power beyond my easy failures,
        released to think
        how so much freedom
45   can keep the broad look of serenity
                and nearly statable balance:

                    ———

not unity by the winnowing out of difference,
not unity thin and substanceless as abstraction,
   uneventful as theory:

50   I think of California's towns and ranges,
      deserts and oil fields,
highways, forests, white boulders,
     valleys, shorelines,
     headlands of rock;
55   and of Maine's
      unpainted seahouses
      way out on the tips of fingerlands,
lobster traps and pots,
freshwater lakes; of Chicago,
60   hung like an eggsac on the leaf of Lake
Michigan, with
its
Art Museum, Prudential Building, Knickerbocker Hotel
(where Cummings stayed);
65   of North Carolina's
Pamlico and Albemarle Sounds, outer banks, shoals,
     telephone wire loads of swallows,
of Columbus County
     where fresh-dug peanuts
70   are boiled
     in iron pots, salt filtering
in through boiled-clean shells (a delicacy
true
as artichokes or Jersey
75   asparagus): and on and on through the villages,
along dirt roads, ditchbanks, by gravel pits and on
     to the homes, to the citizens and their histories,
inventions, longings:
I think how enriching, though unassimilable as a whole
80   into art, are the differences: the small-business
man in
     Kansas City declares an extra dividend

and his daughter
     who teaches school in Duquesne
85 buys a Volkswagen, a second car for the family:
out of many, one:
from variety an over-riding unity, the expression of
variety:

no book of laws, short of unattainable reality itself,
90 can anticipate every event,
control every event: only the book of laws founded
    against itself,
founded on freedom of each event to occur as itself,
lasts into the inevitable balances events will take.

1962 (1965)

Halfway

This October
rain
comes after fall

summer and
5 drought
and is

a still rain:
it takes leaves
straight

10 down: the
birches stand
in

pools of them-
selves, the yellow
15 fallen

———

leaves reflecting
those on
the tree, that
mirror the ground.

1963 (1965)

Interference

A whirlwind in the fields
lifts sand
into its motions
to show, tight, small,
5   the way it walks
through a summer day:

better take time to watch
the sand-shadow mist—
since every
10   grain of sand
is being counted by the sun.

1964 (1965)

Saliences

Consistencies rise
and ride
the mind down
hard routes
5   walled
with no outlet and so
to open a variable geography,
    proliferate
possibility, here
10   is this dune fest
    releasing

mind feeding out,
gathering clusters,
fields of order in disorder,
15 where choice
can make beginnings,
    turns,
    reversals,
where straight line
20 and air-hard thought
can meet
unarranged disorder,
    dissolve
before the one event that
25 creates present time
in the multi-variable
    scope:
a variable of wind
among the dunes,
30 making variables
of position and direction and sound
of every reed leaf
and bloom,
running streams of sand,
35 winding, rising, at a depression
falling out into deltas,
weathering shells with blast,
striking hiss into clumps of grass,
against bayberry leaves,
40   lifting
the spider from footing to footing
hard across the dry even crust
toward the surf:
wind, a variable, soft wind, hard
45 steady wind, wind
shaped and kept in the
bent of trees,
the prevailing dipping seaward
of reeds,

50   the kept and erased sandcrab trails:
       wind, the variable to the gull's flight,
       how and where he drops the clam
       and the way he heads in, running to loft:
       wind, from the sea, high surf
55   and cool weather;
       from the land, a lessened breakage
       and the land's heat:
       wind alone as a variable,
       as a factor in millions of events,
60   leaves no two moments
       on the dunes the same:
           keep
       free to these events,
       bend to these
65   changing weathers:
       multiple as sand, events of sense
       alter old dunes
       of mind,
       release new channels of flow,
70   free materials
       to new forms:
       wind alone as a variable
       takes this neck of dunes
       out of calculation's reach:
75   come out of the hard
       routes and ruts,
       pour over the walls
       of previous assessments: turn to
       the open,
80   the unexpected, to new saliences of feature.

           ✲

       The reassurance is
       that through change
       continuities sinuously work,
85   cause and effect
           without alarm,

gradual shadings out or in,
motions that full
   with time
90   do not surprise, no
abrupt leap or burst: possibility,
with meaningful development
of circumstance:
when I went back to the dunes today,
95   saliences,
congruent to memory,
spread firmingly across my sight:
the narrow white path
rose and dropped over
100   grassy rises toward the sea:
sheets of reeds,
tasseling now near fall,
filled the hollows
with shapes of ponds or lakes:
105   bayberry, darker, made wandering
chains of clumps, sometimes pouring
into heads, like stopped water:
    much seemed
constant, to be looked
110   forward to, expected:
from the top of a dune rise,
look of ocean salience: in
    the hollow,
where a runlet
115   makes in
at full tide and fills a bowl,
extravagance of pink periwinkle
along the grassy edge,
and a blue, bunchy weed, deep blue,
120   deep into the mind the dark blue
    constant:
minnows left high in the tide-deserted pocket,
    fiddler crabs
bringing up gray pellets of drying sand,
125   disappearing from air's faster events

at any close approach:
certain things and habits
   recognizable as
having lasted through the night:
130   though what change in
a day's doing!
desertions of swallows
   that yesterday
ravaged air, bush, reed, attention
135   in gatherings wide as this neck of dunes:
now, not a sound
or shadow, no trace of memory, no remnant
   explanation:
summations of permanence!
140   where not a single single thing endures,
the overall reassures,
deaths and flights,
shifts and sudden assaults claiming
limited orders,
145   the separate particles:
earth brings to grief
much in an hour that sang, leaped, swirled,
yet keeps a round
   quiet turning,
150   beyond loss or gain,
beyond concern for the separate reach.

1962 (1966)

Trap

White, flipping
butterfly,
paperweight,

flutters by and
5   over shrubs,
meets a binary

---

mate and they
spin, two orbits
of an

10   invisible center;
rise
over the roof

and caught on
currents
15   rise higher

than trees and
higher and up
out of sight,

swifter in
20   ascent than they
can fly or fall.

1963 (1965)

The Foot-Washing

Now you have come,
the roads
humbling your feet with dust:

I ask you to
5   sit by this
spring:

I will wash your feet
with springwater
and silver care:

10   I lift leaking handbowls
to your ankles:
O ablutions!

Who are you
sir
15   who are my brother?

I dry your feet
with sweetgum
and mint leaves:

the odor of your feet
20   is newly earthen,
honeysuckled:

bloodwork in blue
raisures over the white
skinny anklebone:

25   if I have wronged you
cleanse me with the falling
water of forgiveness.

And woman, your flat feet
yellow, gray with dust,
30   your orphaned udders flat,

lift your dress
up to your knees
and I will wash your feet:

feel the serenity
35   cool as cool springwater
and hard to find:

if I have failed to know
the grief in your gone time,
forgive me wakened now.

1959 (1965)

Recovery

All afternoon
the tree shadows, accelerating,
lengthened
till
5   sunset
shot them black into infinity:
next morning
darkness
returned from the other
10   infinity and the
shadows caught ground
and through the morning, slowing,
hardened into noon.

1964 (1964)

Two Motions

I.

It is not enough to be willing to come out of the dark
    and stand in the light,
all hidden things brought into sight, the damp
    black spaces,
5   where fear, arms over its head, trembles into blindness,
        invaded by truth-seeking light:
it is not enough to desire radiance, to be struck by
    radiance: external light
throws darkness behind its brilliance, the division
10   nearly half and half:
it is only enough when the inner light
    kindles to a source, radiates from its sphere to all
points outwardly: then, though
    surrounding things are half and half with
15   light and darkness, all that is visible from the source
    is light:
it is not enough to wish to cast light: as much

darkness as light is made that way: it is only
enough to touch the inner light of each surrounding thing
20   and hope it will itself be stirred to radiance,
eliminating the shadows that all lights give it,
        and realizing its own full sphere:
it is only enough to radiate the sufficient light
        within, the
25   constant source, the light beyond all possibility of night.

II.

However;

        in separating light from darkness
                have we cast into death:
        in attaining the luminous,
30   made, capable self,
                have we
                        brought error
        to perfection:
        in naming have we divided what
35   unnaming will not undivide:

        in coming so far,
synthesizing, enlarging, incorporating, completing
(all the way to a finished Fragment)
                have we foundered into arrival:

40   in tarring, calking, timbering,
                have we kept our ship afloat
                        only to satisfy all destinations
        by no departures;
                        only to abandon helm,
45   sailcloth, hemp, spar;
                        only to turn charts
        to weather, compass to salt, sextant
                to sea:

as far as words will let us go, we have
50   voyaged: now
we disperse the ruin of our gains
to do a different kind of going
that will
become less and
55   less
voyaging

        as arrival approaches nowhere-everywhere
        in gain of nothing-everything.

                                    1962 (1964)

Composing

        An orchestration of events,
        memories,
        intellections, of the wounds,
        hard throats, the perils
5   of the youthful private member:
        a clustering of years into phrases,
        motifs, a

        keying to somber D-flat
        or brilliant A:
10   an emergence
        of minor meanings,
        the rising of flutes, oboes, bassoons:
        percussion,
        the critical cymbal

15   crashing grief out
        or like a quivering fan unfolding
        into spirit:
        the derelict breakage of days, weeks,

hours, re-organizing,
20   orienting
to the riding movement,

hawklike,
but keener in wings,
in shadow deeper:
25   a swerving into the underside
gathering
dream-images,
the hidden coursing of red-black cries,

darkness,
30   the ghosts re-rising,
the eyeless, crippled, furious,
mangled ones:
then two motions like cliffs
opposing, the orchestration at
35   first

too torn, but going back
finding new lights to doom
the dark resurrections
until the large curve of meaning
40   stands apart
like a moon-cusp or horn
singing with a higher soundless sound.

1958 (1965)

Ithaca, N.Y.

When the storm passed,
we listened to rain-leavings,
individual drops in

fields of surprise;
5   a drop here
in a puddle;

———

the clear-cracking
drop
against a naked root;

10   by the window,
the muffled, elm-leaf drop,
reorganizing at the tip,

dropping in another
event to the ground:
15   we listened and

liveliness broke
out at a thousand quiet
points.

1963 (1965)

Consignee

I have been brought out of day,
out of the full dawn led away;
   from the platform of noon
I have descended.

5   To death, the diffuse one
going beside me, I said,
   You have brought me out of day
and he said
No longer like the fields of earth
10   may you go in and out.

I quarreled and devised a while
   but went on
having sensed a nice dominion in the air,
the black so round and deep.

1951 (1965)

February Beach

Underneath, the dunes
    are solid,
        frozen with rain
    the sand
5   held and let
go deep
without losing

    till a clearing freeze
left water the keeper of sand:

10   warm days since
have intervened,
softened

    the surface,

evaporated
15   the thaw
    and let grains loose: now

the white grains drift against the dunes
and ripple as if in summer,
hiding the hard deep marriage
20   of sand and ice:

fog lay thick here
most of the morning
    but now lifting, rides
in low from the sea,
25   filters inland through the dunes
but
    over the warm and
sunny sand rising
loses its shape out of sight:

30   the dense clumps of grass, bent
                      over,
        still wet with fog,
                      drop
                dark buttons of held fog on thin dry sand,
35   separately, here, there, large drops,
        another rainsand shape:

        distant, the ocean's breakers
        merge into high splintering
                      sound,
40   the wind low, even, inland, wet,
        a perfect carriage
                      for resolved, continuous striving:

                    not the deep breakage and roar
        of collapsing hollows:
45   sound that creation may not be complete,
        that the land may not have been
        given
        permanently,
                    that something remains
50   to be agreed on,
        a lofty burn of sound, a clamoring and
                            coming on:

        how will the mix be
                      of mound and breaker,
55   grain and droplet: how
                long can the freeze hold, the wind lie,
        the free sand
        keep the deep secret: turn: the gold
                            grass will come
60   green in time, the dark stalks of rushes
        will settle
                    in the hollows, the ice bridge

dissolving, yielding
will leave solid
65   bottom for summer fording: the black bushes
will leaf,
hinder
the sea-bringing wind: turn turn

here with these chances
70   taken, here to take these chances: land winds will
rise, feed
back the sands, humble the breakers: today's
high unrelenting cry will relent:
the waves will lap with broken, separate,
75   quiet sounds:
let the thaw that will come, come: the dissolved
reorganizes
to resilience.

1963

Self-Portrait

In the desert a
clump of rocks
sang with hidden water:

I broke in &
5   water spilled:
I planted trees:

wild animals from the hills
came at night
to tame water
10   and stood still:

the air gathered
hoverings of birds

from
drought's celestial trees:

15   grass sprouted
and spangled into seed:

green reaches of
streams went out:
the rabbit that
20   had visited,
dwelled:

this was a dream.

1964 (1966)

Passage

How, through what tube, mechanism,
unreal pass, does
    the past get ahead of us
to become today?

5   the dead are total mysteries, now:
their radiances,
    unwaxed by flesh, are put out:
disintegrations

occur, the black kingdom separates, loses
10   way, waters rush,
    gravel pours—
faces loosen, turn, and move:

that fact, that edge to turn around!
senselessly, then,
15   celebrant with obscure
causes, unimaginable means, trickles

of possibility, the cull beads
catch centers, round out,
    luminescence stirs,
20   circulates through dark's depths

and there—all lost still lost—
the wells primed, the springs free,
    tomorrow emerges and
falls back shaped into today.

1964 (1966)

Peak

Everything begins at the tip-end, the dying-out,
    of mind:
the dazed eyes set and light
dissolves actual trees:

5   the world beyond: tongueless,
unexampled
burns dimension out of shape,
opacity out of stone:

come: though the world ends and cannot
10   end,
    the apple falls sharp
to the heart starved with time.

1964 (1966)

Zone

I spent the day
differentiating
and wound up

with nothing
5 whole to keep:

tree came apart from tree,
oak from maple, oak
from oak, leaf from leaf,
mesophyll cell
10 from cell
and toward dark
I got lost between
cytoplasm's grains
and vacuoles:

15 the next day began
otherwise: tree
became plant, plant
and animal became
life: life & rock,
20 matter: that
took up most of
the morning: after
noon, matter began
to pulse, shoot, to
25 vanish in and out of
energy and

energy's invisible
swirls confused, surpassed
me: from that edge
30 I turned back,
strict with limitation,
to my world's
bitter acorns
and sweet branch water.

1964 (1966)

Muse

From the dark
fragmentations
build me up
into a changed brilliant shape,

5   realized order,
mind singing again
new song, moving into the slow beat and

disappearing beat
of perfect resonance:

10   how many
times must I be broken and reassembled! anguish of becoming,
pain of moulting,
descent! before the unending moment of vision:

how much disorder must I learn to tolerate
15   to find materials
for the new house of my sight!

arrange me
into disorder
near the breaking of the pattern
20   but

should disorder start to
tear, the breaking down of possible return,
oh rise gleaming in recall,

sing me again towering remade, born into a wider
25   order, structures deepening,
inching rootlike into the dark!

1959 (1965)

Sitting Down, Looking Up

A silver jet,
riding the top of tundra clouds,
comes over
maybe from Rio:
5   the aluminum sun shines
on it
as if it were a natural creature.

1964 (1965)

Belief

for JFK

1

drums gather and humble us beyond escape,
propound the single, falling fact:
time, suspended between memory and present,
hangs unmeasured, empty

2

5   erect,
disciplined by cadence into direction, the soldier
obeys the forms of rumor:
the riderless horse,
restive with the pressure of held flight,
10   tosses the hung bit,
worries the soldier's tameless arm—
sidling, prances the energy out

3

ahead, unalterable, the fact proceeds,
and the bit holds:
15   the fire-needle bites,
training the head on course

4

the light, determined rattle
of the caisson
breaking into sunlight
20   through the crystal black ribbons of trees!
the slack traces,
weightlessness at the shoulders of horses!

5

if we could break free
and run this knowledge out,
25   burst this energy of grief
through a hundred countrysides!
if bleak through the black night
we could outrun
this knowledge into a different morning!

6

30   belief, light as a drumrattle,
touches us and lifts us into tears

1964 (1964)

Song

Merging into place against a slope of trees,
I extended my arms and
took up the silence and spare leafage.
I lost my head first, the cervical meat
5   clumping off in rot,
baring the spinal heart to wind and ice

which work fast.
The environment lost no self-possession.
In spring, termites with tickling feet

10   aereated my veins.
       A gall-nesting wren took my breath

       flicking her wings, and
       far into summer the termites found the heart.
       No sign now shows the place,
15   all these seasons since,
       but a hump of sod below the leaves
       where chipmunks dig.

Orientale

       The pebble spoke and down
       came the sun
              its plume
       brushing through space as

5   over smooth sea-reaching stream
       bent reed
              lets sodden leaf
       arrow-ripples cut

       and acorn husk wind-whirled
10   ran out and caught the sun
              in its burred cup
       and said Look

       to everyone standing on
       edge of fern leaf watching
15   the other edge
       become imaginary as

       waterbirds low-flying through
       islands snake-long dark offshore
              Acorn husk got
20   no attention and even

       ———————

the universe could sundering
hold no ear
    What somebody asked did
the pebble say

25   and sea colander washed
aland said Nothing
    nothing exists
and everybody watched to

see if fern leaf could
30   re-appear with its lost edge
    and when
snow fell went in

1958

Mays Landing

I sit in sun
light
on a white

yard-bench:
5   the sparse great
oaks

cower the county
buildings:
a bumblebee

10   works a head
of marigolds: the
jail back

there, keys rattle
a sheriff
15   by:

———

people stand about
in twos and
threes talking,

waiting for
20   court:
a drunk man

talks loud as
if sobering to
alarm:

25   an acorn leaps
through leaves and
cracks the ground!

1963

Sphere

In the dark original water,
amniotic infinity
closed
boundless in circularity:

5   tame, heavy
water,
equilibriant,

any will forming to become—
consistency of motion
10   arising—
annihilated
by its equal and opposite:

an even, complete extent:
    (there
15   an eden: how

foreign and far away
your death, rivulets
        trickling
through ripe bowels,

20   return to heavy water,
infinite multiplicity, in

the deepening, filtering
earthen womb
that bears you forever
25   beyond
the amnion, O barrier!)

A warm unity, separable but
        entire,
you the nucleus
30   possessing that universe.

                              1960 (1964)

First Carolina Said-Song

(as told me by an aunt)

In them days
        they won't hardly no way to know if
            somebody way off
        died
5   till they'd be
            dead and buried

        and Uncle Jim

hitched up a team of mules to the wagon
and he cracked the whip over them
10   and run them their dead-level best
the whole thirty miles to your great grandma's funeral

down there in
Green Sea County

and there come up this
15   awfulest rainstorm
             you ever saw in your whole life
             and your grandpa
             was setting
             in a goat-skin bottomed chair

20   and them mules a-running
      and him sloshing round in that chairful of water

                till he got scalded
                he said

                and ev-
25   ery
      anch of skin come off his behind:

      we got there just in time to see her buried
             in an oak grove up
             back of the field:

30   it's growed over with soapbushes and huckleberries now.

1962 (1965)

Second Carolina Said-Song

(as told me by a patient, Ward 3-B,
Veterans Hospital, Fayetteville, August 1962)

             I was walking down by the old
      Santee
             River
                one evening, foredark
5   fishing I reckon,

＿＿＿＿＿

　　　　　　when I come on this
swarm of
bees
　　　　lit in the fork of a beech limb
10　　　　　　and they werz

　　　　jest a swarming:

　　　　it was too late to go home
　　　　and too far
and brang a bee-gum

15　　　　　　so I waited around
　　　　　till the sun went
down,
most dark,

　　　　and cut me off a pinebough,
20　　　　dipped it in the river
　　　　　　and sprankled water

on'em: settled'em right down,
　　　good and solid,
about
25　　　　　a bushel of
　　　them:

　　　　when it got dark I first cut off
the fork branches and
then cut about four foot back toward
30　　　　　the trunk

and I
　　　　throwed the limb over my shoulder and
　　　　carried'em home.

　　　　　　　　　　　1962 (1965)

Discoverer

If you must leave the shores of mind,
scramble down the walls
of dome-locked underwater caves
into the breathless, held

5   clarity of dark, where no waves break,
a grainy, colloidal grist
and quiet, carry a light: carry $A = \pi r^2$,
carry Kepler's equal areas in

equal times: as air line take Baudelaire's
10   *L'Albatros*: as depth markers
to call you back, fix the words of
the golden rule: feed the

night of your seeking with clusters
of ancient light:
15   remember the sacred sheaf, the rods of
civilization, the holy

bundle of elements: if to cast light
you must enter diffusion's ruin,
carry with you light to cast, to
20   gather darkness by: carry A is to B

as A plus B is to A: if to gather darkness
into light, evil into good,
you must leave the shores of mind,
remember us, return and rediscover us.

1962 (1965)

A Symmetry of Thought

is a mental object:
is to spirit
a rock of individual shape,

a flowerbed, pylon,
5   an arbor vitae
to cerebral loam:
is a moon in the mind,
water and land divided,
a crystal, precipitate,
10   separation, refinement,
a victory of being over void,
hazardous commitment,
broken eternity,
limited virtue;
15   coming into matter
spirit fallen
trades eternity
for temporal form:
is a symmetry of motion,
20   can always find its way
back to oblivion,
must move accommodating,
useful, relevant:
is, dead, a perfection;
25   here is its cage
to contemplate; here
time stops
and all its hollow bells
struck loud are
30   silenced in the never-ending sound.

1958 (1959)

Holding On

The stone in my tread
sings by the strip of woods
but is
unheard by open fields:

5   surround me then with walls
before I risk

the outer sight, as, walled,
I'll soon long to.

1963 (1964)

Uh, Philosophy

I understand
   reading the modern philosophers
that truth is so much a method
   it's perfectly all
5   right for me to believe whatever
   I like or if I like,

nothing:
   I do not know that I care to be set that free:
I am they say
10   at liberty to be
provisional, to operate
expediently, do not have to commit myself

to imperturbables, outright
   legislations, hardfast rules:
15   they say I can
     prefer my truths,
whatever
   suits my blood,

blends with my proclivities, my temperament:
20   I suppose they mean I've had more experience than I can
ever read about, taking in
    as I do
possibly a hundred sensations per second, conscious
   and unconscious,

25   and making a vegetal at least
   synthesis
from them all, so that
    philosophy is

a pry-pole, materialization,
30   useful as a snowshovel when it snows;

something solid to knock people down with
    or back people up with:
I do not know that I care to be backed up in just that way:
    the philosophy gives clubs to
35 everyone, and I prefer disarmament:
    that is, I would rather relate

to the imperturbable objective
    than be the agent of
"possibly unsatisfactory eventualities":
40   isn't anything plain true:
    if I had something
        to conform to (without responsibility)

I wouldn't feel so hot and sticky:
    (but I must be moved by what I am moved by):
45 they do say, though, I must give some force to facts,
            must bend that way enough,
    be in on the gist of "concrete observations,"
        must be pliant to the drift (roll with the knocks):

they say, too, I must halter my fancy
50   mare
with these blinding limitations:
        I don't know that I can go along with that, either:
    for though I've proved myself stupid by 33 years
        of getting nowhere,

55 I must nevertheless be given credit for the sense wherewith
        I decided never to set out:
    what are facts if I can't line them up
            any way I please
    and have the freedom
        I refused I think in the beginning?

                                                        1959 (1963)

The Numbers

are
consecutive:
everything is real: no use

to worry: everything comes after everything,
5 safely held in count:

experience, yes:
remember that:
selective memory: but the whole is difficult to
recall, day by day:

10 certain things are so clear:

think of the numbers, they proceed: there are five sparrows
at the feeder:
two are on the ground:
one is descending:

15 of those three on the ground
one is looking off,
toward or through the hedge, considering:

nevertheless, the count
is perfect:
20 942:

do not
worry that anything
is going to go wrong,
please:
25 turn to page 5: count two pages farther: count two pages
farther: count two pages farther:

where we are:
there is no use to worry:
grab the addendum:

30   today when the leaves fell it was
                    brilliant: shadows counted every one:
shadows broke against the limbs,
swept with several degrees of intensity across the grass,
moving
35   not as
                the leaves
                moved:
                that was exciting:

the angles of descent (tho there is no use to worry) were not
40   predictable,
having to do with wind velocities and turns of leaf:

                please turn to page 6:
                all is explicable:

      here are the boxes: 4×4×4×4×4×4×4×4:
45   how many? how many?

how many? how *many?*

many:

the numbers can set you free: square a pear:
                pare a pair:
50   peel a peer:
                a peer? appear
and seem:
                be confident;
                as you turn the numbers
55   veracity
                links segment to segment: a sausage bliss!

      there is no reason:
      for concern:
      falls wear the rock away
60   by a volume of noise: add it up:

———

think, think of the numbers, how they move!

appear and seem:

           the industrial buildings

           are as a shed of apples

65   a truck has crushed through: musiked with

           bees!

there is no cause:

for concern: spell the numbers: gather them: the numbers

are consecutive:

                        1964

Empty

        Prison break!

          the single-idea bolt shot back!

            the grillwork

              of syllogism

5   lake loose!

          the unyielding walls, square,

            sharp-cornered,

              fallen flat out

       to total openness!

10   certain isolations:

                the diminished moon over cold

                sea:

                introduction of rocks

                and shrubs—the

15   multiform land:

guilt diffused in limitless air:

punishment

        glittered dim among turning deep-sea schools:

           the unknown—pointless, vacant, blunt:

———

20   emptiness!

                            say everything again:
                            say everything over:

        cluck the words out of configuration,
        into configuration:
25   remake:

                ramble:

        nothing has been established:
        the forms have not been placed:
        the mixers are not ready:

30   the man will hear no answer:
                    he is not listening:
                    his heart knows shapeless music:
                    he is turned loose:
                    the prison is broken

                                            1964

Unbroken

                Evening falls: earth
                    divides:
                            insects waken
                    as
        5   birds fly to roost:

                out there, nothing
                    happens:
                            everything is
                        the
        10   same.

                                        1963 (1965)

Fall

Summer gauds,
crickets
sing:
the cool-snap
5   quavers their song
beyond
meanings they intend.

(1964)

The Wind Coming Down From

summit and blue air
said I am sorry for you
and lifting past
said you
5   are mere dust which I
as you see control

yet nevertheless are
instrument of miracle

and rose
10   out of earshot but
returning in a slow loop
said while
I am always just this bunch of
compensating laws
15   pushed, pushing
not air or motion
but the motion of air

I coughed
and the wind said
20   Ezra will live
to see your last
sun come up again

I turned (as I will) to weeds and
the wind went off
25   carving
monuments through a field of stone
   monuments whose shape
wind cannot arrest but
taking hold on
30   changes

while Ezra
   listens from terraces of mind
wind cannot reach or
weedroots of my low-feeding shiver

1958 (1959)

Interval

Coming to a pinywoods
   where a stream darted across the path
like a squirrel or frightened blacksnake
I sat down on a sunny hillock
5   and leaned back against a pine
and picked up some dry pineneedle bundles from the ground
and tore each bundle apart a needle at a time
   It was not Coulter's pine
   for *coulteri* is funnier looking
10   and not Monterey either
and I thought God must have had Linnaeus in mind
orders of trees correspond so well between them
and I dropped to sleep wondering what design God
had meant the human mind to fit
15   and looked up and saw a great bird
warming in the sun high on a pine limb
tearing from his breast golden feathers
   softer than new gold that
   dropped to the wind one or two

20   gently and touched my face
        I picked one up and it said
                The world is bright after rain
        for rain washes death out of the land and hides it far
        beneath the soil and it returns again cleansed with life
25   and so all is a circle
        and nothing is separable
        Look at this noble pine from which you are
        almost indistinguishable it is also sensible
                and cries out when it is felled
30   and so I said are trees blind and is the earth black to them
        Oh if trees are blind
                I do not want to be a tree
        A wind rising of *one in time* blowing the feather away
        forsaken I woke
35   and the golden bird had flown away and the sun
        had moved the shadows over me so I rose and walked on

                                                    (1957)

Way to Go

                West light flat on trees:
                        bird flying
                            deep out in blue glass:
                        uncertain wind
        5   stirring the leaves: this is
                        the world we have:
                            take it

                                            1963 (1965)

UPLANDS (1970)

for Mona and Vida

⌒⌒⌒

Snow Log

Especially the fallen tree
the snow picks
out in the woods to show:

the snow means nothing by that,
5   no special emphasis: actually
snow picks nothing out:

but was it a failure, is it,
snow's responsible for
that the brittle upright black

10   shrubs and small trees
set off what caught the snow
in special light:

or there's some intention
behind the snow snow's too shallow
15   to reckon with: I take it on myself:

especially the fallen tree
the snow picks
out in the woods to show.

1969 (1970)

Upland

Certain presuppositions are altered
by height: the inversion to
sky-well a peak
in a desert makes: the welling

---

5 from clouds down the boulder fountains:
it is always a
surprise out west there—
the blue ranges loose and aglide

with heat and then come close
10 on slopes leaning up into green:
a number of other phenomena might
be summoned—

take the Alleghenies for example,
some quality in the air
15 of summit stones lying free and loose
out among the shrub trees: every

exigency seems prepared for that might
roll, bound, or give flight
to stone: that is, the stones are
20 prepared: they are round and ready.

1969 (1969)

Periphery

One day I complained about the periphery
that it was thickets hard to get around in
 or get around for
an older man: it's like keeping charts

5 of symptoms, every reality a symptom
where the ailment's not nailed down:
 much knowledge, precise enough,
but so multiple it says this man is alive

or isn't: it's like all of a body answering
10 all of pharmacopoeia, a too
 adequate relationship:
so I complained and said maybe I'd brush

deeper and see what was pushing all this
periphery, so difficult to make any sense
15   out of, out:
with me, decision brings its own

hesitation: a symptom, no doubt, but open
and meaningless enough without paradigm:
    but hesitation
20   can be all right, too: I came on a spruce

thicket full of elk, gushy snow-weed,
nine species of lichen, four pure white
    rocks and
several swatches of verbena near bloom.

1969 (1969)

Clarity

After the event the rockslide
realized,
in a still diversity of completion,
grain and fissure,
5   declivity
    &
force of upheaval,
whether rain slippage,
ice crawl, root
10   explosion or
stream erosive undercut:

well I said it is a pity:
one swath of sight will never
be the same: nonetheless,
15   this
shambles has
relieved a bind, a taut of twist,

revealing streaks &
scores of knowledge
20   now obvious and quiet.

1969 (1970)

Classic

I sat by a stream in a
perfect—except for willows—
emptiness
and the mountain that
5   was around,

scraggly with brush &
rock
said
I see you're scribbling again:

10   accustomed to mountains,
their cumbersome intrusions,
I said

well, yes, but in a fashion very
like the water here
15   uncapturable and vanishing:

but that
said the mountain does not
excuse the stance
or diction

20   and next if you're not careful
you'll be
arriving at ways
water survives its motions.

1969 (1969)

Conserving the Magnitude of Uselessness

Spits of glitter in lowgrade ore,
precious stones too poorly surrounded for harvest,
to all things not worth the work
of having,

5   brush oak on a sharp slope, for example,
the balk tonnage of woods-lodged boulders,
the irreparable desert,
drowned river mouths, lost shores where

the winged and light-footed go,
10   take creosote bush that possesses
ground nothing else will have,
to all things and for all things

crusty or billowy with indifference,
for example, incalculable, irremovable water
15   or fluvio-glacial deposits
larch or dwarf aspen in the least breeze sometimes shiver in—

suddenly the salvation of waste betides,
the peerlessly unsettled seas that shape the continents,
take the gales wasting and in waste over
20   Antarctica and the sundry high shoals of ice,

for the inexcusable (the worthless abundant) the
merely tiresome, the obviously unimprovable,
to these and for these and for their undiminishment
the poets will yelp and hoot forever

25   probably,
rank as weeds themselves and just as abandoned:
nothing useful is of lasting value:
dry wind only is still talking among the oldest stones.

1969 (1970)

If Anything Will Level with You Water Will

Streams shed out of mountains in a white rust
(such the abomination of height)
slow then into upland basins or high marsh

and slowing drop loose composed figurations
5   on big river bottoms
or give the first upward turn from plains:

that's for modern streams: if sediment's
lithified it
may have to be considered ancient, the result of

10   a pressing, perhaps lengthy, induration:
old streams from which the water's
vanished are interesting, I mean that

kind of tale,
water, like spirit, jostling hard stuff around
15   to make speech into one of its realest expressions:

water certainly is interesting (as is spirit) and
small rock, a glacial silt, just as much so:
but most pleasurable (magma & migma) is

rock itself in a bound slurp or spill
20   or overthrust into very recent times:
there waterlike stone, those heated seekings &

goings, cools to exact concentration, I
mean the telling's unmediated:
the present allows the reading of much

25   old material: but none of it need be read:
it says itself (and
said itself) so to speak perfectly in itself.

1969 (1970)

The Unifying Principle

Ramshackles, archipelagoes, loose constellations
are less fierce, subsidiary centers, with the
attenuations of interstices, roughing the salience,

jarring the outbreak of too insistent commonalty:
5   a board, for example, not surrendering the rectitude
of its corners, the island of the oaks an

admonishment to pines, underfigurings (as of the Bear)
that take identity on: this motion is against
the grinding oneness of seas, hallows distinction

10   into the specific: but less lovely, too, for how
is the mass to be amassed, by what sanction
neighbor touch neighbor, island bear resemblance,

how are distinction's hard lines to be dissolved
(and preserved): what may all the people turn to,
15   the old letters, the shaped, characteristic peak

generations of minds have deflected and kept:
a particular tread that sometimes unweaves, taking
more shape on, into dance: much must be

tolerated as out of timbre, out of step, as being not
20   in its time or mood (the hiatus of the unconcerned)
and much room provided for the wretched to find caves

to ponder way off in: what then can lift the people
and only when they choose to rise or what can make
them want to rise, though business prevents: the

25   unifying principle will be a
phrase shared, an old cedar long known, general
wind-shapes in a usual sand: those objects single,

---

single enough to be uninterfering, multiple by
the piling on of shared sight, touch, saying:
30   when it's found the people live the small wraths of ease.

1969 (1970)

Runoff

By the highway the stream downslope
could hardly clear itself
through rubbish and slime but by

that resistance gained a cutting
5   depth equal to its breadth
and so had means to muscle into

ripples and spill over angled
shelves:
and so went on down in a long

10   curve, responsively slow to the
sizable ridge it
tended

and farther on down, quiet and clear,
never tipping enough to break sound,
15   slowed into marshy landrise and burst

into a bog of lupine and mirrored:
that was a place! what a place!
the soggy small marsh, nutgrass and swordweed!

1969 (1970)

Transaction

I attended the burial of all my rosy feelings:
I performed the rites, simple and decisive:
the long box took the spilling of gray ground in
with little evidence of note: I traded slow

5   work for the usual grief: the services were private:
there was little cause for show, though no cause not
to show: it went indifferently, with an appropriate
gravity and lack of noise: the ceremonies of the self

seem always to occur at a distance from the ruins of men
10   where there is nothing really much to expect, no arms,
no embraces: the day was all right: certain occasions
outweigh the weather: the woods just to the left

were average woods: well, I turned around finally from
the process, the surface smoothed into a kind of seal,
15   and tried to notice what might be thought to remain:
everything was there, the sun, the breeze, the woods

(as I said), the little mound of troublesome tufts of
grass: but the trees were upright shadows, the breeze
was as against a shade, the woods stirred gray
20   as deep water: I looked around for what was left,

the tools, and took them up and went away, leaving
all my treasures where they might never again disturb
me, increase or craze: decision quietens:
shadows are bodiless shapes, yet they have a song.

1969 (1970)

Then One

When the circumstance takes
on a salience, as a

crushing pressure, then one,
addled by the possible closures,

5   the tangles that might
snap taut in a loop

or other unfigurable construct,
then one

pores on drift-logs far at sea
10   where room can wear drifts out

winds change
and few places show one can't

embark
from and then one thinks finally

15   with tight appreciation
of nothingness

or if not that far of
things that loosen or come apart.

1969 (1970)

Further On

Up this high and far north
it's shale and woodsless snow:
small willows and alder brush

———

mark out melt streams on the
5   opposite slope and the wind talks
as much as it can before freeze

takes the gleeful, glimmering
tongues away: whips and sticks
will scream and screech then

10   all winter over the deaf heights,
the wind lifting its saying out
to the essential yell of the

lost and gone: it's summer now:
elk graze the high meadows:
15   marshgrass heads high as a moose's

ears: lichen, a wintery weed,
fills out for the brittle sleep:
waterbirds plunder the shallows.

1969 (1970)

Hope's Okay

The undergrowth's a conveyance of butterflies
(flusters of clustering) so buoyant and delightful,
filling into a floating impression, diversity's
diversion breaking out into under-piny seas
5   point by point to the mind's nodes and needs:

let's see, though, said the fire through the undergrowth,
what all this makes into, what difference can
survive it: so I waded through the puffy disgust
and could not help feeling despair of
10   many a gray, smoke-worming twig, scaly as if alive:

much that was here I said is lost and if I stoop
to ask bright thoughts of roots

do not think I ask for better than was here
or that hope with me rises one leaf higher than
15   the former growth (higher to an ashless fire) or
that despair came any closer than ash to being total.

1969 (1969)

Life in the Boondocks

Untouched grandeur in the hinterlands:
large-lobed ladies laughing in brook
water, a clear, scrubbed ruddiness lofted

to cones and conifers: frost blurs
5   the morning elk there and squirrels
chitter with the dawn, numb seed: clarity,

the eagle dips into scary nothingness,
off a bluff over canyon heights: trout
plunder their way up, thrashing the shallows

10   white: ladies come out in the gold-true sun
and loll easy as white boulders
in the immediate radiance by wind-chilling

streams: I have been there so
often, so often and held the women, squeezed,
15   tickled, nuzzled their rose-paint luxury:

so many afternoons listened to the rocky
drone of bees over spring-water weed-bloom,
snow-water violets, and distant moss turf.

1969 (1970)

Spiel

     I feel sure you will be pleased
with our product: it is
a coil spring comes wintrily into
    as house plants
5   react first to the longer light:

               but begin all
enterprise with celebration: measures
on the sand by
fluttering rush, sail, heart spun in
10   a resonance between
departure, grief and adventure of
    change, the hurry and detail,
sudden calamity
of shoving off, moorless into a hunk of
15   time that may
round back to greet its other edge:
may:

     (nothing is so phony as an incomplete
obscurity—it needs spelling
20   into its deepest outing,
surrounding into its biggest bulging:
when it gets aglitter
it grows black: what to make of a
hinted thing
25   where the mind's not traveled
but a botch: but spelled out any
spiel can pick enough surfage up
to drum a sea loose)

     I just ate a green banana: it is in
30   me now mushed and gushy: there is
nothing small enough to conjure clarity with:

     take the bathroom spider wintered thin:
so thin

bleached out against walls
35   life seems in him a brown taint that
lacking might make him water or crisp:
he spun an open-ended house
(safety, closed up to perfection,
      traps, he knows)
40   in the ceilingwall sharp
angle:

      (well then I will take a mere
suasion!
a drift
45   as of earth into light, the chorus
dancing to the right,
left, a multimedial parlance:
well I will take just the angle
the waves come out of the sea, say,
50   the way they break down their length
in a continuous moving roar:
      I don't care how many drops of
water there are
or how totally they are water or how
55   the ocean is nothing (figuratively
speaking) else: I identify waves,
they have an
action, many actions: I've seen them
come straight in, crest first in
60   the middle, break outward both ways
and leave behind
a pyramid of foam: I've never
seen a drop of water do that:)

at night he rides down to the white
65   sink
and hums in a drop of water's
uptight edge: I try to think
of what he eats
so winter skinny, such a bugless
70   winter: maybe those tiny book lice

leave learning
scoot ceilings sometimes and suffer
the usual
confrontation with reality:
75   or I think dandruff scales soaked in
droplets
drift dripping proteins loose that
drunk skirl spiders into hallelujahs
    of darkening:

80   from the state of distress a pill can
remove you: meanwhile the blue
spruce
is perilously unaffected:

                    it's monsterless here:
85   the
bayberry in a green sweep, breeze
lively:
indifferent as lace:

swipes, swatches, smears, luminous
90   samplers: what is

the existence in the argument of what
the argument
is about: precise but unspecified,
hunted out, turned from, disguised,
95   brunted:

            order, strict,
                is the shadow of flight:
I mean because of the lusterless
structure
100   the wing has rein: fact
is the port of
extreme navigation:

————

where footprints
disappear at the edge of melting snow
105   hesitation breaks mindfully into itself:

        the fairgrounds

        (hill meadows, aslant
        triangular sweepclosings of heights,
        scrub fringes, yangs of woods,
110   lovely sumac and sassafras, golden
        clumps of grass
        rising to a wind line, commas,
        the pheasant's tail, long,
        perfect for disappearance in
115   winter weeds, clumpy printwork
        of rabbits
        over hedge-kept floats of snow . . .

        I don't know what all there is
        but there's more than plenty and
120   that's just it there's too much
        except for, there'd be too much
        except for the outgrowth of soothing
        hills)

        sporting goods

125   nip and tuck

        scoops
        scopes
        scrimps &
        scroungings

                                    (1970)

Guitar Recitativos

1

I know you love me, baby
I know it by the way you carry on around here certain times of the day
    & night
I can make the distinction between the willing and the unrefusable
That's not what I'm talking about
5   That's not what I need
What I mean is could you just peel me a few of those grapes over there
I want to lie here cool and accumulate . . .
Oh about half a bunch
That's what I need
10   —flick out those little seed—
Just drop'em in here one at a time
I'm not going anyplace, baby, not today
Relax—sneak the skin off a few of those grapes for me, will you?

2

Baby, you been stomping round on my toes so long
15   They breaking out in black and blue hyacinths,
Well-knit forget-me-nots
Geraniums are flopping out over the tops of my shoes
tendril leaves coming out along the edges of my shoelaces

Gladioli are steering out of the small of my back
20   strumming their cool stalks up my spine
Zinnias radiating from the crock of my neck
and petunias swinging down bells from my earlobes
All this stomping around on me you been doing, baby,
I'm gonna break out in a colorful reaction
25   I'm gonna wade right through you
       with the thorns of all these big red roses

3

I can tell you what I think of your beauty, baby,
You have it, it's keen and fast, there's this

glittery sword whipping about your head all day
30   and, baby, you make people snap—you condescend

and a surprised little heart splatters or you turn your
cold head away and a tiny freeze kills a few
cells in some man's brain—I mean, baby, you
may be kind but your beauty sweetie is such

35   many a man would run himself through for
hating your guts every minute that he died for you

4

I'm tired of the you-and-me thing
I am for more research into the nature of the amorous bond
the discovery of catalysts for speeding-up, wearing out, and getting it over
        with
40   or for slowing it down to allow long intervals of looseness

Baby, there are times when the mixture becomes immiscible
and other times we get so stirred up I can't tell
whether I'm you or me
and then I have this fear of a surprising reaction in which
45   we both turn into something else

powdery or gaseous or slightly metallic
What I mean is this whole relationship is, lacking further
knowledge, risky: while there's still time, why
don't you get yourself together and I'll

50   get myself together and then we'll sort of shy out
of each other's gravitational field, unstring the
electromagnetism and then sort of just drop this
whole orientation baby

5

You come in and I turn on:
55   freon purrs and the

refrigerator breaks out with hives of ice
The Westinghouse portable electric fan flushes
    my papers all over the room
The waffle-iron whacks down sizzling imaginary waffles
60 One paper glues itself and billows to the back of the fan
    my nerves nervous as newspapers

I tell you you are a walking calamity
And when you sit down there is hardly less activity
The alarm clock breaks out raging its held cry
65 and the oven in the kitchen sets itself for broil
I mean the gas-jet in the incinerator bloops on
and frankly the mechanisms in my legs—I hope you
never find out—jerk:
Oh, beauty, beauty is so disturbingly nice.

1967 (1968)

Laser

An image comes
and the mind's light, confused
as that on surf
or ocean shelves,
5 gathers up,
parallelizes, focuses
and in a rigid beam illuminates the image:

the head seeks in itself
fragments of left-over light
10 to cast a new
direction,
any direction,
to strike and fix
a random, contradicting image:

15 but any found image falls
back to darkness or

the lesser beams splinter and
go out:
the mind tries to
20   dream of diversity, of mountain
rapids shattered with sound and light,

of wind fracturing brush or
bursting out of order against a mountain
range: but the focused beam
25   folds all energy in:
the image glares filling all space:
the head falls and
hangs and cannot wake itself.

1964 (1967)

Virtu

Make a motion
the wind said and
the mountain
strained hard
5   but

couldn't
even quiver:

so the wind curved and shook the poplars:
a slope
10   pebble loosened
and struck

down sharp goings:

the mountain
stunned at being
15   moved nearly
broke with grief

and the wind
whirled up the valley
over the stream

20   and trees
utterly unlost
in emptiness.

1965 (1967)

Choice

Idling through the mean space dozing,
blurred by indirection, I came upon a
stairwell and steadied a moment to
think against the stem:
5   upward turned golden steps
and downward dark steps entered the dark:

unused to other than even ground I
spurned the airless heights though bright
and the rigor to lift an immaterial soul
10   and sank
sliding in a smooth rail whirl and fell
asleep in the inundating dark
but waking said god abhors me
but went on down obeying at least
15   the universal law of gravity:

millenniums later waking in a lightened air
I shivered in high purity
and still descending grappled with
the god that
20   rolls up circles of our linear
sight in crippling disciplines
tighter than any climb.

1955

Body Politic

Out for stars he
took some
down
and we all
5   wondered if he might be
damned to such sinister
& successful enterprise:
we took and
unfolded him: he
10   turned out
pliant and warm
& messy in
some minor way: then, not
having come to
15   much, we
lit into his stars which
declaring nothing dark
held white and high
and brought us down.

1967 (1967)

Apologia pro Vita Sua

I started picking up the stones
throwing them into one place
and by sunrise I was going far away
for the large ones
5   always turning to see never lost
the cairn's height
lengthening my radial reach:

the sun watched with deep concentration
and the heap through the hours grew
10   and became by nightfall
distinguishable from all the miles around
of slate and sand:

———————

during the night the wind falling
turned earthward its lofty freedom and speed
15   and the sharp blistering sound muffled
toward dawn and the blanket was
drawn up over a breathless face:

even so you can see in full dawn
the ground there lifts
20   a foreign thing desertless in origin.

1956 (1958)

Offset

Losing information he
rose gaining
view
till at total
5   loss gain was
extreme:
extreme & invisible:
the eye
seeing nothing
10   lost its
separation:
self-song
(that is a mere motion)
fanned out
15   into failing swirls
slowed &
became continuum.

1967 (1969)

Mountain Talk

I was going along a dusty highroad
when the mountain
across the way
turned me to its silence:
5   oh I said how come
I don't know your
massive symmetry and rest:
nevertheless, said the mountain,
would you want
10   to be
lodged here with
a changeless prospect, risen
to an unalterable view:
so I went on
15   counting my numberless fingers.

1964 (1970)

Impulse

If a rock on the slope
loosens tonight
will it be because
rain's
5   unearthed another grain
or a root
arched for room
and
will a tree or rock
10   be right
there, or two rocks or trees,
to hold the
flashed decision back?

(1969)

Needs

I want something suited to my special needs
I want chrome hubcaps, pin-on attachments
and year round use year after year
I want a workhorse with smooth uniform cut,
5   dozer blade and snow blade & deluxe steering
wheel
I want something to mow, throw snow, tow, and sow with
I want precision reel blades
I want a console-styled dashboard
10   I want an easy spintype recoil starter
I want combination bevel and spur gears, 14
gauge stamped steel housing and
washable foam element air cleaner
I want a pivoting front axle and extrawide turf tires
15   I want an inch of foam rubber inside a vinyl
covering
and especially if it's not too much, if I
can deserve it, even if I can't pay for it
I want to mow while riding.

1968 (1968)

Help

From the inlet
surf a father
pulls in a crab—
a wonderful machinery
5   but
not a fish: kicks
it off the line &
up the beach
where three daughters
10   and two sons take
turns bringing cups
of water

to keep alive, to
watch work, the sanded
15   & disjeweled.

1968 (1969)

Love Song

Like the hills under dusk you
fall away from the light:
you deepen: the green
light darkens
5   and you are nearly lost:
only so much light as
stars keep
manifests your face:
the total night in
10   myself raves
for the light along your lips.

1966 (1967)

Love Song (2)

Rings of birch bark
stand in the woods
still circling the nearly
vanished log: after
5   we go to pass
through log and star
this white song will
hug us together in the
woods of some lover's head.

1966 (1967)

Mule Song

Silver will lie where she lies
sun-out, whatever turning the world does,
longeared in her ashen, earless,
floating world:
5   indifferent to sores and greenage colic,
where oats need not
come to,
bleached by crystals of her trembling time:
beyond all brunt of seasons, blind
10   forever to all blinds,
inhabited by
brooks still she may wraith over broken
fields after winter
or roll in the rye-green fields:
15   old mule, no defense but a mule's against
disease, large-ribbed,
flat-toothed, sold to a stranger, shot by a
stranger's hand,
not my hand she nuzzled the seasoning-salt from.

1958 (1969)

Script

The blackbird takes out
from the thicket down there
uphill toward
the house, shoots
5   through a vacancy in the
elm tree & bolts
over the house:
some circling leaves waving
record
10   size, direction, and speed.

1968 (1969)

Holly

The hollybush flowers
small whites (become of
course berries)
four tiny petals
5   turned
back and four
anthers stuck out:
the pistil low &
honey-high:
10   wasp-bees (those small
wasps or
bees) come around
with a glee too
fine to hear: when
15   the wind dies
at dusk, silence,
unaffronted,
puts a robe
slightly thinner
20   than sight over
all the flowers
so darkness &
the terrible stars
will not hurt them.

1968 (1968)

Small Song

The reeds give
way to the

wind and give
the wind away

(1969)

Possibility Along a Line of Difference

At the crustal
discontinuity
I went down and
walked
5   on the gravel bottom,
head below gully rims

tufted with
clumpgrass and
through-free roots:
10   prairie flatness crazed
by that difference,
I grew

excited with
the stream's image left
15   in dust
and farther down
in confined rambling
I

found a puddle
20   green, iridescent
with a visitation of daub-singing wasps,
sat down and watched
tilted shadow untilting
fill the trough,

25   imagined cloudbursts
and
scattered pillars of rain,
buffalo at night routed
by lightning,
30   leaping,

falling back,
wobble-kneed calves

tumbling, gully-caught;
coyote, crisp-footed
35   on the gravel,
loping up the difference.

1959 (1969)

Cascadilla Falls

I went down by Cascadilla
Falls this
evening, the
stream below the falls,
5   and picked up a
handsized stone
kidney-shaped, testicular, and

thought all its motions into it,
the 800 mph earth spin,
10   the 190-million-mile yearly
displacement around the sun,
the overriding
grand
haul

15   of the galaxy with the 30,000
mph of where
the sun's going:
thought all the interweaving
motions
20   into myself: dropped

the stone to dead rest:
the stream from other motions
broke
rushing over it:
25   shelterless,
I turned

to the sky and stood still:
Oh
I do
30   not know where I am going
that I can live my life
by this single creek.

1966 (1969)

Summer Session

Saliences are humming bee paths
in & out around
here, continuous if
unpredictable: they
5   hang the air with cotton
candy
and make a neighborhood:

we set out four tomato plants a while
ago: good soil
10   where a row of winter-used cut wood was:
I've been out several times to see
but coming dark hinders me,
forcing faith up which
must
15   spindly as high walloping
weeds
outlast the night:

earlier came a shower so
skinny
20   not a coil spring in the glass pond
rang the periphery, for a minute:

walking home from class:
dogs yurping

out from hedge tunnels,
25 jerking to snazzy, skidding halts,
an outrage about the legs,
hairy explosion with
central, floating teeth:
I hope snitching hairy little
30 worms
will thread their eyelids and distending close off
the eyeballs of flagrant sight the way
summer closed up the
hedges to fill
35 us with surprises:

in my yard's more wordage than I
can read:
the jaybird gives a shit:
the earthworm hoe-split bleeds
40 against a damp black clump:

the problem is
how
to keep shape and flow:

the day's died
45 & can't be re-made:
in the dusk I can't recover
the goldenbodied fly
that waited on a sunfield leaf:

well I can't recover the light:
50 in my head—on the
inside frontal wall—the fly waits
and then, as he did, darts upward at an
air-hung companion:

ghosts remain, essences out-skinnying
55 light: essences
perceiving ghosts skinny skinny

percipients:
reverence, which one cannot
withhold, is
60   laid on lightly, with terror—as if
one were holding a dandelion back
into the sun:

all these shapes my bones
answer to
65   are going to go on
consuming, the flowers, venations, vines,
the roots that know their
way,
going to go on taking down and
70   re-designing, are going to go on
stridently
with bunchers & shears
devouring sundry mud, flesh: but their
own shapes will, as will all shapes, break
75   but will with all
others
cast design ahead where possible, hold
figuration in the cast seed:
shape & flow:
80   we must not feel hostile:

the most perfect nothingness affords
the widest play,
the most perfect meaninglessness:
look up at dusk and see
85   the bead fuzzy-buzzy bug
no darker than mist:
couldn't get along
at all except against infinity:
swallow, bat dine
90   in a rush—
never know what hit him
nothing hit him sent him to nothing:

but the temporary marvels!—
getting along against. . . .
95   take it from there:

(to slink and dream with the interior singing
attention of snakes)

prolix as a dream, a stream, sameness
of going
100   but diverse, colorful, sunlit
glints and glimmerings:
can motion alone then
hold you, strange person:
entertainments of flame and water,
105   flame in water,
an honorable, ancient flame
removed in high burning: water
no less a metal of interest, subtly
obeying: sit down and be consoled:
110   the death that reaches toward you has
been spared none:
be enchanted with the shrill hunger
of distant children:
do something:

115   the boughs ripen:
birds falling out
around here like plums,
rolling around, tilting over, turbulent
somersaults, a wrestling with divinity,
120   smooth & mostly belly:
the tail's a mean instrument but
feathered
gives poise, as of
contrary knowledges:
125   the cats frizzling with interest tone
down to pure motion: songs go
such way:

destruction of the world into the
guts: regeneration:
130   the kill is a restless
matter: but
afterwards the fact's
cool as satiation:

we just had lunch at the picnic table
135   under the elm: chunks of cantaloupe,
peach slices, blueberries, all cool
colorings in a glass cup: hotdogs &
pepsi:
brilliant replenishment:
140   icy destructions with the berry
burst, the teeth in a freshet
of cantaloupe juice:
the robin's nest, way out on a pear
limb, nearly
145   overhangs the table: some
worry, of course, a chirp or two:
distant approaches: above, the yellow
triangles of mouths:

up the stairs you go
150   up the stairs you go
beddybye &
snoozy snooze
up the stairs you go
ho ho
155   up the stairs you go

now the lawnmowers of reality are
whirring on the slopes of absent lawns
and sunday is in the world or part
of it: I look across the valley
160   to the otherside big hills and realize
the whole thing's rolling
tumbling in the smoothest quietest

lunge, our
bristlegreen rockship, our clamorous
165   house wherein difference bites so
hard hardly
a man will admit the common nickelodean core
where metals twist in
slow drifts of warping
170   pressure:

nevertheless into raw
space we turn, sun
feeding cosmic drift through,
expelling radiance of cosmic storm,
175   and we are at an
incredible height going round
something:
in the whole coming and going of man
we may not
180   get around once:
at certain levels recurrence is not
a bore: we clip an arc:

buttered batter's better bitter:

what do you know:
185   Western Prong beat Old Dock:
stir up them little wasps and you
have a nest of hornets:

past 21
women suffer
190   unbearably (!)
take bladder irritation: that headachy
backachy feeling:
that burning stitching itching gives them
the weewees, makes them need
195   fast relaxing comfort: what women go
through

to make or lose a buck: in those
ample haunches
greased with sheer illumination's light
200   is a mess of bacterial bloomers: it's
merciful to lust the eye's
small-blind: cultures from average nipples:
knowledge is lovely
but some of it shivers
205   into the blood stream
and undermines the
requirements of the moment: but
desire spills antiseptic gold celluloid
sheathes o'erall
210   and pours pellucid lubricants
down the drains of microfloral
habitations:
the clitoris rises above
surmountings, backs off, and
215   takes a testy peck or so:

we went to the park & John swung on
the swings and swung:
little children, I told my wife,
these little children, some of them
220   will live to say two thousand forty
maybe forty-five, fifty:
I said think of it by that time
we, you and I, will have been dead
so long
225   worms yet will scoff at us:
it makes you think
(twice):
what are
a few vaginal weeds in the teeth
230   compared with the traipsing gluebellies of
candorous maggots: & other worms,
all their noise:
get down, yes:

enwarm to eradication the carnal
235 longings: which are short:

what, then, is the organization of the
soul: scrambles to the peak,
squirts off, slumps back: the
long & short of it:

240 ducks were there, spinning, sputtering
in the glass: popcorn, wiener rolls
floating in the circumstance: but do
they do do underwater:
if a scientist, I'd devise
245 a test
and count the dropping abstractions off:
a glass tank with top
and a careful observer
could keep that duck in there
250 till he had to: yes, but the
test's wrong: suppose the observed's
disturbed & would much have
preferred
to go out upon the ground & hunker up on
255 a hunk of grass:
could turn to billets due
formerly:
following a duck around au naturel
though
260 could wobble a man's weltanschauung:
scientific objectivity puts
radiance on
duckshit even: we used to save
coop chickenshit for choicest
265 garden plants:
a powerful ingredient that
through the delicacies of floral
transfiguration
makes tasty gravy:

270 friend of mine, brilliant
        linguist, told me
        a Southern Gentleman screwed
        himself in the
        penis
275 with a squirrel's
        pizzle:
        puzzling:
        got it hung in there's how everybody
        found out:
280 doctor had to cut it loose:

        let approved channels then be your
        contemplation
        so you will not wind up in a fix
        or fuxy fox, feel the fire asphaltic:
285 do
        not go in for strange devices:
        pins, strangulations or such:
        practices that lead gradually away
        from picnic tables,
290 the trivial fluvial fumes of sunday braziers:

        I'm not going to
        delay my emergence:
        I'm going to plop
        a polyp:
295 I'm going to pupate
        pussycoon:
        I'm going to shoot for the wings:
        I can't tell you how many times with
        stalled interior I've
300 watched the spiders hatch & thrive:
        I'm going to
        get something off my chest—
        incubus or poking heartflipper:
        I'm 42:

305   the rank & file has
    o'errucked me & cloddled on:
    I'm not going
    any longer officially
    to delay my emergence:
310   I want the head of the matter to
    move out of skinny closure:
    I want a pumping, palpable turgidity:
    I want the condition to take on flare:
    I want manifestation silk-dry:

315   I told this fellow:
    I met him out under a soaking
    elm tree:
    I said you're needy:
    you're so needy something's rotten:
320   I told him just because you have a
    mailbox doesn't mean anybody has
    to put anything in it:
    it's your epidermal hole, nobody else's:
    I was getting so much pleasure out
325   of soaking under the elm tree I
    couldn't get interested in the guy's nasty cavity
    and knew without looking I wasn't
    going to put anything in there:
    too bad about the elms being in dutch:

330   Archie:
        Summer Session has agreed (somewhat
    reluctantly) to split 303 into 2
    sections, with one for Baxter. I
    haven't been able to reconfirm with Bax
335   that he does still want a second course
    but I've gone ahead as if he did, with
    the understanding that *someone* will
    teach the plus-23 students and do so
    at the same time (8:00) as you.
340   Barry

seeing in a green yard a sailboat for sale:
worth a morning:
when you consider life
adds up
345   to exactly nothing:

one day I'm
going to go
out & conjure
the clouds down:
350   I'm going to try the cape on:
if they don't
come right down
flubbing their responsive damp bellies over the
ambience
355   I'm going to strip and shit:

as a writing teacher I tell them
revise the world:
they clip, trim, slice:
they bring it in:
360   oh no I say you've just put it on
stilts:
they lob, twist, crack:
oh no I say when they bring it in
you've killed it:
365   reconceive:
they bring in something new:
what's the use, I throw up my hands,
we're already two or three worlds
behind:

370   down this drain, endless
ingestion, getting
bloated with world: anybody toss
an old memo in: it's squirting
milk into treeping squabs:

375 burning's going on down
     there:
     the whole world's a few flakes:
     it's sedimentation through seas:
     those in the heights need
380 substantial bottoms: need the
     sense
     things are leveling off: hate
     wide, especially open, disparities:

     equilibrium fills holes with hills:

385 feed in a grocery list, somebody:
     feed in how to fix a
     telescope on, say, a comet: feed in a
     few large pieces of legislation,
     couple committee reports, some lab
390 notes, triptickets, sailing schedules,
     the dawns & dusks of planets,
     contemplations of squirrels:

     somewhere along the line the computer
     is going to perpetrate a large announcement:
395 then we'll know why the
     imagination's
     winding no scraps up into
     windy transfigurations:
     in our day
400 comfort is sunrise at 5:25:

     couple systems analysts: bushel of
     female ticks, engorged: some dirty
     rats:
     cutworms:
405 nightfeeders that dusk arouses:
     cubic mile of infestation,
     corruption, rust, pus, pus
     caterpillars,

snot:
410 tank of wound weepage:
boxcar of love salt,
fill, siftings, winnowings, dregs,
curds, chips,
aerosols of eagerness, dozen black
415 widows:
a league of universal ivy stone:
choice:
much testament of need: 400
singing horses, a flask of
420 wart-juice from the udders of the awry:

families with a lot of living to do:
should get turquoise, shaded coppertone,
or spanish avocado:
features for fun-loving families:

425 discover for yourselves where
the problems are & amass
alternative strategies:
otherwise it's D– & no pussy:

Archie:
430   Thanks very
much. That's a
real pleasure.
      · Neil

I scribble, baby, I mean
435 I breeze on:
every mile a twist, I
should be back:
a smidgen slit of silence lets all
in:
440 the land's turning tables
greased with the finest silence
money can buy, still, the wind, mine & its,

rattles over the ridges, splits
the cords of wood & gristle:
445   to a cartographer
part of Pennsylvania's a broken record:
curving grooves & ridges in
visual music:

day after day the camels of the rain
450   bear their gray way by: the ditches
bend green grass in:
but then drought enlarges in rapids
the incidence of rocks:
but then flood, so salient, though
455   with muscle swirls, could
scrape you across a single
prominence,
splitting possibility like a paper shell:
it is, even after an 8-day rain,
460   hard to know what to ask for:
a baby robin's been out on the
lawn all day, all day wet and for
many days wet though only one
day out: maybe if it were
465   dry he could get to a low branch at
least, some force from those fumbling
wings, airier dry:

here are the 18-year-old
seedbeds & the
470   19-year-old fertilizers:
they have come for a summer session:
knowledge is to be my insemination:
I grant it them as one grants flesh
the large white needle:
475   what shall I tell those who are
nervous,
too tender for needles, the
splitting of iridescent tendons:

oh I tell them nothing can realize
480   them, nothing ruin them
like the poundage of pure self:
with my trivia
I'll dispense dignity, a sense of office,
formality they can define themselves against:
485   the head is my sphere:
I'll look significant as I deal with
mere wires of light, ghosts of
cells, working there.

1968 (1970)

BRIEFINGS:
POEMS SMALL AND EASY (1971)

for John Logan

❦

Center

A bird fills up the
streamside bush
with wasteful song,
capsizes waterfall,
5 mill run, and
superhighway
to
song's improvident
center
10 lost in the green
bush green
answering bush:
wind varies:
the noon sun casts
15 mesh refractions
on the stream's amber
bottom
and nothing at all gets,
nothing gets
20 caught at all.

1963 (1968)

Mechanics

A clover blossom's a province:
actually: florets cluster helical
villages with visible streets:
down the main arteries a ways

leaffarms produce common sustenance:
a kingbee when all is ready
visits and tries the yellow-doored
purplish houses for virgin
sweet, feeds in winged spells,
10   rumples everything, and leaves behind
not as a gift or fee—seed, seed.

1967 (1969)

Up

A clown kite, my
self rustles
up
to any gust:
5   warps & whucks
the wind: O
my blustering orange
and striped green
immensities!
10   I get sometimes so
good
tickled at my
self I slip
flat down and
15   windless
make no
show of grief.

1968

After Yesterday

After yesterday
afternoon's blue
clouds and white rain
the mockingbird

5   in the backyard
untied the drops from
leaves and twigs
with a long singing.

1968 (1969)

Event

A leaf fallen is
fallen
throughout the universe
and
5   from the instant of
its fall, for
all time gone
and to come:

worlds jiggle in
10   webs, drub
in leaf lakes,
squiggle in
drops of ditchwater:

size and place
15   begin, end,
time is allowed
in event's instant:
away or
at home, universe and
20   leaf try
to fall: occur.

1962 (1963)

High & Low

A mountain risen
in me
I said
this implacability
5 must be met:
so I climbed
the peak:
height shook and
wind leaned
10 I said what
kind of country is
this anyhow and
rubbled
down the slopes to
15 small rock
and scattered weed.

1965

Peracute Lucidity

A perspicuity like a sanctuary: against
the pond a pavilion, led to by a glide
of stairs, set right and accurately

gauged: the bobolink in the dusk bush
5 says a closing say-so: *bunk*
bunk the frog maintains and aims his

tilty eyes: just above the brookfall's
shaggy seams and rags, clarity's chapel
bodied by hung-in boughs: and

10 widening out over the pond, the blown
cathedral luminous with evening glass:
I go out there and sit

_____

till difference and event yield to
perfect composure: then the stars
15   come out and question every sound, the brook's.

1969

Increment

Applause is a shower
to the watertable of
self-regard:
in the downpour
5   the watertable's irrelevant
but after the shower passes
possibility takes on
an extensive millimeter.

1968

Bees Stopped

Bees stopped on the rock
and rubbed their headparts and wings
rested then flew on:
ants ran over the whitish greenish reddish
5   plants that grow flat on rocks
and people never see
because nothing should grow on rocks:
I looked out over the lake
and beyond to the hills and trees
10   and nothing was moving
so I looked closely
along the lakeside
under the old leaves of rushes
and around clumps of drygrass
15   and life was everywhere
so I went on sometimes whistling

1951

Storm

Branches broken,
the clean meat at the branch knot
turned out white,
traveled by cleared
5   white light: certain
consequences are

irreversible, arrangements
lost to
death's and black's
10   scavenging the sweet grain:
well but weakness
went sacrificed to the wind

and the trees, clarified,
compress rootstrength
15   into remaining flesh
and the leaves that shake
in the aftermath shake
in a safe, tested place.

1963

Two Possibilities

Coming out of the earth and going
into the earth compose
an interval or arc where
what to do's

5   difficult to fix: if it's
the coming
out that answers, should one with all
thrust come out and

rise to imagination's limit, leaving
10   earthiness, maximally

to mark the change, much below:
if it's

going in, should one flatten out on
coming, lie low
15   among bush
and rock, and keep the residence

near the palm of the hand, the
gross engrossed and palpable:
well, there is an interval designed,
20   apparently, for design.

1970

Medicine for Tight Spots

Consider big-city
tensions
rurally unwound,

high-tension lines that
5   loft through the countryside,
give off

"wirelings"
and fine-up to houses
cool as a single volt:

10   there are so many ways to approach the problems:
reproach:
best of all the by-pass and set-aside: the

intelligence has never been called for
because as usually
15   manifested it's

———

too formulated to swim
unformulable reality's
fall-out insistences:

just think how woodsy roads
20   shade spangled
wind up big-city printed circuits:

if the mind becomes what it sees or
makes how it works
I know which way I'm headed:

25   won't bushes bust us
mild:
won't the streams

ravel us loose:
won't we be untold
30   by sweetwater tongues.

1969

Brooks & Other Notions

Currents figure
you can see them
they boil out
of themselves &
5   slice in
from both
sides
a downward crease steady at
the moving burial:

10   in the wind too
you can feel them
spell
themselves along the
arm, watch them

15 against an elm
or
multiple on puddles:

below speech
mind
20 figures motion,
plunges or takes
a turn: grief's
a common
form of going:
25 its letters rise &
spiel away expressly
inexact.

1969

Cougar

Deprived like the cougar
into heights

I knew huge
air, rock
5 burn,

lightning, sun,
ice,

gained
insouciance:

10 bend, bend
the stream called high:
but I climbed higher

knowing what
takes rock away.

1965 (1970)

This Black Rich Country

Dispossess me of belief:
between life and me obtrude
no symbolic forms:

grant me no mission: let my
5   mystical talents be beasts
in dark trees: thin the wire

I limp in space, melt it
with quick heat, let me walk
or fall alone: fail

10   me in all comforts:
hide renown behind the tomb:
withdraw beyond all reach of faith:

leave me this black rich country,
uncertainty, labor, fear: do not
15   steal the rewards of my mortality.

1955 (1956)

Attention

Down by the bay I
kept in mind
at once
the tips of all the rushleaves
5   and so
came to know
balance's cost and true:
somewhere though in the whole field
is the one
10   tip
I will someday lose out of mind
and fall through.

1963

Return

1

drought continuing
the stems
drop their leaves

healing hard the pulvinal
5   scars and
dangling buzzards

drop to sleeps
in ledge and
cactus shade, to rockheld

10   reservoirs of night
and
sidewinder from the

stinging air
holds
15   his tongue

2

I have come a long way
without arriving
torn songs up

from the roots of weeds
20   but made no
silence sing:

climbed the peak but
found no foothold
higher than the ground

3

25   should I roll
rocks
down the slope

to learn
the thunder of
30   my being:

should I call out,
echolocation fixing me
against a certain wall:

should I break
35   a switch
and whirling inscribe

a circle round me
to know my
center and periphery

4

40   the leaves drop:
wolves thinning
like moons run through scuds of sage:

moon cloud shadows
sail gulfs
45   through a wild terrain

1958

This Bright Day

Earth, earth!
day, this bright day
again—once more
showers of dry spruce gold,
5   the poppy flopped broad open and delicate
from its pod—once more,
all this again: I've had many
days here with these stones and leaves:
like the sky, I've taken on a color
10   and am still:
the grief of leaves,
summer worms, huge blackant
queens bulging
from weatherboarding, all that
15   will pass
away from me that I will pass into,
none of the grief
cut less now than ever—only I
have learned the
20   sky, the day sky, the blue
obliteration of radiance:
the night sky,
pregnant, lively,
tumultuous, vast—the grief
25   again in a higher scale
of leaves and poppies:
space, space—
and a grief of things.

1967 (1969)

Look for My White Self

Find me diffuse, leached colorless,
gray as an inner image with no clothes
along the shallows of windrows: find

---

me wasted by hills,
5 conversion mountain blue in sight
offering its ritual cone of white:

over the plain I came long years,
drawn by gaze: a flat land with
some broken stems, no gullies,

10 sky matched square inch with
land in staying interchange: found
confusing hills, disconcerting names
and routes, differences locked
in seamless unities:

15 so look for my white self, age clear,
time cleaned: there is the mountain:
even now my blue

ghost may be
singing on that height of snow.

1955 (1956)

Undersea

Foraminiferal millennia
bank and spill but
even so
time's under pressure of
5 diatomaceous event,
divisions a moment
arcs across:
    desperate
for an umbrella, net, longpole,
10 or fan: so much
to keep for paradigm,
so much to lose.

1967

Auto Mobile

For the bumps bangs & scratches of
collisive encounters
madam
I through time's ruts and weeds
5   sought you, metallic, your
stainless steel flivver:
I have banged you, bumped
and scratched, side-swiped,
momocked & begommed you &
10   your little flivver still
works so well.

1967

Wagons

Going west
we finally hit
the sea hills, halted
& went down to
5   see shells, touch
sand and surf, the
peculiar new conditions,
the anguish perfect
that the sun still
10   took its gold away:
the waves harmless
unharmable posed
no shapes we could
wrestle to the ground:
15   turning back like
going down ever
diminishes: we
decided maybe we
would hold but
20   never turn back
and never go down.

1968 (1968)

September Drift

Hardly anything flies north these days
(a jay occasionally makes the bleak
decision): the robin, sitting on a high
dead elm limb, looks melancholy with
5   leisure: he thinks, probably: I wonder
how or of what: small bark-searching

birds drift through the shrubs and trees,
the usual feeding, but in one direction:
I guess I won't go anywhere myself, not
10   that I don't rustle somewhere deep
and remember ice and wolves: I'll stay
to imagine everything can get back.

1968 (1970)

Civics

Hard up for better lays (with
fewer diseases)
a less qualified gliding,
he took
5   amelioration seriously,
thought the poor deserved better
dreams, that
taxes should husband
unwed mothers, house
10   the losing mad,
raised money for
churches
& otherwise by rising
and increasing
15   spent himself so his old
eat-up woman got
little of his coin:
there are a number of possibilities.

1967

He Held Radical Light

He held radical light
as music in his skull: music
turned, as
over ridges immanences of evening light
5   rise, turned
back over the furrows of his brain
into the dark, shuddered,
shot out again
in long swaying swirls of sound:

10   reality had little weight in his transcendence
so he
had trouble keeping
his feet on the ground, was
terrified by that
15   and liked himself, and others, mostly
under roofs:
nevertheless, when the
light churned and changed

his head to music, nothing could keep him
20   off the mountains, his
head back, mouth working,
wrestling to say, to cut loose
from the high, unimaginable hook:
released, hidden from stars, he ate,
25   burped, said he was like any one
of us: demanded he
was like any one of us.

1965 (1969)

Locus

Here
it is
the middle of April
(and a day or so more)

5   and
the small oak
down in
the
hollow is
10   lit up (winter-burned, ice-gold
leaves on)
at sundown,
ruin transfigured to

stillest shining:
15   I let it as center
go
and
can't believe
our peripheral
20   speed.

1966

Circles

I can't decide whether
the backyard stuff's
central or irrelevant:
how matted rank the mint is! and
5   some of the iris stalks are so
crooked rich
the blossoms can't burst
(scant weeds
pop their flowers fast) loose

10 and the pansies keep
 jointing up another blooming tier:
 I can't figure out what
 the whole green wish again
 is, tips pushing hard into
15 doing the same, last
 year again, the year before:
 something nearer than
 the pleasure of
 circles drives into the next
20 moment and the next.

1968

Working Still

 I can't think of a thing to uphold:
 the carborundum plant snows
 sift-scum on the slick, outgoing river
 and along the avenues car wheels

5 float in a small powder: my made-up
 mind idles like a pyramid: oxides
 "under proper atmospheric conditions" become
 acids and rain a fine broad bleaching:

 man's a plant parasite: so I drop
10 down to the exchange, $CO_2 \leftrightarrow O_2$, and
 find dread there, just dread: too
 much care fuddles me dull:

 beef hormones bloom monstrous
 with tenderness:
15 but I won't take up the scaring cause
 and can't think of a thing to uphold.

1969 (1970)

Tooling Up

I cut a new thread on it this morning,
smeared a little dab (a small glob) of
pipedope around (for perfect action,
should the opportunity arise or
5   withdrawal prove premature) and
stuck myself out again: a
formal—possibly too formal—stance,
a willed extension, as if in
expectation of pain:
10   well but I've done my share: my
mind's at ease: I'm
obviously out, my
intentions are obviously firm.

1968

Father

I dreamed my father flicked
in his grave
then like a fish in water
wrestled with the ground
5   surfaced and wandered:
I could not find him
through woods, roots, mires
in his bad shape: and
when I found him he was
10   dead again and had to be
re-entered in the ground:
I said to my mother I still
have you: but out of the
dream I know she died
15   sixteen years before his
first death:
as I become a child again

a longing that will go away
only with my going grows.

1968 (1969)

Sumerian

I have grown a marsh dweller
subject to floods and high winds,
drinking brackish water on long hunts,
brushing gnat smoke
5   from clumps of reeds, have known

the vicissitudes of silt, of
shifting channels flush
by dark upland rains, of mounds
rising no more firmly than
10   monsters from the water:

on the southern salty
banks near the gulf the ducks
and flying vees of geese have
shunned me: the bouncing spider's net,
15   strung wet over narrows of reeds, has
broken terror dawn cold across my face:

rising with a handful of broken shells
from sifted underwater mud
I have come to know how high
20   the platform is, beyond approach,
of serenity and blue temple tiles.

1955 (1956)

Hippie Hop

I have no program for
saving this world or scuttling
the next: I know no political,
sexual, racial cures: I make
5   analogies, my bucketful of
flowers: I give flowers to people
of all policies, sexes, and races
including the vicious, the
uncertain, and the white.

1968

Garden

I have sung
delphiniums
seasonless, seedless
out of debris,

5   stone-white asters
out of shale:
I've made it this far
turning between made sights

and recognitions:
10   and now
if everything becomes,
as it could,

naturalized, returned,
I may pick hyacinths
15 here real and tender
in the ruse.

1965

Hymn IV

I hold you responsible for
every womb's neck
clogged with
killing growth

5   and for ducks on the bay
barking like hounds
all night
their wintering dreams

responsible for every action of
10   the brain that gives
me mind
and for all light

for the fishroe's
birth spawning forage to
15   night eels
nosing the tidal banks

I keep you existent at least as
a ghost crab
moon-extinguished his crisp
20   walk silenced on broken shells

answering at least as
the squiggling copepod
for the birthing and aging of
life's all-clustered grief

25   You have enriched us with
fear and contrariety
providing the searcher
confusion for his search

———

teaching by your snickering
30   wisdom an autonomy
for man
Bear it all

and keep me from my enemies'
wafered concision and zeal
35   I give you back to yourself
whole and undivided

1957 (1958)

The Mark

I hope I'm
not right
where frost
strikes the
5   butterfly:
in the back
between
the wings.

1965

Loft

I live in a bodiless loft,
no joists, beams,
or walls:

I huddle high,
5   arch my back against the stiff
fact of coming down:

my house admits to being
only above the level of most
perception:

———

10   I shudder and make do:
        I don't look down.

1965

Poetics

I look for the way
things will turn
out spiralling from a center,
the shape
5   things will take to come forth in

so that the birch tree white
touched black at branches
will stand out
wind-glittering
10   totally its apparent self:

I look for the forms
things want to come as

from what black wells of possibility,
how a thing will
15   unfold:

not the shape on paper—though
that, too—but the
uninterfering means on paper:

not so much looking for the shape
20   as being available
to any shape that may be
summoning itself
through me
from the self not mine but ours.

1965 (1969)

Working with Tools

I make a simple assertion
like a nice piece of stone
and you
alert to presence and entrance
5   man your pick and hammer

and by chip and deflection
distract simplicity
and cut my assertion
back to mangles, little heaps:

10   well, baby, that's the way
you get along: it's all right,
I understand such
ways of being afraid:
sometimes you want my come-on

15   hard, something to
take in and be around:
sometimes you want
a vaguer touch: I understand
and won't give assertion up.

1968 (1968)

Doubling the Nerve

In the bleak time look for no cooperation
from the birds: crows show up, black blatant
clarions in the gawky branches, to dominate
the rain's dark: grackles on sprung hinges
5   grate from tree to tree, around:
                  remember
the redbird then in the floral plum, the
bluebird nesting in the apple bough:

remember the white streak in the woodpecker's
10   wings against shadblow:
                            expect abundance
to yield nothing to privation, no easing
off by contrary song: the quiet world, so
quiet, needs to cut its definitions wide
15   so snow can rinse across the hard lake.

                                       1969 (1969)

Making

     In wingbar light
     the mockingbird
     takes the day into
     making
5   takes the clouds still
     shipping stars
     takes the spring trees'
     black small leaves
     and with staid motions
10   and many threads
     brings into
     view
     lightens
     and when morning
15   shows sings
     not a whit more beautifully
     because it has been dark.

                                           1968 (1969)

Dominion

I said
Mr. Schafer
did you get up to see the comet:

and
he said
Oh no
let it go by, I don't care:

he has leaves to rake
and the
plunger on his washing machine isn't working right:

he's not amused
by ten-million-mile tails
or any million-mile-an-hour
universal swoosh

or
frozen gases
lit by disturbances

across our
solar arcs

1965 (1970)

Round

I sat down
from too much
spinning & spun
the big spin's calm:
I said
this is
like it is:

bluebirds
stripped my shoelaces
for nesting:
pill bugs took the cool

under my shoesoles
and weeds, sprung up,
made me their

15   windbreak:
I said
this is
like it is
and got up turning
20   out of the still into
the spinning dance.

1968 (1969)

Tight

I should have had my macadam
driveway re-sealed this fall but
saved a few bucks & let it
go: now the rain pools
5   out there and the pools
graduate toward each other
with long necks of lonesome
longing: but there's a sort
of idle rain, like today's,
10   when the drops, large &

sparse, pop huge bubbles
that cruise around smooth
uneventful country: I sat out
there watching a couple of
15   hours from the garage and got
rapturous trying to think why
that particular show (not to
mention how) ever got devised:
it makes me wonder which way
20   the economy should be sent.

1968 (1969)

The Woodsroad

I stop on
the woodsroad,
listen:
I take myself in:

5   I let go the locust's
burr-squall, pointless,
high in the pine:
I turn all

the clouds crossing
10   above me loose:
I drop free of
the fern's sori:

I zoom home through,
as if hailstruck,
15   caterpillar-pocked
whiteoak leaves:

I take myself
all in, let go &
float free: then
20   break into

clouds, white dots on
dead stalks, robin
mites: then, I'm here:
I listen: call.

1966 (1969)

WCW

I turned in
by the bayshore

and parked,
the crosswind
5 hitting me hard
side the head,
the bay scrappy
and working:
what a
10 way to read
Williams! till
a woman came
and turned
her red dog loose
15 to sniff
(and piss
on)
the dead horseshoe
crabs.

1962 (1969)

Saying

I went out on
a rustling day
and
lectured the willow:
5 it nodded profoundly
and held
out many arms:
I held my
arms up and said things:
10 I spoke up:
I turned into and
from the wind:
I looked all around:
dusk, sunless,
15 starless, came:
the wind

fell and left us
in the open
still and bent.

1965 (1968)

Looking Over the Acreage

I wonder what I should do now:
probably
I should wait
for the onset or oncoming of a large order,
5   an aqueduct perhaps
with an endless (theoretically) echo of arches
but which a valley would
break into individual aqueductal shape:
or perhaps an abecedarian procedure
10   though there are some
problems there
(not everyone is agreed on
what is what)
or I could riffle through the zodiac:
15   then there are
triads, pentads, dodecahedra,
earth-water-air-fire,
the loft
from indivisibility to all-is-one
20   (which is where nothing is anything):
descents are less usual
having associations of undesirability
(cities, societies are
exclusive):
25   the great advantage of an overall arbitrary
order is that one
need not wait until he has earned an order
but may go ahead with some serenity arch
by arch
30   content if minor forms appear:

one may do that:
I don't know what to do:
no matter what I think I'm probably going to wind up
in both wings of another balance:
35   fabulous, ex
        cit
        ing, over
        populated
        Hong Kong: yeah.

1968

Gain

        Last night my mind limped
        down the halls of its citadel,
        wavered by the lofty columns
        as if a loosened door had
5   let the wind try inside
        for what could go:
        dreamed of the fine pane-work
        of lofty windows it
        would not climb to again to see,
10   of curved attics aflight with
        angels it would not
        disturb again: felt the
        tenancy of its own house,
        shuffled to the great door and
15   looked out into its permanent dwelling.

1965 (1969)

Off

        Morning's the woman time of day,
        light rising
        as in a small failure,
        the parting of fog

5   to cloud,
       the casual centerless thunder
       and the rain beginning
       so sporadic
       the eye can hardly weave the evidence
10   and then rain
       deep rain
       windless,
       the iris unshook from its beads,
       the firs like old old
15   men dripping their bottoms wet:
       I catch my breath
       I throw my clothes on
       I have to get out of the house and,
       out, my eyes'
20   concision shoots to kill.

                                    1968

Treaties

       My great wars close:
       ahead, papers,
       signatures, the glimmering
       in shade of
5   leaf and raised wine:
       orchards, orchards,
       vineyards, fields:
       spiralling slow time while
       the medlar
10   smarts and glows and
       empty nests
       come out in the open:
       fall rain then stirs
       the black creek and
15   the small leaf slips in.

                             1966 (1969)

Convergence

My sorrows he said
begin so
deep they join only
at extreme, skinny height:
5   so he climbed

and water fell
smooth, chasms
lifted into ripples
and earth's slow
10   curve

merged, emerged:
he stood capable
poised
on the peak of
15   illusion's pyramid.

1965

Project

My subject's
still the wind still
difficult to
present
5   being invisible:
nevertheless should I
presume it not
I'd be compelled
to say
10   how the honeysuckle bushlimbs
wave themselves:
difficult
beyond presumption

(1970)

North Jersey

Ninth-circle concrete
bending in
high suasions like
formal reductions of
5   perfect fears: refineries
oiling the air:
burnt reeds, a chemical
scald: gouged land &
shoved mounds:
10   and man
burning fast motions along
the steely wreaths,
the steely wreaths.

1968

Ship

Nobody comes here to stay: that's
incredible: and nothing to stay:
the bird tilts tail-up in the high
branch and tilts time away:
5   well, I don't want to think about that:
the phony comfort about timelessness
time is supposed to work back
into: I've seen no sign of that:
nothing on the re-make or comeback: the
10   crest breaks, whatever side the sea's on:
the crest bears in and out in a single
motion, not a single point unmoving:
men and women in your loveliness, I cry
nothing against the wall forever giving in.

1969

Play

Nothing's going to become of anyone
except death:
    therefore: it's okay
to yearn
5   too high:
the grave accommodates
swell rambunctiousness &

ruin's not
compromised by magnificence:

10   that cut-off point
liberates us to the
common disaster: so
    pick a perch—
apple branch for example in bloom—
15   tune up
and

drill imagination right through necessity:
it's all right:
it's been taken care of:

20   is allowed, considering

1969 (1970)

Spinejacking

One of these days I'm gonna leave you, baby:
I know it: I can tell:
my bellyfat shakes and knows:
one of these days I'm gonna just
5   up and outsy: like that:
my dog knows: he
turns around a lot lately:

I don't know if the parrot knows:
it isn't just lately she started scratching:
10 you always were a kind of bushy bitch:
one of these days I'm gonna just pack off:
you get to make some new
arrangements, then: you like to change
things around, change this one:
15 one of these days I'm gonna leave you, baby:
I know it: I can tell:
my bellyfat shakes and knows.

1968 (1970)

Shore Fog

On the cedars and yews
this morning
big drops
(as of rain)
5 held by finny hands
(but not rain):
fog kept the night all
night awake
and left this morning
10 in addition to these
big clarities
a close-worked white drift
too multiple to
prevent some dozing.

1968

Meteorology

Reality's gossed guzzlings,
bristle-eyed
in light
mare's-tails of bleached

5   speech have
unmaimed the handshrunk
blessings,
declotted the conveyances:
the bleakies
10   sung against
sweep soaring (that's
delightful) into
high seed
but come back
15   heebies and harpies
ever
scratching &
fartching:
confine self to
20   "extremities & superfices"
the unenterable core's rusty
lode shut up.

1968

Exotic

Science outstrips
other modes &
reveals more of
the crux of the matter
5   than we can calmly
handle

1968

Hosts

Secrets are slimber black worms
whose appetites are red:
they ball up with searching periphery:
sometimes they string out, roam

5 the body in a panic of mismanagement:
it's nice when they slacken
(wads of worthy long fellows) and go
to sleep: often they're
sleepless:
10 some people have more
than others which
makes a difference.

1968

Crevice

Seeing into myth is
knowledge myth can't sanctify:
separating symbol and
translucence
5 disembodies belief:
still, nothing's changed:
the slope that
falls here toward the lake
has held
10 since the first mind figured
in and out of shape:
but a constant in change
no hand or sight has
given definition to:
15 how are we new from the slow
alterations now:
we stand around dazed
and separate, sunless and eventful:
mind can't charge the slope:
20 again we've fallen wise.

1966 (1969)

Transducer

Solar floes
big as continents
plunge rasping
against each other:
5   the noise
flaring into space,
into thinner & thinner
material means,
becomes two million
10   degrees of heat.

1968

Mean

Some drippage and spillage in
active situations:
efficiency's detritus,
fall-out from happenstance:
5   a, probably calculable,
instrank of frabigity:
people accustomed to the wide terrain
know, with little alarm, some
clumps are dissolving:
10   singular's the terrible view
from which the classy gods
take up glassy lives.

1968

Banking

Sometimes I see an
enormous loveliness:
I say help like a
deprived nation:
5   this loveliness

moves & the motion
starves rivers:
the air where
this motion
10   moves feels
expensive: I go
out where this
is going by and
come back in narrow
15   about the nose
with some
wilted plants & all
my old peeled sticks.

1968

Elegy for a Jet Pilot

The blast skims
over the string
of takeoff lights
and
5   relinquishing
place and time
lofts to
separation:
the plume, rose
10   silver, grows
across the
high-lit evening
sky: by this
Mays Landing creek
15   shot pinecones,
skinned huckleberry
bush, laurel
swaths define
an unbelievably
20   particular stop.

1964 (1969)

Countering

The crystal of reason
grows
down
into my loves and
5   terrors, halts
or muddles
flow,
casting me to
shine or break:

10   the savage peoples
wood slopes, shore rocks
with figures of dream
who struggle
to save or
15   have his life:

to keep the
life and
shape, to keep
the sphere, I hide
20   contours,
progressions between

turning lines,
toward the higher
reason
25   that contains the war
of shape and loss
at rest.

1965 (1970)

The Quince Bush

The flowering quince bush
on the back hedge has been
run through by a morning
glory vine

5   and this morning three blooms
are open as if for all light,
sound, and motion: their adjustment
to light is

pink, though they reach for
10   stellar reds and core violets:
they listen as if for racket's
inner silence

and focus, as if to starve, all motion:
patterns of escaped sea
15   they tip the defeated, hostile,
oceanic wind:

elsewhere young men scratch and fire:
a troubled child shudders to a freeze:
an old man bursts finally and
20   rattles down

clacking slats: the caterpillar pierced
by a wasp egg blooms inside with
the tender worm: wailing
walls float

25   luminous with the charge of grief:
a day pours through a morning glory
dayblossom's adequate, poised,
available center.

1967 (1968)

Square

      The formulation that
      saves damns:
      consequently (unsavable)
      a periphery riffler
5   I thread the
      outskirts of mandate,
      near enough
      to be knowingly away &
      far enough away to
10   wind and snap through
      riddling underbrush.

1968 (1970)

Autumn Song

      The large is gone—well, it
      was mostly vacant: the big
      time,
      a past and future scoop,
5   gone, too,
      but it was too
      big to move much:
      I picked up a wet leaf
      today: it
10   left its shape moist
      on the macadam
      and there was an earthworm
      his arteries
      shining in the brilliant light—
15   it really was brilliant today—and
      he
      panicked at both ends
      with the threat of drying out:
      a basic
20   concern I shared with him

and share with him
for I lifted him with the leaf
and took him to the grass:
I'll bet he knows now
25   he can be seen through and turn
into a little thong:
I knew it all along though I'm
not in grass
and the leaves that fall
30   give me no sense of refuge.

1968 (1969)

Early Morning in Early April

The mist rain this morning made glass,
a glittery preponderance, hung baubles
spangled to birch-twig jewelry,

and made the lawn support, item by
5   item, the air's weight, a lesson as a
various instruction with a theme: and

how odd, the maple branches underlaced
with glaring beadwork: what to make of it:
what to make of a mist whose characteristic

10   is a fine manyness coming dull in a wide
oneness: what to make of the glass
erasures, glass: the yew's partly lost.

1969

Reversal

The mt in my head surpasses you
I said

———

becomes at the base
more nearly incalculable with

5 bush
more divisive with suckers and roots

and at the peak
far less visible

plumed and misty
10 opening from unfinal rock to air:

arrogance arrogance
the mt said

the wind in your days
accounts for this arrogance

1967 (1970)

The Confirmers

The saints are gathering at the real
places, trying tough skin on sharp
  conscience,
endurance in the hot spots—
5 searching out to define, come up
against, mouth
the bitterest bit:
you can hear them yelping
down in the dark greeny groves of
10 condemnation:
their lips slice back
with jittery suctions, cold
insweeps of conjured grief:
if they, footloose, wham up the
15 precise damnation,
  consolation

may be no more than us trudging
down from paunchy dinners,
swatting hallelujah arms at
20   dusk bugs and telling them pure
terror has obviously made them
earnest of mind and of motion lithe.

1968 (1968)

Involved

They say last night radiation
storms spilled down the meridians,
cool green tongues of solar
flares, non-human & not
5   to be humanized, licking at
human life: an arctic
air mass shielded us: had I been
out I'd have said,
knowing them masked, burn me: or
10   thanks for the show:
my spine would have flared
sympathetic colors:
as it is I slept through,
burning from a distant source.

1967

Admission

The wind high along the headland,
mosquitoes keep low: it's
good to be out:
schools of occurring whitecaps
5   come into the bay,
leap, and dive:
gulls stroll
long strides down the shore wind:
every tree shudders utterance:

10   motions—sun, water, wind, light—
intersect, merge: here possibly
from the crest of the right moment
one might break away from the final room.

1966 (1970)

Mission

The wind went over
me
saying
why are you so distressed:

5   oh I said I
can't seem to make
anything
round enough to last:

but why
10   the wind
said
should you be so distressed

as if anything here belonged to you
as if anything here were your concern.

1965 (1967)

Cut the Grass

The wonderful workings of the world: wonderful,
wonderful: I'm surprised half the time:
ground up fine, I puff if a pebble stirs:

I'm nervous: my morality's intricate: if
5   a squash blossom dies, I feel withered as a stained
zucchini and blame my nature: and

when grassblades flop to the little red-ant
queens burring around trying to get aloft, I blame
my not keeping the grass short, stubble

10 firm: well, I learn a lot of useless stuff, meant
to be ignored: like when the sun sinking in the
west glares a plane invisible, I think how much

revelation concealment necessitates: and then I
think of the ocean, multiple to a blinding
15 oneness and realize that only total expression

expresses hiding: I'll have to say everything
to take on the roundness and withdrawal of the deep dark:
less than total is a bucketful of radiant toys.

1969 (1970)

The Limit

This left hand
side is
the clear edge of
imposition: the other the
5 thrusting and breaking to possibility:
in between
a tumbling, folding under,
amounting to downward
progression:
10 the prisoner is not much enamored of compression:
I wonder if this slight
tumbling, brookish, is a large enough motion
to prevent lodged sticks & harrow beavers:
apparently it
15 can
reach out broadly across the page in space-hungry gesture:
the events a stick makes
coming down a
brook

20   scraping the bottom
      of the ledge-smooth spill—such
      events exist in memory
      & possibility as in
      a silver radiance: the salience,
25   in a bodiless arrogance,
      must preserve
      algal tracings or it
      loses further (already scared of loss)
      ground for possible self-imaginings:
30   interwork, interwork, it's interwork
      that pays with mind because mind
      (if an entelechy)—
          shifting over here
          will suggest a tone-gap, slant,
35   a redshift as of direction

                                            1968

Concerning the Exclusions of the Object

          Today I
          looked for myself,

          head full of
          stars,

    5   cosmic
          dust in my teeth,

          and small,
          lost

          as earth in such a
    10   world, I

          fell around my
          cell's space

                        ———

and said
I must be here—how

15   can I get the seeker
home into these jaws:

how
can I expel these roomy stars?

1965 (1969)

The Makers

We slung do out of the rosy alligator
and
finding him somewhat flattened
    opened

5   our kits to engines of more
precise destruction
and set in to settled, intense abuse:

lovers and haters of dragons found
themselves
10   grievously ready to do a little slicing

back:

it was hilarious, stupendous, and quite painful
until
ritualization so overtook us all

15   that the only product dropping out from
    slitting & stitching was
pocketbooks pocketbooks pocketbooks
from the colorful land of the

1968 (1968)

Levitation

What are you doing
up there
said the ground
that disastrous to seers
5   and saints
is always around
evening scores, calling down:

I turned
cramped in abstraction's gilded loft
10   and
tried to think of something beautiful to say:

why
I said failing
I'm investigating the
15   coming together of things:

the ground
tolerant of such
widened without sound

while I turning
20   harmed my spine against
the peak's inner visionless ribs—

heels free
neck locked in the upward drift—

and even the ground I think
25   grew shaky
thinking something might be up there
able to get away.

1965

Medium

What small grace comes must
count hard
and then

belong to the poem that is in need
5   not to my own redemption
except

as the mirror gives back the dream:
since I'm guilty
any crime

10   will do
to pour my costly anguish to:
but

payment is exact,
strict and clear: the purchase
15   never comes

or if so becomes a song
that takes its blessings to itself
and gets away.

1965 (1969)

Transfer

When the bee lands the
morning glory bloom
dips some and weaves:
    the coming true of
5   weight
from weightless wing-held
air
seems at the touch
implausible.

1967

Monday

Windowjarring gusts again
this morning:
the surf slapped back white:
shore cherry bushes
5   trying to
stay put or get away:
the vague storm's
aroused a weekend of
hyphochondria: today
10   the doctors' offices
froth with all
that tried to stay unruffled.

1968

Pluralist

Winds light & variable break
upward out
of cones or drop cones down
that turn up
5   umbrellalike from the
ground

and even the maple tree's large
enough to express contrary
notions
10   one side going west & the
other east or northeast or one
up & the other
down: multiple angling:

the nodding, twisting, the
15   stepping out & back
is like being of two minds
at least

and with the comforting
(though scary) exemplum
20   that maple trees
go nowhere at all

1969 (1970)

Here & Now

Yes but
it's October and the leaves
are going
fast: rain weighted
5   them and then
a breeze
sent them in shoals clear across
the street

revealing
10   especially in the backyard
young maple
branch-tip buds that assume
time as far away as
the other side of the sun

1968 (1970)

The Run-Through

You're sick:
you're on your back:
it's hot:
they take off a leg:
5   you wake up and feel,
both hands:
you develop pride
in the sewmanship
and show it:

———

10   a tube in your skull bursts:
you bleed half
still:
with one arm
you show how
15   the other flops:
you show, show:
speechless with pantomime:

you're on your back:
it's hot:
20   they take the other one off:
then you fail
some
with the difficulty
of redundancy:

25   you're on your back:
you are heavy and hard:
your heart bursts and you are weightless:
you ride to a high stillness:
in death's cure, you exit right.

1969 (1969)

The Put-Down Come On

You would think I'd be a specialist in contemporary
literature: novels, short stories, books of poetry,
my friends write many of them: I don't read much
and some drinks are too strong for me: my empty-headed

5   contemplation is still where the ideas of permanence
and transience fuse in a single body, ice, for example,
or a leaf: green pushes white up the slope: a maple
leaf gets the wobbles in a light wind and comes loose

half-ready: where what has always happened and what
10   has never happened before seem for an instant reconciled:

that takes up most of my time and keeps me uninformed:
but the slope, after maybe a thousand years, may spill

and the ice have a very different look withdrawing into
the lofts of cold: only a little of that kind of
15   thinking flashes through: but turning the permanent also
into the transient takes up all the time that's left.

1968

The City Limits

When you consider the radiance, that it does not withhold
itself but pours its abundance without selection into every
nook and cranny not overhung or hidden; when you consider

that birds' bones make no awful noise against the light but
5   lie low in the light as in a high testimony; when you consider
the radiance, that it will look into the guiltiest

swervings of the weaving heart and bear itself upon them,
not flinching into disguise or darkening; when you consider
the abundance of such resource as illuminates the glow-blue

10   bodies and gold-skeined wings of flies swarming the dumped
guts of a natural slaughter or the coil of shit and in no
way winces from its storms of generosity; when you consider

that air or vacuum, snow or shale, squid or wolf, rose or lichen,
each is accepted into as much light as it will take, then
15   the heart moves roomier, the man stands and looks about, the

leaf does not increase itself above the grass, and the dark
work of the deepest cells is of a tune with May bushes
and fear lit by the breadth of such calmly turns to praise.

1970 (1971)

COLLECTED POEMS 1951–1971 (1972)

To the memory of my mother and father

∼≈∽

The Pieces of My Voice

The pieces of my voice have been thrown
away I said turning to the hedgerows
and hidden ditches
Where do the pieces of
5   my voice lie scattered
The cedarcone said you have been ground
down into and whirled

Tomorrow I must go look under the clumps of
marshgrass in wet deserts
10   and in dry deserts
when the wind falls from the mountain
inquire of the chuckwalla what he saw go by
and what the sidewinder found
risen in the changing sand
15   I must run down all the pieces
and build the whole silence back

As I look across the fields the sun
big in my eyes I see the hills
the great black unwasting silence and
20   know I must go out beyond the hills and seek
for I am broken over the earth—
so little remains
for the silent offering of my death

1955

Chaos Staggered Up the Hill

Chaos staggered up the hill
and got the daisies dirty
that were pretty along the road:
messy chaos I said
5   but then in cooler mind saw
incipient eyes revolving in it
with possibly incipient sorrow
and had to admire how
it got along at all
10   in its kind of weather:
passing, it engulfed me
and I couldn't know dissolving
it had rhizobia with it
to make us green some other place.

1953

Eolith

I give you the wretched sympathy stone
tears there is no end to the common matter
dropped like suds water
   down garbage shutes in places
5   if you wish
Enlil has whipped your thighs with cane
and the possibility of unloading pity is
not greater than my giving it
   there have been days like
10   wasting
               ziggurats while
your past spoils what is quick like river flies
            days like
the sweep of a steppe I have gone out
15   like a northwind over the Nile
                    cavernous
with Florida muddy hellish fountains of me it
is quite terrible

to think of it
20   a shortening of days locusts dark west sounds
of oak limbs under pigeons
        splitting in the night
roof mounting troubling clay gods river wind
I have sketched pyramids for
25   viewing splendid Hamlet
a task waking at night in dark speed
the pelican's over bays
    carrying this eolith

1952

Hymn V

Assure us you side with order: throw
off atomicities, dots, events, endless
successions: reveal an ancient inclination
we can adore and ritualize
5   with sapphirine cones and liturgies,
refine through ages of
canonical admissions and rejections; a
consistent, emerging inclination to prefer
the circling continuum, void receptacle,
10   and eternal now: spare

us the accidents, controversies, novelties,
constant adaptations, the working truths and
tentative assessments, the upheavals and unrest
of an unquiet past shaken by
15   the addition of a modern fact: package

knowledge, square-off questions, let them in
triumphs of finality be categorically
answered and filed: a
constant known yields all time to love: let our
20   words grow out of and strengthen the authority
of old rich usage, upholding what upholds.

Spring Song

I picked myself up from the dust again
and went on
phoenix not with another set of wings but with
no other choice
5   Oh I said to my soul may a deep
luminosity seize you
and my blanched soul smiled from its need and
dwelt on in the pale country of its bones

A field opened on the right
10   and I went in
slipping arms-high through bleaches
of golden broom grass
and whirled with the wind sizzling there

Look said the golden tussocks and I
15   looked down at the rising shoots
Where, if spring will not keep you,
will you go
I said to the broom straws
so I cried
20   and stooping to scold the shoots fell
in with their green enhancing tips
and nearly died
getting away from the dividing place

At dusk the sun set and it was dark and having
25   found no place to leave my loyalty
I slaughtered it by the road and spilled its
blood on sand while the red moon rose

1957 (1958)

Come Prima

I know
there is
perfection in the being
of my being,
5   that I am
holy in amness
as stars or
paperclips,

that the universe,
10   moving from void to void,
pours in and out
through me:

there is a point,
only itself,
15   that fills space,
an emptiness
that is plenitude:

a void that is all being,
a being that is void:

20   I am perfect:
the wind is perfect:
ditchwater, running, is perfect:
everything is:

I raise my hand

1957

Terminus

Coming to a rockwall
I looked back

to the winding gulch
and said
5   is this as far as you can go:

and the gulch, rubble
frazzled with the windy remains
of speech, said
comers here turn and go back:

10   so I sat down, resolved
to try
the problem out, and
every leaf fell
from my bush of bones

15   and sand blew down the winding
gulch and
eddying
rounded out a bowl
from the terminal wall:

20   I sat in my bones' fragile shade
and worked the
knuckles of my mind till
the altering earth broke to
mend the fault:

25   I rose and went through.

1959 (1971)

Back Country

The sun binds:
the small cold
moon
leading spins you,
5   marionette:
the silver ruts of backwoods roads

narrowing
straiten your interests:

   you keep moving:
10   return is to your vitiations:
ahead, the road,
pure of you;
   the pasture hills
fractured with
15   hurls
of white rock,

   unsurrendered to
your spoiling eyes;
plum blossoms
20   uncast at your breath:
   you have come
to back country:
hogweed's hard yellow
heads

25   crowd the ruts
apart: there are
wagon tracks
and, splitting the weed,
   the hoofprints
30   of long-stepping, unshod mules:
the hill people will
not discern

   your wound:
you will pitch hay,
35   .wash your
face in a staved bucket,
   soap your arms with
chinaberry leaves,
rinse
40   well-water clean:

———————

    no: they will know
you:
keep on:
the sun calls:
45   the moon has you:
the ruts
diminish you to distance:
a hill puts you out.

Christmas Eve

When cold, I huddle up, foetal, cross
arms:
but in summer, sprawl:

    secret is plain old
5   surface area,
decreased in winter, retaining: summer no
        limbs touching—
radiating:
everything is physical:

10   chemistry is physical:
            electrical noumenal mind
        is:
(I declare!)

put up Christmas tree this afternoon:
15   fell
asleep in big chair: woke up at
3:12 and it
        was snowing outside, was white!

Christmas Eve tonight: Joseph
20   is looking for a place:
Mary smiles but
        her blood is singing:

she will have to lie down:
          hay is warm:
25   some inns keep only
the public room warm: Mary

is thinking, Nice time
          to lie down,
good time to be brought down by this necessity:

30   I better get busy
and put the lights on—can't find
          extension cord:
Phyllis will be home, will say, The
tree doesn't have any lights!
35   I have tiny winking lights, too:
          she will like
them: she went to see her mother:

my mother is dead: she is
deep in the ground, changed: if she
40   rises, dust will blow all over the place and
          she will stand there shining,
smiling: she will feel good:
she will want
to go home and fix supper: first she
45   will hug me:

an actual womb bore Christ,
divinity into the world:
     I hope there are births to lie down to
back
50   to divinity,
since we all must die away from here:

I better look for the cord:
we're going to
          the Plaza for dinner:

55   tonight, a buffet: tomorrow there, we'll
           have a big Christmas
      dinner:

      before I fell asleep, somebody
      phoned, a Mr. Powell: he asked
60   if I wanted to
      sell my land
      in Mays Landing: I don't know:
      I have several pieces, wonder
           if he wants them all,
65   wonder what I ought to quote:

      earth: so many acres of earth:
      own:
      how we own who are owned! well,
      anyway, he won't care
70   about that—said he would
      call back Monday: I will
      tell him something then:
           it's nearly Christmas, now:
      they are all going into the city:
75   some have sent ahead for reservations:
      the inns are filling up:
           Christ was born
      in a hay barn among the warm cows and the
      donkeys kneeling down: with Him divinity
80   swept into the flesh
           and made it real.

                                        1960 (1970)

Communication

      All day—I'm
      surprised—the
      orange tree, windy, sunny,
      has said nothing:
5   nevertheless,

four ripe oranges have
dropped and several
dozen
given up a ghost of green.

1964 (1965)

The Whole Half

In his head
the lost woman,
shriveled,
dry, vestigial,
5   cried
distantly
as if from
under leaves
or from roots
10   through the mouths
of old stumps—
cry part his
at her loss,
uneasiness
15   of something
forgotten
that was nearly pain:
but the man-oak
rising has grown
20   occupying
a full place
and finding its whole
dome man
looks outward
25   across the
stream
to the calling
siren tree,
whole—woman.

1964

Bay Bank

The redwing blackbird
lighting
dips deep the
windy bayridge
5   reed but
sends a song up
reed and wind rise to.

1964

Money

Five years ago I planted a buttonwood slip:
three years ago I had to fit myself
into its shade, a leg or arm
left over in light:
5   now I approach casually and
lost in shade more than
twice my height and several times my width
sit down in a chair
and let the sun move through a long doze.

1964

Fall Creek

It's late September now
and yesterday
finally

after two dry months
5   the rain came—so quiet,
a crinkling

on
flagstone and leaf,
but lasting:

this morning
when I walked the bridge over
the gorge

that had been soundless
water shot out over rock
15 and the rain roared

1964 (1972)

Utensil

How does the pot pray:
wash me, so I gleam?

prays, crack my enamel:
let the rust in

1964

The Fall

I've come down a lot on the tree of terror:
scorned I used
to risk the thin bending lofts
where shaking with stars
5 I fell asleep, rattled, wakened, and wept:

I've come down a lot from the skinny
cone-locked lofts
past the grabbers and tearers
past the shooing limbs, past the fang-set
10 eyes

and hate-shocked mouths:
I rest on sturdier branches and sometimes
risk a word
that shakes the tree with laughter or reproof—
15 am prized for that:

———

I've come down into the
   odor and warmth
    of others: so much so that I
     sometimes hit the ground and go
20   off a ways looking, trying out:

if startled, I break for the tree,
   shinny up to safety, the eyes and
    mouths large and hands working to my concern:
     my risks and escapes are occasionally
25   spoken of, approved: I've come down a lot.

1965 (1972)

April

Midafternoon
I come
home to the apartment
and find the janitor

5   looking up and
policeman looking
up (said he'd

go call Bill—has
a ladder)
10   and all the old
white-haired women

out looking up
at
the raccoon asleep
15   on the chimney top:

went up the ivy
during the night and
dazed still with
winter sleep can't

---

20   tell whether
to come down
or take
up sleep again—

what a blossom!

1965

Lion::Mouse

Cutting off the
offending parts

plucking out

they were so many I
5   tore the woods
up

with my roaring losses

but kept on
dividing, snipping away,
10   uprooting and
casting out

till
I scampered
under
15   a leaf

and considering
my remnant self
squeaked
a keen squeak of joy

1966

Breaks

From silence to silence:
as a woods stream
over a
rock holding on

5   breaks into clusters of sound
multiple and declaring as
leaves, each one,

filling
the continuum between leaves,

10   I stand up,
fracturing the equilibrium,
hold on,

my disturbing, skinny speech
declaring
15   the cosmos.

1966

Heat

The storm built till
    midnight
then full to quietness
broke:
5   wind
struck across the surf
hills and
    lightning, sheeting
& snapping, cast
10   quick shadows, shook
    the rain loose:

———

this morning
    the flowers on the steep bank
look bedraggled
15   with blessings.

1966

Definitions

The weed bends
    down and
becomes a bird:
the bird
5   flies white

through winter
    storms: I
have got my
interest up in
10   leaf

transparencies:
    where I am
going, nothing
of me will remain:
15   yet, I'll

drift through the
    voices of
coyotes, drip
into florets by
20   a mountain rock.

1966 (1971)

Path

Leaves are eyes:
light through
translucences
prints
5   visions that
wander:

I go for a walk and my image
is noticed by the protoplasm:

I wonder what visions
10   the birch-heart
keeps dark:
I know their cost!
the heart shot
thin that
15   pays winter hard:

I am run so seen and thin:
I see and shake

1966 (1972)

Mediation

The grove kept us dry,
subtracting from
the shower much
immediacy:

5   but then distracted us
for hours, dropping
snaps faint as the twigs
of someone coming.

1966

Snow Whirl

The snow turning
crosshatches the air
into
tilted squares:

5   I sit and think
where to dwell:

surely, somewhere before,
since snow
began to fall,
10   the wind has

managed to turn
snow into
squares of emptiness:

dwell there
15   or with the flakes
on one side of the motion
squareless,

dropping in an
unreturning slant.

1967

Reward

He climbed hard,
ledge to ledge, rise,
plateau,
caught his breath,
5   looked around,
conceived the distances:

———

climbed on
high, hard: and made the peak
9   from which the
major portion of the view was
descent.

1967

Timing

The year's run out
to the tip
blossom on the snapdragon
stalk.

1967 (1968)

Trouble Making Trouble

The hornet as if
stung twists
in the first cold,
buzzes wings

5   that wrench him
across the ground but
take on no
loft or

direction:
10   scrapes with feelers
his eyes to find
clearance

in the crazing
dim of things, folds
15   to bite his tail (or
sting his

———

head) to life or
death—hits the
grill of a stormdrain
20   and drops.

1967 (1968)

Rome Zoo

Subtract from that shower
each leaf's take
and the oak's
shadow is bright dust:
5   great
yellow helium
rabbits with bluetipped ears
stick the mist-weight
rain and, from high
10   tussling, yield
all the way to the ground:
the rhinoceros's back darkens.

1967

Alternatives

I can tell you what I need is one of those
poles Archimedes, thrust
into an unparalleled transform of intellect to power,
imagined dangling on the end of which he could
5   move the world with: he was as much a dreamer
as I was (sic): I thought, given
a great height, I could do it with words:
still in a sense I have the dream, I have
Archimedes's dream, that is, it hasn't been tried yet
10   for sure with a pole: with words, I tried it.

1967

Positions

I can tell you what I need is for
somebody to asseverate I'm a poet
and in an embroilment and warfare of onrushing words
    heightened by opposing views
5   to maintain I lie down to no man in
the character and thrust of my speech
and that everybody who is neglecting me far
    though it be, indeed, from his mind
is incurring a guilt complex
10   he'll have to reckon with later on
and suffer over (I am likely to be
recalcitrant with leniency):
what I need I mean is a champion or even
    a host of champions,
15   a phalanx of enthusiasts, driving a spearhead
or one or two of those big amphibian trucks
through the peopled ocean of my neglect:
I mean I don't want to sound fancy but
what I could use at the moment is
20   a little destruction perpetrated in my favor.

1967

Reassessing

I can tell you what I need, what I need
is a soft counselor laboriously gentle
his warm dry hands moving with a vanishing persistence
to explain to me how I fell into this backwater,
5   verse: oh what is the efficacy of
this lowgrade hallucination, this rhythm not even
a scientific sine curve:
I mean I need him to wave it all away,
syllables spilling through the screens of
10   his soft joints, erasing
in an enchantment similar to that I would evoke

all this primitive tribal hooting
into some wooden or ratty totemic ear:
boy, I need to hear about the systems analysts,
15   futurists, technocrats, and savvy managers
who square off a percentage of reality and name their price.

                                  1967

Renovating

I can tell you what I need is a good periodontist:
my gums are so sensitive, separated and lumpy,
I have to let my cornflakes sit and wilt:
the niacin leaks out before I get it in
5   and the ten percent daily requirement of iron
rusts: I've got so mashed potatoes best
accommodate my desire: my gums
before them
relax and, as it were, smile: I have bad dreams that
10   snap, crackle, and pop (to switch seeds)
have built an invisible wall soggy-resistant: what
I could use with my gum line
is like a new start
or at least a professionally directed reversal or
15   arrest of what has become abrupt recession.

                                    1967

Devising

I can tell you what I need is
money and I don't mean
a few thousand piddling shares of Standard Oil or
Xerox or a chunk
5   of some up-and-coming (now over-the-counter) computer or
computer component stock:
what I need is a kind of expansive diversification
with exploding international implications,

pools, banks, and, in a figure, shoals
10   of residual and seminal coin: what I need
to do is adopt a couple of ministates
and then enforce upon the populace the duty
of eating walnuts (which I'd ship in or
aid in the local growth of) and then
15   the populace would be free
to do anything else it chose before or after or
even while eating walnuts
and then I'd return the fleet (or
else move myself to a ministate)
20   to bring the shells back for my fireplace:
I like a nice walnut-shell fire
on a coolish autumn night.

1968

Emplacement

I can tell you what I need is
a stronger assortment of battleboasts:
I mean I need visions of toothy monsters
so old greens rot their sludgy toes
5   so that meeting such visions (and, indeed,
apparently they cannot be avoided) I could
fetch myself up
on a blood-lilting flinching flight of battleboasts:
for I perceive the great work to be done is
10   too often mismangled in committee, so lacks
all identity, all measuring out into
salient, songster-mongered cherishing:
what I need is for somebody to first of all
point me out a monster and then
15   loosen a word-hoard or two jacking
my spine up to the duty for
to tell the truth my imagination's sometimes
as pale as my spine's always yellow.

1968

Touching Down

Body keeps talking under the mind
keeps bringing up lesser views
   keeps insisting
      but coaxingly in pale tones

5   that the mind come on back, try
to get some rest,
   allow itself to
      be consoled

by slighter rather than slackened
10   thirst: body keeps with light touch
   though darkening
      lines sketching

images of its mortality but not
to startle the mind further off
15   hums
      all right all right

1968

Spring Coming

The caryophyllaceae
like a scroungy
frost are
rising through the lawn:
5   many-fingered as leggy
   copepods:
a suggestive delicacy,
lacework, like
the scent of wild plum
10   thickets:
also the grackles

with their incredible
vertical, horizontal,
reversible
15   tails have arrived:
such nice machines.

1968

Ocean City

Island-end here is
elongated as a
porpoise's nose, all
lawns and houses
5   except one spot
where bending property lines have
turned out odd,
giving this plot
the sanctuary of contention—
10   bayberry, wild
cherry, plum thicket:
a shore hawk
knows the spot,
knows grackles, sparrows,
15   cardinals, even
mockingbirds cluster here:
he drops by &
right here in town
some early mornings wilderness
20   meets wilderness
in a perfect stare.

1968 (1968)

Chasm

Put your
self out
and you're
not quite
5   up to
it or
all in

1968

Bearing Mercy

I spent with her
a
merciful night of
lubes &
5   loblollies,
of goings out
& in &
by & through:
I held her
10   in the teeth of my
need:
I turned her round
smartly
like a fumbled
15   beachball: in
the morning she
got up
& her tiny hand
touched her
20   hair, day's
first flower.

1968

Tossup

This wall interrupts the wind:
sand falls out:
bushes loft vines
& mockingbird &
5 caterpillar have their ways:
is this wall anything more than
an interruption:
nothing outlasts the last things
across the surfaces of Nothing:
10 okay I said
I believe in faith,
this soft determination,
this blasted wall.

1968

Plexus

The knot in my gut's
my good center:
I can trim
off fume & froth,
5 glob & dollop,
come in there and
be
hard as indivisible:
or trusting
10 the locked twist
float off office
buildings of glassy
mind,
confident if they
15 don't land they'll
circle back some day.

1968

Three

The floodcrest of afternoon passes:
the blood smooths:
they say a roar's in the world:
here nothing is loud or incomplete:
5   the yellow iris with a fabulous surrender
has flopped triple-open, available:
sheaves of pointed fingers,
clusters of new holly leaves assume
the air: the redwinged blackbird's
10   jeer's aboriginally whole in the
thicket across the street: if nothing's
broken, then I'm alone for sure.

1968

Miss

Wonder if
you're gross
consider the cosmic
particle so scant
5   it can splink all
the way through
Cheops
nicking nothing

1968

Celestial

The most beautiful, haunting
dusk scenes around here, clumps of
tidal-marsh reeds on a highway's edge
with supple dark-green
5   cedar and tough bayberry and such
full of widges, mean
and manyful, opaque with invisibility:

nature turns so wide it can afford to
spoil an interweaving of scapes or
10   flashing an Icarus by endanger the minds
of several listening millions whose
creation was superb if not special.

1968

Correction

The burdens of the world
on my back
lighten the world
not a whit while
5   removing them greatly
decreases my specific
gravity

1968

Mirrorment

Birds are flowers flying
and flowers perched birds.

1968

Coming To

Like a steel drum
cast at sea
my days,
banged and dented
5   by a found shore of
ineradicable realities,
sandsunk, finally, gaping,
rustsunk in
compass grass

1968

Even

Complexity o'erwhelms the gist,
engravities the grist and grits up
the anflob of the flubile:
hurts:
5   nabs the numbance, fritters the foamost,
fractures the raptors and
rippling rislings:
finding a nut to fit a
bolt is an undertaking.

1968

Windy Trees

You'd be surprised how short the roads
in the air are today:
they twist, drop, burst, and climb:
such roads the sparrows have trouble on:
5   in fact the only thing flying around
here today's the grackle and he
goes over the brush so low looks as if
he's beating something up from hiding:
it's just like reality,
10   the very day you can't get out to fly
there's also no place comfortable to sit.

1968

Photosynthesis

The sun's wind
blows the fire
green, sails the
chloroplasts,
5   lifts banks, bogs,
boughs into flame:

the green ash of
yellow loss.

1968

Making Waves

Some mornings of maximal
frustration—wind,
rain four days old—
your hate waves rise &
5   slap around the walls:
I float, smile, above the
unadmitted show:
but soon, bobbing, send a few
waves out myself and
10   the two sets
sloshing against each other
agitate the environment
or coming into beat
raise waves so big we both
15   get scared and hussle out the
oilslicks of consolation.

1968

Clearing

It's day again, the fourth day,
still overcast and sprinkling:
but the wind's stopped:
the trees and bushes in
5   profound rest
hold beads:
occasionally a bead drops and a
spur of leaves springs upright:
if the sun breaks out an
10   amazing number of things will change.

1968

The Account

The difference, finding the
difference: earth, no heavier
with me here, will be no
lighter when I'm gone: sum or
5   subtraction equals zero: no
change—not to the loss of a
single electron's spin—will
net from my total change:
is that horror or opportunity:
10   should I spurn earth now with
mind, toss my own indifference
to indifference, invent some
other scale that assents to
temporary weight, make something
15   substanceless as love earth can't
get to with changeless changing:
will my electrical system noumenally
at the last moment leap free
and, weightless, will it
20   have any way to deal—or if
there is some thinnest weight,
what will it join with, how
will it neighbor: something finer
than perception, a difference
25   so opposite to ground it will
have no mass, indifferent to mass.

1968

Winter Saint

In the summer I live so
close to my neighbor I
can hear him sweat:

———

all my forced bushes, leafy
5   and birdy, do not
prevent this:

his drawers wrenched
off his sticky butt
clutch my speech white:

10   his beery mouth wakes up
under my tongue: his
lawnmower wilts my cereal:

I do not like to hear him
wheeze over difficult weeds:
15   I don't like his squishy toes:

I'm for ice and shutters
and the miles and miles
winter clears between us.

1968

The Imagined Land

I want a squirrel-foil for my martin pole
I want to perturb some laws of balance
I want to create unnatural conditions
I want to eliminate snakes, rats,
5   cats, martens from dread
I want above the sloping foil regions of
     exceptional deliverance
I want my evening air trimmed bug clear
     (pits of bottomless change
10   shot through the clarifying ambience)
I want design heightened into
     artificial imbalances of calm
I want a squirrel-foil for my martin pole

1968

The King of Ice

Now and then the intolerable crooks
down around my temples
and binds—an ice-vice, you could
say, vice-ice—a crown of ice:
5   kings know how to take matters

casually, so I just sit there cold,
intensely inward, brow bowed,
loneliness universal: I wait:
I'm not going anywhere: I
10   wait for the thing to slip or for

my attention to fix, somewhere on
the inner glacier, on polar bears
in disconcerting romp: I figure
the intolerable not to be dealt with,
15   just set aside: I am going to

wait: look at these interesting
stitches in my robes, I say:
I've already settled my affairs of state;
that is, I'll take the cold when it comes,
20   but I will never believe in ice.

                              1968

Village, Town, City—Highway, Road, Path

Grove, forest, jungle—a thickening motion
accompanied by a sense of loss of control:

swamp: ah, an uncertain or sloppy (hungry) bottom:
flood moccasins lining the bayous, drowning snakes

5   rafting down the gulf-wide river: patch, copse,
thicket—a surrounding tameness with a touch of

---

central wilderness: let a dog belch up worms—
they string from his mouth in a white beard,

his eyes grave, tamed, shamed to affliction:
10   but affliction can storm from shame and

tussle the peripheries of order: but take a word,
there are backward suasions: you may have twice

as much of anything as you ask: my yard maple's
in the open, full of leaf, and single to the wind.

1969

Lonely Splendor

I tell the maple it's unwise—though
it stands open
and alone—to put too much splendor
of leaf on
5   so that rather than stand firm and quiver
to the wind it rolls
raising whole branches on a swell
that plays out into tossing and twisting
at the top:
10   but, of course, it is
difficult to tell
the inner thrust it can't ornament the whole
open universe, such quenchless
putting out and on:
15   I tell the maple, if a wind's taken by
the bounty of your heavy ship,
what may be assumed, what saved:

if I were a maple I'd want neighbors
to keep me skinny and high
20   in windbreaking thickets:

———

but then loneliness can't be cajoled
to give a leaf up
(or keep one in)
and can't believe slim thickets
25   do any slender speaking worthy note.

1969

The Swan Ritual

Yield to the tantalizing mechanism:
fall, trusting and centered as a
drive, following into the poem:
line by line pile entanglements on,
5   arrive willfully in the deepest

fix: then, the thing done, turn
round in the mazy terror and
question, outsmart the mechanism:
find the glide over-reaching or
10   dismissing—halter it into

a going concern so the wing
muscles at the neck's base work
urgency's compression and
openness breaks out lofting
15   you beyond all binds and terminals.

1969

He Said

Speaking to mountains (&
hearing them speak!) assiduously
(though encounteringly)
avoids the personal,

———

5 a curvature whose swerve, however,
   can out-range the scary planets

   and seriously attenuate
   the gravitational
   core which wanting the personal
10 had to give it up:

   being can't always be as it is:
   volcanoes, droughts, quakes,
   natural disasters of all kinds,
   including (heavy rain &)

15 the personal,
   mitigate much fixity, the dwelling
   of mind in its dwelling:

   my immediate sympathetic reaction was
   that I understood all that
20 well in a way

   and said it seemed reasonable that
   mountains, though,
   should attract such voices and
   furnish such replies.

1969

One More Time

I took my likely schizophrenia in hand
and said if
it must be the high places, let's go to them,
muse how they lie about, see how

5 the lessening to immateriality occurs,
   how the peaks, chipping off, folding in, loft
   free to the danger of floating, endure
   the falling away, the unneighboring to high isolation:

the essential reductions to form
10   and to rock, the single substance,
gained, we'll confront puzzling air, from
the strictest consideration to the freest,

and the height made we'll have the choiceless ease
of the single choice, down, and leisure to come on
15   deepening multiplicity,
trifling, discrete abundance,

bottomless diversity, down into the pines,
morning glories and trout streams
(where the lacewing works the evening, marginal air)
20   blueberry brush: high-slope cucumber vines abearing.

1969 (1970)

Drought

Bees turn in a fire
of dry-rich honey,
visit the faucet
for the left, crescent
5   drop: below the faucet
by the cool cement a

webbed bumblebee spins:
the spider, whilom serene,
attacks to feed
10   another filament in: I
can't understand
for a minute why

the bumblebee
works so hard into the
15   straitening maze:
but Lord I know why:

it's to find if not flight
the far end of the dark.

1969

Image   -

The indefinable idol's invisible to the mind:
its visage unmonstrous and unsaintly's unavailable
to the iconoclast who in the whirling wind learns
something of his whirling subduing, which is

5   primary instruction: of course, it breaks down
into griffins, calves, beavers, gargoyles but
re-summed shoulders up again and disappears: because
it disappears, the put-down's universal and complete:

but then the ignorant and stupid, the unerring
10   majority, think something's died and promote the
precision of the visibly defined: the more partial,
the more certain, until partiality collapses under

its exclusions: that's another kind of death
that draws human blood: oh, how I wish the notion
15   of unity could get around: how I wish the idol could
hold summed his attributes, empty free the mind.

1969

Equinox

I went out to cut a last batch of zinnias this
morning from the back fencerow and got my shanks
chilled for sure: furrowy dark gray clouds with
separating fringes of blue sky-grass: and dew

5   beaded up heavier than the left-overs of rain:
in the zinnias, in each of two, a bumblebee

stirring in slow-motion, trying to unwind
the webbed drug of cold, buzzing occasionally but

with a dry rattle: bees die with the burnt honey
10   at their mouths, at least: the fact's established:
it is not summer now and the simmering buzz is out of
heat: the zucchini blossoms falling show squash

overgreen with stunted growth: the snapdragons have
suckered down into a blossom or so: we passed
15   into dark last week the even mark of day and night
and what we hoped would stay we yield to change.

1969

Russet Gold

The shoddy furbishings I pick and choose among,
having, as I have, little hope of the foil brights
shimmering, those ghastly ecstatic blankouts

of rosy coordination in complete deliveries: no:
5   I take the radiance in, for example, rain, or shiver
to drops beaded up on cellophane: I tell you

when the bark loosens on a soggy stick, I can
get into that space and respire: and have thoughts
otherwise difficult, if not impossible, to assume:

10   half the time I'm unable, frankly, from a hurtful
capacity to imagine my own privation: but the other
half, I can wait with a yew drop, whether it will

evaporate or, struck by a rapid augmentation, splish,
presuming that the rain is, as here it often is, light
15   if long: when everything's given up,

———

amazingly, I think, so much stuff to give up,
and reluctantly, appears: everybody's seen a cast
feather, the dislocation: that's something: and when

a zinnia turns all cone, it's certainly not into
20   disorder or waste: I don't expect to busy
much with or in the sun, ghosts my valid glimmerers.

1969

Essay on Poetics

Take in a lyric information
totally processed, interpenetrated into
wholeness where

a bit is a bit, a string a string, a
5   cluster a cluster, everything beefing up
and verging out

for that point in the periphery where
salience bends into curve
and all saliences bend to the same angle of

10   curve and curve becomes curve, one curve, the whole curve:
that is information actual
at every point

but taking on itself at every point
the emanation of curvature, of meaning, all
15   the way into the high

recognition of wholeness, that synthesis,
feeling, aroused, controlled, and released:
but then find the wholeness

unbelievable because it permits
20   another wholeness,
another lyric, the same in structure,

in mechanism of existence, but bearing a different weight,
that is, a different, perhaps contradicting,
bit-nature and assimilation:

25   wholeness then is a condition of existence,
a one:many mechanism, internally irrelevant to scope,
but from the outside circumscribed into scope:

I like the order that allows, say, when
a thousand cows are on a thousand acres,
30   clusters to flow out in single file down a gully,

encirclings of drinkholes, concentrations in a green
bottom, spread-outs, but identifiable, across
a broad rise or scape: I like that just as I

like tracings converging into major paths,
35   untracings of widening out beyond a clump of
trees or small pass:

those configurations, rendered by aerial photography,
would interest me endlessly
in the precision of their topographical relations:

40   the interests of cows and the possibilities of
the landscape could be read (not a single actual cow)
there well: and nothing be as a consequence known and

yet everything in a sense known, the widest paths
the controlling symbols, with lesser resemblances of
45   motion: after a while I could account for the motions of

the whole herd and make interesting statements:
for example, with experience, I bet I could tell
from the wear under a copse

whether a lot of hot sunny days in a year
50   or windy days come: I could tell something obvious already
from the copse whether it constitutes a meaningful

———

windbreak in a cold wind, sand or snow storm, and then
that, though obvious, would tell about cows:
I'll bet in warm climates with heavy, maybe daily, rains

55 there'd be little wear under trees, for the cows
would enjoy being out in the showers:
anyway, there's a time when loose speech has to give in,

come up to the corral, run through the planked alleys,
accept the brand, the medication, surrender to the
60 identity of age, sex, weight, and bear its relationship

to the market: there's no market for most speech, specially
good, and none for loose: that's why I don't care
how far I wander off;

I wouldn't care if I found a whole year gone by and myself
65 not called for: the way I think is
I think what I see: the designs are there: I use

words to draw them out—also because I can't
draw at all: I don't think: I see: and I see
the motions of cowpaths

70 over a non-existent, thousand-acre ranch: (times
frequently recur in good scope in which I don't see):
stop on any word and language gives way:

the blades of reason, unlightened by motion, sink in,
melting through, and reality's cold murky waters
75 accept the failure: for language heightens by dismissing reality,

the sheet of ice a salience controlling, like a symbol,
level of abstraction, that has a hold on reality and suppresses
it, though formed from it and supported by it:

motion and artificiality (the impositional remove from reality)
80 sustain language: nevertheless, language must
not violate the bit, event, percept,

fact—the concrete—otherwise the separation that means
the death of language shows: when that happens abandonment
is the only terrible health and a return to bits, re-trials

85   of lofty configurations: if the organism of the ranch
alters, weeds will grow in old paths and the new waterhole
exist in a new weaving: means, reaching identity too

soon, exclude: mannerism is more suitable to the lyric
than to larger affairs because both lyric and manneristic style
90   are slight completions: dropping back from the completion

to a linear mode can be more engrossing: for example, the
dactyllic hexameter can grind on, entangling, ingesting bits,
threads, strings, lesser saliences into considerable scope: or

iambic pentameter, especially unrhymed, is an infinitely various
95   ployable means: one must be ever in search of the rapier that
holds the world on guard: but the sparrow trap traps a sparrow:

(disquisition is sesquipedalian pedestrianism, tidying up
the loose bits, but altogether missing the import of the impetus):
a center's absolute, if relative: but every point in spacetimematter's

100   a center: reality is abob with centers: indeed, there is
nothing but centers: centers of galaxies, systems, planets, asteroids,
moons, drifts, atoms, electrons: and the center, as of the

earth, where all turns and pressures meet, is inexpressibly light,
still, and empty: the spruce trees at this moment deeply
105   sway with snow and snow is falling, the temperature below

freezing: the muffled morning offered no relief: now, though;
just after noon, small gusts twist the branches: not
the heavy lower branches, too long in their holding, and too wide,

to respond: but twist the lighter, higher branches so they drop
110   falls of snow and those falls, light, their efficacy increased
by falling, strike the lower, heavier loads, dislodging airy

———

avalanches, sketchy with event but releasing: it seems to me
a possibility of unceasing magnitude that these structures
permit these eventualities: small winds with small branches can

115   loosen heavy postures: a miraculous increase, as if heat could
go uphill: but occurring within a larger frame, at great potential
expense: (but energy displacements, switches, translations are

too considerable for calculation in the smallest sector): still,
though the whole may be running down, spills
120   here and there are overspills, radiances: the lyric, then,

has never been found out because at the center it, too, is
empty, still, silent: this is a point of provisional
summation: hence, the *thens*, *stills*, and *buts*:

a point of entangling toward the intertwining of a core, a core
125   involving every thread: so far, we have ranch, snowsquall,
avalanche, ice skates, wind, etc.: but the main confluence

is one:many which all this essay is about: I get lost for fun,
because there's no chance of getting lost: I am seeking the
mechanisms physical, physiological, epistemological, electrical,

130   chemical, esthetic, social, religious by which many, kept
discrete as many, expresses itself into the
manageable rafters of salience, lofts to comprehension, breaks

out in hard, highly informed suasions, the "gathering
in the sky" so to speak, the trove of mind, tested
135   experience, the only place there is to stay, where the saints

are known to share accord and wine, and magical humor floats
upon the ambient sorrow: much is nearly stable there,
residencies perpetual, more than less, where gold is utterly

superfluous and paves the superfluous streets, where phenomena
140   lose their drift to the honey of eternity: the holy bundle of
the elements of civilization, the Sumerians said: the place

where change is mere disguise, where whatever turns turns
in itself: there is no reason for confusion: that is
what this is about: it's simple and impossibly difficult,

145   simple by grandeur, impossible by what all must answer there:
enterprise is our American motif, riding horseback between
the obscure beginning and the unformulated conclusion, thinking

grace that show of riding, the expertise, performance, the intricacy
of dealing: to be about something: history can assign and glean,
150   furnish sources and ends, give grades: that is the

enterprise of history, always best when best accomplished: since
the one thing we learn from history is that we do not learn:
enterprise then's the American salience, rainbow arch,

colossus: but the aristoi are beauty, wealth, birth, genius &
155   virtue who should be gouvernors: enterprise somewhat, though
not necessarily, inconsistent with those, we lack governors:

the definition of definition goes two ways, opposing:
one direction cuts away, eliminating from relevance, limits
into true: take the word *true*: it goes back through ME.

160   *treue, trewe* to AS. *treowe, trywe* to a kinship with G. *treu*
and on to IE. *derew*, meaning tree, in the basic sense of as
firm as a tree: if one could be sure of Indo-European forests

one might add lofty, abundant, straight, strong, majestic:
somewhere then in the essence of *tree* has been found the
165   essence of *true*, including perhaps the perpendicularity or

verticality of true: but while *tree* clarifies the
mind with certain boundaries, it also recalls clusters
of tree-images, memories of particular

trees, and a sense of a translation (separation) in the mind which
170   is trying to distil *tree*, a luminous, ideal image-tree, the truest
tree, from the actual clusters of memory: it is necessary

———

then to turn the essential image of a tree into the truest
rational wordage: truth, then, might be "conformity
with the facts": but then we know that facts have truth

175 when touched, given configuration by transforming,
informing fiction: is this unnecessarily
puzzling: all I mean to suggest is that the reality under

words (and images) is too multiple for rational assessment and
that language moves by sailing over: the
180 other way definition has is to accept the multiplicity of

synthesis: of course, synthesis is at work in certain levels of
analysis, but I mean by synthesis the primary intent: look
at it this way: I am experiencing at the moment several

clusters of entanglement: if I took a single thread from a
185 single cluster, viewed it, explained it, presented it, would
I not be violating my reality into artificial clarity and my

bundles into artificial linearity: but if I broached, as I seem
to be doing, too many clusters, would I not be violating this
typewriter's mode into nonsense: hue a middle way, the voice

190 replied, which is what I'm doing the best I can,
that is to say, with too many linking verbs: the grandest
clustering of aggregates permits the finest definition: so out

of that bind, I proceed a little way into similarity and
withdraw a bit into differentiae: unfortunately, man cannot
195 do better though it might be better done: if I begin with

the picture of a lyre, translate it into a thousand words,
do I have a lyric: what is a lyre-piece: a brief and single
cry: the quickest means to a still point in motion:

three quatrains rhyming alternate lines: let me see if I can
200 write a poem to help heave the point:

At Once

Plumage resembles foliage
for camouflage often
and so well at times it's difficult

205 to know whether nature means
resembler or resembled:
obviously among things is

included the preservation of
distinction in a seeming oneness:
210 I say it not just

because I often have: maximum
diversity with maximum unity
prevents hollow easiness.

poetry, even in its
215 self-rationale aims two ways at once, polar ways sometimes

to heighten the crisis and pleasure of the reconciliation:
getting back to *tree* and *true*, though, I was thinking last
June, so multiple and dense is the reality of a tree, that I

ought to do a booklength piece on the elm in the backyard here:
220 I wish I had done it now because it could stand for truth, too:
I did do a sketch one day which might suggest the point:

I guess it's a bit airy to get mixed up with
an elm tree on anything
like a permanent basis: but I've had it
225 worse before—talking stones and bushes—and may
get it worse again: but in this one
the elm doesn't talk: it's just an object, albeit
hard to fix:
unfixed, constantly
230 influenced and influencing, still it hardens and enters

the ground at a fairly reliable point:
especially since it's its
general unalterability that I need to define and stress
     I ought to know its longitude and latitude,
235   so I could keep checking them out: after all, the ground
drifts:
and rises: and maybe rises slanting—that would be
difficult to keep track of, the angle
     could be progressive or swaying or
240   seasonal, underground rain
& "floating" a factor: in hilly country
        the underground mantle, the
"float" bedrock is in, may be highly variable and variable
in effect:
245   I ought to know the altitude, then, from some fixed point:
I assume the fixed point would have to be
     the core center of the planet, though I'm perfectly
prepared to admit the core's involved
     in a slow—perhaps universal—slosh that would alter the
250   center's position
     in terms of some other set of references I do not
     think I will at the moment entertain
     since to do so invites an outward, expanding
reticulation
255   too much to deal precisely with:

true, I really ought to know where the tree is: but I know
it's in my backyard:
I've never found it anywhere else and am willing to accept
        the precision of broadness: with over-precision
260   things tend to fade: but since I do need stability and want
to make the tree stand for that (among other things)
it seems to me I ought to be willing to learn enough about
theory and instrument
to take sights for a few days or weeks and see if anything
265   roundly agreeable could be winnowed out: that
ought to include altimeters (several of them, to average
instrumental variation), core theory and gravity waves:

but I'm convinced I'm too awkward
and too set in some ways
270   to take all that on: if I am to celebrate multiplicity,
unity, and such
I'll be obliged to free myself by accepting certain
limitations:

           I am just going to take it for granted
275   that the tree is in the backyard:
it's necessary to be quiet in the hands of the marvelous:

I am impressed with the gradualism of sway,
of growth's sway: the bottom limb that John's
swing's on and that's largely horizontal
280   has gradually outward toward the tip
      demonstrated the widening of the leaves
by
sinking: the rate of sinking, which is the rate of
growth, has been
285   within the variations of night and day, rain and shine,
broadly constant
and the branch's adjustment to that growth
      of a similar order: nevertheless, the
wind has lifted, a respiratory floating, the branch
290   as if all the leaves had breathed in, many a
time
and let it fall
and rain and dew have often lowered it below its depth—
birds have lighted bringing
295   varying degrees of alteration to the figurings, sharp
distortions, for example, to the
twigs, slow dips to secondary branches, perhaps no
noticeable effect at the branch root:
           I should go out and measure the diameters of
300   the branch, secondary branches, small limbs, and twigs
and their extensions from base
and devise a mathematics
to predict the changes of located average birds: it

would give me plenty to do for weeks
305   and save me from the rigors of many heights:
or scoot me to them: conceiving a fact stalls the
imagination to its most threatening dimension:

I think now of growth at the edges of the leaves as the
reverse of the elmworm's forage:

310   the elmworm, I haven't seen any this year—one spring
there were millions—is as to weight an interesting
speculation:
as he eats the leaf lessens but of course the weight is
added to himself, so on a quick scale the
315   transformation is one to one:
but the worm makes waste, the efficiency of his mechanisms
average and wasteful: in the long range, then,
worms lighten trees and let in light: but that's
another problem: could it be maintained that
320   the worm lets in light enough
to increase growth equal to his destruction:
    it's a good point, a true variable, but surely
any sudden defoliation by a plague of worms
would be harmful: a re-entry of winter (though possibly
325   with all of winter's possibility): time and number figure
mysteriously here:

one should be patient and note large results,
reserve some time for broad awareness:

broad awareness is the gift of settled minds: or of
330   minds hurt high from painful immediacy: it eliminates
and jettisons
sensory contact with too much accident and event—total
    dependencies at the edge: the man
fully aware,
335   unable to separate out certain large motions, probably
couldn't move: it's better, I think, to be

broadly and emptily aware so as more efficiently
to negotiate the noons of recurrence:

(I have come lately to honor gentleness so:
340   it's because
       of my engagement with
       tiny sets and systems of energy, nucleations and constructs,
       that I'm unnerved with the slight and needful
           of consideration: part of consideration's
345   slightness: it approaches and stands off peripherally
       quiet and patient should a gesture
       be all that's right
               but of course it will on invitation tend:
               it never blunts or overwhelms with aid
350   or transforms in order to be received):

while shade increases equally with surface area of leaf
the net result's
a considerable variance:
leaves inter-shade
355   but the result on the ground's non-accumulative:

in May last year, a month before the above sketch, I did another
briefer thing:

               elm seed, maple
               seed shower
360   loose when the wind
               stirs, a spring-wind harvesting
               (when so many things
               have to be picked—take strawberries,
               stooped to and crawled
365   along before, or the finger-bluing
               of blueberries):
               everything so
               gentle and well

                 done: I sit down not to flaw
370   the ambience:

             the elm seed's winged all round
             and exists, a sheathed
             swelling, in the center: it
             can flutter,
375   spin,
             or, its axis just right, slice
             with a draft or cut through one:
             (it doesn't go very far but it can
             get out of the shade):

380   then there's the maple seed's oar-wing:
             it spins too
             (simply, on an ordinary day)
             but in a gust can glide broadside:

             (dandelion seeds in a head are
385   noted for their ability to become detached
             though attached:
             with a tiny splint-break
             the wind can have a bluster of them:
             the coming fine of an intimation):

390   those are facts, one-sided extensions:
             since the wind's indifferent
             the seeds take pains to
             make a difference:
             praise god for the empty and undesigned:

395   hampered by being ungreat poetry, incapable of
        carrying quick conviction into imagination's locked clarity,

        nevertheless these pieces establish the point
        that a book might be written on the interpenetrations of
        appearance of an elm tree, especially when the seasons could be

400   brought in, the fluff cresting snow limbs, the stars and the
influence of starlight on growth or stunting—I have no
idea how such distance affects leaves—the general surround, as of

wind, rain, air pollution, bird shade, squirrel nest: books
by the hundred have already been written on cytology, the
405   study of cells, and in an elm tree there are twelve quintillion cells,

especially in the summer foliage, and more takes place by way
of event, disposition and such in a single cell than any computer
we now have could keep registration of, given the means of deriving

the information: but if I say books could be written about a single
410   tree I mean to say only that truth is difficult, even when
noncontradicting; that is, the mere massive pile-up of information

is recalcitrant to higher assimilations without great loss of
concretion, without wide application of averaging: things are
reduced into knowledge: and truth, as some kind of lofty reification,

415   is so great a reduction it is vanished through by spirit only, a
parallelogram, square or beam of light, or perhaps a more casual
emanation or glow: when so much intellectual energy seems to be

coming to nothing, the mind searches its culture clutch for meaningful
or recurrent objects, finds say a crown or flag or apple or tree or
420   beaver and invests its charge in that concretion, that focus: then

the symbol carries exactly the syrup of many distillations and
hard endurance, soft inquiry and turning: the symbol apple and the
real apple are different apples, though resembled: "no ideas but in

things" can then be read into alternatives—"no things but in ideas,"
425   "no ideas but in ideas," and "no things but in things": one thing
always to keep in mind is that there are a number of possibilities:

———————

whatever sways forward implies a backward sway and the mind must
either go all the way around and come back or it must be prepared
to fall back and deal with the lost sway, the pressure for dealing

430   increasing constantly with forwardness: it's surprising to me
that my image of the orders of greatness comes in terms of descent:
I would call the lyric high and hard, a rocky loft, the slow,

snowline melt of individual crystalline drops, three or four to
the lyric: requires precision and nerve, is almost always badly
435   accomplished, but when not mean, minor: then there is the rush,

rattle, and flash of brooks, pyrotechnics that turn water white:
poetry is magical there, full of verbal surprise and dashed
astonishment: then, farther down, the broad dealing, the smooth

fullness of the slow, wide river: there starts the show of genius,
440   in motion, massive beyond the need of disturbing surprise, but, still,
channeled by means—the land's—other than its own: genius, and

the greatest poetry, is the sea, settled, contained before the first
current stirs but implying in its every motion adjustments
throughout the measure: one recognizes an ocean even from a dune and

445   the very first actions of contact with an ocean say ocean over and
over: read a few lines along the periphery of any of the truly
great and the knowledge delineates an open shore:

what is to be gained from the immortal person except the experience
of ocean: take any line as skiff, break the breakers, and go out
450   into the landless, orientationless, but perfectly contained, try

the suasions, brief dips and rises, and the general circulations,
the wind, the abundant reductions, stars, and the experience is
obtained: but rivers, brooks, and trickles have their uses and

special joys and achieve, in their identities, difficult absoluteness:
455   but will you say, what of the content—why they are all made of water:
but will you, because of the confusion, bring me front center as

a mere mist or vapor: charity is greater than poetry: enter it,
in consideration of my need and weakness: I find I am able to say
only what is in my head: a heady constraint: and to say it only

460 as well as I can: inventory my infirmities and substitute
your love for them, and let us hold on to one another and
move right away from petulant despair: to broach a summary, I

would say the problem is scientific—how is reality to be
rendered: how is 4,444 to be made 444 and 44 and 4 and 1: I
465 have the shaky feeling I've just said something I don't trust:

poems are arresting in two ways: they attract attention with
glistery astonishment and they hold it: stasis: they gather and
stay: the progression is from sound and motion to silence and

rest: for example, I can sit in this room, close my eyes, and
470 reproduce the whole valley landscape, still: I can see the
southern end of Lake Cayuga, I can see Stewart Park, the highways,

the breaking out and squaring up of Ithaca, I can see the hill-ridges
rising from the Lake, trees, outcroppings of rocks, falls, ducks
and gulls, the little zoo, the bridges: I can feel my eyesight

475 traveling around a held environment: I am conscious that the
landscape is fixed at the same time that I can move around in it:
a poem is the same way: once it is thoroughly known, it contains

its motion and can be reproduced whole, all its shapeliness intact,
to the mind at the same time the mind can travel around in it and
480 know its sound and motion: nothing defined can

be still: the verbal moves, depends there, or sinks into unfocused
irreality: ah, but when the mind is brought to silence, the
non-verbal, and the still, it's whole again to see how motion goes:

the left nest in the shrub has built up a foothigh cone of snow
485 this morning and four sparrows sitting in the quince bush are
the only unaugmented things around: eight more inches are piling

———

on to ten we had and every evergreen has found the way it would
lean in a burden, split its green periphery and divide: John's
old tractor on the lawn only shows its steering wheel: the

490   snowplow's been by and blocked the driveway: it's December 26:
yesterday was Christmas: I got a pair of water-resistant gloves
with a removable woolen lining: I got Phyllis three charms for

the bracelet I bought her in Rome: John got a snowsled, a beautiful
wooden train set, Lincoln logs, toggles, and several things
495   operated by non-included batteries: this morning he has no fever:

he's had tonsillitis this is the fifth day with fevers to 103 and
104: I've felt built over a jerking machine, not quite turned on
or off: this morning John put on his new cowboy hat (he's nearly

four) and I put on his crash helmet, and we searched all the dark
500   corners and closets for thieves and robbers: we jailed a couple:
one teddy bear and one stuffed, long-legged leprechaun: everyone

will find here a detail that is a key to a set of memories:
strings of nucleations please me more than representative details:
(not that the detail is representative—only that it is a detail

505   of numerical dominance in recurrence):

                    subatomic particle
                    atom
                    molecule
                    cell
510   tissue
                    organ
                    organ system
                    organism
                    species
515   community
                    living world

       —————

           or

        observation
        problem
520   hypothesis
        experiment
        theory
        natural law:

                    the swarm at the
525   subatomic level may be so complex and surprising that it puts
quasars, pulsars and other matters to shame: I don't know:

and "living world" on the other hand may be so scanty in its
information as to be virtually of no account: nevertheless,
a drift is expressed in the progressions up or down—organization,

530   the degree of: the control into integration (integrated action)
of the increasingly multiple: the human organism, composed of
billions of cells formed into many specializations and subordinations,

can deliver its total lust to the rarification of sight of the
beloved: for example: and many other high levels of symmetry,
535   unification, and concerted thrust: poems, of human make, are

body images, organisms of this human organism: if that isn't
so I will be terribly disappointed: it sounds as if it ought to
be right: consonants, vowels, idioms, phrases, clauses (tissues),

sentences (organs), verses (organ systems), poems (living worlds):
540   I react to such stuff with a burst of assent resembling for all
I can tell valuable feeling: rubbing a girl also, of course,

produces feeling, I would be the last to deny it, but it may be
precisely the organization-principle in girls that one, rubbing,
is pleasured by: if, as I believe, we are not only ourselves—i.e.,

       —————

545   the history of our organism—but also every process that went into
our making, then, in the light of our present ignorance, we may
safely leave much potentiality to undisclosed possibility: mush,

mush, how friendly: that's what I think, I'll tell you in a nut-
shell: and in poems, the insubstantial processes of becoming
550   form inscrutable parts of the living thing: and then how the

orders of the poem build up and cooperate into the pure heat of
sight and insight, trembling and terror: it makes me gasp aghast:
no wonder we pedants talk about history, influence, meaning

in poems: that's peripheral enough to prevent the commission of
555   larger error, and safe error is a pedantic preference well-known,
widely footnoted, and amply rewarded: I believe in fun:

"superior amusement" is a little shitty: fun is nice: it's what
our society is built on: fun in the enterprise: I believe in it:
I have no faith in the scoffers: they are party-poopers who are

560   afraid they ought to believe in history or logical positivism and
don't have any real desire to do so: they are scarcely worth a
haircut: organisms, I can tell you, build up under the thrust to

joy and nothing else can lift them out of the miry circumstance:
and poems are pure joy, however divisionally they sway with grief:
565   the way to joy is integration's delivery of the complete lode:

the flow broken, coinless, I, the third morning of Ithaca's most
historical snowbind, try to go on, difficult, difficult, the hedges
split open, showing inside the vacancy and naked, bony limbs: snow

up past the garage door handle, new snow still falling, and high
570   gusts roaring through the cold: supplies low or gone: and the stores
closed: that last appeals too much in the wrong sort: like any

scholar, I should, at this point to uncripple the condition, quote,
but first, I must, like a scholar, clear the field: I choose Ruskin
to say what thousands have said: "Art is neither to be achieved by

575   effort of thinking, nor explained by accuracy of speaking": well,
        still, Ruskin, it cannot be achieved without effort, and one level
        of accuracy may be preferred to another: this must be a point of

        clustering because I feel a lot of little things jostling
        to get in where they can be said: for example, I just walked
580   a mile to the store, blowing snow, I was in to my ass practically

        getting out to the plowed road: I got hotdogs, bacon, bread (out of
        eggs), coffee: and on the way back, the wind in my face and snow
        drifted ten feet high along one curve that has an open field behind

        it, I passed two straggly young girls laughing, dogs barking after
585   them, and one carrying her jacket, big boobs jouncing in her short-
        sleeved sweater: I was barking inside myself a little, rosy ideas

        in the blinding snowlight: one guy I passed said "beautiful weather"—
        the kind of thing one, after four days penned up, is grateful to
        say and hear: I quote now to enrich the mix, to improve my stew from

590   the refrigerator of timeless ingredients:

            "A large number of the inhabitants of a mud flat will
        be worms. It is hard to develop enthusiasm for worms, but
        it took nature more than a billion years to develop a good
        worm—meaning one that has specialized organs for digestion,
595   respiration, circulation of the blood and excretion of
        wastes. All organisms perform these functions—amoebas,
        flagellates, bacteria or even filterable viruses; but the
        worms—at least the higher worms—do all these things better.
        They also developed segmentation or reduplication of parts,
600   permitting increase in size with completely coordinated
        function. Contemporary architects call this modular
        construction. It is found in man in the spinal column,
        in the segmental arrangement of spinal nerves, and in
        some other features that are especially prominent during
605   embryonic development."

        The Sea by Robert C. Miller. Random House. New York,
            1966. p. 165.

———

"We may sum up. Carbohydrates, fats, proteins, nucleic
acids, and their various derivatives, together with water
610   and other inorganic materials, plus numerous additional
compounds found specifically in particular types of living
matter—these are the molecular bricks out of which living
matter is made. To be sure, a mere random pile of such
bricks does not make a living structure, any more than a
615   mere pile of real bricks makes a house. First and foremost,
if the whole is to be living, the molecular components must
be organized into a specific variety of larger microscopic
bodies; and these in turn, into actual, appropriately
structured cells."

620   *The Science of Botany* by Paul B. Weisz and Melvin S. Fuller.
McGraw-Hill Book Company, Inc., 1962. p. 48.

                                        poems are verbal
symbols for these organizations: they imprint upon the mind
examples of integration in which the energy flows with maximum

625   effect and economy between the high levels of oneness and the
numerous subordinations and divisions of diversity: it is simply
good to have the mind exposed to and reflected by such examples:

it firms the mind, organizes its energy, and lets the controlled
flows occur: that is simple good in itself: I can't stress that
630   enough: it is not good for something else—although of course

it is good for infinite things else: so my point is that the poem
is the symbolical representation of the ideal organization, whether
the cell, the body politic, the business, the religious

group, the university, computer, or whatever: I used to wonder
635   why, when they are so little met and understood, poems are taught
in schools: they are taught because they are convenient examples

———

of the supreme functioning of one and many in an organization of
cooperation and subordination: young minds, if they are to "take
their place in society" need to learn patience—that oneness is

640   not useful when easily derived, that manyness is not truthful when
       thinly selective—assent, that the part can, while insisting on
       its own identity, contribute to the whole, that the whole can

       sustain and give meaning to the part: and when these things
       are beautifully—that is, well—done, pleasure is a bonus
645   truth-functioning allows: that is why art is valuable: it is

       extremely valuable: also, in its changing, it pictures how
       organizations can change, incorporate innovation, deal with accidence
       and surprise, and maintain their purpose—increasing the means and

       assuring the probability of survival: the point of change, though,
650   brings me to a consideration of the adequacy of the transcendental
       vegetative analogy: the analogy is so appealing, so swept with

       conviction, that I hardly ever have the strength to question it:
       I've often said that a poem in becoming generates the laws of its
       own becoming: that certainly sounds like a tree, growing up with

655   no purpose but to become itself (regardless of the fact that many
       are constantly trying to turn it into lumber): but actually, a tree
       is a print-out: the tree becomes exactly what the locked genetic

       code has pre-ordained—allowing, of course, for variables of weather,
       soil, etc.: so that the idea that some organic becoming is
660   realizing itself in the vegetative kingdom is only partially

       adequate: real change occurs along the chromosomes, a risky business
       apparently based on accidence, chance, unforeseeable distortion:
       the proportion of harmful to potentially favorable mutations is

       something like 50,000 to 1: how marvelous that the possibility of
665   favorable change is a flimsy margin in overwhelming, statistically,
       destruction and ruin: that is the way nature pours it on: once it

has arrived at a favorable organization—a white oak, for example—
it does not allow haphazard change to riddle it—no, it protects the
species by the death of thousands of its individuals: but lets the

670   species buy by the hazard of its individuals the capacity to adjust,
should adjustment be indicated or allowed: that is terrifying and
pleasing: a genetic cull myself, I have the right to both

emotions: along the periphery of integrations, then, is an exposure
to demons, thralls, witcheries, the maelstrom black of
675   possibility, costly, chancy, lethal, open: so I am not so much

arguing with the organic school as shifting true organismus from
the already organized to the bleak periphery of possibility,
an area transcendental only by its bottomless entropy: a word on the

art/nature thing: art is the conscious preparation for the unconscious
680   event: to the extent that it is possible—a fining up of the attention
and filling out of the means: art is the craft and lore of preparing

the soil for seed: no enmity: complementary: is any yeoman
dumb enough to think that by much cultivation of the fields wheat
will sprout: or that saying words over the barren, the seedless,

will make potatoes: son of a gun's been keeping a bag of seed-wheat
in the barn all winter, has sorted out good potatoes and knows how
to cut their eyes out: it's hard to say whether the distinguishers

or the resemblancers are sillier: they work with noumena every
day, but speak of the invisible to them and they laugh with
690   silver modernity: well, as I said, we are more certain that we

are about than what we are about: here is something I have always
wanted to quote:

     "Around the mouths of rivers, where the fresh waters
     of the land meet the salt waters of the sea, live some of
695   the world's densest populations. This food-rich borderland

harbors immense numbers and varieties of living creatures—
protozoans, worms, snails, shrimp, clams, oysters and on up
through the vertebrate fishes. Life in an estuary may be
rich, but it is also almost inconceivably dangerous. The
700   temperature of its shallow waters runs the scale from
freezing to over 100 degrees Fahrenheit. Twice each day
the ebb and flow of the tides drastically alter the conditions
of life, sometimes stranding whole populations to die a
high-and-dry or freezing death. Winds, floods, and tidal
705   currents often bury the stationary bottom animals under
suffocating slides of sand or silt. But the greatest
hazard of all is alien water—water that is too fresh or
too salty. Aquatic animals are sensitive to the salt
content of their water environment. A sudden rain-fed
710   flood of fresh water from a river mouth can be catastrophic
to populations dwelling in the estuary."

    "The Life of an Estuary" by Robert M. Ingle. *Scientific
    American*, May 1954.

                isn't that beautiful: it has bearing in many
715   ways on my argument: it provided me years ago with ideas on

risks and possibilities: well, my essay is finished: I thank it
with all my heart for helping me to get through this snowstorm:
having a project is useful especially during natural suspensions.

                                        1969 (1970)

Plunder

I have appropriated the windy twittering of aspen leaves
into language, stealing something from reality like a
silverness: drop-scapes of ice from peak sheers:

much of the rise in brooks over slow-rolled glacial stones:
5   the loop of reeds over the shallow's edge when birds
feed on the rafts of algae: I have taken right out of the

air the clear streaks of bird music and held them in my
head like shifts of sculpture glint: I have sent language
through the mud roils of a raccoon's paws like a net,

10   netting the roils: made my own uses of a downwind's
urgency on a downward stream: held with a large scape
of numbness the black distance upstream to the mountains

flashing and bursting: meanwhile, everything else, frog,
fish, bear, gnat has turned in its provinces and made off
15   with its uses: my mind's indicted by all I've taken.

1970

Triphammer Bridge

I wonder what to mean by *sanctuary*, if a real or
apprehended place, as of a bell rung in a gold
surround, or as of silver roads along the beaches

of clouds seas don't break or black mountains
5   overspill; jail: ice here's shapelier than anything,
on the eaves massive, jawed along gorge ledges, solid

in the plastic blue boat fall left water in: if I
think the bitterest thing I can think of that seems like
reality, slickened back, hard, shocked by rip-high wind:

10   *sanctuary, sanctuary*, I say it over and over and the
word's sound is the one place to dwell: that's it, just
the sound, and the imagination of the sound—a place.

1970 (1971)

Lollapalooza: 22 February

Lord, have mercy! what a day: what a merciful day:
went to fifty: I listened all day to garage-music:
old roof snow, heavy-bottomed with melt and freeze,

began at sunrise to drop at the eaves, each drop
5   discrete as a plectrum: then the old icicles
loosened at the root and fell into brown chrysanthemum

stalks (and snapdragons, still green!) and then as
morning tided, seeing down the angle of the drops
was like watching a rain section, and then by noon,

10   the wind risen, the eaves swung ragged with sound
and glitter: I felt the roof rise as if to relief,
ten weeks turning casually to water: the afternoon

was lovely and constant (except, wingfeathers in a
ground-melt, I shoved the mound aside to find, as if alive,
15   a pheasant under snow): at dusk, a patch of white

still centered on the roof, I went out to check and
sure enough the motions had lessened: spicule icicles
lengthened into a lessening overflow, the music cold-skimpy.

1970

Satyr Formalist

As the perpetual laugher about the grounds,
the grouped yews and carved high stones (always
in a diminishment, looking for light),

as the caperer of flat stones, their intervals
5   a watery disarray nevertheless along directions, the
light dunker of lilypad leaves (to see the jewels

———

roll in and stand), as the caresser of whatever
gets too far into the dark, the whickerer at
hints of gross intent, sampler of hues and

10   cornices, he touched death for the first time as
the smallest significance of a tremble in the thighs,
the rounding white of the moon in his eyes, stricture

by the thornbush border, and uncomprehending, like
us, uncomprehending, he took to it blank, vacancy
15   to vacancy, brittle, fine, dew-bush's pool drop.

                                        1970

Late Romantic

Change the glacier's loneliness and the ice melts,
streams going off into sundry identity systems,
bog floats, lakes, clouds, seas, drinking water:

flux heightens us into knots of staid tension:
5   we live and go about containing various swirls:
too much swirling improves loneliness poorly:

we take advantage of separateness to unite sensible
differences, the tube in the fineness of its coupling
nearly a merging: well, nothing's perfect: fall

10   away, of course—we have other things to do alone,
go to the bathroom, brush our teeth, reel:
how can we give ourselves away if we're not separate

enough to be received: and, given away, we know
no desire but the other's desire: and given each
15   to each, we're both both, indistinguishably, sort of.

                                        1970

Spaceship

It's amazing all
this motion going
on and
water can lie still
5   in glasses and the gas
can in the
garage doesn't rattle.

1970

Cleavage

Soon as
you stop
having trouble
getting down
5   to earth
you start
having trouble
getting off
the ground

1970

Schooling

Out mountainward, I explained I've already
yielded to so much, truly, an abundance,

to seas, of course, ranges, glaciers, large
rivers, to the breadth of plains, easily to

5   outcroppings of bedrock, specially those
lofted amalgamated magmas, grainy, dense, and

easily to waterfalls double-hands can't halt:
but now I'm looking to yield to lesser

———————

effects, wind-touch of a birch branch, for
10   example, weed-dip, tilting grasses in seed,

the brush of a slipped lap of lakewater
over a shore stone: I think I'm almost

down to shadows, yielding to their masses,
for my self out here, taut against the mere

15   suasion of a star, is explaining, dissolving
itself, saying, be with me wind bent at leaf

edges, warp me puddle riffle, show me
the total yielding past shadow and return.

1970

Space Travel

Go down the left
hand side of the yard,
a contrived bankslope,
down to the corner of
5   the lot, past the
forsythia bushes now
all green, and look
back up toward the house,
the lawn, the young
10   maple, the bushes along
the foundation & you can
practically work up
a prospect: vision adjusts:
feeling roomy is room
15   enough and many a
twenty-mile out-west view
thins to staging:
it's going to be all right
I think, for those

20   who wish to live, at least:
        there are some who do.

1970

High Surreal

        Spit the pit in the pit
        I told the cherry eater
        and see what crumbling
        shoulders, gully washes,
5   & several other bardic
        dimensions can produce:
        possibly a shiny asbestos
        tree with cherry
        nuts—reversal obvious
10   in the formation—but
        if you come to impossible
        productions on
        absent trees, get out the
        bulldozer and shove the
15   whole thing over smooth.

1970 (1971)

Sharp Lookout

        Rain still falls, the wind moves
        the maple branches to
        gestures and patterns reasonable:
        the stream deals with rocks
5   and hollows, slowing or dashing,
        in ways apparently regular: whole
        bushes and even tall trees
        light up as usual with song to
        the songbird out of sight:
10   the clouds that have never taken
        shape are shapely: the bulby,
        engrossing sun splinters red

through the hedge toward dusk:
though I've been expecting
15 a wrench or unpraiseworthy re-ordering
to shock loose any moment from
lost curvatures, I've not been able
today to form evidence of any
trend countering our prospects
20 for a moderate life and a safe death.

1970

Right On

The tamarack can cut rain down to size, mist-little
bead-gauze, hold at needlepoint a plenty
and from the going, blue-sunk storm keep a

shadow, glittery recollection: the heart-leaved
5 big hydrangea bends over blossom-nodding, a few
large drops and a general glaze streaking leaves

with surface tension: the maple leaves
gather hail-size drops at the lobes and
sway them ragged loose: spirea, quince, cedar,

10 elm, hollyhock, clover (a sharp beader)
permit various styles of memory: then the sun
breaks out and clears the record of what is gone.

1970

Rectitude

Last night's thunderstorm's
glancing quick shifts of strong wind and
heavy sheets of tensed up
beating down rain

———

5   have left the snapdragons
velvet-hung in red bead
bedraggled, a
disorientation extreme:

but this morning,
10   the clouds clearing, the sun
breaking its one source out,
light is working in the stems' cells,

drawing up, adjusting, soft alignments
coming true, and pretty soon
15   now the prevailing command "attention!"
will seem to have been uttered suddenly.

1970 (1972)

Object

X out the rondure of
the totally satisfying
and all other sizable areas
near the central scope:
5   that degree, that circumference,
put aside: the leftovers,
though, pips & squeaks,
think to pick up, shovel
up, if possible: that is what
10   is left: stuffing the central
experience into the peripheral
bit overinvests though &
creates aura,
wistfulness and small floating.

1970

Ground Tide

Headed back home from Harold's, we came down
from some Connecticut hills, crossed the
height-slowed Hudson, mounted into the hills

again, the Catskills, made the divide and then
5   picked up a stream that ironed out
in wandering descent as much as possible into

one grade—when we noticed the earth risen,
darkness of lofted hills, every one piled with
woods and possessed to the top, drowning

10   us under the dark line of a weighty dominance:
nothing of the sort, of course! just fall-outs
of the ridge we'd already cleared, and so,

amiably, tilted by grade into a floating,
unearned speed, we eased on out into the open
15   failing slopes, led by the spiritual, risen stream.

1970 (1971)

Translating

This afternoon the thunderstorms were separate and tall,
the intervals blue with clearing and white with icy
summits moiling upward till height could accept no

more and the vast glides called out evenness: so,
5   through the afternoon there were several systems of
shower, the translations of heat vapor lofted to grit-ice,

the falling drafts of grit bounding, gathering into stones, the
further falls through the heavy warmer waters: at first, the drops
in any shower were huge, few, obviously stone water,

———

10   then the narrower rods of slant-thick rain, then even
smaller rain, dense but fine with a half-light following or
a full breaking out of sun: then, it was, the sun come but

the rain not over, I saw under the aural boughs of the elm
the last translation, a fine-weaving gathered by leaves,
15   augmented from tip to tip into big, lit, clear, sparse drops.

1970 (1971)

Sorting

There's not much hill left up from here and after
rains runlets lose head quickly to the least
quiver: height has such poverty of

reservoir, and in a drought poplars will go
5   brittle with yearning and take lightly their usual
mass and rock-hold, while at the bottom of the

ridge, the fountains will still be blinking,
the glade weeds rushed green: well, at least, we get
some view up here and sometimes breezes that miss

10   the valley cut a high sweep across from ridge to ridge
and then most often the drought will break
in time, the trees come back, a branch or two burnished.

1970 (1971)

The Next Day

Morning glory vine
slight
as it is will
double on itself and
5   pile over
a quince bush before

you know it:
so the woodless-stemmed
can
10 by slender travel
arrange its leaves and
take away
light from the wooded:
beholding the rampancy
15 and the
thin-leaved quince
thereunder, I stripped
off an armload
of vine
20 and took it down to
the brushheap
under the pear tree:
the next day
the wilted leaves had
25 given up their
moisture to the
vines that here and
there
to diminished glory
30 lifted half-opened
morning glory blooms.

1970

Extremes and Moderations

Hurly-burly: taking on whatever is about to get off, up the
slack, ready with prompt-copy for the reiteration, electronic
to inspect the fuzzy-buffoon comeback, picking up the diverse
gravel of mellifluous banality, the world-replacing world

5 world-irradiating, lesser than but more outspoken:
constructing the stanza is not in my case exceedingly
difficult, variably invariable, permitting maximum change
within maximum stability, the flow-breaking four-liner, lattice

of the satisfactory fall, grid seepage, currents distracted
10   to side flow, multiple laterals that at some extreme spill
a shelf, ease back, hit the jolt of the central impulse: the
slow working-down of careful investigation, the run

diffused, swamped into variable action: my ideal's a cold
clod clam calm, clam contained, nevertheless active in the
15   digestion, capable of dietary mirth, the sudden whisk, nearly
rollably spherical: ah, but friends, to be turned

loose on an accurate impulse! how handsome the stanzas are
beginning to look, open to the total acceptance, fracturing into
delight, tugging down the broad sweep, thrashing it into
20   particulars (within boundaries): diversity, however—as of

the concrete—is not ever-pleasing: I've seen fair mounds
of fine-stone at one end or the other of highway construction
many times and been chiefly interested in the "hill": but
abstraction is the bogey-boo of those incapable of it, while,

25   merrily, every abstractor brings the concrete up fine: one,
anyway, as Emerson says, does well what one settles down to:
it's impossible anyone should know anything about the concrete
who's never risen above it, above the myth of concretion

in the first place: pulverize such, unequal to the synthesis,
30   the organism by which they move and breathe their particulars:
and the symbol won't do, either: it differentiates flat
into muffling fact it tried to stabilize beyond: there aren't

just problems for the mind, the mind's problematic, residing
here by a scary shading merely: so much so it does seem
35   at times to prefer an origin other-worldly, the dreaminess,
the surficial hanging-on, those interior swirls nearly

capable of another invention: astonishingly, the
celestial bodies are round, not square or triangular, not
dodecahedral, and then they are sprinkled in the void's
40   unusual abundance: if it weren't for light, we wouldn't think

anything here, that scanty a fabric: that is the way it
was made: worse, that is the way it works out: when the lady
said she accepted the universe, it was a sort of decision:
anyway, granted that the matter appears to be settled, there's

45   plenty around for the mind to dwell on: that's a comfort,
but, now, a ghastly comfort: that's the difference:
the first subject I wanted to introduce, because it's
inanimate but highly active, is my marble garden bench down

by the elm—actually, well under the elm: it's in three parts:
50   the seat slab, four to five inches thick, and the two end slabs,
equally thick but, deeply buried, of undetermined length: I
bought this old place a few years ago, so wasn't present for the

setting: but as to length the upper slab is, say, four feet:
some cool seeps up the legs from the ground, but I
55   doubt there's much commission between the legs and the upper
slab: cool nights deeply penetrate the bench, so that on

a flash-hot summer morning, the reservoir of dense cooling
will ooze right through to one's bottom, providing, I must say,
a tendency to equilibrium: the stone never gets as hot as the
60   day and never as cool as the night (maybe it's colder some winter

nights of cold remembrances) so it moderates the environment,
working as a heater or air-conditioner: it has no moving
parts—it's all moving parts, none visible—and yet is
capable of effect, animation: that such a thing can work for

65   us day and night makes us feel, by cracky, that nature is our
servant, though without singular intention: the gift, though,
the abundance! we don't have to pay for, that requires no
matching social security funds, no fringe benefits: the

unutterable avenue of bliss: in spite of the great many works
70   in progress, I feel this is the last poem to the world: every
poet probably feels he is writing the last poem to the world:
man, in motion how avaricious, has by the exaggeration of his

refinement shown what intelligence can commit in the universe:
bleak scald of lakes, underground poisonous tides, air litter
75   like a dusk, clouds not like the clouds: can we give our wild
life a brake: must we keep tinkering until a virus swerves

from our interventions into a genesis consummating us: must
we spew out acids till we're their stew: lead on the highways,
washing into the grass, collecting into lead brooklets bound
80   for diffusive destinations: get your musclebound mercury dose

here: come on, guys: we know how to handle the overpopulation
problem: sell folks carloads of improvement marked uncertain:
progress can be the end of us: how neat: in a way, you might
say, how right, how just, poetically just: but come on, I say,

85   overrefined exaggeration, if you got us into this, can't you
get us out: come on, hot-shot fusion: give us plenty with no
bitter aftertaste: paradise lies ahead, where it's always lain:
but we may reach it, before hell overtakes us: nature, if I may

judge out a law, likes extremes, in some ways depends on them, but
90   usually keeps them short or confined: if we are broadly, densely
extreme, can't we count on the outbreak of dialectical alternatives:
we can count on it: what is a beer party now but a can of cans:

what is wine now but a bottle in a recalcitrant green glow,
empurpling in the sun: nevertheless, the petunias are incarnadine
95   by the hedgebrush: nevertheless, the catbird comes to the plastic
boat the goldfish summers in, fools around looking, then takes

a drink: we are aided by much I will discuss and much as
yet unfixed: it's time I introduced an extreme, but this time
I'm going to pick a moderate one, I think—the gusts before
100   thunderstorms: now the gusts before thunderstorms are sometimes

high enough to trim trees: a bough summer has coaxed overweight,
that splitting riddance, serviceable enough, but more anthropo-
centrically, the shaking out of dead branches: when we are
out walking in the woods on a calm day, we don't want a

105   dead limb to just plunge out of a tree by surprise, striking us,
        possibly, on the cranium: whatever we normally go to the woods
        for, surely we don't go for that: by high gusts thunderstorms
        accomplish the possibility of calm residence: the tree, too,

        counts on nodding times, sun-gleanings, free of astonishment,
110   and to buy them is willing to give up its dead or
        even its living limbs: nature gives much on occasion
        but exacts a toll, a sacrifice: that puzzling suggestion,

        or autumnal impulse, has accounted for much sacred carnage: I
        hate to think of it: I nearly hate to think of it: the Maya
115   hearts pulled out still flicking have always seemed to me gruesome
        separations, attention-getting, but god-like with revulsion's awe:

        of course, even closer home, high gusts can carry hints to the
        hapless by, for example, blowing down a fence obviously too weak
        to stand: that should be good news to the farmer whose cows have
120   been getting out: and who should not be alarmed by an immediate

        problem if the lesson has been well bestowed: nature sometimes
        gets all its shit together and lets you have it: but good farmers
        make good fences and anybody else gets whatever the traffic will
        bear away: I wrote the other day a poem on this subject:

125   Ancestors

                    An elm tree, like a society or
                    culture, seems to behave out of
                    many actions toward a total
                    interest (namely, its own) which means
130   that in the clutter and calamity
                    of days much, locally catastrophic,
                    can occur that brings no sharp
                    imbalance to the total register:
                    for example, dead limbs, white already
135   with mold and brackets, can in

a high storm—the heralding windtwists
of thunderstorms, say—snap and, though
decay-light, plunge among the
lower greens, the many little stiff
140   fingers entangling, weighing down
the structures of growth: ah, what
an insupportable extravagance by
the dead, held off the ground, leaching
white with slow, dry rot: what
145   a duty for the young limbs, already
crowding and heavy with green: well,
I guess the elm is by that much local
waste wasted, but then perhaps its
sacrifice is to sway in some deep rich
150   boughs the indifferent, superfluous,
recalcitrant, white, prophesying dead.

circulations are moderations, currents triggered by extremes:
we must at all costs keep the circulations free and clear,
open and unimpeded: otherwise, extremes will become trapped,
155 local, locked in themselves, incapable of transaction: some

extremes, though, *are* circulations, a pity, in that kinds of
staying must then be the counters: for example, when in spring
a gray sandstorm arises over Indiana, circulation becomes
too free and open: hedgerows, even, are important at such times:

160 they stall the storm just enough for heavy sand to fall out:
but what of the lengthy problem of small sand and, even worse,
of high-rising fine dust: if the storm hits
Pennsylvania, the woods will drag at its foot, then

tilt and capitulate it: heavy suspensions will lose their
165 directions to gravity quickly but even the fine dust slowing will
sift through the equally numerical leaves, be caught by them,
and the air will be breatheable again by Jersey, west Jersey:

———

water's carriages act the same way: high narrow valleys, roomless,
propel water along, loosening sometimes substantial boulders: the
170   mature valleys, wide-bottomed, slow the flow, and
particulate weight falls out: in the ancient flat valleys,

where meanders have cut off into oxbow lakes or little crescents
of difference, the water goes broad and slow and only the
fine stuff in a colloidal float, a high drift, stays out
175   the ride, hanging finally in long curtains in the gulfs and lagoons:

well, I just, for poetic purposes, wanted to point out the parallel:
parallel too in that even Pennsylvania can't get some of the
high dust, the microscopic grit—settles out with the
floating spiders on Atlantic isles and (too bad for the spiders)

180   waves: such circulations are average and quite precious: the
sun's the motor, the mechanisms greased by millions of years
of propriety and correction: the place produced deliciously
habitable, a place we found we could grow into: how marvelous!

lightning is one of the finest, sharpest tensions, energy
185   concentrations: it has to be lean because it leaps far:
how was the separation to be bridged, the charge neutralized,
except by a high-energy construct: gathers the diffuse

energy from clouds and ground and drains it through a
dense crackling: I don't know how it works: it works:
190   the charges rush together and annihilate each other:
or the charge goes one way, to the ground, or to the

clouds: I'll bet it's one way and to the ground: the
lofted's precarious: the ground is nice and sweet and not
at all spectacular: I wonder if I'm really talking about
195   the economy of the self, where an extreme can gather up a lot

of stale stuff and mobilize it, immoderate grief,
or racing terror, or a big unification like love chugging
up to the fold: we never talk about anything but ourselves,
objectivity the objective way of talking about ourselves:

200   O calligraphers, blue swallows, filigree the world
        with figure, bring the reductions, the snakes unwinding,
        the loops, tendrils, attachments, turn in necessity's precision,
        give us the highwire of the essential, the slippery concisions

        of tense attentions! go to look for the ocean currents and
205   though they are always flowing there they are, right in place, if
        with seasonal leans and sways: the human body
        staying in change, time rushing through, ingestion,

        elimination: if change stopped, the mechanisms of
        holding would lose their tune: current informs us,
210   is the means of our temporary stay: ice water at the northern
        circle sinks and in a high wall like a glacier seeps down the

        ocean bottom south: but the south's surface water is going
        north, often in spiral carriages of an extreme intensity, nevertheless
        moderating, preventing worse extremes: as when snow streaks up the
215   summit, up past the timberline where interference is slight, and

        having passed the concision of the ridge, blooms out diffusing
        over the valley, drifts out into the catchments, fills with
        feathery loads the high ravines, the glacier's compressions forming
        underneath, taking direction in the slowest flow of relief, so on

220   any number of other occasions, massive collections and dispositions
        restore ends to sources: O city, I cry at
        the gate, the glacier is your
        mother, the currents of the deep father you, you sleep

        in the ministry of trees, the boulders are your brothers sustaining
225   you: come out, I cry, into the lofty assimilations: women, let
        down your hair under the dark leaves of the night grove, enter
        the currents with a sage whining, rising into the circular

        dance: men, come out and be with the wind, speedy and lean, fall
        into the moon-cheered waters, plunge into the ecstasy of rapids:
230   children, come out and play in the toys of divinity: glass, brick,
        stone, curb, rail are freezing you out of your motions, the

uncluttered circulations: I cry that, but perhaps I am too secular
or pagan: everything, they say, is artificial: nature's the
artwork of the Lord: but your work, city, is aimed unnaturally
235   against time: your artifice confronts the Artifice: beyond

the scheduled consummation, nothing's to be recalled: there is
memory enough in the rock, unscriptured history in
the wind, sufficient identity in the curve
of the valley: what is your name, city, under your name: who

240   are your people under their faces: children of the light,
children of the light: of seasons, moons, apples, berries,
grain: children of flies, worms, stars: come out, I cry, into
your parentage, your established natures: I went out and pulled a

few weeds in the lawn: you probably think I was getting goofy
245   or scared: it was just another show: as the mystic said, it's
all one to me: then I went on over to the University, and there
was Slatoff's new book, fresh from the publisher's: and Kaske

had left me a book he'd told me about: *Ballad of the Bones
and Other Poems*, by Byron Herbert Reece: E.P. Dutton: 1945:
250     $2.00: introduced by Jesse Stuart: and praised, on
the back cover, by William Rose Benet, John Hall Wheelock,

John Gould Fletcher, and Alfred Kreymborg: I do believe I'm going
to enjoy the book: the South has Mr. Reece and, probably,
Literature: I bet I pulled a thousand weeds: harkweed's
255   incredible: it puts up a flower (beautiful) to seed but at the

same time sends out runners under the grass that anchor a few
inches or a foot away, and then the leaves of the new plants
press away the grass in a tight fit: I put havoc into those
progressions, believe me: plants take their cue and shape

260   from crowding: they will crowd anything, including close
relatives, brethren and sistren: everybody, if I may switch
tracks, is out to get his: that is the energy we must allow
the widest margin to: and let the margins, then, collide into

265 sensible adjustments: slow moderations are usually massive:
nature can't heave a lot fast, air and
oceans reasonably unwieldy: true, they work into lesser
intensities, local: maelstroms, typhoons, fairly rapid highs

or lows, the boiling up of deep, cold water: dimension may be
the sorter, although it didn't seem so originally with the
270 garden bench, small and yet efficiently moderating: if
you built a wall across the Gulf Stream, though, the sundering

would be lengthy: and what would it take to bring about a quick
thermal change in an ocean: a solar burst; at least,
unusual effusion: quantity of mass or number (as of leaves) then
275 moderates the local effect: as for cooling an ocean, a lot of

icebergs would have to split off from the caps and plunge before
the change would be measurable: expanded, though, through
sufficient time—a massiveness—the lesser effects could assume
large implications: but, of course, with the icebergs, one

280 would have to investigate the mechanisms that were heating up the
general air, causing the splits in the first place, and then one
would have to deal with the probability that the air, massive to
massive, would warm up the oceans which would then be able to

absorb large numbers of icebergs without cooling: I suppose
285 my confusion is no more than natural, reflecting
the reticulation of interpenetration in nature, whereby we should
be advised to tamper cautiously with least balances,

lest a considerable number, a series or so, tilt
akimbo: even now, though, we apparently cannot let well enough
290 alone: how well it was! how computer-like in billionths the
administration and take of the cure: just think, the best cure

would arise by subtle influence of itself if only we would
disappear: but though we have scalded and oiled the seas and
scabbed the land and smoked the mirror of heaven, we must try
295 to stay and keep those who are alive alive: then we

might propose to ourselves that collectively we have one grain
of sense and see what the proposition summons forth: the force of
the drive by which we have survived is hard to counter, even
now that we survive so densely: and it is not certain the plants

300   would not lose their shape and vigor if they had to stop
crowding: a very hard reversal and loss of impetus: we may
have time to diminish and cope with our thrust: the little patch
of wildwoods out behind my backhedge is even now squeaky and

chirpy with birds and the day is as clear as a missing windowpane:
305   the clouds are few, large, and vastly white: the air has no
smell and the shade of trees is sharp: floods are extreme
by narrowing rain, which can, itself, be quite bountiful:

it's hard to blame floods—useless—because they're just
showing how hard they can work to drain the land:
310   one way a slow impulse works up into an extremity's
the earthquake: coastal land, say, drifts with sea currents

north a couple of inches a year, setting up a strain along a
line with the land's land: at some point, tension gives in
a wrack and wrecks stability, restoring lassitude: or resonance
315   of circulation coming into a twist or "beat": the gathering up,

the event, the dissipation: but that would imply that everything,
massive, slow, or long is moving toward the enunciation of
an extreme: we dwell in peace on the post-tables and
shelves of these remarkable statements: what kind of lurch is

320   it, I wonder, when a comet sideswipes us, or swishes by near
enough to switch our magnetic poles: can the atmosphere
be shifted a few hundred miles: the oceans
would pile up and spill: maybe just the magnetic poles would

switch, that sounds all right: but if the comet hit us and
325   glanced off or even stuck, its impact would affect
our angular momentum and possibly put some wobble in our motion:
somebody said the purpose of science is to put us in control

of our environment, allaying calamity and catastrophe, though
conceivably also making nice days a little nicer: well, all
330   I say (figuratively speaking) is a lot of things are
still in their own control: maybe my point, though, is that

by and large I prefer the other controls to our own, not
forsaking the possibility that still larger controls
by us might bring about a fair, if slightly artificialized,
335   paradise someday: from here, it looks like ruin and

destruction either way, more or less: one thing we will never
do is sit around on this planet doing nothing, just soaking
up the honey of solar radiation: if our problems were
solved, we'd go out of business: (stretch that a little

340   and it will do): it's dry: the weeds in the lawn
are being tested to the limit, some having died: I've just
put a soakhose by the maple: I'll let it go slowly that way
for a few hours: the grass in patches is parched tan:

it crackles underfoot: tight spurs of hay:
345   I didn't see the hornet at first when I went to attach the
hose: he was sucking the spigot: people around here don't
have sprinklers, I can't understand it: I always used to have

one in South Jersey: maybe water's expensive or maybe
very dry spells are rare: seems to me I remember a very dry
350   one last year: the days are shortening: it's sundown
now at eight: maybe a little later officially, but the sun's

down behind the ridge on the other side of the lake by then: any
night could turn sharp cold—read August 21: I've been at this
poem or prose-poem or versification or diversification for three
355   or four days: I'll never get all the weeds

out of the grass: I just know after each day that
there are a hell of a lot fewer weeds in the lawn:
it's evening: seven: I just noticed
a dark cloud coming from the west, so I went out

360 and said, please, rain some here: a few pin drops
 fell, I think though more because of the dark cloud than the
 saying: saying doesn't do any good but it doesn't
 hurt: aligns the psychic forces with the natural:

 that alignment may have some influence: I have found the world
365 so marvelous that nothing would surprise me: that may sound
 contradictory, the wrong way to reach the matter-of-fact: but
 if you can buy comets sizzling around in super-elongated

 orbits and a mathematics risen in man that corresponds to the
 orbits, why, simple as it is finally, you can move on to glutinous
370 molecules sloshing around in the fallen seas for something
 to stick to: that there should have been possibilities enough to

 include all that has occurred is beyond belief, an extreme the
 strictures and disciplines of which prevent loose-flowing
 phantasmagoria: last night in the cloud-darkened dusk rain began
375 gently, the air so full of moisture it just couldn't help it,

 and continued at least past midnight when I went to bed: this
 morning is dark but not raining: recovery's widespread: rain
 comes all over everything: trees, bushes, beans, petunias,
 weeds, grass, sandboxes, garages: yesterday I went with the hose

380 on the hard crusty ground from one single scorched patch to
 another, never able to stay long at one point the other places
 were calling so hard: ocean dumping of nuclear garbage requires
 technological know-how, precision of intention, grace of

 manipulation: devilish competition invades even the dirty work
385 of the world, where, though, the aggressive, intelligent young man
 can negotiate spectacular levels of promotion: we have spilt
 much energy generating concentrations—nerve gas, specific

 insecticides, car polish, household cleansers "fatal if swallowed"—
 we must depend on land, sea, and air to diffuse into harmlessness:
390 but some indestructibles resist all transformation and anyway
 our vast moderators are limited: an oil slick covers every inch

of ocean surface: at the poles pilots see in the contrast the
sullied air's worldwide: because of the circulations, water can
never be picked up for use except from its usages, where what
395   has gone in is not measured or determined: extreme calls to

extreme and moderation is losing its quality, its effect: the
artificial has taken on the complication of the natural and where
to take hold, how to let go, perplexes individual action: ruin
and gloom are falling off the shoulders of progress: blue-green

400   globe, we have tripped your balance and gone into exaggerated
possession: this seems to me the last poem written to the world
before its freshness capsizes and sinks into the slush: the
rampaging industrialists, the chemical devisers and manipulators

are forging tanks, filling vats of smoky horrors because of
405   dollar lust, so as to live in long white houses on the summits
of lengthy slopes, for the pleasures of making others spur and
turn: but common air moves over the slopes, and common rain's

losing its heavenly clarity: if we move beyond
the natural cautions, we must pay the natural costs, our every
410   extreme played out: where we can't create the room of
playing out, we must avoid the extreme, disallow it: it's Sunday

morning accounts for such preachments, exhortations, and
solemnities: the cumulative vent of our primal energies is now and
always has been sufficient to blow us up: I have my ventilator
415   here, my interminable stanza, my lattice work that lets the world

breeze unobstructed through: we could use more such harmless
devices: sex is a circular closure, permitting spheric
circularity above hemispheric exchange: innocent, non-destructive,
illimitable (don't you wish it) vent: I want to close (I may

420   interminably do it, because a flatness is without beginning,
development, or end) with my chief concern: if contaminated
water forces me to the extreme purification of bottled or distilled
water, the extreme will be costly: bulldozers will have to clear

———

roads to the springs: trucks will have to muck the air to bring

425   the water down: bottles will have to be made from oil-fired

melts: a secondary level of filth created to escape the first:

in an enclosure like earth's there's no place to dump stuff off.

1970

Mid-August

Now the ridge
brooks
are
flue-dry, the rocks

5   parching hot &
where sluice
used
to clear roots &

break weeds down brambly,
10   light finds a luminous
sand-scar,
vertical: it will

go to a hundred
today: even the
15   zucchini vine has
rolled over

on its
side.

1970 (1972)

Clearing the Dark Symbiosis

Any entangling however
scandent and weighty

is likely
if it's lasted some eons

5   to show mutuality, fervor
symbiotic, if
in the first trials
unravelingly scary:

for example, the hollyhocks
10   strung out tall,
the peaks heavy with
bud-nub and bloom sway,
I started to look out thinking

thunder, thunder-made or making
15   wind, would down
those highest blooms, or
rain and wind would: but

the morning glory vines,
taking over like sudden guests,
20   built a holding between
all the hollyhock stalks,
a mutual house, an air house:

the storm came, well you know,
but the vines were just

25   sufficient to keep the margin of
extremity off: I said
well in the fall (almost)
when the

hollyhock has very little
30   to lose, it has still itself
to gain: add, for me,
the morning glory blooms.

1970

Viable

Motion's the dead give away,
eye catcher, the revealing risk:
the caterpillar sulls on the hot macadam

but then, risking, ripples to the bush:
5   the cricket, startled, leaps the
quickest arc: the earthworm, casting,

nudges a grassblade, and the sharp robin
strikes: sound's the other
announcement: the redbird lands in

10   an elm branch and tests the air with
cheeps for an answering, reassuring
cheep, for a motion already cleared:

survival organizes these means down to
tension, to enwrapped, twisting suasions:
15   every act or non-act enceinte with risk or

prize: why must the revelations be
sound and motion, the poet, too, moving and
saying through the scary opposites to death.

1970

Precursors

In a little off-water
snaggy with roots
I dibbled

thinking
5   what a brand new place this is—
the surprising fauna,

scribblings
scribbling in water, landing

in mud-dust,
10   the spectacular green moss
creeping down
stump slopes to waterlevel,

and, look, clouds appear
in the ground
15   here, puddles
perfectly representational,
giving day or night
totally back:
it was so new

20   I thought I must've invented
it, or at least said it
first into the air:

but when I looked around
there were a thousand
25   puddles—had been
thousands more—some larger
than mine
in an over-place
called a swamp:

30   over-place led on to over-place
to the one place where
invisibility broke
out vacancy's flawless opacity:

but there, so the story
35   end good,
a turn brought me back

———

to this particular old
dawdling hole,

the wonders greener than they were,
40   the mirror clearer,
the fauna (and flora)
diverser, tangled,

the oldest things freshest,
most in need of being told.

1970

Lonesome Valley

This time of year a bumblebee's
sometimes found off
well away from anywhere
with a ragged wing:

5   seems foreign, probably, to him,
once a smooth bullet shot clear over
untroubling shrubs,
the difficulty of giving
grass and tiny, spangling
10   clover leaves:

as if from anger, a very high blurred buzz
comes and the bee lofts
three inches off, falls one-sided,

perplexed in a perfect scramble
15   of concretion—

immense vines & stalks brushy
interweaving—

———

frost's the solution still
distant
20   but too much effort in the crippled
condition can
do it too

or being dragged down by ants,
the sucked dryness,
25   the glassy wings perfectly remnant
in their raggedness,
the body shell shellacked complete,
the excessive hollowness and lightness.

1970

Delaware Water Gap

Rounding the mountain's rim-ledge,
we looked out valleyward
onto the summits of lesser hills,

summits bottoms of held air, still lesser
5   heights clefts and ravines: oh, I said,
the land's a slow ocean, the long blue

ridge a reared breakage, these small peaks
dips and rises: we're floating,
I said, intermediates of stone and air,

10   and nothing has slowed altogether
into determination and a new wave
to finish this one is building up somewhere,

a continent crowded loose, upwarping
against its suasions, we, you and I,
15   to be drowned, now so sustained and free.

1970 (1971)

Day

On a cold late
September morning,
wider than sky-wide
discs of lit-shale clouds

5   skim the hills,
crescents, chords
of sunlight
now and then fracturing

the long peripheries:
10   the crow flies
silent,
on course but destinationless,

floating:
hurry, hurry,
15   the running light says,
while anything remains.

1970 (1971)

Staking Claim

Look, look where the mind can go
I said to the sanctified
willows
wreathing jittery slow slopes of wind

5   look it can go up up to the ultimate
node where
remembering is foretelling
generation, closure
where taking in is giving out
10   ascent and descent a common blip

———

look going like wind over rocks
it can
touch where
completion is cancellation

15 all the way to the final vacant core
that brings
things together and turns them away

all the way away
to stirless bliss!

20 and the willows,
dream-wraiths song-turned,
bent in troops of unanimity,
never could waken
never could feel the rushing days

25 never could feel the cold
wind and rushing days
or thoroughly know
their leaves taking flight:

look I said to the willows
30 what the mind
can apprehend,

entire and perfect staying,
and yet face winter's
face coming over the hill

35 look I said to the leaves
breaking into flocks around me taking
my voice away
to the far side of the hill
and way beyond gusting down the long changes

1970

The Eternal City

After the explosion or cataclysm, that big
display that does its work but then fails
out with destructions, one is left with the

pieces: at first, they don't look very valuable,
5   but nothing sizable remnant around for
gathering the senses on, one begins to take

an interest, to sort out, to consider closely
what will do and won't, matters having become
not only small but critical: bulbs may have been

10   uprooted: they should be eaten, if edible, or
got back in the ground: what used to be garages,
even the splinters, should be collected for

fires: some unusually deep holes or cleared
woods may be turned to water supplies or
15   sudden fields: ruinage is hardly ever a

pretty sight but it must when splendor goes
accept into itself piece by piece all the old
perfect human visions, all the old perfect loves.

1970 (1971)

The Shoreless Tide

The universe with its
universal principles
was out exact with concision—

but toying, idling—
5   again this morning: that
is, the lemon-yellow

———

lime-veined sugar maple
leaves were as in a
morning tide, full but

10   slow with the slowness
of huge presences, nicking
off the branches and

coming down points up, stem-end
first, centered and weighted,
15   but spiraling nicely,

a dance perfectly
abundant: I got excited,
the universe concentrated

on the small scope of
20   a fall, as if to
expend reserves of

spectacle on the doomed so
we might, I thought, consider
some well beyond all loss.

1970

Grace Abounding

for E.C.

What is the misery in one that turns one with gladness
to the hedge strung lucid with ice: is it that one's
misery, penetrating there as sight, meets neither

welcome nor reprimand but finds nevertheless a picture
5   of itself sympathetic, held as the ice-blurred stems
increased: ah, what an abundance is in the universe

———

when one can go for gladness to the indifferent ghastly,
feel alliances where none may ever take: find one's
misery made clear, borne, as if also, by a hedge of ice.

1970 (1972)

Phase

These still days after frost have let down
the maple leaves in a straight compression
to the grass, a slight wobble from circular to

the east, as if sometime, probably at night, the
5   wind's moved that way—surely, nothing else
could have done it, really eliminating the *as*

if, although the *as if* can nearly stay since
the wind may have been a big, slow
one, imperceptible, but still angling

10   off the perpendicular the leaves' fall:
anyway, there was the green-ribbed, yellow,
flat-open reduction: I just now bagged it up.

1970

Hibernaculum

1

A cud's a locus in time, a staying change, moving
but holding through motions timeless relations,
as of center to periphery, core-thought to consideration,

not especially, I'd say, goal-directed, more
5   a slime- and sublime-filled coasting, a repeating of
gently repeating motions, blissful slobber-spun webs:

---

today's paper says that rain falls on the desert and makes
it fertile: semen slips, jets, swims into wombs
and makes them bulge: therefore, there must be

2

10   a big penis above the clouds that spills the rain:
that is, I think, reasonable, which says something for
reason operating in fictions akilter: reason's no

better off than its ambience, and an ambience can't
alter frequently from its reason: (somewhere, though,
15   along the arm of a backwoods spiral, interchange

and adjustment with the environment are possible but
adjustment likely to be at the surprise of reason,
displeasure included: but then there has to be

3

protection against jolt-change: smashing alterations,
20   kind of cottonpicking conniptions, fail of impulse:)
the thunderbolt, another celestial phallus, though

sterile, peels trees, explodes bushes, ravels roots,
melds sand into imitation lightning, spurry and branchy,
deep into the ground: that sort of thing is

25   not promising, so represents, as with Zeus, authority:
cussed superegomaniacal threat that gets from the outside
in, doing its dirty work bitterest closest to

4

pleasure's fundament: the better it feels, the bigger
the bludgeon: O merciful constructions that are so made,
30   do have mercy: the stuff is sweet, why crud it up

———

with crud: for every fructifying heavenly penis, such as
the rain penis, a ghastly one seres sand:
if there were any way to get around the universe, somebody

would've by now: history informs despair:
35   the lucky young, they don't know anybody's screwed
or perished before: just as well, too: although

5

screwing is nearly worth perishing, and, too, the two not
always concomitant: perhaps, co-terminous: but then the
penis is also (like the heavens) splitting and pleasuring:

while it's in, it is, afterall, commanding and will not,
just because somebody's edgy, withdraw: it will come
out only when it backs off from a puzzled loss or when

something truly spectacular appears, a shotgun or, more
accurately, roused maiden aunt: rhythms, speeding up,
45   build necessity into their programs: I see filigrees of

6

confabulation, curlicues, the salt walking-bush, ah, I see
aggregates of definition, plausible emergences, I see
reticulations of ambience: the days shorten down to a

gap in the night, winter, though gray and vague, not half
50   dubious enough: I see a sleet-filled sky's dry freeze:
I see diggings disheveled, bleak mounds, burnt openings:

what do I see: I see a world made, unmade, and made again
and I hear crying either way: I look to the ground for the
lost, the ground's lost: I see grime, just grime, grain,

7

55 grit, grist: the layers at thousand-year intervals
accumulate, reduce to beginnings: but I see the nightwatchman
at the cave's mouth, his eyes turned up in stunned amusement

to the constellations: from zero to zero we
pass through magnificence too shatterable: sight, touch,
60 inquiring tongue, water spinning into white threads over rocks:

I see the man moving boldly, staking his love on time, time
the slippery, the slick mound stragglers slide into the
everlasting encompassing waters from: not a drop of water

hasn't endured the salt-change of change: how
65 have the clouds kept fresh, the soil kept lively, its
milling microbes, how has the air, drawn into numberless

dyings kept clarity, breatheability: I see quiet lakes
and composed hills: I see the seasonal wash of
white and green: I am alarmed with acceptance: nothing

70 made right could have been made this way, and nothing
made otherwise could have been made right: nothing can
be made to make it right: we're given the works to

purchase nothing: the hardest training of the eye
against this loveliness, what can we make of holding so
75 to what we must give up, as if only in the act of giving

up can we know the magnificence, spent: what are we
here to learn: how to come into our estates before night
disinherits us: dear God (or whatever, if anything, is

———

merciful) give us our lives, then, the full possession,
80 before we give them back: I see the flood-child astir in the
surf, the clouds slowing and breaking into light:

10

what did he buy or sell: what is the meaning of loss
that never lived into gain: the mother, not far off,
flickers in a ditch to the minor winds: how far off

85 she is, past all touch and dream, the child huddled
snug into himself, his decomposition: how the dark
mind feeds on darkness, hungry for the inmost core: but

it is only darkness, empty, the hollow, the black, sucking
wind: this everyone knows: everyone turns away: light,
90 tendril, moon, water seize our attention, make us turn:

11

I think we are here to give back our possessions before
they are taken away: with deliberate mind to say to
the crushing love, I am aware you are here cloaked in

this moment, you are priceless, eternity is between us,
95 we offer ourselves in the sacrifice of time to this
moment become unconditioned and time-evering: I think

we are here to draw the furthest tailing of time round
into the perishing of this purest instant: to make out
the proximity of love to a hundred percent and to zero:

12

100 I see the bitterest acquiescence, the calm eye in the
tragic scene, the smile of the howling mind: I keep
forgetting—I am not to be saved: I keep forgetting this

———

translation from fleshbody to wordbody is leaving my
flesh behind, that I *have* entered into the wordbody but
105   *may* not enter in, not at last: I need a set of practices,

a mnemonics, my fleshbody can keep close to its going:
of those practices the stepping out into love, motion's
glimpse, blanches to the highest burn: I can lose myself:

13

I'm not so certain I can lose you, I'm not so certain
110   you can lose me: but all the others have succeeded, all
the others have tricked on their legs by graves, all

the others have gotten through all the losses and left
the air clear, the bush aleaf, the ground in scent:
after it takes place, there will be a clearing for us,

115   too, we will be in the wind what shape a leaf would take
if a leaf were there: let's join to the deepest slowing,
turn the deepest dark into touch, gape, pumping, at the

14

dark beyond reach: afterwards, shoveling the driveway,
warming up the coffee, going to the grocery store, opening
120   the cookie jar, washing, shaving, vacuuming, looking out

the window at the perilously afflicted, that is, snow-loaded
bent evergreens, watching the pheasants walking across
the yard, plopping up belly-deep in snow, wondering

if one can get the car out or, out, in: the Ceremony of
125   Puzzling over the Typewriter, of swishing off the dishes
and getting them in the washer, of taking out the trash

15

and hearing the trash-can lids snap and bang, opened or
squeezed shut: the considerable distance the universe
allows between brushing the teeth and helping John put

130   his fort together: these small actions near the center
form the integrations, the gestures and melodies, rises
and falls minutes give over to hours, hours to days, days

to weeks, months, and years: it all adds up to zero only
because each filled day is shut away, vanished: and what
135   memory keeps it keeps in a lost paradise: the heroic

16

entangler, benign arachnid, casting threads to catch,
hang and snatch, draw up the filamental clutch, the
clump-core reticulate, to tie energy into verbal knots

so that only with the death of language dies the energy!
140   so all the unravellers may feed! the dissipators go with
some grain to their swill: pleasure to my tribe and

sufficient honor! to lean belief the lean word comes,
each scope adjusted to the plausible: to the heart
emptied of, by elimination, the world, comes the small

17

145   cry domesticating the night: if the night is to be
habitable, if dawn is to come out of it, if day is ever
to grow brilliant on delivered populations, the word

must have its way by the brook, lie out cold all night
along the snow limb, spell by yearning's wilted weed till
150   the wilted weed rises, know the patience and smallness

———

of stones: I address the empty place where the god
that has been deposed lived: it is the godhead: the
yearnings that have been addressed to it bear antiquity's

18

sanction: for the god is ever re-created as
155 emptiness, till force and ritual fill up and strangle
his life, and then he must be born empty again: I

accost the emptiness saying let all men turn their
eyes to the emptiness that allows adoration's life:
that is my whole saying, though I have no intention to

160 stop talking: our immediate staying's the rock but
the staying of the rock's motion: motion, that spirit!
we could veer into, dimpling, the sun or into the cold

19

orbital lofts, but our motion, our weight, our speed
are organized here like a rock, our spiritual stay:
165 the blue spruce's become ponderous with snow: brief

melt re-froze and knitted ice to needles and ice
to snow so the ridges eight inches high hold: the
branches move back and forth, stiff wailers:

the cloud-misty moonlight fills small fields, plots,
170 woodnooks with high light, snow transluminant as
fire: the owl, I'll bet, looks about little from

20

those branchy margins, his eye cleaned of liking in
the soft waste not a mouse burrows or thrashes through,
liking gone inward and sharp into the agony of imagined

———

175   mouseful lands: one thing poetry could be resembled to is
     soup: the high moving into clarity of quintessential
     consommé: then broth, the homogeneous cast of substance's

     shadow: then the falling out of diversity into specific
     identity, carrot cube, pea, rice grain: then the chunky
180   predominance of beef hunk, long bean, in heavy gravy:

21

     last night the eaves from roof heat dripped and the
     drops in those close-holding freezing laminations
     noded the tips of the cedar lobes hammer heavy, such

     ice: today, though, some sunshine and in the mid-forties,
185   the freeing up has been steady, if slow: the blue
     spruce stands isolated out in the yard—nothing drips

     on it except the sky—and since mid-morning it has
     had a little melt-shower in it, a shower canopy:
     from a low-hung dangle the emptied branches have risen

22

190   to near horizontal and the snow left looks edged and
     drained: I think in the marked up annals of recorded
     evolutionary history mind will turn out to have been

     nova-like, say; a pressure of chance built up
     nature had to take, the slide toward the slow explosion
195   of searching risk: some think mind will continue

     growing out of nature until possessed of its own self
     second-nature it will bespeak its own change, turn with
     or against the loam out of which it grew: I'm pessimistic:

23

for my little faith, such as it is, is that mind and
200   nature grew out of a common node and so must obey common
motions, so that dickering with second-nature mind

violates the violation: a made mind can live compre-
hendingly only in a made world and artifice, exact and
independent as it looks, can't, I'll bet, extend intricacy

205   working out through the core of every single atom: I
depend on the brook to look out where it's going:
I depend on the snow to ornament the woods: I depend

24

on the sun to get up every morning rightfully off-time:
I depend on the sea current to find just which way to
210   sway to the thermodynamic necessity: I depend utterly

on my body to produce me, keep me produced, don't you:
the autonomy of the mind! who could desire it, staying
up all night to keep the liver right, the pancreas calm:

I prefer like the sweet brook to be at ease with my
215   findings: I prefer the strictures that release me into
motion: for not even the highest branch is free to wave,

25

it responds as freedom to the wind's tyranny: what have
I to desire of autonomy except slavery, its ware:
I prefer to be offered up by all the designs and musculatures

220   into the liberty of correspondent motions: when the
mind can sustain itself it then may consider sustaining
the universe: meanwhile, I have nothing, nothing to sell:

———

I write what is left to write after everything's sold out:
and also I write not very wide, just to the fence or hedge
225   around the lot (sometimes from my window I take in the

26

neighboring lady's scrap of woods—I hope she
doesn't get word and charge me) but of course I write
straight up and down as far either way as I can reach,

which by sight (but not reach) one way is far but by
230   reach the other way, the ground, is near, if so opaque
only imagination, that frail, filters through: still

it's world enough to take my time, stretch my reason, hinder
and free me: do a section on the garage roof snow and you
will find several strata: I haven't looked but I know

27

235   because I was here when they happened: fluff snow, grit
snow, plain sleet, fluff snow, wet snow, more grit, and
snow (regular): similar sedimentary phenomena might be

expected elsewhere: and I have sat here by the window today
and seen a direct relation between the sunny intervals and
240   the rate of eave-melt off the garage: that close a

pull between the sun and my garage snow stuns me,
though I would be the last to insist it do a thing for you:
I really do not want to convince anyone of anything except

28

that conviction is cut loose, adrift and aswim, upon the
245   cool (sometimes sweltering) tides of roiling energy:
that's not to despise conviction, definition, or other

———

structure but to put them in their place: I hope
you are in the middle income bracket (at least): I
desire to be in the very high upper high outgo bracket:

250   to furnish forth energy out of nothing, except reflection,
a few hard years, several procedures of terror and
astonishment, New Hope Elementary School, assorted

29

mothers and fathers (with the one and the one), fifty
acres of ground, half swamp, half hill, Whiteville High
255   School, the Pacific Ocean, a small sweep through the arc

of the galaxy, one arm of the spiral in particular,
etc.: I know I can't give all that back but so what I
haven't quit trying yet and anyway it's just giving

nothing to nothing: I'm somewhat shocked by clouds
260   of organic compounds in deep space but anticipate
no flagrant reaction: I think it's going to rain:

30

our young don't believe in time as future and, so,
suffer every instant's death: they don't believe
in the thread, plot, the leading of one thing into

265   another, consequence, developed change: without retrospect
or prospect, they seek the quality of experience
a moment's dimension allows: thrill replaces

goal: threat lessens and fractures time, shortening
the distance to the abyss, immediate, a step away:
270   without calm, they can't see tomorrow unfolding: the mind,

31

too, can't move beyond the surface event into the
assimilations of higher, restful suasions where arc-like
staying has beginning and end and smooth curvature

reliable: hell is the meaninglessness of stringing out
275 events in unrelated, undirected sequences: remove danger
(holocaust, suffocation, poisoning) from the young and

their anxieties will unwind into long reaches of easeful
seeking: not that anyone is, has been, or ever will be
more than a hair away from disaster, and the statistics

32

280 on anyone's living forever are unpromising: still,
we have now a Myth of Disaster, and that's harder than
some other kinds of myth: with another snow coming, we

drove out past Route 13 on North Hanshaw this afternoon
to the tree farm for a scotch pine: there was half an
285 acre of perfectly spaced trees tied up to permanent

stakes: that was enough, some of the stakes deserted:
nevertheless, I bought a full, short, four-dollar tree
which I've just put twinkle lights on: now, with

33

the snow still steady, John and Robbie (his little
290 friend) are doing their part, hanging balls and
icicles: Christmas is still five days away, but no

matter—anticipation starts to burst out of little boys
early, and a present to raising the tree must be opened:
vent, vent: we need every trigger and valve we can

———

295   invent to achieve restless deflations: invent vents:
       my enormous, airy self sputters like a balloon at its
       inadequate outlet and shoots off spinning enlarging circles

34

       into the galaxy—or at least over the fence and treetops or
       halfway over the lake: when it gets too dry around here
300   in the summer sometimes, the little creeks nearly creak

       with drought, a dribble of a drop dropping off the
       dry ledges: well, I could use a little of that spareness
       of form and volume: imagine the luxurious lassitude of

       taking five minutes to swell into a drop and then let
305   go with a lengthy reluctance: the last drop bulbing
       from the spent member: but little boys have small

35

       emotional bladders and the pressure's terrific: they'd
       rather have a string of little wows every day
       than build up to one big blast: I see the gully-wash,

310   lineated at the bottom with every stone the flash
       could reach and roll into marcation: the honeybee sings
       by the hard cactus, wings, spines, works his way up to

       the barrel-tip blossom wet, resilient with the roothair
       aperture of giving: somewhere in a dry trunk, the grog-rich
315   honey cushioning the beeswax: I see the industry of water

36

       variously dense and laden, the distributions, the little
       pools, saved lockets: the bead in the ant belly,
       the thread in a cactus vein, the reservoirs of birds'

———

eyes: the droplet concentrations: I keep thinking
320   I'm saved, a shock of mild hilarity! I keep thinking
I'm a pot eternity is dropping coins in! think,

if you will, of that: or I keep thinking these words
translate me into another body less affected by
the weather and time's clicking subtractions:

37

325   public, I have nothing to say to you, nothing: except,
look at the caterpillar under this clump of grass: it
is fuzzy: look at the sunset: it is colorful: listen:

it's hard to compete here in winter: snow makes the
broadest impression, an ineradicable eradication: slows
330   and muffles: you can hear the snow fall, a fizz: if

I cannot look at you, I can look with you: since there
is something between us, let it be a thing we share:
if there is nothing between us, I'm coming up with this:

38

by the time I got the world cut down small enough that
335   I could be the center of it, it wasn't worth having:
but when I gave up center, I found I was peripherally

no bigger than a bit: now, I have decided the former
was the better: I must re-mount the center and force
the world to subside about me: not easy and not

340   promising, but neither is surrender: still, St. Francis
said if you give up everything it's all yours: giving
up is not easy at all: why is everything so perplexing:

39

I feel in the company of the soul, however, nervous:
I grow arch and curt: I talk nasty: I wink and grunt or
345   switch to salacity: I mouth reprovables: I don't

belong here, I try to announce: I am not worthy: I say
to the soul, you know this is no place for me: I am,
besides impolite, flawed: but the soul absorbs my defense

and turns my pain into a pure form of itself, investing
350   my embarrassment with grace: I go out to the hedge bush-vine,
but there is the soul, tangled with curvature: I look at

40

the gaunt maple, but a nest is hung in it: I look
at the points of the picket fence, but there, too, the
snowflakes hold: in between, thinner than sight,

355   returns and compliances give and take: can I take this
in, I ask, stand with it, assume it: can I talk of it just
as it stalls against the garage, bends upward and outward

around the eaves, picks up a drift and walks it to the edge:
is there an accepting it so complete it vanishes, my wills
360   and motions tidings in a tide: ah, soul, I say,

41

awkwardness is being conscious of you: I will move and
do directly as I like and that way correspond to your
liking: the point is just to get this page full so I can

take it out of the typewriter and write some letters: sour
365   cream, yogurt, cottage cheese, chip dip: lizard,
lick-flicking: rancher, ranching: fly, buzzing: tiger,

———

hassling: cicada, burr-grinding: squirrel, leaping:
chicken, walking: fur, flying: day, breaking: dove,
alighting: fish, gulping: sight, seeing: nose, running:

42

370 a poem variable as a dying man, willing to try anything,
or a living man, with the consistency of either direction:
just what the mind offers to itself, bread or stone:

in the swim and genesis of the underlying reality things
assume metes and bounds, survive through the wear
375 of free-being against flux, then break down to swim and

genesis again: that's the main motion but several
interturns have been concocted to confuse it: for example,
the human self risks chaos by breaking down to a flash of

43

single cells in order to plant the full human code early
380 in the beginning: and many other continuities of pattern,
as slowed flux, work through the flux durably: adagio

in furioso: a slow bass line to a treble revel: tell
him he is lost, he will turn in there and show you what
lost is, a positive sight: tell him his iciness is perfect,

385 he will lower the cold till perfection drifts like sleep
to aimless absoluteness: tell him he is thin, he will
become so thin the spiritual will take charge: he will

44

turn into any failure abruptly as into a detour and find
his way to a highway: tell him he knows beauty,
390 he will, going and trying, disclose ugliness: virtue is

———

waiting anywhere to be by concision of dealing established:
chiefly in the virtueless: huntsman, huntsman, how many
hounds arunning: a lead-hound and a following:

breaking, moving, and filling: people who dress up like
395   artists, their art form is dressing up like artists:
the sun came up this morning without clouds before it:

45

what is it, then, that the poem is trying to give us
an image of: the ideal image of the ideal man: invariably:
the realist wants to know ideally the ideal realist: the

400   ragged man and the ragged poem aspire to ideal raggedness:
the loose or fragmented or scopy: the mind can't conceive
any way except into the desired image, the ideal, that's

the only way it works right: let there be, he said
prayerfully though he was only talking, more mass and less
405   direction, so that the propaganda cannot get off the pad

46

and the concision cannot gather to incision and the
over-simplification cannot settle real clear, accumulative
diversity a dreadnought bristling stifled guns: let

there be, he continued, orb-gathered complication, fuzzy,
410   bewildering, so that right carries a heavy bilge of wrong
and wrong looks as if it could sump out right: let—

he moved to the rostrum—certainty wallow iceberg-deep in
confusion: let nobody know very much precisely about
anything in—here, puzzled, he dozed: take that lady:

47

415   her mind is always lying down pleasing the legions: it is
a bow leant in a corner, gaunt with decommission:
how long did that last last last: it's snowing now with

the sun shining: squalls with clearings: today is Tues-
day: yesterday there were 9 hrs and 2 minutes of
420   daylight, sunup to sundown: that means light is

broadening: right here at the edge of winter-beginning's
winter-ending: today will probably be 9 hrs and 3 minutes:
tomorrow will be different, maybe 9 hrs and 4 minutes:

48

what is the prevailing tone: are there minutes of the
425   last meeting: should articles be padded with dummy
footnotes: are there any concepts to circulate: can

anyone form a motion: if we stall, will we sink:
if we run, will thinness split underfoot: the mind's
one: it pre-existed, I think: even before it was

430   mind it was mind plausible: it was the earth: when
it is fully born, it will be another earth, just like
the earth, but visionary, earth luminous with sight:

49

it will be nearly half dark: contemplation dwells on
one thing at a time: it will have lows and highs,
435   basins and high countries, peaks and abysses, naked

seabottoms and naked summits: it will have interior
circulations, crusts in slow flotation: the wind
will blow through it and rock will confront it: it

———

will be oriented to polar transactions: nothing will
440   be left out, nothing, not a thing, and yet it will be
whole: there will be islands, island chains, bays,

50

peninsulas, bottom spreads, inland seas, and mind will
have below its active surface several layers of
sedimentary history, though below that will be the

445   melts in high heat and heavy pressure, the mobility
underlying encrustation and phenomenological flux:
there is one mind and one earth: it was all there

before it was first discovered and nothing will have
been added when it is fully elaborated: and yet it is
450   completely unknown until made out: then the cosmos:

51

why does he write poems: it's the only way he can mean
what he says: you mean, say what he means: yes,
but it's harder for him to mean something than say

something: his sayings are facile, light-headed, and
455   discontinuous: he keeps saying in order to hope he will
say something he means: poems help him mean what he says:

poems connect the threads between the tuft of his head
and the true water: that's important to him, like roots
to a turf: without it, the separation would be awful:

52

460   poems deepen his attention till what he is thinking
catches the energy of a deep rhythm: then he becomes
essentially one: one in thought and motion: then, he

———

means: the recent forward brain is working with the
medulla oblongata: by the time I get to the end of this
465   all, I'll have to have found something to say to the

people: this scratching around in the private self has
to yield something beyond a private waste of time: I
have to say, here is my drop of glue, now, somebody,

53

hold the world together, or just yourself: I have to say,
470   here is a saying, binding: I must not when I get up on
the soapbox wash out: here, I will say, is my offering

to the people, these few words right at the center of my
experience of me and you: the complicated, elaborate weaving
of interconnection: I want to do well: I want people to say,

475   did you hear that, that sounded good: perhaps I will say,
the cosmos, as I understand it, wants you to have fun:
or I will say, your deepest error may be divine:

54

much have I studied, trashcanology, cheesespreadology,
laboratorydoorology, and become much enlightened and
480   dismayed: have, sad to some, come to care as much for

a fluted trashcan as a fluted Roman column: flutes are
flutes and the matter is a mere substance design takes
its shape in: take any subject, everything gathers up

around it: friend of mine is studying barbedwireology
485   and he finds you can marshal up much world and history
around the discipline: barbedwire limitations and

55

intellectual definitions produce about the same
securities and disasters: I think a lot about meter and
right away it becomes the mirror in which I see the face

490 of the times: oh, but the hierarchy of subjects persists,
sociology way above scabology, philosophy a sight beyond
toothbrushosophy: the aristocracy of learning is so much

will: I'd as soon know one thing as another, what's the
difference, it all fits and comes out the same: and I
495 can tell you, I'd rather see a tempest in a teapot

56

than Shakespeare plain: but Shakespeare was all right:
a nursemaid's lip meant as much to him as the king's eye:
but he never got it straight that in talking about the

actual king and the symbolical king he was merely
500 engaging a problem in rhetoric: well, I'm glad because
I can't reconcile the one with the many either—except

in the fuzzy land of radiant talk—and if Shakespeare grossly
surpassing me failed, I don't have to worry about surpassing
others, my place comfortable in the lowerarchy:

57

505 work's never done: the difficult work of dying
remains, remains, and remains: a brain lobe squdging
against the skull, a soggy kidney, a little vessel

smartly plugged: wrestling with one—or those—until
the far-feared quietus comes bulby, floating, glimmer-wobbling
510 to pop: so much more mechanical, physical than

—————

spiritual-seeming grief: than survivors' nights filled
without touch or word, than any dignity true for a state
of being: I won't work today: love, be my leisure:

58

there is something dwelling in too correspondent for
515   haphazardry: I read Plotinus once, a little, and
saw my mind (increased): currents, polar fads,

flash back and forth through a center apparently staid:
we may just now be getting enough lead into time to note
that nothing at all is moving except into the halfways

520   of diversion: what if at the core the final eye's
design's fixed, the vision beaming locked, we the motes
crossing about, breaking into and dropping out

59

of light: what if we're not seeking the light at all,
the transfixion (stare to stare in a bereft learning)
525   but worrying the corners of our confined, held

suasions for the exit we could, from the starved light,
choose: why has the dark taken so much if darkness is
not the satisfaction: and how have we found the will

to thrive through the light from sway to sway: O
530   Plotinus (Emerson, even) I'm just as scared as comforted
by the continuity, one sun spelling in our sun-made heads:

60

I exist by just so much as I am will-lessly borne
along: I am as given up as the boat-sloped maple leaf
on fast water: not a thing remains, not a motion's

———

535   curl, of any desire, and none of the things I desired
    and gathered are with me: I deserve nothing, not
    a glimpse into this world overbearingly rich, this

    hungry, hardly-visionable air: just as empty as I am
    is the just emptiness, not a leaf between here and
540   extinction I have not spent the night in luminous

61

    supplication with: by just so much as a tide flows in
    and lifts me floating, by just so much I can never
    grin the deathgrin at the silver abundance until I must:

    where I never came to self, repletion's an abundant
545   wind (I'm picking out the grains, gritty, between me
    and that abundance): considerable as any least

    burdockflower, I'm alive to the stalk tip: anything
    cries salvation big as capturing a waterfall: by just
    so much as I have given up, I am sustained till finally

62

550   the boat bumps solid, sucks the surface tit, and, bloated, drowns:
    today's the first of the year, icicle, cloud, root
    in a slow procedure, every house re-roofed with snow:

    the biggest numbers represent the finest differences:
    plus or minus two parts of variation in a trillion, as
555   in narrowing down on the inconstant readings of a

    fundamental constant—the mass of the electron, the
    speed of light, or the hyperfine splitting in hydrogen
    proton precessions: nature seems firm with casual

63

certainties (one could say a steel spike is a foot
560   long) but pressed for certainty breaks out
in bafflings of variability, a thousand close

measurings of the spike averaged out and a thousand
efforts to average out the variables in the instruments
of measure or in the measuring environment

565   (room temperature, humidity, the probable frequency
the door to the room is opened): recalcitrance is built
in perfectly, variations thereon perceived as possibility:

64

oh, I'm going to walk right out onto th'elision fields,
eat up gloria in the morning and have it out with her
570   in the evening: I'm going to postpone reality (but for

cheeseburgers) and focus yearning, doubly focus it,
bring into view three-dimensional hopes and hokum:
dying here sour with flesh and sweat—the disposition

of nature's bounty, a bounteous abandonment to sludge,
575   desireless, breathless: otherwise, otherwise to the limit!
if all must come down, make a high possibility for the

65

dependable work, space out an extreme differential,
an illusion for the future: the poet entangles: the
critic untangles: the poet, baited by illusion, figures

580   that massive tangling will give locus to core-tangles
and core-tangles to *the* core-tangle that will
fix reality in staid complication, at that central

———

core's center the primordial egg of truth: ah, what an
illusion: from the undifferentiated core-serum the mind
585 turns back to the definition of its tangles for rescue

66

and then back to the core for clarification, only to
hesitate in quandary's puzzlement: carefully, the critic
unwinds thread from thread, making out the energy and

translating it into ratiocination: but the untangling
590 done, all the untangling done, nothing remains but the
dumb end of the last thread and the opus of statement

that replaces it: illusion! illusion! there are not
two somethings but two nothings: one nothing surrounds,
extends beyond, the fullest entanglement, and the other

67

595 nothing is an infinitesimal dot of void at the center of
the primordial egg: inside calls to outside: in between
is the choice, an impoverishment that does away even with

the egg, or an abundance of entanglement very much like
the world but also nothing: for myself, I would rather
600 wear beads than have no neck at all: the void is the

birthplace of finches, gyrfalcons, juncos (a specialty),
snowy egrets, woodcocks, hummingbirds, crows, jays,
wood ducks, warblers, titmice, and the end of everything:

68

I dreamed Edna St. Vincent Millay's female companion
605 had just arrived on the beach of Europe and was reciting
a moving poem about why had they come back when their old

———

friends had resettled or were lying in the sod: it was
a very sad poem and the lady was sad and wrinkled:
I woke up just before crying myself, impressed with

610   the power of the poetry and life's risky changes:
the morning was cloudless, rosy with atmosphere, the sun
already brightened to appear suddenly over the sudden ridge:

69

a little philosophy never hurt anybody: or else, little
philosophy hurts everybody: takes a lot of philosophy to
615   make a little philosopher: the bubble swells and bursts,

the leavings cherishable, as being of themselves, not
devoted to an organ of use but, as with balloons, dumbly
elastic, shrunk wrinkled, and, often, highly colorful:

constituting an encounter of thing to thing: the bubble
620   bursts and then one participates in the universal energy
of biting an apple, having a tooth filled, turning a

70

corner (the friction and earth-displacement of that) so
that the universe seems available in the
gravity of a ladybug tipped down a blade of grass:

625   there's a difference between division and differentiation:
from the primal energy, much has split away into identity—
toothpicks, yew berries, jungle gyms, pole beans (the

thoughtful differentiations into bell pepper and basil)—
but a little time undercuts these matters into shape (soon
630   they will be shapelessly available again) so that division

71

is, at most, temporal—(mind & body) ha! (mind & nature) ha!
(reality & appearance) ha! (dream & fact) ha!—no, no, this
is not an expression of division, of taxonomy, dogma, bouncy

635 triadic motion, structure, solidification, type, but of
identity differentiation: one of the strongest thrusts,
you might say, is to perish away from unity the fully

discrete, expressed, captured hollybush—the lust to
individuation we've heard so much about: let me, the cry
is, stand like the drop cast back from the breaking

72

640 crest apart and regard the other satisfactory expressions
so there may be action, interaction, contrariety, and sum:
but the rise into differentiation is exactly equal

to the fall, a just compact not too friendly to the
appetite ravingly incomplete, or something, the deflections
645 into limbo: routes go awry but everything anyhow gets

safely, if reluctantly, back into circulation, the
least differentiae nearest the continuum: it's true the
splits sometimes look perfect, the divisions ghastly, severe

73

alienation an agreeing merely with temporality: but actually
650 while the leaf may not answer one's questions, it waves, a
nice language, expressive and complete: and if the ladybug,

traveling across the droppy peaks of grass, seems not my friend,
then I have not understood hanging to cool in shade; or
legs nimbly feeling for grass-hair; or any other

———

655   sight-loud talk: if I pick a leaf, it wilts: if I cap a
       spring, it swells: if I crush a grass-spear, it stains:
       if the quince crowds the hollyhock, the hollyhock

74

       bends away, suffering subtle losses of rectitude:
       what am I to say: my brotherhood's immense, and if the gods
660   have vanished that were never here I do not miss them:

       some universe comes here to my yard every day or so and bursts
       into a fly standing, with six little dents, on water: sometimes
       when I'm shaving, a real small fly, screen-penetrating, gets

       stuck in a bowl-drop of water: but he wiggles and would be all
665   right if something could be done with the whole him, floating:
       but when I touch a tissue to the drop of water, tension pulls him

75

       down, crushing him limp, so he never gets up, no matter how
       dry: a killing rescue: some things will not work: one day
       I poured brine and salt-ice from the icecream freezer onto

670   a strip of ground near the hedge: earthworms walloped up
       rampant and thrashing and then went puffy-limp and
       white: I have killed I can't tell how many thousand priceless

       moths and flies (even goldfinches and bright-streaked warblers)
       sucked up by the grill or radiator grid: all of these lives
675   had been acting in accordance with given principles, identical

76

       to my own: nothing's changed, with all the divisions
       and terrors: the physical drowns and buoys, divides and comes
       together: the bird's song-air's in my range, comes on my air:

       ————

I wrote the foregoing passage in July last year, which accounts
680   for the change of weather and some summery tone: and a
slightly longer line: winter is different, shortening:

if you believe in equivocation as a way then you
must also believe in univocation because that is one
of the possibilities of equivocation: and if you

77

685   believe all is fire why then everything is, including
the stones' dull music, solid, slow, and
cold: and the weatherless moon less is nevertheless

singing blips of meteoric bits, the flash
smirching to glistening moon-tears of solar effusions,
690   the wind, the solar wind, that pours out coronal lacings

into a great space: and then the mud by the swamp
ponds with cloud trails of crawdads scurrying is working
with little cellular thrivings: and the cool fire of

78

ferns climbing tree-footings from the deep freshets:
695   allow, allow for the cryogenic event even, low down
nearly where the atoms give up relation and drift in slow

falls, incredible, spaceless beads: that is an extreme
form of burning, say, but of the fire: I can't
help thinking that what we have is right enough, the

700   core of the galaxy, for example, a high condition,
ample, but here, though, on the surface at least,
toads, picnic tables, morning glories, firs afire:

79

the world seems to me a show closed down, a circus
left standing: the ropes slack, the loose tent
705   bellies and whomps in the wind like a scared gigantic

jellyfish: some stragglers are around but they are
turned inward on their purposelessness: they make up
directions that go nowhere: they turn missing corners:

the clown's paint has worn off: his rags have become
710   rags: his half-bald wig has become his head, his falls
have become his tricks: he now clowns to the universe:

80

now meter is interesting: the prospects are before
us: I feel the need for a realistic approach: we were
promised for today nine hours and six minutes of

715   daylight: we were promised no sunlight and received
none: but can you imagine forty degrees: we have it:
the ground is practically asplatter with eavesdropping:

there are pools under the floating mush: they are not
clearly of a depth: one must know the terrain well or
720   fill his boots: the garage, the cold garage, and the

81

porch still have six inches of snow but the house across
the way whose second floor is all under a slanting roof
is snow-free: the woods, unhung completely,

have resumed an old darkness, whereas yesterday they were
725   still irradiated with snowholdings: the sun,
invisible before, has set into another invisibility and

———

the consequences are darkening here through the clouds:
oh this little time-drenched world! how it jiggles with
flickering! light as history, as relic, light two

82

730   billion years old, moves its ancient telling through
the universe and deposits right here on my grass on a
clear night dim sediment of sizable duration: that

light can be so old and far-traveled, like flint, no
prayerstone that constant, the permanent telling of
735   that quickness: lucky that only by the equalizing instant

anything survives, lucky for us, who can thereby kiss
out time to a full reduction and know everything ravished,
burnt out in a lid's quickness: the total second:

83

sir, I told him, you have so many tones I can't tell
740   which one's prevailing: the dominant from the
predominant: you have so many, they come in chords,

tonic, subdominant, diminished: I can't tell the
significant significances from the insignificant
significances: won't you, I implored, thin out your

745   registration or, at least, give discernible direction
to your componency: it would take a battery of tonometers
just to find out about where you're at: in the

84

contextual sense: have something to say: say it:
need you spray sense and be trusted only in the spray's
750   shape: such enlargements of limitation often

fail into disorientation at the center: boo boo pee
doo: plot a course, Mr. Sulu: let's split: poetic
action mirrors human action: what preserves the

755   absurdist through the enactment of absurdity, what but
the feathery need to touch ideal absurdity: the
ideal's an imperishable validity: the illumination

85

identity takes thrust toward: it is the proposition
how we are to live our lives: the ideal hero and the
ideal anti-hero have ideality in common: heroes may

760   change ways, clothes, directions, moods, but all bear
the pressure of ideality: James, the train robber,
sublime: Appleseed, the life of service, yes:

the vacuum cleaner salesman can, in our time, hardly
give the imagination suction, gather dust into any
765   credible bag: rail splitter, spike driver, done, gone:

86

the sum of everything's nothing: very nice: that
turns the world back in on itself: such as right
when you possess everything, you'd give everything

up for a sickle pear: I hope my philosophy will turn
770   out all right and turn out to be a philosophy so as
to free people (any who are trapped, as I have been)

from seeking any image in the absolute or seeking
any absolute whatsoever except nothingness:
nothingness, far from being failure's puzzlement,

87

775   is really the point of lovely liberation, when
gloriously every object in and on earth becomes just
itself, total and marvelous in its exact scope,

able to exist without compromise out to the precise
skin-limit of itself: it allows freedom to fall
780   back from the thrust to the absolute into the world

so manifold with things and beings: the hollyhock,
what a marvel, complete in itself: the bee,
how particular, how nothingness lets him buzz

88

around: carless in Gaza, with a rocker arm on a valve
785   snapped, I to the gas station made it this morning,
left car, and by taxi so-forthed with son and wife

to University, son and wife going on beyond me to
nursery school: lunch hour nearing, I decided to
hitchhike home and did, first with a lady and baby

790   daughter all in a foreign small car, then with two
toughlooking guys from Virginia, leaned front seat
forward and let me in the back: we talked about

89

the snow, local squalls filling the air even though
the sun was shining: the driver said he had to get
795   back to Pennsylvania this afternoon: I asked if he had

snowtires and he said, No, and said he'd heard he could
get picked up if he got stuck without snowtires:
whereupon, apprehensively bound to be cheerful and useful,

———

I said when it's so cold like today the roads
800   stay dry even with the snow because the cars blow the
snow away as if it were feathers and that probably

90

he wouldn't have any trouble: just then a dog glanced
out onto the road, the driver, pushing back in his
seat, soaked on the brakes, and the car slid hardly at

805   all, verifying, as if by a universal complicity, my
faith's predictions: well, then, as we neared the
Corners, things seemed with me a little brighter, so

I said, that stop sign ahead would be perfect for me:
he would have to stop anyway, and I would know
810   immediately, if the other guy didn't open the door, that

91

I was about to be robbed, killed, or bent out of my will
which seemed about the worst thing: all went well,
ruining the story: I got out, saying thankyous and

wishingwells and walked about the mile down Hanshaw
815   home: just turning the curve in sight of home, I saw,
as in a perfect vision, my wife and son pulling up into

the driveway, driven back from nursery school in someone's
luminous stationwagon: I felt relieved: I said, ah, the
broken and divergent lines of morning are coalescing:

92

820   Wilde in some ways *contra naturam* really was: he loved
Art and set it against Nature, possibly because Art is
overwhelmed by Nature and he identified with being

———

overwhelmed: somewhat *contra mundum*, too: since
social nature had a majority against him: well, he did
825   rather well, a sort of terrier of the mind: he barked,

if mostly in the regions where opposites are clear, not
reconciled: I admire that: why think nature good if it's
against you: if it's against you, then it's hard to

93

approve even what produced you: not to approve what
830   produced you, though, bumfuzzles, since it's a kind
of suicidal vindication to hate nature in order to

love the self: how twisty things are: nature ought to
bear the blame, then, for fumbling, or society
learn to approve nature even when it fumbles, as being

835   also nature: well, I don't know what to hope in that
way, since society is also *contra naturam*, a device, a
convention: but if so how could Wilde come to love

94

convention so, I mean, convention as artifice, not the
conventional: Wilde, Art, Society, Convention—and then
840   convention damned him: that shuts off most of the roads

and suggests not detours but deadends: when a lioness
whelps a defective cub, she whomps it against the
ground till it's dead: well, I think we ought to put

ourselves above the beasts and take care to be respectful
845   where persons move: provided all persons move with
respect: we should exhaust all our virtues, first:

though it's gooseegg zero, morning sunlight hits the
strip of woods broadside and a squirrel is sitting out
pretty still on a limb taking in the direct radiation:

850   enormous jungle-like fronds of ice (and other configurations
like species) have run across possessing the outer windows
but, now, the sun up, thaw like a fungus is making dark

melts in the foliage: the sun's arc rises a little
daily into the world, marking a slightly longer
855   journey along the ridge between rising and setting:

96

yesterday afternoon, right after I had written about
the adventures of the morning, the gas station called and
said my car was ready: I had been thinking how many

days, not how many hours, it would take: so John, that's
860   his name up at Ned's Corners Station, drove the car on
down here to 606, less than a mile, and I made out a

check for him ($19.39), dropped him back at the station,
and took off for the University, free and mobilized again!
the total parts came to $7.79, 1 push rod ($1.25), 1

97

865   rocker arm ($1.35), l rocker retainer ($0.50), l set 2
gaskets @ $2.10 ($4.20), and 1 roll electrical tape ($0.49):
the total labor was $10.50: r & r (remove and repair?)

l. (left?) valve cover, r & r both valve covers, replace
rocker arm, push rod, & retainer on #4 cyl intake valve:
870   all in all I thought I got off easy: one thing interesting

———

is that Ned's Corners Station is at 909 Hanshaw Road
and I'm 606 Hanshaw Road: that's configuration:
today is, as I said, bright and cold: but 9 hrs 12 min.:

98

everyday (somedays, twice) I remember who I am and I
875   metamorphose away through several distracting transformations
till I get myself out in bidable shape on comfortable

ground, and then the shows, the transactions, carry
traces of such brilliant energy of invention that I am
half willing to admire my new self, thrust into its

880   lofty double helices, so winding: well, that's one way
to get out of the dumps, but they say it's wiser to
find the brilliants right in the dumps themselves: but on

99

the show side, there's not only the show itself, bodiless
if arresting, but the honest mechanisms that produced
885   the show: those mechanisms are earnest and work to

conserve their energy through transformations with a
greater efficiency than you can find anywhere in the
dumps: I mean, the quantity of structured mass you have

at the end is almost perfectly equal to that at the
890   beginning: on the dump, though, fire, efficient,
will achieve nothing but ash, heat, and smoke: excellent

100

change, but poor payload: or take rust, sluggish,
but it operates okay, not that you can do much with
ironic dust: the thing is to derive the *jus commune*

———

895   from the *jus singulare*: never must the *jus commune*
      breeze through eradicating the *jus singulare*: the *jus
      commune* must be merely a fall-out from happenstance:

      that way it can find some curvature (if any) with the
      actual: otherwise, the *jus commune* might become clear
900   to itself and propose imposition: never: never never:

101

      I don't think I want to be buried here in these rocky
      hills: once underground, how could I ever get my arms
      free of the silk and steel, how could I ever with those

      feet travel through the earth to my sweet home country
905   where all the flesh that bore me, back through grandfathers
      and grandmothers, lies, and my little

      brothers and my little sister I never saw, born before
      me and dying small: and where will my living sisters
      be put down, not here, and their children who might

102

910   visit me sometime to weep: but, a running weed,
      I've come off up here and started a new offshoot
      nucleus of a family and that sort of act perhaps should

      be run into the ground: I mean, extended, preserved
      into the ground: but this is phantasmagoria: death's
915   indifference will absorb living nostalgias and, anyway,

      earth's a single mother and all who lie in her are brothers
      and sisters: jungle cats and mudcats, sleek and slick:
      the other night on Hee-Haw somebody said, "slick as

103

a mudcat's fin": that's slick: poetry to the people,
920   not that they will ever acknowledge it: well, it's
night now and still fair, the moon full: the temperature

is dropping and the heater picking up: I put John's
tent together in the basement this afternoon: 8 rods
of fiberglass, connected with flexible tubes into 4

925   lengths, those then run through the sleeves, aluminum
sleeves adding support at the joints, and all brought
together at the top: a zipper door: his little house:

104

I looked up man in the dictionary and he was illustrated
and, as it turned out, chiefly muscle, a red fabric, and
930   bone, the whiteness men share: this creature, I

thought, has taken over, I know not whether because of
the freedom of the fingerbones or of the wagging, detachable
jaw, one about as gross and fine as the other: he

depends, ultimately, I thought again, on grass but, my,
935   what a transfiguration from the grass: he sees, his
vision air-clear: he tastes and feels: he thinks, ah:

105

he devours: he falls into necessities, or madnesses, only
his body can untangle: he carries in his lobed, zoned
skull earth's little supernova, the cerebral explosion,

940   somewhat in its stems and exfoliations like a mushroom
cloud: in him is ticking the californium 254 he's
detected in bombs and stars, whether still in its

———

first or some lesser half-life, unknown: but his little
explosion is growing up to equal celestial models: for
945   example, the other night the paper said two nearby

106

galaxies, hidden by our Milky Way, have been found, sight
having made other kinds of sight hunting, eating, loving
had no use for, some high conditions of burning: oh, yes,

we're *in* the explosions and we're going to see them out
950   and no other course could be half as interesting: falling
back can't help us now, returning to nature's lovely

subtle mechanisms: forward to the finish, of course, the
way it's always been or to a knowledge how to avoid the
finish: the possibility seen through to its perfect end:

107

955   the young are earnest, impatient: the older have learned
the alternatives, to be wrecked or reconciled: oh,
but it's not that easy: combinations and degrees make

life rough and rugged: yuck, yuck, the muck-sleet sings
pone the midnight windowpane, and the shattery wind
960   the shutters shudders: the confessor yanks up a belch

of privacy gone to seed: orangutans aren't groupy
as gorillas: cello alto solo pronto: if there is to be
no principle of inclusion, then, at least, there ought

108

to be a principle of exclusion, for to go with a maw at
965   the world as if to chew it up and spit
it out again as one's own is to trifle with terrible

———

affairs: I think I will leave out China, the perturbations
and continuities, transmutations and permutations of
Chinese civilization because, since that is so much,

970 giving it up's an immediate and cordial act of abasement,
betokening readiness to leave the world alone as
currently constituted (but, of course, how could words

109

do otherwise!): but I'm willing also to leave out most,
if not all, of the Amazon basin (all those trees, what
975 a whack), millions of islands I've never heard of and

some big ones I have, all ocean bottoms, all very high
places (whose spirituality blurs me), nearly all clouds
(which come and go lots before they pass through here), and,

if the population of the earth is four billion people,
980 then nearly four billion people: am I safe yet: of
course not: principles of exclusion become inclusive, etc.:

110

hiatuses, non-sequiturs, and indiligences later (nine hours
and forty-three minutes daylight) federal reorganizations
and revenue-sharings, advancings on extremely heavy

985 volume, what is everything about or anything for:
procedure's the only procedure: if things don't add
up, they must interest at every moment: a

difficulty: yesterday, severe, high-altitude winds
took our lower atmospheres in tow, making highly-compressed
990 bottom stirs, thunder at noon, one flash and blam,

111

and an even mixture of snow, rain, and sleet: zero
visibility was visible as near waves and white streams:
today is iron-fist windy and nudging zero: outside the

995   pheasant have lost all fear: they hunker down by the
picket fence, inattentive as the enemyless, or knowing
the enemy, too, must bear the cold: the ground is

assuming the curvatures of wind, flat-open places skinned
clean of snow, interruptions by fall-out being built up
to, mounds with sharp precipices, sometimes a mound

112

1000   breaking loose into strings of fast snow: I am unnerved
by openness and pure prose: the blue spruce is like
sprinkled with white crowsfeet, the inner intensive stems

branching, holding snow the needles can't: and into the
huge, round yew bush starlings light and go two-thirds
1005   under: they peck the frit of snow the wind leaves

and drink: I'm reading Xenophon's *Oeconomicus* "with
considerable pleasure and enlightenment" and with
appreciation that saying so fills this stanza nicely.

1970–1971

Eyesight

It was May before my
attention came
to spring and

my word I said
5   to the southern slopes
I've

missed it, it
came and went before
I got right to see:

10   don't worry, said the mountain,
try the later northern slopes
or if

you can climb, climb
into spring: but
15   said the mountain

it's not that way
with all things, some
that go are gone

1971

Left

Particularly near sundown
other worlds
  (dome on
dome)
5   suggest themselves to longing,

tangerine airs,
violets burnt out emeralds,

time's rush into wind sheet
as the sun nears the ridge,
10   a skinny plane slipping

at the last moment through
the thinnest rift and
away

———————

where the sun locks
15   as with a melting opening
the exact high center

of another possibility—

the self-justifying delusions
of darkening,
20   this inscrutable by clarity
& undifferentiation,

this single-centered single
dome
spent in the mind's-eye
25   gathering of peripheral sight.

1971 (1972)

The Arc Inside and Out

for Harold Bloom

If, whittler and dumper, gross carver
into the shadiest curvings, I took branch
and meat from the stalk of life, threw

away the monies of the treasured,
5   treasurable mind, cleaved memory free
of the instant, if I got right down

shucking off periphery after periphery
to the glassy vague gray parabolas
and swoops of unnailable perception,

10   would I begin to improve the purity,
would I essentialize out the distilled
form, the glitter-stone that whether

the world comes or goes clicks gleams
and chinks of truth self-making, never
15   to be shuttered, the face-brilliant core

stone: or if I, amasser, heap shoveler,
depth pumper, took in all springs and
oceans, paramoecia and moons, massive

buttes and summit slants, rooted trunks
20   and leafages, anthologies of wise words,
schemata, all grasses (including the

tidal *Spartinas*, marginal, salty
broadsweeps) would I finally come on a
suasion, large, fully-informed, restful

25   scape, turning back in on itself, its
periphery enclosing our system with
its bright dot and allowing in nonparlant

quantities at the edge void, void, and
void, would I then feel plenitude
30   brought to center and extent, a sweet

easing away of all edge, evil, and surprise:
these two ways to dream! dreaming them's
the bumfuzzlement—the impoverished

diamond, the heterogeneous abundance
35   starved into oneness: ultimately, either
way, which is our peace, the little

arc-line appears, inside which is nothing,
outside which is nothing—however big,
nothing beyond: however small, nothing

———

40   within: neither way to go's to stay, stay
          here, the apple an apple with its own hue
          or streak, the drink of water, the drink,

          the falling into sleep, restfully ever the
          falling into sleep, dream, dream, and
45   every morning the sun comes, the sun.

1971 (1971)

SPHERE: THE FORM OF A MOTION (1974)

❧

For Harold Bloom

I went to the summit and stood in the high nakedness:
the wind tore about this
way and that in confusion and its speech could not
get through to me nor could I address it:
5   still I said as if to the alien in myself
        I do not speak to the wind now:
for having been brought this far by nature I have been
brought out of nature
and nothing here shows me the image of myself:
10   for the word *tree* I have been shown a tree
and for the word *rock* I have been shown a rock,
for stream, for cloud, for star
this place has provided firm implication and answering
        but where here is the image for *longing*:
15   so I touched the rocks, their interesting crusts:
I flaked the bark of stunt-fir:
I looked into space and into the sun
and nothing answered my word *longing*:
        goodbye, I said, goodbye, nature so grand and
20   reticent, your tongues are healed up into their own
element
and as you have shut up you have shut me out: I am
as foreign here as if I had landed, a visitor:
so I went back down and gathered mud
25   and with my hands made an image for *longing*:
        I took the image to the summit: first
I set it here, on the top rock, but it completed
nothing: then I set it there among the tiny firs
but it would not fit:
30   so I returned to the city and built a house to set
the image in
and men came into my house and said
        that is an image for *longing*
and nothing will ever be the same again

Sphere: The Form of a Motion

1

The sexual basis of all things rare is really apparent
and fools crop up where angels are mere disguises:
a penetrating eye (insight), a penetrating tongue (ah),

a penetrating penis and withal a penetrating mind,
5   integration's consummation: a com- or intermingling of parts,
heterocosm joyous, opposite motions away and toward

along a common line, the in-depth knowledge (a dilly),
the concentration and projection (firmly energized) and
the ecstasy, the pay off, the play out, the expended

10   nexus nodding, the flurry, cell spray, finish, the
haploid hungering after the diploid condition: the reconciler
of opposites, commencement, proliferation, ontogeny:

2

often those who are not good for much else turn to thought
and it's just great, part of the grand possibility, that
15   thought is there to turn to: camouflagy thought flushed

out of the bush, seen vaguely as potential form, and
pursued, pursued and perceived, declared: the savored
form, the known possession, knowledge carnal knowledge:

the seizure, the satiation: the heavy jaguar takes the
20   burro down for a foreleg or so: then, the lighter,
though still heavy, vultures pull and gulp: then, the

tight-bodied black crows peck and scratch: then ants
come out and run around the structure, picking bits:
finally, least bacteria boil the last grease mild:

3

25 so the lessening transformers arrive at the subtle condition
fine, the spiritual burro braying free, overwhelming
the hairy, and so must we all approach the fine, our

skinny house perpetual, where in total diminishment we will
last, elemental and irreducible, the matter of the universe:
30 slosh, slosh: vulnerability is merely intermediate: beyond

the autopsy and the worm, the blood cell, protein, amino acid,
the nervous atom spins and shines unsmirched: the total,
necessary arrival, the final victory, utterly the total loss:

we're haplessly one way the wrong way on the runway:
35 conglomerates, tongues or eyes or heel strings that
keep us, won't keep: we want to change without changing

4

out of change: actually, the imagination works pretty
diagrammatically into paradigm so one can "see things":
and then talk fairly tirelessly without going astray or

40 asunder: for me, for example, the one-many problem figures
out as an isoceles triangle (base:diversity and peak:unity)
or, even, equilateral, some rigor of rising: and this is

not to be distinguished from the center-periphery thing, in
that if you cut out a piece of pie from the center-periphery
45 circle, you have a triangle, a little rocky, but if you

cut off the arc, it sits up good, as (peak:center:unity)
and (base:periphery:diversity): actually, one could go even
so far as (peak:center:symbol:abstraction), etc., and the other:

5

50 this works in the bedrock, too, or undifferentiated gas:
one feels up the two legs of the possibility and, ever
tightening and steered, rises to the crux, to find

there the whole mystery, the lush squeeze, the centering
and prolongation: so much so that the final stone
never locks the peak but inlet:outlet opens unfolding

55 into nothingness's complete possibility, the strangling
through into the darkness of futurity: it is hard at this
point to avoid some feeling, however abstract the circumstance:

if one can get far enough this way where imagination
and flesh strive together in shocking splendors, one can
60 forget that sensibility is sometimes dissociated and come:

6

I wouldn't be surprised if the radiance we talk about isn't
that part of the structureless lust that rising from the
depths gets by all the mechanisms of mediation and, left over,

feels like religion, the heights visited; that is, the route
65 from energy to energy without frigging, an untainted source
with an untainted end: when the professor rises to require

structure in the compositions, he invokes a woman: he wants
shapeliness intact, figure shown forth: dirty old
man hawking order and clarity: but if he would not

70 be dark, what a brightness! though I am not enjoying the
first day of spring very much, it is not with me as it is
with my friend George, spending his first spring in the grave:

7

windbaggery, snag-gaggling, yakety-yak, fuss: if you dig
a well, steen it well: earth's fluid: it moves: any
75   discontinuity imposed, opposing the normal intermingled sway,

must be chocked full of resistance: and with a well, one
can't count on the mechanisms that stay by yielding to the
sway: but if a well, steened well, can stay, it can be

caused to bring together the truly fluid from the so-so:
80   precise imposition leading to separation, an unmuddling of
clarity, a purification and cleansing invested with identity:

from bunkum and hoarse gol-danging surgical nicety can remove
a truth's modest pleasantry: between the mixtures and
distinctions, what is economy to prefer: a cheap bulk of

8

85   slush or a costly drop to drink: it is a choice imposition
imposes: for myself I'm tempted to let the well
cave in at times and the water stand to my thirst: I

never did like anything too well done, a scary invitation
to catastrophe: a bright challenge to the insuperable forces:
90   let it all mosey: there is no final resistance: nor any

endless going along: if nothing in us, under us, or around us
will redeem us, we'd better get used to the miseries: at least,
unbuffaloed about the outcome: well, make the well well or

don't: (it has never occurred to me to face the terror but
95   as to how to hide from it, I'm a virtual booth of information):
come to think of it I don't have much smell in my works:

9

though the surface is crisp with pattern still we know
that there are generalized underlyings, planes of substratum
lessening from differentiation: under all life, fly and

100   dandelion, protozoan, bushmaster, and ladybird, tendon
and tendril (excluding protocellular organelles) is the same
cell: and under the cell is water, a widely generalized

condition, and under that energy and under that perhaps the
spirit of the place: if we sink we go awash: so
105   thanks for the surface if also for the deeps: but if we

pass through the discrete downward to the general, may we
not also pass upward, to the high syntheses of overlyings
and radiances, and may it not be so, extremes meeting, that

10

the heights and depths somewhere join in a near-complete
110   fizzle of the discrete: on either side well-boundaried
by the impassable, our selves float here, as

safely as duration allows, time in its stew mixing as much as
unmixing: I could not say, then, that the earthworm is not
my radical cousin, and I could not say that my veins entering

115   along the cell walls disresemble the transportative leaf:
I mean, if one speaks of mysticism, it makes good science,
which is the best part of science, that it makes mysticism

discussable without a flurry: and yet, too, the discrete
annihilated, suddenly here it is, blandished and available:
120   things go away to return, brightened for the passage:

11

desk chair, wheel-back side chair, armchair, country
corner chair, bedside commode, side table, pad-foot
side table, lowboy, credence table, console, drop-leaf

table, writing table, armoire, refectory table, ladder
125   chair, washstand, pedestal table, tilt-top supper table,
oak coffer, dining chair, settle, bedside table, bureau,

serving table, chest, slant-front bureau, chest-desk,
bureau desk, spindle-back dining chair, kettle table,
corner table, bookcase, chiffonier: in the furniture

130   of the mind, diversity pushed into distinction is enabling,
a pleasant calculation of possibility: the same can be
said for footwear, glassware, software, and willowware:

12

they say when egalitarianism is legislated into ultimate
ramification, legislation and effect click
135   heels into totalitarianism: the smoothest sailing's in

a canal, the water as if abstracted out of itself, slack, mere,
unresisting, aerial: while anything you tried to send
down a ravine of boulders would be substantially altered,

even something as compliant, accommodating, as water,
140   rushed, stirred, whitened, and sprayed, anything more
got-up, say a watermelon, likely to be finished: anyone

who knows sharp lakewater or blasted bay water or
open sea water knows where he wants to sail, prizing the
choppy, difficult, and swift: I do not smooth into groups:

13

145   the shapes nearest shapelessness awe us most, suggest
       the god: elemental air in a spin, counterclockwise
       for us, lets its needlepoint funnel down and gives us

       a rugged variety of the formless formed: and the great
       slow stir of the Sargasso cycles the weed in, a holding,
150   motion's holding: snow from snow kicks up in a fume

       and sprinkles audibly the stripped lilac shrubs: the
       shape of air, deep as material, blunt off a cliff face: fire
       as it crowns out over forests and clings to

       itself exploding as if into a new fire: the gods near
155   their elemental or invisible selves turn or sweep or
       stand still and fill us with the terror of apprehending:

14

       wood, though, a log, rigid with shape, seems
       innocent and meek, accepted, trivial: even starlings,
       grazing in a dark patch, move as a bunch, single flights

160   out or in a small percentage of the potential: the
       ashtray sits with a flat, notched containment, powerless:
       shape, definition, ease: thank the gods for those

       though only the least gods will take them on or those
       gods are least who do: but the real gods, why talk
165   about them, unavailable: they appear in our sight when they

       choose and when we think we see them whole, they stall
       and vanish or widen out of scope: the highest god
       we never meet, essence out of essence, motion without motion:

15

170 in the generations and becomings of our minds, anthologies,
good sayings are genes, the images, poems, stories
chromosomes and the interminglings of these furnish beginnings

within continuities, continuities within trials, mischances,
fortunate forwardings: gene pool, word hoard: the critic
samples the new thing, he turns it over in his consideration,

175 he checks alignments, proportions, he looks into the body of
the anthology to see if the new thing hooks in, distorts, to raise
or ruin: he considers the weight, clarity, viability of

the new thing and reconsiders the whole body of the anthology:
if the new thing finds no attachment, if energy, cementing,
180 does not flow back and forth between it and the anthology,

16

it dies, withered away from the configuration of the people:
but if it lives, critic and teacher show it to the
young, unfold its meaning, fix its roots and extend its reach:

the anthology is the moving, changing definition of the
185 imaginative life of the people, the repository and source,
genetic: the critic and teacher protect and reveal the source

and watch over the freedom of becomings there: the artist
stands freely into advancings: critic and teacher choose, shape,
and transmit: all three need the widest opening to chance

190 and possibility, so perceptions that might grow into currents
of mind can find their way: all three are complete men,
centralists and peripheralists who, making, move and stay:

17

groups form—it's natural—agglutinations, a center shaping,
a core center of command and focus: group attaches to group,
195   some slight delimitation still distinguishing them, and region

to region, till a public is formed, however tenuous and
widespread the binding syrup now: my sympathies do not move
that way, building toward the high consolidation (except in

poems), the identifying oneness of populations, peoples: I
200   know my own—the thrown peripheries, the stragglers, the cheated,
maimed, afflicted (I know their eyes, pain's melting amazement),

the weak, disoriented, the sick, hurt, the castaways, the
needful needless: I know them: I love them: I am theirs:
I can't reach them through the centers of power: the centers

18

205   of power aim another way from them: I reach them out in the
brush in the rangeful isolation, night: I touch them: I
turn my face into the rock walls and say sayings: the rock

jiggles with magic: the black grass burns darkness, fries:
the brush dances: I do the ones I love no good:
210   I hold their pain in my hands and toss it in moonlight:

it multiplies and sparkles: I attack trees and wrestle
them to the ground: I roll rocks into heaps and pull the heaps
down: come, I say, with morning, this is the exact specification

of the account: the leg is inflamed: the tooth is aching:
215   the mind gathers and dissolves, the water is both fast and
deep, the branches are picked clean, but saying is becoming day:

19

oh, it's spring, and I'm more transparent than ever:
I heard the white-breasted nuthatch gurble over the trunk
bark today, and tonight everything is so clear it's

220 going down to zero: my idealism's as thin as the sprinkled
sky and nearly as expansive: I don't love anybody much:
that accounts for my width and most of my height: but

I love as much as I can and that keeps me here but light:
everything is so plain: death is lake-space, crystal dusk:
225 (a morning following, the poet still alive but with

a headache, a toothache, a throatache, a jawache, and a
backache, forges on)—though the snow on the lawn has
receded into a numerous archipelago of small valleys and

20

though the boughs on the south side of the blue spruce
230 hang calm in a heat-holding of the bright sun and though
the garage eave is letting the snow down in a linear rain

still I am not high on the bestseller lists, the Wonderful
Award is gradually being given to someone else (more
deserving) and the money's pouring out: funny, when we

235 were oriented geocentric (with our heads in the harmonious
skies) we became unsettled by locating vaster centers but
made a rescue by bringing our heads down to a geocentric

identity with the earth, the core-mind of the hot moving
metals, the swimming transitional zone between core and
240 solidification, and then, of course, the discrete, cool

21

variegated surface: from a large threat, a concise retreat:
a woman in black dress and gray apron spreads mayonnaise
on a slice of bread: the knife glimmers pushing the pliant

ridge before it: there is lettuce but not much light to see
245   by: maybe ham-and-lettuce-with-mayonnaise (I sometimes
order that): the woman talks softly but urgently to a

heavier woman beside her: they are discussing how the
sandwich is to be made: the procedure is scheduled and, step
by step, must be done right: the dead man who will accompany

250   the sandwich is either in the next room in a box or right
in the kitchen, which could explain why the women whisper:
he does not yet know he is dead: he wakes underground,

22

feels around for the sandwich: he rises to eat or just
goes back to sleep: or the ham-and-lettuce crackle and
255   squish in loud teeth and generate light for the eyes: a

new world appears: light that he can move in swells: are
the women done with the sandwich: is it time to tighten
the lid: last-minute placements, arrangements: has the trip

started: I think of the box, the closure underground: I do
260   not trust the lettuce: eyes of the dead open later in the
dark: I wake: but sail, sail on, oblate spheroid,

feather-light at center, snug about floating dimensions, speed
like a wish in the vacuum, even though for 46 years the
redbird has been red, dropped stones have fallen, beans have

23

265   twined (counterclockwise, again) up the stakes, merry-go-rounds
       have maintained an exhilarating, centrifugal verge: it may
       be the mind can wear out the earth: what a put-down

       for the enterprising, inventive earth: an empty mind on a
       bleached planet: bet on the void: but, of course, nature
270   sheds deadwood and spins commencements out, tendrils,

       surprised to be here and looking forward: a hell of
       a way to keep fresh: you could wish nature would accept the
       challenge to keep us here and keep us entertained: the mind

       has come up with some interestingly inexhaustible quandaries,
275   at least, nodes resistant, wherein as you go in you come
       out, presumably the only stillness a nothingness at the

24

       center: a good task for those so minded who would not prefer
       to be out regarding waves: bugus ecstaticus: hocus focus:
       some things should be forgotten on the grounds that they

280   aren't worth remembering: coelum empyreum that dries up gods
       into luminosities, radiances cooling into sightlessness:
       brine, dearth, desolation, sand, the grand circulation, the

       lesser circulations trivial, the fireball shrinking and
       swelling—bells rung apart from the savagery of a tune, the
285   word bells of dissonance between the harmonious keys—(play

       up the other side a bit, too, some other time), sprite of
       falls, now nothing inspires gladness in breaking water: some
       things are discrete (who stores gathers thieves) if not

25

dichotomous: but if I back off to take the shape of a tree
290   I gather blurs: when does water seeping into the roothairs
pass the boundary after which it is tree: the light, the

surrounding, penetrating, shading light, at what aural
remove from the actual leaf does light cease to be tree: or
do the tree boughs linger all the way into the sun: when

295   the leaves fall, as they are falling now in shoals of variable
intensities, when does the wind have them and the tree give
them up: is the high syrup invisible moving under, through,

and by discretions our true home, not these bodies so much
change makes and ends: but dichotomy, no: I can't divide
300   structure and function: as one loosens, the other fades:

26

we want to go home and exist in a quietude like merriment
but we can't go home as ourselves but wearing the faces
of many answering things until, faceless, we can't tell we're

home because we are: here in a closing house, we have the
305   self to have, wherein, however, dreams of home come and go
as with foreigners and exiles: from implacability and

quandary we make shabby or golden peace: pain at the end will
move us like a willing rocket away: short of the cycle of
the natural ongoing is the human, a stream broken, bent,

310   stalled, re-begun that began back with the first transmissible
molecule and is sticking to time and motion still: if one
adds a point of light to the ongoing mind, one exists with,

27

lodges, a preserved energy, ever able to give energy off,
a great peculiarity, the only immortality known: it is a
315   real translation but the body dies away from it and even

the species must go by going or changing out of itself:
nothing the biggest subject, total comprehension is
a wipe-out: but if one adds a point of light to ongoing

mind, the point may lock a right angle, righteous with
320   rigidity, the identity firm but unavailable to accommodation:
but one's point of light may be a worm wriggling away at

a coordinate constant—destructive creativity: it is not
possible to make an altogether favorable decision: the
rightest mind is shadowed by leftovers' dark carriages,

28

325   the unadducible, the small haunting that tilts
rightmindedness toward the possible: protected from
mental congealing, having finished the pyramid, one recalls

the circle: everything is so clear: the round yew (or
whatever it is) that sits on the lawn like a big green
330   beachball reacted immediately to coolish weather by

reddening in the berries, and then gangs of cedar waxwings
(maybe it's a cedar) came through and softening up to the
bush, a mellow beating, took the berries, but the softening

is because the bush is, however hard-limbed inside,
335   peripherally limber, so the birds combine wingy air with
alighting carefully: when they've fed, they can fly off hard

29

and fast: ecstatic as mating, the transforming's pleasing:
a windy dusk, the clouds low and running, the maple leaves
picking up yellow glows, citron pellucidity: spirits

340 loosen from the ground: unremembered and unresolved are
coming back, breaking free, flapping and gnashing, spooking
the bones of the milling trees, some leaves letting go

skittering streetlight black dances: cats twist frying in
the wind: keep low: the hedges move: there's a lit door:
345 hello: we're pirates: how can and how long can an identity

hold to the skin of the earth: day before yesterday was
brisk windy, blustery, and a lot of leaves fell, some of
them not quite ready couldn't hold on, and I said if it's

30

calm tomorrow (which was yesterday) not a leaf will fall:
350 you know the casual fall when a leaf comes off over nothing:
extremity can move ahead of time: but by today others had

mellowed at the pedicel, ready to unclasp to zephyrs: I'm
in touch with spirits: squeaky she-devils, flapping jacks,
batty left-overs: listen: I know Matthew Arnold is not

355 far off: he's going to come roaring out of the woods, deeply
offended by the briars and limber limbs, and mount up on a
high stone chair and declaim to the woods: he's going to

reinaugurate the distinctions and subordinations that make
sense: he's going to turn the lofty lofty and broad and
360 force the minuscule into its residence: we're going to climb

31

up the low belly of this sow century, through the seventies,
eighties, right on upward to the attachments, the anterior
or posterior fixation, anything better than the swung pregnancies

of these evil years: considering the fluxions, radiations,
365   drifts, malleabilities, considering chance and random (what
could be more just than that a united world take its power

from and bring its power to the person—the widest sweep of
unity taking definition and meaning from the unit) (the pheasants
neck-nicking walk out of the snowthickets and explode over

370   the white paling fence away: it's afternoon, gray, snow:
the eavesdrops a much-intervaled music, alive, unintentioned,
scraggly): considering sensations, rampaging difficulties,

32

poor assessments, it's hard to draw a line, the careful,
arrogant, arbitrary imposition, the divider that blocks off
375   and sets apart, the arising of difference and distinction:

the discrete a bolus of slowed flux, a locus of depressed
reaction rates, a boned and fibered replication: slowed
but not stopped (heightened within its slows): on the instant

of cessation, disintegration's bacteria flare: bloom, puff,
380   and blow with change: much energy devoted to staving off
insweeps of alteration: to slow, defer, to chew up change

into the materials of slowing: until the body, increasingly
owed, is paid: take the mind's radiant works, the ground
changes under them: they lift off into distraction: one

33

385   needs clarities to know what one is baffled by, the small
left- and righthandedness: suppose one saw the nonsupportive
clearly: how could the mind, lit up and possessed, find

energy for salvation's befuddlement: to confront nothingness,
the best baffler, is to disengage monsters and prevent
390   lofty identifications: to be saved is here, local and mortal:

everything else is a glassworks of flight: a crystal
hankering after the unlikely: futures on the next illusion:
order is the boat we step into for the crossing: when we

step out, nothingness welcomes us: inspiration spends through:
395   by the snowroad the boulder floats afire: fir-bark,
skittering under a startled squirrel, falls in flames

34

rattling and flecks the burning snow: the moundhill wintered
lean lifts a shackling of cindery trees into the element
unending: the stream, drawing radiance, collects and casts

400   the light, kindled glancing: mania dries with ash, the
oppressed grows weightless: doze/n th/rough c/and/or man/aged
leg/ions stud/ents: in hill-gold sun, mock orange branches

swim windy shadows, like lean fish in glass, against the
windowpanes: a golden dream swims with the light, schools
405   of thoughts turning, bunching, heading down, up: nothing is

wrong: all is carrying over: the windowpanes flow with shapes,
fish in a glassen clarity: snowsqualls interrupt but return
the shaking moment: the dream sets off for the sufficient journey:

35

the safety engineers complain that the people are numb
410   along the fault line and will not survive if they do not
respond to warning signals: maybe so: but how

have we survived at all but by numb nonchalance: to know
and care is to take victory out of the moment when a
moment's victory is what everything is for, apparently:

415   still, there's no sense in being stupid: floors can
collapse, flopping pancakes, and too much wavering,
even, in the heights can bring files and bookshelves down

on folks: does just a little forethought so diminish the
impulse: must the stadiums, gymnasiums, and grade schools
420   be put right on the line: still the people know: a

36

few thousand can be spared, but life can't be compromised:
there are so many dangers and possibilities of danger that
even if you entertained them one at a time you'd still be

numb to most of them: but there's no need to be perversely
425   careless: according to the World Book, the Jabiru wades
the swamps of South America, and the Jaçana's a relative of,

or looks a lot like, the gallinule, of which I, in a recent
unpublished poem, spoke briefly: *I* which suggests *eye*
really derives from a symbol for the hand: and *K* stands

430   for the palm or open hand: and *J*, you know, is just another
form of *I*: that whole IJK cluster is one of my favorites
in the alphabet, and I specially like the JK vol of the WB:

37

you take me: I never used the word *rink* in my work nor
tosh as in *turgid tosh* nor *slipup, backswing, tocsin,*
435   *discinct, skin-flint, razzmatazz*: thank the Lord:

if the world wears out, there are still shenanigans left in
the lingo, more compiled than the world around here which
is mostly winter: but the old quince bush looking like

a mess of last year's baling wire is putting out the redbud
440   so much that the dry intertwining morning glory vine is
starting to look ridiculous: but those vines outlined so

many beginnings of snow last fall and this spring! and
may yet again so outline the snow, that is, provide a
catchment with configuration no different from the

38

445   catch itself: most of our writers live in New York City
densely: there in the abstractions of squares and glassy
floors they cut up and parcel out the nothingness they

think America is: I wish they would venture the rural and
see that the woods are undisturbed by their bothering
450   reputations and that the brooks have taken to flowing

the way they always have and that the redwing pauses
to consider his perch before he lights in a cedar:
I never saw more birds than this cold spring: they are

intervaled foliages to the branchy bushes and trees, so
455   many comings-in and flyings-out summer and winter mix
in a minute: I don't know their names, leaves that make

39

their own wind of shrieks and whistles: but there's a
bluish small roll of garden wire in the edge of the woods
that shows no sign of sprouting, however naturalized,

460   the robin striking leaves over by it and staring: leave
it there long enough, it will start to function, a
protective tangle, a harbor or arbor to centipede or

vine, a splinterer of gusts: Apollo 16 just blasted
off: it's 1400 miles downrange at 16,000 mph, orbit
465   established: a stirring bit of expenditure there in the

blastoff into freefall's silent, floating speed: hurry back,
boys: look out your window at North America: I'm right
under that big cloud: it hasn't budged in six months:

40

John and I drove out to check the paint job on the propjet,
470   Mohawk merging with Allegheny and losing its emblems and
identifications, such as colors, black and gold, and the

head of the Indian chief on the tail assembly, to the white
and blue streaks, with red lettering, of Allegheny: as
part of his commitment to the baggage man, John stood out

475   by the wire fence in the pouring rain until the second
engine started to spin and the passenger door went up: then
we stood under a shelter with our hands over our ears while

the plane taxied out on the runway: just then it occurred
to me how much I dislike weekends and how pleasant it would
480   be to pull Sundays in particular out of the calendar and

41

add a longish month to June: this measure, maw, can grind
up cancers and flourish scarfs of dandelions, manage the
pulp of hung ticks and be the log the stream flows against

for a whole year: its mesh can widen to let everything
485   breeze through except the invisible: it can float the
heaviest-bloodied scalding dream and sail it into the high

blue loops of possibility: it can comprise the dull
continuum of the omnium-gatherum, wait and wait, without
the alarm of waiting, getting as much being out of motion

490   as motion out of being: multiple and embracing, sweet
ingestion, the world bloat, extension pushed to the popped
blossoming of space, the taking of due proportion's scope:

42

I think my problems no classier than anyone else's, though:
closure ends all shows, the plain strict and the frowzy
495   brilliant: and if we go, separately but all together,

to nondistinction, we might as well make as much distinction
here as we can: the proud fall, right, but the great fall
came before, and when one knows he's going out, can we

blame him for shoving the voltage up: I wake in the morning
500   fairly level with the tide: the dust feels right on my
tongue: but in no time a trifle or two, tardy toast, ice

on the windshield, the crusty vestments of day, I veer off
into classic compensation, a vision or two shot anger-high,
a little gilded scaffolding toward unreal floors, so I get

43

505 home at night and go to bed like a show folding: it's
great to get back in the water and feel time's underbuoys,
the cradling saliences of flux, re-accept and rock me off;

then, in nothingness, sinking and rising with everyone not
up late: the plenitude: it's because I don't want some
510 thing that I go for everything: all the people asleep with

me in sleep, melted down, mindlessly interchangeable,
resting with a hugeness of whales dozing: dreams nudge us
into zinnias, tiger lilies, heavy roses, sea gardens of

hysteria, as sure of sunlight as if we'd been painted by
515 it, to it: let's get huzzy dawn tangleless out of bed,
get into separateness and come together one to one: you

44

who are showless and self-full, be generous, come by, offer
me a chat: I'd trade my shows in any day for the real thing:
meanwhile, amusement, a waiting amusement, is my study—I

520 hope you will take it at no other level: this measure moves
to attract and hold attention: when one is not holding one,
that is a way of holding: dip in anywhere, go on until the

attractions fail: I angle for the self in you that can be
held, had in a thorough understanding: not to persuade you,
525 enlighten you, not necessarily to delight you, but to hold

you: the lofty, shot high by constraint, adopt the rigor
of scary levitation, grow icy by the swirl of fear as much
as by the vacant, sizable view, but sometimes imagine they

45

are flying: but the mirrorments, astonishments of mind,
530 what are they to the natural phenomena, the gross destructions
that give life, we cooling here and growing on a far outswing

of the galaxy, the soaring, roaring sun in its thin-cool
texture allowing us, the moon vacant though visitable, Mars
not large enough to hold an air, Venus too hot, so much

535 extravagance of waste, how can the bluegreen earth look
purposeful, turn a noticeable margin to meaning: what are
mirrorments, then, so shatterable, liable to melt, too

much light, the greasy graying of too much time: man waited
75,000 years in a single cave (cold, hunger, inexplicable
540 visitation of disease) only to rise to the bright, complex

46

knowledge of his destruction! that heaviness weighs down,
lacking an interpenetrating spiritual float: but were men,
starting out three million years ago, calling up to us:

if they were not able to call up to us, what was in them able
545 to call them up: what was the hidden, interior elixir that
glided them along the ground, gave them the speech of staring

into their dumfounded hands: or did they turn in each day's
light, storming the world for food and place, merely and
sufficiently: when we have made the sufficient mirror will

550 it have been only to show how things will break: know thyself
and vanish! and the knowledge not for itself or the self
but so the ambience may call itself vacantly expressed,

47

fully exfoliated, empty! sunrise this morning was not
a fraction: it was self-full, whole in motion: the man
555   falling asleep in the cave winters of time ago swayed

into the fullness, assumed the measure: we are as in a
cone of ages: each of us stands in the peak and center
of perception: around us, in the immediate area of recent

events, the planets make quickly-delivered news and the sun
560   acquaints us of its plumes eight minutes old: but then
the base widens dropping back and down in time through

the spinal stars of spirals and deepens broadening into
the core of our configuration with its ghostly other side:
and then the gulfs and deepenings begin and fall away

48

565   through glassy darkness and shadowy mind: antiquity on
antiquity the removes unveil, galaxies neighbors and foreign
cousins and groups of galaxies into the hazy breadths and

depths the telescope spells its eye to trace: but here
what took its beginning in the farthest periphery of event,
570   perception catches the impact of and halts to immediacy,

the billion-year-old flint light striking chemical changes
into the eye: behold: the times break across one
another like waves in surfy shoals and explode into the

white water of instantaneous being: each of us stands in
575   the cone of ages to collect the moment that breaks the
deeper future's past through: each of us peak and center:

49

who owns nothing has everything and who owns something
has that: snow's a reservoir spring springs with leaks,
interminglings of onrush and withholding: how close *middle*

580   comes to the middle of the dictionary: make a mighty
force, that of a god: endow it with will, personality, whim:
then, please it, it can lend power to you: but then you

have created the possibility of its displeasure: what you
made to be greater than you is and enslaves you and then
585   suppose trying to be free again you begin upward desperate

identifications until those identifications enlarge beyond
you and terrify you and move you out of the frame of actual
gestures: take my advice: the forces are there all right

50

and mostly beyond us but if we must be swayed by the forces
590   then at least let's be the only personalities around, the
sort of greatness a raft in a rapids is and at the top

let's put nothingness, good old: the most open suasion:
a darkness in the method, a puzzling, obfuscating surface,
is the quick (and easy) declaration of mystery, with the risk,

595   though, that should the method come plain, be made out, the
mystery, surficial, its elements jumbled, would disappear,
unless, of course, under the quick establishment of difficult

method the true mystery survived: it's not necessarily true
that things left to themselves go to pieces: without the help
600   of human hand, for example, far from the scaffolding of the

51

human imagination, old (presumed) Chaos stirred in himself,
spirals (cellular whirlwinds), upward swoops of bending aspiration,
collisions high with potentials of linkage, dissolvings and

meldings lengthy and free—these "motions" brought particles
605   into progression often: if the progressions often failed into
tatterdemalions, do-funnies, whatchamacallits, and thingumbobs,

there was time enough in the slow motions of landforms, oceans,
of moon and sun for Chaos to undo and recommence: certain
weaves caught on to random hooks and came into separation and

610   identity: and found ways to cause the causes of origin to
recur with increasing frequency: one must be careful not to bestow
intention where there may have been no more (much) than jostling

52

possibility: keep jiggling the innumerable elements and
even integrations can fall out of disintegrations: in any case,
615   physicochemical phenomena account sufficiently for the

output up to now: but all movements are religious: inside
where motions making up and rising turn about and proceed,
node and come to pass, prayer is the working in the currents,

hallelujahs dive and sculp the mud, mazes of mud melting away
620   from the slurpy lifting loads: when the mob goes wild and thrashes
a bit copulating, shaking the bushes, it is moving in service:

when one screams in terror of the Most High, he is asserting
his hunger for the merely usual and mortal, for the circum-
scription of place: the polar bear snarling or running,

53

625   diving or sleeping, attunes to the accuracy of the imperative:
sketchiness and incompleteness, broken gestures, stuttering
intentions, fact blanching and breaking fiction, seizures

of cold and pied heat, these are prayerful realizations of
disorientation, holy efforts to accept or change: nothing,
630   not even the least (the half-step or stalled intention) is

without the rigor of knowing: how to be saved: what is
saving: come to know the motions with what rightness, accuracy,
economy, precision they move and identify the motions of the

soul with them so as to find the self responsive to and in
635   harmony with the body of motions: morality is not a judgment
on action but acting rightly, truly—total, open

54

functioning: how to make the essential fashionable is the
problem without promoting boredom for there is little variation
day to day in the essential and, worse, when the fashionable

640   hangs on it loses the quality of the fashionable: of course
we are sure that the fashionable relates only peripherally
to the essential so that it is nearly certain that to be

fashionable is not to be essential: there is the aspect,
though, of change that it is constant so that always to be
645   fashionable is to participate in the lasting: problems

problems: the essential without specification is boring
and specification without the essential is: both ways out
leaves us divided but so does neither way: unless—and here

55

650
is the whole possibility—both essential and fashionable can
be surrounded in a specified radial essential, which is difficult:
imagining withered conditions (for company), I think of

settled bulk, the ancient bristlecone, a sprout surviving
fanny: down South there: when they want to say *magnificent* they
say most-maggie-went-a-fishing: does'em good: have atchoo

655
and a couple of belches: when I was a freckle-faced boy, said
they warn't no freckles but fart bran from following cows:
said I was a redheaded woodpecker: I was redheaded: I been

humiliated: now, I'm a redheaded, woody pecker: stand
up, stand up for beauty, thou soldier of the breechjammed hole,
660
garrison gates, thou wayfarer upon the breastworks and

56

ramparts (ram parts), thou regular maker of meter, convivial iamb,
sleuthy sluice: halt, hut, two: what we believe in requires no
believing: if the axe falls on the toe, severance will

follow promptly: put the burner on Hi the coffee will boil:
665
push down the fence it will no longer be standing: walk off
the cliff, air greets you: so much we do not need to

be urged to believe, we're true, true believers with no
expenditure of will: to believe what runs against the
evidence requires belief—concentration, imagination, stubbornness,

670
art, and some magic: the need to disbelieve belief so disbelief
can be believed: there are infidels only of fictions: not
a single temple has been raised to the fact that what is raised

57

falls, yet that is the lesson: here's my credo: if the merry-
go-round goes too fast it will be difficult to hold on: if you
675   pull up the rosestock, you lose your hips: certitude plus:

everything in moderation including moderation: when you come
to know the eternal forces realizing themselves through form
you will need to lay on no special determination to assent

to what demands none: but if truth is colorless, fictions
680   need be supreme, real supreme with hot-shot convincingness
and lashes laid on lavishly for the doubter, and, per

usual, regular dues: gentlemen of the naked vision, let us
see straight: here we are today and here we are not tomorrow:
if you kick the sand you are likely to raise some dust:

58

685   if you bite me in the ear, I will knee you in the nuts:
if you do something nice for me, I will feel encouraged to do
something nice for you: fight on my side, we fight together:

aleatory composition and choral improvisation throwback to
dinosaur lagoons, the much floating, winged sawbills,
690   bankless, ambient figurings, dismemberments of breath by

overhanging fern-spun ramification: I hear the swirls of
morays, I think, breathing undersea, and see shadows
of mantas remora travel in: but which way is this distant—

a throwback or coming: I'm aware of the military-industrial
695   complex and of lust for erosion: I hear in choral breakings
in and out clamoring gulls guzzling a clam shoal washed up

59

rank: I hear us coming to a pass and just beyond the ridge
sawbills chirr circling an outbreak of undamageable light:
a single dot of light, traveling, will memorize the sphere:

700   redemptions despise the reality: when may it not be our
task so to come into the knowledge of the reality as to
participate therein: wherever the imagined lands it's

likely to brush up against a thorn and pop or get hit by
a bus on the freeway or at the minimum be thought flatulent:
705   I wonder where all on what ledges, on what nordic heights

or high sinkages of meadow the aspen grows and where all
poplar breaks out in shivering testimonial under bright skies,
if along irrigation ditches, flat lengths into diminishment,

60

regimentation of strict discipline, or at the edges of backwoods
710   fields, off from the sight of anything save night's night bird or
day's night bird: I wonder where all seagulls follow the plow,

how far inland, or float serene in dislocation on sweetwater
lakes, I wonder where all along the bottoms of what hills the
roses open their brief and failing rages: ardency is a

715   calf, butting and guzzling, let free to the cow: a luminous
saint reeling in the heights of objectless desire: hornets
after rain splitting out for lit flies: my heart shakes,

my eyes concentration's flames, you my attention, absolute:
dust travels, gets up into the wind's limbs and through
720   stirrings and catchments makes itself available to new

61

coherences, settles out, for example, carrying in microscopic
branches paramecium, virus, germ to damp stayings,
boom bloomings, gets going to return: leaves nothing lost:

the field widens—at the same time the essential begins
725   to take shape: an immense victory unfolds before me: my
potassium-laced diet (jiggers of orange juice) will free me

from episodes of irregular heartbeats, premature ventriculations,
and the misimpressions ads for nonprescription painkillers
pain me with: I expect to promote good will and difficult

730   clarities: I'm tired of bumfuzzlement and bafflement: and
I expect to give my friends who have found it impossible to
love me grounds for further trials: a big clinkery is a big

62

cinder field or a clinkery of big cinders: a fish out of water's
out for water: grief is all I know and joy all I understand:
735   news item—search of creek nets no new results: today's

radicalism is tomorrow's triviality: but excellence,
one of the forming principles of the universe, is ever
radical: garrulity is harm enough even when, as here, it

finds harmless way: but novelty, like garrulity, is one
740   of the forming principles, so much waste and ill-conceiving
before invention provides advancement to the ongoing:

for a form to complete everything with! orb: but this is the
procedure: if everything's put in, the boundary bursts and
one is nowhere except picking up havoc's fragments, things

63

745   nowise as shapely in their selfness as before: but
settling in the beginning for fency definition, that straight
reach across the variable field, chokes the pulse, bores

the tame, excludes the free rush of imagination except as
wind or as a small consistency like sand: the only bearable
750   fence is the continuum, the scope of oneness under which

the proud ephemerals play discretely in their energizing
laws and play out, transformations taking their ways, bending
their boundaries, giving and losing: the outface of the

sphere, the skinny seat on infinity, this holding, this
755   gentle stay in the bosom of reconciling but progressing
motions: the universes, they say, warp, bend, plunge into

64

dark centers that blossom white into other spaces, but in
the slope and backwater of some ancient events, the meld
cools into solidifications, white roots lift green leafages,

760   mold blooms pink and orange in the shade, and maggots race
like traveling waves in the stems of brief, huge mushrooms:
in this open form there's room enough for everything to find

its running self-concisions and expansions, its way, its
definition, down to the precious least: (when an image or
765   item is raised into class representative of cluster, clump,

or set, its boundaries are overinvested, the supercharge is
explosive, so that the burden of energy overwhelms the matter,
and aura, glow, or spirituality results, a kind of pitchblende,

65

radium, sun-like: and when the item is moved beyond class
770   into symbol or paradigmatic item, matter is a mere seed
afloat in radiance: it is the mystery, if reasonable, that

when the one item stands for all, the one item is so lost
in its charge that it is no longer bounded but all radiance:
this is the source of spirit, probably, the simple result of

775   the categorizing mind: the mind will forever work in this way,
and the spiritual, the divine, always be with us: in the
comprehensiveness and focus of the Most High is the obliteration

total that contains all and in that we rest, moving as we like
back into change and boundary and back: since these procedures
780   will not change, we may think rescue omnipresent, a calming,

66

and may exist in that really through the last change: a state
of mind can override the worst tendency and not, even in
surrender to the tendency, be false to its state: to live in

the shifts of facts, unorganized and dark, is to know only
785   generation, mindless, fallen, senselessly repeating: things
work in these ways: deliverance a way they allow): what,

April 23rd and still not a daffodil: suddenly as if a
bright bird had passed, one is old: one dozes forgetful of what
one was for: a suspension of interrelationships: the reader is

790   the medium by which one work of art judges another: hypnosis
is induced by focusing the attention: the trinket swings
or spins before the eyes, the normal flood of distractions

that keeps one awake is drained, and the mind sinks into
simplified ease: the poem, its rhythm, is exclusive and hypnotic,
795   too, but the poem keeps enough revelant variety going to interest

the mind from sleep but enough focus to disinterest it in
external matters: a hypnotic focus, then, that is awakening,
a focus of controlled fullness, not over-exclusiveness: but

the purpose of the motion of a poem is to bring the focused,
800   awakened mind to no-motion, to a still contemplation of the
whole motion, all the motions, of the poem: this is very

different from hypnosis: a descent into the subconscious
(tentacles maybe into the unconscious) is prepared for not by
blotting out the conscious mind but by intensifying the alertness

68

805   of the conscious mind even while it permits itself to sink,
to be lowered down the ladder of structured motions to the
refreshing energies of the deeper self: but why is it of use

to be brought through organized motion from chaos and
ephemerality to no-motion: to touch the knowledge that
810   motions are instances of order and direction occurring

briefly in the stillness that surrounds: to touch, to know,
to be measured and criticized by the silence, to acknowledge
and surrender to wholeness and composure: the non-verbal

energy at that moment released, transformed back through the
815   verbal, the sayable poem: spirit-being, great one in the world
beyond sense, how do you fare and how may we fare to Thee:

69

people set out to serve the people become those the people
serve: given the skinny poles of fact to theory, person to
man, event to continuum, how are we to develop intermediacy:

820   what is to be done, what is saving: is it so to come to know
the works of the Most High as to assent to them and be reconciled
by them, so to hold those works in our imaginations as to think

them our correspondent invention, our best design within the
governing possibilities: so to take on the Reason of the Most
825   High as to in some part celebrate Him and offer Him not our

flight but our cordiality and gratitude: so to look to the
moment of consciousness as to find there, beyond all the
individual costs and horrors, perplexing pains and seizures,

70

joy's surviving radiance: I ask because I am terrified of my
830   arrogance and do not know and do not know if the point in the
mind can be established to last beyond the falling away

of the world and the dreams of the world: but if we are small
can we be great by going away from the Most High into our own
makings, thus despising what He has given: or can we, accepting

835   our smallness, bend to cherish the greatness that rolls through
our sharp days, that spends us on its measureless currents: and
so, for a moment, if only for a moment, participate in those means

that provide the brief bloom in the eternal presence: is this
our saving: is this our perishable thought that imperishably
840   bears us through the final loss: then sufficient thanks for that:

71

there is a faculty or knack, smallish, in the mind that can turn
as with tooling irons immediacy into bends of concision, shapes
struck with airs to keep so that one grows unable to believe that

the piling up of figurements and entanglements could proceed from
845   the tiny working of the small, if persistent, faculty: as if the
world could be brought to flow by and take the bent of

that single bend: and immediately flip over into the mirrored world
of permanence, another place trans-shaped with knackery: a brook in
the mind that will eventually glitter away the seas: and yet pile

850   them all up, every drop recollected: a little mill that changes
everything, not from its shape, but from change: the faculty
then can be itself, small, but masterful in the face of size and

72

spectacular ramification into diversity: (the way to have a following
is to get up in front of whatever is moving and start waving your
855   arms): (sir, the piece you have sent me on poetic process and

psychotherapy errs not in being wrong but in being rudimentary: the
poetic consciousness beginning at a center works itself out by
incorporation until through craft, experience, insight, etc., it

brushes in a fulsome way against the fulsomeness of nature so that
860   on the periphery it is so deeply spelt out that it can tangle with
the coincidental: this provides a growing edge to change and surprise

so that unexpectedness is constantly being fed into the engines of
assimilation and probability, giving shades of tone and air
to the probabilities that make them mean slightly adjusted things):

73

865   if raindrops are words, the poet is the cloud whose
gathering and withholding overspills generously and unmissed
from a great keeping: (depression, low pressure area): the

false poet is a white wisp that tries to wrest itself into
a storm: but the true storm moseys on with easy destructions
870   like afterthoughts: how else but by greatness can the huge

presence exist between the gifty showers, twists and blow-outs:
on the way back from Northfield today (April 29, I've been
away a few days to Baltimore) I wrote a poem as follows:

when I go up into the mountains, I like to go up into the
875   mountains: when I come down from the mountains, I like to
come down from the mountains: there has to be something ahead

74

to like: it might as well be what is ahead: I found this
word *repodepo* in the newspaper only to find it, apparently,
a mischance of machinery: I could not myself have invented

880   a nonexistence so probable, insignificance so well made: let
it stand for a made nothing, a pointer with no point: or
for anything about which the meaning is insecure: a heavy

registration: a cluster of empty pods, or a special phonetic
depot, or something that repods pseudopods: a leaf cannot
885   appear on or fall from the branch except via the total

involvement of the universe: you and I cannot walk the street
or rise to the occasion except via the sum total of effect
and possibility of the universe: we are not half-in and

75

890   half-out of the universe but unmendably integral: when we
move, something yields to us and accepts our steps: our
tensions play against, find rightness in, other tensions not

our own: we move into the motions with our tiny oars: there
are seas not oceans but invisible seas: they sustain,
they drown, but the abundance, the intricacy and dispersion,

895   is glorious: hope lends silverness to that edge: having
been chastened to the irreducible, I have found the
irreducible bountiful: the daffodil nods to spring's zephyr:

when the grackle's flight shadows a streak of lawn, constellations
of possibility break out, for example, the multitude of
900   grassblade shadows subsumed in a sweep: for example, an aphid

76

resting in bugleleaf shade must think lost his discretion of
position: (his feelers notice, his eyes adjust): an ant
struck by the flashed alteration stops, the friction of which

event gives off a plume of heat, a small invisible boom:
905   myriad chloroplasts circling the cell peripheries kick out
of photosynthetic gear and coast in a slough and many atoms

of carbon and nitrogen miss connection: if you dyed the grass
at day's end, you'd see a white streak of starchless loss:
thermodynamics is inscrutable here: the coolant wings, heat

910   currents, wind currents fanned into unpredictable motions:
when an immense afternoon darkbottomed thunderhead hoves rearing
over the ridge, you can imagine how unencompassing and flustered

77

I get—night a full coming uninterrupted into difference: at
clarity of zooming, I'm unpassed in Cayuga Heights, unparalleled
915   (nobody hanging on that wing, baby) possibly: at easing

into orbit grease, nuzzling right in there with not a touch
till the whole seal smacks: at that I'm unusually salient,
gritless in curvature with withal enthralling control,

perfection of adjustment, innocence of improvisation beginners
920   and old strumpets of the spirit know: I don't want shape:
I'll have water muscles bending streams (recurrences of

curvature): wind sheets erect, traveling: lips accommodating
muscle glides: identity in me's a black, clear bead: I've
strongboxed and sunk it, musseled and barnacled with locks,

78

925   but it's breathing in there, a dumb eager little botch: I aim
absolutes at it so blasting, recoil and strike unnerve my
stability: (from so small a thing, what distant orbits I've

taken into residence) but it's not now form against that form:
it's motion: the renunciation of boxes, magicless: I'll
930   put the speck in soak, dissolve it, or pump fluids in so dense

flooding will work it out: what is its nature that has caused
so many engines, some fearful: I do not think bat or rat:
it's a sprout child: it coos: it coos pink: the world and I

oppose it: it mustn't see light as itself: it must appear
935   dissolved, transfigured, or go down with the body it meant to
bloom into the various distractions of decay: then the little

79

breath will die: then the locks, so many, will cast: to
that late funeral of my true self, no weeper will come,
hushing attendant, twelve-footed accompanist: then the small

940   self will taste the ruin that has been my only food: (one
whose home is afire wanders): just now it's 7:15 and
thunderstormy, blue deepened evening green, somewhat windy,

rain a likely solution: (when ground trash blooms all ways
at once like a flower, something has descended): though I
945   have a bunch of potential any mush of which could sharpen

into cutting blooms, I sometimes lose definition tendencies
by looking out: look out: the tiny invites attention:
outward concentrations: (the poem reaches a stillness

80

which is its form): crush a bug and the universe goes hollow
950   with hereafter: in the cemeteries a shiver settles: sparrows
played down to speech in the cedar bunch into flowers:

across the valley a one-sided rim rises, highways like
caterpillars climb to the biting edge: the wings of red-ant
queens clamp flat macadam pools, the queens free-climbing

955   mirrored trees to the extinction of overhead boughs: fear's
a reservoir inscrutable rivers feed: I'm at the dammed
gate sizzling utterance: spending fear into any shape that

can manage the investment: cypress, weed, swallow-drink,
serpent-drink: to the huge air's multiple fuzzy tongues
960   I address vague hosannas: evaporation without arithmetic of

81

loss: what a blessing: I have too much to weigh, shape
into meaningful expenditure: I need jars, jugs, hogsheads,
vials: here's a drop to pierce your ear for: have a large

pendant with lesser spangles: send folks over: I have
965   plenty to pass around: the right investment's in decay,
decayable: brothers, fine brothers, be strong, be merry:

girls, she falcons, be thin: let us work ourselves asleep
against you: you are rocks that bend and flow, take in our
nervous edges: be the blossoms we spend into flower: I go

970   on the confidence that in this whole magnificence nothing is
important, why should this be, yet everything is, even this
as it testifies to the changing and staying: as man, singular

82

in certain kinds of feeling (we don't know what shades of
feeling travel the weed) I know importances, love, grief,
975   terror, that can retire nature into strangeness, but until

I get right enough to appreciate the lesser celandine by
the woodsroad, I have not achieved the calm necessary to the
joys of small riches, the briar bud bending out into the path:

feelings, feelings: conceptualization nowhere nears so accurate
980   a source: nevertheless, except within the highrising dome,
canopy, reach of the forming intellect, feeling has no meaning,

no guidance, but stir, rush, the splintering cycles of small
beginnings and endings, the *sui generations* of particularity:
New York City can be grown over by birch brush: south of

83

985   Scranton, birch has covered the slag and shale heaps (terrains
of conical spills), the crevices catching dust and leaves,
roots and ice granulating edges: it will be lovely someday,

if left alone, and have a brook: I feel like a brook shedding
a hill, the glassy wide and the thick white falling, a
990   scud-cover of moss, with a copse here and there of something

quailing, pine in a catchment moved high, a bear's cold red
tongue sloshing in a runlet, and a deer's eye shot with flight:
I am there pondering berries and the bear: my mind furnishes

a clear sky and smart wind: for me, there's more death behind
995   than ahead, though ahead lies the finish endless: the
seventeen-year-old self is gone and with it the well and

84

wellsweep, chinaberry tree, the mother and father, the two
sisters, living but lost back there, and Silver, Doll, all
the jonquils, the smokehouse, mulberry tree, but when I was

1000   last by, the pecan tree's still standing, the same one, big,
the lean growths and lean shades vanished: more death done
than to do, except that memory grows, accumulating strata of

change, and the eyes close on a plenitude, suddenly, directly
into nothingness: so, in a sense, there's more and more to do
1005   with increasing reluctance: a world if not the world:

I am standing by the hill brook with the hill wife: but
where did all the mosquitoes come from: I'm tired of raw
nuts and berries and staying up late freezing with no

85

          television: you can't keep visions selective enough: they

1010   fill up with reality, too gravid grown to keep off the ground:

          as we return to the dust from which we came, the gods die

          away into the sky, the womb of gods: from the common

          universalized materials we ascend into time and shape, hold our

          outlines and integrations a while, then stiffen with the

1015   accumulations of process, our bodies filters that collect

          dross from the passages of air and water and food, and begin

          to slow, crack, splinter, and burst: the gods from the high wide

          potentials of aura, of encompassing nothingness, flash into

          concentration and descend, taking on matter and shape, color,

1020   until they walk with us, but divine, having drawn down with them

86

          the reservoirs of the skies: in time the restlessness that is in

          them, the overinvestment, casts the shells of earth to remain with

          earth, and the real force of the gods returns to its heights

          where it dwells, its everlasting home: these are the mechanics

1025   by which such matters carry out their awesome transactions:

          if the gods have gone away, only the foolish think them gone

          for good: only certain temporal guises have been shaken

          away from their confinements among us: they will return, quick

          appearances in the material, and shine our eyes blind with adoration

1030   and astonish us with fear: the mechanics of this have to do with

          the way our minds work, the concrete, the overinvested concrete,

          the symbol, the seedless radiance, the giving up into meaninglessness

87

and the return of meaning: but the gods have come and gone
(or we have made them come and go) so long among us that
1035   they have communicated something of the sky to us making us

feel that at the division of the roads our true way, too,
is to the sky where with unborn gods we may know no
further death and need no further visitations: what may have

changed is that in the future we can have the force to keep
1040   the changes secular: the one:many problem, set theory, and
symbolic signifier, the pyramid, the pantheon (of gods and

men), the pecking order, baboon troop, old man of the tribe,
the hierarchy of family, hamlet, military, church, corporation,
civil service, of wealth, talent—everywhere the scramble for

88

1045   place, power, privilege, safety, honor, the representative
notch above the undistinguished numbers: second is as good
as last: pyramidal hierarchies and solitary persons: the

hierarchies having to do with knowledge and law, the solitaries
with magic, conjuration, enchantment: the loser or apostate
1050   turns on the structure and melts it with vision, with

summoning, clean, verbal burning: or the man at the top may
turn the hierarchy down and walk off in a private direction:
meanwhile, back at the hierarchy, the chippers and filers

hone rocks to skid together: the bottom rocks have much to
1055   bear: the next level, if buoyed up from below, hardly less:
but the top rock, however nearly in significant flotation,

89

is responsible for the symmetry of the whole, the office of
highsounding purpose, noble gesture, pulling together (by
which is meant pressing up though of course it's pressing

1060   down—but everyone below is willing to bear some weight if
it feels uplifting): the manager's office is 14 × 20 and
the vice president's 16 × 20 and the executive vice president's

18 × 20 and the president's 20 × 20 and the chairman of the board's
the golf course or private jet: for identity and/or effect,
1065   exclude the extraneous, which, though, leaves the identity

skimpy and the effect slight: great procedures move the
other way, inclusively, but with the hold back that when they
have everything they have nothing, an all-ness of identity

90

and no effect, a calm, resolved effect: you can't win: you
1070   can strike balances and, for laughter or sublimity, imbalances
enough to keep the show going, but even at the midpoint of

perfect balances you can suspend oppositions which are no more
than self-cancellations: all identities and effects are
imbalances: but then you get into balancing imbalances,

1075   the effect of most narrative: force mind from boxes to radiality:
the maple buds open into a basket of spangles, a vased bouquet:
greenish-yellow five-petaled flowers, not noticeable or attractive:

I wonder if maples depend on bees: I haven't seen bee one: pulled
the old lawnmower out of the garage after a long winter and it
1080   started right up, two good tugs on the spinning rope: cut the grass,

91

first time of the year: real green grass: been raining so much
people can't get to mowing and then when they do lawnmower chokes
up with blackgreen chunks and clumps, muffling the blade and stalling

the motor: yesterday (May 6) we drove up to Phil Booth's house
1085   and there he was: his wife, Margaret, too, his youngest daughter,
three dogs (all different kinds) and one cat: what a great day: he

cooked outdoor hamburgers and hotdogs: he has fossils in his rocks:
George (P.E.) was there, good old George, and Mary Emma: and others
all come to the picnic: a brook runs right through Philip's

1090   yard and falls over rocks, gets up and goes on: you can
stand on the rocks and not fall off in the water: the youngest
dog runs around and looks up at you as if wondering what

92

is so surprising: intense and quizzical: I wonder why dogs
haven't learned more in all these years: they take the proper
1095   attitude: what is true service: the true question: or of

the many services, which ones are most nearly true: it
must be a service that is celebration, for we would celebrate
even if we do not know what or how, and for He is bountiful if

slow to protect and recalcitrant to keep: what we can celebrate
1100   is the condition we are in, or we can renounce the condition
we are in and celebrate a condition we might be in or ought

to be in: should we like the saint, ascetic, or priest spurn
the world, sensuous and sensual, and celebrate those longings
in us, sweet heights, that seem the potential of a necessary

93

1105   coming: or should we fall to the pleasures and raggednesses
so relentlessly and opulently provided here, the flappings of
the flesh, the ghostly agonies, the long bleak streaks, commitment

to love's threshing flesh brings on: do we celebrate
most truly when we fall into our limitations, accept our
1110   nothingness of years, spawn, beget, care for, weep, fail, burn,

slobber, suck, stroke, dream, shake, sleep, eat, swim, squirm:
does He forgive us, does he accept our celebration, when we turn
away from the fruits given and hunger after Him—the

arrogance!—His silver and immortal agencies: will He not afflict
1115   us with loss of life in life with nothing later of another kind:
when we take the needy hand in hand, when the tear humbles

94

us with horrible splendor, when tenderness is fully placed
in the human eye, we find service exceeding body into sky:
when anxiety rises words too start to stir rising into schools,

1120   moving into sayings (a recourse, though delusional) like winds
making up before a mild May-evening thunderstorm, the winds
spilling across the trees, then like surf sucking back in a

growing tug: at such times, I pick up a tape, stick the end
into my typewriter, and give everything a course, mostly
1125   because in a storm course is crucial and in proportion to the

storm must be fought for, insisted on: I've weathered a batch
of storms: the words rising from behind the palings of
the back fence, getting loose and showering up from the points

95

1130

of maple leaves, shaking loose in wind-defined drifts
of elm seed, take on configuration of motion and spiel
out into spelling: the few drops of rain have put a fizz

on the street and the cars go by in splitting noticeability:
I just finished planting the pole beans, the zucchini and
cucumbers and transplanted the pepper plants, asters, and

1135

petunias: I had the best time: and after the first shower,
the catbird lit on the top bar of the jungle gym and ripped
off a few bars, as if a surprise announcement: but I know

where that bird's nest is and how quiet it's been around
there this month: I like to think the bird just went

1140

out of his mind with all the rising and fell afloat of it

96

with a singing: that's the way I do it when I do, and I
know the bird's meaning at least in coming to my own: all
the greens, a company of differences, radiant, the source

sunk, the mellowing left-over light suffusing: I thought

1145

I saw a piece of red paper in the grass but it was a
cardinal: and I thought I saw a clump of quince blossoms

move but that was a cardinal: one morning three orioles
were in the green-red quince bush: that was what it was:
the pear tree looks like lime sherbet with whipped cream

1150

topping: the bottom part all leaves and no blossoms and
the top part all blossoms and no leaves: a green sailboat
or a spring mountain, from tree-green to conic, glacial white:

97

the work of the staying mind is to burn up or dissolve the day's
images, the surface falling of pear petals or of hailstones
1155   from the blue bottoms of thunderheads at sea, the curling up and

vanishing or the plopping and melting: for the mind, large as its
surface is, hasn't room for the spreading out of each day's
images to the hard edges: so the subterranean fires of the mind

float upward into the day's business and here and there like
1160   volcanoes burn through into dream meldings, the hard
edges turning inward then moving out assuming their own

foliages and lineations, essentialized: the white hot mouth spewing
up islands recovered to the conscious mind: in this way all the
sensory bits are made available in symbolical assimilations ready to

98

1165   train the mind through its surprises and commonplaces: I am
waiting for the evening star to appear in the windowpane but
the sun's still a ruddy burnishing fire in the lower branches of the

tamarack: this afternoon I thought Jove had come to get me: I walked
into a corridor of sunlight swimming showering with turning shoals
1170   of drift pollen and not yet knowing it was pollen thought perhaps I

was being taken or beamed aboard but saw over the roof the high
   swags
of the blue spruce swaying and felt stabilized from wonder:
I would still rather beget (though I can't, apparently) than be

begotten upon, I think I'm almost sure, but I don't know that a vague
1175   coming of a shimmery gold floating would be so bad: I sneezed: my
eyes watered: the intimacy was sufficient: nothing is separate:

99

there's the evening star and two jets blazing sunlit vapor trails:
stentorian: tendentious: sonorous: orotund: the moon's up:
however provisional the procedure, tentative the thought, the

1180   days clang shut with bronze finality: days wherein we wavered
studiously with uncertainty, went this way a way and that way a
way, thought twice, take on the hard and fast aspect of the

finished, the concluded fact, thus misrepresenting us: and then
there is at the end the stone that makes it all look purposeful
1185   and deliberate, what was hesitation, gaping, and wondrous

turning around: life takes on the cast of decision and seeds
the ground with marmoreal memento: stone outcroppings in the
pasture like sheep resting: I'm glad the emphasis these days

100

is off dying beautifully and more on a light-minded living with
1190   the real things—soap, spray-ons, soda, paper towels, etc.—for
indelicacy taints taking oneself too seriously and saving life

up to close with a serene finish: I expect to die in terror:
my mother did: old songs (hymns) erupted from her dying
imaginations: they say she sang them blurred for two nights

1195   before the interval of clearing that preceded her majestic
drawing away: my father's heart burst finally and he coasted
off, a cool drifting out of course: these destinations we

think we do not wish to attain: unsettling flurries and
disconnections, hurries and worries, strictures and
1200   besiegings like preparations for camping out: driven, I go

101

into high and drive as fast as I can: driving faster than
I'm driven I can keep the forces aligned and taut but if
a holiday comes along and I try to slow down for vacation,

I swerve a lot, meander and hassle, my driver drives over
1205   my driving, an overdrive taken over by overtaking, hopeless,
hapless helplessness: better trim the quince bush now before

the thorns of new growth harden: or come fall there'll be a
further periphery-thicket of spines: maybe one isn't supposed
to trim while the shoots are still purplish and tender:

1210   doing it now may bleed and depress the bush to death: but
meanwhile, while doing it, I find the placid quince rage
enticing: by now the old periphery of blossom and nub-green

102

quince is inward in an exceeded stratum: even though the bush
has put on the strain of blossoming and fruiting, it has
1215   at the same time shot out shoots all over, threatening the

upcoming hollyhock and lemon lilies: a green rage to possess,
make and take room: to dominate, shade out, whiten: I
identify with the bush's rage, its quiet, ruthless, outward

thrust: whatever nears me must shrink, wither up, or widen
1220   overlarge and thin with shade, ambition the size of the room
I need to unfold into: but cunning and deviousness are at

work at the quince bush: morning glory stock is underground,
ready to shoot up a spear of leaving through the quince's
underbrush and by fast moving to overcrown the bush tops

103

1225   and take the light away: look at the smooth-cut lawn, how
even and gentle: but finger through the turf, the nap,
and there are the brown twists of clover, veronica, plantain,

grass in a striving: it is hard to stand up crowding full
into a full unfolding: being's terror: I wonder if we
1230   should pick the gems out of the reliquary crowns and

give to the poor, boons and munificences showering, plenty
of meat, wines medicinal, soothing beer, classic pretzels:
I wonder if we should shave the gold from the gold reliquary

beards and cast it to flurries of gleaning: or melt down
1235   the artful forms, float off the dross, and mold the gold
or stamp it into guinea suns: then the poor could have

104

their operations, pay off their loans, and thrive with comfort:
the babies could get fresh milk and the lovers could propose:
(but if we demolish the past's imposing achievements, hold

1240   away only the lyre upon which we can plink immediacy): scared
sacred: how dark it gets before the hail starts! lightning
fries in quick crisps, thunder splits and cleaves open into

booming crumbling walls that jar the ground: then the perfect
ice spheres from the high world come down in a bounding
1245   rustle, some remnants of thunder far along the periphery

grumbling: lightning strikes close and lightbulbs sear
in their sockets and flick out: then the heavy rain brushes
in on wind gusts at the windows: a drenching too demonstrable

for poppies, all twenty-eight heads half-closed with bending
1250   over and drooping: for a long time the eaves-gutter,
lightening, keeps a mesh of seed-ice, the milky cores:

because of the holdings of its many needlepoints, every one
drop-bulbed, the long shags of the blue spruce lie into one
another like shoals of high moss and a weatherless shower

1255   ticks on for hours after rain: slowly the boughs lighten,
loosen, jar and sprinkle apart: a thousand acres of those
trees could suspend a shower and turn it into an all-day

soak: that would be good for the brooks whereby the rocks
had refused all but a wetting: mediations soften the
1260   extremities without changing their quantities, merely

106

translating times: getting to know your philosophy, finely
rational and small, is like coming into a city and finding
a trellis, precise, consistent, which after all only holds

up a bush: some people when they get up in the morning see
1265   the kitchen sink, but I look out and see the windy rivers
of the Lord in the treetops: you have your identity when

you find out not what you can keep your mind on but what
you can't keep your mind off: mind, many sided, globe-like,
rich with specification and contrariety, is secure from

1270   slogans, fads, starved truths, and propaganda—defeats itself,
meanwhile shoring itself up with sight and insight: how to
devise a means that assimilates small inspirations into a

107

1275

large space, network, reticulation complex (almost misleading)
but moved forward by a controlling motion, design, symmetry,
suasion, so that harmony can be recognized in the highest

ambience of diversity: in a single day, one may "hear" a small
connection, an interesting phrase, but to what can each day's
stock be added: what is the measure to accommodate the

1280

diverse impressions, moods, intuitions: in the right scope
any fragment fits: since we can't, apparently, have whole
motions of mind through the higher reaches (sufficiently

impregnated with the concrete), we turn to the unit to
represent the universal: but while we can hope to arrive at
the definition of essence through the unit, we can never in

108

1285

that way satisfy the other capacity of the mind to achieve
definition by ordered accumulations, massive suasions: if
nothing shaped stays and shapelessness is dwellingless, where

can we dwell: as shapes (bodies) we dwell only in the flow
of shapes, turning the arcs of mortality: but the imagination,
though bodiless, is shaped (being the memory or imagined

1290

memory of shapes) and so can dwell in nothingness: the human
being is as inscrutable and unformulable as a poem, or, if
possible, more so: the gas station attendant has a bottomless

well in him, too—shoots from his brain down his spine, breaks
into incredible ramification, the same as bottomless: we
have our definitions, imperfect, but all we have: around them,

1295

109

though, and running through, and immensely more vast, the
indefinable, the source of possibility: acme came: speaking
with "the flower of the mind" gets pollen up my nose: how

1300 to give up the life of words for life: just now (June 6 in
the dusk) only a few dozen flowers are left on the honeysuckle
bush, the flowers like the pink, sprung mouths of tiny vipers:

thunder shakes pennies out of stack: if one follows the western
littoral of Africa northward, one moves up past Walvis Bay
1305 to Sorris Sorris and, rounding out westward and turning back

in again, to Benguela and Lobito and then way on up, swerving
out again slightly westward, to Port Gentil and then sharply
west to Cape Palmas and on up and around to Sidi Ifni and

110

past the gaping Strait and on up past Oporto and, crossing
1310 water, to Brest and then through certain colder finaglings
one turns into the other side of the world along Siberian

shores to the Bering Strait and, switching, descends along
the western littoral of North America: if all else fails,
try hocus-pocus to bring your writing into focus: for sun,

1315 moon are out of joint until you bring them to a point: cry
Muse! and if you cannot reach her, bleed some juice from a
writing teacher: bad images are bad but what is worse is

verse loose where it should be terse: verse would be, except
for magic, dull as life and twice as tragic: the shortest
1320 route to adulation is to skirt your education: in need to be

111

diminished, I sought out peaks and stars and at my cost
sang them high and bright: you don't have to be superhuman
to survive—let go and let your humanity rise to its natural

height, said the star, and you will in that smallness be as
1325   great as I: so I sat down and sang and mountains fell and
at last I knew my measurable self immeasurable: the weak

rigs a universe against himself, then overstrives to keep
himself—but nothing is set up, nobody cares, it's all right
for him to come out, shine a little and love his light:

1330   aspirations (misdirections) move in the upper branches of
the mind like vine vipers, slender, loopy, slithery:
notice the highest cranes reach into the deepest pits:

112

therefore, if my slat-steel triangulations of abstraction
and strict cables surprise and dismay you on the landscape,
1335   think how from under the foundations the waters of life

may rise to meld with mirrors and wave the cranes away:
think of that: for such the elegance of my uprisings: what
is deep to come to, being overlaid with too much stone of

fear, suggests high drills: the little red squirrel dashes
1340   out onto the thin branches, picks a maple seed, and dashes
back to the cover of bigger branches: nibbles out the

greenmeal seed then drops the wing into asymmetrical flutters,
not the nosewing-spin of the true event: semblance with no
journey: terrors bluster with undercutting sweeps, or pelt

113

1345   with staying fragmentation (hail on the spring garden) through
or in the mind, the swirlings of imbalanced loops between
highs and lows, just like weather predictions and actual

storms over average landscapes: one terror mind brings on
itself is that anything can be made of anything: if there are
1350   no boundaries that hold firm, everything can be ground into

everything else: the mind making things up, making nothing
of what things are made of: scary to those who need prisons,
liberating to those already in: that this dismissal is

possible, no more recalcitrance within or without, slides our
1355   surfaces and disturbs our deeps: the poppies are all gone:
the tulips were all gone last week: we have lemon lilies now,

114

some iris, some spirea still white where it's mostly brown: we
have four hills of mound-building ants: two hills are on the
lawn and regularly get their hills sliced off: one hill is

1360   under the four-legged merry-go-round: I have to clip under
there so I leave it alone: one mound is just between the
blacktop and shrubs, on a slight incline, so it's safe from

the lawnmower: I notice the ants have two primary visible
duties: some ants bring little dried bits, castings from maple
1365   bloom, dried strips of grass, even green clover leaves and deposit

them on top of the mound: meanwhile, other ants bring up pellets
of soil, and a weaving betwixt them takes place which the rain,
short of destroying, glues and seals: they are interesting ants:

115

          I was pulling veronica out of the lawn when this hornet came
1370   up upon my squatted self, buzzed around my anklebones inquiringly
          and then buzzingly persisted about my face and neck: that was

          a few days ago: then he did it the next day: and the next: but
          today when he did it, I retreated into the house: he followed me
          and got caught between the door and the screen: the screen door

1375   was ajar and when he got in the groove, I closed the door crushingly:
          I took him by the wing to the mound builders: they hassled him
          down the side part way, for some reason, and commenced to pierce

          and suck him: I am sorry, of course, but the veronica has to
          be pulled, as I don't want to use funny sprays that might poison
1380   the worms and birds: killing to save perplexes: just facts,

116

          just bits: let's, as if sore, grab a few things from the flood,
          from the imagination's burning everything up into the contours
          of staying: or let us, before the transfusions commence, hamper

          the imagination with full freightages of recalcitrance, cripple
1385   it short of any transmutation that avoids the massive registration:
          if the burn's to be true, let it be the real: nor let us guide

          too much the proceeding but be carefully in it when it goes: we
          must come out on the other side, on our feet and ready to ride:
          this drawn fellow said he was quartered, split two ways,

1390   horizontally and vertically, by the horizontal into height and
          depth and by the vertical into left and right: said he tried
          to live in one half only to find it halved: these terrible

117

partitions interested him in unity: he wanted all of himself
together but each quadrant felt defiant and exclusive: he
1395   looked for the coordinate only on finding it to find it

represented by zero: a terrible bind that made him at least
attentive: very much aware, he could give many sides to any
argument: we all thought that largeness a spark of divinity:

we told him everything has a cost but he rejoined he would
1400   settle for something less expensive: the poem insists on
differences, on every fragment of difference till the fragments

cease to be fragmentary and wash together in a high flotation
interpenetrating much like the possibility of the world: the
poem wants every fragment clear but a fragment until, every

118

1405   fragment taken into account, the fragments will be apprehended
to declare a common reality past declaration: a fragment is
a person, edgy with difference, fearful of broadsweep

elimination: interpenetration is a welling up of fresh deeps
of tolerance and consideration: I beg the liberty of such
1410   edges and wells to function and of fearful concision to relax

its boundaries inclusively: if one would preserve the integrity
of his going, his taut conveyance (bright and trim), he must
be willing to give over to indirection: if in the South

Atlantic one selects the prime meridian as an ideal northward
1415   voyage, one runs into difficulty in the progression: at Accra
or thereabouts one must abandon ship and hire elephants or

119

Fiats and proceed at a lumbering or sizzling pace: and
somewhere around Upper Volta it will be necessary to get
camels ready (and do something with the elephants, put them

1420   in keep for the return trip or dispose of them by sale,
shot, or wilderness), packed with figs, dates, and curd,
and around Oran find a marketplace to trade the spitting

camels off for ships again, a short voyage, and then onto
land: before ships again, there will be dogsleds and
1425   finally seals slipping off chunks of sea-ice: bend out

and around and in in order to keep familiar rudder and sail
at hand: when poetry was a servant in the house of religion,
it was abused from all angles, buggered by the fathers,

120

ravished by the mothers, called on to furnish the energies
1430   of entertainment (truth) for the guests, and made, at the
same time, a whipping-post for the literal: poetry is not

now a servant in the house of religion, the matter having
become clear who got what from which: if you wish to get
religion now you will have to come and sit in poetry's

1435   still center, bring your own domestic help, and resort to
your own self-sustainment: if, leaving center, you make
uses of poetry, you must represent them as uses, not as the

true life, and in recognition of that you must dress your
uses in rags as an advertisement that violations are underway:
1440   no more hocus-pocus derived from images and lofty coordinations:

121

if you want to drain a place, don't begin on the marshy side:
you'll get your feet wet and every time you trench, water will
run in hiding your trench depth: begin on the other side

of the clog where the ground may be crumbly dry and where you
1445   can work without sloshing and then you can at last break into
the water and see it start from dead holding into motion's

declarations and extensions: if you do everything with
economy and attention, the work itself will take on
essentialities of the inevitable, and you will be, if causing,

1450   participating in grace: the aspects will concur in one motion:
when the water breaks into the trench, notice spells of
jerking in the water's head, caused by the uneven angles and

122

depths of shoveling: but soon the water will find a smooth
current compensating for the ragged edges, and you may feel
1455   that the water itself, as if grateful, is joining to complete

your work: attention enters in: I can't understand my readers:
they complain of my abstractions as if the United States of America
were a form of vanity: they ask why I'm so big on the

one:many problem, they never saw one: my readers: what do they
1460   expect from a man born and raised in a country whose motto is *E
pluribus unum*: I'm just, like Whitman, trying to keep things

half straight about my country: my readers say, what's all
this change and continuity: when we have a two-party system,
one party devoted to reform and the other to consolidation:

123

1465   and both trying to grab a chunk out of the middle: either we
reconcile opposites or we suspend half the country into
disaffection and alienation: they want to know, what do I

mean *quadrants*, when we have a Southeast, Northeast, Southwest,
and Northwest and those cut into pairs by the splitting
1470   Mississippi and the Mason-Dixon line: I figure I'm the exact

poet of the concrete *par excellence*, as Whitman might say:
they ask me, my readers, when I'm going to go politicized or
radicalized or public when I've sat here for years singing

unattended the off-songs of the territories and the midland
1475   coordinates of Cleveland or Cincinnati: when I've prized
multeity and difference down to the mold under the leaf

124

on the one hand and swept up into the perfect composures of
nothingness on the other: my readers are baffling and
uncommunicative (if actual) and I don't know what to make of

1480   or for them: I prize them, in a sense, for that: recalcitrance:
and for spreading out into a lot of canyons and high valleys
inaccessible to the common course or superhighway: though I

like superhighways, too, that tireless river system of streaming
unity: my country: my country: can't cease from its
1485   sizzling rufflings to move into my "motions" and "stayings":

when I identify my self, my work, and my country, you may
think I've finally got the grandeurs: but to test the center
you have to go all the way both ways: from the littlest

125

1490 to the biggest: I didn't mean to talk about my poem but
to tell others how to be poets: I'm interested in you, and
I want you to be a poet: I want, like Whitman, to found

a federation of loveship, not of queers but of poets, where
there's a difference: that is, come on and be a poet, queer
or straight, adman or cowboy, librarian or dope fiend,

1495 housewife or hussy: (I see in one of the monthlies an astronaut
is writing poems—that's what I mean, guys): now, first of
all, the way to write poems is just to start: it's like

learning to walk or swim or ride the bicycle, you just go
after it: it is a matter of learning how to move with
1500 balance among forces greater than your own, gravity, water's

126

buoyance, psychic tides: you lean in or with or against the
ongoing so as not to be drowned but to be swept effortlessly
up upon the universal possibilities: you can sit around

and talk about it all day but you will never walk the tightwire
1505 till you start walking: once you walk, you'll find there's
no explaining it: do be afraid of falling off because it is

not falling off that's going to be splendid about you, making
you seem marvelous and unafraid: but don't be much afraid:
fall off a few times to see it won't kill you: O compatriotos,

1510 sing your hangups and humiliations loose into song's
disengagements (which, by the way, connect, you know, when
they come back round the other way): O comrades! of the

127

1515

seemly seeming—soon it will all be real! soon we will know
idle raptures (after work) leaning into love: soon all our
hearts will be quopping in concert: hate's fun, no doubt

about that, tearing things up and throwing them around and
ending some: but love is a deep troubling concern that rises
to the serenity of tears in the eyes: prefer that: hold

1520

hands: help people: don't make a big fuss and embarrass
them, and if your empathy is right you won't, but help people
where the message is that it's called for: and when you're

tired out, write songs about hate's death and love's birth:
you'll get it straight, you'll see: the mind: a periscope
in the perilous scope, rises from comforting immersions in

128

1525

what sways good and feels fine, the plush indulgences like
ledges or canyon scarps rimmed with spring's finery of bush,
the creams and jellies of reverie, and looks abroad for a

reassuring scope to sweetness or for the oncoming, if
distant, catastrophe that will return it to the pudding

1530

of change, the mind's own describing and roving fire

drowned from shapening: the mind studies the soil, wedges
out spudeyes and plants them, attends, devours with its body,
and yet declares itself independent of the soil: like a

Portuguese man-of-war, the mind shakes rustling tentacles

1535

down into the nutriment: it wants to survive: as storms
of zooplankton pour up onto the shelf at dusk, it swarms

129

to feed: (I want to be declared a natural disaster area:
I want my ruins sanctioned into the artifice of ruins: I
want to be the aspect above which every hope rises, a

1540   freshening of courage to millions: I want to be, not shaved
marble in a prominence that cringes aspiration, but the
junkyard where my awkwardnesses may show: my incompletions

and remains tenable with space: I want to be the shambles,
the dump, the hills of gook the bulldozer shoves, so gulls
1545   in carrion-gatherings can fan my smouldering, so in the

laciest flake of rust I can witness my consequence and times:
I want to be named the area where charlatan rationality comes
to warp, where the smooth finishes bubble and perk, where

130

aerosol deodorants lose their breath: when the freeze of
1550   this century retreats, leave me the slow boulders and
smashed pebbles arbitrarily disposed: whatever was bright,

clever, chic, harmonious in my time took plane from mind's
tricky shallows and too quickly found plastic rightness
distant from the winding center: declare me an area

1555   prohibited where the wind can come among the grasses and
weeds, robins nest in high wheels under the whole look of
heaven:) chaos, pushed far, gives up chunky sleaziness and

in the milling mastication of change assumes pale light
in a diffusion and on the periphery gives off golden
1560   illuminations of unity and, beyond, becomes the merciful,

131

non-instrumental continuum: the continuum allows at the
outermost thinnings skimpy weavings tearing into the surrounding
uterus of nothingness, a way to go: from this womb

separations appear, the land from water, the sky departs
1565   upward, the water breaks up into seas, lakes, rivers, runlets,
a few noticeable configurations, short of perplexing multeity:

the mind rides the cycle from all things enchanted and
summoned into unity, a massive, shining presence, to all
things diffused, an illimitable, shining absence, confusion

1570   the wrong zone of intermediacy, a lack of clarifying extremes:
the week of windy cold comes and removes the last hangers-on
from the trees and heaps them against hedge, fence: rake

132

the leaves or a still morning's inch of snow will weight
every disposition disposed, the pheasant moving about dazzled
1575   with the sudden loss of ground: I am like the earth about

twenty-three degrees off, which gives me summer and winter
moods, sheds hopes and sprouts them again: what are my hopes:
it's hard to tell what an abstract poet wants: my hopes

are for a context in which the rosy can keep its edges out of
1580   frost: my hopes are for a broad sanction that gives range
to life, for the shining image of nothingness within which

schools of images can swim contained and askelter: my hopes
are that the knots of misery, depression, and disease can
unwind into abundant resurgences: forces other than light

133

1585   give shadow: the leaves under the maple tree are flattened
in an overlapping elliptical, headed southward, the sun
itself subsided southward: after a long northwind, the leaves

are the wind's shadow: a solid shadow with no shadowing
leaves on the tree, just northward splinters of nakedness:
1590   a shadow of former substance transmigrated into shadow-substance,

not shadow but a redisposition of substance: the redisposition's
form is the shadow of all the redisposing forces, a shadow
of the universe! a record and perfect summary, signs of

gusts in scatterings-out at the shadow tip: I wonder if one
1595   can pay too much attention, as one can pray too much and
forget to shop for dinner: legible, the evidences propose

134

no text: dwelling over ashes, the bitter, spent spirit recovers
the taste of desertion, the sense of scripture: meanwhile,
in calm, a thousand shows wind to manifestation and a thousand

1600   others loosen ropes and take down their poles: how much
attention can we pay, count the snowflakes or flurries, the
clouds or blue intervals: is celebration to pay no attention

but go along with the ongoing, buoyed up by accuracies
beyond receipt: if geese can see low, the leaf shadow will
1605   show them which way to go: light patches on the floating

hill across the lake stand up into columns when half a
snow-flurry, giving medium, brushes through: interpenetrations
of gray and blue with breaking luminescences, streamings

135

	skirting whirls: the column stands but moves over the hill,
1610	the foot walking up and down ravines, and sometimes leans

skirting whirls: the column stands but moves over the hill,
1610 the foot walking up and down ravines, and sometimes leans
a broken top as if held up by the sun: time enough to think

of death when there's no time left to think: big ditties:
the poem is love: love is fictional only where it can't
grow, but always supreme: making the poem makes the body

1615 that makes love: the abstract poem reaches too far for the
body, love bodiless there, better, if scarier, burns nearby:
or having loved nearby, the abstract poem turns to the spirit,

bodiless and frightless: or the abstract poem, searching
breadths and heights of fiery ease, trains its way down to
1620 settle in the woman's eye: we have so many ways to go wrong

136

and so often go wrong, we must read rightness written in the
face of wrong: if the abstract poem goes out and never
comes back, weaves the highest plume of mind beyond us, it

tells by its dry distraction, distraction: love is better
1625 awry than any other quantity true: the abstract poem, yearning
into the lean-away, acquires a skeleton to keep it here, and

its jangling dance shocks us to attend the moods of lips,
the liquid changes of the spiritual eye: the abstract poem
cleaves through the glassy heights like the hump of a great

1630 beast, the rising reification, integration's grandest, most
roving whale: in this way Enlil became a god and ruled
the sky: in this way earth became our mother: in this way

137

angels shaped light: seek the whole measure that is ease
and ramble around without constriction or distortion
1635 (debilitating exclusion) until the big sky opens the freedom

between design and designed airiness: the rational mind
absorbed, structures float in plenitude rather than in
starved definition: order, the primeval hillock, is a

lessening from chaos, chaos the ampler twin: the visible
1640 resides within the invisible: the coherent within the
incoherent: the discontinuous, the discrete, occurs within

the continuous: the visible, coherent, discrete dwell
in flotation which faces out on the illimitable: the power,
he said, to invent and sustain great structure is uncommon,

138

1645 dibs and dabs, driblets and tail-ends defeating minds, those
incapable of the see-through intermingling: but there are
minds, he maintained, nervous of structures, especially the

impressive, minds requiring the see-through to act as liquid
of flotation outside the structures, such a flotation no
1650 structure could hem in but many structures could sort out

their destinies fairly freely in: I don't know about you,
but I'm sick of good poems, all those little rondures
splendidly brought off, painted gourds on a shelf: give me

the dumb, debilitated, nasty, and massive, if that's the
1655 alternative: touch the universe anywhere you touch it
everywhere: man's a scourge not because he is man but because

139

he's not man enough: how public like a smog publicity is:
in spite of the spectacularity of the universe (even in the
visual reception) it appears to those who have gone above our

1660   atmosphere that the universe is truly a great darkness, light
in the minority, unsurrendered coals sprinkled in the thinnest
scattering, though, of course, light, even when seen from

afar, attracts the attention most: but out on the periphery
the lights are traveling so fast away their light can't get
1665   back to us, darkness, in our dimension, finally victorious

in the separation: I have dreamed of a stroll-through, the
stars in a close-woven, showering bedazzlement, though
diamond- or ruby-cool, in which I contemplated the universe

140

at length: apparently, now, such dreams, foolish anyway,
1670   must be abandoned and the long, empty, freezing gulfs of
darkness must take their place: come to think of it, though,

I'm not unfamiliar with such gulfs, even from childhood, when
the younger brother sickened and then moved no more: and
ahead lies a gulf light even from slow stars can never penetrate,

1675   a dimension so endless not even the universal scale suits it:
the wise advise, don't get beyond yourself into foolish largeness,
when at my step is a largeness the universe lies within:

to be small and assembled! how comforting: but how perishable!
our life the tiny star and the rest, the rest: this extreme
1680   flotation (it and us) this old, inconstant earth daily born

141

new into thousands of newborn eyes—proceeding by a life's
length here and there, an overlapping mesh of links proceeding:
but, for me, turning aside into rust, reality splintering the

seams, currents going glacial and glassy with knowledge, the
1685   feared worst become the worst: meanwhile, once again the world
comes young, the mother follows her toddler around the cafeteria

and can't see him her eyes so keeping in touch with the admiring
eyes of others: (the old mother, thin-white, thick-jawed, feels
her way, but barefooted, out to the mailbox: nothing: all

1690   the fucking finished, all the sweet, terrifying children grown
up and blown away, just the geraniums in the tire watered
every day, fussed at, plucked:) let me tell you how I get up

142

in the morning: I get up, take a step or two, and morning jars
and pauses me, and I look down into the bottom of my grave:
1695   shaken, I move, though, as if through iron, on when my life,

my real life, wakes up in a tantrum and shakes me like last
year's beanstakes: I lean against the doorjamb until my life
gags into despair, and then I proceed: I proceed, how, into

what: I say, if I can get through this hour, I won't come to
1700   another one but to life: with a front left, I erect a smile
on it, and right away everybody starts laying his troubles on me:

I say in myself, don't lay any more trouble on me: when here
comes another youth anxious for fame and sorry he doesn't
have it: what can I do, he says: well, I say, why not try

143

1705   whatever you can: by the time you amount to something,
the people you meant it to mean something to are dead and you
are left standing there, your honors in your hands: the

ribbons wilted: the cheese melted: the sausage running:
there at the end (which may be anywhere) after dullish
1710   afternoons and vacant mornings, after settlement from the

disturbance of sex, when you were coward, clown, fool, and
sometimes lord, there saved for the end, a novelty, death,
infinite and nonrepeating, an experience to enter with

both eyes wide open, the long play that ends without boredom:
1715   its unexpectedness such you don't have the materials for
a rehearsal, more surprising than with girls where one

144

approach run through can profit a later one: you go in,
your mouth stretches so wide it turns you inside out,
a shed skin, and you gulp nothingness, your biggest bite,

1720   your greatest appetite, stuffed with vacancy: who knows
whether in the middle years, after the flashing passions
seem less like fountains and more like pools of spent flood

metal, one may not keep on partly because of that black sucker
at the end, mysterious and shiny: my skull, my own skull
1725   (and yours) is to be enclosed—earpits, eye sockets, dangled-open

mouth—with soil, is to lie alone without comfort through
centuries and centuries, face (if any) up, as if anticipating
the return of the dream that will be only the arrival of

145

        the nova: how sluggish consciousness, when in death the
1730   nova is a wink away! the rational, the formed, defined,
        directional is the male principle: the cushioner, the female

        principle, the pudding within which the rational plays:
        these two principles give birth to mind: one could not want
        all pudding (pudenda) nor all shape but an interworking,

1735   a whole generating: this poem is an elongated cylinder
        designed to probe feeling, recognition, and realization,
        to plunder the whoozies of the world sensationally and cause

        to come to bear what is and may be: I am not a whit manic
        to roam the globe, search seas, fly southward and northward
1740   with migrations of cap ice, encompass a hurricane with

146

        a single eye: things grown big, I dream of a clean-wood
        shack, a sunny pine trunk, a pond, and an independent income:
        if light warms a piney hill, it does nothing better at the

        farthest sweep of known space: the large, too, is but a
1745   bugaboo of show, mind the glittering remnant: things to do
        while traveling: between entrance and exit our wheels

        contact the ribbon of abstract concrete: speed-graded curves
        destroy hills: we move and see but see mostly the swim of
        motion: distance is an enduring time: here, inside, what

1750   have we brought: between blastoff and landing, home and
        office, between an event of some significance and another
        event of some significance, how are we to entertain the time

147

and space: can we make a home of motion: there is a field
of sheep, vanishing: something terminal may be arriving to
1755   that house, but we are leaving: mortgage payments, water rent,

phone bills, medical insurance, steep steps imprisoning an old
man: but we are fueled and provisioned: motion is our place:
history lists and you know by the difficulty of getting around

at an angle all day that something is too much or amiss: your
1760   awareness begins to take shape, to obtrude, to call attention to
itself, a warp or persisting tension: you are reminded

to go below and check the ballast: how is it that what was
enough for both sides has become too much for one side and not
enough for the other: you gather a force and go down to make

148

1765   correction: history uprights, sways to the give and take in
a touchy balance, so active, lively, so responsive: nevertheless,
a wind may come up subtle or sudden and persist and you may

have to go down and change the ballast, only to find when the
wind does cease that uprightness in an imbalance is imbalance:
1770   fire, instructive flame, foliate saprophyte, consumer,

criticism at the wafered edges of form, master of shape, god
of a kind, traveling wave of the imagination, fire line,
waster of the old that gives destruction's ash to the future,

we are assembled, what is the instruction: the instruction is
1775   in perceiving the principle itself, the god, his action: by
this instruction we are reduced, our works ashes in the wind,

149

but the field, gone through, is open and in the woodburn
the jackpine cone flicks open and ejects seed: ferns rouse
subsoil curls: birds accept the brush margins of feeding

1780   grounds and hawks police the new actions for waywardness:
the gods of care and economy of motion, the grass gods, the
god of the killdeer arrive, and the old god of the forest

begins to take everything away again: from other planets,
as with other planets from here, we rise and set, our presence,
1785   reduced to light, noticeable in the dark when the sun is

away: reduced and distanced into light, our brotherhood
constituted into shining, our landforms, seas, colors
subsumed to bright announcement: we are alone in a sea that

150

shows itself nowhere in a falling surf but if it does not
1790   go on forever folds back into a further motion of itself:
the plenitude of nothingness! planets seeds in a coronal

weaving so scant the fabric is the cloth of nakedness:
Pluto our very distant friend skims a gulf so fine and far
millions and thousands of millions of years mean little to—

1795   how far lost we are, if saving is anywhere else: but light,
from any distance or point we've met it, shines with a similar
summation, margin affirmational, so we can see edges to the

black roils in the central radiances, galaxies colliding in
million-year meetings, others sprung loose into spiral
1800   unwindings: fire, cold space, black concentration:

151

harmonies (in my magnum hokum) I would speak of, though
chiefly as calling attention to neglected aspects of fairly
common, at least overreaching, experience: with considerable

rasping along the edges, bulgings of boundaries, we made
1805   and tamed into play each of these States: if the States
kept falling into lesser clusters about lesser points of

focus (and then the long division, so costly), still we
checked and balanced and, incorporating as much sin as grace
with each holding, kept the mobile afloat, together, each

1810   dangle with good range to dip and rise and convey itself
roundly with windy happenstance, communicating, though, its
position throughout the network and receiving from the sums

152

of the network just adjustments: yes, we got it all together,
ocean to ocean, high temperate to low temperate, and took
1815   in so much multiplicity that what we hold person to person

in common exists only in the high levels of constitution or
out to the neighbor's fence, an extreme, an extreme pity,
with little consolation in the middle after all: still,

it holds and moves within the established rigors: now, with
1820   the same rasping and groaning, we try to put the nations and
communities of nations together and there, too, only by

joining tenuous extremes, asserting the dignity of the single
person above united nations: we pray this may succeed and
correct much evil in the dark edges of dislocation and

153

1825   distraction: lately, we've left out the high ranges of music,
the planetary, from our response, though the one sun is here
as usual and the planets continue to obey holy roads: the

galaxy is here, nearly too much to speak of, sagely and
tremendously observing its rotation: we do have something to
1830   tune in with and move toward: not homogeneous pudding but

united differences, surface differences expressing the common,
underlying hope and fate of each person and people, a gathering
into one place of multiple dissimilarity, each culture to its

own cloth and style and tongue and gait, each culture, like
1835   the earth itself with commonlode center and variable surface,
designed-out to the exact limit of ramification, to discrete

154

expression into the visible, specific congruence of form and
matter, energy moving into the clarification of each face, hand,
ear, mouth, eye, billions: still with the sense of the continuous

1840   running through and staying all the discretions, differences
diminished into the common tide of feelings, so that difference
cannot harden into aggression or hate fail to move with the

ongoing, the differences not submerged but resting clear at
the surface, as the surface, and not rising above the surface
1845   so as to become more visible and edgy than the continuum:

a united, capable poem, a united, capable mind, a united capable
nation, and a united nations! capable, flexible, yielding,
accommodating, seeking the good of all in the good of each:

155

to float the orb or suggest the orb is floating: and, with the
1850   mind thereto attached, to float free: the orb floats, a bluegreen
wonder: so to touch the structures as to free them into rafts

that reveal the tide: many rafts to ride and the tides make a
place to go: let's go and regard the structures, the six-starred
easter lily, the beans feeling up the stakes: we're gliding: we

1855   *are* gliding: ask the astronomer, if you don't believe it: but
motion as a summary of time and space is gliding us: for a while,
we may ride such forces: then, we must get off: but now this

beats any amusement park by the shore: our Ferris wheel, what a
wheel: our roller coaster, what mathematics of stoop and climb: sew
1860   my name on my cap: we're clear: we're ourselves: we're sailing.
1972–1973

DIVERSIFICATIONS (1975)

for Richard Howard

❦

Transcendence

Just because the transcendental,
having digested all change into
a staying, promises foreverness,

it's still no place to go, nothing
5   having survived there into life:
and here, this lost way, these

illusory hollyhocks and garages,
this is no place to settle: but
here is the grief, at least,

10   constant, that things and loves
go, and here the love that
never comes except as permanence.

1973 (1974)

Insouciance

You notice
as
the flowering spike
of the
5   forget-me-not
lengthens
with flowering it
leaves
behind a drab notation (namely
10   seeds even
smaller

than the flowers)
which does not
say
15   forget me not
because
it means to
be back

(1973)

Narrows

Constrictions, gross substantialities (the lifting
of form) figure definitions: narrows govern seas:
like there at Gibraltar, an enrichment,

landforms, Africa's good-sized mountain easily as if
5   seeing across the Straits, looking into Iberia, the
Mediterranean touching the Atlantic in a seeable

scape: that ruffling of surfaces, Atlantic weather
mixing with Mediterranean, the winds of each weather
buttressing, reconciling their systems: awareness frantic

10   with things and differences, the forces of great matters
brought into concisions of resolution: the meeting
of differences, a sexual stir: (I liked it there: I

was amused and somewhat afraid:) strictures clarify:
the rock, coarsened with form, has an edge, at least,
15   like relief: the mulling ocean, au contraire, seldom

shows an island, whale, or glacier, its mounts of
a watery likeness, however majestically they lift,
roll, suck under, and kill: get at the stone in the

duct, though, and you know why the bladder swells:
20   bolus in the artery, quickly damaging: but the ocean's
fine, in a way, with a life of its own apart from

inlets and outlets: knots, tangles, twists draw
attention, provide milieu, engrossing turn and contrariety,
give circulations focus, wield greatnesses unspecific:

25   how can we leave the narrows firm, surveyable, and
prefer undifferentiations' wider motions: how can we
give up control into being controlled: the suasions.

(1972)

Salt Flats

I need this broad place to work because I'm
    not certain what design wants
to emerge: I have to have room to work in various
places
5   with minor forms
        reconciling multiplicity here and there

a little at a time
before unity, subsuming all lesser curves and devices,
    can assume perimeter:
10   the blue-air mountains
on the plain's edge jingled with vanishment:

I set to work: here is this, I said, drawing from
    a center certain yearnings into line:
and here is this, wavy: I ran several miles
15   across the sand, roughed an area off, then
        informed it deeply with glyph and figure:
when
a single wind arrived, set
down its many hands, whirled, and made me out.

Full

I retire from
the broad engagements,
leave the line
and go
5   back into the woods
to openings of

hillslides and lakes:
l do not want
to be
10   loud with emptiness
a hundred years
from now: the

simple event
suffices—complete—
15   when fall
hawkweed spindling
lifts a single
adequate blossom.

1963 (1973)

Uppermost

The top
grain on the peak
weighs next
to nothing and,
5   sustained
by a mountain,
has no burden,
but nearly
ready to float,
10   exposed
to summit wind,

it endures
the rigors of having
no further
figure to complete
and a
blank sky
to guide its dreaming

1974 (1975)

Lightning

Once a roving man
tired of roving
took a place and
planted a tree

5   which grew
year by year—
its

roots deepened, complicating,
its
10   branches filled out

holding, figuring
space:

and the man,
mirrored, stood
15   in the tree:

one day the causes of
his roving
found him and struck:

he turned to the tree:
20   it held
and could not go:

tired of roving but
unable to stay,
where could
25   he go:

he hangs from the tree.

1965 (1973)

The Marriage

The world is wound round
with theorems, a winding:
syntax in thickets meshing:

coalescences of ongoing
5   darkening with thread of
thought, unraveling: tangles

of hypothesis weaving
semantic currents: spools
of possibility feeding

10   spun cotton balls: caps
of *a priori* with zones of
steamy incipience: the mind's

spider laying into the natural
motions binding filaments
15   of sight, the orb sustaining

warps of motion under
heaving, forced declarations:
ah, this caught thing!

it can't get loose from
20   meanings and the mind
can't pull free of it.

1974 (1974)

Self-Portraits

Though I have cut down, pulled up, and
plowed you under, don't, weeds, spurn
my more usual love:
that others have hated you
5   costs my love not a quality:
because others have hated you
my imagination, at home with dirty
saints, gets sand in its eyes:
if this lessens neither your horror nor mine,
10   if this lessens neither your hardiness nor mine,
still it adds my pip to the squeak:
the rejected turn strange
to get their song through: I'm familiar
with byways: I've worn
15   paths out of several unlocated woods.

Double Exposure

Flounderlike, poetry
flattens white
against bottom mud

so farthest tremors can get
5   full-ranged to the bone:
but on the side it flowers

invisible with blue mud-work
imitations, it
turns both eyes.

1968 (1973)

Currencies

I participate
with rain:
precipitate at twig-ends

    and come
5   down:
drop from the bellies of galls:

elbows of branches accumulate
trembling nodes
that

10   flash fang-silver
into
snow-soaked ground:

I participate with
rain's
15   gathering and coming down:

hear me, gathered into runlets,
brooks, breaking over falls,
escaping with the silver of seeing.

1964 (1972)

Bonus

The hemlocks slumped
already as if bewailing
the branch-loading

shales of ice, the rain
5   changes and a snow
sifty as fog

———

begins to fall, brightening
the ice's bruise-glimmer
with white holdings:

10   the hemlocks, muffled,
deepen to the grim
taking of a further beauty on.

1974 (1974)

Emerson

The stone longs for flight,
the flier for a bead, even
a grain, of connective stone:
which is to say, all
5   flight, of imaginative hope or
fact, takes accuracy from stone:

without the bead the flier
released from
tension has no true
10   to gauge his motions in:
assured and terrified by
its cold weight, the stone

can feather the thinnest
possibility of height:
15   that you needed
to get up and I down
leaves us both still
sharing stone and flight.

1973 (1973)

Meeting the Opposition

The wind sidles up to
and brusquely in a swell flattens
lofting one side
of the spirea bush:
5   but the leaves have

so many edges, angles
and varying curvatures that
the wind on the other side
seeps out in a
10   gentle management.

1973 (1973)

Appearances

I could believe water
is not water
and stone not stone
but when

5   water comes
down the brook
corresponding with
perfect

accuracy of adjustment
10   to the brookbed,
spreading like a pane
over slate

or wrinkling into
muscles to skirt
15   a tilt
or balking

———

into a deep loss of
direction
behind a tangled dam
20   and when

I feel those
motions correspond
to my own, my
running quick and

25   thin and stalling broody,
I think a real
brook and I in some
missing mirror meet.

(1973)

Measure

for Robert Morgan

I said there must be someway
to determine
what good
a stalk of grass is—what

5   other measure but man?

In the hierarchy of use
to us
sea-oats are
inconsequential. But since

10   they exist, they
exist in the measure of
themselves
and promote the measure.

1963 (1964)

Delight

The angels who in innocent if
not painless intelligence
fly around a lot (sometimes away)

flew down one day
5   to the pastures of men
and said

"look, this one's a stone
brunted
and there is one turning in himself

10   like a burnt-over viper
and look, this one's
broader in his eyes than the world"

and the angels grew surprised
with the quantity
15   of contortion, misplacement, and mischance:

the stone cried
"if I am not to take myself
as I am, by

what means am I to be changed" and the viper
20   said
"the fountains of myself are a vision

I will not behold" and others grown old in
pain
cried out "who am I"

25   and the angels said "shall we give advice"
and said "should we
bring water

———

or bread or should we at least slay
selected ones"
30   but knowing neither whether to accept

the pastures as they were nor, if not, any
means to change them
veered off again

in broad loops and sweeps through the skies
35   and out of sight brushed
stars in their going by atwinkle.

(1973)

The Stemless Flower

A big majestic poem, consummation,
could be written on the gradations
of flow from the gross to the fine:

but who would read it: no matter:
5   brevity's self-justifying: take
the energy of flow in diamonds,

rocks, trees, brooks, cyclones, in
light, feeling, mind, spirit:
of course, it's not just

10   the energy of flow, it's
constant energy operating in a
diminishing substance, so the sum

total of change in a diamond is
slight, but in a thought, how little
15   matter and how much speed: somebody

could hit the physicochemical texts
and come up with a nice rise on this
subject, a massive compilation and

registration, a book of order for the
20   disgruntled, misapplied times: and
motion would then sway all—as it does.

Imperialist

Everybody knows by now
that the weeds are mine
& knows I don't feel
altogether sorry for them:
5   but they I think
resent being owned or
written into roses.

(1975)

Poem

In a high wind the
leaves don't
fall but fly
straight out of the
5   tree like birds

1973

Imago

I refuse the breakage:
I hold on
to the insoluble knots
I've circled for years
5   turning in contradictory
wildness, as
safe with center as
jugs and stars: what
I can't become keeps me

10 to its image: what
can't be reconciled is
home steady at work.

1968 (1972)

Light Orders

Sometimes maple leaves come all of an angle,
stacked planes, resembling glimmery schools
of fish caught in dazzling turns: of course
leaves are a kind of fish the wind swims
5 its ocean through, and the glimmering—dislocated—

of a school might be no more than staid leaves
the ocean riffles like a wind: but a spider
out there on one leaf's built a surface web
over a lake of space, top of the leaf, stiffened
10 into a drought fold, sloop, and he's filtering out

whatever motion brings—the kill intended
exact, unglancing into metaphor: I feel
coming the rise of nets and flow and
the possibility of a further sea-wind summation
15 and many things have died since that was old.

1969

History

The brine-sea coupling
of the original
glutinous molecules

preserves itself all
5 the way up into our
immediate breaths:

———

we are the past
alive in its
truest telling:

10   while we carry it,
we're the whole
reading out of consequence:

history is a blank.

(1973)

Self-Projection

The driest place in the yard's
under the faucet:
where there is hose,
length will move
5   the source away
from its own critical drought:
hesitate and
undo: unscrew
and turn the undisciplined faucet
10   on: what more than the self
sometimes needs the self.

1968 (1972)

Outside-the-Household Hint

When picking
pears
off a hanging
pear-limb
5   start picking at
your highest
reach
and then pick

down into
10   the limb's rise:

if you start
picking
from
the bottom the
15   limb in
rising
will bear
the high pears beyond
you.

Metaphysic

Because I am
here I am
(nowhere)
else

1969

Tussock

From high
winds the gulls
lie low: as the self

crouches from the
5   ragings of its
high mind:

hunkers down
into all that
silence can advise.

(1973)

The Make

How I wish great poems could be written about nothing
you know just sitting around a comet coming
leaves falling off a bush in a cliff
ducks flicking their tails, a driblet spray,
5   the universe turning over or inside out
small prominences on the ocean wind-smoothed into waxen scallops
how I wish there could be the most exciting line ever going nowhere
or traveling making money spending it messing around
a warp in pure space just a warp unwarping
10   a stone losing three molecules into a brook's edge
or the point of a leaf trying to fall off by itself
how I wish that instead of poetic tensions there could be dreaming
shales of mind spilling off (with a little dust rising) into deep cones
a gathering and spinning out
15   into threads some so fine the mind rescues them with imagination
little bits of lightning when the wind bends them through the light
how I wish there could be such poems
about nothing doing nothing

1973 (1975)

Juice

I'm stuck with the infinity thing
again this morning: a skinny
inexpressible syrup, finer than light,
everywhere present: the cobweb becoming
5   visible with dust and the tumblelint
stalled in the corner seem worthy.

Terminations

Sometimes the celestial syrup slows
into vines
stumps, rock slopes,

it's amazing in fact how
5　　 slow it can get—diamond:

but then sometimes it flows
free in a flood
and high
so procedure drowns out
10　　perception

practically, a roof showing
here and there
or a branch
bobbing:
15　　as skinny

wind it recalls
and promises everything
but delivers nothing
except the song that
20　　skims the mountains

and makes no sense
(except all sense)
to us
slowed discrete
25　　out of following.

(1973)

Fundamental Constant

The clouds,
from what possible formations,
nudged and shaped
to what directions,
5　　came this
way
and the rain, hardly breaking

free from the
larger motions,
10   occurred:

I look through the window now
to the hedge
leaf
unsettled by a drop
15   that quivering to fall
blinks a prismatic
code
several kinds
of change sorting
20   through eons have
failed to change or break.

(1973)

Making It

Entering the dark sounds
all right
if promising radical
loss of diversion
5   and going down into
dwelling through the dark
that sounds okay a
deepening into profundity
but at the giving
10   up into the dark of the dark
the loss of
the sight of sightlessness
a cry begins
to tear
15   that tears till it tears free

1973 (1974)

Scope

Getting little
poems off (clusters
of them) hits
centers—if lesser centers—
5   quicker and
set-wise like the rocks
of kaleidoscopes
makes infinite
combinations possible whereas
10   the long job's
demand for consistency
levels,
though the one center it
shoots for
15   may be deeper
(if hit
or if not moved away into
disintegration
by the fulsome carriages)

Weight

He loved cloud covers,
went into woods
to hide from stars: he
wept under bridges,
5   noticed weeds, counted
frog calls
till a stone in
his belly hardened
against infinity, the
10   grievances of levitation.

1965 (1976)

Ballad

I want to know the unity in all things and the difference
between one thing and another
    I said to the willow
and asked what it wanted to know: the willow said it
5   wanted to know how to get rid of the wateroak
that was throwing it into shade every afternoon at 4 o'clock:
        that is a real problem I said I suppose
and the willow, once started, went right on saying
I can't take you for a friend because while you must
10   be interested in willowness, which you could find nowhere
        better than right here,
        I'll bet you're just as interested in wateroakness
which you can find in a pure form right over there,
a pure form of evil and death to me:
15   I know I said I want to be friends with you both but the
willow sloughed into a deep grief
and said
if you could just tie back some of those oak branches
until I can get a little closer to mastering that domain
20   of space up there—see it? how empty it is
and how full of light:
        why I said don't I ask the wateroak if he would mind
withholding himself until you're more nearly even: after
all I said you are both trees and you both need water and
25   light and space to unfold into, surely the wateroak will
understand that commonness:
        not so you could tell it, said the willow:
        that I said is cynical and uncooperative: what could
you give the wateroak in return for his withholding:
30   what could I give him, said the willow, nothing
that he hasn't already taken:
        well, I said, but does he know about the unity in
all things, does he understand that all things have a
common source and end: if he could be made
35   to see that rather deeply, don't you think he might
        give you a little way:

no said the willow he'd be afraid I would take all:
would you I said:
or would you, should the need come, give him a little way
40   back:
        I would said the willow but my need is greater than
his
and the trade would not be fair:
maybe not I said but let's approach him with our powerful
45   concept that all things are in all
        and see if he will be moved

                          (1973)

Three Travelogues

I.

Off backwoods macadam
swinging back at a sharp angle
onto the sandy road
downwoods
5   laurel in hung cloud clumps opening
the sprung anthers
ready to shoot loose
multitudinous into the air
floats of pollen
10   gazes of yellow along the pinkribbed floral bowls:
a grouse hen
sanding
in sun at the road's edge,
not stirring, enthralled,
15   interruption
a disbelief,
the car's motion safety enough
and on along the ribbed rubbling road
to the white small bridge
20   at the turn's downward curve:
got out to see,
saw on the stream's bank

in full sun
the arching fern, its
25   cinnamon
rod lifting high, set off,
tall and honest,
waterbeetles swimming upstream,
darting, "standing" in flow:
30   on the other side
damselflies, blackwinged,
needle bodies
enameled, oriental green,
at the wingtips, strutted open,
35   a white dot, star,
the wings closed upward,
drawn open downward four white stars,
the lacy pumping of
amazement and desire

II.

40   Fell ashore in high seas,
the blackwet, weed-slickened canes of my raft
loosened by the surf approach:
rose between rocks and hit ground
beyond the sea's way:
45   held an armful of reeds from my breaking ship:
gleaned from swell and foam
slack straws to keep:

and went higher among sprayless rocks and stiff shrubs
and rested,
50   the stars available, multitudinous, the dark
wide, deeper than sight:

I lived there, treasuring
the rainpool in the scalloped rock,
stretching my clothes to showers, gathering
55   rain,

wringing the pool full,
drinking from the twisted fountain:

there I lived, preying
on gulls' nests,
60   splashing minnows from the runlets of caves,
sleeping,
the straws of my ship bedded under
stones from the wind's lift, dreaming,

tomorrow wings,
65   the cautious, off-circling eyes,
the water clear, dotless far as light
into the tunnels of rock,
fire's simmering,
a white-sailed cloud's blue hull of rain:

70   nude, brush-burned, alone: underwater, land and
vegetation, hostile, oily luxuriance,
the deep, windless surges, quiet, proliferation:
sang on the moon-bleached highest rock
the bell-less hours of night,
75   time-starved in the plenty of time

III.

An interruption makes a world: descent of
energies, failure of equilibrium: an unevenness,
imbalance:

in late March I went for a walk along the
80   margin of fields and woods
(margins are places for things to happen:
a line of difference there, disparity,
discernible change)
and could hardly bear the sight of the small events
85   happening in fullness, occurrences of promise or terror:
a green flake of weed between two larger flakes,
the dark wet ground clumpy, rising here or falling,

weed leaf curling to crowd into the sun,
that great body, furious and radiant, relating
90   directly to billions of events
too common to notice or too small: wild
plum blooming under the edge of pines,
a hold of ground and grass
saved along the ditchbank from the spring plow,

95   the extra green in a rye blade where a rabbit dropped
dark pellets (leaching out and lightening
to rain and sun): the placement
and width of brackets on a soggy stump:
these events:
100   I can hardly tell about them: they seem so
worthless yet are undiminished: so independent,
throwing back our meanings:

and followed the ditch down the wood's edge,
across the bottomland field, and
105   into the woods at the other side
and on down through the woods to where
in the branch the small ditch-flow lost
its separate saying: found a dry, high log, held
from the ground by the circle of turf it turned
110   in falling, and sat down
to see if I could take on the center of a filled out
world but heard from another fallen tree
a branch-trickle whose small music
from breakage and hindrance brought the world
115   whole and full again and to itself.

1962 (1969)

Sight Unseen

Take some prose and build
fairly shabby metrical dikes
around it, so it seems
firm enough, if empty, like

5   scaffolding (that was an
unintentional rhyme) and
(also unintentional) you have
a good representation of

the frame (pun unintended)
10   of mind most of us prefer—
at least, adopt: (here
see visions of people

like tendrils forming into
trellises growing up into
15   (unintentional) crane-like
triangulations, noble structures

that attain workable loft:)
nobody needs, apparently, or
apparently desires monstrous
20   extrusions of energy,

maniacal spools, jungle growths
of ascendancy that could
crunch the held spaces and
finger, in wobbly failures,

25   the sky (the sky of sky and
sky of mind): I am against
something but I don't know
what: failure, a fatigue

of the metal (or bracket loose),
30   enters into every means and
proposition, just as some little
success can be expected nearly

anywhere: I have no beef:
take a fairly unselfconscious

35   prose style, in a prosy day,
        and fail to get excited

        about its median flaws and
        flows and sort of relax
        into an adequate object: the
40   privileged moments confine

        their privilege to moments
        while we have to live, somehow,
        all day: well, here we are, unlost,
        advanced beyond being found:

45   there in the mirror is
        a half-engaged willingness
        to comply, an interest
        we can practically claim.

1973 (1978)

Facing

        I take your hand:
        I touch your
        hair, as if

        you were going away
5   to be a long time
        away, as

        you must someday go
        forever away:
        lust burns out high

10   into light: I walk
        away and back: I
        touch your hair.

1966

Glass Globe

I woke up (merely) and found
myself
inside a bulb of pain:
I said
5   everybody else looks all right,
it must be mine:
I kept it & kept it
shined invisibly clear.

1968 (1972)

Separations

Looking for clear water he
came from murky lowlands
to the desert and
after high plains & higher mesas

5   saw a white mountain
and going up into the sharp reaches

fell down and drank melt:
the cold water bore no
dream: he perished,
10   swilling purity.

1965

Circling

Occurrence is continuous (and in
continuum)

(mind
ever making) and unmaking: the star

5 burns to the brim:
water moves:

motion organizes, parallel motions
echo along
parallels
10 and break out (or are broken out)
to oppose
other motions, confluences:

the white flakes of
rue anemone
15 spindled up
break into light

and broken

snow
against a surf of motions: (occurrence
20 continuous) and in
continuum.

1966 (1975)

Fix

Stumped again, I
sit and radiate
loss like
the message finally
5 come:

in truth, though, I
don't know what
to do: if
there were any

———

10   way out of this,
      I'd, giving up
      the sphere,
      assume the linear,
      smart as a bullet.

                                        1971 (1977)

Weather

Guilt's been circling
my head all morning
waiting for the crime

to be defined
5   so conscience can drop
and punish the black meat out:

but all morning I haven't been able
to conjure up a single
wrong: the vulture rides

10 in the fairest weather:
light and warmth
send him higher, abler.

                                        (1975)

Coward

Bravery runs in my family.

Crying Out

Cool peripheries, raw
interludes of hedgerows,
confusions of ditchbanks,

brush weedstalks
5   standing: testing the mesh
for a rupture, I
trouble the rims
and distances of possibility
because
10   my center is vacant,
its hallelujah in a shambles.

(1973)

Certainty

I have certainly felt the documentation of terror:
I have certainly known my
insides to turn all hands
and rush to the surface for help
5   and felt the hands go loose:
I certainly have come to believe in death:
my head rustles with footnotes and
quotation marks
that pinpoint places where my blood
10   has certainly stopped cold and certainly raced.

1968 (1972)

The Flaw

I never saw anything like it—
such a day:
coolish, dry, bright,
the sky deep blue,
5   trees and bushes a hard
dark green:
now
an hour before sundown
were it not
10   for the robin's song

rippling out along the pear limb
everything would be glass.

1967 (1968)

Triplet

Iris leaves
threes-in-one
cut
broadside into sun and rain
5   to send high
flop loose the
hairy huzzy
iris bloom

Design

It's actually six-thirty:
we've already been to
Scotch Hall for dinner:
I had tired flounder,
5   the whitest meat, in
every flake
extremest finery of black
lace, once bloodways:
now of course the
10   flounder has
completely foundered.

1968

Rocking

The cock sparrow with a sweet
tweetering
did it on-and-off
fluttering four times quick

on the porch eaves:
the hen sparrow seemed
moved no further than
injunction's
"propagate the species":
10 well, the sun's breaking
out, maybe she'll like that,
or maybe she means her
propriety to send
that earnest little
15 rooster off again.

1968

Ars Poetica

The gods (for
whom I work) are
refreshing realists:

they let you into
5 paradise (which is
the best pay—

and pay they
know's the best
equalizer,

10 disobliging
all concerned)
and say, sing:

that's all: they
have their own
15 business: and

you can't begin
by saying, I've
been in

―――――

Hudson, Partisan,
20   and *Poetry*: the
gods are

jealous of their
own judgment: and
you can't say, I

25   feel sort of
stove-up today, just
got rejected

by *Epoch*: the
gods, as with other
30   species, don't give

a damn about
you, only the song,
and song is all

protects you there:
35   tough: but the
pay is good enough.

1959 (1974)

Course Discourse

Brief histories, scribblings,
are permitted to snow:
in winter woods, the
trees generous with open ground,
5   the parchment gets
through and, settling, sheets
the leaves:
and there's the legibility,

clumps of rabbit tracks
10   tracing through the trees,
the leap off a mound
onto the frozen, snow-hidden
puddle, the broad skid,
the skirmish of recovery
15   and the clumps again.

(1975)

Obtrusion

The leaf has to be thick
enough to catch the light
and thin enough

to let it through:
5   the double governance, bind,
leads to precise adjustments,

optimum advantages within
constraining and releasing
possibilities: reason,

10   caught between holding to
know and letting go,
adjusts to the exact taint,

introducing into the medium
just so much of itself as
15   will construe but not destroy

the essence it seeks:
limit against limit
plays accuracy into procedure.

1974

Louise

I drove down to Aurora
at 4:15 and picked up
Louise from work
and Louise's hair, what a deposit,
5   and her eyelashes and teeth,
her shoulders hung
with all that seemed to be
getting away with her sweater,
and I suggested McDonald's
10   for dinner but thought we
should stop off somewhere
first and get it over with:
Louise and I love relaxed
dinners and that's the
15   kind we had: Louise's
shiny fingers pulled
french fries out and her
stomach and hips and thighs
appreciated the hamburger: by
20   then I was feeling real loose
and easy and thought as we
left of Louise's ankles and
toes getting her out of the
place and of the way her
25   mind put it all together
without even thinking.

(1973)

80-Proof

A fifth of me's me:
the rest's chaser:
35 lbs.'s
my true self: but

5   chuck 10 lbs. or so for bones,
what's left's
steaks & chops &
chicken fat,
two-over-easy & cream-on-the-side:
10   strip off a sheath of hide,
strip out nerves & veins
& permeable membranes,
what's left's a greasy spot:
the question's
15   whether
to retain
the shallow stain
or go 100% spiritual
and fifth by fifth
20   achieve a whole,
highly transcendental.

(1964)

Having to Do with Birth

I've always been impressed with the word *incunabulum*:
even put a little off: *cun* immediately seems to be working
up to something—a kind of dash of feeling: and then

in cun suggests an actually ruffling stress or imminence
5   hard to turn back on: *nab*, however, seems practically
imperative, following so close upon, as if ready will

were enduring the nudges of insistent, jabbing impulse: but
then *nab u* personifies the thing out of figurative reason,
activating recall of a clutter of ideal images, set in

10   glow: *bul* is only an *l* short of the ideal presence of my
own hope in the piece: but I don't know that I like to be
stirred where I'd counted on the safety of lexical drought:

a *p* would complete *lum* to the afterwards feeling all
too puzzlingly well; the lassitude and disorientation
15   that while blessing the magic are half-relieved it's gone.

1971 (1977)

Limp Lump

Glubgullies in the fricassee:
careful: circling things are
out: terminals, too, scare me & I'm
alarmed at the coils beginnings imply:
5   let's shove one
another:
impotence comes when need
exceeds seed: much is needed here:
one feels overworked working over
10   the same old worked over work.

Mind

After the complex reductions come
the simple reductions, the apple
firm in the hand, weightless in the mind,

the elms drifted out of their roots, strung
5   into a green-wind wear, a sense of
seeing through never ending

in the endings, a piling into the sun
of the mind's sun returned: and then,
high with reductions, the chill that

10   we live where we can't live but
live there if we live, a house of mind
we never quite get the door open to.

1970 (1973)

Attenuations

Fantasies that do test the periphery of consciousness
let us have then, if death's the solid center absolute
but death's not, the center as much in the rufflings

of nothingness as the peripheries: for example, rock,
5   whole ragged ranges, that fells us with surficial weight,
weighs at the center of the earth nothing, becomes

outward flotation cast into poise by its opposite
radial: whichever way we move from the exact, we become
less like the local but more like the sphere: this

10   morning I turned a disintegrating ray on myself and
glimmered into mist, broke down further into limelight
and then became nothingness, continuum transportable.

1971 (1973)

Turning

From reality's flowing flurry
take out a glass bead
and steer round &
round
5   it, an everlasting:
the center's in there,
its invisibility seen through.

(1973)

Swipe

In the useless study of uselessness one
gets cramps, twinges of contradiction—
how spiritless, in a sense, that contradiction
leads to wholeness, perhaps wholesomeness,

in that if anything can be presumed to have
     been divided, contradiction can seem to be

     taking both quotients into account: how
     quickly uselessness makes a useful comment
     on usefulness; for example, that mere usefulness
10   is useless, the useless less available
     to the hacking divisions of definition,
     a positive value: everything pays off a little.

Paradise

     Rot richness, sticky, feverish,
     that clears and thins, worm-gum globs
     rinsing in rain,
     the ripe garbage truck, odors
5   lacing the wind,
     dispersing, molecule standing miles downwind
     from molecule,
     naked, odorless—the translation:
     the mind has seen a clear place
10   beyond the reach of any molecule.

                                        1965

Satisfaction

     Still I'm for upper
     buzzardry: the high
     easy fix
     of the actual meal:
5   hunger lofts:
     descent's a nasty dinner.

The Unmirroring Peak

What changes:
the changeable which
everything, including

the universe swelling
5 and shrinking from
bang to

bang, is: but
a summit in the
mind

10 holds expansion &
contraction to its
lesser heights,

changelessly out-and-in even there:
but in
15 the highest heights

where the converging loft
reaches past
material's finest

wash to immaterial
20 staying,
a land, the mind's,

where nothing comes
to pass,
lies, abides, untouchable

25 and unyielding:
down the slopes
changeable forms and colors

———

assume their fictions,
dread, joy,
30   despair but lie, press against

the rise whose angle
is invariant and whose
completion is final.

1971

Pray Without Ceasing

I hear the low falling from the
highlands of hog-pasture, a music
of spheres, a couple: whatever is

done is to be
5   undone:
call me down from the
high places: I have achieved much
of the difficulty of my translation:

        stock in trade
10   gunstock
        stockings
        stocks & bonds & good
        stock
   put no stock in that
15   a stock case
       in stock
        stock the soup

3, the mystical figure, comes through:
the alternating, suspended,
20   opposing spheres undirected and
the directed unity, reconciler and

putter to sleep—
milt on
the levees of rationality:

25   "O Aegypte,
Aegypte, of thy religious rites nought
will survive but tales
which thy children's children
will not believe;
30   nought
will survive but words graven upon
stones that tell of thy piety."
               (Trismegistus)

and in sleep, as in a natural sleep,
35   prone, face turned as if into breath,
he had about him needments, bottles of
rare glass, bowls: we wrapped him
in reed mat, rose from decomposing,
generating waters, went up on
40   the plateau
and put him in
sand: hereafter has
not·changed since for him:
but his head's
45   magnificence and funny-stuff, those
epicycles of motion, rituals of
turning, dancing, the wind
has taken, nothing
changed into grass: all the way
50   out of the rise and fall:

O Egypt I sometimes hear the
future of the universe
speaking in a moonwheel's
turning of sand and light:

55   we set out a withe of silver grass and
it remains: it
has interfered with the natural wind,
fractured the paralleleity of
moonbeams and disturbed
60   lesser sandstorms: mimicry
so often far more succeeds:

you heal back from napalm: the
flame-scars pull chin to chest,
the fingers stick: the mercy

65   of sand's
scarless:

when the sand roars, a lion
rouses in the center, his eyes,
as if in a hollow, headless:
70   recognition is
the fiercest imperative:

a pararox, couple achers: the
real estate of the imagination:

whatever is—
75   terror, pity, grief, death,
rising—a child sits in explosion's
clutter, homeless, his small
driftwood legs, his eyes inventing
an equal rage & dark, white smears
80   of burn
the mask
his face must fit:
whatever is, brutality, the inner siege,
the mind orange, blue with
85   desolation's mold, something
thin & high

cuts through whatever is
and makes no difference of difference:

my mouth, become eyes, weeps
90   words: words spill
into
hyacinths: for my acquaintance
with grief is
intimate, lost voices my credentials:
95   singing's been sung: the same
body is crying:

fatigues snagged by wire,
bodies sag in their buttons, collars
flutter, surf jogs, the wind
100   all outside and usual:
blue dusk fills up under the gold smoke:
the sky violates nothing to intercede:

I held her
by the rose and
105   intruded: the petals
slickened, silken: I shaved
my head &
offered it there:
O rose
110   the microflora along your hinder walls
are fast bloomers: tunnel-scapes
beady with stiff
moss: who keeps the saltsea keeps
its plankton, not reasonable?
115   microflora, reproducing, don't mind
the long glider that
coming shoulders out the wind to
fundamental suction: collapsible
I live with
120   spherical walls:
everyway I look leaning in, leaning in's

the style &
passing over: I pick pockets of
perse pansies, poesies, posepays,
125   powder palls & wary:

I had a little pony:
his name was Dapple Gray:
and every time I had him,
he tried to get away:

130   who will eat from such a garden
let him have an oedipal situation
and my rights and privileges:

that the triadic Hegel could have been
evidencing his
135   genitals is a notion of
such cracking solemnity
birds fail to fly:

some are spring harvests: today,
April Fools', a squirrel in the leafless
140   elm gathered torn bark and inner tissue
from dead branches, wadding them
into her mouth then going limb by
thinning limb to leap onto the heavy
electric wire, then going upstreet to my
145   neighbor's streetside spruce: I
think that's
where the nest will be:
waste assimilated into
use: the result a neatness
150   unpremeditated, a re-ingestion of
process:
so arranged it is that my wasted
life becomes words
that through complexity and
155   unstructured swirl

seek the fall-out of
comparable enhancements:

occurrences
   recognitions
160   surroundings

           tensions sprung free
           into events

happenstance & necessity
   prediction & surprise
165   moment & forever

and the gloomy, oh the melancholy,
remorseful
falling back and away
of time-sunk persons and places,
170   ragged knots
of a grounded, celestial kite:

yesterday robins
on the dark edge of dusk sang like
peepers:
175   I went out to listen
and they were robins:

and on the cold edge of spring
though on a warm day
we went out into the woods for
180   hepaticas up
along Six Mile Creek: we
found one spring-beauty and
by sun-warmed logs
a few clusters of hepatica,
185   hundreds of plants
but few bloomers: the
backfall of creekwater was

interesting, countercaps, and
compensating, the up-creek water
190   along eddying banks:

peripheries:
the dance about the fire,
utterance of tongues,
parlance of feet:
195   griefs can't be removed,
only altered, caught up into the
timed motions
of bearable sway:

fall in love with yourself
200   where it's shallow:
don't
thwart shriveling up by
suddenly drowning:

if change is certain, as say so many,
205   certainty is where there isn't any:

          pop gun
       soda pop
         pop art
         popsicle
210   mom & pop
         popinjay
         pop in
         popeyed
         population

215   I can't get that star carted I said:
flooded carburetor, cracked voltage
regulator: I didn't realize at once
it was apt: a Starchief: and
one day a man said looking at
220   the dash word, it has

your name in it: S*tarchie*f: he
was a good abstractor:

I had a little pony:
his name was Dapple Gray:
225   and when I tried to trim him,
he had a lot to bray:

an inch of snow last night but
mid morning is bright and melting:
the shadows are white:

230   napalm isn't falling here:
so what is it:

first, an explosion near the ground:
then a tarry rain,
soft and afire, falls, crumbles, & sticks:
235   sticks to trees, houses, children,
things like that: if
it hits it's 94.3% effective:

I see my death, my horror, the radical,
real, senseless pain,
240   as a coming afloat,
rocking in a mastery of oceans:
what time caricatures should
time keep:
to those busy making themselves
245   great, with grave music and
solemn looks, a thorough using up and
setting forth of language's materials,
I send
empty statements, slip-shoddiness,
250   incredible breeziness and such:
the wind we go to
understands everything:
I sing, though, in a way, the best I can,

for I may be understood
255   where I do not understand:

around the aureola matters get touchy:

confusion erodes the ice-glass
steel office buildings of rationality:
anti-rationality only makes another
260   kind of thrust: complexity
blurs the sleek towers, wilts the
phallus of mistaken direction:

welcome to your unattended,
coin-operated, do-it-yourself
265   laundry:
bring and use your favorite bleach,
soap, and starch: if
machine is
defective, please use another machine:
270   to start washer put money in coin meter
and
(1) if slide type meter—slowly push
slide all the way in: then slowly
pull slide all the way out:
275   (2) if rotary knob type meter—
turn knob:
tub
will start filling not later than ½
minute after operating coin slide:

280   stopcock
                  cock & bull
            ears cocked
                  cocktail
            peacock
285   cockle
                  cockney

                    cockiness
                    cockscomb
             poppycock
290   cockeyed
                    cockroach
                    cockpit
                    cocksure

         dryclean wash 'n wears, even cotton
295   items: use this
         handy clothing guide: follow
         these simple steps:
         brush away loose lint
         and other soiling matter: turn sweaters
300   inside out: turn down cuffs of
         trousers: insert the
         necessary coins:

         rubbers, after several drycleanings,
         tend to lose elasticity: plastic-coated
305   fabrics often become stiff:
         beware sequins, beads, and other fragile
         ornaments, can get you into trouble:

         remove wear wrinkles and sharpen creases
         and pleats: some spots refuse
310   to come out, rust, mildew, dried paint,
         indelible ink:

         little artery, couple inches long,
         branching into cardiac muscle: it pops
         and you give up philosophy and
315   ultimate concern, car payments, son and wife,
         you give up the majors & minors,
         the way you like your egg cooked, your
         class ring, lawn,
         sparrows nesting in the garage, the

320 four crocus bulbs (maybe more next
year), toenails and fillings:

I wouldn't want to happen up on any
critters of eternity, absolutes that
end the world: fellow said one star
325 up there in our galaxy is mostly
gadolinium, a rare earth;
nobody knows how the concentration occurred:
then there are other surpluses and
scarcities
330 that uneven the tissue:
I wouldn't want anything
to get known tight: ignorance is our
boat giving us motion: or, capsized,
knowledge is our ark which is more in
335 line with the tradition:
  the ocean would then
  be what it
  is:

spirit, though
340 it encompasseth mightiness, etc., however,
cannot, like a motor,
raise and lower
toast:

nothing matters, believe me, except
345 everything: to sift & sort, magnify
& diminish, admit & renounce, impairs
the event:
what the mind can't accept's obscene:
the rest shines with an
350 additional, redeeming
light,
the light in the head
of language in motion:

———

the wave coming in, running, gathers,
355   lofts, curls—the instant of
motion's maximum
organization: then: then one is
forty & hollow: the curl's reach
redeems the hollow, equals it, till
360   the curl touches over: what is the
use: the crashing, the hollow coming
topside into wide prevalence,
the flat waters skinnying out and
rushing back—is merely endurance
365   until the next wave lifts:
as for what's left,
dip it and ship it: to have made
it here is not to have it made:

entering is lovely:
370   such delicacies, scents, the
feminine source, perfumes: cookies
in the oven, delights:

mixmaster, maxmister,
mast me a mix, ur,
375   mix me a mist, ur . . .

the mixers and blenders chew up
differences: chomp & whirl
to knotless paste: the spurt for
equilibrium:
380   to compensate for which somewhere root,
bark, leaf must make a walnut, some
skinny saint rail through the cosmos,
shot from earth by penury and dread:
what is more costly or
385   needed than a mind shot to space by
shiny thrust, a renunciation of
earth, a negative blast away:

———

I have seen all the way in with
a white bang that they
390 are spheres, round solids, sprinkled,
lightly, in a medium, not
empty, called space and that
these round bodies go round
different orders of center
395 that swoosh away burning
their peripheries and sucking
their centers through virgin space, neither
up nor
down—the
400 terror that that is
the way it is,
that particular way, a
pure flower of terror:

ancient souls sitting on
405 the bright banks of forever
in
raptures of old acquaintance: for every
never again,
an always again: and young souls
410 from their quick missing
quick as branches and glittering:
where the lost remains, immortal in
the foreverness of the lost:
say good morning, say buon giorno,
415 say hi
to infant brother, to mother, father,
sit down under the golden pines on
the slopes of no further parting:

the Buddhist nun burns for the peace
420 her ashes will achieve:

the village woman coming home finds
her shack afire, her

son & husband shot: she bends down
where she is:
425 she is given tokens of the dead but
her left arm like a sickle reaps at the
air
for the harvest
already taken:

430 through the reeds somewhere, as by a
paddy or ditch in her head,
wind burrs
a leaf: the woman flutters,
her grief absolute and
435 not a mystery:

how can I know I
am not
trying to know my way into feeling
as

440 feeling
tries to feel its way into knowing:
it's
indifferent what I say: the motions
by which
445 I move
manifest
merely a deeper congruence
where the structures are:

run my poem through your life and
450 exist, decommissioned,
like rubble,
innocent, slouchy on the uptake:

the scramblers, grabbers, builders—
rubblerousers: sticking stone to
455 false stone in a unity of walls which

wants to come apart: let
weeds and grasses move in among a
scattering, make a little shade, hide
mice, give burrows to ground bees,
460   byway hideouts to the engines of spiders,
stones the
owl can come and sit in moonlight on:
we
should all be in a shambles, shacked up,
465   peeping round the grasshoppers,
preserving a respectful quiet:

don't snatch & grab: grab snatch:
laboratory tests attest,
when a system of two bodies
470   charges and discharges itself
it's peaceful as tulips:

can a 41-year-old man living on dandelion leaves
from the cool edges of junkyards
find
475   songlore enough
in the holocausts, boggy garbage,
fly swarms, lamb bones, and rust-floral
cans
of his weedy search
480   to sustain interest:

the continuum, one
and visionless, within
which
the breakdown of pure forms,
485   arising of skyscrapers, laws,
the high crystal-clear arising
of theory:

the evening blue-purple, the trees
black,

490   the birds can't quit singing: damp
        heat built
        and rose through the golden towered afternoon,

        broke finally into motion, as of
        descent, rain beating
495   straight down
        between racks of thunder:

        can anything be erased: can this day's
        praising hold to the day it praises
        down the slopes of total entropy:

500   pray without ceasing:

        we found hailstones in the grass
        and ate them to cool:
        spurred stones
        with interior milkwhite halos,
505   an arrested spangling:
        the high hard water
        melted
        aching our tongues.

                                        1967 (1973)

THE SNOW POEMS (1977)

for my country

༄

Words of Comfort

Words of comfort,
a railing before the fray,
mumbling shock
away from seizure,   between mts
5   a drone, narrative, longer   wind runs
than mourning, going on over
past the waters of
every expense of care

can modes, syntaxes, rhetorics,
10   folkways compete
with equanil (I think not)
to put you away) to sleep
(contemporary verse excepted)
(pick up this week's
15   feelings at your local drugstore)

today misty drizzling (around seventy)
the pleasant pheasant
disappear
drippy-humble
20   into the shrubs and few
birds bother: crows emphatically find dead
trees to sit in,
skinned branches, line up
into the wind,
25   a black countercurrent
drippy but cool

get a poem big enough
ocean-sea rivers
stream around it

———————

30   by the time
a poem is the world
the author is
out of town

pushing fifty—
35   those years you waited to fill out, you
aren't going to fill out, your
biceps firm up:
past fifty the muscles
string free, lean separations into thew and bone:
40   pushing fifty, you notice that the
crest due or normal to arrive has
arrived or isn't coming, not
ever coming, not at all, but something else
quite different, that is certainly coming

45   my friend said
if you can
learn to swim
or fence at
forty or crochet
50   at forty-two age is just numbers

I go back	odd that
over and often	death the evidence
to repeat myself:	for which is
where repetition is	absolute
55 imperfect	is completely
possibility clears	incredible

each of us
exception's single

One Must Recall as One Mourns the Dead

One must recall as one mourns the dead
to mourn the dead and so not mourn too much

thinking how deprived away the dead lie
from the gold and red of our rapt wishes

and not mourn the dead too much who having
broken at the lip the nonesuch

bubble oblivion, the cold grape of ease at
last in whose range no further

ravages afflict the bones, no more
fires flash through the flarings of dreams

do not mourn the dead too much who bear no
knowledge, have no need or fear of pain,

and who never again must see death
come upon what does not wish to die

Things Change, the Shit Shifts

Things change, the shit shifts,
byways and sideways,
break out, horn in,
step in the same do twice

I followed the swamp
hogs off, I picked meat
with cousinly buzzards,
I got rotten meat out
of the ears of old
raccoons while under
the skin next to the

ground, maggots rippled
85   in the heat like breezy water

the levelest look's the jaguar's
peccary gaze (deadset to flare)
or the weaving thermal gaze of
the viper for the small mammal, mama
90   mia, cute frisky little rascal

the curvature of the necessity rides
no more skyward but rounds off,
a comedown comeuppance: in a fallish time,
the birds' gatherings and flights
95   skim treetops, not
much entering in now, no nests, pausing to consider
or dwell, the wide
storm winter coming

.Envy

100   Let your friend have
as much of the
world as he can
have, what does
he have: the
105   wind blows it
away and your friend
also and
you, freeing all
from any trace of taint
110   ❀
but because the dust
mills all looks,
tastes, honors fine,
because of that the
115   small hope
cannot extinguish itself
that some flavor

of the self, indelible
in dust,
120   qualifies the common end
        ✿

we are abandoned
here to found
our lives on gossamer
125   distinctions
where steel rusts
& rock cannot hold

My

my
long   slobberer
130   palaver &   belaborer
palaverer

(biggest old ugliest
awfulest-looking thang)
    Price Slashed (whew)
135   For . . .
        QUICK SALE

treetops twittering
birds windily gathering
heading south for
140   the scallop, scallop-through, in the ridge:
    the jay
    quince-sits
    a minute
    and flies north
145   into the coloring thicket

when we learn we are trash   I'd rather be
flimsy, flowable, our holding   the flakey

trivial and slight, we must
not say, if that's what
150   the universe thinks of us, so
much for the universe:
it should be the benefit of our
experience here to realize trash
the just groundwork
155   of marvelous devising, feeling,
touching, tasting, looking,
beauty's unbelievable contrary

fool of hope
than the
smartass
of the
small and mean

Here I Sit, Fifty in the

Here I sit, fifty in the
mid-seventies, the 28th of the 9th, cedarberries
160   reddening a veil, vine leapage
and leafage red or yellow flame tips in the trees,
the sky mixed
after pure days of rain,
coolishness and windyishness, most
165   birds gone,
hi-flo hieroglyphic geese going over,
a day and decade like most any other
if you put in the wind, sun,
believe the brook's fuss,
170   trees nodding, yessireeing,
the mixture of identifiable hunks of
historicity with permanences and continuos
like geese stringing singings,
the clash and intermingling
175   within the boundaries of the momentary
and instantaneous of the
perception of the, ah,
all the wavelengths of time, ah, bending in
& out of themselves like coil worms
180   or worm coils

———

byways and sideways
forth and back
outsight and inlook

(in a time of)
185   failing powers, physical,
sexual, intellectual, artistic,
belleslettristic, optimistic, etc.,
it's hard (a hair firm)
to keep the slant of the curvature
190   above horizontal   coelum
without bobbing and dozy dipping
below
into the languorous waters of letting
things take their course & get on by:
195   no use to wait on you today
nohow, baby, because with the fallings
off of spatiotemporal apples and leaves
and seeds and pods
and skinnyings up for winter, in the
200   and because, ah, of the apple cider and
aster honey and the blue glaze on the
brook slowed distillation-column clear
    and the yellowjackets
    hummed up quiet in the
205   stump
    waiting for snow to feather to the door

hard to think of going back into spring,
buds, slender parts, sprigs putting
out, early green and preparation,
210   then summer filling out, making up,
might as well rush right on through into
ripeness rotten
where like summation or artistic
compression
215   seeds velvety in the dried-up pulp
summarize recommencement, time's compression

would, some will say, there were
a plain simple thing with a fence round it
　　I don't know it seems
possible don't you think plausible a
bit plausible
or perhaps a few
plain simple things with small fences
you say around them
　　a cluster or lay-out of them
organized to cardinal points or rated,
axiologically
　　　　rated
　　　　according to

I cut the quince down the other day into so
many stalks it all made a big bundle
upon the lawn high as my head I'd say

but then today I took the pile
thorny limb by branch down to
the limb&branch pile in the bottom yard

I don't care I think for quince, the
thorns, I mean, I am pricked and itchy
here and there including the shanks

some branches got to in the carrying
off well so back and forth which is up
and down (the yard) I went forty times

I think till I began to sweat and stink
and there under the pear tree was a dead
jay, poor thing, which stank in a stream of

whiff which I hit eighty times,
the universal smell of rotten meat not
really an attractive smell when you get

———

right down to it. . . .

I do not, can not, will not
250   care for plain simple things
with straightforward fences round them:
I prefer lean, true
integrations of ongoing
with recurrences,
255   resemblances, half-adventitious or fortuitous
or as some would say accidental,
half-accidental,
not under a third

a live jay lit on the pearlimb (pearl imb)
260   over the dead jay,
looked down and flicking shrieked & squawked
directly into the dead ear
two minutes (I don't insist
on the meaning, only the facts)
265   a scolding for dying
or grief trying to make itself heard;
it looked like grief's rage,
a protest like revenge,
grief's blue wings and bright cries!

270   money can't buy happiness   neither one nor the other
happiness can't buy money   either one or the other
(misery can't buy either)   both (misery loves company)

hark! in my across-and-down-the-street
neighbor's yard, his apple grove all loaded
275   with red half-rotten apples
smelling good and souring the wind,
a mockingbird singing!
I saw three majestic weeds of ragweed
growing in the ditch and
280   slipped'em right up out

of the mud and turned their roots onto
the macadam to dry
    this part is called
    the old Intimidation Rag
285   it is never right to play ragtime fast
it is never right to play ragtime
it is never right to play
it is never right to
it is never right
290   it is never
it is
it

surface amenities aside
we have little to
295   go on
except violence and brutality (the long, flat light
of this bright day comes slicing through)

may love	words strip
and least	a man's bones
300 harm	
prevail at	
times forever	naked

My Father Used to Bring Banana

My father used to bring banana
stalks home from town
305   and place them in the chicken coop
so chicken mites would stick
to them
    & a few years ago we had
    a flare-up in the local
310   papers here about feeding layers
crushed oyster shells
to thicken egg shells

forty years ago in Carolina
we used to
315   bring home a towsack full
of oyster shells every time we went
to the beach

and we had this big old anvil and
big old hammer to
320   beat up the oyster shells with
         I don't know what became
         of the roosters
         that ate them
         broke out an
325   extra set of teeth
my father sure was a mess

this part of my poem is
called chicken (gravy, shit, wing, liver)

sometimes I notice my
330   shadow and think
there's my father
but I'm fifty now
and it's me

Have You Seen the Severe Waters

Have you seen the severe waters
335   (how they flow)
have you seen the nodes of high

glass standing or the sharp slants
by the bank where the bank looks for
itself

———

340   I care not what is is   it's up
             what is seems is is   to you
             enough for me

             I went to the brook and inquired
             what do I have now
345   how do you mean the bank bushes replied

             oh I said
             oh I said
             and the brook broke saying speak up

             so the saying of that day was not
350   said and the turn that might have been
             added to the mind turned away

                       clear all day the foliage
                       coloring etc. the jay loud
                       the mockingbird still at it
355   thickage

Early October

             Early October,
             fally, papery, yellowy,
             watery, raggedy, high
             skimmy clouds, brooky
360   (last week's rains,
             now run off, brookly,
             cool glass flowing,
             metal over slate sweeps)
             I'm at fifty Octobery,

365   not frantic with commencements,
             preparations, seedings, searchings
             for ways of spring and not

        the rage of
        summer, clumpy fulfillingness,
370   but a throwing of the self out
        of gear into gliding's mild astonishment,
        letting up into freefall on
        rise's other side,
            the leaves still green or
375   holding hints hang,
            no longer feeding on light,
            an indifference to purpose,
        purpose complete, now
        color and high view:

380   inner purpose given over,
        other purposes not one's own start to
        clear the stage:

        nothing to dwell on, astonishment right
        into startled grief,
385   the rising of settled knowledge that
        in a short time all here will
        clear and go

        why speak of that now,
        the pears
390   hard green after frost's first smart
        and the apples
        purple-ruddy, burnt onesided:
            still one pauses
            to reflect shallow bemusements,
395   recall honey,
        the inner light of wine,
        cold's tang and burn
        (good as ever but not as often)

Terror of

terror of
400 interval
(even with
bridge-note reassurance) the slicing
away into
(dentaljuice)°
405 depthless discontinuity, whorey bottom
or bottomless horrid,
 too many intervals break up
the road
the sinuous continuous look
410 out for slides land snow rock
tree blows freshets bridge-outs

neck wires
 hair ties
 sorghum broomcane braided
415 (vines' rising risks) down
to handles
 log planters
nothing necklaces
cowtooth dangles
420 I'm in the swamp I
 must have followed
 the hogs off
awkweird to go to bed with the
chickens and wake up laid

Ivy, a Winding)

425 Ivy, a winding)
an area, specimen one can keep
coming back to,

° Betelgeuse

a place where, as to school, one can
try out one's explanations
430   (exegesis is better than no gesis at
all)   but
       what
          got me
       about   give
435   the   up
       tree
          today
was that
       the leaves
440   after a season's
service, their span, serve
fallen: flatten out black
and limber wet and put a film of
chitinous structure on the
445   ground so nothing
not even a winding vine, can come up and
take nitrogen, carbon dioxide, water, or
room from the tree:
            (they say walnut shells
450   falling to the ground
          release an antiplant
          ingredient) imagine!
writing something that never forms a
complete thought, drags you
455   after it, spills you down, no barrier
describing you or dock lifting you up:
imagine writing something the CIA would
not read, through,
the FBI not record or report,
460   a mishmash for the fun-loving,
one's fine-fannied friends!
            imagine, a list, a
puzzler, sleeper, a tiresome business,
conglomeration, aggregation, etc.
465   nobody can make any sense of:

                    a long poem, shindig,
          fracas, uproar,
          high shimmy uncompletable, hence like
          paradise, hellish paradise,
470   not the one paradise where the points
          & fringes of
          perception sway in and out at once
          in the free interlockings of
          permanence:
475   roots and moles (and grubs) (and
          a microorganism that feeds on
          carbon monoxide) live in the ground: fish and
          ribbonswale and —worms live in the sea:
          birds carrying stable mite colonies
480   and crop-worms live in the air: we, we,
          carrying fungal and bacterial residences, our
          numberless silent populations, flashy molds,
          angry, flashy molds, live, though mainly
          in the light, a fine fluid
485   fragmentation breaks into presence: (any
          high consistency, of course,
          lacks the differences to know
          itself by—hence is unheard, invisible,
          unknown, etc) so we are here in a very
490   great blackness except when the fluid
          surfs against a pumpkin, thinning willow,
          boulder (any whole thing in space such as
          earth) and the disturbance communicates
          itself dispersing through molecular
495   air, a frizzling wide static of sight,
          and then the eye's central blackness
          none can read or follow creates a
          disturbance of color to pick up light
                              disturbances: O
500   fine fluid, fluency,
          and then the
          finest highest fluids we've
          learned to live in on occasion or for short

visits, the sheeting pulses of the spiritual
505   intelligence which
                  when it breaks
                  against & thru us
                  declares its nature:
if you would shed light upon a thing
510 smash it: or adore it, leave it whole,
                hold to it in darkness:
who will remember us
we cry
yet we will forget
515 before we are forgotten

if you would explain That Which Is by
structure you would have to locate
the spurs and main beams, sills, joists,
of the put-together, whereas anything
520 worth taking apart is so put together
it is assimilated
beyond edge, angle, or joint:
niche, cranny, or nookie:
                you can erect skeletons of
525 structure for their own sake and then
analogize freely: hermeneutic
                propaedeutic:
good thing June peas
come loose from the continuum:
530 make a moongate of an
oeil-de-boeuf, make the frangible-invisible
infrangible:

the mind buries to let lie:
times, stations, planes
535 and overlappings of felt-events give
base and height, structure, to feeling:
vindictiveness, jealousy, greed, alarm,
hostility adjust to deep
dispositions so that reconciliations

540 and motions at a greater height can be
released as tenderness, concern, delight:
 the error not that the deep
 feelings, found, are heaved up
 but that
545 heaving as a form destroys the
forms of modesty, gentility, and
modulated delight:
 at three I realized
 that my interpersonal relationships
550 considered for example as a cottonball
of interweavings and
closenesses (a warmth, as of a
mother-centered, father-peripheried
group) were going to be sheared off,
555 cut through
and that I was going to be a bit of
lint blowing in the irrelevancies of
dissociation: as I grew older
I learned this
560 more thoroughly:
I write for those who have
no comfort now and will never have any:
I'm delighted that the comfortless are
a minority and
565 that rosy tales amble otherwise for others:
 I'm not making a fuss:
 I note the determination:
 it is a strict script
written in the injustice of
570 necessity: I forgive
the injustice, nearly: I no longer cry
to be another, not myself, or seldom:
you who have no comfort
are welcome here, here
575 with the chaff
alongside the abundant reaping, among
the weeds, after the gleaners:

———

I am the writing of what was to be but
did not become: your writing
580　strangled mine:
I make seeing because I have nothing else
& nothing to do in the seen:
bitterness
compels me
585　to roll my
tongue and spit
a saying
to the loneliness of my unbecoming
unbecoming:
590　I bring you　　　no harm that
no harm but　　　is not nothing
I bring you
nothing

this is "lake country" too: I hadn't thought
595　of that: indeed, "finger lake country": see
you top that one (has a small extra finger or

so): course I'm *country* and *western*: I like
music that plinks and means it: *western* New
York: the poetry isn't as good either

The Hieroglyphic Gathered, the Books

600　The hieroglyphic gathered, the books
numbered and shelved each
to its interior singing, the hum
broken in on or left in high loft
unattended, the quill-conversions to
605　mock permanence, so many acts
feared, committed or hoped, regretted—
what a relief to go outside away from
the rooms, seminars, policy-committees
to where stability's mode is movement, wind

610   working with leaves and trash
    across the asphalt, windings and
    scatterings, starlings flying
    into the ivyvine-skein leafless
    against the Music building and picking
615   berries, the clouds fluffy,
    pulling apart here and there into blue
    sliver-troughs: the freshness
    of breaking down, picking,
    churning through
620   versus the artifice
    ungathered after all anywhere
    except into the fluidities of currency
    forever: (that happened yesterday
    and only gathered hieroglyphics can
625   keep it):
            distinguish the long
            arm of the law from
            the member in good standing:
    it's pouring rain but I went walking:
630   the first rain on Dr. Ensworth's dog's
    grave, now mounded among the hedge shrubs:
    whiff of earthworm
    (I almost said earthroom), puddles
    fragrant and in the puddles ornaments,
635   stars of green weed bottom-clear:
    from every needletip of spruce
    bough, bough on bough, spruce on spruce,
    hung a drop-bulb, gray lit:
            will equanil and elavil replace the
640   trances and spells of religion, philosophy,
    art, and madness, theories of depth
    psychology or depth theories of the deep:
    for, altogether, miltown can do more than
    Milton can: luncheon muncheon: more
645   than fluff and   (l)anguish
    less than effluvium: milk is white
    blood:

---

           clouds giving way, the sun broke
        out and turned up the voltage
650   in the bulbs: my fingers are so
        cold from the walk (another one) I can
        hardly type: chez fuck'n'suck: also no
        book like a frigit: and no poem
        with a bush you could fly your bird in:
655   forecast for today
           were snows and blizzards
           but we may
           have a mere
           high, empty with glory:
660   would a collection
              of clarities
              be clearer than a clarity
              or as the collection
              grew would the
665   single clarities remain
              clear and
              a great darkness commence
              to surround
              or would opposite lobes of clarity
670   annihilate themselves
              into continuum emptiness:

        FINGER LAKES PAINTING

        I don't like any bush
        water won't drip off
675   except the
        two-legged bush, of course, how happy, and
        the golden bramble-bush in whose
        branches the Sumerian goat's horns, vexed,
        tangle:
680   desert crows,
           picky, and the deep desert hawks and
        flight-lean eagles, but
        walking predators, too, cautious,

big-eyed, and "possessed of a gnawing
685   hunger to destroy and ingest" as we
artists, so to speak, would create &
dump, only the hunger remaining likewise
stuck in the bush
and mama goat gone and papa off:
690   leaves fall from the thornbush,
hair and meat from the
goat: skeleton, branch,
the slackened-free entanglement:
the goat thrashes and bleats at midnight
695   and overhead the desert stars,
big brights (not helping)
and oil underground, the
goat chafing with sharp hooves to
peel and worry down the bush:
700   the good of images is
that they make no
statement and the bad
is that they make (evoke)
numberless statements:
705   (or is that good, too:
meanwhile, the statement
makes one statement: except
in the clump, thicket,
or cluster of statements
710   is the image again)
I could write forever, I mean, I could:
I never would
because boundaries, terminations,
determinations give class to held and holding:
715   but the imagistes should have
known that the Golden Calf
narrows, confines, straitens,
identifies, and lessens the Spirit
too much which is shape without
720   shape, timeless time,
visible and never to be seen:

poems should imitate the spirit's motions from
the fabulous limitation, so
golden because so
725   striking off temptation, of
the means, uh:
I can speak big and high
(but to which end?)
I can hone the severe metric,
730   incision's incendiary:
but honing misses broadcast:
anyway, who would have one around
speaking big and high:
over dishes: filling the vaporizer:
735   emptying the trash:
prefer chitchat to
swales of the austere unknown:
    neighbor down the street stakes
    his dog out on the lawn, chain
740   twenty feet, pretty
    good run: I notice a path of peripheral
lawnwear, a ring of loss
where the chain, run out, runs
round: the central self unattended,
745   unworn while the untouchable
other, far and away calls forth
the bark, the slaver, slobber,
scenting: to pull up stakes!
I can talk big: I come
750   from a land of bigtalkers and
big talkers: what one needs is
the address of relief (relief of
address): (*King Kong* is on—
Thanksgiving classic): summer
755   for dogs is a conflagration of
smells while winter is the ashes
(snow), a sprig of smoke
rising here and there:
all this poetry
760   in Thanksgiving on Thanksgiving

Your Full-Service Mover, Madam

Your full-service mover, madam:
your full-service madam, mover:
arouse, attract, specify,
identify, concentrate, propel
765   and release unmixed, mixed
emotions: I can package
reactions, lob, locate, and lure
centers, keys, knobs,
slots and play upon you as with
770   or upon an organ:

                      go off to a
country, you see things done
different ways: you distinguish fashion
from nature, an educational
775   distance: but, educated, you're
into fashion more than nature,
a change loosening, shallowing:
             overcast forecast a
true cast but this afternoon is
780   to open sunny periods, dashed
dashes, clearing exclamation
points, followed by
colonic etceteras:

we need a basis for argument,
785   argument always we have enough of,
although probably never more
than we need, but though we have
experienced tugging
this way and that
790   and though we have chipped, honed,
polished, dug and double-dug,
we have failed to find
the single, the first, not to mention
mountain or continent, grain (tiny mew) of
795   unyielding reality:
    what a pity, many will sigh,

having argued at length over nothing:
but many will be grateful,
locating the necessary recalcitrance
800 in the unyieldingness to explanation, that
is, finding centers of operations
where, as with juggling, nothing is,
and in contrary motions finding
balance's informed harmony:
805 explanation explains nothing *away*: get
up the next morning and recalcitrance
has shaded up to opacity again:
think of the medium, the medium's
malleability, explanation works in,
810 wordy nothingness: then how reassured
we are to risk castles only air and how
delighted to know
that explanation changes just itself,
an arrived-at nothing: whereas,
815 the work of art (here come the boss)
establishes an empty-centered space,
spiral stabile, wordless where words
may not go,
a recalcitrance of a kind explanation
820 can only sharpen itself against:

    lukewarm   stand to reason

    the elm I write of is
not the doomed elm, the dutch,
but the siberian,
825 small-leaved, resistant: the two doomed elms
I had were cut down
and hauled away: just now,
a snowbead shower: the beads fall,
springing, on the greenroofed garage
830 and roll off the eaves some
but when fall pauses
melt scrubs the white away

_____

        (somedays a mist
        too fine

835   to form drops
        at the eaves
        or shine the highway)
        darkens things a
        little, though

When in Early

840   When in early
      December everything should be
      naked
      except spruce, cedar, yew,
      here and

845   there down the side
      of a hill or in
      a hill's hollow
      will be found
      a willow's fragile clothes,

850   yellow dress dropped,
      showing the green slip's
      shift
      of hiding   snow rhymes
                  soundwise but

855   contrariwise
      (being alike in   colorwise
      one set of   with crow
      terms and
      unlike in the other

860   make   oh, my father, you
      one whole form   said, "someday
      overmastering   your mouth will
      the one polar   get you in trouble"
      unlikeness)   you were (I've

865   made you)
                     right

the sheet of
snow, thin,
missing,
870 mingled with loft,
under cedars and
such
    under the mailbox
    a wind-mingled
875 thinning

and you said,
"you'll be a preacher,
like your uncle,"
close enough, in that
I try to give the
word life:
oh, my father,
I am one of the few
left to miss you
I do not miss you much

mostly representing the reachable or
available sky
like sky like ground
880 except for interruptions:
snow's itself's scripture
but in addition
written in it
accumulate actions
885 reading re-enacts—
the pigeon-toed pheasant,
a hen, I think, walked across the driveway,
short toe inward, long toe, you know,
one foot almost in front of
890 the other—a mystery and
contemplation, the beautiful, plain hen
color-coded, her signs

our door mouse
houses between the concrete
895 step and a bottom shingle: every now and
then I catch him streaking for
concrete crack or door crack: yesterday
morning, there was an inch of snow,
(remember)
900 just enough the mouse could nuzzle under:
he inscribed eventuality on the lawn,
a limber line of snow-collapse showing

behind him: and today, little snow left,
there is the dribble of his feet
905   over the white blacktop: if it doesn't
warm up more
the paperboy will see
his yesterday-afternoon, snow-pressed,
delivery bike trail

910   after snow
when evening clears and
night settles
cleared and cold,
crisp forms
915   on the snow
midforest
and along starry pond margins
and flavors,
scents dry up, lose their stems to sources,
920   where the dogs
cracking crisp
run:
cold cleanses,
brightens, thins:
925   if one could save a cubic mile
of this for August!
(magazines advertise
themselves in themselves)

a year, what a year: *anus mirabilis*:
930   what can you do: the inner ring of
relatives in trouble with
their teeth, fixing, lumbago,
running off in Dusters,
and a wider ring of relatives,
935   regular mishpucha, coming up for
advice backed up with a loan,
so-and-so's cousin's pill
in the wrong end: what is it:

—————

making baskets

940   tonight to meet Kammen's guest
Bailyn, the historian, such a nice
man: there were the Novarrs: they
knew Bailyn way back and Ruth calls
him Buddy, imagine, the National
945   Book Award winner, Buddy, also
the Pulitzer

The Arc

The arc
of
the
950   loop, the
cradle
of
sway
      to be
955   rocked
       in the heights
       (not dropped,
inert, in
earth)

960   oh, to carry out the byways of
reverie
(the cedars teardrops
before impact)
(something to feel
965   not just the
discursive unwinding of
feeling)
born we scream

fed we ummm and smack
970   beboweled we grunt
fucked we groan
and so with death do we tussle and
groan
but why
975   when in moments of importance
we hold
our tongues
do we give
significance to articulation that
980   only waits the next
seizure out

oh, to be rocked in the arm
of the dwelling, to be
cuddled and cooed to,
985   to whisper and sip, slur
and loll in the long
unwindings and squdgings,
the honey, the honey, oh,
the honey high,
990   oh, the
air-clear, beer-lit,
oh, the bright drop,
retsyn:

eat a pig dinner sometimes and sit
995   down in a deep chair that rightangles
your uplumping belly out
cuts off the avenues of circulation
and boluses of air
form promoting gastric
1000   distress:
if it gets severe take a sip
of water, will dislodge
the gasball enough to ease off the

pain but then walk about
1005   to re-establish the circulations
also lift your arms, your hands clasped
behind your head and
let go of your belly or heave out your
chest and meanwhile swing slowly from
1010   side to side this may ease the bubble
up, also it is important to think you
may not be dying, although you will be feeling
like it, because added
tension forms another airball
1015   over itself like those scared, foam-nesting
insects

good reception

fair this morning, much
warmer, over fifty, but
1020   cloudy and rainy in the afternoon
with a falling off of temperature down
to where a few snowflakes flew and
so today was mostly dark and lowering
and blustery but nice

There! the Light of Human Reason!

1025   There! the light of human reason!
issues from the crevasse of that black
hump of hill-line, rounds a
        pastoral fallacy,
is lost behind the Dark Wood,
1030   the thicket treacherous,
but reappears as two, the one
light and its dropped reflection
in the Cavity of Eternal Depth (the
dentist's dream) which is or filled

1035   with water or with a liquorish air of
    consistency so the
    light will not penetrate it but
    throw back up into the world
        but now there goes the progress
1040   around that awful pit but note
        the light now introduced
    into a lantern, flat-sided with panels
    in grapy glass, to make it
    past
1045   the gash of gorge that strikes
    down from the hills through the earth
    in a plunge the wind observes
    to howl through so that none may pass
    unhouseled up (long wait) but there
1050   the faithful light reappears on this our
    edge, the long going down into and
    arising from, and proceeds onward to
    meet us: the light flickers and sometimes cannot
    in the whole dark scene be seen but
1055   with tendance and awful looking we may
    severally be reminded that reft of this
        bright bit
    we sink into greater toothiness and squinting
    but so much for the story if
1060   no end to the story's glory (glory's story?)

                what is
    matter's project here, is it, where every
    hub is afire with spinning and every
    axle taking on the resonance of a
1065   dissonance, where every next instant has
    a twelve-ton meteorite or thousand-foot
    ledge-drop in it, where everything
    one once loved drains backward away into
    a common hole, where underfoot one
1070   feels time's shimmy, the sludge- and

sledgeweight of gravity's maw,
where nothing that in this fair
day takes on brilliant delimitations
and delights will miss tomorrow's
1075 indifferent spill, waste, or fill or gravid
mud

(I can hardly care a paragraph for such
fidgeting)
          (when the downswoop collects us
1080 will we look into the sky's
mild mien or
back on an
earth we haven't learned to lose)
          matter
1085 projects
the breeding of races crusty, to fall
asleep in calamity's bosom, power
too self-effacing to bear its own
strength, that can be the patient nurse . . .

1090   The X Press
          The X Press Press
          The ReXPress

bound and determined
metes and bounds   sky-high
1095 ground meats   meets

Mr. Spilldiddler
Mr. Dillspiddler

          rough day
          stuff tough

Hard Lard

1100   Hard lard hard fact
     hard wind hard core
     hard ball hard time
      hard hard

    the clouds lower low dipping almost
1105   skirting skinny-brittle treetops
    but drop a ground-brightening!

    the snow, pleasant flakes, dry
    enough to worm in the wind
    before touching down
1110   or brushing stopped against bush, brush,
    garagedoor handle or what, even the
    clothesline a skinny, longwinded catcher:
    people are good for you if nothing
    much ails you but if people (cruel
1115   and insensitive, survival pluses) ail
    you nature is a rescue, go to it,
    nonpersonal, decommissioned, an
    indifference big enough to cool off or
    melt down
1120   your differences: sometimes,
    when it seems the mind will hesitate,
    swell in a realization and break,
    and one thinks that perhaps one may
    fall down or wobble past resilience,
1125   then one turns with relief to nature,
    the verbal empire's blocks, pigeonholes,
    axioms, pronunciamentos, and stuff (stuffiness)
    chewed up in the simplest
    wind-sand design or snow flurry: oh, to
1130   break through the strangling entanglements,
    binds, clusters of wordy mentality and
    feel the luster of woodsfloor under snow!
     vitiated by arrogance, jubersome

of seriousness, my language
1135 will hardly touch stumps or stump: if words
hurt me, why do I
come to them to move a saying through:
am I saying in words how I wish nature
in fact were, though impersonal: fluent,
1140 yielding, showy, a dance of mind not
words (though in words) but things:
I could get something straight but
it would stop winding:

with words to make nature sound off,
1145 speak up
till we find the place where it
will say nothing further,
be of no further use, an example to
no further imposition,
1150 an illustration of, allegory of, nothing

so that we can achieve the podium of
inhumanity, the clearing, wherefrom
we can look back and away to the
astonishing thing, man's rise and demise,
1155 and then what, the crazy universe here,
here, here for thousands, even millions
of years, going on with purposes, if
any, not ours: room
enough for every correction of view,
1160 where perspective is never sold out, utero,
utero, the
commencement before the commencement:

snow sounds like gritty pellets
on the panes:
1165 I thought it was a mouse in my paperbox:

here's a little poem I jotted down this
morning: it's about a complete action,

ah, except for the purple do: the starlings,
having hung sideways on the music building's
1170 ivyvine collection while picking the berries,
sit meditatively high in the branches of the
oak to rest and then the berries
that had not fallen from the vines fall
from the lofts of oak, empurpling do's
1175 sparse rain:

 the starlings barely
 got the berries
 off the vines

 before snow
1180 lineations loaded
 them up again

once there was a maple tree: during
the summer it produced lots of
maple seed: when the leaves fell,
1185 clusters and clusters of dry maple seed
were left, ruffles, hanging in the tree:
when the first snows came, squirrels
were often in the maple tree eating seeds
and, soon, most of the branches were
1190 empty: one day a dog came by and startled
a squirrel as he was eating from a cluster
of seed far out on a branch: the squirrel,
leaving one seed in the cluster, stopped
eating and ran back to the trunk to go
1195 up higher in the tree: but the dog went
on and the squirrel turned back to eating:
but not back to the single seed
far out on the branch: hard cold set in
one day and for weeks no squirrels came
1200 out: then on a warm windy day in March,
two maple seeds, the only two left on the
tree, softened in their stems and blew

away: one seed fell on the macadam and
the tires of a car crushed it: the other
1205   seed, the one the squirrel, interrupted
by the dog, had left behind, fell next to
the garage between two rosebushes: that
was the sunny side of the garage, and the
rosestocks helped hold the warmth, so the
1210   seed germinated and soon was a tiny tree
with a leaf of its own: I thought, my
goodness, all the maple tree's seeds
produced one tree, but I
couldn't have a tree that close to
1215   the garage so I pulled it up

a poem is a machine made out of worlds
a poem is made of words fed to machines

hard fart   hard tack   I feel so much
hard ware   hard sell   better on my
1220   hard head   hard boil   feet provided
I have something
to lean against

Hard Fist

Hard fist
hard turd
1225   cool whip
soup dip
freezer queen
candy 6pack
full quart
1230   good thru
strawberry preserves
boneless ham
personal butcher
save more

1235   windshield washer
       raisin bran

   will all   rarely has so much
   my talk   been said over so
   not dissolve   little unsaid
1240 reticence's pellet,
   dishonorable silence's   big wig
   unwanted bead

      pay attention
      pay no mind

1245 "up yr nose   "up your dick
   with a rubber hose"   with a toothpick"

   in yr ear
   with a hornet's rear "up yr ass
           with a blade of grass"

1250 many fears are born of
   fatigue & loneliness

   scraps from, the trash of, the verbal
   environment
   saved, retention's waste, waste's
1255 retention, the scary, sublime,
   heavy musk anal honey, but also
   the collection, munitions
     for colonic assault

   save a life
1260 return my dog
   my brown and white
   female dog was taken Record
   from the Straight
   Lobby Friday Dec 5 My wife, the
1265 she is my closest   weightlifter,

companion and I am   smiles and three
destroyed without her   tons
    (from a bulletin board)   rise from my back

1270

Go   lemon juice
           crabmeat claws
Old age swiss slices
gets   salad shrimp
set   lean roast
to sit   baking mix

1275

down   apple sauce
           pie filling
           ground chuck
           minced clams
           corned beef

1280

the elm
also (like the   in
willow) late   this
to lose   our
its leaves   own

1285

has (like   day
the willow)   and
lost them   time

arrange these words so that they make
sense

1290

                       people, self-centered,
inconsiderate,
cheer news of a darkness darker
than theirs, a deeper gouge
into a wound more rotten:

1295

least can they bear news
of a happiness close to them

I side
a minority of myself
with the majority

1300 against the majority
of myself
which is a minority

there it is
equation-tranquil
1305 mesh it   make little
with life and   of much
it can (almost   make much
unfailingly will)   of little
break   or
1310 down   make little or much
or short circuit   of much
and little

I won't weep
though:
1315 the rhetoric
"make a big fuss over nothing"
is not a good poetic,
not even a
good idea,
1320 not even
"make a big fuss over something"

make molehills
of mountains

8:45 A.M.—Doorbell Rings: Wife

8:45 A.M.—doorbell rings: wife
1325 answers: voice says, "Good morning,
I have a chest for you."

wife says, "Right up the stairs."
I'm right up the stairs on the stool,
door and butt cracked; here they come:

1330   conceptualization is
          self-correcting (don't worry)
          and not as bad as I've made out, I've
          made out: for example, imaginative
          forms derive from bioforms, take the
1335   maindrifts and subtleties: the big
          channel moves away from the heart of
          the matter directly and sizably (as
          to volume) but then, moved away, begins
          to correct itself
1340   to the pressure
          to break down, lessening in—
          to distinction so as
          to become available
          to organs, tissues, and cells,
1345   to establish deep and wide application
             and relevance: but there rationality,
             though at its sharpest ramification and closest
          to its immediacy, commences
          to break down, the mind unable
1350   to bear so much division of matter
             with no lessening of rationality as
             "form": the mind reacts with dullness
          to
          too much subtlety and falls asleep:
1355   but just as rationality has lost its way in—
          to contact with every body cell, there it
             corrects itself, having achieved an
             ocean presence, where distinctions are
             so slight and multiple, they assume
1360   the wide look of universal constitution:
          the mind, refreshed by that playing
          out, at least, returns slowly
          through the capillaries, regathers
          itself in—
1365   to its main drifts and
          considerable matters and, announcing

itself, returns
to the circulations:
I think I already wrote about (or
1370 thought about) this but
the alimentary canal as river with falls, lakes,
etc. is a good form, also the form
expansion-contraction: lot
of them, probably, all finding
1375 ways to play in the imagination,
too: how delightful:

I saw through the earth once:
a clearing-through as if of light:
terror made the light, drilled it through:
1380 the earth spindled, insubstantial as life:
another fellow saw through, once:
I hope the shakes did not shake him long

kill time

expect turmoil, gusts, shifts in stone,
1385 expect the arms of change to spin
but allow the Singing Sage
to slip by on his Big Boat singing
                Turmoil is Illusion
                at the Heart of
1390   the Great Peace

bedrock nestles
in flow
and flow rides
highways
1395 tips of flame plume:
but under that,
deeply within,
the most fluent fluid, motion,
establishes the citadel

———

1400   I can see but little,
           and that with much leaning,
           of the elm from this window and
           indeed no part of that attached to the
           ground but outbuoyed branches only,
1405   mostly tips
           nevertheless
           possessing curvature of definition
           in the uttermost, the tips ending in an
           invisibly inscribed continuity or
1410   configuration of nothingness:
                if I worked in the other room
                next to the elm
                (a winter-sunny room)
                I'd get to know more about
1415   the elm
                but so much more would dominate
                the poem: to want a poem about
                an elm is not to want a poem
                too much so, or too much poem
1420   too much so: if I need more
                elm to say, I can
                mosey over and peer
                out into further information)

           overwhelm whelm helm elm

1425   this day bluedog clear
                I stood in it absolutely
                unoccupied a minute and
                said how sharp the world
                that cares nothing for
1430   us is
                but now at dusk,
                billows come up
                over the west looking
                solider than hills
1435   and black and blue with

snow, I think
how is it possible the world
so entertaining and extravagant
has nothing to do with us (on a personal
1440   basis) though we
in the formation of gene arcs, contours,
sweeps, saliences, and spirals
were tested bit to bit by
billows, swell of snowwind,
1445   bright our sandy river,
and found to survive the astonishments,
coping, throwing them back:

    behind bars

when I have studied the elm
1450   I hope to devote myself to the weather,
majors and minors of substance, the high
substance nothing is done about, the
low showers narrowed into washouts,
the happy variabilities day to day
1455   winding round the deep variabilities of
season (reason, treason): the year
cycles, sunspot cycles,
micro, meso, macro: bi:

it's too dark to see to write:
1460   gather it up and rip it off

Shall Will Be Used Properly or Will Shall

Shall will be used properly or will shall
    here near
    midDecember
    grayworks   (if we have
1465   hit the deep   a falling off
    dismal,   we'll fall

                    days clipped   into a
                    off on   falling out)
            both ends till you can
1470   hardly find the middle
            but then comes a winter
            festival (festival
            estival) inaugurating
            longer light

1475   the city that cares
                for tares   (egad,
                has no need   gasso,
                for weeds   glorybe)

            the **M** Sea bore
1480   Civ, unhappy
            daughter
            (dumping the dump from 400
            million sets of human guts
            plus industrial scours, washes,
1485   rinses) now killing
            the mother,
            a daughter who unless made a Bridegroom
            of Intelligence
            must swoon away into
1490   self-poisoning unredemptive guilt,
                whereas
                with Wisdom for the weed,
                Care for the ground cricket
            (whatever is good for the ground cricket is
1495   good for the country)
                Concern for the undersea
                rocky ledges of octopuses
                the mother might
            still have lineations of
1500   life left which, clearness drawn deeply into,
            would begin to show again
            an image Mother Mediterranean:

                              but nothing is to be
                              expected of man, his
1505   intentions tedious &
                              mean: by accident
                              he is wise or noble:
                              he sees not his life
                              one life among many
1510   kinds of life, every
                              kind attuned to a
                              careful impulse
                              that lets it boom
                              and loll in its own
1515   dwelling: Civ,
                inconsiderate daughter, maker of weeping,
                unnaturalizer, fabricator of
                fabrications, pretender to feeling, huzzy,
                it would hardly be unfair if
1520   Sea gobbled you up so you could not harm
                Forest, Icecap, Deep Trench, or Friendly
                Breeze again, baby:

                natural gas is okay on a cold night and
                antibiotics are so fine when you need them:
1525   but man's fabrications aren't as subtle
                and resilient, flexible, accommodating
                as natural complexes: why can't we proceed
                but show the proper respect:

                    FreshLARGEEggs
1530   This carton is bio-degradable
                a contribution to environment

                (also, what are we to do with it if
                you bring it back) a contribution, tribute,
                offering, tithe
1535   as if to the new god: ok then a few more
                worshippers will do it:
                              playacting:

                    playoffs:
                    (Redskins, Raiders, Steelers,
1540   Colts, Dolphins, Cowboys)
                    (look, cavity, no moms)
                    poeticules shrink up
                    into starved strategies
                    and strive to prove
1545   skinny devices significant,
                    but I, I mean . . .
        nothing works without a nearly
        equal tug the other way:
        and then one is fifty and feels oneself
1550   (if no one else will) (no one else will)
        in the tug of
        a tendency, as if one were an
        impurity rushed through
        various waters
1555   to the kidney of selection
        where the organism engages in certain
        abandon:
        but the mind, imagination, is only getting
        fresh at last, wind free, ready for
1560   treetop castle or diamond waterfall,
        recalcitrance flowing loose, a clear honey
        to the embrasures of sight:
        truth's a show,
        a good one one that does not end before
1565   the audience leaves: that holds
        up a cranesweep of meaning,
        snakes or eels or noodles, great
        wound-up unwindings, heavy, light: that
        lets no direction or effect grow pure
1570   without contrariwisdom, counter-purity:
                    say not what
                    I have made
                    say what made
                    I have cut
1575   free of:
        Sumerian, Egyptian, Greek, Roman,

European, Holy-Roman, Anglican: we have
hills old-low,
     lines of windbreaking lombardies:
1580   windrows:
     thickets wind-settling:
     spruce nook moving nothing, resident
authorities
                                        big rig
1585   spoontang   big zig
     spoontongue   big cig
     dongtong   big fig
     dungtongue   big MIG
     tightassed tightend: big dig
1590   eternal journal: big pig
                                        big gig
                                        big jig

mindgoggling:
     the poet abandons a
1595   place to the reader

I sometimes catch myself
fearful I've
let out the news of death,
told more than people will
1600   please to hear,
a news, though, nowhere to be
kept still:
it flies loose and about
and is (must be) told in
1605   every ear till
told too loud
no one's there to hear

ass/mind balls/heart
ball loose flag down

1610   it's 4:20 dusk coming
the Redskins have a touchdown
to go with their fieldgoal

Phyllis made seven fruitcakes
undetermined square or round

No Tirement Like Retirement

1615   No tirement like retirement
no floppage like stoppage
busy busy boys and girls
old geezers,
strungout ninnies (no
1620   treads
               like   threads
               retreads)
having made avocation vocation
I must now
1625   rise through
making vocation avocation
so I can spend
    my
time rusting   (l)agony

1630   dressed, undressed, redressed

use is the best polish
(drooping thru the chills of the
                          sorghum to
where the spinnet's broke)

1635   after so many days of
        mingling, cloud and hill,
        mists, skirts of vapor
        dripping and valley-dragging, fringes,
        brushing ghosts
1640   through hillbrush, moon
        and soon
        I mean sun
        clorox twins

———

everything lifted this morning and there
1645   between the devil and the deep blue
between a rock and a hard place
between a cliff and a sharp slope
was the source bright,
                looking central

1650   a warmish morning walkable and how musty
I'd grown far off from the lean, mean
brook
its quick scars of light
its breaking, regathering,
1655   ledges and clear heights underwater,
its mosslawned banks, rock terraces,
tangled vestment vine
    (choked trees
    deadwood trellises)
1660   (those with
            inclinations to
            sprawl on
            you, spurn,
            sprawl on them)
1665   if you come into the world
with an unspeakable structure or
stricture to speak,
a weird move to the freak fringe,
then you got an insoluble
1670   problem, an
"immedicable woe"
you got a sore with a lifetime supply
of scabs, you is, in other words, in
business
1675   the average person is average
  the common people is common
  the straight people is straight
  you gone be the crooked weird
  rare intelligent bird creep type
1680   that what you gone be, honey

you gone look funny
when they put you in your
coffin
like you something
1685   unright
like you ain't
worth dying
like every day when they passes out the
honey
1690   you gone get a little vial of fear and
you gone drink it yes you is
cause tomorrow when they passes out
    the honey again
you gone git another one of those little vials
1695   and what you gone do with them vials
honey better go head drink up one at a
time
    cause you gone have something to
    shake about too
1700   while the others is shaking with
    the sweetness
    you gone be breaking out in the high
    jives of terror
shaking like you done met up with some'm:
1705   I hope no young'un mine
go through with that
(salt talk with a dash of pepper)

being there is the next best
thing to long distance

1710   may I by
being me be
you for you
                  trust money
or will you   and trust people
1715   take my I   to try to get it
to be you   away from you

———

for a minute
as I will
take you
1720   looks like an
        to be I   all-day gray
        when I can
        maybe your you

Light Falls Shadow and Beam through the Limbo

        Light falls shadow and beam through the limbo
1725   limbboughs, short and long mixtures,
        lineations,
        staff and heading, balling the
        boughs, clusters, white bass clefs
        churning rotund
1730   thunder and up there sparkling and
        bellying out
        skeins and scads of treble felicities,
        cones and points:
        tree as music in the light,
1735   the scoring of the permanent
        enchantment,
        a presence not regular but hastening
        or not like the imagination or
        the wind
1740   and telling

        nothing but that though the gorge roars
        and though
        sodden swatches of forest spill
        from a high ravine and though
1745   a beaver is shut in by a boulder time
        will slowly budge
        and though we ourselves see and do not
        know what we see and cannot tell why
        we are here attracted to enchantment
1750   and scriptures intermingling substance

and light—
        oh, the hillways, passes, the peaks
        of the thoroughly achieved!
some such dwelling in the light,
1755   hardness in the ray,
        the interpenetration
        that in leaving, separating out,
        never leaves out,
        that bringing things still again runs away
1760   also with everything into night

Mist Curtains Lower and Dissolve

        Mist curtains lower and dissolve
        the ridges halfway down
        (imagine
        a thunderstorm predicted
1765   for midDecember,
        55 but
        no thunder yet: rain,
        though)
                1:01
1770   1:00
                :59   downspouts

        the threequarter
        moon at midnight
        shining from a
1775   high sky's well
        on this host of
        hills, the lake
        off to the side
        there glimmering
1780   in a big space,
        a Christmas tree
        crystalline with

```
           colored lights
           down a near slope,
1785       way over the valley
           a string
           of glitter, a
           highway, ropes a
           slope: how can we
1790       be here: how is
           it possible, here
           with earth moon sun
           these people these
           myths and dreams:
1795       were we not here
           we could never
           be
           thought of:
                          oxbows of
1800                      highway rise
                          like a
                          small elation
                          over the opposite
                          ridge
```

The Snow Is Fine-Sightless Today the Ground

```
1805   The snow is fine-sightless today the ground
       brightens white for no cause
       and the green garageroof
       is all at once side-white

       the elm's grooves and streaks
1810   of bark are highlighting: it's 28
       again to be 10 tonight
                               make
       all the fuse that's lit to glint   a
       one handy tool (ah)                 difference
```

1815   arm milk   when we
          eye cunt cheese have nothing
          hip shit   significant
          leg come   to say
          ear blood   spelling it
1820   toe wax   right matters
          lip eye cracklings   (makes a
          jaw snot   difference)
          rib spit

          I reckon
1825   cornholers get dooky
          on their tools (and yucky blood)
          time's dust is a rinse
          nothing resists

          to get the spook off language,
1830   the microphone, pulpit, lectern, the high
          whines and
               broad moans out,
               scald and rinse every word
               till it takes on and gives off
1835   the exact hue (drift)
               for for
               the most part
               language moves our lips while
               we grind, hiss, haw—
1840   let the words have no rich soup
          they cannot themselves generate

          if fellows burr, hum, buzz, loop
          break out strict shears
          snip ropes from the heavy molasses to
1845   hang those fellows with

          tipping from pole to pole
          we flash through uprightness, stability,

truth but
        unchanging reality
1850   is the polar extreme's
        intolerable
        exaggerated weather

the temperate zone the land of soft announcement

one desires leisure, ease, if
1855   those are to be desired, when one
        might desire action, stress, doing
        as being, too, ideal

I write this to be writing,
wife gone off with a stationwagonload
1860   of women to Rochester in the snow,
son at school,
        office hours this afternoon,
        meeting,
        Christmas coming,
1865   me home

                go through

I'm not sure there's enough light
out there to make a day of
        but look
1870   a patch of blue the size of a man's hat:
it could grow into a radiant clearing,
blue inanition, dome of
high feeling, starvation

when a father dies
1875   the sky comes unlooped from the stars

The Hen Pheasants Streak Out of the

The hen pheasants streak out of the
thicket
down the hedgeline through the
yard

1880   selfcentered shortsightedness

fag pag jag
feg peg jeg   trouble
fig pig jig   shovel
fog pog jog
1885   fug pug jug   stir-fry

is life a   is life a   a puzzlement
show death show truth a bit of
corrects   kills   a difficulty
  or is   or is
1890   death a   truth a
show life   show life
corrects   kills

as you go into life (some say they
wish they were alive or dead) you must
1895   forget where you're going
which is into death
but as you go into death you must begin
to take a more general and perhaps
generous view of life, and not be
1900   so particular
but that may be the difficulty
that we are heavy
to relinquish our made selves,
mirrorments, to the trust of the
1905   great unwieldy, unspecific self:
          in these transmissions
          we are not like to be consulted:

                    our talents turn to attitude:
          verbal flak:
1910   (a bishop or royal personage
                          displays his
                          flabella, a touch to the
                          human that he sweats)
          picking up brilliants, bowerbirdwise,
1915   etc., or as with the builder
          of beercan palaces, tidbits, also, of
          tile, mirror, sherd, whatever with a
          paste, mortar, of cogitation, sealing
          throughout making of-a-piece: but if
1920   you seek brilliants it's
          no matter what shines:
          the value is apparent in apparent shining
               but those who dwell upon
               and on the invisible
1925   value not the visible
          apparency
          not diamond-shine
          but rarity or hardness
          so invisible

1930   to deal with muddlement
          which is not
          just a mixture but
          a single speaking of multiple clarities
          (very puzzling unless the
1935   clarities are so small
          as with sand
          they will lose their special identities
          to a general view)
          to deal with muddling or muddlement
1940   confine the currency of inquiry
          within fairly narrow banks urging
          and also guiding flow
          so that means can go out among the
          areas and question closely

1945	so to speak
	or drop bits of matter at the roots
	of things so that answers may grow
	(we need have faith
	only
1950	that of course currency is
	winding
	that can never wind away,
	cannot go far without returning,
	an observation
1955	so succinct
	faith
	is perhaps too high a shelf to bother)
	when I look death
	in the eye
1960	my pavilions quiver
	and my crystal battlements
	and walls of high castle
	dance in the afternoon breeze
	this one
1965	death swept
	shape
	broken off from the
	earth broken off
	from the mother
1970	spent now except
	for the flicker of
	burning out
	supposed to get cold tonight
	the ephemeral lasts because
1975	it's back fast

Dawn Clear

	Dawn clear	
	by sunrise	
	hazes riffles	you want to be
	furrows and floats	bullfucked when
1980	of fluff	mine is no longer
	appear	than a penguin
	so the sun	
	has too much	
	to come through	quilt raffle
1985	to come through	antiques
		handcrafted gifts
	make verbal	live country music
	things tangles	whimsies, furbelows, and
	mazes puzzles	sundries
1990	clusters	
	consonances	bitter winds
	dangles knots &	clink the tinkle
	stuff to have	bell in the tree
	something	and find
1995	to fool with	cold's exact key:
	when time has	the big male
	a bigger presence,	pheasant sulls
	margin, than	low on one foot
	things or actions	
2000	I make things	
	and abandon	
	them for you	
	the sun didn't do much for us today	
	but it de-snowed the garage roof	
2005	and left a crop of	
	smallish icicles down the eaves-row	

If You Were Standing under the Elm and

If you were standing under the elm and
looked up it would be dark
but if you were above it (flying?)
2010   and looked down it would be
white:
     dust or flurry snow, the fine
sifty stuff, has not missed a twig,
hiding it from the sky: but if it
2015   gets windy and wrenching or if a
crow lights somewhere and flaps his
wings squawking, then
darkness may be noticeable

In the Old

In the old
2020   days
of vaginal, or coincidental,
sprays
     hairpie diners
     could have plum
2025   tart, peach or
     strawberry
tart (in the old days words didn't buy
much)
     get more   pedazo
2030   out of   de
     going out   burro

authentic theatrical
forms with
mimes, masks,
2035   puppets, processionals, players
         (singers
keep   groups

         my   bands
         word   writers
2040   composers)

               islets and islettes
         informal (isles)   formal (tisles)
                  soup aisle
                  aisle de soup
2045   do-ahead dough

         super bargains in vinyl flooring
         roll-ends for bathrooms, entryways,
                     pantries, laundry rooms

         grind

2050   she said this afternoon that
         because of the snowsqualls she
         might have to put a damper
         on her shopping expeditions

         the sun came out enough
2055   to moon
         behind the snowclouds
            so, everything loaded,
            there'll be no unloading
         today
2060   unless by dusk the wind comes unsprung:
         the hemlocks,
         sculpture all day, now
         nod in the breezy free-ends
               ohyesohyes

2065   so many whales plundering through,
            more whaleback than water

         hemlocks made to order
         to hold snow

were also made
2070   limber to sway snow
loose
or at least hang unsplinteringly
in white
holding:

2075   lamb sandwich

Namath, ribs bruised, limped off the cold
field today, Shea Stadium snowy, windy,
four days before Christmas, Namath who
broke all showing-them-how's expectations!

2080   if we are reluctant   if only one could
to step into the field   make or find a bit of
when it is our time   wisdom that turned
we may be reluctant to leave   through a situation
the surroundings   or two would hold
2085   when our time   still or still hold
has passed

it's after sunset
cloudy
cold and gray
2090   but tomorrow is
to reach the mid-thirties

Forecast for Today (Winter's Firstday)

Forecast for today (Winter's Firstday)
(you may
recall) was
2095   thirty-five or so (which hasn't seen
twenty yet)
beefed up this morning by a promise of
sunny spells
but now at five minutes to one the drifty

2100 tinkle of snowflakes
    merely continuos: a few minutes ago,
    in truth,
    a blue patch appeared sky-high but the sun,
    wintering elsewhere, wasn't there so
2105 nothing hit the ground here:
    couple three months ago
    I cut a grapevine out of the big cedar
    to reduce weight's becluttering darkness
    but here the snow's
2110 getting into the tree as much as
    grape leaves shaded light out:
      at dusk a flock of pheasant
    will be-wing, shrieking rusty flanges, up
    and beheist themselves,
2115 belaboring beswung boughs:
      the squirrels in the thicket
      had such a good time this fall
      up-and-down winding
      chasing each other
2120   I bet there isn't a flake
      of loose bark unfallen
      on a trunk
      in the whole blame thicket

      all I ever know is
2125   rigor between the shoulderblades,
      lumber in the gut,
      hard theory-light in the head:
      I process life by shaking,
    I'm a sifter: I wish I were limber
2130 and relaxed, able to affirm the self
    and take from the world a small taking

    limberer than lumber

    I swerve attention out of the mix of
    myself into the outerness where otherness
2135 can conjoin my outerness whereas

only I can look into myself
and I spend enough time doing that

the sun broke out before setting
but set behind new clouds moving
2140 in: the Christmas tree's up and
John & I have bought presents,
everybody has bought everybody presents

I Come in from the Snowy World

I come in from the snowy world
of muffled roads and she says
2145 how's the outside world
and I say
still outside (gotterdattoom)

Giants Beat Saints

you can't step forward with
2150 both feet on the ground

proverbs suck up recalcitrant reality
and spit out a beam of light but
emerge among them
systems of conflict, divergence,
2155 contradiction: too many
proverbs obstruct the view
but enhance the reality:
not the wisdom but saying's finding:

the middle regions

2160 toilet paper chinks cracks
against excessive windiness:

jocundity

the beswirling elm this morning was attacked
by white bees

2165   last night after sunset the weather
warmed up, night-snow-blue clouds
heaped on the horizon,
holding, glowing underneath in earthshine

in winter here
2170   the sun arcs a
southern circle of small compass
and has
slight surface relation
to temperature
2175   except
ice will melt off a car or
highway great
in direct radiation
but it warmed up last night after sunset
2180   to twenty-five and the fronds and
jungle foliages (that make
in teens climates)
ran off the windows, thaw's
deconstruction:

2185   how does a running back hold it

sight
feeds on a
medium
whose
2190   source blinds
but no big
sound gives
off little
earfuls
2195   although the ear can be exploded

(not death
but life can   one forgets
be   before one
missed)   is forgotten

2200   the squall   a bit of
        comes on   dried hydrangea
        from the west   blossom
        across the lake   comes loose and
        with the sun   the wind
2205   behind it   rolls it
        suffusing it,   over a yard of
        oblivion melting   snowcrust the wind
        everything   variable
                            enough to
2210   play
                            the blossom with us,
                            no, there it
                            goes behind
                            the garage

2215   on the way down
        but then the
        squall hits
        with fierce soft
        mingling

2220   snow
        ghosts stand up
        and walk off the roof

Poetry Is the Smallest

Poetry is the smallest
trickle trinket
2225   bauble burst

	the lightest	f
	windseed leaftip	r
	snowdown	e
	poetry is the breaks	e
2230	the least loop	d
	from	o
	the general curvature	m
	into delight	
	poetry is	
2235	the slightest	f
	hue, hint, hurt	r
	its dance too light	e
	not to be the wind's:	e
	yet nothing	d
2240	becomes itself	o
	without the overspill	m
	of this small abundance	

•

you don't mind, do you, I
2245 said to the mountain, if
I use this ledge or, like,
inspiration pavilion to say

a few things out over the
various woods, streams, and
2250 so on: by all means, said
the mountain: I was a little

concerned, I said, because
the speech is, like, about
the individual vs the major

only
where
we

2255 structures and, like, I

was thinking of siding with
the individual: but, of

are
to
lose

course, said the mountain: all

2260   well, but, I said, it   are

    we

doesn't make any difference   to

what I say if it doesn't   have

make any difference: please,   here

2265   said the mountain, be my guest   and

    there

•   a

    trifle

a slice of clearing   only

2270   widened over the ridge at   where

sundown and the sun   we

stood in it a minute,   are

full glow flapping up against   to

the garage and trees   lose

2275   and through the windows against   all

the walls and it was very nice   are

say around four twenty,   we

gold effluvia gone   to

by four twentyseven   be

2280   here

•   beholding

    everything

poet friend of mine's

dick's so short   still his fat wife's

2285   he can't pull it long enough   radiant every morning:

to pee straight with: he humps well, probably,

not to pee on   stringing her out far and

anybody by surprise   loose on the frail hook:

sideways, he hunkers   and, too, I notice she

2290   into the urinal so far   follows his words

he looks like, to achieve,   closely like one who

relief: knows what a tongue can do

Christmas Eve Morning

Christmas Eve morning
a sifting of snow
2295   blurry clouds
with near-clear spans of western blue
still at nine
nothing coming through in beam from
the east
2300   the hemlocks rocked and
        winded yesterday
hold their old darkness back today

to have fun you have to need it
so little you don't need any

2305   you fear the grave   if you won't
    so much it is   change yourself change
    possible before life is   the world
    done with you you
    will beg for it   change the world you
2310   won't change yourself
    this year's been
    so horrible even the
    thought
    of improving it
2315   is frightening

then the sifting thins into a sheen of
micro-lights, pane crystal flints,
twinkling down like fog-fuzzy bugs through
beams of early sun,
2320   derived not from clouds but a haze
that barely pales the sky

weather is continuo to the clustral or choral
the deep through-going that adds a middle
to islands, glaciers, ponds, fields, woods,

2325   to rain, or snow, or wind or
      the sun's weather is
      continuo
      to earth and Mars and
      elsewhere
2330   or the galaxy's (here we go again) shine is
    continuo
    within which gather and move chords,
    concerts, aggregates, configurations,
    tangles, thickets
2335   which in turn turning feed into and move the
                        continuo:
    clapper-hung bulls tinkling bells
    balls on icy highweed

        spot of marsh there
2340   in the meadow
        cattails and redwings
        artesian source
        a bog going
        around saved

2345   the tree-mingling mists
    on the high gap's ridge
    seem not a nature
    my self, too, inhabits, brushing up
    against the rockface,
2350   leaking from boughs
      but another dimension, intention, or
    working that asks neither my
    compliance nor participation

    buried yesterday afternoon
2355   today Uncle Emory
    begins his first
    full day in
    the grave, the
    whole round of

2360   the dark service,
        the wageless hours
        and hourless wages

                but what a brilliant
                finish to the snowstorm
2365   (another due tonight)
        so much sun I sat with the jade
        plant half an hour
        while sheaves of brightness
        fell across its deep leaves
2370   and, eighteen the high, here and
        there direct light caused icicles
        to form out of hung snow,
        the ridge on my
        metal mailbox turned into a single
2375   long icicle, dog's tail

Analysis Mines and Leaves to Heal

Analysis mines and leaves to heal
clouds, coasts along the way but comes
to recourse's nothingness to heal itself

                during the night
2380   the wind pulled
                up a cloud cover

        patchworks
        aprons   my wife says
        hotpads   you can't learn
2385   place mats magic by magic
        skirts
        lunch bags

intercourse is better than no course at all

————

2390   hardly able to take a frail wind
or thin change in altitude or
attitude, we measure riffles,
waves, ounces, vibes for power,
scrupulous tissue

axioms, postulates, theorems, hypotheses,
2395   hypotenuses, conclusions, paradigms in
neat blue conic sections, curved lines, dots,
lines, and planes, cubes, prisms, cylinders,
spheres, all that good stuff

temperature goes up, snow falls:
2400   break out the stars,
cold shines them: stir up a southern breeze,
here come the windchillindex

here, indeed, we're eating dead chicken (stuffed with
stuffing) cranberry sauce, applesauce,
2405   white potatoes, broccoli, salad with
dressing including one dark olive, cookies
and ice (dark olive how I luf you) cream
and cake and the snow outside coming down

Snowed Last Night a Lot but Warmed Up

Snowed last night a lot but warmed up:
2410   today has been cloudy
unsnowing and up to 40 maybe 45:
icicles have dived off eaves:
the hemlocks
which keep fine clumps
2415   are unsnowed
tipsy with breeze

I got a plant collection
for Christmas, jars, cups, liqueur & other glasses,
potted and planted,

2420   but I'm doing tiny plants
I like my loyalty
and their precariousness

                        the big round yew
                        has five thick floes
2425   indoor green   of snow on top
                        too central
                        to angle off, fall
                        away
the maple's fleshy underlimbs look spooky,
2430   more light bounding up from the
snow than falling from the gray near-dusk:
          I shoveled
          wet-bottomed snow out to
          the garage, where I got the peat moss,
2435   then out into the yard
          where I dug soil
          from John's old sandlot
          soil mixed about half with sand
          that half and half with peat moss:
2440   then I dribbled bits
          into my finestemmed glasses
          and reluctant jars
          poured dabs of water in
          to settle the roots
2445   and left them to heaven

Those in Ledge Fright Seek

Those in ledge fright seek
the complacencies of the high Way
for who
given the apple of life
2450   wants a different sweetness

          low marsh
          where water heads or sulls
          is common but

high holdings,
2455   marsh lofts, prevented into height,
kept where all that can run runs,
high marsh,
sedge, weed, grass, tiny flower!

snow upside down and/or backwards spells
2460   mons, the
mountainous part where snow falls
gniwolp wons
one of the wons

with herbicides, pesticides,
2465   the penetration, saturation become
systemic, what for us,
the children of Mithridates's   run, the end is
poison prick   narrowing in for
                                     a close, the saying
2470   midroad and midway the Way   is gaining
change, disturbance's daily loss,   concision to
shock, grief,   slash and slashing
looks illusory   slash itself off
but the world's vanishing as we
2475   stand tiptoe at the rim of
a world never to come

water runs
but the ripple
dwells

But If the Way Will

2480   But if the Way will
not answer common feet,
we hack through thickets,
winding vine-nodes, and
befuddling treebranching

```
2485        offshooting
            divisions that divide us
            bringing no lessening to
            the investigated material
            but if like the emu we
2490        cannot fly we can
            run fast or while we scramble up
            fright's sharp ledge we can
            contemplate the skyWay,
            treetopless, hightensionlineless,
2495        peakless, stormcloudless
            but who would be there except
            as relief from here
            here the pond muscles in a flash,
            cracks, sprinkles, circles and
2500        produces a disengaged item,
            shining fish
            delicious simmering

            freedom, freedom

            some people think it's going
2505        to stop snowing
            someday

            today glazed because it went up
            to 45 yesterday: stuff
            melted and ran, and last night went
2510        down to twenty or twenty-five:
            the motion slowed, piling up, slowing,
            then stopped into slick hard terrain:
            today not having gone above
            twenty-five, crystal-drawn
2515        configurations, tire figurings, dry,
            crunchy, are holding tight: now, forty minutes
            past sundown, the dark evergreens
            fall away in a white sea, clouds
            above, behind, between,
```

2520 only a shade lighter than
the trees:
all day the sun found two blurs
to come through, each a few seconds
wide: people who have a life
2525 to live don't notice weather: the rest
of us study it like a feast, eating
the windshifts and coolings,
the details, main shows,
fringe events, chewing and wolfing:
2530 who dines on clouds, drinks
the wind, gets loose mouthfuls, has
for fanfare stripped willows and
grumpy hemlocks: outriders
not regular, he should
2535 address himself to the center
folds, vertical drapes, entryways
wherein to go straight: it is
one thing to tongue pussy and another
thing not to: well said, nature
2540 lover: less polluted these
days than acid wind or leady sleet:

                                                    the future
"let's come and eat"   will carefully
                                                    husband and
2545 Dallas at Minnesota   draw out
                                                    strands of
I hope dianthus that through   the natural
platycodon simple engagement hesperis   to weave the
with diverse lychnis materiality   controlled
2550 I calendula will be able   artificial
ageratum to wipe dusty
miller the shitty salvia
grin off my cockscomb face   I need a
                                                    constellation
2555 where all lose, one   to set a
must study gain, move into   few sharp
herd-appraisal and praise, announce   stones in

energy and direction,
not slouch behind
2560   tempting wild animals:
        the business is serious
but wipes away,
chalk on slate, the scribbling
powdery: hunger, greed, fear,
2565   anger write themselves out
through and with things,
then dissolve,
the things themselves also

I carry an extra
2570   pouch on the hip, around
the neck, over the shoulder
it's awkward and burdensome,
in it a piece
of paper
2575   with the heaviest
directive
    find
    something to save
    us, if
2580   not a lot, a little
(tell us, at least, there
is no equivocation between
necessity and necessity)
    or if
2585   you can find nothing to
    save us,
    cheer us up
or give us a good rubdown
or put us after a problem
2590   worth pursuing

the admiration of can-do
the basic structure
out of its holster,

admired, received—this
2595 enlarged and multiplied
into aspects of day

hello from one who knows nothing
(and never lets you hear
the end of it)

The Sun Climbs Daily Higher

2600 The sun climbs daily higher
into a longer arc:
lows ride
thaws in from
the south for a day or so
2605 but the
long summer dissolve and making
this daily increment unfolds and cinches

that I	that's what I	I have to do some
take it	take it it	light writing
2610 is what	takes	so I can do some
it takes		light reading

taking thought

poets add
obscurity
2615 to the
inexplicable
for critics
who can't
get their
2620 tools sharp on
the obvious

A Seventeen Morning &

A seventeen morning &
the maple, lit below,
looks as if it's

2625 in pearl fire
   the high-luminous snow
catching every branch
I may change rooms
because I can't see

2630 the main subject
from here
   I can't continue
to proceed indirectly:
in the other room I wd

2635 be able
to see a frowzy jay light in
it (my subject)
or watch a winter wind
whistle it

2640 or behold the coming & going
of snow leaves,
nature-witnessing,
attention-getting poetry

all the fit that's news to print

2645 what's a sphere: (you ask)
a nucleus
prowled by circumferences:
a moon or sun

or asteroid, orange, tangelo,
2650 grapefruit, or
two selves or sexes
clustral: a mere

———

bead, seed, marble, an
irreducibility gathered
2655   about itself, or a
radial awareness, more

blocked off on one side than
the other but about
as fluid and penetrating in
2660   rock as air: awe or ire:

clearly the question is what
one does from there: the
spiral drills a more
majestic form, centralizing

2665   spheres, binaries, clumps,
arms and windings into
vast discs turning but more
open to variety on the

edge than spheres, a malleability
2670   outward to diversity:
moving to sweet heaps as of
rocks or garbage in spill:

every lawn,
sandy path effects, influences
2675   the weather: every bush's
held-air temple,

cooler or warmer or more or
less humid: every fringe
of bank grass alters the
2680   wind's rill,

spill, the way
thunderstorms roil white-ice
high with stricken
majesty: I

2685 know how things go one
way and then the other
without separation, tenacity
continuous throughout

the measure: I
2690 know how the big wind falls,
the winds of hollows,
thickets, ponds

adding or subtracting huff
or lag, easing or blocking,
2695 lofting or snatching down:
clear progressions and puzzling

intermixtures: so much
stability or quiet change in
fantasies of motion: wind vane,
2700 rain gage, barometer . . .

1 look at the people in the graveyard	**2** look at the people in the graveyard

2705   they   the
    don't seem to   sweet north wind
    mind

3 look at the people 2710 in the graveyard	**4** look at the people in the graveyard

    unfailing   a cardinal
    attraction   singly singing

5 look at
the people
in the
graveyard

memory
slips

6 look at
the people
in the
graveyard

disturb the
peace

7 look at
the people
in the
graveyard

stone recalls
last

8 look at
the people
in the
graveyard

when dawn comes
no one stirs

9 look at
the people
in the
graveyard

shade
trees

10 look at
the people
in the
graveyard

quiet
celebration

fucking forefront
rump humper
bang spangler
wart wrestler
butt fucker

belly wormer
crawdadhopper
spider spitter

shoot the breeze
people who worry about
things have something
to worry about

I have behind enough but

kitty cornered   suffer from foreshortening
cattywompus
cattybiarsoned

2745   diagram of eclipse
          paradigm of ruin
            figure of flood
          bustnut of wind
   sketches, fit-ups for
2750   the cataclysm

   name and number   (my culture agriculture)

   sense decays when it moves too
   far toward statement, concept,
   abstraction, or theory where
2755   generalization, synopsis, or
   summary has taken on wide
   prevalence but left
   behind, or digested away, any
   experience of example,
2760   concretion, or sensuous
   actuality; or, toward the
   coincidental, the single
   example, event, or thing
   without context or placing,
2765   the isolated particular:
   poetry operates, not to deny
   the abstraction or the
   particular and not to diminish
   the distance between them but
2770   to hold in relation the
   widest play between them

   shooting iron   today, fair, saw the sun
   don't riot bade lions all the way down
   flowers flow   till, arc lost, it

2775　　flower bowls　　　　touching scattered up
　　　　　　　　　　　　and down the ridge,
　　　　　　　　　　　　bulbs and spherules glowing
　　　　　　　　　　　　coals crumbling and I think
　　　　　　　　　　　　it was 4:30 before the
2780　　　　　　　　　　operation ended: this adds
　　　　　　　　　　　　a minute or two
　　　　　　　　　　　　to the hold of light

The First Morning in a Few

　　　　　　　　The first morning in a few
　　　　　　　　the windows haven't been
2785　　　　　　ice-befrizzled, bestreaked,
　　　　　　　　befoliaged, or befrilled,
　　　　　　　　the numerous fronds & species: today
　　　　　　　　is mostly plain
　　　　　　　　pane invisibility: but at 33
2790　　　　　　and snowing, sleeting, and
　　　　　　　　raining, a few driblets stick
　　　　　　　　to the panes still ice, clear
　　　　　　　　as ice or water, a bomb gone
　　　　　　　　off at LaGuardia
2795　　　　　　and 11 people killed:

　　　　　　　　　　the snow scanty, slow,
　　　　　　　　big-flaked, I went out
　　　　　　　　into a reality
　　　　　　　　audible with unsuspected
2800　　　　　　sleet:

　　　　　　　　　　round and square
　　　　　　　　　　　　dancing and
　　　　　　　　dancing undetermined
　　　　　　　　　　square or round

　　　　　　　　　────────

2805   I care not a fig
            for a fag in a fog
               fog in a fug
               fug in a fig
            fug a jug
2810   (jig a fig)

sphincter of Oddi in
your face!

it was supposed to be warm today
up to 40 or 45
2815   but it wasn't and more sleet
fell than ice melted
now we have six new inches of
snow

This Is

          This is
2820   the great
          man's skull:
          we saved
          it from
          the fire
2825   so you
          might see
          the light
          in it

any part of the day you
2830   move out of the accuracy
of honor you waste
for honor, in no need of
sanction, moves in its own
self-evidence, necessity:

2835 if we prove
 unworthy of tenure
 on earth earth will
 give us notice

 the force of necessity
2840 merely operates
 (but lay a log across
 the flow, you have
 a bridge)

 poison earth, eat poison

2845 I get so much good out of my
 neighbors: they don't
 speak or visit
 but they come
 home from a trip
2850 and put on the lights or I
 look out the window on a cold
 night and see one or two
 of their windows lit and get
 neighborly feelings

Quilted Spreads

2855 Quilted spreads

 pigeons every morning prowl
 and rove
 the hills at
 fifty
2860 miles an hour:
  out walking, prowling, I
 hear them coming
 a soft, intense muscling

                    then the visual speed,
2865   cushioned rigor

            constitutional

            quarter to ten and the sun's
            nothing, more in the south
            than east,
2870   leftover moon

            are you looking for a minute,
            second in the welter,
            grain of what-for, nit of
            news, bind of delight
2875   just this way

            may a fart pule brown billows
            about your earlobes

            may your teeth acquire anal
            longings and fly home

2880   may your rump-grooving nose
            plunge into the shot pot

            towels pillows & bath rugs
            polyester fiberfill
            jumbo welt
2885   hand-knotted fringe trim

            C ALL US FOR YOUR
            NEW YEA SEVE GALA
            an increased middle region
            answers polarities
2890   the pode which be
                de (pod) foot and antipode
            which gwine ter natcherly be

de head, baby do,
some lard, though, hung and
2895   swung about the organs,
subcutaneous rugs, blankets,
drapes, curtains, stuffed
liver, swoll'n gut,
(with a railyard of fuming,
2900   fussing, foaming, and verting)
these enlargements, equatorial
intensifications, of
content between the mouth
and so forth:

2905   forget the colorless, clear,
frigid, polar life:
come to
where the   puddentang
zonky wohwoh
2910   pleasure is

will one waft whither wind
winds forever
    the current moves with
necessity's inner accuracy
2915   but mind what will it do
it will not accord
as if a native element
indistinguishable: it will
not have currency
2920   but come into a state of
its own
terrain decision settles
choice disposes
some influence as to what will
2925   and will not be
    for example choice though
will need to choose what
cannot be unchosen what is

like stone grain
2930   constitutional
for example loneliness
one need not look forever
out of windows or into
adjoining offices
2935   or mailboxes
for the thing that will
not come, the face from
wax-museum memory
            no
2940   one may say loneliness if
with me
it is myself
it will not remove
it is mine
2945   I hold it to myself
I will not let go of it
it is clothes on a certain
person it is a sharp watch on
a hemlock jay
2950   it is the long tunnel of
memory personalized with
murals and hangings
it is where I must
hacking go
2955   there will be some terror
I accept
it is mine
it comes
and when it goes
2960   leaves furious fragrances
one will dispose
the disposable

I will not for example love
a new person
2965   not with that force's full

focus
I will love sweeps, banks,
and glances
and lengthy spaciousness but
2970 I will not
grant an extended reach
or stir to fill a need
the decision is a new knowledge,
the matter shaped and settled

2975 monthly payment

the last day of seventy-five
some sun this morning mostly
gray this afternoon
fairly warm some melting
2980 say thirty-five

having missed the calisthenics
of maturity
I practice early and late
to catch up with what is
2985 gone

I am not wise
please forgive me for writing
even so
correct me with your own
2990 deep acceptances of
condition and self
I call attention
I enliven when I can

to open press here

2995 string out the old
string in the new

happy new year

Dung Ball, Round Graveyard

Dung ball, round graveyard,
wax ball, this sphere, nest
3000   cell-laced with permanent eggs,
these dead moving loose
in vines through branches,
this orange body and apple body
devoured, our mouths
3005   the substance of millings:

the sabertooth's big-game furnace
burned forty million years:
elephants, rhinoceroses stoked
it: look in his skull, cool,
3010   polished:

the hominid ancestor dreamed
him through entanglements of fire,
the polishes of volition: the
more recent, the thinker, the banquet,
3015   observed him go closely by:

     have you heard
     the mockingbird: those who
                        have nothing
     mark   have nothing
3020   the woodlark: to lose

words, a sculpture, let us
see wind:

the cart after a time
goes not on as a cart

3025   rock the boat in a calm sea: people
in storm wildernesses hold on,
balance against, empty out,
a mindlessness resembling the

conservative: the revolutionary
3030   is stable in it and
cannot bear it:

the upland bog!
a flat clearing
means pond-water snowed under,
3035   and brown-shambled fringe
broken high from
by right cattails
smart and clean as pricks

    bog
3040   clearing
    prick freud
    ruined everything

tops in scoring and rebounding:
violence, suspense, and non-stop action:
3045   strikes, spares, and splits:
    fireplace specialist:
    carpentry, masonry, plumbing,
    painting, roofing, wiring, heating:

    it looks like today
3050   though it commenced
the   a year isn't going
    to amount to much
first   gray skies
    meal-like gritty
3055   comes   snow enough
    to make running whirls and curls
right   on the highway: we
    just went to FAYS:
after   bought a plant: the death of god
3060   sort of jointy   the god of death
the   cactus put it in

                    a big glass jar   cleared off late
          last   had pretty good   the flat light
                    roots reckon   comes underwood
3065   if   they'll root all   like a fire
          right   right the others I
          before   got last week did
          the
          served   the content of the obsession
3070   changes but the form returns

          lay across the multiple
          polymorphous
          defining inventions
          that limit and
3075   accentuate so as to say
          we, too, exist

          I'm one fourth as
          old as the country

I See Downhill a Patch

               I see downhill a patch
3080   mixed in the tops of two or
               three cedars—the lake,
               a mile's breadth hardly wider
               than cedars' tips

               when we dam sluices
3085   in river gaps
               we don't violate
               the accuracy of flow
               but build a temple
               to flowing nature,
3090   housing for the river god,
               our structure interpreting river nature

```
                    ————

    time out        time up
    in time         down time
             outage


3095    yesterday the west cleared by
        sunset and the sun
        went down
        a bright spot in an exact place
        but as it went deeper
3100    glow widened up and down
        the ridge
        until half an hour later
        the storm had broadened
        and caught up the earth
3105        in a rising fire


        but it was only nothing
        because here we are today
            (one who makes much
            of little
3110        makes much of little
            aches and pains,
            trivial inconveniences,
            slight delays, and is
            a pain
3115        to work with or
            be around)
        in a full radiance
        morning having broken from
        the very skin of sunrise
3120    bright and
        unrelenting and here just
        past now
        the windows beam,
        the floor scattered with
3125    the fallen lumber of light:
            thousands in wars have lost
        their hands and/or feet—
```

specially in recent wars
where things picked up or
3130   stepped on
have exploded
(if you can bear to feel it
you will never cause it)

Big Old Thang

3135   She stuffed vulvas in the
cracks, hammered the main
labiums together with
vaginas and stapled
the clitorises up till it was
3140   to the point he
couldn't get a thing in there.

this is your spotty reporter
folks
putting one on

3145   first day after the first
look like it all gone down

(criticize in general
praise in particular)

The Stomach Is Quite

The stomach is quite
3150   a development
on the esophagus and
if cross-country is
efficient
           the small intestines
3155   represent a winding

parlousness
                    so I don't think
                    we will be
                    concerned if the
3160   continuo's overwhelmed
                    underground
                    by appallingly
                    pretentious blocks of
paydirt
3165   it goes on trinkling under
        there, eventually reappearing
        enunciating

        Big, BIG savings on all
                    units

3170   low mileage
        fully equipped
                    mint condition

                    houseflies are spongers

My Neighbor Shakes Feed along

        My neighbor shakes feed along
3175   the spruce thicket fringe and
        keeps the pheasant plopping on
        down, their central heating,
        main ramp to life's roots:
        lucky for the pheasant they
3180   have a big ass and long
        tail to sustain them above the
        snow when their legs blop through

        you have to feel pretty
        good to have a good time:

3185   the aspirant spiral: you remember
the aspirant spiral

the limbs' topside catches the
eye today
    high-lit with downsnow
3190   brighter than snow's
underglow

the	scads
ordinary	arpeggios
realm	obbligatos
3195 of	& cadenzas
the	of detail
ready-to-wear	

(though the pentameter's heaved we're
splinter assertions of the great iamb)

Nature As Waterfalls

3200   Nature as waterfalls,
lives, or generations
spills fast,
not fashion-fast

nature as ridge is deep
3205   stay:
        these the oldest
        mountains in the
        world,
        authority fills the
3210   clearings
        under cedar
        thickets

———

or writes precisely as the ridge
across the blue dusk coelum

3215   authority's springs and
white-scaping falls, the responsive
rounding off of hills,
creek- and riverways
are a spelling out no
3220   character muddles but
characters, the wind's many
motions, inscribe,
a telling not of one
thing to another, pen
3225   to paper, chalk to slate,
skyscraper to groundbase,
microinscription to fossil
but undivided telling:
    this writing
3230   makes bowls
and fills seas: man older
than the megalith faced
unstoried stone, deep
priority, as this about here,
3235   now after a hundred years its
millions hardly broken into:
here in America the
fashion, the scale or
intellectual sheet, sorts
3240   against a chasm without time
and one the other criticizes
to digest but, the reach not
commensurate, the maw
can't feed: this not an
3245   evening land but a
morning too early to make anything out:
the ridge fills our moment
and, time's fill, fills time:

there's no news like snow news:

3250   the tongue stuck out,
tongue tip, sticky:
then teeth, mouth, the
shaping back and the business
of swallowing: the
3255   slender esophagus, bottomed
with a valve, followed by a
great opening out, containing
another valve, then subsidiary organs,
duodenal and pancreatic, and
3260   interpenetrated systems,
blood and air, followed by
a meandering of
guts that roil and shift,
then the water system and
3265   larger hunks of gut (nice, necessary,
so precisely made) finally
the mechanisms of holding
and releasing

man is a motion through
3270   variations on a tube

Larry Brown

those who fret to generate
intensity don't understand
those who thrash in lakes
3275   of fire for the cool banks

vice versa

The Wind Picks Up Slick

The wind picks up slick
bounding upslope
on the slippery freeze

3280   "build your own worksop bench"

insulation services
tile and formica contractor
welding
upholstery service
3285   bath remodeling
gutter installation
heating and air conditioning
concrete construction
ceiling installations
3290   fireplace and chimney service

the indigestible
unaired into meaning

    area rugs

saxony plush broadloom
3295   speaker systems

    Ed White

Steelers & Cowboys

    grain off the old pebble
    pebble off the old stone
3300   stone off the old rock
      rock off the old boulder
   boulder off the old range
    range off the old divide
   divide off the old tectonic
3305   jerk off the old jerk

    arrrive

Cold Didn't Keep the Stuff

Cold didn't keep the stuff
kissed back last
fall & forsythia &
3310   pear florets couldn't
sleep, woke up blooming
in winter's skirts

spring'll spring blossom-light

know your onions

3315   a sprung spring can't
unspring and spring again
till devices and
rondures have clicked
through and gone round

3320   ramrod concept

you would think it
easier for happiness to
happen than for
unhappiness to unhappen

3325   words' windy feed

in perilous times one needs
for diversion
clipped, unsustained
lyrics with no
3330   drama (stifled cries)
vehicles to stir reality
a touch away,
to hold the unnamed nameless
back,
3335   till when times ease one may
creep into focus on sharp

rims, the alleyways of
the long arisings

                          water

3340   squall largely   to
           shapeless   plants
           the flakes   is
           repeat the crystal   air
                            to

3345   balloons
           adultery
           infantry

accomplish a designation
dense for though

3350   we would understand   get
           the world we would   this
           not have it stop
           or disappear

our doorstep mouse

3355   travels little
           this time of   a snow
           year, waits for a dry   mole
           snow and tunnels
           under the surface,

3360   a furrow burrow which
           collapses behind into
           permanent waves and windings,
           exact histories
           till high wind blows

3365   or the sun looks

defining terms was Socrates's
way of not knowing himself

if one's hopes
cease to rise

3370   so will one's peccadillo

———

I think I may not write much
today
I didn't write much before
breakfast
3375 and during breakfast I was
busy eating
and right after breakfast
I had to go, the setting good
for getting things out but
3380 short on things to write
them down with or on,
memory my shortest instrument:
I drove John to school, so
cold and windy,
3385 and it took me twenty minutes
to get my pollution control
equipment overload to let up
on the choke and smoke
so I wrote practically nothing
3390 during that time maybe a note
on a matchbook or map or
gasoline ticket (whatever,
I lost it)
so by mid-morning the time
3395 up to then was a perfect loss
as far as writing goes
so since I had the car
already warm I went over
to the University, picked
3400 up a few things,
arranged them, and, nothing
doing, came on back
and by the time I got the
coffee heated up began
3405 to think of lunch
so Phyllis and I had a
great lunch composed of
soup with turkey strippings
in it, I mean we added the

3410   turkey, it was delicious, a
delicacy, and I didn't write
a word the whole time, then
after lunch I rushed off to
be in on this thesis-defense
3415   having to do with David Jones
and that lasted you wouldn't
believe how long
and I didn't get anything down
on paper
3420   to speak of
but after that, late in the
day, the sun having broken out
clean into a perfectly clear
sky, I just came home and hung
3425   in there, meditating on that
happy brightness
and as anyone knows you cannot
meditate properly if you
interrupt yourself to write
3430   what you're thinking down
so even though we have
a quarterhour left to
sundown I don't think I'll get
much done today
3435   toodleoo

Teeth Out

Teeth out   og   u
toenails in   lu   gl
                        dy   y

when you're
3440   up you're
out of this   le mismo
world and when   difference
you're down   chickweedo
you're out   gone

3445   to
                               goodness

                 poetry is the life of criticism

When I Think of "the Poet

            When I think of "the Poet
            paramount"
3450   how nature narrowed
            through him without
            loss of breadth

            through one past the aspiration
            of envy,
3455   free of the fidgetings,
            picky dispositions, effects
            of lesser men (giants
            themselves)
            one in no need of praise
3460   for why thank
            a tree whose leaves inscribe
            the sun's doings,
            one better left unpraised
            where praise falls away
3465   from its object   my premature
                                     sex life

            entangling poet   came before
            untangling critic   my mature
                                     sex life

3470   weeds don't read books
            (or write them) so I sing
            of weeds and they
            don't turn red or pale
            with embarrassment or   if That
3475   gratitude or turn me   Which Is
            singing pale or red   spoke it
                                     wd say

```
                big rigs                      That Which
                big digs      tookus          Is speaking
      3480      bosoms
                few & far between

                                               when duh
                when the                       going git
                "voice"                        tough duh
      3485      (the                           tough git
                assimilator)                   gone man
                is too
                strong it consumes the
                particulars (words,
      3490      images, tones, meanings)
                a clearing
                in bulrushes as if an
                elephant had paraded
                through, more opaque
      3495      than voice
                but no pushier


                shoving every drift with oar


                my poetry has                  (some weeds
                fallen off a                   that stand
      3500      little, it has                 through winter
                slackened                      collect
                from standing                  snowblossoms
                right up in                    bigger
                there                          than their summer
      3505      and doing it,                  blooms)
                it has weakened away,
                it's soft


                a hollow
                log's as            (( ϙϙ ))
      3510      good a                 • •
                place as              ⟙⟙
                any for
                a long hole     Sigmund took our
```

888

                    head out of
3515   the clouds and
    gum   hung it between
    surgery   our   legs
                      hello
                      in
3520   there

        a lot of sunshine today now falling in
        gold vertical striping against
        the garage and breaking to
        fall on up the roof
3525   a glorious coldness
        and brightness antibacterial as saliva or vulture shit

You Can't Get It Right

        You can't get it right:
        if it doesn't slide off the   from side
        track on one side   to slide
3530   it will on the other or
        find an unsuspected
        side to slide off: it will not
        go right down the slender middle
        long:

3535   stabilize political
        matters by turning them
        over to permanent agencies
        and how do you
        protect yourself against
3540   the stability:
        return the matters to politicians and,
        every election re-stirring the ambience,
        you lose continuity

        things, tilt acquired,   he has her
3545   achieve acceleration: all sewed up

—————

the tongue, powerful,
moving organ, will in the
dark find bliss's button,
describe its contours,
3550   buffet gently and swirl it,
and then swarm warmth (and
grease) into other areas
equally touchy and astonishing
suffusingly

3555   we are to several
organisms, micro
and macro, in their
billions,
as islands, archipelagoes,
3560   isthmuses, regions, elevations,
continents, seas: the mouth's
pit folks, so many kinds, the
friendly anaerobe
(honey, see your bacteriologist
3565   twice a night)
yes
vultures (and other
        scavengers) will
eat up the ruptures, lesions, gashes,
3570   dissolving sores of dead
animals
and gut-cleanse the disease till
shit's reductive bit, which may
stink, is (as the world
3575   is made) pure   like so
                  so like
poets probe and punish out
dark eruptions or
invasions of the
3580   public mind and deposit in clear

anthologies
lean germicidal turd of the just
word restored

the poet wants	the poet, torn by
3585 to govern, sway;	maximum knowledge,
he wants	makes the best
a difficult	possible decision,
dialectical test,	tradeoff in recent
particulars forming	times—governs,
3590 into motions and	imitating the
parties: he wants	real thing & the
contention, compromise,	enterprise of each
sneak plays, judgments,	of us to himself
surprises wherein he	

3595   whatever the body knows
or teaches,
the known, found through the
body, can exist other than in
the body, the dancer, for
3600   example, the single body
never out of itself, writes
a story entangled, interlocking,
unfolded on the stage which
lasts in the head when
3605   the dancer has gone, a rondure,
a tendency and completion,
whose composure memory finds
and forms and imagination
redisposes and revisits at will

3610   if you could write much
superlatively beautiful
like reaches of
snow in the Rockies no
one visits

3615   imagine high-lying
writing unread wasted on
ridges and peaks

separate as word is from
thing, the motions of the language
3620   system correspond to
the motions of the world system
rather closely one, taking first one
and then, to the extent
possible, the other side into account,
3625   thinks

    the woodlark,
the lilt and liquid
upward-breaking spiral,
sound's artesian spring (the
3630   dogs get excited in the thicket
rushing up the pheasant, making
plain hens fly off
chirping) but
I love the mockingbird, childhood's
3635   bird, most, and
weather changes or winter feed
has brought him to live here
where till this year I had
not seen him and now
3640   with everything down white
(and mockingbird quite silent)
I see him flash across the
snow
into the big round yew or
3645   cedar bush
whatever it is
and pick the leftover
shriveled or half-shriveled
red cedar or yew berries
3650   and he seems fat enough

dealing with the cold long
nights (I put out a cage of
suet but he will not light on it)
I wonder when in spring
3655   musing he'll
dropping burst the first note,
sweep a cluster of shatters into song,
and then fire the air with
a fire-line glinting unwinding

3660   (the days lengthen, this morning's
rim-sky rosy at seven:
last evening
the great orb tucked in
a last slice at 20 to 5!)

3665   the crow I think
has smelled my suet
but surely he
won't come to it

hanging on a nail near the
3670   ceiling of the backporch

press the incidental
to assume the general
(any particular general)

most people don't like to think
3675   of the stuff in their livingroom
as sitting there, chairs,
lamps, end tables, vases, tables:
they think they ought to have a focal
point, so they get something big &
3680   noticeable, like a philodendron,
and plunk it down where nobody
can miss it
and that is not what a focal point is

I declare the crows have
3685   come right in to hanging
around in the maple tree
and I jest bet you five
dollars since it's over
thirty today they got the
3690   scent of that suet and
they jest a waitin' that's
what they doin' they jest
a waitin' sooner or later
they gonna plunk right
3695   there on the porch and
start a grabbin' and a
tearin' well I thought this
year I was goin' to make up
my mind to do somethin'
3700   good fer nature but that
warn't the nature I meant to
do any good fer that's a
fact and I don't keer who
knows it them crows is a
3705   eating up what little bit
of stuff people has and if
they ain't something done
about it I'll tell you they
won't be a thang left around
3710   here that them crows ain't
fooled with I bet
you five dollars on that

see see see you can
see it for a pennis

3715   come come   will teen wind
        (unlikely)   slice the yellow
        come, come   peaks off acne
        (more likely)

———

I have not been out to stand
3720 near or touch the elm
recently so though I see it
occasionally through the other
room's window
I lack heavy information that
3725 it remains substantial and yet
by faith I have no doubt
if I went out there
to hang myself on it
it would do well enough

The Perfect Journey Is

3730 The perfect journey is
no need to go

another nothingly clear day and
I went
to walk between the pine
3735 colonnades
up the road on the hill and there
hill-high in dry cold
I saw the weaves of glitterment
airborne, so fine,
3740 the breeze sifting
figurations from the snow
reservoirs of the boughs

Snow of the

Snow of the
right consistency,
3745 temperature, and
velocity will
fall in a lee
slope

building out over
3750   space a
promontory of
considerable
reach in
downward curvature:
3755   and snow
will do this
not once
but wherever possible,
a similarity of effect
3760   extended
to diversity's
exact numeration

. . .

here a month of snow,
3765   more January than
February, intervenes
during which
I wrote
nothing: it is
3770   the winter-deep, the
annual sink:
leave it unwritten,
as snow unwrites
the landscape

3775   . . .

The Prescriptive Stalls As

The prescriptive stalls as
to when to take effect:
the admonishment loses the
color of certainty: the
3780 recommendation lies down like
a mule and rolls in the sand:
the traders arrive with their
incredible auctioneer and
commence to squabble
3785 and at the end of the day
nothing has been sold or
bought: in having found no
imbalance into a way out
as yet, an imbalance that
3790 throws the leaves and
hangings of imbalance into
balance, I stand for
whatever will not come round
or be whole
3795 or made out or reduced:
here breakdown allows
the small solution to
operate on the local problem:

this morning I got up early
3800 and took the wetsack off my
foot, toe healing:
I went down and
turned up the heat, so
everybody could get up warm,
3805 then I made coffee, cooked
an egg, had toast:
it was glorious enough:
but anyhow the man said it
will truly go to fifty today:
3810 it's already 30: when all

the hills' holdings and the
trees' and ridges' loosen and
commence to trickle or
slide, gouge out and roar,
3815 we may have a thaw
disturbance, that aspect
to happiness and warmth:
I hope it will take on
slow-moving

3820 •

or after shoals of selloffs,
options, shorts, long-terms,
after heavy-risk purchases
and quick turnovers, the
3825 unspeakable auctioneer having
fed in his energy and taken
his toll, there at the day's
end is my portion: crust:
I just got back from the
3830 University: so many
matters of great interest and
no moment:
but in the moment the general
world assigns,
3835 the special person, the
one taking the brunt,
finds the ultimate explosion:
a former student, now
representing a book publisher,
3840 stops by: he is engaged:
soandso calls that soandso
will not keep the appointment
because her father has died:
soandso left her dog
3845 at home shut up
because he runs after
bitches and winds up

in the pound:
a University writes offering
3850   me a job: one who
wants to apply for the job
won't get it:
    the turn of the day:
    the spill, waterfall, shed:
3855   impossible to make
any version
(perversion better than no
version at all)
adequate to the circumstance:
3860   one enlarges the scope
and increases the fill-in:
deepens, dumps, delineates
the fill-in:

who or what is watching over
3865   the waterfall (the waterfallwatcher)
where the
spill picks up, the urgency
takes on muscle and speed,
the fast overshoot with
3870   giddy, weightless fall,
and the splintering disturbance
against bottom, rock, water:
things pick up, of course,
from there and go on in a new
3875   mildness but strange setting:
some things pass into
unrecognizable strangeness:
    is no one watching, of
    course not,
3880   not even a gentle, universal
principle with a calming circularity,
a soft persuader reminding us
of the marvels, the high
concerns and yearnings over
3885   us, the realms luminous our

we can be okay
socially and
know that the
same moral laws
are operating
as before, as
usual, and still
grind crudely at
the circular
edge between
human and natural
law, one harmony
not disclosing
how it
meshes with
another
harmony

understanding
need only bend for comfort to:

are we here, single things,
lifted up into clarity and
3890   recognition
by the same powers and forces
to be struck down, the calm
coasting going quite on beyond
us: or is it here precisely
3895   that sleeve enters sleeve
so we see the interpenetrations,
to live to die, not to
die not to live, this is
the motif, announcement,
3900   deep conditioner, the knowledge
from which there is no
freedom and no freedom
except in the knowledge,
the hardest, most bitter
3905   schooling beauty and decay
could have devised,
allowing, though, ironic sweets
highest invention is humbled by:
    one is helpless: one weeps: e
3910   terror raves beyond the tear: q
    one is without help: u
    and then one sees or recalls   a
that on the balance line between   n
purchases and payoffs   i
3915   indifference looks neither this   l
way nor that:
our help is the call of
indifference that says
come where there is no
3920   need of help
and have all the help you need:
so we rock (and roll) between gratitude
and terror (burns the cheek)

so we commend ourselves to
3925 what is to be and what must be
so we celebrate dome's day, the
big theatre, we came to see
and so we quail
at show's end, the going back
3930 into forgotten dark,
the stripping off of illusion's privileges:
the sleep beyond the
edge of the deepest sleep

•

3935 my fears of the
piling up of too
much fluency
in high-rise temperature were,
I think, ill-founded
3940 for though the radio says it is
now 42
the drips from the garage eaves
slow winter down:
you could write a sonnet
3945 between one drop and the next

•

insecurity of registration in
a terrain measures the
potential, that susceptible
3950 to disposition or re-disposition,
but to the extent that potential is pure
potential, with not a skimming
of announcement or definition,
it is nothing, who needs
3955 potential: and yet who does
not, not need "give", border
or boundary stone
relocateable: if you could,

for example, set poetry off
3960   into 10 orders of this and
that, subsidiary systems spelled out, lifted into
interpenetrative connection
with what is perceived to be,
you could call it preserved
3965   territory, a public or private
garden, identity certain:
but poetry resists this, yielding to erosion,
horse manure, bird droppings,
pine needles, the wind, moss,
3970   bracket, bract, stone of change,
a troublesome, marvelous garden:
fertility inexhaustible, a milling:

After the Dissolve

After the dissolve,
under cedars and black and blue
3975   spruce,
hemlock thickets,
crescents of coverless
ground where
if pheasant eat grass
3980   pheasant can
plick chilly uprights of
green grass
or sort through the
vegetal remains, rubble for seed or
3985   seed-like knobs,
clusters, or pods, roots, or
whatever
contributes generating to
the possible: but now
3990   my class over for today
traces of white airiness
mean-sprinkling are expanding
into hard lightness

again, temperature falling,
3995   new snow on old
melt-rinsed-to-ice snow

limited visibility
yield ahead
yield
4000   stop
frost heaves
merging traffic

	at most dusk
bill of goods	the ringneck
deepdown clean	as if reluctant
I saw enough	to fly up to roost
of the real	walks about
to flee and	on the meltshade
found enough unreal	under the cedar,
to return to	his feet on the
see the real	ground for the first

(4005, 4010 mark the rows "deepdown clean" and "to return to")

time since midDec: he walks elegantly,
slowly, now and then bends
to peck:
4015   of course, he sleeps
on warm legs and feet
but all day every day he's
snow-plopping barefooted:

scouring ugliness
4020   and bathing beauty

my friend the	drover
poet is no	oversold
longer attracted	oversoul
to any	lover
center of which	mover
he is not	shover
the attraction	

(4025 marks the row "center of which")

A Sift, Sprinkling, or Veil

A sift, sprinkling, or veil
of snow came
4030   last evening sun after dusk
but ended soon:
today, though, is bright!
I got up at 6:30 to turn up
the heat and the
4035   east was brightening: oh,
I said, the sun may come up
this morning and now it is
bursting pointblank against
the thicket

Structureless Rage, Perhaps

4040   Structureless rage, perhaps,
pure energy of motion, volition, lies
alongside or moves under
and upfloats appetite: blah, blah:
an energy that we should have   one with no
4045   been put here among these   community has
bounties and possibilities,   only the world
crippled with these walls and
spoons:
       rage then flares into fear
4050   that resentment has destroyed
our chances with the good
makings, the father dispraised:
       it is a circumstance
medicine cannot surround or
4055   work preservingly to the core
of: we must be and be
destroyed at once: rage and
love, fear and love, these
work themselves
4060   out so that we become

accredited lovers and fearers
with no loss to either wing:
with no cancellation into
boredom or indifference:
4065   harsh: harsh: with the
fate-like calm acceptance
that no other mix could keep this stir:
            in a bush's
            fine division
4070   the sparrow lights free
from the hawk's broad shoulder:
            tie one on:
         another matter:
there is not
4075   at the moment   y
one single flake   e
of snow on   a
the garage roof:
a warm day again up to 45,
4080   good old February
and there are wide circles
of dark ground under evergreens
and oblongs and funny
strung-out clustral darknesses
4085   under groves, along hedges,
the woods in untouched natural color
but it's gray again
    (it's gray again
    like clay again!)

4090   uyyl   lggu ugyu lygl
glug   yuly yllg guuy

Tell What Will Not Tell Direct

Tell what will not tell direct
encompassingly:
the bindings of avoidance

4095   gather terrain
manysided and cushioning,
should the direct route of
the direct saying emerge,
should the furrows of
4100   circumference, hills
and dells, the wild,
off-the-mark talk,
lead to the very place unspoken
standing out where the stand
4105   must be taken,
avoiding avoidance

      go out of your
        out of your
      way to help
4110   others
      help others

but watch it what you raise into
strength may suspect you of
strength withheld and raid you
4115   down and out loose, windy

since before day
and all day
the wind's rolled billows across
us, the soundlessness,
4120   rising roar, crash,   weave is what it is:
muffling, sucking   no matter the wisdom,
against the house   perception: the truth,
and this   yes, but only because
with the sky gray gray as   attendance to truth
4125   before as usual   enlarges complexity:
well but even so it's good   but is one wave of the
weather for February   weave balanced by an
                         equal & opposite: that
great weather's   is important: is
4130   destruction, though: everything stressed but

the blue dry high
radiant inanition
shrinks brooks to crisp
routes
4135 burns grass
upholds dust

in its proper place:
is consideration
observed in the
dispositions: not an
ailing net but
adequate weave

find reality
find duplicity
two bows of a single knot

4140 my feelings are caught
gauze in a strong wash

with the prevailing snow
and full moon
nothing prowls through here
4145 at night
without prowling declarations

raccoon prissy
used sway

Spread It Thin

Spread it thin
4150 zip it in

give me a ring
go back up for a lay
(better laid than never or up)

today continues the tropical
4155 extravaganza—up to 45,
the circle of under-cedar melt having
widened halfway across the
yard and the pheasant pecking here &
there significantly

———

4160 an interim free of spring
   madness and summer dangers
   a protectorate of warmth
   midway winter's wars

   bees body cells of the animal, hive

4165 today you couldn't get a sprig
   of hemlock to wiggle
   where yesterday
   bounding sloped green
   surfs
4170 permanent as breaking
   entanglements: when the wind
   does not arrange to have
   tongue, much is tongueless,
   as great distance

Dark Day, Warm and Windy

4175 Dark day, warm and windy,
   light breaking through
   clouds
   coloring the sides of tall
   furrows, thaw decaying
4180 snow, the wind stirring
   time up to a rush, I come home
   from work midmorning
   dark with contemplations,
    that the infant finds
4185 his hand unopened
    and the old man forgets
    his has closed—that rondure:
   I sit down at the piano
   and try the "Fuga 1" in *The*
4190 *Well-Tempered Clavier* and

my feelings lighten,
the melody so incredible,
the counter-melody incredible,
the workings in and out
4195   precise and necessary

Like Fifty

Like fifty
I'm fifty

                ditch water,
                spring caterpillar,
4200   ripples downhill,
        an eager
        thermometer,
        the volume of motion a direct
        reading of melt
4205   and melt keyed to the temperature

        so during the time of thaw
        correction made for
        shrinkage of reservoir,
        the ditch
4210   with some variable constant
        lag tells:

        I don't care much about the
        language these days (!)—turn this upside
                            down and you have
4215   I want   the happiness
        to make a point: without measure
        the point is essential,
        the connection: the language
        should be adequate:
4220   (I've felt, might as well admit
        it, other ways (not

necessarily opposite (
sometimes opposite) ways)
before)

4225   if mush were slush   dud
        meep could sleep   dad

        scruffy lines between me & my
        neighbors, lean thickets,
        spirea brown fine-bush and
4230   overhangings of maple, silver
        and sugar, big spruce,
        honeysuckle bush-stump, ground
        cover, and my own kept ant
        hills: a stringy wilderness
4235   inhabiting civilization's
        straight lines

        a half-century inscribed
        birthday cake, promises
        of presents, a wheelbarrow
4240   (red, rained on) and stereo!

A 41 Morning, Still Cloudy

        A 41 morning, still cloudy,
        rainy, gray, vague, the only
        snow left
        skinny archipelagoes, once
4245   drifts, or stalls, as by (before)
        (or after) garages or thickets:
            the forecast is for
            skin temperatures dropping
            through the day
4250   into snow flurries
        with no significant
        accumulation:

———

still three months away to leaves:
for us now there
4255   is a discontinuity in the
flow of energy from the
physical which we still can
trust some to the metaphysical
now exploded: ideally, the
4260   physical would be the roots
or trunk and the metaphysical
would arise easily and smoothly into
the subtleties of embranchment
allowing, when leaved, flows
4265   and wavings of light, variable
shades, tones and atmospheres
like the spiritual temper of a time:
for us now, we dig in to
see if the trouble with the
4270   boughs is not some trouble
with the roots and so we have
nearly killed the tree:

still, however long it is to
leaves, the grass has from
4275   this warm spell taken
the hint, sprung its leaves
up into the cushions of air
and given out a tint hint:
imagine, the readiness
4280   of it all! the unwearying readiness
to cycle, eagerness all over
fresh, as if for the first time:

now the tree is cracked off
at the ground: a peel of
4285   cambium holds the boughs:

the boulder columns
of the temple
   hold

                    up (arbor-skinny
    4290   roof)
                    eternal emptiness

                    I brought in the garbage
                    cans, there was
                    (at this temperature)
    4295   a faint smell in them:
                    it was
                    nearly pleasant:
                        spring's first
                        midwinter
    4300   fragrance:

                    we eat the dead, swirling decay into
                    such a fret it gives energy off
                    to us, saprohumanists:
                    we can't go on long eating and shitting and
    4305   beshitting the world before,
                    eaten, we are beshat:
                    the banqueter's the banquet:
                    (well, then, dine!)
                    look you to it:

    4310   will not the wolfer be wolfed:

                    can there be a dwelling for man
                    with no cock to cry the days
                    in: I hear from across the lake
                    in quiet spells
    4315   dogs barking or crows cawing: or,
                    even, though terribly early,
                    geese going over, high over:
                    in any case, it is not the
                    rooster, wing-thubbing and crowing:
    4320   do you not miss the biddies:
                    yellow butterballs

peeping about the hen's legs
and beak:
do you dwell securely where
4325   there is no cackle to the lay
      and no offal dog neither
       nothing
good Lord not even a guinea:
I need pig and fowl: company:
4330   and the goat!
how I need a goat!
what is the flavor
of anything without
the bright-eyed,
4335   astonished,
big-balled billy: or the
fucking sheep: who can do
without it: what we have is
      the radio blaring
4340   a flat high level
       of disaster this
       and disaster that:
when I lived in the world
there was nothing worth doing
4345   doing

Produce and Fuctifry

Produce and fuctifry

a snow so misty, melty,
and thick
only careful looking sees it:
4350   it does not resemble itself
on garage or grayass: my
      teeth and victory stick
      dream of being

hard on
4355   cavities

guys with things so fine
they consider noses
or so blunt   (earful,
they blunder ears   getting an)

4360   stuprum   stream   new snow
          stupulose mill run   on old
                      wash   melt narrows
                      brook brooks
                      creek
4365   branch
           mill race
           mill
           mill town
           mil town
4370   Mil ton
           Milton

geese did fly over yesterday!
northward along the east shore
harkking & honnking
4375   in the accustomed ways:
seeing believes even if belief
can sustain seeing

an inch of snow fell during the night
drawing lines in the trees and
4380   filling bushes with snowberries, big ones,
fork blossoms

                               at least
                               more fell
                               than rose

I Look Up Guff and Find the First

4385 I look up *guff* and find the first
 thing I learned about Babylon, the
 gufa, the round wicker boats
 in the fourth-grade reader! and I
 remember the camels slinking high
4390 against the flat, low line in the
 background
 with the aerial twist of leafage
 at the palm top:
 I can taste the sand now that I could
4395 taste then, the muddy yellow river,
 I feel the gristy hot soup of it now
 that I did then!

  mean business

 the split between us

4400 snow remains (remains
 of snow) out under
 the woodsedge brush
   and lee of the put-out
   Christmas tree, there a dab
4405   (white scab)
 and up here before the big yew
 which brought the wind
 paused to a crescent fall-out

 histories of past
4410 motions thawing away into motions,
 runlets and trickles,
 histories of redispositions

 I cry nothingness nothingness as long
 as the inadequate, the issuistic, is
4415 proposed: I cry nothingness nothingness

to open space for the more nearly
adequate should it be deeply spoken for or of:

the dialectical
sways
4420   in on the clarification of
oversimplification
and falls in to opposite or
indifferent tendencies:
and after heavy losses on both sides
4425   burns itself out in error and
grief and astonished self-correction
only to go a little way
too far the other way,
take on concentration,
4430   force, and direction,
lean down into an assertion
that challenges, tests others
and then the opposite sway
falls into motion
4435   with heavy losses, etc.
       nothing achieved apparently but excuses
       to form energies idly potential, test
       belief, swell the capacity to tolerate tragedy:

the economies, the allowances and costs, are so
4440   finely adjusted, broadly and thoroughly applicable,
it is hard to believe the absurd design, haphazard:
though it would be dialectically just for economy to
be grounded in happenstance because only at the level
of absolute freedom of bit could swells of new
4445   information rise to alter the valuations of the economies

the weather today continues
recent trends: 35 at dawn,
near 40 now at 10:37 a.m.,
supposed to go maybe to 45:
4450   high for tomorrow 40:
the tiger lilies are green

nubs standing in ice:
I see a hollyhock leaf
or so lying on the ground,
4455   still green, the snow cover
having kept it: they say
there are snowdrops up
(a switch from the downs) and
crocuses are heaving off
4460   shelves and roofs

One at One with His Desire

One at one with his desire
slurps not the bone soup
of syllables
    but rises to the other's
4465   rose and falls immediately
    from
feeding desire
to recollection or anticipation
of desire
4470   the business of the day
    not bending the contour
    out of circle

one not at one with his
desire has not a whole
4475   intention
    and consequently no place
    to go unqualified
    or any single thing to
look for but one aspect
4480   of himself knows the
otherness of another aspect
    so that he cannot become
    disentangled
    into other otherness

———

4485   all singers are blind, of course,
for the same reason that they
do not see the world
     but thickets of
     complication between
4490   themselves and their desire:
so much loss for the little
rescue of a lilt, a passing
fine turn, a modulation
     practiced and true:
4495   art's
     nonbeing's

dark consolation:
what a nice stanza! imagine just going
on: I think I've invented
4500   rooms to walk through
     or stand amazed
     or lie sleepy in:
it is no place, though,
to rehearse the flesh
4505 of the beloved,
     it is no place to touch
     or taste
     enter or leave:

it is dry delight, whatever
4510 service remains when
the church closes:
     the sweepstakes of
     no desire
     whole as fulfillment:
4515 the sweetest passer of time
scheduled for emptiness:
the drug that makes erasure
     bliss: an illusion some
     of the uneasy can cover
4520   misery with:

still when you think of the
nourishment of such delight as
over starvation,
    what a numb pale

4525   paradise! how constant
    the music
dwelling among the constant
bushes, the deathlessness only
lifelessness can know

4530   one not at one with his
    desire still has to desire
    so much more than nothing

    this stanza compels
    its way along: a

4535   break will humble it:

form consumes:
form eliminates:
form forms the form
that extracts the elixir from

4540   the passages of change:
well, we mustn't let this
    form reverse itself
    into an opposite
    though parallel

4545   largely similar insistence:
must we?

a marvelous morning
dull gray aflood with the possibility of light

live unknown!

4550   (the protean density   a pane's
    of that!)   mirror
    unmonitored by   lets
    the clichés of praise   everything

                                              through
4555   well, no, the light changed
        away into indistinguishable   if you froze
        gray, flicking wet dashes,   a fog, that's,
        gravity-sprung ellipses, on   turned loose on
        the windowpane: a bluster, how
4560   colder, foggier, suddenly: snow-fine's
        a front entering us doors   the stuff today

                    / /
        we have become now in
        the afternoon balled up
4565   horizonless in pearly
        mist, a billion bits of snow
        jostling this
        way and that, coming
        down and putting
4570   differentiation down downy:

        the temperature dropped
        in an hour twenty degrees an hour
        an hour

        sheet-deep in sleet
4575   I haven't written as
                many words as an hour's
                grains of sleet
        and so far only a scattering
        impression of white
4580   has risen from the lawn:
        one should go on till one's
        hue is
        unmistakeable

        nature goes so far to make
4585   us one of a kind
        and treat us all alike

Dull Lull

           Dull lull
           palustral
               mule

4590   logging a
   swamp   sull
     pompous
     ramps
      amperage
4595   palatial
        labial
       mull
        gulls

    dropped to eenzie teens last
4600 night and snowed
    three inches
       now at noon it's
       the biggest teen

    the car was crunchy and
4605 crusty with
    frozen rain in the windshield
    wipers, stuck,
    and the door wouldn't break
    open and every window was
4610 snowed white,
    tribulation's Parian wreaths
    (hark, a footnote)

    hurdygurdy hurlyburly
    loveydovey

4615   with the snow white
      as snow and the light
      bright as day
      one sees too much to see
        outside

4620   //1:50 p.m.
                though it is
                warm by the
                window and though
                the garageroof snow
4625   cannot but melt
                and tinkle twinklefree
                at the eaves
                still the thermometer
                has not budged up a bit
4630   all day
                standing right where it
                is regardless of what-all
                the sun pours it on day
                and (elsewhere) night
4635   but the air masses will come
        variably from here and there
        and they warm and cool in
                cycles longer than a day
                longer than a week maybe
4640   even longer than a year
                as long maybe as the 11
                year sunspot cycle or
                sunspot cycles well
                you get the point
4645   just because you
                have a fair day you
                can't expect the
                temperature to
                shoot right up
4650   to seventy like
                I told this
                writing
                student of
                mine who
4655   was a real
                tomato

I said you don't say to a
tomato you just set out make me
a tomato you say to it
4660 make leaves and stems and
roots and branches, acquire
an abundant presence, and
then easy as pie you will be
able to make lots of tomatoes
4665 and I think this girl got the
point that a Platonic form is one
thing and a piece of ass
something else
and nobody with that kind of
4670 awareness will stay puzzled
long or talk to teachers
queer for tomatoes

enough horse do for today
ltho prhps ct shrt

The Temperature Rose 15 Degrees over

4675 The temperature rose 15 degrees over
the sunless, unaided
night: clouds like freight
cars packed the heat in
here and like tarpaulins
4680 held it in place: high
winds today will change the
pacings and placings, only to add heat
to heat: high

winds shake out from scruffy
4685 snow-disorganized bushes
crosslimbs, tangles, and
dead twigs and comb every

long branch out into its
separate space and possibility,
4690   a ruffling and swaying
that brings cleansed motions
to high alignment!

rhythm is the spreading out
of sense so that curvatures
4695   of intonation, gestures of
emphasis, clusters of
relationship can find disposition
and placement within the
enclosing identity of the sense scope
4700   (as metrics eats
away at motion
it loses its identity
and becomes like motion)

metrics aside, though (and
4705   why not, though relevant) much
of the power of motion resides
in the reliability (see dict.)
of the repetition (al fine
senza repetizione): at some point
4710   in the whole
scope of an act
of congress, encouraging
trust, there ought to be a
plateau, a plateau before the
4715   peak: it needn't be a flat
plateau: it can be building
at an angle into buoyancy:
but for this part of the act,
a regular rhythm or a regular
4720   progression (generally
accelerating) ought to be
established as the highest
feeling comes on stressful

entering or unstressful
4725   withdrawing: but aside from
the regularity of duration, timing,
between stresses (c'est à
decir, a poem or novel must
achieve identifiable motion
4730   as the highest contour above
its many motions): it follows
from the reliability of these
stresses and durations that
the pleasures that lie ahead
4735   are available, can be reached,
ought to be entertained:
reliability gradually
accelerated could then explode
into huge releases of, umm,
4740   expression, into dissolving,
stressless gliding, unwrinkled
calm

expression through issue   creelo o no
is not too bad   creelo o yes
4745   if clusters of plurality
balance counterbalances:
that way, all expressions
are tolerable but
meaningful change is slow,
4750   an undercurrent forming past
calculation in accuracy:
      the unwilled will
      will the future
      more truly than the
4755   willed will:

10:10 a.m.: it has cleared
up sunny and warmed to the thirties:
the snow's not rushing into melt
but clumps have damp edges: one thinks

4760   the buds and flower-clusters
have swelled but actually one
has only thought of spring
and noticed the buds for the
first time: they've been about
4765   so big all winter:

        prey bolts, whines
        but overtaken is pulled down,
        dignity of design
        forgotten in dust and the
4770   fastest heart beat, grace
        of motion
        broken down into dinner

(have so many things to do that you
rarely do them)

4775   //5 p.m.
my first walk to the brook
this year and though
it was only 15 minutes
including taking out the garbage
4780   it was exhaustingly delightful
        the brook by the way
        by the way ay ay
        is sassy
        up to roaring
4785   the water melt-muddy with
road runoff (salt, ash, cinders,
& gravel) and cutting gullies:

good to see a streak of water oozing
in caterpillar ripples across
4790   the dry highway and to notice
farther up
the forsythia thicket letting its
holdings of groundsnow go

———————

4795   I would love to get the poetry just
the way it happens, the way it comes
on, heavy and thick like
a thunder tangle or empty as high
blue, weaving, stalling,
a little bit of all the
4800   progressions including the
unstirring:

hunt   high
wild   ass

on the walk a fart worked its
4805   way loose
probing through like a variable
long balloon seeking
till
wind to wind it broke free
4810   so generous & satisfying

As for Fame I've Had It

As for fame I've had it
before I've
had it: meanwhile,
others grow vast on
4815   very little
(but it has
by wise men
often been
spoken: less is
4820   more or
less more)

while the more
I give the fewer

tangles of
4825   attention to me
unwind

I suppose I've
worried too much
about the outbreak
4830   of destructive
clarification:
when most folks
are in such confusion
any slight light
4835   falls into far illumination

in darkness will we
heed too much
the twinkling of a tiny
twinkler when on the
4840   mountain
chasms, gulfs, ravines,
ledges and weighty slides wait:

to be made of steel!
so bullets and aches and
4845   pains and sorrows
the sorrows of knowing and
not knowing and witnessing
bing off you
that would be so fine
4850   provided you did not
remain stiff and
uneducated

meanwhile the day has been
beautiful from sunlight binging
4855   right off the horizon
through bright to now 3:15:

not as warm as yesterday but
warm enough, 40, 45:

poetry has become an outing
4860   (outage), church social, a picnic of
huggy self-embracing, small hopes
and a tremendous capacity to bear
up under daily disappointment,
no mail, no state funds, no
4865   fed funds, no city or county
funds, no scholarship or fellowship
today, no
subsidy on this issue, no
programs for the public
4870   or public schools this week, no
improvement at all, I'm sorry,
we can't offer you a
reading engagement this year,
no, not now:

4875   take up slack
choose cheese

When One Is a Child One Lives

When one is a child one lives
in helplessness, in terror
of arbitrary force, and in the
4880   fear of death

when one is young one lives
in helplessness of the
passions, in terror of the
ultimate vulnerabilities, and
4885   in the fear of death, passion's
opposite

———

when one is grown one lives
in helplessness of the webs
of demand and responsibility,
4890   in terror of failing, and
in the fear of death, the temptation

when one is old one lives
in helplessness, in terror, and
in the fear of death

4895   a windy, almost flashingly
changeable morning, the
clouds ripping across
influxes of light, that moist
blue in the clouds, temperature
4900   50 but failing, the willow
yellower, perhaps, than
usual, or more noticeable
against the rank clouds

instability is a loss into
4905   motion but the best integrities
move, the coming out
of "sense" from sound
progressions: the
"flow" on the court to a swish:

4910   crows sit in the thicket
hushed mainly in the noon
cloudiness:
when the great geese
fly over
4915   the crows appear strange
as if separated into their
contemplations

———

most anything, stopped, falls
apart: motion
4920   is the world's glue
    holding-together
but time eventually underslips
the whole thing

it is so lovely, the world,
4925   so full of change and death
    how can we find ease
    in the uneasy
    stability and calm
    in the rushing
4930   where is our stay
    that is in a holding
    higher
    than motion's formings

here, we know a stillness that will
4935   not work, and, there, a
stillness we can't stir from:

hold on to your self and your things
as long as there is
hope of holding: then swirl
4940   loose into the mercy of others, set
your sights on having nothing,
staying nowhere: rest home:

who lets go needs not even
the need to hold on
4945   he is free with nothing
which is in to everything,
these strange and comforting
contradictions, emollients,
ointments, and
4950   soothing sanctions for the lost:

———

swashbuckling bushwhacker

the weather cooled and calmed
into 4 o'clock
sunny, nice

4955   I look out   bang bang
         the window   yr're dead
         but the only   brush your teeth
         thing coming   and go to bed
         is another
4960   tooth out

         if I had   language says
         more fight in   wise and
         me there   sobering things
         would be less   but in
4965   run   real binds
                     nobody reads

         I picked up lost wood under   sores run
         the elm yesterday afternoon   scabs
         limbs airy with light rot   stay put
4970   bark expanding to separate
         speckled white with decay

         high winds trim the tree
         into the continence and
         security of calm

4975   frijolillo

Cloud Strays Rounded Up

Cloud strays rounded up
in a windy direction before

dawn, a hustled, rustled
        clearing

4980   as the stone buildings at the
        university get older
        life seems more and more
        like whitewater over an
        architectural rapids

4985   slope soak
            seeps (spews up)
            through a
            highway chuckhole
            late at
4990   night and
            freezing through
            early morning
            builds up ice
            which
4995   when dawn brings out
            the cars
            grinds fine
            under the tires
            and looks
5000   like a bucket
            of dumped
            gook

        a curiosity to pedestrians admiring
        the sunny morning

5005   newlyweds: honeyback guarantee

        can your father stuff it

            the Rangers can't
            seem to do
            anything in their

5010   own end
something outside the bedroom
maybe a shutter
burrs in gusts and
another thing, an electrical
5015   attachment, squeaks at the
corner of the house as if
someone were squeezing
a bird or turning over on a
spring

5020   (at nigh on to three the wind
has died down but the
temperature has gone right on up to
sixty)

tulip leaves are up
5025   green spears of lilies show
an inch of daffodil is
up
the hollyhock clump that was
aleaf under snow
5030   having lost those leaves now
to naked frost
has unfolded held small leaves
precaution freed from caution

maybe the Lord troubles
5035   people's knees so they
will pray short and get on
with what must be done
//it's getting late &
we had a shower
5040   (enough to lay the salt
and silt on snowroads):
Bernie's coming to dinner & Don
couldn't quite get the
backboard up on the face of

5045   the garage and I have pulled
       out old spirea stalks and
       picked up sticks till I'm
       pooped nevertheless let's see
       if we can approach the
5050   brushpile principle: now
       a brushpile is by nature a
       place to throw things
       but you must be careful
       when you throw armloads of
5055   this or that on the pile—
       some pieces will slide
       down and off the pile or you
       will dribble a stalk or so
       of something just before you
5060   get to the pile
           which is only to say that
           in normal usage
           you will start to blur the
           line between the brush pile
5065   and the periphery
       this should not be permitted
       because pretty soon you'd be
       kneedeep in junk before you
       could get to the pile with a
5070   load: right:
       principle: be sure to police
       the periphery of your fucking
       brushpile
       or you will wind up with
5075   nothing but a mess,
       an undifferentiated junkyard:
       is that what you want:
       do you want that:
           lines sometimes help the mind
5080   take steps from
           one thing to another
           possibly ascending steps

to the tall place
where nobody
5085   walks around

leap year

It's Half an Hour Later Before

It's half an hour later before
a spring shower
gets all the way down
5090   to hemlock ground

last night it rained easy
all night till dawn the rain
got white and
the dawn world, stained this
5095   or that, came up white
coming up on white

they's a limit, he said:
she cracked up,
   mother nature's response
5100   to male weaknessdomination

and all morning up to now
heavy stuff, white and sticky,
right on the rain line,
has been falling in a
5105   calmness no tree quivers

winter trees aren't good
winnowers: nevertheless,
fine branches snatch flakes
and big branches take
5110   single ridges: the chaff
   hits the ground
   but the caught

          turns to lit melt beads
          that light up
5115   trees in a different light:
          march one and   march   one and
          in the clear   in the   clear
          thicket highchoired   thicket   highchoired
          grackles grate squeak, grackles   grate squeak,
5120   dissonant as   dissonant   as
          a music school   a music   school

      not much verse today but we
      got the backboard & hoop up

This Poem Concerns

          This poem concerns
5125   the elm over past
          the windows of the other room

          the elm includes the weather

          this poem is largely about
          the weather because
5130   weather is a major influence
          on elms

          you've heard I know that the dutch elms
          are gone
          this is to remind you
5135   that they are still gone
                              but I heard
          we come from up   a man once
          to 30 billion yrs   whose thing
          of oblivion but think was done and
5140   of not even a   whose race
          little more lightly   run say
                              he was ready

the great flash their selves
onto, obliterating, surroundings:
5145   they are normal:

cutting back, undercutting, schools
us to lessenings, including
the total lessening, nothing:

from what bin more gigantic than stars
5150   could the diet be doled:
doled! poured out!
when the biggest thing, the grand repository,
we have is oblivion, slick with emptiness

will the fed few
5155   feed on
cut-aways
from the schooled starved

we applaud the loudmouth who
breaks through into the feast of our portion!

5160   could shed your shingles
could shingle your shed

today was a fair day all day
and most of the snow got
mopped up except
5165   here and there next to
trees, fences, in thickets
hard to get at

I turn to the word and it brings me
anything:
5170   I no longer go to look about in the world:
I have become so lonely
that only the word
is free enough and large enough to take my

                    mind off
5175   the world going day
                    by day over the brink
                    used up but unused:
                how thankful I feel
                bent gutless over
5180   the vomited void
                to have at least the word
                going anywhere fetching anything:
                pretty soon it may have
                brought so much
5185   it will not need to go off again
                and then the word will
                draw me up about it

The Word Cries Out

            The word cries out
            and I fetch

5190   a thing or thought is noted
            and from need or in
            response to pressure
                urgency for a verbal version arises
            and words dash in
5195   taking trial positions,
            sort and re-sort themselves   wor(l)d
            into provisional clusters
            and whole strings:
                a marshal, severest linesman,
5200   shouts out down the ranks
            and ta-tum
            the verbal version
            with last minute stumbling or twitching
            on the edges
5205   declares itself   there was a heavy
            its trimmest   frost of snow on the garage's

                                    roof scales but the sun
I hunt and peck   wiped it off
leaf through   or the garage crawled away
5210   check alignment
        do it again
        start over
        wait a while
        look up
5215   reconsider, readjust:
        friendly word, image,
        you hold my attention:
        even as attention fails
        and revives with work,
5220   stirring and re-doing:

        now as many snowflakes as you would find
        bees working a quince clump, flakes big
        as mayflies, run or stall or turn or rise
        in the wind all together, flocks, swarms,
5225   droves of things: this may be where fish
        got the notion of turning in a single
        action (it snows over oceans)

I Woke Up at 6 and It Was

        I woke up at 6 and it was
        light enough
5230   to shell peas or water begonias:
        midwinter, fine-work would
        have had
        to wait till eight:
            two days off from spring,
5235   two hours of light
        attached to both ends of the
        day, the middle position
        will enlarge, going on
        to four hours either end,

5240   sixteen dark switched to
             sixteen light:

             the reason it makes
             no difference what people
             think
5245   is that they don't think
             enough to make any
             difference

             the weather got us this week:
             Tuesday an alldayer, a
5250   heavy snow with the temperature
             dropping, dropping (from the
             shales of the morning) so low
             that last night, low teens,
             jungle escalations, ropes,
5255   vines, fronds, seized the
             windows crystal-blind again:
                    today
                    the sun came up
                    in light,
5260   to warm to thirty: that will do
             in the garage snow (an inch
             on the windy side, one to three
             inches on the hemlock side):
             yesterday at the university as, my
5265   wont, I mused out my window,
             I saw a certain twist and
             horny warp
             registered in the deep-long
             eaves icicles and since
5270   Tuesday night had been windy
             I thought, my word, icicles
             summarize the rate of melt
             and wind direction, are a glacio-spiral
             version of a wind-rose: nature
5275   that will uproot an eavesload

of history
can be so careful of history

A Flock of My Days

A flock of my days
either gone already or to
5280   come rises up
in a flurry and flies into
itself
setting off
a maelstrom descent, whirlpool bloom
5285   with a fine hollow stem figuring for a
bottomless source

in yesterday's dusk hickory,
a flicker black on skylight,
not a grackle but a
5290   robin! the behavior exact,
     year's first!
pecking his breast, grooming,
regarding the groundcover of
snow unsharply
5295   (but today the temp is to go
to 60, worm raising weather)

yesterday when melt was
commencing late
in the afternoon
5300   one icicle with a fringehold
on the eaves
waved back and forth
windily
as if hinged,
5305   its hold become so light

but now this morning
the temperature nearing fifty

the eaves rain with
melt, rooftiles starting to show

5310   radiance's darkness
(too much light on too much snow)

I guess the lady next door
when she had the elm thinned
from the thicket
5315   didn't know
snow would cap a hemispheric cone
on the left stump

they say it took some days
for the cries in No Man's Land
5320   to die down: first
there was a noise
of pain
but a few dawns and dusks
settled things
5325   down to here and there
a filament of dissent
and then the dawn came wherein
the peace was incredible

You Can't Imitate

You can't imitate   the extent to
5330   anybody really   which you can't
and the extent   imitate anyone
to which   really is enough
you can't is   originality
enough originality

5335   one gains   after another blow
with immortality   I pick up
a lasting   loose wood
tomb   under the elm,

                                                    hard branches, the
5340   skinny bones
                                                    of a flesh
            if you caught a   left
            dusk-glimpse   that was leaves
            as a first seeing
5345   of the thin-tapering
            hemlocks (a row   ringneck &
            of raving beauties)   redwing
            you'd think they'd,   (redneck &
            waggled and whipped,   ringwing)
5350   worn off in the
            wind that way

            Stevens, you should be here
            now with the ringnecks
            and rigorous rednecks
5355   and the green billows
            of grass with drained
            hunks of black-old
            snow floating in them
            and the ringnecks
5360   stirred by a nosey dog
            racing into the thickets!
            if you could hear the
            brook like a bear breaking
            through the thicket

5365   (the thicket floor
            a manuscript patches
            of snow illuminate)

            yours truly
            yours treely

5370   "live unknown" is
            no fun unless
            you have to work at it

———

why kill
yourself when
5375   you can
die
without
your help   trees fall to
    the wind
5380   and falls'
    murmuring
    trees the wind
the comet mingling
with us this
5385   week (a
windy week)
will
be back in
fifty
5390   thousand years   the grave may
    not be its
    goal but that's
    where it lands
the world's too serious
5395   to take seriously &
too funny to take lightly   faint &
    fall over

Old Milling

say to the race
5400   your run's
run its race

say to the run
your race's
race's run

Spring's Old Hat Is Older

5405 Spring's old hat is older
than hills:
but spring's skinny shade
(as old)
gives cedar, pine, spruce,
5410 upstart and low-profile,
the jump on maple,
elm, latecomer

my yew ball
is ten feet high and wide
5415 (it doesn't roll in
but unrolls the wind)
you can stand behind it
when there're insistent breezes
and it's like standing
5420 on the bank of
a current and even if the wind
is sucky
blowy with variability
the whole
5425 context
is diminished in a matrix
of holding

The Temperature Fell

The temperature fell
through yesterday afternoon:
5430 big clouds came
and winds rose: and fell
and the clouds came and went
and the temperature fell on
through the night
5435 plunging into the teens

from a daytime high
above seventy

today though the sun is out at
times and
5440   though the wind, steady,
has lessened,
the temperature is staying
where it fell,
snowflakes feeling
5445   their way (more
numerous than far-off legions)
through the air
in fabrics too fine for "snowing"

goalless as a ping
5450   pong table I'm
as a free-versite
also netless
(courtless)

systems, structures,
5455   big hunks of culture
do not melt and flow
directly
one to the other but
        turn
5460   articulate
        dis-poise
often on single glints of
perception,
the exception sharply noticed
5465   become the groundwork
of the next familiar:
        as one who looks
to the mechanisms and costs
(sad joy
5470   breaking away into acceptance)

in the "flow" of systems and
structures
I cannot stop to see if
at any point a thing
5475   still moving was
satisfactorily complete:
the sky's stabiles
hasten and churn:
    I befriend, or hope to,
5480   gently,
motion: it is my slow veracity
and belief:
the conveyance of discard is
the arising of beauty:
5485   perception, flat, impersonal, out-of-context
perception disfamiliars, erupts motion:

my life (pent)
misspent &
(piddling pity)
5490   unspent
has poured itself off into
a big jar, jug, cistern, pool,
bog, mere, lake, bay, or
ocean of grief but
5495   this was a morning, like
    any other, for anything,
    a whistling colleague,
an assignation finally
accomplished, a birth,
5500   death, a pheasant screeching

achieve an identity,
find a direction, such achieving
leaves behind as much as it finds

choose short-term goals and having
5505   realized them, wait for the grave

wandering afloat the landscape
to find you

have long-range, even impossible,
goals and
5510   you will complete no work
but you will,
eyes on the sky, stumble astonished
into the grave,
your work left
5515   to others, an inheritance

imbalance providing the
illusion of direction,
the loops, sways
of exaggeration, we can, ah,
5520   and, therefore

could a shady
spot of the peace
everlasting patch
the wretched ways
5525   and byways of the
lusty & hard-to-take!

oh, but we should not rail!
everything but our understanding
is flawless

5530   the hemlocks are
sensitive wind instruments
    you can
      judge by the thicket
    that it's calm
5535   but just then the tips of
hemlock branches pick
up the frailest motions,
    the long branches, you

                    know, rise out in high
5540   bow-boughs from the trunk
                    and secondary branches
                    branch off,
                a dense replication and
                registration so that
5545   when the wind blows branch
                tip and branch tip
                try out the sways and lofts
                of space and
                        sure enough
5550   here and there
                branch tips intermingle
                and where they often
                intermingle (summarizing
                prevailingness)
5555   the tips lose needles,
                fray,
                and, no way proved to go,
                the tip dies
                and growth takes place at
5560   another tip:
                each way won or free:

                a little past four
                it has turned so clear
                the sky bright blue
5565   cold
                        the blacktipped brown
                        caterpillars
                        lured out
                by yesterday's heat
5570   circle crinkled in the grass
                now (one on the garage floor)
                the teens cold working on
                them: spring steps up
                warmly saying

5575   bud bloom sprout shoot
and arctic highs
mow the answering down:
to endure
a thing must speak
5580   more slowly than
highs & lows

You Can

You can
walking with the wind
think yourself
5585   becalmed
but turning to return
find yourself
in a ten-mile-an-hour gale
and on a great
5590   bright
cold morning like
this that
calm thirty degrees
drops
5595   chilling windchill degrees:
but the birds
are a chorus,
the jay's big vocabulary:
the sparrow
5600   is hauling straw
up to a streetlight
(nitelite)
sheets of ice standing in
v-bottomed ditches
5605   and a vapor-ice
of white haze
on grass near water:

                    grackle, crow, cardinal,
                    robin, birds but no bees:
5610   according to the weather forecast
                    here comes another warm
                    spell up to the sixties:
                    lately the temperature
                    has been up & down on
5615   a four-day cycle,
                    teens to seventies,
                    really rolling differentials,
                    spiraling through dragging
                    nordic or tropic skirts:
5620   let's not get into that:
                    cunt is disturbing

                    today if it goes to 45
                    caterpillars run down outside
                    may nick away in the sun
5625   the lilyshoots
                    though
                    or also,
                        deeply puzzled,
                        rush out firm
5630   to sixty degrees
                        but bend stain-limp
                        to the teens
                    scare crows
                    raise money
5635   field mice

                    they said I ought to get
                    a stereo because
                    when from seventy you subtract
                    fifty it only leaves
5640   you twenty mo'
                    for stereo
                    (lessen yall gits lucky)
                    you do do do, too

The Wife's Plaint

5645 There may be
more room on
the outside than
on the inside but
there's more

5650 room on the
outside outside than
on the
outside inside.

   may hernias

5655 rot in your
soup! the disgusting
husband said:

may
cocksuckers ululate on

5660 your doorstep! the
precious wife replied:

may the worms
in your round worms
need worming & may

5665 a great Swish
swallow your Knob!

french-freud

Cunit

Cunit

   close as i can

5670 come without being there

———

cuneus is okay and cunette
fellow said he got his
tongue hung
in one
5675 once (which I never believed)
and said whenever he did
the rest of it
started in to pecking on him
is what he said
5680 till he couldn't tell
whether he was coming or
going
and his whole tongue got
covered with red-peckered
5685 welts like you never seen
cunnythumber
slurp slop
I never met a man
with a dirty mouth
5690 (delicacy governs true passions)
that had any real
respect or deserved any

everybody well-adjusted
to sex keeps his mouth shut

5695 the elm is darkening
with mere
budbead

I saw this morning
come out on the porch steps
5700 and on a leaf of periwinkle
a beadblack bug
hemispheric so as
nearly to stick flat
to leaf or slate
5705 two red eyes
one on either wing

It's a Wonder the Body

It's a wonder the body
goes on making
things not thought
5710   well of, saliva, for example,

wondrous devising
containing
water, mucin, protein, salts,
and a starch-splitting
5715   enzyme
      that has been accorded little
common knowledge and small
applause, like great servants
who flawlessly
5720   disappear
into their work

eyes spread around
inside scraps,
tips, filaments of
5725   brand new or newly
worn attraction

                  the bigeye belly
aphids that eat up the   is
roses are   love's Polyphemos
5730   as pretty
as roses   maggots like
    twice as green,   undertakers (too)
    their dew honey,   work dead stuff
    and their petals fly but are unlike
5735   livelier
a gray warm
day with sprinkles
not met on concrete

I just went for a walk by the brook
5740   (high brooks are interesting,

the collections aimless
above the slope drop)
geese again

Today Was Like Vomiting

Today was like vomiting:
5745 all morning and until
midafternoon
the wind scoured the trees
like the dry heaves
blustering dust and pollen
5750 till finally it brought
the clouds up
and by four the smallest
rain came with a quieting
wind and then later the
5755 true tensions found themselves
and wind and cloud
delivered the shaking
spouting flood we'd been
waiting for
5760 now there will
 be some ease
 the birds can settle
 we can have dusk,
dinner's smooth time

5765 because winter cut a deeper
trench this year than usual
 I feared last year's
 mockingbird might not make
 it back or through
5770 but there
down in my neighbor's
orchardlike yard
 I saw the bird dive

                    spread those barred
5775   rounded-off wings
                    and splash into trilling song:
            I saw that yesterday:
            you know how a robin can get
            variable in a pellucid dusk
5780   and sound remarkable
                    but not quite make it, as
                    the mockingbird
                    can hold no vocal candlestick
                    to the woodlark
5785   sound's most beautiful song

            Showers

            The grass is
            green by
            the time the
5790   clouds are blue

            how much
            more blowing
            will establish
            spring

It's April 1

5795   It's April 1
                    the willow's yellow's
                        misting green:
            adding white maybe
            tonight or tomorrow

5800   Canadian air 30 below above
            the clouds has

settled into the midlands
and is moving eastward
   this will bring
5805   ground temperatures
within range
of the structural
flare-out snow

       (ọ (ọ   a look-see
5810   (ọọ)   slightly more direct
       (- (-   shut-eye
       ($ ($ American dream
       (° (°   34" bust

great logs
5815   dragged to the fireplace are
with ashspoon dipped away

earthworms are only
little long people

I'm Unwilling

I'm unwilling
5820   to write this
morning but
       things
keep nudging me
to sidle with
5825   them into
words,
    what is it, even a tension
   in the mind
wants to play
5830   itself
through the lit stage
wing to wing,

across and through
severe illumination,
5835 burning every crick
and hue
of the hidden out;
to be announced!
pronounced!
5840 shaped, made, attended
to, to have occurred as
an item of what was,
to be a thing that is

the bloom shed of the
5845 maple is
spring's
first fall   the maple itself
a falls
the milling fall making
5850 of bloom parts
to hold through winter
and open
to spring's first warmth
and fall
5855 (so early this year!
midFeb)

the syrup keeps
rising through the trunk,
wooden fountain,
5860 and always from
the replications and
rondures, slope heights,
of the tree
spill
5865 the bloom parts
the sent
wide reaches of pollen, the
lightgathering, dismissed

leaves, hunting, spinning
5870   seed

        the tree,
        holding to one place,
        moves as far
        as possible
5875   abroad, away, away
        to other holdings

it is not for the poet to
speak the speakable
that which long known & said
5880   requires no energy
of finding or forming but to
murmur, stammer, swear, and
sing on the edges of or around
or deep into the unspeakable—
5885   the unspeakable, silent sorrow!
the unspeakable, silent joy!

there was a time in January
when the light was barren
moving in blurs and glows
5890   between clouds and falling
on the snow-and-ice-enameled
hills, the streaks and
thickets
of ice-brush
5895   like ink brushwork
     ornamentation:
the ridge, I thought,
moves, flows, and
I was held by a power
5900   beyond all but silence
to contain

a joy inexpressible,
inexcusable

standing not away or at an
5905   opposite pole but
in the midst of which
grief
like high icy ghosts of
lombardies
5910   slow-swayed!

things arranged
at their centers so
that when we
grasp them
5915   they turn slightly
(like a dishwasher
dial) and go into
another tone or slant
or cycle or flatly
5920   from kind to kind

quandary lies centrally in balancing wings
so much so that as we draw near, the directness of
our sight blinds us to the full facetal radiality
so we are not likely ever to dissolve the knot because
5925   we work against ourselves when we hope to for if
we did, behold, the world and we would stop: how
grateful we must be that as we reach to take the
much desired in hand it loses shape and color and
drifts apart and must be looked for all over again
5930   so are we shoveled
forward half unwillingly
into the future (where futurity is lost)

praise or railing—
these two the sky equally
5935   takes up unlimited
and lets vanish

The Sky Clabbered Up with

The sky clabbered up with
blue-clabber clouds
and
5940   (meanwhile the temperature
    falling off)
the whey-gray whey rose
shutting off from earthly
view the fine white
5945 cumulus heights (yogurt)
    but still whereas and
    whenever he did
the cold kept coming and
pretty soon drops
5950 of rain
lost sharp swift
substance
    and blurred their way
    down white
5955   (white down)
    big clumpy snow mixed with
    rain, one thing popcorn
    and the other popcorn popped

there's no accumulation
5960 anywhere
on hemlock, garage, lily
shoot, yew, nor in crocus
cup, nor forsythia bell
    whenever it did & any
5965   flake touches anything
    it crumbles, shrinks,
    a little bit
    of nearly nothing

A Single Fact

A single fact
5970   inadmissible into
sound generates
billows of volubility
whereas said out
it would turn
5975   small as
a drop of rain   I looked down the
    brook at the outblanking
    high glaze
    running water gets when light
5980   falls (into) against it
    and thought how polished
    water lofts ripples stone still
    almost

and about how the dullish gold
5985   gets down between the
radiant-gray ledge shoulders
and holds color over each brook-step
ledge to ledge down the hill
    until of course (!)
5990   everything narrows
    and disappears going down
into the burial of itself
slope-lowering
burial from my sight though
5995   for others beneath me
it makes sights and tunes

It Does Not Rain in

It does not rain in
air-conditioned rooms
and the fan-wind blows

6000   (dust weaves in the rooms
    looms and glooms
    of loom-gloom) leaves
    pittering across
    dome-locked, skyless pavilions
6005   are grocery tickets or nasal
    tissues

        (the brown
        bushbrush
        here
6010   though hazes greenly
        dense)

    snot rags

    I feel like a master:
    nothing happens here that I
6015   do not wish and
    everything responds

        (when we arrive at the
        center
        a wing-gate flies open
6020   and turns
        us into new material
        out)

    like water in
    eddy
6025   about to find
    restful rondure
    then sliced
    from its widest
    circumference
6030   downstream

    cold
    currents settle

from polar ice
bottomward
6035   like falls

motion holds moving—
(the ripple I spoke of the
other day,
now the eddy,
6040   but also the millennial
deep bends &
sweeps of rock forms
and sea currents)

there's ice under ice in
6045   Antarctica so old
it's lost to count
but is still pressing down:
    the earth, mantle-deep or
    crust adjustment,
6050   is responding to that:

I see into so much every day
(sd the obstetrician)
my breakfast nooky quivers

mostly cloudy at sunrise but
6055   now turning clear blue in
spots and a turning up and down
of light (we may go to
McDonald's for lunch!)

One Loves

One loves
6060   absolutely and   in wax museums
forever   men have
    anything else is · wax balls
something else   but in fire

                                museums
6065   I know only one   balls of fire
        thing to talk
        about (poetry)
        and that
        covers everything

6070   (even on a moist morning
        midMarch, the street
        showered still-wet,
        flocks of birds foliating,
        defoliating shrubs and
6075   trees, the cardinal singly
        chirping, even on such a
        morning, the word, pliant,
        suppliant,
        wrenching shinnies up the
6080   ash-damp heights
        and higher cries out in the
        cindery desert for an
        answerer)

        headstone-shade snow
6085   melts slowly

        it still can't quite clear off
        or get cloudy—
        dwelling mixed
        in between
6090   some of both and not much of either

The Miltonic (Miltownic) Isn't

The miltonic (miltownic) isn't
milty or come
to think of it   all you can do
tonic   with a day like today is

6095   either   slice it and eat

it, cake

blue, radiant,

frill green, also

the maple   just-right cool

6100   bloomparts, cast millings,

have shrunk into meal, so

dry, granola, forsooth,

that stepped on they turn

snuff-dusty, a

6105   prepared, engineered reentry:

I do not wish to speak too

highly of nature where only

what can work works,

only the possible possible

6110   (though I like brooks

better than diamonds)

        (no wonder things work in and

        out so well together because

        if they didn't they wouldn't

6115   work long)

(the mind wishes to design other works)

that so much should come

to nothing, an abundance!

so much design be dust!

6120   at-onceness

startles marveling

my head, the

skull grown

brittle thin,

6125   I hold it

in my hand:

it is the world

to me: I

turn it some

6130   as if
        it were a
        precious object:
        but it is
        mainly hollow
6135   without longitude
        or latitude,
        good for lolling
        and wobbling
        when I
6140   open a book
        to a strict or
        famous verse

My Father Used to Tell of an

        My father used to tell of an
        old lady so old
6145   they ran her down and knocked
        her in the head with
        a lightered knot
        to bury her (then
        there was another
6150   one so old
        she dried up and turned
        to something good to eat)

        what my father enjoyed
        most—in terms of pure,
6155   high pleasure—was
        scaring things: I remember
        one day he and
        I were coming up in Aunt
        Lottie's yard
6160   when there were these
        ducks ambling
        along in the morning sun,

a few drakes, hens, and a string of
ducklings,
6165   and my father took off his
strawhat and
shot it spinning out sailing in
a fast curving glide over the
ducks so they
6170   thought they were being
swooped by a hawk,
and they just, it looked
like, hunkered down on their
rearends and slid all the
6175   way like they were
greased right under the house
    (in those days houses
     were built up off the ground)
my father laughed the purest,
6180   highest laughter
till he bent over
thinking about those
ducks sliding under
there over nothing

6185   my father, if you could rise
up to where he was at, knew
how to get fun straight
out of things
    he was a legend
6190   in my lifetime

I remember when he was so
strong he could carry me and
my sister, one leaning to
each shoulder, with our
6195   feet in the big wooden slop bucket:
he died with not a leg
to stand on

———

yesterday afternoon it snowed &
I scribbled: "more
6200   uncertain (showery) glory,
flurries and sunshine, the
ground dry because as the
flakes melt on touch the sun
gives the moisture back to
6205   the wind, also uncertain, the
flakes steeply or widely
rising almost as much as
falling but so thin-scattered,
so fine hardly
6210   more than an uninformed
bluster—really nice, the
sun cracking stark bright off
one cloudhead and plunging
paling and dissolving like a
6215   flake into a new blue summit"

today's spanking bright blue
(gold willows and green evergreens)
and chilly, a
little fresh-windy, great day for a walk

Arm's Length Renders One

6220   Arm's length renders one
helpless
   (stiff and loud)
where one cannot intimately
and warmly tickle tits
6225   or drive to bust
balls
      one must seek
      out the subtleties
      and rapid
6230   adjustments, suggestions, and

speed of the middle way,
using the extreme only as a
total realization of
potential (punch in face):
6235   spring drought,
no significant
precipitation for ten days at
least, has persuaded the
brook down to a wink here
6240   and there (lust or
rebellion) and
the ground has cracked as if
to swallow birds or fire,
not seed: it's warming up
6245   this morning, to 40, but
forecast for tomorrow is
cold, blusters, and snow flurries:

the poem hangs
on like winter,
6250   words flying out and dropping
to greet
the leftover flurries and
chills:
night before last was 19 but
6255   nothing was killed, just hit
scorched with the blahs:
    one Sunday when I was
    eleven my father and
    I found the "mineral"
6260   spring back
    below the Hinson Field in
    the woods
    and we sat down where
    the little hill fell away
6265   toward the swamp and talked:
    I carved my father's
    initials and my own in

a treetrunk and 1937:
I would not want to see that
6270   work again

I'm the Type

I'm the type
FARM BOY MAKES GOOD
(not farming)

or, with more development tho
6275   still very commonly,
Redneck Kid Grows Up On
Farm Goes Through Depression
But Thanks To Being In
Big War Goes To College
6280   Gets Big Job Making
Big Money
(relatively speaking)

so that I am not much of a
person after all and
6285   do not need be, the
lineations of the type
include egregious individuality

broaden lineation or
replicate included space

6290   because of last fall's
late bloom-thinning
the forsythia is
this year not a
golden bulwark but a
6295   yellow sprinkle bush

———

when the wind blows through
my round yew
it changes direction so many
times to get round the branches
6300 and needle leaves
it wears itself out
half way through:
eventually, though, demolished
smooth, really put together,
6305 it floats on through and out,
a massive, indifferent
tranquility available to give
substance to quick turns or
swerves

6310 REDNECK FARM BOY WRITE GOOD
(doesn't sell much)
WRITE VERY GOOD
(but misses
farm, etc., also other rednecks)
6315 MAKE NO MONEY
BUT
WRITE NICE
(tries hard)
(misses the mules and cows,
6320 hogs and chickens, misses
the rain making little
rivers, well-figured with
tributaries, through the
sand yard)

6325 REDNECK UNDERSTAND OTHERS
WRITE A LOT
(books too good
to sell, leave on
shelf in bookstore)

———

6330   REDNECK START TO SOUND LIKE
           INDIAN

           him remember Indian burial
           mounds in woods, sandy pine woods,
           also used to plow up arrowheads
6335   and not think much of it

           HIM REDNECK
           OPERATE UNDER TOTEM
           WASP
           (barefoot all summer)
6340   (get hookworm)
           (pale neck)

Snow Showed a Full Range

           Snow showed a full range
           today, showers at six
           this morning with
6345   the temperature falling
           through sleet and grainy,
           gritty, and, now, dusty
           snow
              a tying-off action with
6350   cold striking, congealing, the
           last skirts of action

           the lawn is whiter than green
           the hemlocks hold touchy sprays

No Matter

           No matter
6355   how
              driving

                    fast or
                    dense
                       (to speak of
6360   whited air, indeed, the lake
          was wiped out, and the
          opposite ridge's
          fields,
          house-clusters, dairy barns
6365   and silos
          fell under) the flakes all
          afternoon,
          the ground would take no
          steady impression
6370   and the highway not stay wet:
              big icicles hung off the
              car like the brocade and
              strings of epaulets but
          the temperature held just
6375   where an outflash of sun
          would thaw them loose
          so the sun and clouds
          needled sewing and unsewing
          the white sheets
6380   dyeing and bleaching

          so it snowed and snowed
          the wind blew and the
          flakes flew
          and it added up to a
6385   passing

          the lily shoots
          hold scoops and sloops of
          snow
          (keeps off the grass)

6390   and the hairy hollyhock's
          young leaves and the hairy

green tongues of oriental poppy
had the right way to
hold snow so it would last
6395   fluffed up on stiff hairs
(hairy tongues)

I hope winter will not
end like a Beethoven symphony
with big bams and
6400   flurries into June but that
it will ease off
like something by Debussy
so you hardly miss it

It's So Dry the Brook, Down

It's so dry the brook, down
6405   to nearly nothing to do
falls as if asleep, coasting,
between ledge spills

(some old men walk sloped
forward in a stumble-run,
6410   the regular, keyed rhythm
surpassed
into a soothing high dance)

spray churned from the
commotion of a slight ledge
6415   spill, though, can sprinkle
overhanging branches
so they freeze loaded in cold
weather, big ice nodes and
chunks interweaving branches so
6420   as to ride in hard
high separation

from the central rush,
melt lasting from one cold spell
to the next

6425 there is by the gorge
a slope so steep
no one interferes with its
brush and trees
(unshaken by height chills)
6430 nature is not a
palimpsest there but a clear book

vine
limber enough to move
entangles a high branch
6435 which, snapping off,
sways, held, in the
great tree's
windy shoals

that which rising
6440 takes over can break
down and, no longer
to be let go, no longer uphold

nature's message is, for
the special reader,
6445 though clear, sometimes written
as on a tablet underwater,
the message will blur and
seem to run but
declare itself in a smooth
6450 moment to great attention

Today Will Beat Anything

Today will beat anything:
a full day of clarity
up to seventy: but
still no rain
6455   (bright skies starving skies)
and the last precipitation
which was snow, though it
fell blanking out the
world, all but the very
6460   immediate, had no effect on
the ground, a dampening that
did not close up the
cracks, riffles of snow on
the lawn quickly evaporating:
6465   I declare I started to get
out the hose and commence
to water, because that
fertilizer I had the young
man sprinkle about
6470   the hedges and under the trees
has been lying out there feed-dry
for two weeks:
       when you consider how
       dry it is
6475   it's amazing the brook still
runs, clips, brook-brisk: the
ground must be holding
at a height plenty:

it is so odd, upon waking
6480   from a nap, to think that
one's body, including the
back of one's hand, one's
fingernails, the calves
and ankles, the face, these
6485   things one's own, are also

implicated and will die,
too, with one, each
its going away

oneself I sing,
6490   a person apart,
shoved aside,
silenced

cross references

seems the bushes are being
6495   sprayed from a distance green

will the universe become
forever dark:
    once in a lifetime

Sight Can Go Quickly, Aerial, Where

Sight can go quickly, aerial, where
6500   feet can go not at all

scale clouds out of
prison windows,
splash from heights into lakes
(not drowning, not even
6505   getting wet)

from high boughs can
spot rescue in the hills
though marshlands intervene

oh, sight! sight!
6510   how light you make us
and how heavy!

———

         say now
         pay later

         spring drought's good for being
6515   bad for molds
         and fluffy funguses that leap
         snarl-red in dampness or gross blue:
         good for giving the roots
         of young sprouts occasion to
6520   lengthen into the soil and
         be ready for rain when it
         comes: good probably
         for slowing and toughening
         growth so it can better
6525   resist frost
         sure to be back: good
         for killing off anything
         too much or too weak: good
         for getting early pollen
6530   up into the atmosphere:

         if butterflies wrote letters
         of recommendation their wings
         would crack: ripples on brooks
         don't advise or recommend
6535   other ripples, and shale spills
         to and finds alignment with
         brook flow

         supposed to go to 80
         today, probably did:
6540   the early tulips, three
         scarlet-velvet red, opened
         this morning just in
         time to be rained in by
         a trivial shower: all
6545   that negligible
         clouding up and passing over!

These Days Most

These days most
any brown stick
sprouts a green tip

6550   how could you, walking in the mts,
be as big as the mts: only by
wandering: aimlessness
is as big as mts

The Cardinal, Slanted Watershed

The cardinal, slanted watershed,
6555   in sprouting treebranch
singly singing

and some small bird, grayish
with yellowish back feathers,
dipples and dabbles in the
6560   hemlock boughs, flies almost
hard-still into the willowy
withery boughs and hangs
softly on:
the delicate greenworm haunts
6565   terminal tips

unseasonably this
unseasonably that   my
                        tendency
                 to exaggerate
6570   has
                vastly diminished

why, a lady along the way
inquires, is your motor running
so fast:

6575   and I say, is there nothing
to catch or flee:
she says, you're too slow now,
anyway, aren't you, to catch anything
fine: and whatever has not
6580   already overtaken you is
not coming:

madam, I say, I am not
frail and
the weather may improve: she says,
6585   you know those sunny rooms,
enclosed porches, that lie
off the sides of kitchens,
those long rooms with
lounge chairs and hanging green
6590   blades and tongues of
cactus and big-eared begonias:
that is what you have caught,
has caught up with you: come
in: the afternoon sweeps
6595   through here on a good day:

madam, I say, the long
boxes of empty afternoons, I
had anticipated fierier affairs:

come, she said: you
6600   thought you saw something:
it was nothing:

I, he said, going in, am
barely able to conceive . . . or
concede belief

One Desires the Cutting

6605 One desires the cutting
glassy edges of
nearly-wordless poems

but one yearns
for the openness of context,
6610 too, so as to tell

what urn or bottle broke:
restore nothing:
we want nothing back:

contexts (enclosures) show
6615 what ruin we're wrecking in
or passing by,
passers-by or guides

the flawless evidence favoring
death leaves us
6620 unconvinced
and we're ready
on no evidence
to believe we live forever

flasher   laser   lasher
6625 slasher   maser   masher

in long views
even great traditions
are often bulges
from a main line

I Wonder if Pagan Is

6630   I wonder if *pagan* is
        unfairly defined in the dictionary,
        a shade too much lean to bacchic
        as if it were not serious or moral, or
        as manifested by early man,
6635   nature-boy innocence, not true:
        look it up:

        suspicions confirmed!
        oh, well, it takes a while
        to turn or bust up
6640   a current
        (without affecting the climate)
        here is room
        in this long poem's thickets and byways,
        flybys, big timber, high marsh, and
6645   sea lane, for one to turn the wrong way
        around this hedge, streamfork
        or that, boulder,
        pavilion ledge
        and take on
6650   unnoticed a different coloring
        as if one had come
        surprisingly suddenly from
        a pure place or belief:
        if you cannot choose,
6655   here I will lose (hide) you,
        wind and unwind you till you
        will be a found astonishment: you
        will be sitting on a stump
        by a brook and a beautiful woman will
6660   come by and say, who are you,
        and you will say, I am a new man:
        (then you will have completed
        pilgrimage, and begun):
        let us not patch up anything:
6665   let us have it or tear it out:

one or two will get lost
perhaps in a ravine and
forget it is not Eden:
they will concentrate
6670   one on the other: nature
will align its major
forces through them and every
morning shove itself into
their mouths, a fresh
6675   apple!
my outrage, my anger is
oceanic: it is free as
my verse: lovingly I empty
myself of it: lovingly I write
6680   out my loathing:
I would sell my book to
millions to find one to love

slender willowy
in a waterfall

Rage Spells More of My Words Right

6685   Rage spells more of my words right
than any other feeling

the big red sun just set
under two vapor trails that
diverge from a crossing in
6690   the sky, the planes so high
they can't be heard—but
I have found, I think, a
copy of the northern hermit
thrush and I've been trying
6695   to read it—a frailer, less
fluid, less crystalline-breaking sound
than the southern woodlark

but still plaintive,
liquid bell-clarity, glade music:

6700 my crazy rage, depression,
my insulted silence, along
with all my dissolving talk,
my playing tensions out while
others twist believable
6705 tensions tight:
all nothing! when it goes it
leaves
behind inexpressible beauty!
the happiness of lingo

On This Day Noteworthily Warm

6710 On this day noteworthily warm
fossil fuel is 3¢ a ton or vat

the tough sweet element in
man . . . the newsman, no matter
how he feels, comes up
6715 with news, the weatherman
with weather, the
bread&milk man doesn't come anymore

the forecaster for today
forecasts
6720 einen thunderstormen may
blusterbufferoomen through:

gossamer-in-the-wind glint,
(three sheets)
trees-in-the-breeze sneeze,
6725 spruce worms, little greenies,
dangling, squirming

———

say it was 93 downtown
yesterday: about as hot
today: but I think
6730   there's cooling
in the evening breeze

Some Nights I Go Out to Piss

Some nights I go out to piss
among the big black scary shrubs:
the tinkling stars
6735   don't seem to mind:

cruddy crude   stars & stones
ruddy rude   silent & naked

odd that where no one is to have
anything, not even his
6740   own life,
   having is the game:
that where no one is to win
but indeed lose losing
   itself
6745   the game is winning:
and where not a single love,
mother-child, lover-girl, man-son,
is to hold,
   love settles in:
6750   odd, odd that as the days go
by so rich, so lost, one fool, trying to save it,
wastes the day

contradiction is a center
turning around makes
6755   another place to go

nasty century! whose
enlightenment
fills the air with smoke,
darkens the day

My Structure Is, Like the

6760 My structure is, like the
   bug's, external:
   rubbing up against others, I
   acquire form: mingling
   my speech with that of others,
6765 I annex scaffolding:
   like a man in a well, I kick
   one wall, brace my back
   against the other, to work my way up:
   inside, I am too soft to point
6770 a piling, my hard walls
   wet sheets on a line:
     Phyllis and John
     have gone off
     for a few days,
6775   which they need, I suspect,
     and I am,
     alas, alone:
   (terror, my pet lion)
   the catkins
6780 (small lions)
   hard-sharp have
   lengthened fluffy-long and waggly:

   it's better to be tough
   and free than
6785 to bawl and chain

————

I notice on my
walks that when
I move everything
moves!—
6790   so much seeming
to the one motion!

    pollen burn

had a voice and
couldn't place it

6795   my neighbor's dog (big shaggy
black&white) died late last
fall in cold's fringe
and was buried in a
small clearing in the hedge:
6800   this spring
I've expected the ground
to spew, corruption
work up,
but the mound has given
6805   notice neither outward nor inward:

there's a slope-lawn down by
the brook whereon a young
birch frilly in early-girlish
leaf seems to have been caught
6810   raining, catkins icicle long and thick:
girlish or boyish, in case one
is one and the other, other:
up the street a bit, a man
has set out two birch, one
6815   three-trunked and the other four-

sometimes I twist out a roll
of nearly-dry white snot and it

unwinds some in my fingers
so disgusting

6820   star stump stone stare stub stem stob
post oak
white oak
ghost oak
           so much works flawed
6825   it makes you think
           perfection not one of
           nature's hangups: the
crow gets by with a feather-gap
or so in his wing,
6830   the robin is full of worms, and
I have teeth missing trailertrucks
ride through: still, nature
doesn't lose count: it puts
away
6835   everything it brings to life—
           to perfection:

You Think of the Sun That It

You think of the sun that it
burns to burn
and that the soul for its own
6840   brightness burns

but the sun burns right to
the brim of necessity,
its floes dipping and
plunging to averaged effect,
6845   sun spots, flares, in-feed
of interstellar trash, outflow of
radiance through whatever
cloth of radiance, an

historical burn, one-way,
6850   out with surrounding
accidence wide open, stray
chunk pulled in, suns
driving to meet at a fast
sharp point, so many necessities,
6855   so many sides
that the sun cannot burn for
a reason for any reason but
to burn
as the soul burns
6860   to show and shed its brightness

being is the summary
of incalculable interpenetrant
necessity

     motion
6865   itself is the fine
tuning by which the earth
flies neither into space
nor the sun:
however
6870   fine and open the adjustments
though
the structures of motion
exceed all strength of steel
woven, stainlessly wound:

6875   rock whereon much
is founded will
split but motion
is
polished by millions of years
6880   (the foundation
in nothingness, deeply
based, towers highest)

I thought, to water the bees,
hornets, wasps, &c., I would
6885   put a bucket under the faucet
outside that leaks so little:
but I thought if I set it flat
I will have a full bucket,
the brim brimming wet all
6890   around: so I thought I must
slant the bucket (but not
enough to exclude the drop) and
leave a part of the
brim-arc dry so the things can
6895   light: but what, I thought,
will hold a bucket at 45 degrees:
everything hassles me: the truth
is I do not know
how to water wasps: a good
6900   try, though, would be the
slightest slant, a mere lean,
to dry off a crescent, a
fine moon; then,
the things could land on the
6905   high rim and walk as deep as
need be into the refreshing
flood: intricacy has as many
ins as outs:
(the good part about leaning
6910   the bucket is that if the bee
fell in he would gradually
mosey over to the lip-spill
where his legs would catch
rimbottom: then he could loft
6915   and shake his wings and
tiptoe to safety)

if people who can think of
nothing to do would
water bees

6920 they would find themselves
working with the principles
of the universe, a mind-blowing
and consciousness-raising
experience, I suspect)

6925 }}}
short-winged swallows
#
using round nails
↙↙↙↙↙↙↙

6930 turkish birds
↓↓↓↓↓↓↓
enslaved turkish birds
👁👁👁👁👁👁👁
ain't that purty

6935 OO
longing for deconstruction
OO
some other time
(OO)

6940 frameworked

if I could write a poem a
thousand pages long my point
would be established: every line
delightful but all you wd have

6945 to do is lift it to discover
its weight and irrelevance!

6950 unevenness had begun to
establish itself in my lawn
when I got out the mower
and, for the small, let
a lot of room in from the top

6955 (so much for income tax)

———

sweet clarity
reconciled at
great depth
                        regular rational
6960   discourse is good for
taking care
of highways, pick up the trash,
trim the hedges, oil the
cracks, while the imagination
6965   works on giving birth to some
other form of travel

am I law and outlaw, pope and
pensioner, sage and fool,
writer and reader, male and
6970   female, am I, sir, a small
town (in microcosm) where
this one and that one is
sometimes mayor, where at
any rate, government
6975   concerns all:

it's five o'clock, brightly
cold and somedeal chilly: I
have just awakened, having,
after cutting the grass and
6980   getting sweaty, fallen
asleep, sweat-chilled, in the
big chair: I am hungry: I
do not know whether I will go
downstairs and scramble a
6985   couple of eggs, then have a
bite at Neil's later (where
I'm invited to be with Harold
and others at 7:30 but where,
since I was too nervous to
6990   attend the afternoon sessions
of lectures, I may not go) or

go to McDonald's for a Big
Mac (I think I'll do that)
and have a bite later at Neil's
6995   or not have anything till I
get to Neil's—most unlikely

I already came home at 2:30
and fed my city a fresh
banana dunked milky in frosty
7000   flakes: I should not be
hungry: but it is cold and
I cut the grass: and Phyllis
and John are not here, and I
feel the need of something it
7005   is so bright:

I do not care what anybody
thinks of anything, really:
that is to say, I have not
found the flavor of orange
7010   juice diminished or increased
by this or that approach to
Heidegger or *Harmonium*: I
believe the constituency of
water has remained constant
7015   since the Pleiades:
I don't think that any
attitude I take to spider webs
will faze flies: have you seen
Stanley Fish in the flesh:
7020   words sweep around but then
just miss to form their own
world: think what a
caterpillar thinks: he holds
the universe between his
7025   horny toes and eats it in
worky swatches!

---

sublemonade
sublimeade

not only can we not look into
7030 the sun but it sweeping out
its light as if eliminates
what it illuminates: that
the center of light
should be blind! well, I
7035 must go off hamburgerward:
(delicious)
on full alert
massive layoffs
hurt his chances (a strong
7040 case for continuing its
existence)
positive developments
(receptive to such a move)
normalize relations
7045 totally fallacious allegation (lie)

death secures us from
death, words slug for our redemption
always a swing and a miss, meanwhile
it's balls & bacon as usual, conception
7050 and decay, laughter and tears,
the explosive, incredible mix

Snow

Snow   wons
            mons

since we must die,
7055 sweet completeness will
not have us wait in attendance
on our bodies
while workers fatten

and disperse and find
7060   slick tunnels to
flight and the rich (or poor)
man's table,
while roots explore the
forehead and settle in the
7065   ears, while the burrowing
beetle swims through or
around the eye (like a planet)
while the water rises and
the body log
7070   spins, the bottom-gazing
face: how, I mean,
nice that though we know this
we need not witness the
knowing of this

7075   life, that can be death
enough, *that* we need
and know, so that as we
enter into death we slip
out of it
7080   like wrapping off the
chocolate:

wooden boxes eventually "give,"
the rain finds a hole and bores
through, milling the bones and mound
7085   gravel: on such a day of happenings,
those who love go here and there

four days of clouds, two days
of rain, the temperature
steadily falling, this morning
7090   before dawn the rain ran into
deep temperatures that popped
it white and the spruce,
cedar, grass, roofs, and all
tolerable surfaces took on

7095 the accumulation of white and
when everybody got up today
he had something to talk
about: from 93 to 30:
some of the snow lingers in
7100 the cedar hedges almost at
the freezing mark: it has
changed from white to look
almost like water but there is
still ice enough to hold
7105 it in the boughs, so it cannot
fall, held water, islands of
snow:

then there is the presence in
the head, a figure that never
7110 speaks, immortal, apparently,
who, even in one's death, has
nothing to do with what is
taking place and will not credit
its reality, too bemused for
7115 assent or concern

grit, flakes, sleet, fluff,
all day the snow snowed in
vain
nothing but green in the
7120 grass nothing but leaves
in the trees

It Snowed All Night Snow

It snowed all night snow
like pear-petal snow and has
snowed all
7125 morning, skimpy flakes,
solitary, wandering schools:

the clouds, just discernibly
clouds from the general gray,
move on in a brisk
7130   wind: the buttercups,
leant over, have surrendered
their sturdy forms to limp
wastrelness: the birds have
vanished into bushes:

7135   what has come over you

if a rope were tied between
two posts
there would be most play in
the middle: coming out
7140   of the middle, the play
diminishing, one faces
the attached fact, the hard
narrowing and shortening,
the play gone out:

7145   who who had
anything else
to be interested
in would be
interested in
7150   the weather

we mill in a room where
a conveyor belt now and
then entangles and brings down
one who, mindlessly, is carried out:
7155   the others mill
and scramble, touching bottom
lightly, getting high
on the archy:
verse the room's ventilator

———

7160   light showers soak my shoes
verse writers croak my nerves

hard feelings

you know when
something is wrong
7165   how grateful you
have not been

how many
shocks of enlightenment
burn out
7170   a tradition!

after I have been
myself enough I will
die and go
on being universe

7175   modren friend when dil thou do
reaching from end to end
cripes that my bed were in my arms
and I in my love again

Drip Drip

Drip drip
7180   truck it

in our galaxy alone
(billions of others)
extraterrestrial
noncelestial life

7185   S P A C E

the reality man has lately
tried to conceive
in which, however,
solid ground,
7190   scaffolding

ten billion people
may dance on the
pinhead of the earth's
center

7195   undercut

footings, literally, what is
our footing,
not rock, motion, space—
nothingness!
7200   (and the realization,
            tho hard,
            that that
is the strongest
footing, providing most
7205   options, the greatest
range of possibility) how
        fortunate that we
        did not have it
        the way we thought we
7210   wanted it:

        the primate touching
        down lightly on
        the ground
now, three million years later,
7215   ready to give up the ground

THE GROUND ERA

THE SPACE ERA

the heavens acquire another
side, a landing

7220   both feet on the ground
no feet on the ground

there is an animal, louse-like,
but smaller, antennaed, grazing
the winter month of dust on
7225   the bathroom windowsill:

I love a plant
I think too much
I bought it
I placed it by my bed
7230   I think
I love it too much

a ray of sunlight just (11:44 a.m.)
broke through and hit
across the leaves of
7235   my plant whose hunger and
pleasure I feel I think

some sit home and think
about their feelings but
others land elsewhere

7240   the land grows peripheral
and less secure
and secure nothingness moves
centerward

my plant!
7245   what is it sitting on,
the center of the galaxy,

a composition of centers
of galaxies!
the bedsidetable:

7250   drip drip
           the sky is drying
           hot snow

the sky like water
standing in a rowed field!
7255   the furrows of cloud pull
           apart and show
           the sky filling the ruts
           blue and clear

           mucous   it cannot snoo
7260   vomit   at forty too
           gush

Some Fluffy, Long-Swaggly Catkins

Some fluffy, long-swaggly catkins
have fallen to the ground, heads
swung round in looped resentment
7265   or resignation, fashionable cousins
to the earthworm:
    the brook has moved into
higher flow, sustained by last night's
slow-soaker: this morning
7270   the sky's rinsed
blue, the hazy blue of color informing
itself, interrupted here and there
by ranges of white mountains:

           if, as appears likely,
7275   reality is not a wit solid
           but a dream another

head, perhaps, is dreaming,
why, then . . .

what difference does
7280   what we think and say make:
have the mountains responded:
is there word from
the sea: has the sky
looped down to question us:

7285   broadcast gathers coincidence:

people have
scoffed, perhaps,
because from my
upland upstate shelter I've
7290   looked out on the universe:
but in time it will appear
mean to have looked out on less:
the grave quits
speculation:
7295   feel the astonishment
of buried roominess!
a twinkledom in the deep!

roots
would coil
7300   and nest
in the eye
sockets

why but
clapper-like
7305   the hard point
of the catkin
unopened sways
a tip of weight
so the fuzzy

7310   mechanisms and
gold pavilions
of dispersal can
catch and tangle
with the wind,
7315   the ocean whose
currents find
otherness

I think I am sick with a pure
interest in beauty,
7320   a joy skinny as a fountain
that erupts
through entanglements
for real loft before gravity
unfurls fall's umbrella

7325   the wind's rinse over ice-enameled
hill-ridges! how beautiful
all winter, the light flowing
and riding, the dark sharp
lines of hedgerow! too
7330   spare, so lean!

after sunrise this morning the sky
cleared and the sun
hit the windows with light,
the indoor plants standing as if
7335   in celebration:
and all day has been
beautiful, the redbud blooming,
apple trees blossoming, so
many scents and colors, the
7340   brown fingers of spruce
shaking dust, so much and
water trickling in the
ditches, trickling
disconcerted like ridge water

7345   I break poetry off
I have not earned very much
I am not worthy of the
energy that winds up
spruce tops and floats off
7350   into the air still winding,
also I am denied much,
this beauty, though very
beautiful, is an inconsiderable
feast,
7355   a snack enlarged to
astonishment where love
has little meeting

My Father, I Hollow for You

My father, I hollow for you
   in the ditches
7360   O my father, I say,
and when brook light, mirrored,
worms
   against the stone ledges
   I think it an unveiling
7365   or coming loose, unsheathing
of flies
O apparition, I cry,
   you have entered in
   and how may you come
7370   out again
   your teeth will not
   root
   your eyes cannot
unwrinkle, your handbones
7375   may not quiver and stir
O, my father, I cry,
are you returning:

I breathe and see:
it is not you yet it is you

I Knew

7380   I knew
if I

went for
a walk

I'd get
7385   my feet

wet but
only so

I Cannot Re-wind the Brook

I cannot re-wind the brook,
back it up and make
7390   it flow through again ten
times till
it achieves the highest
compression, the concentrated
essential, of being a brook,
7395   brookness finally found and
held away from all brooks:

but the brook shoots muddy
with perfect
accuracy the morning after
7400   rain and in
a dry season
tinkles clarity, the
truest music birds know:

I never want to throw out
7405   the brook because it is
nearly dry or too noisy
so long as it
tells the truth, an
accuracy of all the other
7410   dispositions, hills, marshes,
declivities, undergound ways
of the terrain surround, an
instantaneous, just summary
and announcement:

7415   art is not nature
but the flow, brook-like, in the mind
is nature
and should it be
superhumanly swollen
7420   to art's grandeurs when the accuracies
(absolute) of nature please
suitably to our context: an
ear of corn too high or heavy
is not worth planting:
7425   art too strong or weak
betrays the living man:

    poetry that wrestles
    down all but a few
    has its holding: but
7430   the people, where they
    turn their attention,
that is humanity:

our chief light
will put out
7435   its light by
first putting too
much light out

————

     I should be buying something
     I go on paying

7440   spells narrow in   if all is appearance
         on sayings and   it is still without
         catch the feeling   liberty for we must
                              say the exact air
                              of this & that mere
7445   illusion

     gardeners aren't fairweatherers
     for weeds work
     the cold, damp, cloudy days

     like weeds as
7450   much as roses
     and you never
     lack for liking

Considering the Variety

     Considering the variety,
     nicety, formal hardness,
7455   careful contours of things
     (how sight is filled with
     the apparency of these) one
     wonders about the byways of flow,
     not much yelling of change
7460   noticeable, dead trees (live
     housing—will vines start
     to dead trees) standing
     hard, sun- and wind-rinsed:
     the rumor of flow, one
7465   wonders if invisibility
     suppresses that, wind, water
     carrying on, rearranging,

both clear, sometimes muddy,
dusty, leaf-shown: and
7470   underground, a stirring,
melting:
    is flux invisible to be
    kept out of sight
    or to emphasize the made:
7475   would designed
finery lose its strut and hard
joyousness if it
lost majority: still, not an item,
not even the stones, has not been often
7480   milled away and away, if come
back in a stone or divided
participating in many stones:
(the time at the heart of
stones is no greater, but purer,
7485   than that of the wearing surface)
but whatever flow dissolves
flow also brought the
nourishment of, the great
spirits flow through our forms,
7490   declaring themselves through us,
the freedom of sequence, the leap
from one to another, the
essential preserved:
    but considerable lamentation,
7495   though most scenes are quiet,
lamentation of the inexplicable,
lamentation against recalcitrant
fact, that though nothing is lost,
nothing, still the particular
7500   is, that self or shape, so
carefully contrived,
crumbled, collapsed, its flow
lost in flow:
in this contemplation not a
7505   wall, board, or splinter
yields: the alternatives,

side to side, are blank:
here, with breakdown,
gaiety, contrivance, and
7510 immortality are sustained:
earth turns the bitter, sour,
known
to the bright sweets
born of the dead:
7515 for us, it is a life, a
death, okay, take or leave it:
we
hang steadfastly on:

fresh out

7520 kingdoms of light answer
to the fact

Variable Cloudiness Windy

Variable cloudiness windy
and cooler this afternoon
with showers occasionally
7525 mixed with snow flurries

•

when I was young the silk
of my mind
hard as a peony head
7530 unfurled
and wind bloomed the parachute:

the air-head tugged me
up,
tore my roots loose and drove
7535 high, so high

———

I want to touch down now
and taste the ground
I want to take in
my silk
7540 and ask where I am
before it is too late to know

     •

big aurora last night, a beam
of light, then an aurora, with
7545 a crown!
the end of the world!
every day
in a million eyes

   Unisex

7550 These days there's
only one sex and
I am neither one

a blue cloud went over and ice
poured down like hail for a minute

7555 this combo day mixed January
and May, sleet and tulips

On Walks I Go a Long Way along

On walks I go a long way along
a side-shallow, hardly a ditch,
dandelions grow right down
7560 with grass (separating out the
stones) into the pebbly bottom
and I think if I

were struck down there
it would not be so bad,
7565   perhaps; some weed stubs might
dig into my cheek but I understand
that: the stones might rustle
a little, dry, if I stirred: and
grass might half-tickle my nose
7570   but I am familiar with grass:
I would not like being
held down long but
after death finished, the grip
would slacken, birds would
7575   fly over indifferent as a corpse,
a worm would find a bit
to stir here and there,
the sinews would loosen and
bone spill from bone:
7580   I am familiar with dandelions
between my fingers, slugs
cool in the sockets' dark domes:

today was so beautiful, hazy
blue, cold, cold nectar in
7585   the blossoms, the leaves limp
cold: fellow said to me this
morning a man has been known
to mow his lawn and shovel snow
here the same day in May

7590   penetrate and get the
ball down low

One Trains Hard for

One trains hard for
inadvertency

———

the terrain falls away:
7595   love like a flowering quince
or crabapple bush nowhere
erupts: local green
mixes with stone becoming
on the periphery
7600   casket gray: though this is true
(I care nothing
but to tell what is true)
I am astonished
with gladness
7605   to find the brook clear,
the ripples dark-backed,
scriptures of light
working the slate
floor,
7610   flat scales opaque with revelation:
a grackle stands in the water
and drinks from between his feet:
I can hardly
forget the sound of the
7615   nameplate that squeaks and clangs
on Mrs. Day's mailbox there
when the wind blows:
I bend over clasping my
knees and the old fellow,
7620   friend, frizzled schnauzer
runs out of the driveway
and whines grievous
pleasure
stretching up toward my face:
7625   he knows me: we were
friends last fall:
I am myself:
I am so scared and sad I can
hardly bear to speak
7630   and yet delight breaks
falls through me

and drives me off laughing
down a dozen brooks:
nothing, not anything, will
7635   get over into the high land
and while some may die
as if community-ward
none, not one, will miss
unpeopled oblivion:
7640   (except that in not imagining
oblivion one
cannot enter it)
what a dancer the stem of the
whirling down will be!
7645   I am free:
I feel free, I think:
my chains have healed into me
as wires heal into trees

the saving world
7650   saves by moving,
lost, out of
the real world
which loses all

Will Firinger Be Kissed: Will

Will Firinger be kissed: will
7655   Cézanne's house be itself or
melt into the mountains: will
art have liberty from government
help: how will things
proceed: how will other things
7660   proceed: (provide, provide):
modern industrial debris!
acid thunderheads! nitric, sulphuric
rain! salamander
eggs burnt out in farm ponds: Whitman,

7665   the midwestern flues, effluents,
       Carl, spill crud into the processes,
       the lakes, ponds, and ditches of the
       northeast and who knows what
       the northeast does: Walt,
7670   the greatest country
       isn't wide enough to
       dilute greed or bridge it:
       put a drop of
       water in baby's soreeyes,
7675   acid will scour th'infection out:
       this billowing age enlightened
       with smoke, our eyes open(ed) at last
       to airy cinders: if
       salamanders die,
7680   flies will stifle corporate suites:

       what do those little
       critters with dust-fine
       wings do on a drizzly damp day
       like this
7685   (hold their noses)   home ice

       the dance is the narrative of
       figuremotions the dancer
       inscribes on the memory

       the dancer is the dancer (stylus, pen)

7690   that is one way how
       the other way is never
       I'm tired of loving alone

       roots go to water
       leaves to light
7695   pulling the trunk hard
       between them

———

mist-drizzly cold
the clouds brush hillbrush:
the horizon slips
7700   through

If Walking through Birdy Trees

If walking through birdy trees
you stop, several still birds will burst
into flight, your motion, conserved,
communicated into lesser, faster speeds:
7705   the more familiar
hemisphere, that if having been still you
move and birds or other animals
startle and fly, why I have
not decided what to make
7710   of that: make something of it:
think it over and out:
hold the same thread through numerous terrains,
transfigurations, etc.
and see to how many
7715   oceanic possibilities a strand
applies:
not to hold onto the strand you have is to seem
dismissive, cutting, as if you
liked not all of reality's
7720   clothes but only
certain patches or
threads, whole cloth, a
cheapening: no matter what
intelligence went into making
7725   the maze if
the one thread leads you out

They Say It Snowed

They say it snowed
a few days ago
a bit, one of
7730   those rainy cold
days when skinny droplets
flurred into feathery
fluff,
whitening streaks
7735   out of the dismal
downward descending

the lords of volition slice
down Hanshaw
in the after midnight (close
7740   to dawn, now) hours,
toss beer cans, cigarette
packs, liquor bottles into
the ditch without a thought
for any nature than their
7745   own: and specially into the
bushy border by the brook
the alarming discards of
passion fly: the early
day, when passion is spent,
7750   pent, or bent
shows the brook circling
silver canfish:

the lords of volition care for
the brooks that burst their
7755   breasts, the churning and flowing
there, the spills and stalls,
urgencies not of matter, wind
ripplings
I pick up after them and find
7760   the slug has made a home under

the gumwrapper or grass is
holding and hiding a
Schaefer can
filled with the plump, pulp
7765   bellies of mosquito larvae:
        the lords of volition
        caring for their own
        natures care for nature
around them; they expend,
7770   satisfy, create: I pick
up, tearing their doings out
of time and context, for a
neat ditch with clipped banks

lunch reservoirs on our rears

7775   overlook   to set our feet
        look over   on symbolic rock,
                     solid space—
                     that is the heave

        I am so backward   how many
7780   in my correspondence   should I
        I have to stand in line   put you
        to hear from myself   down for

we(l)come

Fall 1975–Spring 1976
(See the notes for each
section's date of
composition.)

HIGHGATE ROAD (1977)

These poems are dedicated to my son, John, with all my love.

✑

Shuffling

A centipede, the many legs,
will go straight away a way
and cut
back at an angle acute
5   to the course as if
to avert calamity
but then,
    suspecting
his move anticipated,
10   loop round completely,
reversing his way,
disheveling accidents and
probabilities into
cool shambles ahead.

(1976)

Enterprise

A fish, fin
ichthy about the mouth, prim
or
dially
5   neat, translucent hinges
extending toothless
rims,
fans
his gills

For Louise and Tom Gossett

After a creek
drink
the goldfinch
lights in

5   the bank willow
which
drops the brook
a yellow leaf.

1974

Significances

After brief heavy
rain at two o'clock,
he listened at
the wood's edge
5   and could tell by
the clusters and sheets of drops
that some drops, summarizing
the leaves they'd
fallen from,
10   were larger than
others or had
fallen farther,
and when the wind waved
wide like a conductor,
15   a rustle of events,
cool, keyless, spilled:
he listened,
his body sweetened level to
the variable nothingness.

1971 (1977)

Release

After a long
muggy
hanging
day
5   the raindrops
started so
sparse
the bumblebee flew
between
10   them home.

1975

Modality

A grackle
flicks
down from
the cedar
5   onto
the shiny
alley
to see
if the
10   shower softened
the garbage
bags.

Meanings

1)

a grackle lands on a honeysucklebush
limb which sways too deep
(arching like a crossbow)

and sidling up
5   corrects the spill

2)

the hollyhock summer-weighty
leaned over nearly out
of its roots but leafless now
stands winter-stiff to the wind

3)

10   the pheasants leave tracks, an
abundance, in the snow:
icicles grow for the ground

Handle

Belief is okay
but can do
very little for
you unless you
5   would kill for
it in which
case it is
worth too much
to have or not
10   worth having.

Speechlessness

Coming to the windy
thicket I
said a brook
must be here and lay
5   down to listen
to the rustle but

fell asleep:
when I woke
the wind

10   was empty and
the brook had
turned into a poplar.

(1976)

Gardening

I'd give bushels of blooms
to bank my hardy cover
into your cushion mums

1968

Blue Skies

If I leaped
I would
plunge over the
pinetops into

5   the deepest sea

1974

Camels

I like nonliterary,
uneducated people,
beach riffraff:
they are so aloof and

5   unengageable: you
can rope them with
no interest of your own.

Immediacy

On the way to
the eternal sea,
I looked for coins

in the gutter:
5   looked at the sea,
a deep summary;

returned along
the gutter
looking for coins.

Recording

I remember when freezing
rain bent the yearling
pine over and stuck its
crown to ground ice:
5   but now it's spring
and the pine stands
up straight, frisky in
the breeze, except for
memory, a little lean.

1975 (1975)

Early Woods

I think
I have
a tick
on my
5   tock

Enough

I thought the
woods afire
or some
house behind the
5   trees
but it was
the wind
sprung loose
by a random
10   thunderstorm
smoking pollen fog
from the
evergreens

North Street

I tipped my head
to go under the
low boughs but

the sycamore mistook
5   my meaning and
bowed back.

1974 (1974)

Reading

It's nice
after dinner
to walk down to
the beach

5   and find
the biggest

thing on earth
relatively calm.

1975 (1975)

One Thing and Another

It is one
thing

to know one
thing

5   and another
thing

to know another
thing.

1975 (1975)

Self

I wake up from
a nap
and sense a
well in myself:
5   I have
dropped into
the well:
the ripples
have just
10   vanished

(1974)

For Doyle Fosso

I walked at night and
became alarmed
at the high lights and amplitude
but passed a brook
5   the sound of whose
breaking water
took my whole attention.

1974

Generation Gap

    limber body
    stiff dick

    stiff body
    limber dick

1968

Natives

    Logos is an engine
    myth fuels,
    civilization
    a pattern,
5   scalelike crust
    on a hill
    but the hill's swell
    derives from
    gravity's
10   deep fluids
    centering elsewhere
    otherwise

Catch

Near dusk: approaching
my house, I see
over the roof

the quartermoon
5   and, aiming, walk it
down my chimney flue.

(1977)

Lofty

No use to make any more
angels for the air,
the medium and residence of such:
gas is no state
5   to differentiate:
come down here to
bird and weed, stump
and addled fear and swirl up
unity's angelic spire,
10   rot lit in rising fire.

1964 (1965)

Famine

Starving is so funny:
the cow, can
you imagine, the last shuck

gone, moos lean: the
5   mule shrinks up and
walks small:

———

isn't that funny: the
chickens are slices
of feathers on

10   razor sandwiches: can
you imagine: children's
hands become

knucklebone games:
the wind shakes
15   humping to harvest.

Imaginary Number

The difference between
me &

nothing is
zero.

1977

Fortitude

We should think
we can get
by with a
setback or two:

5   the lawn makes
a life of
starting over and
swirly bugs

in dusk air,
10   prey, get where
they're going
changing course.

Ghosts

When first snow
hits
the woods-edge
bushes, it's as

5   if the leaves,
recently lent
the ground, were
returning from

the sky to
10   catch
the branches and
hold on again.

Soaker

You can appreciate
this kind of rain,
thunderless,
small-gauged
5   after a dry spell,
the wind quiet,
multitudes of leaves
as if yelling
the smallest thanks.

NOTES

A Note on the Text

For most of the early poems, the copy-text is the text published in the fourth and final hardcover printing of *Collected Poems 1951–1971*, with emendations listed here in the notes. For each of the ten early poems omitted from *CP51–71*, the copy-text is the text in the first printing of the book where the poem first appeared, with emendations listed here. For each poem first collected in a book published after *CP51–71*, the copy-text is the text in that later book's first printing, with emendations listed here.

Poems reprinted in *CP51–71*, *The Selected Poems* (the 1977 edition and/or the 1986 expanded edition), the *Selected Longer Poems* (1980), and *The Really Short Poems* (1990) appear here in their original sequences in their original books. However, they include all revisions Ammons made before reprinting them in those retrospectives. Generally such revisions were small, but there are a few exceptions, some of which involve changing a poem's title.

Annotations and Emendations

The following notes give some basic information that may be of interest to scholars and general readers. If Ammons recorded a date of first composition for a poem, that date—as specifically as he recorded it—appears here immediately after the poem's title. If a poem appeared in a periodical or other venue before its collection in one of his books, that publication information appears next; for much of that publication information, I am greatly indebted to Stuart Wright for his excellent *A. R. Ammons: A Bibliography 1954–1979* (Winston-Salem, NC: Wake Forest University, 1980). Afterward come emendations, as well as other notes about the text, including brief explanations of names and non-English words and phrases. I have assumed this edition's readers will not consist entirely of specialists in poetry or American literature, but I have also assumed that all will have access to a standard dictionary. Absent from the notes are poems with no recorded date of composition, no publication prior to collection in one of the poet's books, no need of emendation, and no details that—left unannotated— seem likely to impede a general reader's understanding.

Given Ammons's linguistic playfulness and fondness for earlier spellings, an editor should not assume that irregularities are errors. For instance, though recent American dictionaries define "mucus" as a noun and "mucous" as an adjective, in the poems collected here Ammons uses the latter spelling three times (and never the former) for the noun; since his spelling is consistent, and since the *Oxford English Dictionary* does document that spelling's use for the noun in eighteenth-, nineteenth-, and early twentieth-century sources, it stands here. Another example is "arrrive," which concludes "The Wind Picks Up Slick" in *The Snow Poems*. One might assume that the third *r* is an accident; however, it does appear in Ammons's typescript, and when he reviewed the proofs for the book and found that the word had been corrected to "arrive," he circled it and insisted, "3 r's in arrrive." He used that spelling only that once, correctly spelling the word and its variants fifty-one times elsewhere in the poems. Whatever the purpose of the irregular spelling in that instance (I offer one idea in the notes), it should and does stand here.

Some irregularities in the books *have* been simple mistakes. Typically they have been spelling or punctuation errors introduced at some stage of production, and fixing them has usually been a straightforward matter of consulting Ammons's typescripts for the correct text. In a few instances I have made other kinds of emendations. For example, the poet sometimes formed a plural of a nonpossessive noun by adding an apostrophe before the *s*, and that construction occasionally made its way into print; in this edition those apostrophes are deleted.

Unless a note indicates otherwise, all references to "typescripts," abbreviated "TS" in the singular and "TSS" in the plural, are to typescripts Ammons produced himself on a typewriter.

Ammons's book titles are abbreviated in the notes as follows:

O	*Ommateum with Doxology* (1955)
ESL	*Expressions of Sea Level* (1964)
CI	*Corsons Inlet: A Book of Poems* (1965)
TTY	*Tape for the Turn of the Year* (1965)
NP	*Northfield Poems* (1966)
SP68	*Selected Poems* (1968)
U	*Uplands: New Poems* (1970)
B	*Briefings: Poems Small and Easy* (1971)
CP51–71	*Collected Poems 1951–1971* (1972)
S	*Sphere: The Form of a Motion* (1974)
D	*Diversifications: Poems* (1975)
SnP	*The Snow Poems* (1977)
HR	*Highgate Road* (1977)
SP77	*The Selected Poems 1951–1977* (1977)
CT	*A Coast of Trees: Poems* (1981)
WH	*Worldly Hopes: Poems* (1982)
LEC	*Lake Effect Country: Poems* (1983)
SP86	*The Selected Poems: Expanded Edition* (1986)
SV	*Sumerian Vistas: Poems* (1987)
RSP	*The Really Short Poems* (1990)
Ga	*Garbage* (1993)
BR	*Brink Road: Poems* (1996)
Gl	*Glare* (1997)
BF	*Bosh and Flapdoodle: Poems* (2005)

§

"Finishing Up": Oct. 1985. TS held at Cornell. Previously unpublished. This is an alternative, perhaps early version of "Painlessness, to Pain, Is Paradise," which first appeared in *Brink Road* (1996) and is therefore collected in Volume II of this edition.

§

OMMATEUM WITH DOXOLOGY

Ammons's first book was published by Dorrance & Co in 1955. Its dedicatee, the poet Josephine Miles (1911-1985), taught at the University of California at Berkeley and was an important early supporter of Ammons's poetry. Concerned that publication with Dorrance, a vanity press, might jeopardize his credibility as a poet, he asked Miles if he should proceed; she advised him to do so. For details, see Zofia Burr's "Josephine Miles and A. R. Ammons: The Early Correspondence," in *Epoch*, vol. 52, no. 3 (2004); see also Roger Gilbert's preface to W. W. Norton's 2006 republication of the book.

An *ommateum* is a compound eye, as of an insect. The book included Ammons's foreword, which highlights the idea of multifaceted perception:

> These poems are, for the most part, dramatic presentations of thought and emotion, as in themes of the fear of the loss of identity, the appreciation of transient natural beauty, the conflict between the individual and the group, the chaotic particle in the classical field, the creation of false gods to serve real human needs. While maintaining a perspective from the hub, the poet ventures out in each poem to explore one of the numberless radii of experience. The poems suggest a many-sided view of reality; an adoption of tentative, provisional attitudes, replacing the partial, unified, prejudicial, and rigid; a belief that forms of thought, like physical forms, are, in so far as they resist it, susceptible to change, increasingly costly and violent.
>
> In manner the poems are terse and evocative. They suggest and imply and rather grow in the reader's mind than exhaust themselves in completed, external form. The imagery is generally functional beyond pictoral [*sic*] evocation of mood, as *plateau*, for example, may suggest a flat, human existence, devoid of the drama of rising and falling.
>
> These poems, then, mean to enrich the experience of being; of being anterior to action, that shapes action; of being anterior to wider, richer being.

Except for "Doxology" (which, as the book's title suggests, is a work to be distinguished from the rest of the collection), the poems were designated by number, 1–30, with no titles; when Ammons reprinted most of them in *Collected Poems 1951–1971* and in the three *Selected Poems* he himself assembled, he titled the poems with their first lines, or with truncations of their first lines. He explains his thoughts on his poems' titles (these and others) in an August 4, 1979, note to Stuart Wright which he inscribed in a copy of the book now in the Overcash Literary Collection at East Carolina University:

> At first, titles seemed to me unnecessary members to the integrity of the poem, but Lillith Loraine when she accepted my early poems for *Flame* and

Different, I think, asked for titles. I gave in—trying later either to come up with a truly transforming title, as with *Hymn*, or to make the title instantly & merely a tag.

When I put together the *Selected* in 1967 [the 1968 *Selected Poems*, his first], I considered making the titles consistent throughout, so went back to the *Ommateum* poems. I found that the titles I would come up with sounded "poetic" and out of character with the poems. So, finally, I made the titles just tags of the first lines.

The titles of the *Ommateum* poems in this edition are the "tags" Ammons used in *CP51–71* and in his *SPs*. Two of the poems, those beginning with "Behind the I" and "I should have stayed longer idle," were never reprinted after *O* and so never appeared with titles; in lieu of titles, their first lines appear here in brackets.

༄༅

"So I Said I Am Ezra": 1951. In a May 20, 1955, letter to Josephine Miles, Ammons writes, "The name Ezra is one of those private associations which poets would be much kinder to leave out. I take it from the name of a class-mate in elementary school. His name was Ezra Smith, like me a country boy in a wooden school. I think he was killed in the war. But, to me, anybody with the name Ezra would never do anything but wander. I think of the character as wiry, evaporated, leathern, a desert creature, much soul and bone, little flesh. Too, the word itself is just a little twisted, restless, but soft and mystical to the ear. After having used the name for a while, I went to the Book of Ezra to see if I could find interesting parallels but found none useful. In 1951 I knew only the name of [Ezra] Pound and was saddened that his name might interfere with me."

"The Sap Is Gone Out of the Trees": 1951.

"In Strasbourg in 1349": 1951. In a September 26, 1956, letter to the poet John Logan, Ammons said that the source of this poem and "At Dawn in 1098" was *The Portable Medieval Reader* (Viking Press, 1949).

"I Broke a Sheaf of Light": 1951.

"Some Months Ago": 1951.

"I Went Out to the Sun": 1951. First appeared in *The Hudson Review*, vol. 7, no. 1 (Spring 1954).

"At Dawn in 1098": 1951. See note to "In Strasbourg in 1349," above.

"The Whaleboat Struck": 1951. First appeared in *The Hudson Review*, vol. 7, no. 1 (Spring 1954). In a September 26, 1956, letter to John Logan, Ammons said that the source of this poem was the narrative of Miles Phillips in *The Principal Navigations, Voyages, Traffiques, and Discoveries of the English Nation* (1589–1600), by Richard Hakluyt.

"Turning a Moment to Say So Long": 1951.

"Turning": 1951.

"Dying in a Mirthful Place": 1952.

"When Rahman Rides": 1952.

"With Ropes of Hemp": 1952.

"Coming to Sumer": Sumer, one of the world's oldest civilizations (fourth–second millennium BC), located in southern Mesopotamia, now southern Iraq. In a September 26, 1956, letter to John Logan, Ammons said that the sources of this poem and "Gilgamesh Was Very Lascivious" were Sir Leonard Wooley's *Ur of the Chaldees* (first published in 1929) and *Digging up the Past* (first published in 1930), "as well as other reading on Sumer, particularly the work of S. N. Kramer," author of *Sumerian Mythology* (1944).

"Gilgamesh Was Very Lascivious": Gilgamesh is the hero of an eponymous Mesopotamian epic that is one of the world's oldest recorded stories. See note on "Coming to Sumer," above.

["Behind the I"]: An early example of the poet's fondness for aligning instances of a given letter (here, the pronoun "I") from line to line—a practice facilitated by a typewriter's monospacing. Such alignments appear frequently in his TSS of *The Snow Poems*.

"In the Wind My Rescue Is": 1954. In *SP68* the poem appeared under the title "I Set It My Task" and without what had been its first eight lines in *O*. When he reprinted the poem in *CP51–71*, *SP77*, and *SP86*, Ammons restored those lines and gave the poem the title under which it appears here.

"A Crippled Angel": Josephine Miles, the dedicatee of *O* (see above), was wheelchair-bound and also did not have the full use of her arms and hands.

"Doxology": 1952. The word derives from Latin and ultimately from Greek, and means "an utterance of praise." In Christian liturgy it designates a short formula of praise of God, commonly one beginning, "Praise God, from whom all blessings flow. . . ." In line 20, *"thirty-second's"* is here corrected to *"thirty-seconds."* The reference is to thirty-second notes.

§

EXPRESSIONS OF SEA LEVEL

Expressions of Sea Level was published by the Ohio State University Press in 1964. The book bore a copyright date of 1963 but actually appeared the following year.

Ten of the poems had appeared together in *The Hudson Review*, vol. 13, no. 3 (Autumn 1960), and later in 1960 were privately printed as a not-for-sale chapbook titled *Ten Poems*. The chapbook was sequenced as follows and with these titles:

"Silver"
"Prospecting"
"Jersey Cedars"
"Bourn"
"Canto 1:" (retitled "Guide" for *ESL*)
"Canto 7:" (retitled "Risks and Possibilities" for *ESL*)
"Canto 8:" (retitled "Hardweed Path Going" for *ESL*)
"Canto 10:" (retitled "Terrain" for *ESL*)
"Canto 12:" (retitled "Bridge" for *ESL*)
"Canto 17:" (retitled "River" for *ESL*)

∽∾∾

"Raft": c. 1955–60. First appeared in *The Hudson Review*, vol. 16, no. 2 (Summer 1963).

"Hymn": Apr. 2, 1956. First appeared in *The Hudson Review*, vol. 10, no. 3 (Autumn 1957).

"Risks and Possibilities": June 1959. First appeared (as "Canto 7:") in *The Hudson Review*, vol. 13, no. 3 (Autumn 1960).

"Terrain": Aug. 3, 1959. First appeared (as "Canto 10:") in *The Hudson Review*, vol. 13, no. 3 (Autumn 1960).

"Nelly Myers": Apr. 4, 1961. First appeared in *The Hudson Review*, vol. 16, no. 2 (Summer 1963). In his 1992 interview with Alex Albright, Ammons said his family was helped on the farm by someone named Sally Tyree, "an old woman who lived on the farm, not related, but [she] had been taken in by us." In a copy of *CP51–71*, he struck through the poem's title, wrote "Sally Tyree" above it, replaced "Nelly Myers" in line 50 with "Sally Tyree," and replaced "Nel" with "Sal" in line 51—but then wrote "STET" next to those changes.

"Bridge": June 1959. First appeared (as "Canto 12:") in *The Hudson Review*, vol. 13, no. 3 (Autumn 1960).

"Requiem": May 1957. First appeared in *Accent: A Quarterly of New Literature*, vol. 19, no. 4 (Autumn 1959).

"Guide": June 1959. First appeared (as "Canto 1:") in *The Hudson Review*, vol. 13, no. 3 (Autumn 1960).

"Expressions of Sea Level": Jan. 21, 1962. First appeared in *Poetry*, June 1963. Line 79 ends with a period in *ESL* and also in *CP51–71*. As printed in *Poetry* and in *SP68*, however, the line ends with a comma, and that punctuation is restored here.

"Unsaid": Aug. 31, 1959. First appeared in *The Hudson Review*, vol. 16, no. 2 (Summer 1963).

"Mechanism": June 1959.

"Batsto": Nov. 3, 1957. First appeared (as "Ghost Town, N. J.: Batsto") in *Chicago Choice*, vol. 1, no. 1 (Spring 1961). Ammons truncated the title to "Batsto" when he re-collected the poem in *SP68* and *CP51–71*. Batsto Village is in Wharton State Forest, in southern New Jersey, and is on the National Register of Historic Places.

"Mansion": Apr. 19, 1959. First appeared in *Poetry*, Nov. 1960.

"Close-Up": Aug. 10, 1958. First appeared in *Poetry*, Mar. 1959.

"Mountain Liar": First appeared in *Accent*, vol. 18, no. 3 (Summer 1958).

"Prospecting": Mar. 16, 1958. First appeared in *The Hudson Review*, vol. 13, no. 3 (Autumn 1960).

"Jersey Cedars": Mar. 16, 1958. First appeared in *The Hudson Review*, vol. 13, no. 3 (Autumn 1960).

"Hardweed Path Going": July 15, 1958. First appeared in *The Hudson Review*, vol. 13, no. 3 (Autumn 1960).

"Bourn": Nov. 22, 1958. First appeared in *The Hudson Review*, vol. 13, no. 3 (Autumn 1960).

"Grassy Sound": Sept. 21, 1958. First appeared in *Poetry*, Mar. 1959.

"Silver": July 10, 1958. First appeared in *The Hudson Review*, vol. 13, no. 3 (Autumn 1960). Silver was the Ammons family's mule; other poems in which she appears include *TTY* (chiefly the "22 Dec:" section) and "Mule Song."

"Concentrations": Dec. 1959. First appeared in *The Literary Review*, vol. 5, no. 4 (Summer 1962).

"River": c. 1955–60. First appeared (as "Canto 17:") in *The Hudson Review*, vol. 13, no. 3 (Autumn 1960).

"Motion for Motion": Apr. 23, 1961. First appeared in *The Hudson Review*, vol. 16, no. 2 (Summer 1963).

"Identity": Jan. 17, 1961. First appeared (as "Canto 29:") in *Impetus*, no. 7 (Spring 1963).

"What This Mode of Motion Said": Feb. 4, 1961.

"Still": June 14, 1962. First appeared in *The Emerson Review*, vol. 1, no. 1 (Winter 1963).

"The Golden Mean": June 1959. First appeared (as "Canto 13") in *Accent*, vol. 20, no. 4 (Autumn 1960).

"Nucleus": Feb. 6, 1961. In line 105, *CP51–71*'s "specialities" is corrected to "specialties," following the text in *ESL* and Ammons's TS for *CP51–71*. Line 5: The French explorer Jacques Cartier (1491–1557) claimed Canada for France. Line 19: The Laurentian was a passenger train that long ran between New York City and Montreal. Lines 28–30: Nick Bottom is a character in Shakespeare's comedy *A Midsummer Night's Dream*—a play in which Theseus, Duke of Athens, declares that "as imagination bodies forth / The forms of things unknown, the poet's pen / Turns them to shapes and gives to airy nothing / A local habitation and a name." Lines 33–34: The French translates roughly to "the floor with the meeting, third floor, please."

§

CORSONS INLET

Corsons Inlet was published by Cornell University Press in 1965.

⌁⌁⌁

"Visit": July 2, 1961. First appeared in *The Nation*, Jan. 20, 1962.

"Moment": Mar. 9, 1963. First appeared in *Epoch*, vol. 13, no. 1 (Fall 1963).

"Winter Scene": Dec. 4, 1963. First appeared in *Epoch*, vol. 13, no. 3 (Spring 1964).

"Corsons Inlet": Aug. 16, 1962. First appeared (as "A Nature Walk") in *The Hudson Review*, vol. 16, no. 2 (Summer 1963). Corson's Inlet is in southern New Jersey, just south of Ocean City; Corson's Inlet State Park was established in 1969. Ammons reprinted this poem in *SP68*, *CP51–71*, *SP77*, and *SP86*, and each time, as in *CI*, he omitted the apostrophe in "Corson's"; his omission is retained here.

When "Corsons Inlet" was reprinted in *CP51–71*, that book's first three hardcover printings omitted the "of" in line 105. The error was corrected in the fourth and final hardcover printing of *CP51–71* but appeared again in the 2001 paperback edition of the book, and was repeated in the Library of America *Selected Poems* (2006).

"Dunes": Feb. 2, 1963. First appeared in *Epoch*, vol. 13, no. 1 (Fall 1963).

"Street Song": Sept. 19, 1963. First appeared in *Poetry*, Sept. 1964.

"Lines": Mar. 10, 1960. First appeared in *Epoch*, vol. 13, no. 1 (Fall 1963).

"Coon Song": June 27, 1959. First appeared in *Epoch*, vol. 13, no. 1 (Fall 1963). Line 14: Fyodor Dostoevsky (1821–1881), a Russian author best known for his novels *Notes from the Underground*, *Crime and Punishment*, and *The Brothers Karamazov*.

"Portrait": Nov. 30, 1963. First appeared in *The Nation*, Nov. 2, 1964.

"Jungle Knot": Feb. 11, 1961. First appeared in *Discourse*, vol. 6, no. 2 (Spring 1963). Line 21: William Beebe (1877–1962), a distinguished American naturalist.

"Dark Song": Nov. 21, 1963. First appeared in *Poetry*, Sept. 1964.

"Resort": First appeared in *Epoch*, vol. 13, no. 3 (Spring 1964).

"Upright": Mar. 10, 1963. First appeared in *Epoch*, vol. 13, no. 1 (Fall 1963).

"Catalyst": Sept. 15, 1960. First appeared in *Poetry*, June 1963.

"Loss": June 1964. First appeared in *The New York Times*, Sept. 10, 1964.

"World": Nov. 29, 1963. First appeared in *Poetry*, Sept. 1964.

"Butterflyweed": Sept. 11, 1963. First appeared in *Epoch*, vol. 13, no. 3 (Spring 1964).

"Configurations": June 1–3, 1963.

"Glass": Apr. 23, 1963. First appeared in the *Quarterly Review of Literature*, vol. 13, nos. 1–2, 1964.

"Morning Glory": Sept. 27, 1963.

"The Strait": Apr. 16, 1960. First appeared in the *Quarterly Review of Literature*, vol. 13, nos. 1–2, 1964.

"Spindle": Dec. 1, 1963. First appeared in *The New York Times*, May 9, 1964.

"The Yucca Moth": July 1, 1962. First appeared in *Shenandoah*, vol. 15, no. 3 (Spring 1964).

"Anxiety": Dec. 4, 1963. First appeared in *Chicago Review*, vol. 17, no. 1 (1964).

"Four Motions for the Pea Vines": Jan. 20–Mar. 1962. First appeared in *Chicago Review*, vol. 17, no. 1 (1964).

"Hymn II": Nov. 30, 1954. First appeared (as "Hymn V") in *Accent*, vol. 18, no. 3 (Summer 1958). In *CI*, this poem appeared as part I of "Two Hymns."

"Hymn III": First appeared (as "Hymn X") in *Accent*, vol. 18, no. 3 (Summer 1958). In *CI*, this poem appeared as part II of "Two Hymns."

"Open": Sept. 11, 1960. First appeared in *The Hudson Review*, vol. 16, no. 2 (Summer 1963).

"Epiphany": Fall 1959. First appeared in *Poetry*, Nov. 1960.

"Prodigal": June 1959. First appeared in *Discourse*, vol. 7, no. 1 (Winter 1964).

"Motion": July 18, 1962. First appeared in *Chelsea*, no. 14 (Jan. 1964).

"The Misfit": Feb. 15, 1961.

"The Watch": Apr. 3, 1956. First appeared in *The Hudson Review*, vol. 10, no. 3 (Autumn 1957).

"Libation": Summer 1951. First appeared in the *Quarterly Review of Literature*, vol. 13, nos. 1–2 (1964).

"The Wide Land": July 23, 1957. First appeared (as "In the Wide Land") in *Compass Review*, no. 2 (Apr. 1958).

"Thaw": May 1, 1958. First appeared in *Accent*, vol. 19, no. 3 (Summer 1959).

"Whose Timeless Reach": Apr. 13, 1955. First appeared in *Accent*, vol. 16, no. 4 (Autumn 1956). See the note to "So I Said I Am Ezra" for more on the Ezra persona.

"Ritual for Eating the World": July 19, 1957. First appeared in *Accent*, vol. 18, no. 3 (Summer 1958).

"Driving Through": June 29, 1955. First appeared in *Accent*, vol. 16, no. 4 (Autumn 1956).

"March Song": Mar. 8, 1957. First appeared in *Partisan Review*, vol. 26, no. 3 (Summer 1959).

"Gravelly Run": Feb. 17, 1958. First appeared in *Poetry*, Nov. 1960. Gravelly Run is in southern New Jersey, northwest of Ocean City. Line 26: Georg Wilhelm Friedrich Hegel (1770–1831), German Idealist philosopher. Ammons's Cornell friend and colleague M. H. Abrams explains the relationships between German Idealist philosophy and English (and other) Romantic poetry in *Natural Supernaturalism* (1971).

§

TAPE FOR THE TURN OF THE YEAR

Tape for the Turn of the Year was published by Cornell University Press in 1965. Its dedicatees, the poets Josephine Jacobsen (1908–2003) and Elliott Coleman (1906–1980), were friends and supporters.

Ammons typed the poem on a long adding-machine tape, beginning on December 6, 1963, and ending on January 10, 1964. The tape's width defined the maximum length of its lines, and its length defined the poem's.

The Cornell archive holds three TSS of *Tape*: the original (the tape itself), here designated TS1, titled simply *Today*; a bound one, here designated TS2, titled *Fugue for the Turn of the Year*; and a hole-punched but unbound one, here designated TS3, with the typed title *Fugue for the Turn of the Year* corrected in pen to *Tape for the Turn of the Year.*

In a July 22, 1964, letter to Bernard Kendler at Cornell University Press, Ammons explains his reasons for deciding on the word *Tape* rather than *Fugue.* He writes, "*Fugue* doesn't sound American: the word is squeezed in the mouth and finally swallowed. And something I read years ago has caused me to smart at analogies between music and poetry. . . . The word [*Tape*] is matter-of-fact, alliterates well with *Turn*—and summons such modern things as ticker tape, scotch tape, tape recorder, etc." This letter, which includes other comments about the poem, is reprinted in full in *An Image for Longing.*

A copy of the book Ammons marked "corrected copy" includes, in addition to corrections of errors, a few minor revisions here and there. However, there is no indication of when he made those revisions, and there is no way to tell whether they represent firm judgments or merely briefly appealing possibilities. They did not appear in the poem's 1993 reprint. This edition does not incorporate them, but they are documented among the notes below.

❧

6 Dec:

Lines 13–37: Ammons here refers to various classical Greco-Roman figures and places associated with poetic inspiration: the Muse, any one of the sister goddesses thought to be the daughters of Zeus and Mnemosyne (Memory); Apollo, god of light, order, and poetry; Parnassus, a mountain in Greece thought by some to be the Muses' home; the Pierian Spring in Macedonia, sacred to the Muses and thought to inspire whoever drank from it; Hippocrene, a fountain on Mount Helicon also regarded as sacred to the Muses and having the same inspiring properties as the Pierian Spring; and Pegasus, a winged horse associated with inspiration, since the Hippocrene was supposedly created when his hoof struck a rock on Mount Helicon. The unconscious is mentioned in line 29 as a nod to modern psychology's understanding of creativity.

Lines 276–82: The events described take place in Book X of Homer's *Odyssey*.

8 Dec:

Line 407–8: In what he labeled his "corrected copy" of *Tape*, Ammons strikes through "trunk," "it," and "turns," and replaces them with "balls," "they," and "turn," respectively.

9 Dec:

Lines 540–52: Pan Am Flight 214 crashed on December 8, 1963, after being hit by lightning while flying from Baltimore to Philadelphia. None aboard survived.

Lines 553–54: In Book IX of the *Odyssey*, Polyphemus the Cyclops (a one-eyed giant) eats members of Odysseus's crew.

Line 554: In TS3 a colon at the end of the line appears to have been whited out and then rewritten in pen; the colon did not appear in publication. It is reinserted here to help clarify the fact that the clause ends with that line.

11 Dec:

Line 1360: The French phrase "sans merci" means "without mercy," and appears in the title of one of John Keats's best-known poems: "La Belle Dame sans Merci."

Line 1393: The word "if" is corrected to "it," following TS3. The book referred to is *Expressions of Sea Level*; two days later he celebrates its arrival.

13 Dec:

Line 1930: Regarding "my book," see the note on line 1393, above.

Line 1985: Agathon (fifth century BC) was a Greek tragic poet and playwright whose work is now almost entirely lost. His victory at the festival of the Great Dionysia is the occasion of the banquet in Plato's *Symposium*.

14 Dec:

Line 2154: In Ammons's "corrected copy" of *Tape*, he contracts "we are" to "we're."

Line 2300: The word "their" is corrected to "theirs," following TS3.

Line 2305: The word "life" is corrected to "lift," following TS3.

17 Dec:

Lines 2620–24: In Greek mythology, Sisyphus is doomed in the afterlife to roll a great stone up a hill, only to have it immediately roll back down; the cycle repeats unendingly. He and his futile task are mentioned in Book XI of the *Odyssey*.

18 Dec:

Line 2916: "Chacun à chacun" is French for "each to each."

19 Dec:

Line 3111: Praxagora is the heroine of *A Parliament of Women*, by the Greek playwright Aristophanes (fifth–fourth century BC).

26 Dec:

Line 3497: The art historian Bernard Berenson (1865–1959) specialized in the Italian Renaissance.

28 Dec:

Line 4146: The word "thallopyte" is corrected to "thallophyte," following TS3.

30 Dec:

Lines 4411–15: William Carlos Williams had died earlier that year, on March 4.

Line 4478: A colon is inserted at the end of the line, following TS3.

3 Jan:

Line 5669: A closing single quotation mark is here corrected to a closing double quotation mark.

8 Jan:

Lines 6252–53: In his "corrected copy," Ammons strikes through "it's out of order to / be passionate with" and writes "passion is out of order / with."

Line 6328: In TS1, TS2, and TS3, the "1:31 pm" section begins thus:

> Johnson's "State of
> the Union" address:
> unity & diversity: how
> to have both: must:
>   it's Coleridge's
>   definition of a poem:

The reference to Lyndon Johnson's speech was deleted for the book.

Samuel Taylor Coleridge comments in many places on the aesthetic value of balance between "unity & diversity." One such place is Chapter XIV of his *Biographia Literaria*, where he writes that "a legitimate poem . . . must be one, the parts of which mutually support and explain each other."

9 Jan:

Line 6555: In his "corrected copy," Ammons strikes "where the banks also flow" in favor of "the banks flow also."

Lines 6675–82: When Ammons writes that "before long / the red edge will / rise / from the floor," he is referring to a ¼-inch-wide band of red ink along the right edge of the tape, beginning about three feet from the end. At the end of line 6933, the beginning of the parenthetical exclamation "(there's / the red ink / turned into the light!)," he types the word "there's" through the beginning of that red edge.

§

NORTHFIELD POEMS

Northfield Poems was published by Cornell University Press in 1966; its dedicatees are Ammons's father, who died that year, and his father's third wife, who is not to be confused with Ammons's Aunt Blanche mentioned in section 114 of *Glare*. (His mother had died in 1950.) The book is named for Northfield, New Jersey, where he lived from 1952 to 1954 and then again from 1959 to 1964, before moving to Ithaca, New York. Nearly all of the poems in *NP* date from his second residence in Northfield.

"Kind": Aug. 31, 1964. First appeared in *The Trojan Horse*, vol. 5, no. 3 (Nov. 1964).

"Height": Sept. 1, 1964. First appeared in *The Trojan Horse*, vol. 5, no. 3 (Nov. 1964).

"Joshua Tree": Mar. 23, 1958. First appeared in *Poetry*, Mar. 1959.

"Reflective": Aug. 29, 1963. First appeared in *The Hudson Review*, vol. 17, no. 4 (Winter 1965).

"Landscape with Figures": Nov. 15, 1963. First appeared in *Poetry*, July 1965.

"The Constant": July 11, 1962. First appeared in the *Quarterly Review of Literature*, vol. 13, nos. 1–2 (1964).

"Contingency": Sept. 26, 1963. First appeared in *The Hudson Review*, vol. 17, no. 4 (Winter 1965).

"One:Many": June 1962. First appeared in *Chelsea* no. 17 (Aug. 1965). Line 86: "Out of many, one" is a translation of *E pluribus unum*, the Latin motto that appears on the Great Seal of the United States.

"Halfway": Oct. 20, 1963. First appeared in *Poetry*, July 1965.

"Interference": July 8, 1964. First appeared in *The Hudson Review*, vol. 17, no. 4 (Winter 1965).

"Saliences": Aug. 18, 1962. First appeared in *TriQuarterly*, no. 5 (1966).

"Trap": Sept. 27, 1963. First appeared in *The New York Times*, Mar. 21, 1965.

"The Foot-Washing": June 12, 1959. First appeared in *Kayak*, no. 3 (1965).

"Recovery": July 7, 1964. First appeared in *The New York Times*, Sept. 30, 1964.

"Two Motions": July 2–11, 1962. First appeared in *Chelsea*, no. 14 (Jan. 1964).

"Composing": 1958. First appeared in *Poetry*, July 1965.

"Ithaca, N.Y.": July 1963. First appeared in *Poetry*, July 1965. The poem is dated July 1963, the same month the poet gave a reading at Cornell (at poet David Ray's invitation) and made the contacts that led to his employment there beginning the following year.

"Consignee": 1951. First appeared in *Niobe*, no. 1 (1965).

"February Beach": Feb. 6, 1963.

"Self-Portrait": Aug. 16, 1964. First appeared in *Modern Occasions*, edited by Philip Rahv. Farrar, Straus and Giroux, 1966.

"Passage": Aug. 27, 1964. First appeared in *Modern Occasions*, edited by Philip Rahv. Farrar, Straus and Giroux, 1966.

"Peak": Aug. 22, 1964. First appeared in *Modern Occasions*, edited by Philip Rahv. Farrar, Straus and Giroux, 1966.

"Zone": June 9, 1964. First appeared in *Modern Occasions*, edited by Philip Rahv. Farrar, Straus and Giroux, 1966.

"Muse": Dec. 6, 1959. First appeared in *Poetry Northwest*, vol. 5, nos. 3–4 (Autumn–Winter 1964–65).

"Sitting Down, Looking Up": Feb. 16, 1964. First appeared in *The Hudson Review*, vol. 17, no. 4 (Winter 1965).

"Belief": Mar. 1, 1964. First appeared in *Of Power and Power*, edited by Erwin A. Glikes and Paul Schwaber. Basic Books, 1964.

"Orientale": Dec. 16, 1958.

"Mays Landing": Oct. 23, 1963. Mays Landing is a New Jersey community near Northfield. In lines 17–18, "two's and / three's" is here corrected to "twos and / threes."

"Sphere": Oct. 6, 1960. First appeared in *Chelsea*, no. 14 (Jan. 1964).

"First Carolina Said-Song": Sept. 5, 1962. First appeared in *Red Clay Reader*, no. 2 (1965).

"Second Carolina Said-Song": Sept. 6, 1962. First appeared in *Red Clay Reader*, no. 2 (1965). Fayetteville is in southeastern North Carolina, not far from Whiteville. It is home to Fort Bragg, a major U.S. Army base, as well as the Fayetteville VA Medical Center.

"Discoverer": May 1962. First appeared in *Damascus Road*, no. 2 (1965). Lines 7–10: Although most readers will remember that a circle's area is the product of π and the square of its radius, fewer will know Johannes Kepler's second law of planetary motion: the fact that, however elliptical a planet's orbit, the area of its sweep will be the same over any given period of time. "The Albatross," a poem by the nineteenth-century French poet Charles Baudelaire, draws an analogy between that seabird's life and a poet's.

"A Symmetry of Thought": Apr. 1958. First appeared in *Accent*, vol. 19, no. 2 (Spring 1959).

"Holding On": July 27, 1963. First appeared in the *Quarterly Review of Literature*, vol. 13, nos. 1–2 (1964). The poem appears here as revised for *RSP*, with "tread" replacing "tire" in line 1, and a comma replacing a dash between "sight" and "as" in line 7.

"Uh, Philosophy": Sept. 20, 1959. First appeared (as "Canto 44") in *The Carleton Miscellany*, in vol. 4, no. 1 (Winter 1963). The semicolon at the end of line 30 was changed to a colon in *CP51–71*; however, Ammons's TS for *CP51–71* retains the semicolon, and that is restored here. In line 58 "anyway" is here corrected to "any way."

"The Numbers": Oct. 1964.

"Empty": Sept. 14, 1964.

"Unbroken": Aug. 18, 1963. First appeared in *The Hudson Review*, vol. 17, no. 4 (Winter 1965).

"Fall": First appeared in the *Quarterly Review of Literature*, vol. 13, nos. 1–2 (1964).

"The Wind Coming Down From": June 19, 1958. First appeared in *Accent*, vol. 19, no. 2 (Spring 1959). For information about the Ezra persona, see the note on "So I Said I Am Ezra."

"Interval": First appeared in *The Hudson Review*, vol. 10, no. 3 (Autumn 1957). The eighteenth-century Swedish naturalist Carolus Linnaeus developed our modern principles of classifying organisms, as well as our system of binomial Latin nomenclature (e.g., *Pinus coulteri* for Coulter's pine).

"Way to Go": Aug. 18, 1963. First appeared in *The Hudson Review*, vol. 17, no. 4 (Winter 1965).

§

UPLANDS

Uplands was published by W. W. Norton in 1970; the dedication ("for Mona and Vida") is to the poet's sisters. The book's title suggests the hills of Ithaca and surrounding Tompkins County, which the Appalachia Regional Commission recognizes as one of the northernmost counties of Appalachia.

〰

"Snow Log": Jan. 13, 1969. First appeared in *Southern Poetry Review*, vol. 10, no. 2 (Spring 1970). There are several early TSS of "Snow Log" (including one Ammons sent to his sister Vida with other recent poems in April

1969); in all of them, line 15 ends with "I take in on myself," and the poem appeared thus in *Southern Poetry Review*. In the galleys for *Uplands*, however, Ammons indicated that "in" should be changed to "it," adding a note now lightly crossed out: "mistake in MS—but must be changed." That the original phrasing, so consistently typed and retyped, was a mistake seems unlikely: he probably simply changed his mind about using that construction. He reprinted the poem three times (in *CP51–71*, *SP77*, and *SP86*), never reverting to the earlier text.

The revision stands here, but the earlier version is worth considering. Compare "I take in on myself" to two passages in "The Woodsroad": "I take myself in" (line 4) and "I take myself / all in" (lines 17–18). See also the opening to "Vehicle": "I take myself, in / the goal of my destiny, / the way the wind takes / me. . . ."

"Upland": Apr. 2, 1969. First appeared in *Pebble*, no. 3 (1969).

"Periphery": Mar. 9, 1969. First appeared in *Southern Poetry Review*, vol. 10, no. 1 (Fall 1969).

"Clarity": Mar. 9, 1969. First appeared in *Apple,* no. 4 (Autumn 1970).

"Classic": Mar. 7, 1969. First appeared in *The Hudson Review*, vol. 22, no. 2 (Summer 1969).

"Conserving the Magnitude of Uselessness": July 18, 1969. First appeared in *Poetry*, Feb. 1970.

"If Anything Will Level with You Water Will": July 17, 1969. First appeared in *Poetry*, Feb. 1970.

"The Unifying Principle": July 9, 1969. First appeared in *Poetry*, Feb. 1970.

"Runoff": June 30, 1969. First appeared in *Poetry*, Feb. 1970.

"Transaction": June 27, 1969. First appeared in *Poetry*, Feb. 1970.

"Then One": Apr. 14, 1969. First appeared in *Poetry*, Oct. 1970.

"Further On": July 11, 1969. First appeared in *The Hudson Review*, vol. 22, no. 4 (Winter 1970).

"Hope's Okay": June 11, 1969. First appeared in *Southern Poetry Review*, vol. 10, no. 1 (Fall 1969).

"Life in the Boondocks": May 30, 1969. First appeared in *The Hudson Review*, vol. 22, no. 4 (Winter 1970).

"Spiel": First appeared in *Poetry*, Feb. 1970.

"Guitar Recitativos": Fall 1967. First appeared in *The Hudson Review*, vol. 21, no. 1 (Spring 1968). Ammons reversed sections 3 and 4 when he reprinted the poem in *CP51–71*, and the text here retains that reversal.

"Laser": Aug. 30, 1964. First appeared in *Foxfire*, vol. 1, no. 1 (Mar. 1967).

"Virtu": July 30, 1965. First appeared in *Apple*, no. 1 (Summer 1967).

"Choice": Summer 1955.

"Body Politic": June 2, 1967. First appeared in *Kumquat*, no. 1 (1967).

"Apologia pro Vita Sua": Apr. 1956. First appeared in *Compass Review*, no. 2 (Apr. 1958). The title, Latin for "Defense of His Life," is best known as the title of English theologian John Henry Newman's 1864 spiritual autobiography.

"Offset": June 26, 1967. First appeared in *The Quest*, vol. 3, no. 2 (Winter–Spring 1969).

"Mountain Talk": June 1, 1964. First appeared in *Poetry*, Oct. 1970.

"Impulse": First appeared in *The New York Times*, Feb. 10, 1969.

"Needs": May 24, 1968. First appeared in *Stony Brook*, nos. 1–2 (Fall 1968).

"Help": May 26, 1968. First appeared in *The Hudson Review*, vol. 22, no. 2 (Summer 1969).

"Love Song": Aug. 10, 1966. First appeared in *Poetry*, June 1967.

"Love Song (2)": Aug. 10, 1966. First appeared in *Poetry*, June 1967.

"Mule Song": Nov. 1958. First appeared in *The New York Times*, June 8, 1969. Other poems in which Silver appears are "Silver" and *TTY* (the "22 Dec:" section).

"Script": Apr. 14, 1968. First appeared in *The Hudson Review*, vol. 22, no. 2 (Summer 1969).

"Holly": June 4, 1968. First appeared in *New: American and Canadian Poetry*, no. 8 (Fall 1968).

"Small Song": First appeared in *The New York Times*, June 16, 1969.

"Possibility Along a Line of Difference": Apr. 1, 1959. First appeared in *TriQuarterly*, no. 15 (Spring 1969).

"Cascadilla Falls": July 7, 1966. First appeared in *The Quest's* "Poetry Pamphlet Number One: Poetry Extra" (1969). Cascadilla Falls is on Cascadilla Creek, which runs through Ithaca's Cascadilla Gorge.

"Summer Session": 1968. First appeared (as "Summer Session 1968") in *Epoch*, vol. 19, no. 3 (Spring 1970). Restored here is a colon at the end of line 10 that appears both in the *Epoch* text and in *U*, but did not print on the photocopy from *U* used in setting up the poem in *CP51–71* and was likewise omitted in *SLP*. In line 167, the word "nickelodean" is not a misspelling of "nickelodeon": the intended meaning seems to be "made of nickel." In line 194, "the wee-wee's," which is not possessive, is here corrected to "the weewees."

    Lines 330–40: Baxter Hathaway, a colleague in Cornell's English Department, founded the creative writing program as well as the literary magazine *Epoch*. Barry Adams was chair of the department at the time Ammons wrote the poem.

    Lines 429–33: The note is from Neil Hertz, long Ammons's colleague in English at Cornell, now professor emeritus at Johns Hopkins.

§

BRIEFINGS: POEMS SMALL AND EASY

Briefings was published by W. W. Norton in 1971. Its dedicatee, the poet John Logan (1923–1987), was a friend and an important supporter.

❧

"Center": May 19, 1963. First appeared in *The New York Times*, Nov. 25, 1968.

"Mechanics": June 28, 1967. First appeared in *The New York Times*, Apr. 21, 1969.

"Up": Apr. 23, 1968.

"After Yesterday": May 1, 1968. First appeared in *The Hudson Review*, vol. 22, no. 2 (Summer 1969). The poem appears as revised for *RSP*, with "blue" replacing "strungled" in line 2.

"Event": May 1962. First appeared in *Epos*, vol. 14, no. 4 (Summer 1963).

"High & Low": May 25, 1965.

"Peracute Lucidity": Mar. 15, 1969.

"Increment": June 9, 1968. Ammons added the hyphen in line 3's "self-regard" for *RSP*.

"Bees Stopped": 1951.

"Storm": Nov. 13, 1963.

"Two Possibilities": Jan. 24, 1970.

"Medicine for Tight Spots": Apr. 19, 1969. The expression "fine-up" (line 8) is not an error for "fire-up"; see "fining up" in line 680 of "Essay on Poetics," as well as "fines up" in line 125 of "Religious Feeling" (in Appendix B, in Volume II).

"Brooks & Other Notions": June 7, 1969.

"Cougar": Nov. 3, 1965. First appeared in *Poetry*, Oct. 1970.

"This Black Rich Country": Aug. 14, 1955. First appeared in *Epos*, vol. 8, no. 2 (Winter 1956).

"Attention": July 27, 1963.

"Return": June 29, 1958.

"This Bright Day": May 1967. First appeared in *Poetry*, Mar. 1969.

"Look for My White Self": Sept. 9, 1955. First appeared in *Epos*, vol. 8, no. 1 (Fall 1956).

"Undersea": May 1967.

"Auto Mobile": May 1967.

"Wagons": June 14, 1968. First appeared in *Southern Poetry Review*, vol. 9, no. 1 (Fall 1968).

"September Drift": Sept. 8, 1968. First appeared in *Poetry*, Oct. 1970.

"Civics": 1967.

"He Held Radical Light": May 17, 1965. First appeared in *The Quest*'s "Poetry Pamphlet Number One: Poetry Extra" (1969).

"Locus": Apr. 17, 1966.

"Circles": May 20, 1968.

"Working Still": Mar. 21, 1969. First appeared in *Poetry*, Oct. 1970.

"Tooling Up": June 11, 1968.

"Father": Apr. 12, 1968. First appeared in *The Hudson Review*, vol. 22, no. 2 (Summer 1969).

"Sumerian": Jan. 24, 1955. First appeared in *Accent*, vol. 16, no. 3 (Summer 1956). See note to *O*'s "Coming to Sumer," above.

"Hippie Hop": June 9, 1968.

"Garden": July 10, 1965.

"Hymn IV": Nov. 21, 1957. First appeared (as "Hymn VI") in *Accent*, vol. 18, no. 3 (Summer 1958).

"The Mark": Sept. 28, 1965.

"Loft": July 6, 1965.

"Poetics": Sept. 1965. First appeared in *The Hudson Review*, vol. 22, no. 2 (Summer 1969).

"Working with Tools": June 5, 1968. First appeared in *Southern Poetry Review*, vol. 9, no. 1 (Fall 1968).

"Doubling the Nerve": Apr. 3, 1969. First appeared in *Pebble*, no. 3 (Nov. 1969).

"Making": May 3, 1968. First appeared in *The Hudson Review*, vol. 22, no. 2 (Summer 1969). See the etymological note on "The Makers," below.

"Dominion": Oct. 21, 1965. First appeared in *Poetry*, Oct. 1970.

"Round": Apr. 18, 1968. First appeared in *The Hudson Review*, vol. 22, no. 2 (Summer 1969).

"Tight": Sept. 10, 1968. First appeared in *Lillabulero*, Second Series, no. 7 (Summer–Fall 1969).

"The Woodsroad": Aug. 19, 1966. First appeared in *The Quest*, vol. 3, no. 2 (Winter–Spring 1969).

"WCW": Aug. 7, 1962. First appeared in *The Quest*'s "Poetry Pamphlet Number One: Poetry Extra" (1969). The title abbreviates the name of William Carlos Williams, whom Ammons visited and took for drives during the elder poet's last years. In a 1996 interview with Steven P. Schneider, Ammons said, "I have never cared that much about the content of William Carlos Williams's own writing, although I have borrowed so much from him in terms of form."

"Saying": Mar. 21, 1965. First appeared in *The New York Times*, Dec. 28, 1968.

"Looking Over the Acreage": Nov. 30, 1968.

"Gain": Sept. 25, 1965. First appeared in *The Hudson Review*, vol. 22, no. 2 (Summer 1969).

"Off": May 16, 1968.

"Treaties": Apr. 2, 1966. First appeared in *Poetry*, Mar. 1969.

"Convergence": June 30, 1965.

"Project": First appeared in *Poetry*, Oct. 1970.

"North Jersey": Spring 1968.

"Ship": Apr. 4, 1969.

"Play": Mar. 5, 1969. First appeared in *Poetry*, Oct. 1970.

"Spinejacking": June 1, 1968. First appeared in *Choice*, no. 6 (1970).

"Shore Fog": June 9, 1968.

"Meteorology": Apr. 21, 1968.

"Exotic": Spring 1968.

"Hosts": Spring 1968.

"Crevice": Dec. 29, 1966. First appeared in *The New York Times*, Mar. 22, 1969.

"Transducer": May 28, 1968. Ammons added the comma at the end of line 8 for *RSP*.

"Mean": Apr. 1968.

"Banking": June 10, 1968.

"Elegy for a Jet Pilot": Feb. 26, 1964. First appeared in *The Quest*'s "Poetry Pamphlet Number One: Poetry Extra" (1969). The poem is dated one day after the February 25, 1964, crash of Eastern Airlines Flight 304; all passengers and crew members were killed. Another recent crash was Pan Am Flight 214: see the note to "9 Dec:" in *TTY*. Mays Landing is in New Jersey, where Ammons lived at this time.

"Countering": July 12, 1965. First appeared in *Poetry*, Oct. 1970.

"The Quince Bush": July 7, 1967. First appeared in *Abraxas*, vol. 1, no. 1 (1968).

"Square": May 23, 1968. First appeared in *Poetry*, Oct. 1970.

"Autumn Song": Oct. 20, 1968. First appeared in *Lillabulero*, Second Series, no. 7 (Summer–Fall 1969).

"Early Morning in Early April": Apr. 5, 1969.

"Reversal": Mar. 21, 1967. First appeared in *Poetry*, Oct. 1970.

"The Confirmers": July 14, 1968. First appeared in *Abraxas*, vol. 1, no. 1 (1968).

"Involved": May 1967.

"Admission": June 9, 1966. First appeared in *Poetry*, Oct. 1970.

"Mission": Mar. 11, 1965. First appeared in *Poetry*, June 1967. In a July 27, 1966, letter to the poet and translator Richard Howard, Ammons described this fourteen-line poem as a sonnet.

"Cut the Grass": July 10, 1969. First appeared in *Poetry* (Feb. 1970).

"The Limit": Nov. 28, 1968.

"Concerning the Exclusions of the Object": Jan. 12, 1965. First appeared in *The Hudson Review*, vol. 22, no. 2 (Summer 1969).

"The Makers": July 14, 1968. First appeared in *New: American and Canadian Poetry*, no. 8 (Fall 1968). The word "poet" derives from the Greek verb *poiein*, meaning "to make," and many poets have embraced the idea that they are "makers." (See too the poem "Making.") In the Chrono IV notebook at Cornell, an early TS of "The Makers" has in line 1 the word "shit" rather than "do."

"Levitation": July 21, 1965.

"Medium": July 1, 1965. First appeared in *Lillabulero*, Second Series, no. 7 (Summer–Fall 1969).

"Transfer": June 26, 1967.

"Monday": May 27, 1968.

"Pluralist": July 14, 1969. First appeared in *Poetry*, Feb. 1970.

"Here & Now": Oct. 20, 1968. First appeared in *Poetry*, Oct. 1970.

"The Run-Through": June 25, 1969. First appeared in *Southern Poetry Review*, vol. 10, no. 1 (Fall 1969).

"The Put-Down Come On": Sept. 13, 1968.

"The City Limits": Feb. 22, 1970. First appeared in *Modern Occasions*, vol. 1, no. 2 (Winter 1971).

§

PREVIOUSLY UNCOLLECTED POEMS
FROM *COLLECTED POEMS 1951–1971*

Collected Poems 1951–1971 was published by W. W. Norton in 1972; it won the 1973 National Book Award for poetry. Ammons included most but not all the poems he had gathered in his books up to then: he excluded the untitled poems beginning "Behind the I" and "I should have stayed longer idle" from *Omma-teum*; "Portrait" (the only poem in *SP68* not included in *CP51–71*), "Resort," and "Morning Glory" from *Corsons Inlet*; "The Numbers," "Empty," "Unbroken," and "Fall" from *Northfield Poems*; and all of *Tape for the Turn of the Year*. It also included a number of poems, some recent and some not, that Ammons had not yet collected. With some exceptions, the poems were sequenced by order of composition, without reference to the books in which they had originally appeared. The table of contents was broken into four sections, each representing roughly half a decade. The poems' sequence, section by section, was as follows, with the titles of those first gathered in *CP51–71* in bold type:

(1951–55)
So I Said I Am Ezra • The Sap Is Gone Out of the Trees • In Strasbourg in 1349 • I Broke a Sheaf of Light • Some Months Ago • Bees Stopped • **Rack [later retitled "The Pieces of My Voice"]** • **Chaos Staggered Up the Hill** • I Went Out to the Sun • Consignee • At Dawn in 1098 • The Whaleboat Struck • Turning a Moment to Say So Long • Turning • Libation • Dying in a Mirthful Place • When Rahman Rides • With Ropes of Hemp • Doxology • My Dice Are Crystal • Having Been Interstellar • **Eolith** • When I Set Fire to the Reed Patch • Coming to Sumer • I Struck a Diminished Seventh • In the Wind My Rescue Is • A Treeful of Cleavage Flared Branching • I Assume the World Is Curious About Me • Gilgamesh Was Very Lascivious • The Grass Miracles • I Came in a Dark Woods Upon • One Composing • A Crippled Angel • Dropping Eyelids Among the Aerial Ash • I Came Upon a Plateau • Sumerian • Whose Timeless Reach • Driving Through • Song • Choice • Interval • This Black Rich Country • Look for My White Self

(1956–60)
Apologia pro Vita Sua • Hymn • Hymn II • Hymn III • Hymn IV • **Hymn V** • The Watch • March Song • Requiem • Ritual for Eating the World • The Wide Land • **Spring Song** • Batsto • **Come Prima** • Composing • Mountain Liar • Gravelly Run • Prospecting • Jersey Cedars • Joshua Tree • A Symmetry of Thought • Thaw • The Wind Coming Down From • Return • Silver • Mule Song • Hardweed Path Going • **Terminus** • Close-Up • Grassy Sound • Bourn • Orientale • Possibility Along a Line of Difference • **Back Country** • Mansion • Prodigal • Mechanism • Guide • The Golden Mean • Risks and Possibilities • Bridge • The Foot-Washing • Coon Song • Terrain • Unsaid • Raft • Uh, Philosophy • Sphere • Epiphany • Muse • Concentrations • River • Lines • The Strait • Open • Catalyst • **Christmas Eve**

(1961–65)

Identity • What This Mode of Motion Said • Nucleus • Jungle Knot • The Misfit • Nelly Myers • Motion for Motion • Visit • Four Motions for the Pea Vines • Expressions of Sea Level • Discoverer • Event • One:Many • Still • The Yucca Moth • Two Motions • The Constant • Motion • WCW • Corsons Inlet • Saliences • First Carolina Said-Song • Second Carolina Said-Song • Dunes • February Beach • Moment • Upright • Glass • Center • Configurations • Ithaca, N.Y. • Holding On • Attention • Way to Go • Reflective • Butterflyweed • Street Song • Contingency • Trap • Halfway • Mays Landing • Storm • Landscape with Figures • Dark Song • World • Spindle • Winter Scene • Anxiety • Sitting Down, Looking Up • **Communication** • Elegy for a Jet Pilot • **The Whole Half** • Belief • Mountain Talk • Loss • Zone • Recovery • Interference • **Bay Bank** • Self-Portrait • Peak • Passage • Laser • Kind • **Money** • Height • **Fall Creek** • **Utensil** • Mission • **The Fall** • **April** • He Held Radical Light • High & Low • Convergence • Medium • Loft • Garden • Countering • Levitation • Virtu • Gain • Poetics • The Mark • Concerning the Exclusions of the Object • Dominion • Cougar

(1966–71)

Saying • **Treaties** • **Lion::Mouse** • **Breaks** • Locus • Admission • **Heat** • Cascadilla Falls • **Definitions** • **Path** • Love Song • Love Song (2) • The Woodsroad • **Mediation** • Crevice • **Snow Whirl** • Reversal • This Bright Day • Auto Mobile • Involved • Project • Impulse • Undersea • Transfer • Body Politic • Offset • Civics • Mechanics • The Quince Bush • **Reward** • **Timing** • Guitar Recitativos • **Trouble Making Trouble** • **Rome Zoo** • Small Song • **Alternatives** • **Positions** • **Reassessing** • **Renovating** • **Devising** • **Emplacement** • **Touching Down** • **Spring Coming** • Father • Script • **Ocean City** • Round • **Chasm** • Mean • Meteorology • Up • **Bearing Mercy** • After Yesterday • Making • **Tossup** • **Plexus** • Working with Tools • **Three** • Off • Circles • **Miss** • Square • Needs • **Celestial** • **Correction** • **Mirrorment** • **Coming To** • North Jersey • Exotic • **Even** • Hosts • Help • **Windy Trees** • Monday • Transducer • **Photosynthesis** • **Making Waves** • **Clearing** • Spinejacking • **The Account** • Holly • **Winter Saint** • Hippie Hop • Increment • Shore Fog • Banking • Tooling Up • Wagons • Summer Session • **The Imagined Land** • The Confirmers • The Makers • September Drift • Tight • The Put-Down Come On • **The King of Ice** • Here & Now • Autumn Song • The Limit • Looking Over the Acreage • Spiel • Snow Log • Play • Classic • Clarity • Periphery • Peracute Lucidity • Working Still • Upland • Doubling the Nerve • Ship • Early Morning in Early April • Then One • Medicine for Tight Spots • **Village, Town, City—Highway, Road, Path** • **Lonely Splendor** • Life in the Boondocks • Brooks & Other Notions •

Hope's Okay • **The Swan Ritual** • **He Said** • The Run-Through • Runoff • The Unifying Principle • Cut the Grass • Further On • Pluralist • If Anything Will Level with You Water Will • Conserving the Magnitude of Uselessness • **One More Time** • Transaction • **Drought** • **Image** • **Equinox** • **Russet Gold** • **Essay on Poetics** • Two Possibilities • **Plunder** • **Triphammer Bridge** • **Lollapalooza: 22 February** • The City Limits • **Satyr Formalist** • **Late Romantic** • **Spaceship** • **Cleavage** • **Schooling** • **Space Travel** • **High Surreal** • **Sharp Lookout** • **Right On** • **Rectitude** • **Object** • **Ground Tide** • **Translating** • **Sorting** • **The Next Day** • **Extremes and Moderations** • **Mid-August** • **Clearing the Dark Symbiosis** • **Viable** • **Precursors** • **Lonesome Valley** • **Delaware Water Gap** • **Day** • **Staking Claim** • **The Eternal City** • **The Shoreless Tide** • **Grace Abounding** • **Phase** • **Hibernaculum** • **Eyesight** • **Left** • **The Arc Inside and Out**

∽∼∽

"The Pieces of My Voice": 1955. Appeared as "Rack" in *CP51–71*; the poet changed the title for *SP77* and *SP86*.

"Chaos Staggered Up the Hill": 1953.

"Eolith": 1952.

"Spring Song": May 2, 1957. First appeared in *Compass Review*, no. 3 (Summer 1958).

"Come Prima": Dec. 12, 1957. Italian for "as before," pronounced *KOHmay PREEma*—used as a direction in music.

"Terminus": Aug. 4, 1959. First appeared in *Harper's Magazine*, Jan. 1971. A terminus is a boundary or an ending point; the Roman god Terminus was the god of boundaries. Ralph Waldo Emerson wrote two poems titled "Terminus"; the one beginning "It is time to be old" is frequently anthologized.

"Christmas Eve": Dec. 24, 1960. First appeared in *The Hudson Review*, vol. 22, no. 4 (Winter 1970).

"Communication": Feb. 16, 1964. First appeared in *The New York Times*, Jan. 13, 1965.

"The Whole Half": Feb. 26, 1964.

"Bay Bank": July 9, 1964. As revised for *RSP*, with "redwing" replacing "redwinged" in line 1.

"Money": Sept. 4, 1964.

"Fall Creek": Sept. 27, 1964. First appeared in *Epoch*, vol. 21, no. 3 (Spring 1972). Fall Creek runs through Ithaca's Fall Creek Gorge and empties into Cayuga Lake.

"Utensil": Nov. 1, 1964.

"The Fall": Mar. 13, 1965. First appeared in *Abraxas*, no. 5 (1972).

"April": Apr. 10, 1965.

"Lion::Mouse": Apr. 10, 1966.

"Breaks": Apr. 10, 1966.

"Heat": June 1966.

"Definitions": July 9, 1966. *Lillabulero*, Second Series, nos. 10–11 (1971).

"Path": July 29, 1966. First appeared in *Abraxas*, no. 5 (1972).

"Mediation": Aug. 27, 1966. The comma at the end of line 1 was added for *RSP*.

"Snow Whirl": Mar. 21, 1967.

"Reward": Aug. 2, 1967.

"Timing": Fall 1967. First appeared in *The Nation*, Dec. 23, 1968.

"Trouble Making Trouble": Fall 1967. First appeared (as "Front") in *Foxfire*, vol. 2, no. 1 (1968).

"Rome Zoo": Fall 1967.

"Alternatives": Dec. 19, 1967. The reference is to a remark attributed to the Greek mathematician Archimedes (third century BC), whose interests included the physics of levers: "Give me a place to stand, and I will move the Earth."

"Positions": Dec. 1967.

"Reassessing": Dec. 1967.

"Renovating": Dec. 1967.

"Devising": Jan. 3, 1968.

"Emplacement": Jan. 15, 1968.

"Touching Down": Feb. 4, 1968.

"Spring Coming": Mar. 1968.

"Ocean City": Apr. 14, 1968. First appeared (as "The Gardens") in *Contemporary Poets of South Jersey*, a small 1968 anthology listing no publisher or place of publication. The anthology grew out of a series of poetry events sponsored by the Ocean City Cultural Arts Center.

"Chasm": Apr. 18, 1968.

"Bearing Mercy": Apr. 25, 1968.

"Tossup": May 3, 1968.

"Plexus": May 3, 1968.

"Three": May 9, 1968.

"Miss": May 22, 1968. Cheops is the Greek name for Khufu, a twenty-fifth–twenty-sixth-century BC king of Egypt who brought about construction of the Great Pyramid (also called the Pyramid of Khufu or the Pyramid of Cheops) in Gaza. Here the reference seems to be to the pyramid itself rather than the man.

"Celestial": May 1968. Line 10: In Greek myth, Icarus was the son of the master craftsman Daedalus; both were held prisoner by King Minos of Crete, until Daedalus fashioned wings with which they could escape. Ignoring Daedalus's warning not to fly too close to the sun (which would melt the wax holding the wings together), Icarus fell into the sea and drowned.

"Correction": May 1968.

"Mirrorment": May 1968.

"Coming To": Spring 1968.

"Even": Spring 1968.

"Windy Trees": May 27, 1968.

"Photosynthesis": May 28, 1968.

"Making Waves": May 28, 1968.

"Clearing": May 29, 1968.

"The Account": June 2, 1968.

"Winter Saint": June 8, 1968.

"The Imagined Land": July 7, 1968.

"The King of Ice": Sept. 1968.

"Village, Town, City—Highway, Road, Path": May 18, 1969.

"Lonely Splendor": May 26, 1969.

"The Swan Ritual": June 14, 1969.

"He Said": June 15, 1969.

"One More Time": July 18–20, 1969. First appeared in *Harper's Magazine*, Oct. 1970.

"Drought": Sept. 6, 1969.

"Image": Sept. 14, 1969.

"Equinox": Sept. 28, 1969.

"Russet Gold": Oct. 11, 1969.

"Essay on Poetics": Dec. 24–28, 1969. First appeared in *The Hudson Review*, vol. 23, no. 3 (1970). As reprinted in *Selected Longer Poems*, the poem includes an unfortunate error: the tercet beginning with "simple by grandeur" (lines 145–47) appears a second time as lines 169–71, in place of the tercet beginning "trees, and a sense."

 Lines 159–61: "ME.," "AS.," "G.," and "IE." are abbreviations for "Middle English," "Anglo-Saxon" (i.e., Old English), "German," and "Indo-European," respectively.

 Lines 423–24: "No ideas but in things" was a motto of the poet William Carlos Williams (1883–1963).

 Line 471: Ithaca is at the southern tip of Cayuga Lake (Ammons transposes the name), the largest of New York's Finger Lakes. Stewart Park is a lakeside city park.

 Lines 573–75: The quotation from the English art critic and painter John Ruskin (1819–1900) is from his 1868 lecture "The Mystery of Life and Its Arts."

"Plunder": Jan. 30, 1970. See Emily Dickinson's poem beginning "This was a Poet" (no. 446 in R. W. Franklin's edition).

"Triphammer Bridge": Feb. 19, 1970. First appeared in *Modern Occasions*, vol. 1, no. 2 (Winter 1971). The bridge spans Fall Creek Gorge in Ithaca.

"Lollapalooza: 22 February": Feb. 22, 1970.

"Satyr Formalist": Mar. 14, 1970. In an unsent letter to Harold Bloom, dated "Ides 1970," Ammons includes a draft of the poem, explaining that he wrote it after beginning Bloom's book *Yeats*. He explains the thought behind the poem: "The tragedians by moaning and groaning think they purchase knowledge of and immunity from death but they, like us—and like the satyr—will meet it merely uncomprehendingly: so why shouldn't we be like the satyr and meet it for the first time when it is uncomprehendingly there and meanwhile spend our lives pinching broads in the dark? That way it would be like any other event in the garden."

"Late Romantic": Mar. 14, 1970.

"Spaceship": May 2, 1970.

"Cleavage": May 4, 1970.

"Schooling": June 15, 1970.

"Space Travel": Jan. 26, 1970.

"High Surreal": June 26, 1970. First appeared in *Lillabulero*, Second Series, nos. 10–11 (1971).

"Sharp Lookout": June 29, 1970. In an unsent letter of the same date to Harold Bloom, Ammons explains the poem was inspired by playing with John, who, pretending to be a lifeguard, had announced he was keeping a "sharp lookout."

"Right On": July 3, 1970.

"Rectitude": July 4, 1970. First appeared in *Epoch*, vol. 21, no. 3 (Spring 1972).

"Object": July 6, 1970.

"Ground Tide": July 12, 1970. First appeared in *Lillabulero*, Second Series, nos. 10–11 (1971).

"Translating": Aug. 1, 1970. First appeared in *Lillabulero*, Second Series, nos. 10–11 (1971).

"Sorting": Aug. 1, 1970. *Lillabulero*, Second Series, nos. 10–11 (1971).

"The Next Day": Aug. 8, 1970. Ammons includes the poem in an unsent letter (dated August 13, 1970) to Harold Bloom, noting that he wrote the poem on Phyllis's birthday.

"Extremes and Moderations": Aug. 18–23, 1970.
> Lines 114–16: Pre-Columbian Mayan religious ritual included human sacrifice; victims sometimes had their still-beating hearts extracted.
> Lines 247–54: The first book referred to here is *With Respect to Readers: Dimensions of Literary Response*, by Walter J. Slatoff, one of Ammons's colleagues in the Cornell English Department. Another departmental col-

league, Robert Kaske, would be the person who gave Ammons a collection by the north Georgia poet Byron Herbert Reece (1917–1958). Like Reece, Jesse Stuart (1906–1984) was a southern Appalachian poet; William Rose Benet, John Hall Wheelock, John Gould Fletcher, and Alfred Kreymborg were poets and editors of note.

"Mid-August": Aug. 15, 1970. First appeared in *Abraxas*, no. 5 (1972).

"Clearing the Dark Symbiosis": Aug. 14, 1970.

"Viable": Aug. 16, 1970.

"Precursors": Aug. 26, 1970.

"Lonesome Valley": Aug. 28, 1970.

"Delaware Water Gap": Sept. 7, 1970. First appeared in *Lillabulero*, Second Series, nos. 10–11 (1971). The Delaware River, which runs between New Jersey and Pennsylvania, makes an S-shaped pass through mountains. The Gap is at the south end of what is now the Delaware Water Gap National Recreation Area.

"Day": Sept. 19, 1970. First appeared in *Lillabulero*, Second Series, nos. 10–11 (1971).

"Staking Claim": Sept. 27, 1970.

"The Eternal City": Oct. 9, 1970. First appeared in *Harper's Magazine*, Apr. 1971.

"The Shoreless Tide": Oct. 26, 1970.

"Grace Abounding": Oct. 31, 1970. First appeared in *Beyond the Square: A Tribute to Elliott Coleman*, edited by Robert K. Rosenburg. Baltimore, MD: Linden Press, 1972.

"Phase": Nov. 8, 1970.

"Hibernaculum": "Solstice 1970–1971." Early titles for this poem were "Cud" and "Up and Around and Down and Out." *Hibernaculum* is a Latin word meaning "winter residence." The term refers to a structure protecting a bulb or a bud through winter; it also refers to the shelter of a hibernating animal. Ammons wrote the poem in the winter of 1970–71.

Section 3:
    Line 21: In *CP51–71*, the line ended with a comma after "though." Ammons's TSS of the poem include that comma, but in his marked copy of the book, he indicates uncertainty about its appropriateness. He dropped it when he reprinted the poem in *Selected Longer Poems*, and so it is omitted here.

Section 18:

Line 156: In Ammons's TSS of the poem and in *CP51–71*, the line ended with the colon after "again," so that the verb "accost" beginning line 157 was imperative. In his marked copy of *CP51–71*, however, he added the subject "I" at the end of line 156, and that pronoun does appear (in that position) in the poem's reprint in *SLP*—so it is included here.

Section 20:

Line 177: "Consomme" is here corrected to "consommé."

Sections 28–29:

Lines 252–55: Growing up in Whiteville, North Carolina, Ammons attended New Hope Elementary School and Whiteville High School, and his Navy service during World War II was in the Pacific.

Section 33:

Line 291: Following TS, "christmas" is corrected to "Christmas."

Section 35:

Line 308: Nonpossessive plural "wow's" is here corrected to "wows."

Section 38:

Lines 340–41: St. Francis of Assisi (1181–1226) believed that forsaking material wealth was essential to spiritual growth.

Section 58:

Line 515: The philosopher Plotinus (205–270), author of the *Enneads*, studied for eleven years under a philosopher named Ammonius.

Section 59:

Line 530: Ralph Waldo Emerson (1803–1882), the Transcendentalist essayist and poet.

Section 68:

Lines 604–8: The poet Edna St. Vincent Millay (1892–1950) met the sculptor Thelma Wood in Paris in the early 1920s and had a brief relationship with her before marrying Eugen Jan Boissevain.

Section 84:

Line 752: The order to "plot a course, Mr. Sulu" alludes to the first *Star Trek* television series, which aired from 1966 to 1969. Mr. Sulu was the helmsman of the Starship *Enterprise*.

Section 85:

Lines 761–62: The reference is probably to Jesse James (1847–1882), though his brother Frank James was a member of the same outlaw gang. The "Appleseed" who lived a "life of service" is the nurseryman and preacher John Chapman (1774–1845), widely known as Johnny Appleseed.

Section 88:

Line 784: The phrase "carless in Gaza" echoes "Eyeless in Gaza," the blinded Samson's description of himself in John Milton's *Samson Agonistes* (1671).

Section 92:

Line 820: The Irish author Oscar Wilde (1854–1900), a proponent of art for art's sake, was convicted in a British court of "gross indecency with certain male persons" (i.e., homosexual activity) and sentenced to two years of hard labor. "*Contra naturam*" and "*Contra mundum*" (in line 823) are Latin for "against nature" and "against the world," respectively.

Section 100:

Lines 894–95: The Latin term *jus commune* refers to common law or rights, whereas *jus singulare* refers to laws or rights established for special cases. See "One:Many" in *NP*.

Section 102:

Line 918: *Hee Haw* was a popular television variety show featuring country music and comedy, airing from 1969 to 1992.

Section 105:

Line 941: Californium 254 is a radioactive isotope.

Section 112:

Line 1006: Xenophon (c. 430–c. 350 BC) was a Greek historian and philosopher.

"Eyesight": Feb. 7, 1971.

"Left": Feb. 7, 1971. First appeared in *Abraxas*, no. 5 (1972).

"The Arc Inside and Out": Feb. 20, 1971. First appeared in *New American Review*, no. 13 (1971). The literary critic Harold Bloom encouraged and advised Ammons and became one of the most passionate champions of his work. See also "For Harold Bloom," the dedicatory poem to *Sphere: The Form of a Motion* (1974). In a February 27, 1971, letter to Bloom, Ammons comments at some length on "The Arc Inside and Out," beginning, "My little thesis is that within every circle, however infinitesimally tiny, is the bit of emptiness, void, nothingness, and beyond every circle, however great, is a great deal more of the same."

§

Sphere: The Form of a Motion was published by W. W. Norton in 1974; it won the 1975 Bollingen Prize in Poetry. Ammons included the dedicatory poem, "For Harold Bloom," in both his 1977 and 1986 *Selected Poems* without indicating its relationship to *Sphere.*

Sections 1 through 10 first appeared in *Diacritics*, vol. 3, no. 4 (Winter 1973). Sections 71 and 72 first appeared, under the title "Providences," in *Granite*, nos. 7–8 (Spring 1974).

Between them, Cornell and East Carolina hold three TSS of the poem, all undated. Cornell holds an early TS with very few handwritten revisions; that version has 250 numbered sections that, like those of the book as published, consist of four tercets each. East Carolina holds an intermediate TS that has many sections struck out, but also has TSS of shorter poems interspersed and marked to be spliced into the poem. Cornell holds the final TS, the one with 155 sections that was the basis for the book as published.

The published poem's final section, section 155, is section 215 of the earliest of the three TSS. Its concluding punctuation was an exclamation point ("we're sailing!") all the way up to the book's galley proofs, where Ammons decided to use a period instead.

For a consideration of the differences between the poem's early and final versions, see Susannah L. Hollister's article "The Planet on the Screen: Scales of Belonging in A. R. Ammons's *Sphere*," which appeared in *Contemporary Literature*, vol. 50, no. 4 (Winter 2009).

Although the TSS are undated, letters collected in Kevin McGuirk's *An Image for Longing* indicate the period of the poem's composition and revision. In a June 25, 1972, letter to Josephine Jacobsen, Ammons writes, "I've done 166 twelve-line stanzas of a new poem in the last three months." In an August 12 letter to Bloom, he announces, "I finished my long poem a few days ago. It's called The Form of a Motion." He then sets the poem aside for some time, but on November 22, 1973, he informs Bloom, "I have begun to do some new writing for the long poem. And I am slowly making other changes that I think will improve it." On December 28, he submitted *Sphere* to John Benedict, his editor at Norton; the galley proofs, which are held at East Carolina, are dated April 19, 1974.

The Cornell archive holds undated TSS of an unpublished poem about *Sphere*:

Bookish Bookseller

Roll
up the edges of
the squared-off, flattened-out

two-dimensional
mind,

pull
the corners up and tie them off
at the top into a sphere or bag,
so that anyone thinking
will

have
to think about more
sides at once than one,
get volume into his
definitions,

and
become less certain
that summer with him is summer
elsewhere or that his ice cap is feeling's sole
mood:

so
I recommend my new poem
Sphere: The Form of a Motion
with the hope that it will ensphere good and do somebody
some.

❧

Section 17:

Line 195: Following TS3, "distingushing" is corrected to "distinguishing."

Section 36:

Lines 427–28: Ammons is referring to his poem "Shit List," which ends with the word "gallinule." By the time of *Sphere*'s 1974 publication, "Shit List" actually *had* been published (in a 1972 issue of *Abraxas*), but Ammons did not collect it in one of his books until 1982's *Worldly Hopes*.

Section 39:

Lines 463–64: Apollo 16 launched on April 16, 1972. It was the fifth— and next to last—mission to succeed in putting humans on the moon.

Section 42:

Line 501: Following TS3, "toaste" is corrected to "toast."

Section 59:

Line 707: Following TS3, "popular" is corrected to "poplar."

Section 73:

Line 872: The reference to Northfield is to Northfield, New Jersey, where Ammons resided for part of the 1950s and '60s before moving to Ithaca.

Section 74:

Lines 877–79: Ammons seems to think "repodepo" an interesting typo ("a mischance of machinery"). Thanks to William Harmon for pointing out that the word is actually a widely used term for depots of repossessed vehicles.

Section 77:

Line 914: Cayuga Heights is a village just north of Ithaca.

Section 82:

Line 983: The term "*sui generations* of particularity" is based on the Latin phrase *sui generis*, which means "of a kind all its own" (i.e., unique).

Section 84:

Line 998: Silver was a mule on the family farm of Ammons's youth. Her other appearances include the "22 Dec:" section of *Tape*, "Silver" in *ESL*, and "Mule Song" in *U*. Doll, one of the family's cows, appears in no other poem; Ammons mentions her in his 1992 interview with Alex Albright.

Section 87:

Line 1040: For an articulation of "the one:many problem" (also referred to in lines 1456–61), see "One:Many" in *NP*.

Section 98:

Line 1168: "Jove" is another name for Jupiter, the Roman king of the gods and also god of the sky.

Sections 109–10:

Lines 1303–13: This imaginary trip sets out northward from Walvis Bay, in what is now Namibia. Sorris Sorris is still in Namibia but inland; Ammons seems to have thought it was coastal. Benguela and Lobito are both on the Angolan coast, Port Gentil is in Gabon, and Cape Palmas is in Liberia. Sidi Ifni is on the North Atlantic coast of Morocco; one would pass the Strait of Gibraltar ("the gaping Strait") to the east as one continued to Oporto, on the west coast of Portugal. Brest is on the western tip of Brittany, in north-west France. Rounding Europe and following the Siberian (i.e., North Asian) coast, one would eventually pass through the Bering Strait, which divides eastern Russia from Alaska, and thus divides Asia from North America.

Section 119:

Line 1422: Oran is on Algeria's Mediterranean coast.

Section 122:

Lines 1460–62: Following TS3, *"plurisbus"* is corrected to *"pluribus."* *E pluribus unum*, a Latin phrase on the Great Seal of the United States, means "Out of many, one." Although Ammons calls it the national motto, since 1956 the national motto has officially been "In God we trust." Walt Whitman (1819–1892) wrote poetry and prose about the state of the nation— its promise as well as the challenges it faced.

Section 125:

Lines 1491–93: Ammons here caricatures Whitman's view that a strong democracy must be founded on bonds of intimate male relationships.

Section 136:

Line 1631: Enlil was the Sumerian sky-god.

Section 141:

Line 1688: Following TS3, "thicked-jawed" is corrected to "thick-jawed."

Section 148:

Line 1770: "Foliate saprophytes" would be leafy myco-heterotrophs— plants that parasitize fungi to supplement the food they make through photosynthesis.

§

DIVERSIFICATIONS

Diversifications was published by W. W. Norton in 1975. Its dedicatee, the Pulitzer Prize-winning poet and translator Richard Howard, wrote several important appraisals of Ammons's work, and devoted a chapter to it in his landmark 1969 study *Alone with America: Essays on the Art of Poetry in the United States since 1950.*

❧

"Transcendence": July 15, 1973. First appeared in *Epoch*, vol. 23, no. 3 (Spring 1974).

"Insouciance": First appeared (as "Insouciant") in *Salmagundi*, nos. 22–23 (Spring–Summer 1973).

"Narrows": First appeared in *Chicago Review*, vol. 24, no. 3 (Winter 1972).

"Full": Oct. 8, 1963. First appeared in *Diacritics*, vol. 3, no. 4 (Winter 1973).

"Uppermost": Apr. 5, 1974. First appeared in *Brim*, no. 3 (Winter 1975).

"Lightning": June 30, 1965. First appeared in *Diacritics*, vol. 3, no. 4 (Winter 1973).

"The Marriage": Jan. 19, 1974. First appeared in *American Review*, no. 21 (Oct. 1974).

"Double Exposure": Aug. 9, 1968. First appeared in *Diacritics*, vol. 3, no. 4 (Winter 1973). Line 1's "Flounder-like" in *D* became "Flounderlike" in *RSP*.

"Currencies": Dec. 10, 1964. First appeared in *The New York Times*, Sept. 27, 1972.

"Bonus": Jan. 19–20, 1974. First appeared in *Poetry*, Sept. 1974.

"Emerson": June 10, 1973. First appeared in *Diacritics*, vol. 3, no. 4 (Winter 1973).

"Meeting the Opposition": Apr. 19, 1973. First appeared in *Diacritics*, vol. 3, no. 4 (Winter 1973).

"Appearances": First appeared in *The New York Times*, Mar. 16, 1973.

"Measure": Feb. 3, 1963. First appeared in the *Quarterly Review of Literature*, vol. 13, nos. 1–2 (1964). The poem's dedicatee, the poet Robert Morgan, is a fellow North Carolinian who joined the Cornell English Department in 1971.

"Delight": First appeared in *Harper's Magazine*, Dec. 1973.

"Imperialist": First appeared in *The New York Quarterly*, no. 17 (1975).

"Poem": Nov. 1, 1973.

"Imago": May 1, 1968. First appeared (as "Model") in *New Letters*, vol. 39, no. 2 (Winter 1972).

"Light Orders": Sept. 7, 1969.

"History": First appeared in *Diacritics*, vol. 3, no. 4 (Winter 1973).

"Self-Projection": Apr. 16, 1968. First appeared in *New Letters*, vol. 39, no. 2 (Winter 1972).

"Metaphysic": June 11, 1969.

"Tussock": First appeared in *Diacritics*, vol. 3, no. 4 (Winter 1973).

"The Make": Oct. 25, 1973. Appeared in *Mademoiselle*, Oct. 1975.

"Terminations": First appeared in *Antaeus*, no. 9 (Spring 1973).

"Fundamental Constant": First appeared in *Diacritics*, vol. 3, no. 4 (Winter 1973).

"Making It": Oct. 13, 1973. First appeared in *The Georgia Review*, vol. 28, no. 3 (Fall 1974).

"Weight": June 24, 1965. Appeared in *The New York Quarterly* no. 18 (Fall 1976).

"Ballad": First appeared in *Diacritics*, vol. 3, no. 4 (Winter 1973).

"Three Travelogues": 1962. First appeared in the *Quarterly Review of Literature*, vol. 16, nos. 1–2 (1969). Although one might expect the word in line 12 to be "standing," "sanding" does appear to be the intended word. The *Oxford English Dictionary* defines "sand" when used as an intransitive verb to mean "to become clogged or bunged up with sand."

"Sight Unseen": May 6, 1973. Appeared in *New Letters*, no. 20 (1978).

"Facing": Aug. 10, 1966.

"Glass Globe": May 22, 1968. First appeared in *Raven*, vol. 2, no. 3 (Fall 1972).

"Separations": June 30, 1965.

"Circling": Apr. 10, 1966. Appeared in *Mademoiselle*, Oct. 1975.

"Fix": Aug. 23, 1971. First appeared in *Café Solo*, no. 10 (1977).

"Weather": Appeared in *Mademoiselle*, Oct. 1975.

"Coward": On a photocopy, Ammons notes that he wrote the poem before 1973.

"Crying Out": First appeared in *Salmagundi*, nos. 22–23 (Spring–Summer 1973).

"Certainty": Nov. 5 or 6, 1968. First appeared in *New Letters*, vol. 39, no. 2 (Winter 1972).

"The Flaw": June 26, 1967. First appeared in *The New York Times*, Oct. 19, 1968.

"Design": June 5, 1968.

"Rocking": May 29, 1968.

"Ars Poetica": Nov. 29, 1959. First appeared in *Epoch*, vol. 23, no. 3 (Spring 1974). The title, Latin for "Art of Poetry," is most often associated with the Roman poet Horace's instructive verse letter to the Pisos—but Archibald MacLeish's poem "Ars Poetica" would also have loomed large for Ammons. In TS, the colons in line 20 and line 28 were unitalicized, and so they are unitalicized here. Lines 19–20: *The Hudson Review*, *Partisan Review*, and *Poetry* were prestigious venues for poetry during the poet's lifetime. Line 28: *Epoch* is a literary magazine published at Cornell.

"Course Discourse": First appeared in *Brim*, no. 4 (Fall 1975).

"Obtrusion": May 16, 1974.

"Louise": First appeared in *Granite*, no. 4 (Autumn–Winter 1972–73). Line 1: Aurora is a New York village north of Ithaca, on Cayuga Lake. The episode is probably fictitious, the narrator an invented persona.

"80-Proof": First appeared in *Epoch*, vol. 13, no. 3 (Spring 1964).

"Having to Do with Birth": July 9, 1971. Appeared in *The New York Quarterly*, no. 19 (1977). In TS, the colon at the end of line 1 was unitalicized, and so it is unitalicized here.

"Mind": Jan. 29, 1970. First appeared in *Diacritics*, vol. 3, no. 4 (Winter 1973).

"Attenuations": Mar. 5, 1971. First appeared (as "Attentions") in *Diacritics*, vol. 3, no. 4 (Winter 1973).

"Turning": First appeared in *Diacritics*, vol. 3, no. 4 (Winter 1973).

"Paradise": Jan. 12, 1965.

"The Unmirroring Peak": Apr. 9, 1971.

"Pray Without Ceasing": Spring 1967. First appeared in *The Hudson Review*, vol. 26, no. 3 (Autumn 1973). In I Thessalonians 5:17, Paul tells the church at Thessalonica, "Pray without ceasing" (King James Version). Lines 25–33: Hermes Trismegistus is an eastern Mediterranean mythical figure, allegedly the author of an influential body of ancient philosophical and theological writings. A period at the end of line 305 is corrected to a colon, following TS. Also following TS, in line 373, "mixmaster, mixmaster" is here corrected to "mixmaster, maxmister."

§

THE SNOW POEMS

Written from the fall of 1975 through the spring of 1976, *The Snow Poems* was published by W. W. Norton early in 1977. The title suggests a collection, but Ammons made clear that he considered the book one long poem: although his

1980 *Selected Longer Poems* omitted it, in that book's preface he included it in a list of his long poems, and in the 1994 *Paris Review* interview he said that of all his long poems, *The Snow Poems* was his favorite. In recognition of that concept of the book, the line numbering here is continuous from beginning to end. Every line on which any typing appears is counted—with the exception of the section headings, each of which merely repeats its section's first line.

The poem appeared with the dedication "for my country." Early on, Ammons considered writing a sequence of "Fifty Statements," with each section headed by the name of one of the fifty states. As the total work evolved into something much longer, those titles were set aside. In the end, *The Snow Poems* included most of those sections; each of the state titles is given in the notes below.

Ammons's father, W. M. ("Willie") Ammons, died on November 25, 1966. His death looms large in this book, which was begun as the poet, who had become a father himself, neared turning fifty. Dates of the individual sections are given below; as the note on it indicates, Ammons wrote the "Like Fifty" section on his fiftieth birthday, February 18, 1976.

◡◠◡

"Words of Comfort": Undated. Line 11: Equanil is the brand name of an anti-anxiety medication.

"One Must Recall as One Mourns the Dead": Sept. 13, 1975. One of the "Fifty Statements": "Missouri."

"Things Change, the Shit Shifts": Sept. 18, 1975. One of the "Fifty Statements": "Oklahoma." In line 77, "sawmp" is corrected to "swamp," following TS. The embedded "Envy" poem (lines 99–127) is dated May 23, 1976.

"My": Sept. 19, 1975. One of the "Fifty Statements": "Idaho."

"Here I Sit, Fifty in the": Sept. 28, 1975. One of the "Fifty Statements": "Indiana." In line 199, "skninyings" is corrected to "skinnyings," following TS.

"My Father Used to Bring Banana": Sept. 28, 1975. One of the "Fifty Statements": "Wyoming."

"Have You Seen the Severe Waters": Sept. 29, 1975. One of the "Fifty Statements": "Rhode Island." Line 353: Here "etc" is emended to "etc." (with a period), in keeping with Ammons's usual practice.

"Early October": Oct. 5, 1975.

"Terror of": Oct. 18, 1975. One of the "Fifty Statements": "Montana." Betelgeuse, one of the brightest stars in the night sky, is part of the constellation Orion.

"Ivy, a Winding)": Nov. 20–23, 1975. One of the "Fifty Statements": "West Virginia."

"The Hieroglyphic Gathered, the Books": Dated "Thanksgiving" (presumably 1975). One of the "Fifty Statements": "Alabama." Line 715: The "imagistes" (French for "imagists") were early twentieth-century poets committed to the precise evocation of an image, usually in free verse. Line 716: Impatient for Moses to come down from Mount Sinai, the Hebrews made a golden calf and worshiped it (Exodus 32).

"Your Full-Service Mover, Madam": Nov. 28, 1975. One of the "Fifty Statements": "Connecticut."

"When in Early": Dec. 1–5, 1975. One of the "Fifty Statements": "Ohio." In line 938, "what it is" is corrected to "what is it," following TS. Line 929: *Annus mirabilis* is the Latin for "miraculous year" (and the title of a poem by John Dryden); by dropping one *n*, Ammons jokingly suggests that the year had been awful. Lines 940–46: Michael G. Kammen, a Cornell history professor, won the Pulitzer Prize for *People of Paradox: An Inquiry into the Origins of American Civilization* (1973). By the time of the poem's composition, Bernard Bailyn, a professor of history at Harvard, had won the Pulitzer Prize for *The Ideological Origins of the American Revolution* (1968) and the National Book Award for *The Ordeal of Thomas Hutchinson* (1974); he won a second Pulitzer later, for *Voyagers to the West* (1986). Ruth Novarr was the wife of David Novarr, a colleague in the Cornell English Department.

"The Arc": Dec. 6, 1975. One of the "Fifty Statements": "Maryland."

"There! the Light of Human Reason!": Dec. 8, 1975. One of the "Fifty Statements": "New Hampshire." In line 1036, "consistency so that" is corrected to "consistency so the," following TS.

"Hard Lard": Dec. 9, 1975. One of the "Fifty Statements": "Iowa."

"Hard Fist": Dec. 10, 1975. One of the "Fifty Statements": "South Dakota." Lines 1263–64: Willard Straight Hall is the student union building at Cornell.

"8:45 A.M.—Doorbell Rings: Wife": Dec. 11, 1975. One of the "Fifty Statements": "Hawaii."

"Shall Will Be Used Properly or Will Shall": Dec. 13, 1975. Lines 1539–40: National Football League teams.

"No Tirement Like Retirement": Dec. 14, 1975. One of the "Fifty Statements": "New Jersey."

"Light Falls Shadow and Beam through the Limbo": Dec. 14, 1975. One of the "Fifty Statements": "New York."

"Mist Curtains Lower and Dissolve": Dec. 15, 1975. One of the "Fifty Statements": "Colorado."

"The Snow Is Fine-Sightless Today the Ground": Dec. 16, 1975. One of the "Fifty Statements": "Nebraska."

"The Hen Pheasants Streak Out of the": Dec. 17, 1975. One of the "Fifty Statements": "New Mexico."

"Dawn Clear": Dec. 18, 1975. One of the "Fifty Statements": "Arkansas."

"If You Were Standing under the Elm and": Dec. 19, 1975. One of the "Fifty Statements": "Florida."

"In the Old": Dec. 21, 1975. One of the "Fifty Statements": "Oregon." Line 2076: At this time, Joe Namath was the quarterback for the New York Jets.

"Forecast for Today (Winter's Firstday)": Dec. 22, 1975. One of the "Fifty Statements": "Pennsylvania."

"I Come in from the Snowy World": Dec. 23, 1975. One of the "Fifty Statements": "Illinois." Line 2148: In an NFL game played on December 14, the New York Giants defeated the New Orleans Saints 28–14.

"Poetry Is the Smallest": Dec. 23, 1975. One of the "Fifty Statements": "Mississippi." After line 2268½ (the right column), one life of space after "trifle" in TS is here restored. Also following TS, the dots in line 2243 and line 2267 are here restored. The embedded poem beginning "you don't mind, do you" (lines 2244–65) was originally a separate poem titled "Freedom 1976," dated June 22, 1975.

"Christmas Eve Morning": Presumably Dec. 24, 1975. One of the "Fifty Statements": "Wisconsin."

"Analysis Mines and Leaves to Heal": Dec. 25, 1975. One of the "Fifty Statements": "Tennessee."

"Snowed Last Night a Lot but Warmed Up": Dec. 26, 1975. One of the "Fifty Statements": "Arizona."

"Those in Ledge Fright Seek": Dec. 27, 1975. One of the "Fifty Statements": "Kentucky." In line 2454, the comma at the end of the line in TS is here restored.

"But If the Way Will": Dec. 27, 1975. One of the "Fifty Statements": "Maine." Line 2545: The Dallas Cowboys and the Minnesota Vikings (NFL teams) were scheduled to play each other the next day, December 28.

"The Sun Climbs Daily Higher": Dec. 28, 1975. One of the "Fifty Statements": "Louisiana."

"A Seventeen Morning &": Dec. 29, 1975. One of the "Fifty Statements": "Alaska." Line 2744: Thanks to Michael McFee for pointing out that the word "cattybi-arsoned" is probably related to "catabias," which the *Dictionary of American Regional English* defines as "out of line, askew" or "diagonally; positioned diagonally from." Thanks too to Shelby Stephenson for confirming that he heard "cattybiarsoned" (but more often "cattybisoned") used to mean something like "askew" while growing up in rural eastern North Carolina about a decade after Ammons did.

"The First Morning in a Few": Dec. 30, 1975. One of the "Fifty Statements": "Nevada." Lines 2793–95: A bomb explosion at New York City's LaGuardia Airport the evening of December 29, 1975, killed eleven people and injured many more. The perpetrators were never identified.

"This Is": Dec 30, 1975. One of the "Fifty Statements": "Georgia."

"Quilted Spreads": Dec. 31, 1975. One of the "Fifty Statements": "Washington."

"Dung Ball, Round Graveyard": Jan. 1, 1976. One of the "Fifty Statements": "Vermont."

"I See Downhill a Patch": Jan. 2, 1976. One of the "Fifty Statements": "North Carolina."

"The Stomach Is Quite": Jan. 2, 1976. One of the "Fifty Statements": "Texas."

"My Neighbor Shakes Feed along": Jan. 3, 1976. One of the "Fifty Statements": "Delaware." Line 3198: In *The Cantos* (No. 81), Ezra Pound writes, "To break the pentameter, that was the first heave." Lines 3198–99: Ammons's statement that "we're / splinter assertions of the great iamb" is both a comment on prosody and a joking reference to Exodus 3:14, in which God tells Moses, "Thus shalt thou say unto the children of Israel, I Am hath sent me unto you" (King James Version).

"Nature As Waterfalls": Jan. 4, 1976. One of the "Fifty Statements": "California." Line 3271: At this time, Larry Brown was a running back for the NFL team the Washington Redskins.

"The Wind Picks Up Slick": Jan. 4, 1976. One of the "Fifty Statements": "Massachusetts." Line 3296: At this time, Ed White was an offensive lineman for the NFL team the Minnesota Vikings. Line 3297: The Pittsburgh Steelers and the Dallas Cowboys are NFL teams. Line 3306: The spelling is "arrrive" in TS, and when the galley proofs were sent to him with the spelling corrected to "arrive," Ammons circled the word and wrote, "3 r's in arrive." Given the context, this may be an onomatopoeic joke referring to the sexual sense of "coming."

"Cold Didn't Keep the Stuff": Jan. 5, 1976. One of the "Fifty Statements": "Virginia." Lines 3366–67: In Plato's dialogues, Socrates recommends—and explores the meaning of—the aphorism "Know yourself." Line 3415: The Welsh painter and poet David Jones (1895–1974), author of *In Parenthesis* and *The Anathemata*.

"Teeth Out": Jan. 5, 1976. One of the "Fifty Statements": "Utah." Lines 3441–42: "le mismo / difference" is a macaronic and grammatically garbled passage mixing French, Spanish, and English; Ammons seems to mean something like "same difference." Line 3447: In *The Study of Poetry* (1880), Matthew Arnold says that poetry should offer "criticism of life." See also "Theory Center" in *RSP*.

"When I Think of 'the Poet'": Jan. 6, 1976. One of the "Fifty Statements": "South Carolina." Lines 3448–49: The quotation is from Henry Wadsworth Longfellow, who in his sonnet "Shakespeare" dubs the poet and playwright "the Poet paramount, / Whom all the Muses loved, not one alone."

"You Can't Get It Right": Jan. 7, 1976. One of the "Fifty Statements": "North Dakota."

"The Perfect Journey Is": Jan. 10, 1976. One of the "Fifty Statements": "Michigan." An early title was "The Parkway."

"Snow of the": Jan. 11, 1976. One of the "Fifty Statements": "Kansas."

"[here a month of snow]": Undated.

"The Prescriptive Stalls As": Feb. 10, 1976.

"After the Dissolve": Feb. 11, 1976.

"A Sift, Sprinkling, or Veil": Feb. 12, 1976.

"Structureless Rage, Perhaps": Feb. 13, 1976. In lines 4044–46, following TS, the passage in the right-hand column begins one line earlier than in the book as published.

"Tell What Will Not Tell Direct": Feb. 15, 1976. In line 4127, "blanced" is here corrected to "balanced," as it appears in a handwritten draft.

"Spread It Thin": Feb. 16, 1976.

"Dark Day, Warm and Windy": Feb. 17, 1976. Lines 4189–90: *The Well-Tempered Clavier* is a collection of solo keyboard music composed and compiled by Johann Sebastian Bach (1685–1750).

"Like Fifty": Feb. 18, 1976 (the poet's fiftieth birthday). In line 4234, the "a" before "stringy wilderness" is restored, following TS.

"A 41 Morning, Still Cloudy": Feb. 19, 1976.

"Produce and Fuctifry": Feb. 20, 1976. Lines 4366–71: As "mill race" gradually transforms into "Milton," it passes through (at line 4369) the brand-name anti-anxiety medication Miltown.

"I Look Up Guff and Find the First": Feb. 21, 1976. In line 4456, "kept it :they" is corrected to "kept it: they," following TS.

"One at One with His Desire": Feb. 22, 1976. In line 4514, a period following the colon has been deleted, following TS.

"Dull Lull": Feb. 23, 1976. Line 4611: Parian is a kind of porcelain. The allusion is to Ralph Waldo Emerson's poem "The Snow-Storm," which says of the snow-blowing north wind, "Mockingly, / On coop or kennel he hangs Parian wreaths." Line 4666: In Plato's thinking, everything in the material world is an imperfect copy of an ideal or form.

"The Temperature Rose 15 Degrees over": Feb. 24, 1976. Lines 4743–44: Spanish for "believe it or not" followed by Spanish mixed with English for comic effect, "believe it or yes," also suggesting "believe it—oh, yes."

"As for Fame I've Had It": Feb. 27, 1976.

"When One Is a Child One Lives": Feb. 28, 1976.

"Cloud Strays Rounded Up": Feb. 29, 1976. Line 5007: the New York Rangers, a professional ice hockey team, ended the 1975–76 season with 29 wins, 42 losses, and 9 ties. Line 5035: "peoples' knees" is here corrected to "people's knees."

"It's Half an Hour Later Before": Mar. 1, 1976. In line 5107, a comma is added to the line's end, following TS.

"This Poem Concerns": Mar. 10, 1976.

"The Word Cries Out": Mar. 11, 1976.

"I Woke Up at 6 and It Was": Mar. 18, 1976.

"A Flock of My Days": Mar. 19, 1976.

"You Can't Imitate": Mar. 19, 1976. Originally headed "a jumble of jottings." Line 5352: Ammons addresses Wallace Stevens (1879–1955), thinking perhaps of Stevens's poem "The Bird with the Coppery, Keen Claws," which introduces its readers to "a parakeet of parakeets."

"Spring's Old Hat Is Older": Mar. 21, 1976.

"The Temperature Fell": Mar. 22, 1976.

"You Can": Mar. 23, 1976.

"Cunit": Mar. 24, 1976.

"It's a Wonder the Body": Mar. 25, 1976. Line 5729: In the *Odyssey*, Polyphemos (more commonly "Polyphemus") is a one-eyed giant, a Cyclops, who eats members of Odysseus's crew.

"Today Was Like Vomiting": Mar. 27, 1976.

"It's April 1": Apr. 1, 1976.

"I'm Unwilling": Apr. 2, 1976.

"The Sky Clabbered Up with": Apr. 2, 1976.

"A Single Fact": Apr. 3, 1976.

"It Does Not Rain in": Apr. 4, 1976. In line 6036, "motion holding moving" is corrected to "motion holds moving," following TS. In line 6045, "Anarctica" is corrected to "Antarctica."

"One Loves": Apr. 4, 1976.

"The Miltonic (Miltownic) Isn't": Apr. 5, 1976. Line 6091: The adjective "miltonic" can refer either to the work of the poet John Milton, author of *Paradise Lost*, or to others' work that resembles Milton's. Again Ammons playfully juxtaposes Milton's name with that of the anti-anxiety medication Miltown.

"My Father Used to Tell of an": Apr. 9, 1976.

"Arm's Length Renders One": Apr. 10, 1976.

"I'm the Type": Apr. 10, 1976.

"Snow Showed a Full Range": Apr. 11, 1976.

"No Matter": Apr. 11, 1976.

"It's So Dry the Brook, Down": Apr. 13, 1976.

"Today Will Beat Anything": Apr. 14, 1976. Line 6489: "One's Self I Sing" is a poem by Walt Whitman. Line 6490: Section 4 of Whitman's "Song of Myself" includes the line "Apart from the pulling and hauling stands what I am."

"Sight Can Go Quickly, Aerial, Where": Apr. 15, 1976. In line 6526, "to be be back" is corrected to "to be back," following TS.

"These Days Most": Apr. 16, 1976.

"The Cardinal, Slanted Watershed": Apr. 17, 1976.

"One Desires the Cutting": Apr. 18, 1976.

"I Wonder if Pagan Is": Apr. 18, 1976.

"Rage Spells More of My Words Right": Apr. 18, 1976.

"On This Day Noteworthily Warm": Apr. 19, 1976.

"Some Nights I Go Out to Piss": Apr. 19, 1976.

"My Structure Is, Like the": Apr. 20, 1976.

"You Think of the Sun That It": Apr. 23, 1976. Line 6992: "MacDonald's" is here corrected to "McDonald's." Line 7012: Martin Heidegger (1889–1976), German philosopher. *Harmonium* is the title of Wallace Stevens's first book; italics are here added. Line 7015: "Pleides" is here corrected to "Pleiades." Line 7019: At the time, Stanley Fish was best known for his work on literature of the English Renaissance.

"Snow": Apr. 26, 1976. In line 7116, a comma is added to the line's end, following TS.

"It Snowed All Night Snow": Apr. 27, 1976.

"Drip Drip": Apr. 28, 1976.

"Some Fluffy, Long-Swaggly Catkins": Apr. 29, 1976.

"My Father, I Hollow for You": Apr. 30, 1976. First appeared in *The Iowa Review*, vol. 8, no. 1 (Winter 1977).

"I Knew": May 1, 1976.

"I Cannot Re-wind the Brook": May 2, 1976.

"Considering the Variety": May 2, 1976. In line 7466, "supresses" is corrected to "suppresses."

"Variable Cloudiness Windy": May 3, 1976. The embedded poem beginning "when I was young the silk" (lines 7527–41) first appeared in *The Iowa Review*, vol. 8, no. 1 (Winter 1977). Dots setting off that embedded poem, though present in TS and the galleys, were omitted from the published book; they are here restored.

"On Walks I Go a Long Way along": May 4, 1976.

"One Trains Hard for": May 5, 1976.

"Will Firinger Be Kissed: Will": May 7, 1976. Line 7654: Thanks to William Harmon for pointing out that the opening question is an example of *metathesis*—in this case a slight scrambling of the question "Will Kissinger Be Fired?" At the time of the poem's composition, Kissinger was serving as U.S. Secretary of State under President Ford, as he had under President Nixon; the following November, Ford lost the election to Jimmy Carter, who replaced Kissinger with Cyrus Vance. Line 7655: Paul Cézanne (1839–1906), French Post-Impressionist painter. Line 7660: "Provide, Provide" is the title of a poem by Robert Frost. Line 7666: Possibly a reference to the Midwestern poet Carl Sandburg (1878–1967). Lines 7686–89: This seems to be a response to the final line of William Butler Yeats's poem "Among School Children": "How can we know the dancer from the dance?"

"If Walking through Birdy Trees": May 9, 1976. Line 7722: Following TS, "whole colth" is corrected to "whole cloth."

"They Say It Snowed": May 22, 1976. Line 7738: Ammons and his family lived in a house on Hanshaw Road in Ithaca from 1966 to 1992.

§

HIGHGATE ROAD

Ammons self-published *Highgate Road* in July 1977, in consultation with his friend Stuart Wright, publisher of Palaemon Press, under the name The Inkling X Press. (See *The Snow Poems*, lines 1090–92 for references to "The X Press.") The edition was limited to 200 copies. Hoping to sell the book as a collector's item, the poet priced it at $100 per copy—but only a few copies sold. In 1979 he decided to destroy the remaining majority of the edition, explaining in a letter to Wright that by doing so he expected to raise the market value of the existing copies, and thus reward those who had bought the book.

☙❧

"Shuffling": First appeared in *The New York Times*, Aug. 13, 1976.

"For Louise and Tom Gossett": Probably drafted in the fall of 1974, given its placement in the Chrono V notebook. Louise and Tom Gossett were professors emeriti of the English departments of Salem College and Wake Forest University, respectively; they were Ammons's neighbors during the 1974–75 academic year, when he held a visiting appointment at Wake Forest. Louise Gossett is the author of *Violence in Recent Southern Fiction* (1965); Tom Gossett's books include *Race: The History of an Idea in America* (1963) and *"Uncle Tom's Cabin" and American Culture* (1985).

"Significances": July 24, 1971. First appeared in *The Nation*, Mar. 19, 1977.

"Release": Apr. 29, 1975.

"Speechlessness": First appeared in *The Grapevine*, Nov. 23–29, 1976.

"Gardening": Apr. 21, 1968.

"Blue Skies": Oct. 17, 1974.

"Camels": The poem appears here as it does in *RSP*, without the hyphen in what in *HR* was "non-literary."

"Immediacy": The poem appears as it was revised for *RSP*. The earlier version was as follows:

> I looked for coins
> along the street's edge
> on the way to
>
> the eternal sea:
> looked at the sea,
> a deep summary,
>
> and returned along
> the street's other edge,
> looking for coins.

"Recording": "Spring 75—Equinox." First appeared in *The New York Times*, May 12, 1975.

"North Street": Aug. 10, 1974. First appeared in *Ocean City Sentinel-Ledger*, Aug. 16, 1974.

"Reading": June 20, 1975. First appeared in *The Vineland Times Journal*, June 26, 1975. The poem appears here as it was revised for *RSP*. In *HR* it appeared thus:

> It is nice
> after dinner
> to walk down to
> the beach
> and see
> that the biggest
> thing on earth
> is
> relatively calm.

"One Thing and Another": Mar. 31, 1975. First appeared in *The Nickelodeon*, a poetry broadsheet Ammons edited while in residence at Wake Forest University, no. 15 (Apr. 8, 1975). The poem appears here as it appeared in *RSP*. In *HR* it appeared thus:

> It is one
> thing
> to know one
> thing
> and another
> thing
> to know another
> thing.

"Self": First appeared in *The Sewanee Review*, vol. 82, no. 4 (Fall 1974).

"For Doyle Fosso": Nov. 13, 1974. Long an English professor at Wake Forest, Fosso taught the department's course on Shakespeare. Among his publications are two books of poems, *Parabola Rasa* (1984) and *Astralogos* (1987).

"Generation Gap": Apr. 22, 1968.

"Natives": The poem appears here as it was revised for *RSP*, with "civilization" instead of "civilzation" in line 3 and "scalelike" instead of "scale-like" in line 5.

"Catch": Appeared in *Choice*, no. 10 (1977).

"Lofty": June 23, 1964. First appeared (as "For the Lofty") in *The New York Times*, Jan. 25, 1965.

"Imaginary Number": Nov. 28, 1977.

§

Index of Titles

Index of First Lines